CREATED TO LEARN

CREATED TO LEARN

WILLIAM R. YOUNT

B&H
ACADEMIC
Nashville, Tennessee

978-0-8054-4727-9

Published by B&H Publishing Group
Nashville, Tennessee

Dewey Decimal Classification: 380.15
Subject Heading: EDUCATIONAL PSYCHOLOGY \ RELIGIOUS
EDUCATION—PSYCHOLOGY

5 6 7 8 9 10 • 17 16 15 14 13

To Barb—
Blessings to you for watching my back this year,
literally, as I sat hours at a time,
poring over texts and tapping this book into my computer.
Words cannot express my thanks
for your encouragement, support, and love.

TABLE OF CONTENTS

UNIT 4: Educational Psychology and Motivation

UNIT 5: Educational Psychology and the Brain

FOREWORD

In 1989 I taught my first class in educational psychology at Southwestern Seminary. At that time, following the lead of my esteemed professors, I used the best secular textbook in educational psychology I could find. Then I spent that semester and the following years trying to adapt it to the needs of my Christian education students. It was laborious, identifying the applicable aspects of each theory and adjusting the suggestions for those who teach in schools where attendance is compulsory and motivation is often extrinsic to the unique classrooms of Christian learning and teaching, where attendance is voluntary and motivation is intrinsic.

One of the most helpful resources during those days was the class notes that Rick Yount shared with me, his student. I knew then that he had a gift for infusing abstract concepts with real life application, and this knowledge was confirmed when the first edition of *Created to Learn: A Christian Teacher's Introduction to Educational Psychology* was published in 1996.

Since its first publication, I have used *Created to Learn* every year in my teaching at three institutions, including both masters' and doctoral classes. Rick Yount's clear and precise writing, along with his gift for analogies and stories, has made his work a favorite of my students. While it serves as an introduction, students return to *Created to Learn* for clarification and explanation of foundational teachings and review the suggestions for applying educational theories. This book is on my must-read list for every Christian education student.

This new revision builds on the strengths of the previous edition. Yount's engaging, readable writing style; his continuous and creative application of the concepts presented; and the objectives and learning activities that surround each chapter are still present. However, the addition of new material, such as chapters on constructivism and brain-based learning—as well as the added experiences of Yount's international teaching and updated research and statistics examples—bring it up-to-date and solidify its position as the premiere textbook in educational psychology for Christian teaching.

Throughout this text, Yount passionately conveys that God has created each person with the capacity to learn, and that capacity includes the ability to know and follow Jesus. He also convincingly communicates that Christian teachers can know, understand, and appreciate how students learn and can use empirical research to make good decisions about teaching, whether in an academic setting or in the church.

Dr. LeRoy Ford, in his book *Design for Teaching and Training*, proposed that a gap exists between what we know about the way people learn and what we actually do in the classroom. A standard book on educational psychology might focus only on the theories—what we know about the way people learn. But Yount has bridged the gap identified by Ford by taking the theories of teaching and learning and bringing them to life in the classroom. You will enjoy using *Created to Learn* to help your students become bridge builders for learning in the kingdom.

—Norma Hedin, Ph. D.
Fellow and Professor of Foundations of Education
B. H. Carroll Theological Institute, Arlington, Texas

PREFACE

Second Edition

Welcome. Come in. Have a seat here at the table. There's a warm fire in the corner. Sufficient light for making notes and drawing diagrams. Pleasant food and drink to sustain a long conversation. I cannot tell you how glad I am to see you. There is nothing I'd rather do than sit here and discuss the ministry of equipping and discipling others with you. But I am curious. *Why* have you come? What brought you to this place? The answers to these questions make a difference in the way we handle our time together.

How Come We to This Place?

The path bringing me to this place sprang from a life of Bible study and passed through academic studies of philosophy, theology, and psychology. The philosophies of Idealism, Realism, Neo-Thomism, Pragmatism, and Existentialism—particularly as applied to religion and education—still dance across my mind. Even after nearly forty years, I find myself playing with the philosophies as they intersect educational problems: the nature of the learner, the teacher, methodology, intended outcome, and social impact. Yet formal philosophy did not lead me here.

I have little desire to engage in discussions that have little apparent purpose other than the glorification of the intellect of the participants. I think of the two philosophers who, sitting by a quiet brook, spent the afternoon debating the essence of wetness. A young boy came wandering by; listened for a moment; and then, bored by the abstract banter, simply plunged his hand into the water. Ah, wet! I am that young boy. While I enjoy wrestling with various philosophical views from time to time, I do not consider myself, personally or professionally, a philosopher.

The path to this place passed through studies of systematic, historical, and comparative theology. I certainly benefited from the Greek compartmentalization of biblical Truth (God, man, sin, Christ, Holy Spirit, salvation, Church, last things); but formal theology did not lead me here. The endless quoting of essays, books, and monographs; the categorizing and re-categorizing of theological thoughts, views, arguments, and counter arguments can be exhausting and, at times, spiritually demoralizing. While I strive to live out biblical theology in my everyday decisions, I do not consider myself, personally or professionally, a theologian.

The path to this place passed through studies in psychology—especially that strain of psychology given to the educational process. I have taught masters' courses and doctoral seminars in issues of educational psychology for thirty years, but it is not psychology *per sec* that brought me here. While I see the value of psychological insights into human thought, affect, and behavior, I do not consider myself, personally or professionally, a psychologist.

I am a Christian teacher. It is my calling, my focus, my personal passion. You will see this teacher-first focus throughout the text. I am thrilled that you care enough to share my musings, to question and explore them with me. Sharing these discoveries with teachers—disciplers, pastors, missionaries, parents—has been a great joy for most of my adult life.

By teacher, I mean something more than commonly accepted concepts of teacher-teller, teacher-facilitator, or teacher-coach. Teaching embraces nothing less than personal life change. It anchors into concepts of personal engagement, discipleship, equipment, and transformation of learners. It is from this perspective that I began using the term discipler to emphasize the distinction in my very first book on teaching[1] (*The Disciplers*, self-published, 1977). Discipler and teacher are not synonyms.

God calls us as disciplers to shape our learners—their thinking, values, and behaviors—by His power, toward His ends, through His Word. Without that call, we reduce the study of educational psychology to bits and pieces of conflicting theories. Without the desire to use these discoveries to help others grow in their sense of *spiritual being*, we are left with little more than incomplete, and often irrelevant, viewpoints from history. These viewpoints can leave us unsatisfied, even depressed.

Erik Erikson carries us through eight stages of personality development, ending for most, it seems, in a state of despair at the end of a broken life. We all suffer fractures in one way or another, at one time or another, in life. But as *disciplers*, we can use Erikson's stages to attack problems all along the human lifespan—in terms of educational ministries in local churches, in church schools, or even seminaries—to support the Hope only the Lord can give. When we study Erikson through the filter of Christian discipleship, he helps us in ways he never dreamed.

Jean Piaget explained the mechanism by which the mind constructs a mental representation of the world we experience. He sorely misrepresented early developmental stages of children as negative by emphasizing their lack of adult cognitive abilities. Yet, as *disciplers*, we can use his mechanisms and stages to help learners of every age move, according to their ability, beyond personal perception to Truth, beyond personal reality to God's Reality—to His view of our world and His kingdom, which is at hand. Piaget helps us in ways he never dreamed.

Lawrence Kohlberg's work on moral reasoning helps explain the mechanism by which human beings make moral choices. His focus is *process*, however, not outcome. He provides no help with what is right or wrong. Rather, he describes ways we determine what to do. Let me put a finer point to this: What we actually do was not Kohlberg's focus but how we determine what we do. Yet, as *disciplers*, we find his six stages helpful in connecting real world moral decisions (positive and negative, right and wrong) with biblical truths. How do we help learners move beyond religious clichés to determine the Right in the practical moral dilemmas they face? Kohlberg helps us in ways he never dreamed.

Edward Thorndike reduced human growth and learning to stamping stimulus-response bonds into the nervous system through repetition and satisfaction. B. F. Skinner focused on pellets, pigeons, and ping-pong to achieve desired behaviors in learners through prompt, cue, and reward. Thorndike and Skinner rejected the very ideas of mind and person in favor of nervous system and organism. We struggle to find in these theories any glimmer of human virtues: love in the face of hate, integrity in the face of corruption, courage in the face of danger. Yet as *disciplers*, we can use principles of behavioral learning to set patterns and reward success for behaviors that honor God. We can motivate first attempts at proper action where self-motivation does not exist. Thorndike and Skinner help us in ways they never dreamed.

Abraham Maslow emphasized the centrality of personal needs and choice in the lives of learners. *Deficiency needs* hinder learning. *Growth needs* enhance learning and personal development. Children should be free to choose what is best for them. Carl Rogers underscored freedom in the classroom, allowing learners to share their personal stories, questions, and answers with each other. But where do we find truth in these personal stories? If we focus always on needs, where do we find joy? Mere love for a subject—the humanists' dubious and often unrealized ideal—does not often translate into mastery of that subject. Three decades of educational testing have proven that humanistic classrooms produce few scholars. Though Humanistic Learning Theory has all but disappeared from contemporary textbooks, the tenets of *self* remain strong under new names such as radical constructivism. Despite fifty years of increasing social chaos—created by self-centered and self-focused individuals, we can, as *disciplers*, embrace effective principles of learning to connect with learners heart-to-heart, to build relational bridges in the classroom. Maslow and Rogers help us in ways they never dreamed.

How did I come to this place?

It was as a discipler, a Christian teacher. My desire in writing *Created to Learn* (1996) was to share with Christian teachers in Sunday school classes, cell group Bible studies, church schools, Christian colleges, and seminaries what the Lord had been teaching me through years of personal experiences and study. I come here today, with anticipation and joy, to share changes that have occurred since we published the first edition.

The Intervening Years

It has been more than fourteen years since May 1995, the month the last words to the first edition of *Created to Learn* were penned. The following November, a ministry door opened, one set before us more than thirty-one years before—in July 1964.

My wife Barb and I met at an associational youth camp in Waukegan, Illinois. Somewhere during the week, sitting with a hundred others at a campfire, we fell in love. We were almost 16. At the end of the week, facing the beginning of our junior year of high school, we decided we would marry in six years and then go to the Soviet Union as missionaries. The idea was prompted, no doubt, by a picture I saw in an early newsletter published by Richard Wurmbrand.[2] The picture showed Baptists standing knee-deep in snow at the edge of a small frozen pond, deep in a forest. Six adults were dressed in white, waiting to be plunged into the icy water as soon as others finished chopping a rough hole in the ice. They were meeting in secret, breaking Soviet law, in order to baptize, and be baptized, in the name of Jesus. I saw that picture when I was ten, but I have never forgotten it. Barb had seen a full-color picture of St. Basil's Cathedral in Red Square, and somehow the Lord used that picture to draw her to the idea of going there. As we left the camp grounds, we did not know that missionary work was forbidden in the Soviet Union.

In November 1995, thirty-one years after our call at camp, Charlie Warner of *Barnabas International* unexpectedly visited Southwestern Seminary, looking for professors willing to teach at Odessa International (Baptist) Seminary in Odessa, Ukraine. I left that meeting with an invitation to teach. In May 1996—after years of college studies in electrical engineering, psychology, and counseling; after years of deaf ministry and seminary study; after years of educational ministry in churches and seminary—we found ourselves, by God's grace, in the former Soviet Union, teaching educational psychology. The just-published *Created to Learn* provided the course material. The next year, June 1997, I taught the same course at Moscow Baptist Theological Seminary. I have taught in both schools several times since.

In November 1999 I attended the annual meeting of the Eur-Asian Accrediting Association (EAAA) in St. Petersburg, Russia. Andrei Chumakin, one of my Odessa seminary students—serving at that time as academic dean of the Baptist Bible Institute in Almaty, Kazakhstan—introduced me to two Baptist Union pastors. They invited me to teach in their Bible Institute. God miraculously provided the means to go.

I taught sixteen students in Almaty in January 2000. Nearly half of the class had driven 200 miles from Bishkek, Kyrgyzstan, to attend the course. Alexander Schumilin, a student in the class and a Baptist Union leader, invited me to teach at the Bishkek Bibelschule the following year, in 2001. I returned in June 2003 and yet again in June 2007. In May–June 2009, I returned to Kyrgyzstan to lead three-day seminars on Adult Small Group Bible Studies in three cities and to Almaty to teach the educational psychology course.

In 2000 EAAA selected *Created to Learn* as one of ten western texts to be translated into Russian for use in member schools. Bibles for Everyone, an evangelical publisher in St. Petersburg, Russia, published the Russian version in 2001 as *Созданы, чтобы учиться*. I have used the Russian version in all my Russian-language courses since that time.

Yaroslav Pyzh, academic dean at Western Ukrainian Baptist Theological Seminary (Borislav) and one of my students in the 1998 Moscow course, invited me to teach. I taught courses of educational psychology and principles of teaching in June 2002, 2005, 2007, 2008, and 2009. Other teaching opportunities came from Donetsk Christian University (Ukraine) and two teaching visits to the first Baptist church (or House of Prayer—as churches are called there) in Tyumen, Siberia, Russia. In August 2008 I traveled to Lisbon, Portugal, where I taught nine Ukrainian pastors and teachers who are ministering among Ukrainian worker-immigrants. In February–March 2009, I taught both courses in Baptist seminaries in Odessa, Kiev, and Borislav, Ukraine.

I had no inkling while writing the first edition of this text in 1994–95 that the Lord would open the door for such an extensive teaching ministry in the former Soviet Union. Yet each one of the trips—each one of these classes—provided fresh opportunities to observe, over and again, how students process the ideas of this text. Hundreds of experiences in these classrooms—as well as those at Southwestern Seminary—have helped to clarify the most potent principles of learning and teaching worldwide. This edition folds these twelve years of practical experiences into the mix.

The Design of the Text: Emphasizing the Changeless in a Changing Field

The original design decision—to focus *Created to Learn* on classical psychological issues in discipling and equipping—was intentional. I attempted to emphasize fundamental principles over the merely new. The insights provided by the theorists selected for the text have staying power because they connect to basic human learning design—*God's design*—that has been discovered by science. In 2005 I analyzed ten recently published educational psychology textbooks and found the major emphases of the original *Created to Learn* were as relevant as ever.

But changes have occurred. Piaget's ideas on cognitive development focus on individual development and fit western thinking well. A contemporary of Piaget, Russian psychologist Lev Vygotsky, emphasized the *social* dynamics of cognitive learning. His work was slow in coming to the West but has been widely discussed in the last decade. Vygotsky's thinking, which provided support for a new kind of man—a super-man (an ideal of Soviet Communism now rendered moot), holds interesting views concerning *communal issues of learning* in church and family; and I've added them in this edition.

The past decade has seen an addition to Erik Erikson's classical psycho-social theory. Erikson died in 1994. In 1997 his wife Joan revised her husband's 1982 book, *The Life Cycle Completed,* and, working with Lars Torstam, added a *ninth stage* to Erikson's eight. Torstam called the stage gerotranscendence, defining it as a step beyond personal integrity in which the personality embraces the world at large.

We investigate gerotranscendence, finding comfort in this: what we have always believed as evangelical Christians is now being promoted by others—albeit in secular forms. Christ sent disciples nearly two millennia ago, as He sends us today, to embrace the world: "Go, therefore, and make disciples of all nations, baptizing them . . . teaching them to observe everything I have commanded you" (Matthew 28:19-20). We understand that our *lives* exist beyond our *selves.* Jesus proclaimed this truth boldly: "And whoever doesn't take up his cross and follow Me is not worthy of Me. Anyone finding his life will lose it, and anyone losing his life because of Me will find it" (Matt 10:38–39).

Not only do we hear Jesus calling us to look beyond self to the world; we hear Him calling us to embrace life, His life, beyond physical death. Without the Christian's assurance of life beyond death, the secular notion of life beyond self merely mocks human mortality. With the assurance of life beyond life, we find eternal meaning in teaching, learning, and spiritual growth that continues to the end of our days and beyond.

We included a chapter on Information Processing theory in 1996, which has been updated for this edition; but a startling revolution in the field of neuroscience over the last two decades provides far more detail about brain functioning. Advanced medical technology, such as fMRI scanning[3], provides the means to measure brain changes in real time—at far more complex levels than ever before. An entire educational industry, brain-based learning, has grown up in the last decade around the idea of teaching the brain. We address the revolution in neuroscience, the importance of mental attention in learning and growth, and implications for educational practice in a new sixteenth chapter.

Finally, the entire original text has been revisited, revised, and rewritten. Very few sentences escaped unscathed. New illustrations have been added. Old ones dropped. Material that has found its way into other books[4] has been condensed here. Material found to be less than helpful has been dropped altogether.[5] Original references, which continue to reflect contemporary thinking, were carried over from the first edition. Extensive research provides support for evolving ideas in the field, particularly regarding cognitive and humanistic learning theory systems, designing instructional objectives, and the revolution in brain science.

It is my prayer that you will find in this text many useful ideas for your use in teaching, equipping, learning, and preaching ministries around the world. Our goal here echoes that of the apostle Paul: to help learners of every age and every kind to "grow in every way into Him who is the head Christ" (Eph 4:15). Paul's Spirit-breathed discipling goal gives supernatural meaning to the study of theology, philosophy, and psychology of education. While this text cannot accomplish this overarching spiritual goal, it is intended to carry you to the One who engages us in accord with these principles every day.

A Return to the Original Question: Why Have You Come?

I return to my original questions. What brought *you* to this place? Why did you come? If you come as a student in a formal class, I believe with all my heart that these pages will help you in tangible ways as you teach others—in your family, among your friends, in small groups, in worship, and formal classrooms—here at home and around the world.

If you came out of a desire to teach more clearly, more warmly, more skillfully, we will spend many enjoyable hours together. We will leave this place changed by our interactions.

If you came for other reasons . . . well, the Russians would say *pah-smoh-treem*—"we will see" where our conversations lead. Perhaps you will catch the fever of teaching—discipling and equipping others—along the way. That is my prayer for you, and nothing would bless me more.

May God richly bless you in the process. May He give you wisdom, passion, and expertise as you freely devote yourself to Him in preparation—as discipler, pastor, or missionary—to facilitate the learning of others that *they may grow up into Him.*

Rick Yount
Fort Worth, Texas

ACKNOWLEDGMENTS

I wish to thank Southern Baptists for their support of my teaching ministry in local churches, associations, and teacher conventions since 1969 and as a faculty member at Southwestern Baptist Theological Seminary since 1981. My sabbatical leave this past year enabled me to work full-time on this second edition (fall 2008 through summer 2009) and then apply this new research in multiple classes in seven different teaching venues in three former Soviet republics (spring 2009).

I wish to thank John Landers, retired from B&H Publishing Group, for his support since we first met in 1994 to discuss chapters in the original *The Teaching Ministry of the Church* (Eldridge, 1995). John encouraged me to write and, after editing my chapters for *TMC*, asked if there was anything more I wanted to write. There was, and the result was *Created to Learn* (1996). John was instrumental in the publications of *Called to Teach* in 1999 and *Called to Reach* in 2007. Since John's retirement in 2008, I have received great encouragement from B&H's Jim Baird and Ray Clendenen and my new editor Dave Stabnow. Their support has been an incredible blessing to me. Thank you, B&H Publishing Group, for enabling me to extend my teaching ministry to readers I will never meet this side of glory.

Many thanks to the North American Professors of Education association for its untiring efforts in promoting a broad range of issues in the field of Christian Education. The organization and its members have enriched my thinking, year after year, since the early 1990s when Daryl Eldridge and Warren Benson welcomed me to my first annual convention.

I am deeply grateful to Norma Hedin, Ph.D., faculty colleague in the Foundations of Education Division at Southwestern Baptist Theological Seminary from 1990 to 2006, for her helpful comments and suggestions. Her perspective comes from the standpoint of years of experience as a seminary professor, minister of education, and teacher training specialist. I am most grateful that she was willing to write the *Foreword* for this edition. Her quiet professionalism in the classroom, her team spirit among faculty colleagues, and her participation and leadership in the North American Professors of Christian Education (NAPCE) association are well-known among Christian educators.

My thanks to Baltazar Alvarez, Shirley Moxley, Debra Pauley, and Jacob Johnson, Ph.D. students in the Fall 2007 educational psychology seminar, for their research and presentations on *Teaching the*

Brain. Their work, and especially our class discussions, helped clarify major themes in a bewildering array of resources. I wish to further thank Baltazar and Jacob for their additional contributions of research made through a Ph.D.-directed study in selected educational psychology topics during the spring of 2008.

Unit 1

Educational Psychology and the Christian Teacher

Teaching is both art and science. The best teachers weave together competing elements—content and communication, justice and grace, control and nurture, challenge and support—in order to help learners grow. *Teaching is art* in that this weaving of elements happens spontaneously, in the heat of battle, in the very acts of engaging human learners. *Teacher-artists* paint colorful mental landscapes, frame questions on the spot, respond warmly to learners "in the moment," and use humor to dispel tension or drive home a point. Such an artistic weaving of elements flows out of the personality of the teacher, making the process unique for each teacher.

Teaching is science in that the best teachers employ widely accepted principles for establishing knowledge, expediting understanding, facilitating attitude change, and shaping behavior. These principles are grounded in tangible processes, discovered through scientific investigation and empirical observation. *Teacher-scientists* investigate the most effective ways to create positive learning environments, address learner differences, engage learners head, heart, and hand,[1] explain terms and concepts clearly, question learners appropriately, and set reasonable expectations through measurable instructional objectives. Scientific fundamentals flow out of the field of educational psychology and anchor teachers in a common process.

Educational psychology presents the scientific framework for the art of teaching. The word *education* comes from the Latin *educare,* ["bring up, to rear"][2] and refers to the process of developing "the faculties and powers of a person by teaching, instruction, or schooling."[3] The word *psychology* combines the Greek words *psyche-* and *logos. Psyche-* means "soul, life,"[4] and *logos* means "1) Discourse, expression or 2) Science, theory, study."[5] Psychology is the study or science of the soul, the person, the individual—particularly with regard to mental processes and behavior. *Educational psychology,* then, is the study of the *individual as learner.*

God created us to learn and provided the Church as the context. God reveals Himself as Creator (Gen 1–2). He created humankind in His image, male and female, (Gen 1:26–28)—created us to learn of Him. He is Teacher, enlightening us, guiding, training, and lifting us (Deut 4:1–14).[6] Jesus, the express image of God in flesh, was known best as a Teacher, Master, and Rabbi as He taught how to live as citizens of His kingdom.[7] The Church is primarily a reaching-teaching institution, drawing people to faith in Christ, and then growing them to full citizenship in the kingdom,[8] through the power and presence of the Holy Spirit, our Teacher. Through its associated classes, schools, colleges, and seminaries, the Church expands its discipling and equipping functions to both citizens and leaders in God's kingdom.

The teaching task is both nurturing and instructive. The apostle Paul writes "[Christ] gave some to be . . . pastors [shepherds, nurturers] and teachers [trainers, instructors] for the training of the saints in the work of ministry, to build up the body of Christ, until we all reach unity in the faith and in the knowledge of God's Son, growing into a mature man" (Eph 4:11–13).

Educational psychology stands as one of the foundational disciplines of the teaching-learning process. Anyone who desires greater effectiveness as a teacher will benefit from the findings of educational psychologists. But *what,* you may ask, can *we,* as *Christian* teachers, learn from *secular theorists?* And yet we engage spiritually neutral things every day. We order our days by weather forecasts anchored in the science of meteorology. We speed our travel by trusting our lives to modern jetliners, built according to the scientific laws of aerodynamics. We manage our diets according to the latest findings on nutrition, derived from the science of biology. Many of us get our news by way of computers, cell phones, and the Internet, all produced by the science of microelectronics. None of these tools are *Christian.*

Moreover, we regularly seek help from nonspiritual sources. When our cars needs repair, do we seek a pastor or a mechanic? When our teeth need work, do we look for a theologian or a dentist? When our drains are clogged, should we consult a seminary professor or a plumber? When we want to know which highways to take from *A* to *B,* do we consult the Bible or a recent map? The answers are obvious.

In the same way, discoveries made by men and women who have given their lives to the study of human learning can help us as well. Why should we *not* study what researchers have to say, "taking every thought captive to the obedience of Christ" (2 Cor 10:5)? What have dedicated men and women discovered through scientific investigation and educational observation? How might we transfer these discoveries into a Christian context? Unit I addresses these issues by first establishing the Disciplers' Model as the Christian context for the study of learning and then analyzing the scientific approach to knowing.

Chapter 1: The Disciplers' Model

The seven elements of the Disciplers' Model provide a philosophical and theological framework for the remainder of the text. "Eternal Truth speaking to contemporary Need" are the two elements of the foundation. The three tangible systems that energize the discipling process are rational, emotional, and social. The ultimate goal of the process is maturational. The Primary Enabler of the process is the Holy Spirit.

We connect six of these biblical elements with their counterparts in educational psychology: content, individual differences, cognitive development, affective development, social development, and maturation.

Chapter 2: Knowing, Science, and the Christian Teacher

The grand scope of philosophy sets before us three Great Problems. The second of these, and the one most important to us here, is called epistemology[9] and defines several distinct ways that human beings achieve knowledge of the world. Educational psychology is a scientific discipline and uses scientific means to define educational truth. How does knowledge discovered by science differ from other ways of knowing?

Chapter Two investigates seven ways we gain the knowledge we have: common sense, tradition, authority, intuition and revelation, experience, deductive reasoning, and inductive reasoning. The chapter then defines scientific knowing and describes how it functions. Finally, we compare and contrast faith and science as ways of knowing.

1

The Disciplers' Model

And He personally gave some to be apostles, some prophets, some evangelists, some pastors and teachers, for the training of the saints in the work of ministry, to build up the body of Christ, until we all reach unity in the faith and in the knowledge of God's Son, growing into a mature man with a stature measured by Christ's fullness. Then we will no longer be little children, tossed by the waves and blown around by every wind of teaching, by human cunning with cleverness in the techniques of deceit. **But speaking the truth in love, let us grow in every way into Him who is the head—Christ.** *From Him the whole body, fitted and knit together by every supporting ligament, promotes the growth of the body for building up itself in love by the proper working of each individual part.*

Ephesians 4:12–16

The actual well seen is ideal.

—Thomas Carlyle[1]

Chapter Rationale

The Disciplers' Model provides a biblical and theological framework for the remainder of the text. Chapter One defines the seven elements of the Model and explains how they work together. We conclude the chapter by associating elements of the Model with secular counterparts in Educational Psychology. The goal of the chapter is to provide a Christian teaching context for secular theories of learning and development.

If you have read my earlier books,[2] you are familiar with the Disciplers' Model. There I provided a brief overview of the Model as an organizing tool for the texts. Here you will find a more extensive discussion of the Model's seven elements. These elements define a synergistic answer to the question, "How do I teach so that my learners grow in the Lord?" Understanding these elements will provide you a biblical framework for the study of the secular ideas of educational psychology.

Chapter Overview

➤ The Left Foundation Stone: The Bible

➤ The Right Foundation Stone: The Needs of People

➤ The Left Pillar: Helping People Think

➤ The Right Pillar: Helping People Value

➤ The Center Pillar: Helping People Relate

➤ The Capstone: Helping People Grow

➤ The Circle: Holy Spirit as Discipler

➤ The Relationship between the Disciplers' Model and Educational Psychology

➤ Faith in Scripture—Suspicion of Science

➤ *Chapter Concepts, Chapter Objectives, Discussion Questions*

Introduction

In 1971 I began teaching a Sunday school class for deaf college students attending Gallaudet College (where my wife and I worked as dormitory counselors) at Columbia Baptist Church in Falls Church, Virginia. There were no books on teaching deaf adults, and so I began to pray: "Lord, how can I teach so that these learners will grow up in You?" In response to this constant prayer, the Lord brought many experiences into the classroom sessions. In 1973 I began formal studies in educational psychology and philosophy at Southwestern Seminary. I was called as minister to the deaf at First Baptist Church, Irving, Texas, where I continued to teach deaf adults (1973–1976). In December 1976 I accepted the call to return to Columbia Baptist as their minister of education. In January 1977 the personal experiences and formal studies coalesced into what I called "The Disciplers' Model." The first publication of the Model appeared in the spring of 1977 as a series of eight articles in the church's weekly newsletter. Over the next two years, materials were added from teacher training meetings and teacher conferences. In 1979 the self-published *Disciplers* was produced and sold to nearly 1200 churches. In 1981 the text was revised and renamed *The Disciplers' Handbook* and has served as my basic text for Principles of Teaching classes at Southwestern since then.

Discipler's Model

The Model has been reinforced through nearly forty years of serving on church staffs as minister of education, teaching seminary students here and in the former Soviet Union, and leading church-based teacher conferences across the nation. I have found the Model to be an excellent bridge between secular psychological theories and a biblical worldview. We begin with the foundation: the left foundation stone is the Bible, God's eternal Word.

The Left Foundation Stone: The Bible

The left foundation stone of the Model represents the Bible, the Word of God. Unless our teaching produces a clearer understanding of the Bible, with its call to personal commitment to Christ and His Church, all our teaching efforts produce little more than "wood, hay, or straw" (1 Cor 3:12). For education to be rightly called "Christian," it must be built upon the sure foundation of God's Word.

How Does the Bible Define Itself?

Theories of inspiration thrive, and conflicting interpretations abound, but God's Word still speaks across the ages to people today. How does Scripture define itself?

Divinely Inspired. Scripture emphasizes that the Lord, not man, speaks through Scripture. "Take a scroll, and write on it all the words I [the Lord] have spoken to you" (Jer 36:2). "The word of the LORD came directly to Ezekiel the priest" (Ezek 1:3). "The Scripture had to be fulfilled that the Holy Spirit through the mouth of David spoke in advance" (Acts 1:16). "All Scripture is inspired by God and is profitable for teaching, for rebuking, for correcting, for training in righteousness (2 Tim 3:16). "Because no prophecy ever came by the will of man; instead, moved by the Holy Spirit, men spoke from God" (2 Pet 1:21). The Lord spoke, and man recorded the message. The Lord revealed Himself, and man recorded the messages.

Sacred. Scripture warns its readers and teachers not to alter it by adding to or taking away from it. "You must not add anything to what I command you or take anything away from it, so that you may keep the commands of the LORD your God I am giving you" (Deut 4:2). "Every word of God is pure; He is a shield to those who take refuge in Him. Don't add to His words, or He will rebuke you, and you will be proved a liar" (Prov 30:6). "And if anyone takes away from the words of this prophetic book, God will take away his share of the tree of life and the holy city, written in this book" (Rev 22:19). Handle Scripture carefully. It is sacred.

Powerful in Its Influence. Scripture is more than words and symbols. God's Word is an extension of God's power: "the gospel . . . is God's power for salvation to everyone who believes" (Rom 1:16). "Take the . . . sword of the Spirit, which is the word of God" (Eph 6:17). "For the word of

God is living and effective and sharper than any two-edged sword. . . ; it is a judge of the ideas and thoughts of the heart" (Heb 4:12). When we teach God's Word, we convey God's power.

Written for a Purpose. Scripture has a purpose, and that purpose is life in Christ. "But these are written so that you may believe Jesus is the Messiah, the Son of God, and by believing you may have life in His name" (John 20:31). That purpose is hope. "For whatever was written before was written for our instruction, so that through our endurance and through the encouragement of the Scriptures we may have hope" (Rom 15:4). That purpose is to warn us. "Now these things happened to them as examples, and they were written as a warning to us" (1 Cor 10:11). That purpose was to equip us for ministry. "All Scripture is inspired by God and is profitable for teaching, for rebuking, for correcting, for training in righteousness, so that the man of God may be complete, equipped for every good work" (2 Tim 3:16–17). That purpose is assurance of eternal life. "I have written these things to you who believe in the name of the Son of God, so that you may know that you have eternal life" (1 John 5:13).

Reveals Eternal Truth. Scripture moves us upward from our daily experiences to eternal principles. "Lord, Your word is forever; it is firmly fixed in heaven" (Ps 119:89). "The word of our God remains forever" (Isa 40:8). "My words will never pass away" (Matt 24:35). When we teach Scripture, we engage eternal blessings and consequences.

How Do Teachers Use the Bible?

God's Word is Eternal Truth. While Christians argue over various interpretations of Scripture, few argue about the eternal nature of Scripture. And yet, even among those who are most conservative in their view of Scripture, a significant question remains, "How do we handle Scripture as we teach?" Even with the highest regard for Scripture, we may not help our learners grow in the Lord. What makes the difference?

"Talk about it." A popular way to handle Scripture is to talk about it. I can remember spending hours each week preparing to "teach the lesson" on Sunday. I read the assigned passage, studied the accompanying teaching helps, and wrote out several pages of notes: my "lesson." On Sunday morning I stood behind a podium or at a desk and "taught my lesson." I can remember Sundays when I taught so hard (using sign language with deaf college students) that I sweat through my suits! Yet several days later, members of my class remembered little of what I had worked so hard to teach. How could they become "doers of the Word" if they couldn't remember what the Bible said?! Telling people about the Bible is a good first step, but there is a better way to help people grow as they learn.

"Let the Bible Speak!" A better way to handle Scripture in the classroom—and the approach I have found effective in changing learners—is to *let the Bible speak!* Teachers do well to ask thoughtful questions and lead learners into God's Word for the answers. Learners remember what they study far better than when we simply give them our own ready-made answers. The Bible, God's eternal Truth, is the sure foundation of discipling Bible study. Let the Word speak, that it may convict and comfort, warn and console, revive and refresh us—so we might become all He intends and do all He commands.

The Right Foundation Stone: The Needs of People

The companion foundation stone in the Model represents the needs of learners. Jesus taught people the meaning of Scripture by focusing it at their point of personal need. Zacchaeus was lonely. Jesus asked to have dinner with him (Luke 19:10). Jairus grieved at the death of his daughter. Jesus raised her to life (Mark 5:21–24,35–43). Nicodemus the Pharisee sought Jesus' words on the kingdom of God. Jesus gave him specific instructions (John 3). Jesus did not dine with everyone, nor raise all dead people, nor give special instructions to all. He met needs in the lives of people—the leper, the lame, the deaf, the blind, the lonely and the religious—and in doing so, taught us in tangible ways how much the Father loves us.

Jesus pointed to soils, light, salt, and sheep. He illustrated eternal truths with basic things that were familiar to those who pressed close to hear Him teach. He had no need of attendance prizes or candy or free trips to manipulate interest or enthusiasm. He spoke the Words of Life most of us hunger for! He shared with learners a caring Father Who wants the best for them. Jesus did not simply teach the truth. He taught truth in such a way that it became "truth that matters to me!"

What the Bible says is unchanging (Left Stone), but how we explain it varies from learner to learner (Right Stone). Why? Because our learners have different needs that are both general and specific.

General Learner Needs

A *general* need refers to a common characteristic of people in a given group. Age is one such factor. Preschoolers learn differently from children, children differently from youth, and youth differently from adults. Even various groupings of adults—singles, young marrieds, median adults, seniors—learn in distinctly different ways.

Learners within given age categories experience similar situations in life: growing, school, adolescence, marriage, family, home, career, retirement. Similarity of life experiences helps groups focus on the relevancy of Bible teachings.

Life situation is another general need. Children from dysfunctional or broken families learn differently than children in healthy families. Single adults differ from married adults of the same age.

Blue-collar workers see things differently from professional workers. Teachers do well to study the general life needs of their students and apply what they learn to their preparation and instruction.

Specific Learner Needs

A *specific* need refers to an individual characteristic of a single member of a given group. Specific needs include such experiences as personal failures or successes, past tragedies, present struggles, and times of spiritual drought. In any classroom, one finds emotional aches, pains, and scars. We discover the specific personal needs of our learners as we become better acquainted with them as individuals, persons, friends. Teachers do well to provide opportunities for learners to share themselves with the class—prayer concerns, personal experiences, and personal struggles. *How* we do this will be discussed a little later. *That* we do this demonstrates our concern for the needs of our learners and opens the door to deeper learning experiences.

The Two Stones Side by Side

Both foundation stones are required for the model to be stable. If either crumbles, the Model falls, reflecting teaching that does not result in spiritual growth, that is, growth "in the Lord."

When we spend too much class time emphasizing Bible content—recounting historical details, providing verse-by-verse explanations, analyzing language nuances, dissecting doctrinal principles—little time remains for connecting Eternal Truth to general or specific learner needs, or to what learners actually experience at home and at work. Learners leave the classroom feeling that they experienced a factual, but irrelevant, history lesson.

When we spend too much time emphasizing learner needs or concerns—allowing them to share personal opinions, tell personal stories, or chase personal rabbits—little time remains for connecting individual needs to Eternal Truths, to the answers found in Scripture. Learners hear each other's problems, but hear little of God's solutions.

Learners leave the classroom feeling that they have experienced little more than a superficial "group therapy" session. We need to connect learners' needs and experiences to Scripture, letting God's Word speak clearly to the discussion.

Neither irrelevant history lessons nor superficial sharing leads to spiritual growth. Teachers do well to intentionally build on both foundation stones to create an environment in which Truth speaks to contemporary need over time. Such an environment produces a personal teaching ministry that is both eternal and relevant.

I say "over time" because the balance between "Bible" and "needs" is not a 50–50 proposition. There are times when the meaning of a passage of Scripture requires more time than its personal application. When studying the prophet Hosea, for example, teachers would do well to provide a solid historical context to God's command that Hosea marry a prostitute (to illustrate Israel's unfaithfulness to God). This is not the time for group work and learner hunches. The Sermon on the Mount and the book of Revelation are other examples of heavy Bible emphasis.

On the other hand, there are times when the meaning of the passage is well-known and more time is required for personal reflection and application. When studying the Good Samaritan story, for example, teachers would do well to refrain from a verse-by-verse exegesis in favor of two sets of affective questions. The first set focuses on those who have been Good Samaritans to them: "Think about people in your life who have been Good Samaritans to you. What did they do for you? How did their help change you?" The second set focuses on their own experiences as Good Samaritans to others: "Think about times you have been a Good Samaritan to others. What did you do for them? How did helping them change you?" Details of the passage can be explained in the process of sharing testimonies. Those without testimonies may well consider doing more for others, becoming more of a Good Samaritan personally.

"Over time," teachers address both eternal truths and personal needs in a relevant, biblical teaching ministry. We clearly see this balance of Word and needs in the Gospel accounts of Jesus' teaching.

The Stacking of Stones?

It might be helpful to consider one other way to look at the relationship between Bible and needs. This particular suggestion was first made by a Russian Baptist pastor in a course taught in Almaty,

Kazakhstan, but I've had American students raise the same issue. During my summary of the Stones, the pastor raised his hand and said, "I think your model is inadequate. May I change it?" He was seated on the front row,[3] and I handed him the marker: "Certainly," I said. He stepped to the white board and re-drew the Model.

Satisfied with himself and his changes, he turned, snapped the cap back on the marker, and said "God's Word is fundamental to everything else. It provides us all the answers we need. Even the needs of our lives are drawn from a proper understanding of Scripture. I believe this is a better perspective. How can our changing needs be considered equal to God's eternal Word?"

It was an excellent question, and he was certainly correct in his analysis. But the class was stunned by his audacity and sat in silence waiting to see how the professor would respond to his correction. I began with praise. "I really like the changes you have made here. It emphasizes the eternal nature of God's Word and makes the Bible the basis for discussions of 'real needs' in the lives of learners. But, may I ask you a question?"

"Yes, of course," the student responded, now sitting at his desk, smiling.

"In your version of the Model, if I pull the Bible stone out of the Model altogether, does the Model fall?"

He looked at the whiteboard and slowly shook his head "No." The smile was gone. He was thinking.

"Or the Needs stone? If I completely disregard the needs of the learners in my class, does the Model fall?

More quickly this time, he said, "No."

"That's the problem. We are not equating God's Word with learner Needs. We are saying for spiritual growth to occur, we need to connect God's Truth with the relevant needs of learners. We are saying both Truth and Need are necessary for relevant changes to occur in individual learners.

He looked back at the board, slowly nodded his head, and said, "I agree." He smiled again, more enthusiastically. And the class breathed a sigh of relief.

The Left Pillar: Helping People Think

Learners grow in the Lord when they understand, clearly and correctly, the meaning of God's Word. Such understanding grows from analysis of texts, asking and answering questions, weighing the opinions of others, and deriving biblical principles that confront personal views. The objective focus of the Thinking Pillar emphasizes the translation of Bible passages into principles, standards, and ideals, which in turn informs the decisions they make in everyday situations. How do we teach so that thinking skills are improved?

Three Stages of Thinking

The city of Colossae, situated in the Lycus Valley in southwestern Asia Minor, was home to early gnostic philosophy that emphasized knowledge as the means to God. The apostle Paul wrote the Colossian church, using the words of early gnostics—knowledge, understanding, wisdom, mystery—while drawing distinctions between Christian and gnostic thinking. In making his case for the gospel, Paul accentuated the role of rational thought in spiritual growth: "We haven't stopped praying for you. We are asking that you may be filled with the knowledge of His will in all wisdom and spiritual understanding" (Col 1:9). Here Paul presents us with three rational components of spiritual growth. These are knowledge, understanding, and spiritual wisdom.

Filled with the knowledge of His will. Educators define *knowledge* specifically, differentiating between "knowing" and "understanding." To *know* refers to the ability to recall facts or to identify appropriate facts from a list. *Knowledge* consists of collections of facts that one can recall. Philosophers define knowledge more broadly, referring to facts, concepts, and principles accumulated through personal study or experience. Paul's term in Colossians reflects this latter definition—and more.

There are three major Greek words translated *knowledge* in Scripture. These are *oida* (intellectual or academic knowledge), *gnosis* (knowledge accumulated through personal study or experience), and *epignosis* (full or accurate knowledge, or knowledge which "goes beyond"). Paul did not use *oida* because he knew first hand that knowledge of God's will does not come through mere academic study. He was a graduate of the University of Tarsus and a zealous student of Gamaliel. Academic knowledge of his religion led him to persecute Christians, opposing God's will in Christ.

Paul used *gnosis* in his earlier letters, but this word became the moniker for the heretical gnostics[4] (*men of knowledge*, see 1 Tim 6:20). False teachers in Colossae reflected an early form of Gnosticism and assumed, as *knowing ones*, superiority over the "simple faith" proclaimed by Paul. So Paul employs here *epignosis (epi-gnosis)*, a knowledge that emphasizes experiential learning derived from a personal relationship[5] with Jesus Christ. Paul was confronting early gnostics who taught that salvation required more: special knowledge, obtained through secret rituals, ceremonies and *mysteries*.[6]

Curtis Vaughn[7] once explained the term this way: *epignosis* reaches out and grasps its object, and is in turn grasped by that object. When my wife and I married, I knew very little about football. But her family loved football, and I began to learn about the game. As I began to grasp the essentials of the game, football took hold of me. As I have studied brain research these past two years, brain science has taken hold of me. To possess the *epignosis* of God's will means to take hold of His will—personally and relationally—and for God's will to take hold of us.[8]

But Paul goes further. He prays that we be "filled with" *epignosis*. The phrase carries the idea of being *fully equipped*—a ship ready to sail or a soldier ready for battle. Further, the term means *to be controlled by.* One filled with anger is controlled by anger. One filled with the Spirit is controlled by the Spirit.[9] Paul's prayer is that Christians will grow in Christ to the place that they thoroughly equipped and controlled by God's will.

Spiritual understanding. Paul reinforces *epignosis* with *sunesis*—a "mental putting together,"[10]—which speaks of clear analysis and decision-making in applying this knowledge to various problems.[11]

Educators define understanding as the process of organizing knowledge (facts) into concepts and principles that can be used outside the learning environment. Learners who *understand* can explain fact-based concepts in their own words. They can give correct examples of what words mean, as well as what they do not. They can create fresh examples and illustrations to clarify meanings. Paul certainly means all of this but adds the adjective *spiritual.* "Spiritual understanding" stresses the ability to "act and think spiritually."[12]

We mentioned Paul's academic studies (*oida*) earlier. But when he met the Risen Lord on his way to Damascus, his academic understandings became unhinged—he saw things in a new way. During three years in an Arabian desert, he restudied the Old Testament in light of the Resurrected Lord. Before salvation, as one "circumcised the eighth day; of the nation of Israel, of the tribe of Benjamin, a Hebrew born of Hebrews; as to the law, a Pharisee; as to zeal, persecuting the church; as to the righteousness that is in the law, blameless" (Phil 3:4–6), he *knew what the Old Testament says.* He met Christ and began to *understand what the Old Testament means.* As his spiritual understanding blossomed into full-bloomed faith, he declared that "everything that was a gain to me, I have considered to be a loss because of Christ" (Phil 3:7).

Wisdom. Paul reinforces "full knowing" (*epignosis*) yet again with *sophia*, a term that refers to practical know-how that comes from God.[13] Such wisdom allows disciples to apply general knowledge to particular occasions, and to suit it to all emergencies.[14] James describes biblical wisdom as "first pure, then peace-loving, gentle, compliant, full of mercy and good fruits, without favoritism and hypocrisy" (Jas 3:17). James' focus is biblical *action.*

Wisdom is biblical understanding put into action in practical ways. At least, this is my understanding of Jesus' definition in Matthew 7:24–26: "Everyone who hears these words of Mine and *acts on them* will be like a sensible [*wise*, NKJV] man" and "everyone who hears these words of Mine and *doesn't act on them* will be like a foolish man" [*emphasis mine*—RY]. We may *know* the Bible, and we may *understand* the Bible, but we are considered "wise" by Jesus only when we practice biblical truths, living by them. Jesus clearly distinguishes between knowing the Bible and living biblically.

Rational Growth Is an Upward Spiral in Transformation

The process of spiritual, rational growth is continuous. We grow in personal, experiential knowledge of God and His kingdom (*epignosis*). We clarify our own perceptions and perspectives about life and the world in light of God's Word (*sunesis*). We live out what we know and understand in everyday problems and situations (*sophia*). Knowledge begets understanding, understanding begets wisdom, and wisdom begets further knowledge in an upward spiral. The result is life "transformed by the renewing of your mind" (Rom 12:2).

Paul defines the purpose of this growth, this spiral, this life transformation as follows:

So that you may **walk worthy** of the Lord, **fully pleasing** to Him, **bearing fruit** in every good work and **growing** in the knowledge of God. May you be **strengthened** with **all power,** according to **His glorious might,** for all **endurance and patience, with joy** giving **thanks to the Father,** who has **enabled you** to share in the saints' inheritance in the light. He has **rescued us** from the domain of darkness and **transferred us** into the kingdom of the Son He loves, in whom **we have redemption,** the **forgiveness** of sins" (Col 1:10–14).

We teach in a way that helps learners think biblically, in class and in life. The result, over time, are lives that are *worthy of the Lord. Lives pleasing to God. Fruitful* lives. *Strong and enduring, patient and joyful* lives. *Rescued, redeemed, and forgiven* lives. Why? Because learners continually grow as they know what the Bible says, understand what it means, and live as it commands.

The factor that produces life-centered growth and prevents self-serving academics is the focus of the process: *God's* will. Paul prays that the Colossians will be filled with the *epignosis* "of His will." God wants us to know His will (Acts 22:14) and to understand His will (Eph 5:17). We are not the Lord's robots. We are His friends, to whom He makes known the things of God (John 15:13–15). This is the learning process of the Left Pillar.

The Right Pillar: Helping People Value

Learners grow in the Lord when they embrace biblical truths personally, confronting their own attitudes with God's Word and rearranging personal priorities according to God's Word. The subjective focus of the Valuing pillar addresses emotional aspects of Christian growth and maturity. Jesus wore no pious mask to hide His inner feelings, nor did He gush frothy feelings for all to see. He was not controlled by emotions, nor did He repress them. He owned them and used them to manage

life's circumstances. He directed them into tangible expressions of love and concern for others. Jesus was authentic in the way He reacted to life. He was neither a pessimistic prophet of doom, nor an optimistic Pollyanna.[15] Jesus faced the world realistically—meeting life as it was—and responded appropriately to the events of His life.

When His good friend Lazarus died, Jesus didn't shout "Praise the Lord Anyway!"[16] He wept (John 11:35). When His disciples were exhausted by the press of the crowds, Jesus did not stir them up with false enthusiasm. He led them to a place of rest and recuperation (Mark 6:31). When suffering personal agony on the cross, He had the presence to arrange for the care of His mother (John 19:26). We'll look at other specific examples from Jesus' life in the sections to follow.

The apostle Paul was a rugged theologian-missionary. And yet he wrote of spiritual sacrifice (Rom 12:1), humility (12:3,16), belonging to one another (12:5), love (12:9; 13:8–10), family affection (12:10), fervency (12:11), rejoicing, patience, and persistence (12:12), sharing with others, hospitality (12:13), empathy (12:15), peace with others (12:18), benevolence toward others (12:20), submission to authorities (13:1), and acceptance of others (14:1) All of these are heart issues, decisions to be made in our personal relations with each other. These personal attitudes move beyond settled doctrine and stand above ritualized actions.

Disciplers help learners develop a well-balanced emotional life, one which reflects positive attitudes toward life and others, as well as priorities that God Himself controls. While we are powerless to impose our values and attitudes on others (Rom 14:13–23), we can teach in ways that allow the Spirit to quicken biblical attitudes and change personal priorities. Let's look at some of these ways.

Emotional Freedom

Growth in emotional characteristics requires an environment conducive to emotional processes. Such an environment is safe from humiliation or anger. It is a place where self-protective masks can be removed without fear of attack. A place where "real in-the-now life" can be discussed and God's answers found. Two essential qualities of such a warm environment are class openness and a personal willingness to share.

Openness. Attitudinal learning proceeds better in a safe and caring atmosphere than in a cool and indifferent one. Learners do better when they are open to one another. Teachers have control over how open learners will be. I knew a seminary professor who would begin every class by saying, "You are here to learn from me. I am not here to entertain your ignorance. So, please do not interrupt my lectures with your questions." What level of openness do you think existed in his classrooms? He obviously did not want openness in his classes, which might lead to interruptions to his lectures. He wanted his students to sit quietly. Not surprisingly, he achieved this every semester.

Jesus changed the life of the woman at the well by bridging the cultural chasm between them. Racial and gender conventions created the chasm: a male did not speak to a female in public. A Jew did not speak to a Samaritan at all. But Jesus placed little value on social conventions that kept people from the Truth. So He built a bridge between them. He talked about her major interest: water. He was open to her, a Samaritan woman. She became open to His words. He then told her of the Messiah, the Thirst Quencher, the Water of Life. She opened herself to His teaching, learned from Him, believed Him, and told others about Him (John 4:1–30).

Openness grows as individuals within the group become willing to share themselves, appropriately, with others. Teachers create this by modeling personal openness toward students and encouraging student questions, explanations, and "interruptions."

Willingness to share. A second essential for emotionally warm classrooms is a willingness to share with others. Willingness to share is a strong indication of the level of trust in the class. Teachers weaken trust when we create tension in the classroom. We do this by putting learners on the spot to pray or answer questions, embarrassing learners with sharp replies, standing behind a podium or sitting behind a desk, excessive lecturing, or responding to questions or comments with frustration. We also weaken trust levels when we fail to protect members from one another: sharp disagreements, personal attacks, and even heavy sighs can hurt others to the point they refuse to share, or worse in the case of voluntary Bible studies, refuse to attend at all.

Disciplers build trust between themselves and learners by caring for them, listening to them, and responding in kind ways. We stand beside a podium or sit beside a table, otherwise they become psychological barriers between us and our learners. We engage learners with subjective questions[17] throughout our lectures in order to stir them up to share personal experiences related to the topic. If possible, we seat learners in a semi-circle or U-shape so they can see each other and more easily interact with each other. We protect learners from each other, making peace when disagreements arise. In most cases, we lead by example. In some cases, we may have to instruct learners in how to disagree "agreeably," or help them understand how to express opposing views without attacking others. In all these ways, we lay a foundation for civil discourse and, eventually, trust. In that environment of mutual trust, sharing will increase.

Removing Emotional Barriers

In every class we teach, we will find learners who have emotional barriers that keep them from trusting, sharing, and growing. It is the subjective side of the Model that touches them—not doctrine, nor logic, nor words. The old bromide "Jesus cared before He shared" is, in fact, true, for God so loved the world that He sent His only Son (John 3:16) to "give His life—a ransom for many" (Matt 20:28), and to rise again to be our sole Mediator before God (1 Tim 2:5). Emotional barriers are lowered by the gentle touch of caring, listening, and loving. There are learners in every class who have personal hurts, secret burdens, or heavy hang-ups that keep them from coming to the Lord or growing in the Lord. It is the empathetic side of teaching that makes the difference in these situations.

Emotional Growth

Most conflicts and disputes in classes or congregations grow out of symptoms of emotional immaturity: rash comments, fickle conduct, irritability, fear, anxiety, short temper, ambition, and self-interest. The subjective focus of the Model reduces the effects of these destructive traits as learners develop love for and trust in one another. Eventually, learners will grow out of these negative traits as they replace them with alternatives that are more positive.

Subjective teaching strengthens positive emotional traits as learners honestly accept themselves and others. These positive traits include such things as working well with other learners, managing temperamental impulses, expressing good feelings without embarrassment, refraining from worry, and accepting constructive criticism.

Jesus brought unity to the fragmented personality of the Gadarene demoniac (Mark 5:1–20). He can also bring emotional coherence out of the chaos of uncontrolled feelings. Such growth is ever more needed in the face of a society increasingly broken by excessive emotionalism and selfishness.

Balance Left and Right Pillars

The Left (objective thinking) and Right (subjective valuing) Pillars work together to support the Capstone of the Model. Both are necessary because we were created in the image of God as thinking-feeling beings. Maintaining balance between rational and emotional dynamics in learning is not easy. We naturally drift toward one pillar or the other, and in the extremes, spiritual growth wanes. One extreme produces an unfeeling dogmatism that rejects the emotional and distorts the rational. The other produces an unthinking superficiality that rejects scholarship and distorts the emotional.

If teachers consistently over-emphasize the objective side of learning—memorizing facts, explaining concepts, creating illustrations, deriving principles, making judgments—while neglecting the sub-

jective, their classrooms inevitably become cold, theoretical, and overly structured. There is little room in such an environment for personal stories, personal questions, or concern for the feelings of others. There is little time or opportunity for learners to build community in the context of the class. This is a serious distortion because Jesus declared we are not to be identified as His disciples by doctrinal explanations, but by our love for each other. "By this all people will know that you are My disciples, if you have love for one another" (John 13:35). Jesus calls us to be "as children" (Mark 10:15) in terms of our humble trust and dependence on the Lord for righteousness and strength.

On the other hand, if teachers consistently overemphasize the subjective side of learning—freedom, spontaneity, sharing personal stories and opinions, interaction with minimal structure—while neglecting the objective, their classrooms inevitably become warm, superficial, and chaotic. When learning is based on personal experience alone, the result is unstable, emotional "fluff." Without understanding God's Truth, learners are vulnerable to false teachers, which Jesus warned were nothing less than ravenous wolves in sheep's clothing (Matt 7:15). The Ephesian Christians were immature believers who were tossed back and forth by smooth-talking false teachers who used deceitful methods to entrap them in their schemes (Eph 4:14). Immature believers have been entrapped in similar ways throughout Church history. Freedom comes by knowing the Truth (John 8:32), becoming "shrewd as serpents and as harmless as doves" (Matt 10:16).

It is not a matter of being childlike *or* wise, but childlike *and* wise. Not cynically wise, nor callously wise, but lovingly wise. Not childishly trusting, nor naively trusting, but realistically trusting. Paul captures this objective-subjective tension when he writes, "speaking the truth (Left Pillar) in love (Right Pillar), let us grow in every way into . . . Christ" (Eph 4:15).

We are not to shout the truth so harshly or argue our positions so strongly that it breaks bruised reeds or puts out smoldering wicks of faith (Matt 12:19–20). Nor are we to "love" others so sentimentally that we lose our integrity in the name of graciousness by winking at sin. We are to speak the truth in a loving, loyal manner. We are to love others with integrity. In this tension, we find favor with both God and mankind (Prov 3:4).

As with the Stones, we balance Left and Right Pillars *over time*. In any given session, we may emphasize deep scholarship or personal openness to the exclusion of the other. Teachers determine the appropriate approach for any given session based on the particulars. These are the specific nature of the passage and the needs of the learners. Over time, however, teachers do well to balance rational and emotional approaches to learning. Like steel-belted radials, the rational provides strength; the emotional provides comfort.[18]

The Center Pillar: Helping People Relate

When Pharisees challenged Jesus to name the Greatest Commandment, He condensed the Law and the Prophets into two statements of relationship: "Love the Lord your God with all your heart,

with all your soul, and with all your mind. This is the greatest and most important commandment. The second is like it: Love your neighbor as yourself" (Matt 22:37–39).

Our relationship with the Father ("Love the Lord your God") begins with faith in Christ (John 14:6). Spiritual power for repentance and renewal, praise and thanksgiving, worship and service, come through this vital link with the Lord.

Relationship with others ("Love your neighbor") involves fellowship, befriending, ministering, equipping, witnessing, and going. Jesus established the Church to establish and strengthen relationships with God and with fellow believers. As we worship God, study His Word, share joys and concerns as "brothers and sisters," and reach out to others, our lives are joined together. A retired army colonel and godly Bible teacher once described the church to me as "People with people with Jesus in the middle." We build "community," the "Body of Christ," the "Church Family." Of course, this relational dynamic extends to the Christian classroom, even in formal educational settings. This is the central pillar of the Disciplers' Model.

Masks on the Fringe

In every group—congregation or class—there are those who live on the fringes of community. In churches, they come to services from time to time, but avoid commitments that would usher them into family life. They keep up appearances but never build bridges to others. They have nowhere to lay aside emotional masks or discuss the real in their lives with others. Then some tragedy strikes: a death, an illness, a divorce. They search in vain for "the church" and for "God" and wonder why neither can be tuned in like their cable vision. The *koinonia* of Scripture and Church cannot be manufactured in the moment of tragedy—it grows over time. There are no shortcuts. Jesus established the Church to reach the world with the gospel (Matt 28:19–20), but this mission is anchored in the family network of "brothers and sisters," caring for one another. The Church is a living laboratory of human relationships.

Raw Materials of Relational Growth in the Church

Having served as a minister of education in six Baptist churches over a span of eighteen years—in various regions, of various sizes, with various structures—I realize that the irritations, conflicts, and confrontations that occur to some degree in every congregation of believers are a normal part of Christian growth. This social dimension of learning is an essential part of the growth of *koinonia*, of relationship, of family. We are called into the Family because of a mutual love for Jesus. But we are people with varying backgrounds, cultures, languages, and interests. Conflicts are part of the supernatural process of becoming "one family in Him." These social dilemmas and people problems are the raw materials of Christian character and community. God works in and through these human situations to grow us into the image of His Son, for "all things work together for the good of those who love God: those who are called according to His purpose" (Rom 8:28).

One day years ago Barb and I were walking along a beach near Clearwater, Florida. We saw people bending down to pick up something from the sand. When we looked closer, we discovered the sand was dotted with small black stones. They were smooth and well-polished. As we walked around the beach and into the bay, we noticed rough, black rocks dotting the sand. Closer inspection revealed that the smooth stones of the beach were made of the same material as the rough rocks. The elements that made the difference between dull and polished, rough and smooth, and unattractive and beautiful were the pounding of the surf and the grinding of the sand.

Learners who choose to remain aloof from others are like the stones in the bay, undisturbed and unchanging. Learners who risk relationship and share with others despite disappointments and occasional mistakes become like the polished stones. Spiritual unity develops in believers as they gather in small groups to study the Bible, to share with each other, to affirm each other, to minister growth to one another.

Relational Growth in the Classroom

The foregoing discussion focuses on the Church family because it is here we find relational resources for long-term spiritual growth. We can, however, draw lessons from these principles for building relationships in semester-long classes.

Relational bridge building remains a goal of discipling, but disciplers have much less time within a single semester for relationships to develop. When the class environment promotes freedom and openness, willingness to share with others, personal safety, and time for interactive experiences, learners have many more opportunities to connect with classmates. Teachers do well to provide intentional opportunities for interaction among students by using frequent, small-group discussions as well as longer-term group projects.

The three Pillars of the Model reflect three kinds of human growth. The rational helps learners process the facts and concepts of a course objectively. The emotional helps learners process the values and priorities of the course personally. The relational helps learners process course content in community with others. These three stand firmly on the Foundation Stones and, in turn, support the Capstone of discipling Bible study, which is "growing up" in the Lord.

The Capstone: Helping People Grow

The Capstone of the Model represents the process of growing individual believers in the Lord, of helping them become like Christ through a relevant and practical study of God's Word. In the begin-ning of the chapter, I shared with you my constant prayer as I struggled to teach deaf college students in the 1970s: "Lord, how can I teach so that learners grow up into You?"

Over the next eight years, the Lord taught me ways to disciple my learners through dramatic experiences in classrooms in Virginia and Texas and formal educational studies at Southwestern Seminary. During the early days of my first full-time church staff position,[19] the Model coalesced into the seven elements you find here. The previous five elements of the Model exist to support the Capstone, which is growth in Christ. This element finds its biblical anchor in Paul's glorious description of spiritual growth in Ephesians 4:11–16.

Paul's Treatise on Growth

Paul begins his focus on maturational growth with leaders. "And He [Christ] personally gave some to be apostles, some prophets, some evangelists, some pastors and teachers . . . ." (Eph 4:11). When God wants something to be done, He provides leaders to make it happen. The first three kinds of leaders were itinerant leaders: "apostles" (*sent ones*), whom we might call "missionaries" today .Prophets are gifted speakers who proclaim God's Word with clarity and power. Evangelists are gifted speakers who draw listeners to faith. "Pastors and teachers," or "the pastor-teacher" (*The Message*), are local church leaders who provide care (shepherd) and instruction (teacher). These leaders are gifts to the Church ("And He personally gave").

Why was the Church "gifted" with these leaders? What is the primary task of these leaders? Paul says, "for the training of the saints in the work of ministry" (12a). The work of pastor-teachers is the training ("full equipping" *Amplified Bible*) of saints ("Christians" *Message*) in the work of ministry. As military leaders train and equip their units to wage war, so pastor-teachers equip their flocks to wage spiritual war.

What is the purpose of this equipping for ministry? "to build up the body of Christ" (12b). The term "build up" does not refer to church *size*, but to church *maturity* ("growing into a mature man," 13b).

What is the nature of this maturity? Spiritual unity is demonstrated by "unity in the faith and in the knowledge of God's Son" (13a). Christian maturity draws individuals into a common faith in Christ and into an intimate relationship with Him. Paul uses the term *epignosis* ("knowledge that goes beyond") that we discussed earlier regarding Col 1:9.

How mature does the Church have to be? How long must we teach, shepherd, and equip? Our task is done, says Paul, when everyone in the Church is as mature as Jesus—"with a stature measured by Christ's fullness" (13c).

What is the result of this growing maturity? "Then we will no longer be little children, tossed by the waves and blown around by every wind of teaching, by human cunning with cleverness in the techniques of deceit" (14). We will no longer be childishly immature, or emotionally fickle, or rationally gullible—tricked by religious con artists who mouth spiritual words, but lust after worldly power.

Instead, we will know and understand the Truth (Left Pillar), and we will speak it and live it in a loving way (Right Pillar). By doing so, we will grow up into Christ (Capstone) (15). Further, Christ, the Head, draws us together into oneness, a *koinonia*, a Body of loving relationships (Center Pillar) "by the proper working of each individual part" (16).

When these elements—Truth, love, koinonia, spiritual growth—are present in a Christian classroom, learners have every opportunity to grow in Christ, to discover and use their gifts, and to have life-changing influence in the lives of others for Jesus' sake.

The Circle: Holy Spirit as Discipler

The final element in this discussion of the Disciplers' Model is the surrounding Circle, which represents the surrounding and indwelling Presence of the Holy Spirit of God. It is the Holy Spirit Who breathes life into lifeless lessons.

We have seen the extremes that teachers create by overemphasizing one element of the Model over another. More Bible instruction than learner care, over time, produces sessions of "irrelevant history." More learner care, over time, than Bible instruction produces sessions of "group therapy." More structured thinking than spontaneous sharing creates an impersonal, unfeeling "dogmatism." More spontaneous sharing than structured thinking creates a personal, unthinking "superficiality." It is the Holy Spirit, the Spirit of Christ,[20]

Who holds these elements together in balanced tension—"Eternal Truth speaking to personal needs," and "Speaking the truth in love"—to produce spiritual growth. It is the Holy Spirit Who leads us beyond shallow socializing to the mutual ministry of *koinonia*. It is the Holy Spirit Who moves us beyond words and feelings to Christian action.

How do disciplers engage the Holy Spirit to teach? What do we do to open up spiritual communication lines? Three essential attitudes answer these questions: prayer, priority, and position.

Prayer

It is easy for Christian teachers to assume the presence of the Lord in our classrooms. After all, isn't God omnipresent? Aren't we serving Him? Are we not conducting our teaching ministries in churches and Christian classrooms? Although the Lord is everywhere, He does not demonstrate His presence, or make Himself tangibly present, unless we intentionally invite Him to participate. The self-sufficiency of the church of Laodicea shut out the Lord through their presumed self-sufficiency, wealth, and health. The Risen Lord Jesus was nauseated by the church's tepid religiosity (Rev 3:16). He called individuals to fellowship with Him. "Listen! I stand at the door and knock. If anyone hears My voice and opens the door, I will come in to him and have dinner with him, and he with Me" (3:20).

Teachers can, in the same way, shut classrooms and pulpits to the Lord's presence through self-sufficiency. Whether the self-sufficiency flows from educational training, doctrinal purity, or personal status, it locks spiritual doors against the moving and transforming work of the Lord. Fellowship with Him is not automatic. Teachers who wish *the Lord* to teach learners must intentionally welcome Him. This is done through prayer: "Lord Jesus, come!"

We pray for class members by name, asking the Lord to focus their hearts and minds. We ask the Lord to use personal life experiences in learners to reinforce truths that will be addressed. We ask the Lord to prepare ready learners for their study.

We pray for our own preparation—spiritually, as we depend on the Lord and study the Word and educationally, as we prepare lesson plans (objectives, learning readiness, structure, conclusion, and assignment)—so that we will be able to help learners grow in the Lord. We invite the Lord into our own study and preparation. We ask Him to correct our mistakes, to suggest better approaches, and to generally guide us to teach more effectively than we can teach *in the flesh*.

We pray for our own execution of teaching plans, and for the real changes that the Lord will make in learners' lives. After the sessions, we invite the Lord to guide our review and critique of what happened during the session, and how we can improve the process.

At every step of the process, we welcome the Lord of Life into the life-changing process of engaging learners with God's Word and leading them to live out its message. "If anyone hears My voice and opens the door, I will come in." It is the Lord's presence, and only His presence, that transforms history lessons into spiritual transformations.

Priority

A Christian's first priority is God's kingdom. "But seek first the kingdom of God" (Matt 6:33). It is an essential command, since "accepting Christ" means surrendering personal agendas to His (Matt 16:24–26). Despite the Lord's clear command and Scripture's clear demand, Christian teaching is often plagued by the very human notion of turf. The term refers to *personal* kingdoms that teachers build "in the name of the Lord."

Such personal turf is often found in adult Sunday school organizations where teachers work with classes for years. Somewhere along the line, classes become the personal possessions of teachers. *My* room. *My* members. *My* position. The only antidote is an intentional focus on the absolute priority of God's kingdom.

Disciplers see their work as part of the larger work of God. Teachers avoid tendencies of turf by supporting decisions that strengthen the larger good (of the department, the division, and the church as a whole), even if those decisions cause us some inconvenience. Room changes.[21] Literature choices.[22] Organizational structures.[23] Enlistment of teachers from within our classes.[24]

Issues of turf exist in Christian schools as well. Personal kingdom building takes the shape of specialty degrees, departments, and course structures. Human turf focuses on "me and mine," securing resources and priorities for personal interests at the expense of "His and ours."

Disciplers are mature enough to forego personal kingdoms as they maintain the proper priority of God's. Such humility opens the door for the Holy Spirit to work—to teach, to equip, to call—among learners in our classes and churches.

Position

"If anyone wants to be first, he must be last of all and servant of all" (Mark 9:35). This was Jesus' response to the Twelve, who had been arguing among themselves about who among them was greatest (Mark 9:34). From the human tendency of turf grows another, more ominous human tendency, which is the desire to be great. Rank Hath Its Privilege is common among human beings and speaks of a position of control over others.

Talk of sacrifice and service is common. How often have we heard leaders make personal demands of their followers out of a sense of sacrifice? But the desire for power infects any leader who does not consciously and continuously surrender to the Lord. Jesus came to earth "to serve and to give His life—a ransom for many" (Matt 20:28). Jesus occupies the most powerful position in history, and yet He served. Satan twists this and encourages Christian leaders to serve by means of forcing others to do their will. The choice is clear. Leaders either grasp positions of power over others ("It must not be like that among you!" Matt 20:25–26), or they serve as examples to the flock and are lifted to positions of power by God (1 Pet 5:6).

Teachers do well to check themselves intentionally and regularly: are we controllers or servants? Where the Spirit leads, there are servants. Spiritual leaders have influence as they serve others, but they eschew human power and position. Spiritual service does not expect special treatment, nor does it engage in political control. Spiritual servants hold positions of influence loosely, ready to move on to other work, wherever and whatever that may be, at the leading of the Spirit. It is obvious that Holy Spirit can work in and through such servant leaders to do kingdom work more than He can through political bosses who push personal agendas and build personal kingdoms *in Jesus' name*. "If anyone wants to be first, he must be last of all and servant of all" (Mark 9:35).

Spiritual Teaching

These aspects of spiritual teaching—prayer, priority, and position—rise directly out of dependence on and submission to the Holy Spirit. Programs come and go, plans succeed and fail, educational fads thrive and fade. But through all our efforts runs the Golden Threads of God's educational goals: to draw, win, mature, and equip people in Christ. This holy work proceeds best with surrendered disciplers, teachers who find true success as they fasten their eyes on Him.

As we have seen throughout this introductory chapter, our calling reaches higher than transmitting lists of religious facts. We are called to make disciples (Matt 28:19): "to train the saints in the work of ministry, to build up the body of Christ, until we all reach unity in the faith and in the knowledge of God's Son, growing into a mature man with a stature measured by Christ's fullness" (Eph 4:12–13). This is our spiritual mandate as Christian teachers. What does the field of educational psychology have to offer in helping us understand the processes of human learning?

The Relationship between the Disciplers' Model and Educational Psychology

If the Disciplers' Model appeals to you, then educational psychology will enhance your perceptions, attitudes, and skills as a Christian teacher, a discipler. Educational psychology speaks to six of the seven elements of the Model directly. We introduce the links between the Model and educational psychology here. The rest of the text is devoted to establishing the place of educational psychology in Christian teaching.

The Left Foundation Stone and Content Mastery

The left foundation stone of the Model represents the Bible, God's Eternal Word. The focus is on letting the *Bible speak* to learners' needs, concepts, attitudes, and lifestyles. The analogy in the secular field of educational psychology is educational content, the *subject of study*. Teachers provide learners substantially more in content mastery when they demonstrate fluent understanding of the subjects they teach. Fluency in one's subjects is shown in tangible ways by the clear use of vocabulary, course concepts and principles, hierarchies of ideas, distinctions of categories, and the relationships among them. Of particular importance are the ideas of Jean Piaget (conceptual organization, Chapter Four), Jerome Bruner and Constructivism (cognitive structure, Chapter Eight), and Information Processing Theory (meaningfulness, Chapter Nine).

The Right Foundation Stone and Individual Differences

The right foundation stone of the Model represents the needs of learners. Educational psychology addresses the importance of individual differences and individual development. We will focus on Erik Erikson (personality development, Chapter Three), Jean Piaget (cognitive differences, Chapter Four), Lawrence Kohlberg (moral reasoning differences, Chapter Five), as well as the remains of Humanistic Learning Theories (Growth of Self, Chapter Ten), and motivational differences (Chapter Thirteen). We will analyze ways to target learner needs through writing and using instructional objectives (Chapter Twelve).

The Left Pillar and Cognitive Theories of Learning

The Left Pillar represents the process of helping learners think biblically. Educational psychology addresses the rational process of thought in the cognitive development theories of Jean Piaget and Lev Vygotsky (Chapter Four), and Jerome Bruner and Constructivism (Chapter Eight). We will also highlight Albert Bandura's Observational theory of learning, which has become increasingly more cognitive over the years (Chapter Seven).

The Right Pillar and Humanistic Theories of Learning

The Right Pillar represents the process of helping learners unmask and share themselves—experiences, perspectives, values—with others. Educational psychology addresses these issues in humanistic theories of learning and motivation, which emphasize emotions, values, and personal experiences. We will differentiate among classical humanism, secular humanism, and educational humanism, discussing the strengths and weaknesses of the theories of Abraham Maslow and Carl Rogers for Christian teaching (Chapter Ten). We will also chronicle the demise of Humanism as a theory of learning, and the synthesis of self-development in Constructivist theories of learning (particularly "radical constructivism," Chapter Eight).

The Center Pillar: Social Learning, Constructivism, and Cooperative Learning

The central pillar represents the building of relationships—community, *koinonia*—among learners. Educational psychology addresses these issues in the work of Lev Vygotsky (social learning, Chapter Four), Constructivism (group dynamics, Chapter Eight), Cooperative Learning processes (Chapter Fourteen), and the impact of social relationships on individual development (Erik Erikson, Chapter Three).

The Capstone and Maturation

The capstone of the Model is growth in Christ. Educational psychology addresses the issue of growth in terms of human maturation through learning. We will study implications of selected theorists—behavioral (growth of skills), cognitive (grow of understanding), and humanistic (growth of one's value system)—for human growth through learning.

The Circle and _____

The Circle of the Model represents the infilling and surrounding power of the Holy Spirit in the teaching process. As a secular discipline, educational psychology does not address the issue of spiritual growth. As science, educational psychology defines learning processes without reference to God. This exclusion of the supernatural should not surprise us, since science limits itself to natural processes. The truth is that we cannot put God in a test tube. The Holy Spirit is like the wind, blowing where He will (John 3:8). When science attempts to formulate definitions of human spirituality, the results bear no resemblance to what we have experienced as people of faith.[25]

Faith in Scripture—Suspicion of Science

Scripture declares that God designed us in specific ways to learn of Him. We are created to learn. To understand the Grand Design of humans as learners is to open doors to more effective teaching—the effective engagement of human heads, hearts, and hands—for the goal of growing in the Lord. Jesus "knew what was in man" (John 2:25) because He was God in Flesh. We are not Jesus, and therefore need to study God's design for human learning. Educational psychology helps us. Nothing has convinced me of this more than my teaching and preaching experiences in the republics of the former U.S.S.R.

On the first day of every class I teach in the former Soviet Union—and this has been true since 1996—I face students with two common characteristics. One is their absolute confidence in Scripture as the Source of Truth. The other is their deep suspicion of science in general and psychology in particular. For the next 32 hours of class time, students study many of the psychological theories you find in this text: Erikson, Piaget, Kohlberg, Bruner, Skinner, and Maslow. They view these theories, with my help, through the lens of Scripture, aided by Model and Triad. At the end of the course, students find their absolute confidence in Scripture confirmed, and their views of teaching, learning, and spiritual growth greatly expanded.

The Disciplers' Model and Educational Psychology

The **Bible**, God's Eternal Word	**Content Mastery** The structure of the subject matter
The **Needs of Learners**	**Individual Differences** The personal needs of learners
Helping Learners **Think**	**Cognitive Development** How learners process information and think
Helping Learners **Value**	**Affective Development (Humanistic theories)** How learners develop values and attitudes
Helping Learners **Relate**	**Social Context, Group Dynamics** How social interaction deepens learning
Helping Learners **Grow in the Lord**	**Maturation** How learners grow and change
The **Holy Spirit** as Teacher	-- There is no spiritual counterpart

Educational psychology provides us tangible evidence of God's design by means of decades of scientific discoveries. These discoveries help us become better teachers—whether we teach a Bible study class of 10 or a graduate seminary class of 100. We will see how science does its work, its strengths and limitations, in the next chapter.

Chapter Concepts

Cold dogmatism	Overemphasis on "Thinking": affect is ignored and real thinking ceases
Content mastery	Secular counterpart to "Bible" in Disciplers' Model

Fellowship: *koinonia*	Mutual help, caring for one another. Related to Center Pillar of Model
Group therapy	Overemphasis on "needs": sharing of personal stories to the exclusion of Bible
Growth as upward spiral	Knowledge leads to understanding leads to action leads to greater knowledge
Holy Spirit as Discipler	The Circle of the Disciplers' Model, holding other elements in balanced tension
Individual differences	Secular counterpart to "needs" in Disciplers' Model
Knowledge: *Epignosis*	Knowledge that is full or accurate knowledge, knowledge that "goes beyond"
Knowledge: *Gnosis*	Knowledge that is accumulated through personal study or experience
Knowledge: *Oida*	Knowledge that is intellectual or academic
Learner needs: General	Characteristics people of a certain group have in common (e.g., age)
Learner needs: Specific	Needs specific to individual members of our classes (illness, loss of work, divorce)
Tepid fluff	Overemphasis on "feeling": thinking is ignored and emotions are superficial
The Disciplers' Model	Synergistic representation of seven elements essential to biblical spiritual growth
Unrelated history	Overemphasis on "Bible": needs are ignored and Bible is reduced to history lessons
Wisdom	Putting God's Word into practice in daily decisions and actions

Chapter Objectives

Learners will demonstrate knowledge of the Disciplers' Model by drawing the model, and labeling its components with component names and associations with educational psychology.

Learners will demonstrate understanding of the components of the Disciplers' Model by properly categorizing educational issues by component.

Learners will demonstrate appreciation for "a discipling approach to teaching" by recounting learning experiences that reflect selected components of the Model.

Discussion Questions

1 Consider your own teaching style. Where are you on the continuum of Bible and Needs? How do *you* balance Eternal Truth with contemporary learner needs?

2 Are you more a thinker or a feeler? Would you rather listen to a lecture on the historical context of a passage of Scripture, or hear a personal experience illustrating that passage? Would you rather explain a biblical concept, or tell of a time when you experienced that biblical concept for the first time? What implication does your answer have for the way you teach others?

3 How do you encourage relational bridge-building between yourself and your students? How do you encourage interaction among students?

4 Consider teachers who have helped you grow spiritually through Bible study. How have they reflected the Disciplers' Model?

5 Consider for a moment that you are a professor in a Christian college teaching a non-biblical subject (e.g., mathematics, biology, or economics). How would the Disciplers' Model help you as a teacher?

KNOWING, SCIENCE, AND THE CHRISTIAN TEACHER

"You are to have honest balances, honest weights, an honest dry measure, and an honest liquid measure; I am the Lord your God, who brought you out of the land of Egypt."

Leviticus 19:36–37

"Rivalry between scholars improves science."

—Chinese Proverb[1]

Chapter Rationale

Educational psychology is a scientific discipline and seeks to define educational truth by scientific means. This chapter describes seven ways we gain the knowledge we have: common sense, tradition, authority, intuition and revelation, experience, deductive reasoning, and inductive reasoning. The chapter defines scientific knowing and describes how it functions, and how knowledge discovered by science differs from other ways of knowing. Finally, we compare and contrast faith and science as perspectives on knowing.

On an unexpectedly cool day in September, six seminary students discuss the issue of "preferred Bible translations" as they eat lunch under the trees.

Student 1: "I use the New International Version because that's the translation I grew up using in our church back home." (common sense)

Student 2: "I use the King James Version because it's the original English translation and has been used for hundreds of years by those who hold to the ageless power and poetry of God's Word." (tradition)

Student 3: "I use the New King James because my pastor always uses it in his study and preaching. He says it offers the best of beauty and modern scholarship." (authority)

Student 4: "The New American Standard is the version I use. It is so clear in its language. It just feels right." (intuition)

Student 5: "I've tried five or six different translations for devotional reading and teaching and have found that the Revised Standard Version is best for me." (experience)

Student 6: "The essence of Bible study is the understanding of a text. Therefore, I use different translations depending on my study goal." (deductive reasoning)

Student 7: "I use the New International Version because most of my congregation is familiar with it. In a recent survey, I found that eighty percent of our members use the NIV in their Bible study classes." (inductive)

Which student most closely reflects your view?

Chapter Overview

➤ Ways of Knowing

➤ Science as a Way of Knowing

➤ Five Ideals of Science

➤ Hindrances to Scientific Knowing

➤ The Weakness of Scientific Knowing

➤ Faith and Science: Forever Enemies?

➤ *Chapter Concepts, Chapter Objectives, and Discussion Questions*

Ways of Knowing

The grand scope of philosophy sets before us three Great Problems. Philosophers state these problems as questions. The first question—"What is real?"—is designated metaphysics.[2] The third question—"What is valuable?"—is designated axiology.[3] The second question, and one most important to us in this context—"What is truth?" or "How do we know?"—is designated epistemology.[4] We cannot engage an extensive analysis of epistemology in the few pages of this chapter, but we can provide snapshots of the ways we come to know the world. We look at seven approaches to knowing, and then contrast them with scientific knowing, the foundation for educational psychology. These seven approaches, reflected in the statements of students in the text box, are common sense, tradition, authority, intuition and revelation, experience, deductive reasoning, and inductive reasoning.

Common Sense

We learn the customs and traditions that surround us by absorbing them, unintentionally, naturally, from family, church, community and nation. We assume this knowledge is correct because it is familiar to us. We seldom question, or even think to question, the correctness of this knowledge because it reflects what we've personally experienced[5]—it *just is.*

Unless we make an intentional, at times uncomfortable, effort to study the views of others, there is little to challenge our personal perspectives. The response of Student 1 reflects this common sense kind of knowing: "That's the translation I grew up using."

There are obvious problems with this kind of knowing. Common sense said that "dunce caps and caning are effective student motivators" until educational research discovered the destructive aspects of emotional and physical punishment in the classroom. What we "commonly know," personally know, may well be wrong.

Tradition

We hold traditional knowledge as true simply because long-standing ideas and enduring assertions have survived over time.[6] We seldom question, or even think to question, the correctness of tradition because it reflects what many have "known" for a long time—it *just is.*

Unless there is an intentional effort to look beyond established views, there is little to challenge these historical perspectives. The response of Student 2 reflects traditional knowing: "used for hundreds of years."

There are obvious problems with this kind of knowing. The age of an idea does not establish its truthfulness. Traditional neuroscience held for a hundred years that the structure and neural wiring of the brain are fixed ("immutable") by early childhood. Years of research to the contrary, dating back to the 1960s, was ridiculed *by scientists* in light of knowledge fixed by time. It took *scientific* advances in medical technology in the 1990s to demonstrate that basic brain structures, organization, and neural wiring change *for as long as we live.*[7] Traditional knowledge may simply be wrong.

Authority

Authoritative knowledge is established through an uncritical acceptance of another's expertise. We defer to the credentials and training of others, trusting them to tell us what is accurate and true.[8] When sick, we seek a doctor's advice. When in need of legal help, we consult a lawyer. Once we accept experts as valid, we take what they say as true since we cannot verify it for ourselves. It would be foolish to argue with a doctor's diagnosis, or a lawyer's perception of a case. This is "uncritical acceptance."

The only alternative we have to one authority's advice is to seek advice from another. We consult a second doctor, a different lawyer. Yet these second opinions do not prove the truth of our situation—they simply provide another expert opinion. The response of Student 3 reflects authoritative knowing: "my pastor says."

As Christians, we believe that God's Word is the written, objective authority for our lives and work. The Living Word—the Lord Himself Who lives within us—confirms the Truth of the Written Word. The Written Word confirms our experiences with the Living Word (John 20:31). Scripture is a valid source of authoritative knowledge.

Scriptural *interpretations,* however, are another matter. Over the last thirty-five years, I've seen some very heated debates among seminary students. While they always begin discussions with their own points of view, they quickly move to a higher authority—*their pastors!*—who, of course, disagree. It was obvious that both pastors cannot be correct, but that doesn't keep these quarrels from escalating to crackling tension. Future spiritual leaders who fall prey to these unwinnable debates miss Paul's warning to young Timothy: "But reject foolish and ignorant disputes, knowing that they breed quarrels. The Lord's slave must not quarrel, but must be gentle to everyone, able to teach, and patient, instructing his opponents with gentleness. Perhaps God will grant them repentance to know the truth" (2 Tim 2:23–25). The real question facing us is whether the authority is correct. Despite postmodern proclamations to the contrary, Truth exists ("to know the truth," v. 25). Since authoritative knowing does not question the source of knowledge, how do we test the validity of an authority's testimony? Experts may simply be wrong.

Intuition

Intuitive knowledge is true because it "feels right." There is no need for proof or testing or experimentation. Such knowledge comes as a sudden flash of insight and often provides an immediate feeling of certainty.[9] We simply "intuit" the truth.[10] Student 4's response reflects intuitive knowing: "I just know it's right for me."

Intuition is also defined as knowledge that is "self-evident." Propositions are true because it is clearly obvious that they are true.[11] Geometry provides a good example of this kind of knowing. Let's say that line segment *A* is the same length as line segment *B*. Also, line segment *B* is the same length as line segment *C*. From these two truths, we know immediately, and with certainty, that line segments *A* and *C* are equal. Or, in short hand,

IF *A* = *B* and *B* = *C*, THEN *A* = *C*

We do not need to draw the three lines and measure them. We need no expert to tell us. The mind immediately grasps the truth of the statement.

Revelation reflects a spiritual intuition, a spiritual knowledge that God reveals about Himself. We need not test this knowledge, or subject it to experimentation. When Christ reveals Himself to us, we know Him in a personal way. We did not achieve this knowledge by our own efforts, but received the revelation of the Lord (see Matt 16:16–17). We cannot prove this knowledge to others, but it is Truth to those who have received it.[12]

Problems arise, however, when we apply intuitive knowing to educational programs. "It is obvious that note-taking improves achievement." It sounds correct, but is it? Research has shown some students decrease their achievement when taking notes. They concentrate on writing words on paper more than understanding what teachers actually say. "I toss peppermints to people in my conferences when they answer a question. I believe it motivates more participation." Research shows that tangible rewards like candies or stars on a chart motivates learners who are disinterested, but actually decreases interest in those already motivated to learn.

Experience

Experiential knowledge is established by doing something new and analyzing the consequences. It is often called trial-and-error learning. As a minister of education, I experienced this kind of pragmatic knowledge often—especially when suggesting a new way of doing things. There were always people who would warn me ominously, "We tried that before and it failed." They were confident in their opposition to whatever, because they *knew from experience*. It took time and diplomacy to convince these opponents that this time was different from *that* time.

On the other hand, we tried several approaches to providing Vacation Bible School for the children in our area—early summer, mid summer, later summer, mornings, and evenings. We found that holding Vacation Bible School during the third week of August, just before school started, and in the evening, was best for our church. The children were bored with summer play and ready for structured activities and learning. Volunteers—both women and *men*—were much more easily secured for evening activities. We learned this by experience, by trying various approaches and observing the results. Our VBS truth-in-scheduling might not apply to any other church in the area, but it was true for us. It might not be true today, but it was true then. Student 5's response reflects experiential knowing: "I've tried five or six different translations . . . and found . . ."

New ideas in teaching and ministry often come to us recommended by success in other places. We assume that success *there* in *that* context will translate into success *here* in *this* context, but that assumption is often wrong. The only way to determine the viability—the *truth*—of an idea is to try the idea for ourselves, in our own time and context. Such knowledge can never be absolute ("Truth") but does provide contemporary "truths" for given times and places.

Deductive Reasoning

Deductive reasoning begins with general principles and moves to specific applications. General overarching statements of intent and purpose are established. From these overarching statements, specific actions are derived, or "deduced." Student 6's response reflects deductive reasoning: "I use different translations depending on my study goal." The goal is general; the appropriate translation is specific. The general goal determines the specific translation.

We determine purpose, goal, or "worldview" first. Then we engage in specific actions that logically flow from this perspective. If the goal is to teach for understanding (general), then only principles of cognitive learning—examples, questions, problem-solving, explanations—will suffice. Principles for skill development (repetition with feedback) or attitude change (openness, personal sharing) will not achieve understanding.

When a church decides to become a "Great Commission"[13] church, then *it logically follows that* all ministries will be evaluated by their support and reinforcement of Great Commission goals. It also means that programs and ministries that do not support Great Commission goals will be modified or eliminated. The Ceramics Club, where church members gather to make ceramic knickknacks for personal enjoyment or gifts for family or friends, may be changed into a ministry to shut-ins or those in the hospital. Or, it may be changed into an evangelistic outreach to unchurched people who enjoy ceramics. Or, failing that, the "club" may be eliminated altogether.

Deductive reasoning is not, of course, foolproof. How do we determine the overarching generalizations? Humanistic approaches to education—self-esteem, personal experience, and choice—have dominated American education for forty years.[14] It should come as no surprise, then, that high school graduates are weak in content mastery (cognitive learning) and job skills (behavioral learning). When educators are more concerned about student feelings than student mastery and competence, achievement suffers for all but the most self-motivated learners in the school system. One nearby metropolitan school system maintains a grading policy that states "Students may not receive an official test grade lower than 60%, regardless of their performance on a test." The reason for this is to prevent "the loss of self-esteem," which results from receiving very low scores. It also produces low achievement rates among those protected from the truth of what they can actually do.

Inductive Reasoning

Inductive reasoning flows from specific facts to general principles and stands as the logical opposite to deductive reasoning. In an inductive approach to Bible study, we analyze several passages related to a single concept—say, holiness—and then define the term in light of key concepts drawn from specific verses.

If we want to determine, objectively, the general concerns of a group of people—church, faculty, employees—we can do so through an inductive process. We begin by collecting individual statements of concern (specifics). These statements are synthesized into attitudinal statements, which are written in both positive and negative forms. Equal numbers of positive and negative statements are randomly selected and used to construct an attitude scale. Members of the group express their level of agreement or disagreement with the statements. When properly scored, the results of this process provides, in rank order listing, the general concerns *of the group*. The specific concerns of everyone in the group have been translated into statements of general concern of the group-as-whole.[15] Logically, we see the flow from specific statements to general perspectives.

The response of Student 7 reflects inductive reasoning: "80% of our members use the NIV." What will happen when most of the congregation begins using another translation? We might infer from this statement that Student 7 will change his preference to match. "Group consensus" establishes truth.

Science as a Way of Knowing

Science is inductive in its approach to gaining knowledge. Scientific studies focus on specifics—by means of experiments, observations, and measurements—in order to formulate theories to answer intentional questions and offer explanations of how the world works. The scientific community tests these theories under differing conditions to establish the degree to which they can be generalized. The result is temporary (not absolute) truth, open-ended (not settled) truth, and naturalistic (not super-naturalistic) truth.

Scientific truth is open for inquiry, further testing, and modification. For this reason, researchers employ such phrases as "the data *tends* to indicate," "research *suggests*," and "recent studies *add weight* to the argument that." Science does not engage absolute Truth,[16] leaving this to philosophers and theologians. Science assumes that the world is a law-based mechanism existing without Maker or Lawgiver.

Despite these limitations, particularly from a Christian perspective, the scientific method—the methodology by which science gains knowledge—is valid and in many ways superior to other, more subjective approaches. Honest[17] scientific knowing, based on specific data from the natural world, can provide precise information about how our world works. Honest science builds a knowledge base in a neutral, unbiased manner, intentionally controlling sources of personal and subjective bias. Honest science publishes findings publicly, in reports and journals, in operationally-defined[18] language, so that others can duplicate the studies. Honest science forms its conclusions from empirical data. Honest science can test the loftiest ideas—whether drawn from common sense, tradition, or authority—against real data drawn from a real world.

Science Bests Common Sense

Science bests common sense as a way of knowing because it questions commonly accepted truths and seeks objective answers to problems. Common sense tells us that "practice makes perfect." That is, the more we practice a skill, the more competent we become. Research has shown that practice makes no difference at all unless it is accompanied by corrective feedback.

Science Bests Tradition

Science bests tradition because it tests long-held propositions to see if they are true. Many Christians believe that the *King James Version* of the Bible is the best translation of Scripture, even for children. Dr. Gail Linum found in her doctoral dissertation research that fourth, fifth, and sixth grade children had much more difficulty understanding the *King James* than either the *New International* or *New Century* versions. Children had significantly greater difficulty re-telling Bible stories from both Old and New Testaments when read from the KJV than from either the NIV or NCV.[19]

Science Bests Authoritative Knowing

Science bests authoritative knowing because it questions the positions authorities hold, collecting real-world data to support or refute them. In recent years, a nationally-known marriage counselor has become famous for his theory of love languages. One of our doctoral students enthusiastically embraced the idea promoted by his books and tapes—when husband and wife learn speak the love language of the other, marital satisfaction will grow. She decided to empirically test this thesis for her dissertation. After analyzing hundreds of couples in terms of personal love language and whether "my spouse speaks my love language," she found, much to her chagrin, there was no statistically verifiable difference in marital satisfaction between couples who did, and couples who did not, "speak the love languages" of their spouses. Was it because all the couples in the study were Christian? Was it because they were all Texans? Perhaps couples who remain married over a number of years learn "to be content" despite the love language question. Perhaps those who were not content due to love language conflict were no longer married, and therefore not eligible for the study. Or, perhaps the whole concept of "love languages" is flawed, a philosophy based in personal counseling experiences and not in empirical data. Why the two groups did not differ in marital satisfaction cannot be answered from this initial study. But in the Texas Christian couples of this study, the major tenet of a national best-selling therapist was shown to be false.[20]

Science Bests Intuition

Science bests intuition because researchers are personally neutral and objective in their pursuit of truth, intentionally avoiding hunches and "feelings," and replicating studies to generalize findings beyond any single study. My Disciplers' Model has been used in classrooms and teacher conferences for nearly thirty years to focus attention on "how to teach so that learners grow in the Lord." As I said in Chapter One, the Lord led me through a series of experiences, observations, and studies that eventually distilled into the Model. It felt right then, and it has continued to feel right for forty years. It logically fits all that I have experienced in Sunday school and seminary classes. But it has never been subjected to scientific analysis. One of our doctoral students has been working on a proposal to do so this year. I'm looking forward to seeing the results.

Science Cannot Speak to Biblical Revelation

There is no way to empirically test whether Jesus walked on water or turned water into wine. Dishonest scientists can ridicule the idea of miracle, but by definition, "miracle" stands outside the purview of science. Honest scientists do not even try to put God in a test tube. As Jesus said, "The wind blows where it pleases, and you hear its sound, but you don't know where it comes from or where it is going. So it is with everyone born of the Spirit" (John 3:8). Science defines itself as limited to the natural. It cannot speak to the supernatural.

Science Bests Experience

Science bests experience because it objectively seeks relationships between variables or differences between groups that lie beyond personal experiences. John Dewey's pragmatism defined "truth as what works."[21] Science looks beyond utilitarianism for cause and effect connections in the natural world.

Science Bests Deductive Reasoning

Science bests deductive reasoning because the a priori truths upon which the logic depends may be flawed. Given a flawed beginning point, deduced particulars will also be flawed. "Note taking during lectures and discussions supports greater student achievement." This certainly qualifies as a good, overarching truth. How can students succeed in learning if they do not have a complete set of notes from instruction? Given the truth of that statement, we deduce that "students who take careful, clear notes will achieve better than those who do not." Research has shown, however, that the very practice of note taking can interfere with learning. Some students concentrate so much on getting the words into their notebooks that they miss important meanings of the words they're writing. For these students, achievement will be higher if they write less, listen carefully, and jot down key terms and meaningful phrases.

Five Ideals of Science

If our concern is to investigate the world in which we live, the scientific method provides us a means to test our viewpoints, practices, and outcomes. We have addressed some of the characteristics of science already. Let's turn to the five ideals of honest scientific knowing.

Objectivity—the Reduction of Bias

Human beings are complex. Personal experiences, values, backgrounds, and beliefs make objective analysis difficult unless effort is made to remain neutral. Optimists are biased—they tend to see the positive in situations. Pessimists are biased—they tend to see the negative. Honest scientists are neutral. They look for objective reality—the world as it is—uncolored by personal opinion or feelings.

Scientific knowing attempts to eliminate personal bias in data collection and analysis. Honest researchers take a neutral position in their studies. That is, they do not try to prove their own beliefs. They are willing to accept results contrary to their own opinions or values. Dr. Thatcher fully anticipated a difference, based on Love Language theory, between couples who did and did not speak the love language of their spouse. She was surprised by what she found in the couples she objectively studied. She let the data speak and wrote her conclusions accordingly.

Precision

Reliable scientific knowing requires precise measurement. Researchers carry out experiments under controlled, narrow conditions. They carefully design instruments to be as accurate as possible, and use instruments—instruments, tests, attitude scales, checklists—that demonstrate reliability and validity in their measurements. They use pilot projects, which are trial runs of procedures, to identify hidden sources of measurement error. This is important because undefined conditions, unreliable instruments, and untested procedures produce data that lacks precision. Lack of precision renders the separation of true differences, if they exist, from unsystematic and ambiguous differences impossible.

Church programs are usually evaluated by affective factors—personal feelings of participants and leaders, the level of excitement generated, and the ever popular "How many attended?" Programs are considered successful if participants like them, express interest and enthusiasm about them, and if more people participate. Precise measurements are seldom if ever made of actual outcomes. Objective examinations, properly written to test level of understanding, are far more precise in their measurement of learning than more ambiguous essay examinations or self-chosen project assignments.

Replication

Science analyzes, by definition, natural processes in the world that are systematic and recurring. Researchers report their findings in a way that allows others to replicate their studies—to check the facts in the real world. Research reports provide readers the background, specific problems and hypotheses of studies. Also included are descriptions of the samples of subjects and the populations from which they were drawn, definitions, limitations, assumptions, as well as procedures for collecting and analyzing data. Writers do this intentionally so others can evaluate the degree that findings can be generalized—applied to persons beyond their study—and perhaps replicate the study. Replications may confirm the original findings, or refute them.

Since science limits itself to naturally recurring events in the physical world, it is inappropriate for scientists to address theological questions of God's existence or life after death issues. When they do, they cease to be scientists and speak as philosopher-theologians.

Empiricism

Empiricism is the "philosophical theory that attributes the origin of all our knowledge to experience." Science bases its findings on empirical data—data derived from "observation and experiment."[22] Direct observation is the staple of scientific investigation. Researchers document directly observed behaviors of planets (telescopic photography) and bacteria (microscopic photography), as well as communication styles, group dynamics, and classroom interactions (audio and video recording). Observations can be made with the naked eye and a simple checklist. But "observations" are also made with paper-based instruments—such as questionnaires, tests, and attitude scales—and with controlled experiments.

Goal: Theory Construction

Much is made of vast knowledge systems, derived from collections of natural discoveries produced by hundreds of thousands of studies. But these specific studies stand at the *beginning* of the inductive process of science. At the *end* of the process we find the goal of scientific research: the construction of coherent theories that explain how the natural world works. What causes cancer? What makes it rain? What is the best way to relieve anxiety? What factors influence marital satisfaction? How do attitudes develop? What are the most effective approaches to learning a foreign language? What factors improve mathematical reasoning?

While science is limited to natural processes, there is much in Christian life—teaching, learning, leading, organizing, motivating—that is intrinsically connected to natural humanity, and therefore open to scientific investigation. When Christian teachers violate effective human principles of learning, they teach less effectively—even though they may cover themselves "in Jesus' name"—than Christian teachers who use effective principles. When Christian leaders manipulate followers who trust them in order to gain power over them, trust is destroyed, even when this is done ostensibly "according to God's will." Power corrupts, even in Christian circles.

For more than thirty years I've helped doctoral students develop dissertation studies both biblically anchored and scientifically credible. Dissertations have focused on issues of marriage, teaching, learning, age-group characteristics, community-based evangelism, counseling, poverty, parent-child relationships, adolescent discipleship, Christian college attrition, home schooling, spiritual maturity, Bible translation comprehension, critical thinking, and nearly a hundred others.

Science is a highly effective way to gain knowledge about the world in which we live, and there is nothing in science itself that prevents Christians from using its tools to further ministry effectiveness. It is for these reasons that I selected the Scripture passage for the head of the chapter: "You are to have honest balances, honest weights, an honest dry measure, and an honest liquid measure; I am the Lord your God, who brought you out of the land of Egypt" (Lev 19:36–37). This is the first word from the Lord about honest measures. Other warnings are found in Deuteronomy, Proverbs, Ezekiel, and Micah.[23] God's command warns against businessmen who used one set of (heavier) weights for their scales in buying grain, and another set of (lighter) weights in selling grain, a dishonest practice. The self-correcting processes of scientific knowing help keep human beings honest about perspectives on the way the world works. We will see that the original theories of Erikson, Piaget, Kohlberg, Bruner, and Maslow all changed as they responded to critique and continued to research. Further adaptations have continued long after their own research ended. Their work continues to suggest questions to be studied, which, in turn, deepens our understanding of the truths they gave their lives to distill. But science can be as flawed as other kinds of knowing because it is a human process, and humans are flawed by nature. We turn our attention to human hindrances to valid scientific knowing and then how such knowing can be intentionally improved.

Hindrances to Scientific Knowing

The five ideals of science—objectivity, precision, replication, empiricism, and theory construction—help establish empirically sound theories concerning our world. However, there are hindrances to gaining this kind of knowledge. These are selective observation and recall, closure, overgeneralization, and personal involvement.

Selective Observation and Recall

We live in a world of information overload. So much information surrounds us that we cannot adequately process it all. Selective *observation* filters out "non-essentials" as we *investigate*. Selective *recall* filters out "nonessentials" as we *remember*. In either case, the filters are biased by human characteristics.

Selective observation filters out nonessentials as we search. You stand at the airport waiting for a friend to deplane. One by one passengers file out the door. You glance from face to face, looking for your friend. You look at them just long enough to eliminate them from consideration. Finally, you see your friend walking toward you. There is immediate recognition, and you will remember very little about the faces you checked. Undercover agents escape detection because they dress and act like criminals or terrorists. Magicians master slight-of-hand skills that permit them to distract us in one direction while they do their tricks in another. The danger of selective observation to scientific knowing is that collected data is filtered and biased by personal expectations. "Nonessentials" are part of the data set. To eliminate these data points is to distort the data itself.

Selective recall filters out nonessentials as we remember. One of my great aunts was married to a man who treated her shamefully for years. Within just a few weeks of his funeral, she began speaking of her departed husband in surprisingly kind ways—"recalling" what a good man he had been. She repressed many dark memories and brought forward the few bright ones. Researchers can do the same thing in experiments by remembering "helpful" events and forgetting unexpected events. The danger of selective recall is that filtered, *biased* memory distorts the data.

Science combats selective observation by taking random samples of data and analyzing all elements collected. Science combats selective recall by recording data immediately and mechanically by means of checklists, inventories, attitude scales, tests, and videotape.

Closure

Closure is the "tendency to see an entire figure even though the picture of it is incomplete, based primarily on the viewer's past experience."[24] What would you call the two figures below?

If you said "triangle" and "circle," you have experienced closure. You filled in the three dots with lines, creating a triangle in your mind. You filled in the 355° arc, creating a circle. Psychological closure refers to mentally filling in gaps of perception with imagination in order to create a complete picture. While selective observation overlooks data that exists, closure fills in data that is missing.

Science combats closure by collecting as much data as is needed to provide a thorough analysis. Science does not rush to make determinations of meaning from partial data sets. Rather it methodically collects data to provide an empirical foundation for hypotheses and theories.

Overgeneralization

To generalize is to shift one's focus from specific objects to classes of related objects. Earlier, inductive reasoning was defined as moving logically from specifics to generalizations.

"Scottish terrier" is a (specific) breed of dog. "German Shepherd" is another (specific) breed of dog. "Dog" represents a class of animals including Scottish terriers, German shepherds, and scores of other breeds. While differing breeds display a wide variety of colorings, sizes, and temperaments, all animals in the class are dogs. Breeds are specifics. "Dog" is a generalization. "Ford" and "Chevrolet" are specific makes of cars. "Car" is a generalization. With sufficient experience, one can identify unfamiliar types of dogs and cars correctly, or, as we might say, one can generalize accurately.

To overgeneralize means to judge a class of people or events by a few examples. It is a natural human tendency to project experiences with a few individuals or events onto the whole class to which they belong. We see this in prejudices of various kinds, and stereotyping of people and ideas. This tendency is a hindrance to scientific knowing because such projections are based on personal attitudes and have little to do with reality.

Science combats overgeneralization by conducting research with randomly chosen samples that provide data from a cross-section of a population. Large samples provide protection against projecting inappropriately from small data sets. Replication of experiments allows for cross validation of research findings.

Personal Involvement

As human beings, we have a personal set of values, beliefs, and prejudices, developed as a result of prior experiences and study. Researchers are, obviously, human beings. Their studies are important to them. They have hunches about what they want to find. Their personal hopes and fears, their biases and expectations, not only distort the data as it is collected (selective observation), but constantly threaten to distort the research process itself. Even most sophisticated analysis of invalid data can produce valid findings.

Science combats personal involvement by emphasizing objectivity. Two eye-witness accounts are considered objective if they report the same thing. A test is objective if subjects receive the same scores regardless of who grades them. An observation checklist is objective if two observers report the same data in an experiment. Objectivity provides person-neutral data regarding the subjects under study—data that is unrelated in any way to the researchers' personal biases. Commonly used tools include double-blind experiments, validation panels, and data gathering instruments that demonstrate both reliability—*accuracy, consistency*—and validity—*appropriateness*—for the study at hand. Moreover, the more vested researchers are in the subjects they study, the more difficult it will be to maintain objectivity in the study.

The Weakness of Scientific Knowing

As we have seen, the process of scientific investigation is an objective process when pursued in an open, honest, neutral manner—one that rejects personal biases and prejudices. But all scientific research begins with a question. From that question, a hypothesis is derived. Testing the hypothesis leads to empirical answers. The very question that initiates *objective* research may be distorted by *subjective* bias. This is "a reflection of the necessary fact that science is, at bottom, a human endeavor."[25]

But there are other weaknesses as well. Assumptions can be distorted by personal values. Subjects can be drawn in non-random ways, which produces its own kind of bias. Instruments used to collect data can be invalid and unreliable. Statistical analyses can be mishandled. Recommendations can go beyond what the data actually says. Narrow findings can be over-generalized. In all these instances, human characteristics distort scientific procedures and render the findings suspect. Researchers guard against personal bias and perspective, or they produce findings as subjectively flawed as other forms of knowing.

Perhaps the greatest advantage of honest science is that it is self-correcting.[26] The biases of one study are often countered by others through replications of the study. Declarations of one study provide questions for further research. This heuristic value of science is helpful in filtering out human distortions in what we know about the world.

In the end, scientific knowledge, like all forms of human knowing, is flawed, because human beings are flawed. The flaws of human knowing should not hinder the desire to know or prevent us from learning. The scientific method is an excellent tool for analyzing the world in which we live.

Faith and Science: Forever Enemies?

Can Christian pastors and teachers learn from the discoveries of secular psychologists without compromising the Church or our faith in Christ Jesus? Can secular scientists and psychologists embrace or even consider biblical truths concerning life without compromising their integrity as scientists? The answer to that question depends on our definition of science.

Definition One: Science as a Way of Knowing

One definition of science focuses on a methodology of gaining knowledge about the world in which we live. Stephen Hales, English founder of the science of plant physiology, wrote (1727) the following. "Since we are assured that the all-wise Creator has observed the most exact proportions of number, weight and measure in the make of all things, the most likely way therefore to get any insight into the nature of those parts of the Creation which come within our observation must in all reason be to number, weigh and measure."[27] Hales's commitment to scientific methodology in no way compromised his faith in the "all-wise Creator." The bust of Maria Mitchell, U.S. astronomer and the first woman elected to the Academy of Arts and Sciences (1848) carries this quote, "Every formula which expresses a law of nature is a hymn of praise to God."[28] Within this context, *there is no conflict between scientific understanding of the way the world works and faith in the One Who carefully and lovingly designed and made it.*

The Bible is not a textbook on teaching, but by example and instance it provides us a perspective of teaching that is intellectually clear, emotionally warm, and competently, skillfully active. We might think of these emphases as *thinking, feeling, doing.* This triad corresponds to the three major learning theory systems of educational psychology: the cognitive (knowing and thinking), the affective or humanistic (feeling and valuing), and the behavioral (skillful doing). There are numerous examples of how biblical faith and secular psychology agree, because both focus on human beings.

Here are a few examples of this agreement.

1. Both would agree that teachers should model the behaviors and skills they expect their learners to develop. (Science:) Albert Bandura's Social Learning theory emphasizes the role of teacher as model, demonstrating the skills they expect students to master. (Faith:) Before Jesus died, He washed the feet of His disciples. "Now that I, your Lord and Teacher, have washed your feet, you also should wash one another's feet. I have set you an example that you should do as I have done for you. (John 13:12–15). Peter writes that pastors (teachers) should to be an "example to the flock" (1 Pet 5:3). The apostle Paul provided the Thessalonians an example to follow. "It is not that we don't have the right to support, but we did it [worked to support himself] to make ourselves an example to you so that you would imitate us" (2 Thess 3:9–10).

2. Both would agree that teachers should be well-prepared, the material well-organized, and presentations clearly made. (Science:) Information Processing Theory teaches the importance of meaningfulness and organization in effective teaching and learning. (Faith:) The apostle Paul writes to Timothy, a pastor, "Do your best to present yourself to God as one approved, a workman who does not need to be ashamed and who correctly handles [cuts according to the proper pattern] the word of truth" (2 Tim 2:15). Concerning clear speech, Paul writes: "Again, if the trumpet does not sound a clear call, who will get ready for battle? So it is with you. Unless you speak intelligible words with your tongue, how will anyone know what you are saying? You will just be speaking into the air. Undoubtedly there are all sorts of languages in the world, yet none of them is without meaning. If then I do not grasp the meaning of what someone is saying, I am a foreigner to the speaker, and he is a foreigner to me" (1 Cor 14:8–11).

3. Both would agree that the classroom should be emotionally warm and that learning should be both pleasant and effective. (Science:) Humanistic learning theory promotes care and nurture for the student. (Faith:) Jesus taught us "Love your enemies" (Matt 5:43–48). Even though students can feel like "enemies" to us, we are to love them—that is, do what's best for them. Paul instructs Christian fathers: "Do not embitter your children" (Col 3:21). Teachers, who are surrogate parents, should not embitter their students! The Fruit of the Spirit—"love, joy, peace, patience, kindness, goodness, faithfulness, gentleness, and self-control" (Gal 5:22–23)—produces a warm, safe learning environment.

4. Both would agree that teaching in the classroom should relate closely to life outside the classroom. (Science:) Cognitive learning theory, especially the theories of Jerome Bruner and Kurt Lewin, emphasizes transfer of learning and the importance of learning being useful in the world. (Faith:) Jesus chose twelve "to be with Him" to learn by observation and experience, to connect His teachings with life as God intended it to be. Paul wrote that learning should lead to worthy living. (Col 1:9–10).

5. Both would agree that teachers should clearly establish and communicate what is expected of students. There should be no dishonesty in testing or grading. (Science:) Behavioral learning theory emphasizes a systems' approach to the teaching-learning process in which classroom methods are chosen in order to help students achieve instructional objectives. Expectations are communicated through behavioral objectives. Emphasis is placed on objective testing. (Faith:) The Bible records God's standards concerning honesty in business: "Do not use dishonest standards when measuring length, weight, or quantity. Use honest scales and honest weights, an honest ephah and an honest hin. I am the LORD your God, who brought you out of Egypt" (Lev 19:35–36). Honesty in dealing with each other extends to the classroom.

Definition Two: Science as Naturalistic Worldview

The second definition of science reflects the philosophy of naturalism, which proposes that nature is "all there is." The fundamental doctrine of natural science is evolutionism, which teaches, according to Harvard paleontologist George Simpson (1967) that "man is the result of a purposeless and natural process that did not have him in mind."[29] Douglas Futuyma wrote (1983) that "the human species was not designed, has no purpose, and is the product of mere mechanical mechanisms."[30] Such statements reflect the prediction of Karl Marx (1844), "Natural science will in time incorporate into itself the science of man, just as the science of man will incorporate into itself natural science: there will be one science."[31]

Naturalists assume that God exists only in the minds of religious believers, who are in fact deluded. They believe that Man created God, rather than the other way around. Rationality requires the recognition that God is an imaginary Being, and that we rely only on things that are "real," (defined as the material world). Reliance on the guidance of an imaginary supernatural Being is superstition,[32] or worse, mental illness.

Theists believe we were created by God, a supernatural Being Who cares about what we do, and Who has a purpose for our lives which is fulfilled in life and eternity. If God really does exist, then to lead a rational life requires a person to take account of God and his purposes. A person or society who ignores the Creator is ignoring the most important part of reality, and to ignore reality is irrational. That is why the Bible says the fear of the Lord is the beginning of wisdom.[33] What can we say, then, as we begin to apply scientific theories of learning to Christian education?

Faith and Science Are Enemies in their Worldviews

It is helpful to understand that, as Christians, the essence of theism (faith) and naturalism (science) differ too much in their perspectives to allow a suitable synthesis. One is God-centered, the other man-centered. One embraces the supernatural creation of the world from nothing by an eternal loving God; the other the natural creation of the world out of eternal matter by random chance. One emphasizes practical action in the world based on God's love, the other theoretical speculations about the world based on human analysis. One is linked to revealed Truth, the other to evolving ideas. One declares "In the beginning, God," and the other "There is no beginning, only Eternal Matter." One holds that God created Man in His image; the other that Man creates gods in many images. There can be no synthesis of these two positions.

Faith and Science Overlap in Human Life

When we focus on life—human rationality, attitudes, and behavior—we find areas of common ground in what is revealed in Scripture and discovered by scientists. Jehovah God is not a Behaviorist, but He has guided people throughout history using principles of reinforcement. Jesus is not a Humanist, but He cared for and nurtured His disciples while He walked the earth, and continues to care for and nurture His followers today. The Holy Spirit is not a Cognitive Theorist, but He helps believers understand supernatural truths that naturalists cannot see, as well as natural truths that they can. There is overlap between the truth of Revelation and the truths of scientific discovery.

No Conflict between Faith in the Lord and Analysis of the World

There is no conflict between giving hearts and minds to the Lord, and logically pursuing truths about the ways the natural world works. Educational psychology is a scientific discipline that focuses on the nature of the teaching-learning process. It does not—it cannot by definition—speak to the supernatural issues of faith, salvation, or spiritual growth. It does, however, provide wonderful insights into helping people learn, and these insights make the subject well worth our study time. The purpose of this text is to investigate the discoveries of science within the context of biblical faith. The Disciplers' Model (Chapter One) provides the biblical context.

Summary

In this chapter, we looked at eight ways of knowing. We discussed specifically the nature and characteristics of scientific knowing, as well as its weakness. While faith and science are "forever enemies" in terms of worldview, human learning and growth is a place where both overlap, offering rich dividends for pastors, teachers, disciplers, and missionaries.

Chapter Concepts

Authoritative knowing	Knowledge accepted uncritically from others with expertise,
Common sense	Knowledge accepted naturally from family, friends,
Deductive reasoning	Knowledge derived logically from an established principle or purpose
Empiricism	Ideal of basing knowledge on observations of the world
Experience	Knowledge gained from trial and error, attempts and consequences
Inductive reasoning	Knowledge derived logically from a synthesis of discoveries
Intuition	Knowledge derived from formal logic
Objectivity	Ideal of pursuing truth undistorted by the subjectivity of personal preferences
Overgeneralization	Distortion caused by judgment of a class of people or events by a few examples
Personal involvement	Distortion caused by personal experience, study, values, beliefs, and prejudices
Precision	Ideal of measuring world events or processes accurately
Replication	Ideal of confirming or refuting research findings by repeating studies
Revelation	Knowledge from spiritual intuition, a knowledge that God reveals about Himself
Selective observation	Distortion caused by bias or prejudice when collecting data

| Selective recall | Distortion caused by bias or prejudice when remembering observations |
| Theory construction | Ideal of using data to create cohesive explanations of how the world works |

Chapter Objectives

Learners will demonstrate understanding of ways of knowing by explaining each of the seven ways of knowing.

Learners will demonstrate understanding of science as a way of knowing by . . .

- explaining the five ideals of science;
- explaining the weaknesses of science; and
- contrasting science and faith as foundations for one's worldview

Discussion Questions

1 Define each of the seven "ways of knowing" in your own words.

2 Describe at least two "ways of knowing" that you have personally experienced. How did this knowledge change you?

3 Define in your own words five characteristics of the scientific method.

4 What was your perspective on science before reading the chapter? Did your perspective change as you reflected on the "faith versus science" material? In what ways? Are you more comfortable with science as a way of knowing for Christians? Why or why not?

UNIT 2

Educational Psychology and Learners

The learner is central in the teaching-learning process. The importance of the learner outweighs the content to be learned, the teacher who facilitates learning, or the process by which content is communicated. Jesus emphatically underscored the importance of learners in His teaching ministry (see Matt 20:28;16:26). John reinforced the importance of individual learners when he declared that the purpose of his writing was to insure that individuals could learn of Jesus, the Christ, the Son of God, and believe—and that by believing, have "life in His name" (John 20:31).

As we begin our journey into the principles and processes of educational psychology, we anchor our efforts in this central truth: *the role of Christian teachers is to give themselves away for the good of their learners.* Jesus stated this premise quite clearly:

> "You know that the rulers of the Gentiles dominate them, and the men of high position exercise power over them. It must not be like that among you. On the contrary, whoever wants to become great among you must be your servant, and whoever wants to be first among you must be your slave; just as the Son of Man did not come to be served, but to serve, and to give His life—a ransom for many" (Matt 20:25–28).

First, the principle: "To become great . . . serve." Second, the example of His own life: "the Son of Man . . . a ransom for many." Our students do not exist to provide us a place to serve. Our place to serve exists because of our students. They are not in the classroom for us. We are in the classroom for them. The congregation does not exist to edify the pastor; the pastor exists to edify the congregation. This is the example Jesus left us—it is the road to greatness as kingdom citizens. So the fine-tuned focus of Christian teachers must be their students.

Who are these individuals who sit before us in classrooms and sanctuaries? How did they come to be who they are? What experiences do they carry with them? In what ways have they been shaped by life's forces? What prejudices do they carry? How open are they to learning? To change?

These questions point to realities in the teaching-learning process overlooked by many teachers. An adult teacher once said, "The church didn't elect me to be a social worker or counselor. I teach the

Word of God, 9:45 on Sunday mornings. So, don't expect me to visit or call my members. My job is to teach." Teachers like this may present lessons. They may fill teaching or preaching time. But they will do little in the way of nurturing classes or congregations, of intersecting lives and helping believer-students grow in the Lord. The next three chapters focus on key issues regarding the nature of learners.

Chapter 3: How We Develop as Persons

Erik Erikson's Theory of Personality Development

Teaching-learning processes are intensely social. Success is secured through the ability of teacher and learners to relate to each other, to speak clearly and listen attentively to each other, and to participate together in learning experiences. Christians grow spiritually as they learn to depend on the indwelling Lord of Life. We grow emotionally and socially as human beings, according to human dynamics that are both positive and negative. We establish relationships in an environment of trust and mutuality, or not. We are subject to the effects of abuse or neglect. Erik Erikson helps us consider this self-other dimension of growth and learning in families, churches, and classrooms.

Chapter 4: How We Develop as Thinkers

Jean Piaget and Lev Vygotsky: Theories of Cognitive Development

Jean Piaget described a process by which minds are developed and organized to understand the world. His contemporary, Lev Vygotsky, described the social component of cognitive development. The proper understanding of God's Word and world—the left pillar of the Disciplers' Model—is essential to Christian growth. The insights of Piaget and Vygotsky will help Christian teachers in our efforts to guide learners into a biblical worldview.

Chapter 5: How We Develop as Moral Decision Makers

Lawrence Kohlberg's Theory of Moral Reasoning Development

Teaching and learning are dynamic moral processes. At a basic level, rules are necessary to govern classroom discipline and order, fairness, equal opportunities to succeed or fail, and honest measures of evaluation. Personal life issues such as parental support, nutrition, drug or alcohol use, promiscuity, violence, abortion, and racism affect learning, achievement, and growth.

One might think that teaching in a Christian context is, in itself, moral. But faith in Christ and morality are two different issues. If we do not make a conscious effort to teach our children principles of moral decision-making—principles that reflect our biblical faith—then whose principles will they learn?

Lawrence Kohlberg extended the work of Jean Piaget into the area of moral reasoning. Kohlberg's stages provide a framework by which we can help learners analyze their own approaches to solving moral dilemmas.

HOW WE DEVELOP AS PERSONS

Erik Erikson: Psycho-Social Theory of Personality Development

> *"And Jesus increased in wisdom and stature, and in favor with God and with people."*
>
> Luke 2:52

> *"As a twig is bent the tree inclines."*
>
> —Virgil[1]

Chapter Rationale

Teaching-learning processes are intensely social. Success is secured through the ability of teacher and learners to relate to each other, to speak clearly and listen attentively to each other, and to participate together in learning experiences. Christians grow spiritually as they learn to depend on the indwelling Lord of Life. We grow emotionally and socially as human beings, according to human dynamics that are both positive and negative. We establish relationships in an environment of trust and mutuality. We are not immune to the effects of abuse or neglect. Erik Erikson helps us consider this self-other dimension of growth and learning in families, churches, and classrooms.

Chapter Overview

➤ Historical Roots: Sigmund Freud
➤ The Prenatal Foundation of Personal Development

Historical Roots: Sigmund Freud

At the beginning of the twentieth century, children six years of age and younger were commonly thought to be too young to know or experience anything of substance. They were considered "mindless creatures, more like animals than humans."[2] Sigmund Freud conducted clinical research into adult personality disorders. From that work, using hypnotism and free association,[3] he concluded that much of human personality development occurs in the first six years of life. Adult personality could only be understood, thought Freud, by analyzing the experiences and relationships adults had had in childhood. His theory was shocking, even scandalous, to the Victorian sensibilities of his day, primarily for his open discussion of sexual drives and fantasies. Despite the fear and anger his ideas generated, he laid out an approach to human development famously summarized by the phrase "the child is the father of the man." Freud's primary message was that parents must stop treating their children in ways that "mangle, distort, inhibit, and break" them.[4]

Freud divided the first six years of life into three stages. The first he called the "oral stage," which extends from birth through eighteen months. "Oral" refers specifically to breastfeeding, but generally to the quality of care received by the child. Proper care leads to trust and dependence on a stable caring world. The second stage he called the "anal stage," which extends from eighteen months to three years of age. "Anal" refers specifically to toilet training, but generally to issues of self-control that lead to independence. The third stage he called the "phallic stage," which extends from three to seven years of age. "Phallic" refers specifically to the discovery of sexual identity. Freud hypothesized a latency period until adolescence, at which time the adult character is formed from a synthesis of the previous stages.[5]

Erik Erikson was a student of Freud but believed Freud's focus was too narrow. First of all, psychoanalytic theory, which fixes adult personality parameters at age six, was too deterministic for Erikson. He preferred a broader, more balanced framework, including stages through childhood and adolescence to adulthood. Second, Freud emphasized the negative aspects of personality, while Erikson preferred balance between positive and negative aspects of each stage. Third, Freud emphasized the sexual aspect of human nature in driving personality development, producing a psycho-sexual theory. Erikson replaced the sexual orientation with cultural and social factors in the developmental process, a psycho-social theory.[6] Finally, Erikson concluded that Freud's insistence on remaining in Vienna, "interacting only with a small, select group of individuals," ignored the impact of differing values, attitudes, and customs on personality development. Erikson's goal was to develop a theory based in psychoanalysis yet able to take into account these cultural and social differences.[7]

The Life of Erik Erikson

Erik Erikson was born in Frankfurt, Germany, on June 12, 1902. Shortly after his birth, his parents separated. About three years later, Erikson's mother married his pediatrician, Dr. Theodore Homburger. Through his childhood he carried the name Erik Homburger.

When eventually told of his real father, his own struggle with role confusion and identity problems began. These early experiences became the driving force behind his later thinking.

His role confusion was demonstrated in the years after he left high school before graduating. He traveled around Europe, enrolling in art schools. After three years in two art schools, he moved to Florence and joined a group of young artists. He soon gained a reputation as a portrait artist, particularly his portraits of children. A major turning point in his life occurred in 1933 when he was invited to a villa in Vienna, Austria, to paint a child's portrait. When he arrived, he met the child's father, Sigmund Freud.

A few weeks later Erikson received an invitation from Freud to enroll in the Psychoanalytic Institute in Vienna. There he found his vocational identity as a child psychoanalyst. He did such outstanding work that he was given full status upon graduation, rather than the usual associate status. In 1936, as Hitler gained power in Germany, Erikson and his family immigrated to the United States.

He took a teaching and research position at Yale University. In 1939 he moved to the University of California at Berkeley and worked with a research team involved in a longitudinal study of child development. He studied American Indian tribes, normal and abnormal children, and soldiers returning from World War II. These experiences convinced Erikson of the importance of social and cultural factors in personality development.

In 1950 he wrote his first book, *Childhood and Society*, in which he introduced the Eight Ages of Man. His theory was adopted this same year by a White House conference on children. Other books include *Identity and the Life Cycle* (1959, 1980), *Insight and Responsibility* (1964), *Identity: Youth and Crisis* (1968), and *Vital Involvement in Old Age* (1986).

Erikson died on May 12, 1994, at the age of 91. The *New York Times* (May 12, 1994) noted in its obituary that Erikson's theory "represented a quantum leap in Freudian thought, suggesting that the ego and the sense of identity are shaped over the entire lifespan and that experiences later in life might help heal the hurts of early childhood."[8]

Erikson likened the development of personality to that of a baby in the womb. All the major subsystems of a human child are present in the first weeks of the pregnancy. But there are critical periods, or stages, in which the various subsystems develop best. Erikson held that human personality grows the same way, through eight basic stages, each with its own crisis of development. Not randomly, but by design. Not automatically, but by a built-in drive toward a more complex system. If a child has a healthy interaction with others, and if the basic crisis of a given stage is resolved appropriately, then the child is ready for the next stage. If the crisis is not resolved, it will become increasingly difficult to resolve it in the future.[9]

Biologists use the term "epigenetic" (*lit.,* beyond, full + genetic) to describe the process of human development in the womb—the "approximately stepwise process by which genetic information [of an embryo], as modified by environmental influences, is translated into the substance and behavior of an organism."[10] In short, *epigenetic* refers to the way in which organs appear at specific times and eventually combine to form a child. Erikson certainly borrowed the term, if not the concept itself, and called the driving force behind his theory "the epigenetic principle." The formation of human personality occurs "as the ego progresses through a series of interrelated stages."[11]

The Prenatal Foundation of Personal Development

Human personality grows as a result of interaction between a child and others in his or her environment, beginning with the mother, and then proceeding to father, siblings, family, friends, and community. The foundation for this outward growth, which Erikson calls "involvement," is established **before birth**: "Involvement is related to the prenatal containment in our mother's vulva, where, modern research suggests, we were not just passively wrapped up but already had to prove our truly 'inborn' capacity for involvement, which means our being alive, by stimulating the 'environment' as it stimulates us."[12]

As babies grow in the womb, they push outward against it ("stimulating the environment"). The womb pushes back ("as it stimulates us"). This *push out-pushed back* interaction is the root, says Erikson, of human personality formation. Throughout the rest of our lives, we push outward into the world—family, community, region—and the world pushes back. This human *push-pushed* interaction, the very heart of personality development, this essential beginning, this central maxim of Erikson's last word on the subject, is hard to find in contemporary educational psychology texts. One can only suppose his ideas have been suppressed, intentionally or not, by forces dedicated to defining human life as beginning at birth and not conception. Erikson's writings speak loudly in favor of *human* growth in the womb, but one searches in vain for any mention of this outside his own, last book.[13]

The Eight Stages of Erik Erikson

Personality development can move in a positive and healthy direction, or a negative and unhealthy direction. The desired outcome of each stage is to develop positive characteristics: trust, autonomy, initiative, industry, identity, intimacy, generativity, and integrity. Abusive influences can produce negative characteristics: mistrust, shame and doubt, guilt, inferiority, role confusion, isolation, stagnation, and despair. These eight characteristic pairs form Erikson's eight stages of personality growth.

An old bromide says, "The best place to start is at the beginning." But I find in my classes that a much more interesting way to unwrap Erikson's Original Eight is to begin at the end and work backward.[14] So we begin at the end, with the last stage and final stage, and make our way back toward conception.

Stage 8: Integrity-Despair

How do we come to the end of our lives? The years of senior adulthood, beginning at retirement, form the final stage in Erikson's theory. During this stage adults reflect on their lives and accomplishments as they move toward death.[15]

The positive resolution of this stage is **integrity**, which produces a general feeling of **well-being**, a **satisfaction with life**,[16] an acceptance of what they have done and who they are, including failures and limitations.[17] There is a sense of **dignity and wholeness** in one's life.[18]

The negative resolution of this stage is **despair.** Those who cannot resolve this stage appropriately look back on a life of disappointments and unachieved goals.[19] **They regret the things still undone** and worry that **time is running out.**[20] They harbor bitterness in the shortness of life and the fact that they cannot start over.[21] For me, the haunting phrase "if only . . ." echoes the despair of those who can now only wish they had made different choices through life.

The goal for Stage 8 is to embrace life with satisfaction, reflecting on ways one engaged relationships, experiences, and achievements larger than self. The basis for attaining this goal is the **resolution of the seven other stages.**[22] Senior adults are confronted, however, with the fact that life on this earth will soon be over. There is nothing we can do as pastors, ministers, or teachers to change the choices individuals made over a lifetime. But we *can* help people prepare for this last stage of life. Choices made in Stage 7 have a major impact on a positive resolution of Stage 8.

Stage 7: Generativity-Stagnation

The median adult years, ranging roughly between thirty and sixty-five, form the seventh stage of Erikson's theory. This stage, by far the longest, involves the crises of parenting and teaching children, giving oneself to community concerns, and caring for aging parents.[23]

The positive resolution of this stage is **generativity**, which provides adults a sense of productivity and accomplishment. The primary development task at this stage is **contributing to society.**[24] Erikson emphasized the family context, "the interest in establishing and guiding the next generation"[25] where parents lovingly **pass on their values and priorities** to their children.[26] Beyond the family, however, generative adults **care about their communities**[27] and **contribute to others** and society at large.[28] Generative adults engage in creative, productive efforts, such as teaching, which have a positive effect on younger generations.[29]

The negative resolution of this stage is **stagnation**, or self-absorption. Rather than giving themselves to others, self-absorbed adults tend to hoard their possessions and gifts. They become **self-centered.**[30] They possess little interest in improving themselves or making a contribution to others.[31] Self-absorbed adults find little meaning or purpose in life other than their own **self-indulgence.**[32] They are characterized by apathy and boredom.[33]

The goal for Stage 7 is to develop an interest in helping others: caring for family, serving in one's church, working in the broader community, expanding one's influence to the world. The basis for attaining this goal is the **achievement of a rewarding personal life.**[34] Median adults will either give themselves away in service to others, attaining generativity, or they will center their attention on themselves, attaining self-absorbed stagnation. The former leads to integrity, while the latter leads to despair.

How, then, do we encourage median adults to serve? How do we prepare them along the way to establish relationships with others, and to rearrange personal priorities in order to give their time, and money, and energy to help others? Choices made in Stage 6 have a major impact on a positive resolution of Stage 7.

Stage 6: Intimacy-Isolation

The young adult years, ranging roughly between eighteen and thirty, form the sixth stage in Erikson's theory. During this stage adults resolve the issue of giving themselves to significant others in meaningful, long-term, reciprocal relationships.[35] An essential component of these relationships is the ethical strength to abide by those commitments, despite sacrifices.[36]

The positive resolution of this stage is **intimacy**, which results in the ability of one individual to **form an intimate relationship with another.** Erikson, writing in an earlier age, had **marriage** foremost in mind, defining intimacy as an individual finding **one significant other** to give self to, giving for the sake of giving, expecting nothing.[37] Good (1990) defined intimacy as "long-term sexual relationships."[38] Dembo (1994) identifies intimacy as "sexual union and close friendship."[39] Today's textbooks use more general phrases, such as "learn how to give and take love unselfishly" (2002)[40] and "establish close ties with others" (2007)[41] and "close and committed intimate relationships" (2009).[42] Ormrod (2006) references Erikson's focus on marriage by saying "intimate, reciprocal relationships (e.g., **through marriage or close friendships**)."[43] Perhaps her use of italics underscores the sexual nature of relationships—she does not say—but common usage of the word suggests this is so. Generally speaking, Stage 6 finds young adults establishing long-term, reciprocal, mutually trusting relationships with each other. Older adults are able to establish personal relationships based on openness and mutual confidence.

The negative resolution of this stage is **isolation.** Young adults who are unable to form such reciprocal relationships will, in time, develop a **sense of isolation** from others.[44] They **fail to connect with others** in a meaningful way,[45] and move into greater seclusion and loneliness. Young adults become emotionally isolated, unable to give or receive love freely.[46] Older adults tend to be emotionally isolated and have difficulty giving or receiving love.

The goal of Stage 6 is for individuals to establish and maintain meaningful, reciprocal relationships with others without losing their own identity. The basis for achieving this goal is **personal confidence, openness to others, and rewarding experiences with significant others.**[47] Young adults will either learn to give themselves to another (as in marriage) or to a select group of personal friends (as in intimate, mutual, trusting, and sacrificial friendships), or they will pull away from others and become increasingly isolated. The former leads to generativity, while the latter leads to stagnation.

How, then, do we help young adults enter into mutually beneficial, close relationships with a select group of others? Or, ultimately, with that one they will marry? Choices made in Stage 5 have a major impact on a positive resolution of Stage 6.

Stage 5: Identity-Role Confusion

The adolescent years, ages twelve to eighteen,[48] form the fifth stage in Erikson's theory. While a strong case can certainly be made for adolescence extending through the college years,[49] and even to the late twenties,[50] textbooks maintain Erikson's original "12–18" range. Perhaps this is because they target K–12 educational institutions.

Adolescents undergo major physical, emotional, social, and psychological changes. In fact, change is the key word of this turbulent stage, which Sprinthall describes as "the most radical of the eight."[51] Adolescents are seeking an identity of their own, caught in the psychological no man's land between childlike dependence on adults and adult inter-dependence with peers. "Who am I?" and "Who will I become?" are core questions during this period.[52] Adolescents begin to question the value system, beliefs, and attitudes they received from their parents,[53] and begin to form a new perception of self, an identity of their own.[54] The question "How do I understand what is happening to me when so much is different?"[55] reflects the struggle of this stage.

The positive resolution of this stage is **identity**, which produces a sense of **being at home with oneself,** a feeling of **stability,** of **knowing who one is** and what one **will do with life**. Identity comes from reactions from significant others—parents, respected teachers, and especially friends—as they experiment with various roles and behaviors[56]—working on cars, baby-sitting, sports, academics, church activities. Identity is also reinforced by the kind of role models adolescents choose for themselves. Adolescents experiment with fads, clothes, music, hairstyles and special code words to provide them an identity of their own, separate—but not yet independent of—their parents.[57] Adolescents need firm, caring adults who understand them and listen to them while providing security by enforcing limits of acceptable behavior.[58] As adults, they know who they are, and live—not overly dependent on others, nor completely independent from others—in a state of confident interdependence with others.

The negative resolution of this stage is **role confusion**, which is reflected in teenagers' sense of **confusion about the future, worries** about what they will become, what they'll do, who they'll marry: it is a **basic uncertainty about who they are**.[59] Adults who do not resolve this stage lack confidence and tend to reject authority.

James Marcia[60] made a significant contribution to the phases of identity development through interviews with college students. His interviews consisted of three basic questions. First, he asked about their political ideology: "How would you compare your own political ideas with those of your folks?" Second, he asked about religion: "Is there any time you've doubted any of your religious beliefs?" Finally, he asked about occupation: "How have you come to be interested in—career?" He and his staff were able to ask a series of open-ended questions that provided "a good sample of each student's worldview."[61]

From this data he isolated two major questions. First, "Has there been a crisis of identity for this adolescent?" Or, put another way, "Has this person engaged in an active search for identity?"[62] The answer is "Yes" or "No." Second, "Has the adolescent made a decision regarding his identity?" Or, Has this person made a commitment to life choices?"[63] The answer is "Yes" or "No." These two questions and their dichotomous responses create a 2x2 matrix of four cells. Into these four cells, Marcia places his four identity statuses: identity diffusion, foreclosure, moratorium, and identity achievement. The chart below summarizes the four statuses.[64]

Identity diffusion. Adolescents in this status have made no commitment to a belief system, worldview, or career. While there may be some experimentation with various roles, there is no serious exploration of self-definition.[65] Adolescents in diffusion live for the moment, doing whatever feels good, with little thought of who they are or what they will become.[66] "Mom wanted me to be a minister of music, and Dad wanted me to be an engineer. For a long time—for several years—I wasn't sure what I should be."

IDENTITY STATUSES: JAMES MARCIA

CRISS?	COMMITMENT?	
	YES	NO
YES	**IDENTITY ACHIEVEMENT** Secure sense of self. Commitments to career, religion, political views are self-directed and self-chosen	**MORATORIUM** No clear commitments to society No clear sense of identity Seriously seeking an identity
NO	**FORECLOSURE** Commitments to views adopted from others (parents, teachers). Little evidence of personal questioning	**IDENTITY DIFFUSION** Unconcerned with career, religion, political views Lacking direction

Foreclosure. Adolescents in foreclosure have made a commitment to a career or worldview, but they have not experienced an identity crisis.[67] Their commitments are based on the expectations of others: teachers, significant friends, and "especially parents."[68] "Mom and Dad always wanted me to take over their restaurant. I've never wanted to do anything else."

Moratorium. Adolescents in moratorium are actively exploring various professions and considering worldviews and belief systems, but they have not yet made a firm commitment to a particular occupation, or a specific set of beliefs.[69] There is no clear sense of identity.[70] "I've looked into joining the Army Green Berets or Navy Seals, and also given thought to going to Bible College first and becoming a military chaplain. I also like the idea of starting my own computer company. I'm just not sure yet."

Identity achievement. Adolescents who reach identity achievement have experienced a crisis of identity, explored options, and chosen, for themselves, who they are and what they'll do.[71] They have emerged from a period of moratorium with a commitment to particular political or religious beliefs, a clear choice of career, or both.[72] "I've decided to attend Bible College and seminary, and pursue chaplaincy with the U. S. Army." Identity also has cultural implications. Jung Ki Choi conducted research (2008) showing a relationship between cultural identity and spiritual maturity among Korean Christians.[73]

The goal of Stage 5 is for adolescents to establish a satisfying sense of personal identity and direction. The basis for attaining this goal is **social acceptance and recognition.**[74] Those who positively resolve this stage are less self-conscious, more open to others, more logical in decision-making, and able to work effectively under stress as well as establish close interpersonal relationships.[75] Adolescents who do not resolve this stage lack confidence and tend to reject authority. They doubt their own sex role[76] and can easily change their ideas about career, gender roles, and values through feedback.[77]

Adolescents will either seriously search for a personally satisfying worldview and life's work, or they will wander from one perspective to another without any sense of direction. The former leads to identity and purpose, while the latter leads to confusion and aimlessness.

How, then, do we help adolescents seize proper role models and roles? How do we provide them with an opportunity to achieve a sense of self-worth and ability? Choices made in Stage 4 have a major impact on a positive resolution of Stage 5.

Stage 4: Industry-Inferiority

The elementary years, ages six to eleven, form Erikson's fourth stage. Children push outward from home to the neighborhood school, expanding their social environment from family to friends and teachers. The focus of the child in this stage is developing physical, emotional, and academic skills.[78]

The positive resolution of stage four is **industry**, or competence, which garners recognition for successful doing.[79] This, in turn, produces a sense of diligence in working, a persistence to complete tasks, and putting work before pleasure.[80] Teachers help children negotiate this stage by engaging them in learning activities appropriate for their age and abilities, by helping them successfully complete the activities, and by praising them for their effort. Success leads to success in an upward spiral.[81] As adults, they will continue to develop new skills as they engage an ever expanding world.

The negative resolution of this stage is **inferiority**, which develops as a result of repeated unsuccessful experiences.[82] Children, unable to compete with others or succeed on assigned tasks, even with help, fall farther behind in development. Failure to meet the expectations of teachers in the classroom, or parents at home, leads to a sense of being a "failure at everything."[83] If children are derided or treated as bothersome, feelings of self-doubt and inferiority increase.[84] These feelings of failure impair more than academic studies, but extend to hobbies, sports, and even making friends.[85] Adults who fail to resolve this stage tend to be timid and overly obedient. They tend to be observers more than producers and frequently question their own abilities throughout life.[86]

The goal of Stage 4 is for children to master the physical, emotional, social, academic, and personal developmental tasks of childhood. The basis for attaining this goal is **success and recognition of progress.**[87] Children will either apply themselves diligently to a given task—a science experiment in a Western classroom, or hunting for food in a preliterate society[88]—and persist until success is achieved, or, they will shrink back from the task from fear of failure. The former leads to industry, while the latter leads to inferiority.

How, then, do we help children engage the many learning tasks that confront them as they enter school? How do we stimulate their initiative so that they will attempt new assignments with optimism? Choices made in Stage 3 have a major impact on a positive resolution of Stage 4.

Stage 3: Initiative-Guilt

The preschool years, ages four and five,[89] form Erikson's third stage. Fours and fives like to show off and try new things. The constant questions of "Why?" and "What?" can be quite tiring to adults, but they are essential in personality growth.[90] They want to help their parents and need assurance that the help is welcome. They are curious and "into everything."[91]

The positive resolution of this stage is **initiative**, producing children who **attack a task**, who **use their freedom in socially appropriate ways.** Children use language and newfound abilities to aggressively explore physical and social environments.[92] If they are supported and treated warmly during this time, and given guidance from parents concerning appropriate and inappropriate exploration,[93] they develop **confidence** in undertaking new challenges.[94] As adults, they continue to take the initiative to learn new things and meet life's challenges with confidence.

The negative resolution of this stage is **guilt**, the result of parents rejecting or punishing the self-initiated activities of their children.[95] Guilt leaves children **inhibited and afraid** to try new things on their own.[96] Adults who fail to resolve this stage are easily depressed, self-abrasive, and tend to exhibit low energy levels.[97]

The goal of Stage 3 is for preschoolers to vigorously engage the world around them. The basis for attaining this goal is **tolerance, encouragement, and reinforcement**[98] from parents. Preschoolers will either try new things—selecting their own clothes, making their own breakfast, or cutting their own hair[99]—with parental support and guidance,[100] or they will refuse to try new things because of over-control or criticism from parents.[101] The former leads to initiative, while the latter leads to guilt.

How, then, do we help preschoolers try new things with vigor? How do we help them establish self-control so they attempt new tasks safely? Choices made in Stage 2 have a major impact on a positive resolution of Stage 3.

Stage 2: Autonomy—Shame and Doubt

The toddler years, ages two and three, form Erikson's fourth stage. Children in these years gain increased muscular coordination and mobility.[102] They exert a new sense of independence.[103] The focus of the child in this stage is doing things on their own, such as feeding and dressing themselves.[104] They crawl, walk, run and climb. In general, they change from helpless infants to self-controlled children.[105]

The positive resolution of this stage is **autonomy**, a sense of independence from Mom and Dad, of being able to do things **"my own way" within limits.**[106] Toilet training is the best example of this, but a larger issue is that adults begin imposing rules and expectations that call for self-control and self-denial.[107] If parents handle these situations appropriately—with advice, reassurance, and confidence[108]—children can adjust to new demands without losing their sense of personal autonomy.[109] As adults, they can adjust to changing external demands without losing their sense of self-control.

The negative resolution of this stage is **shame and doubt**, the result of parents who make too many demands, or who force issues too early. When parents are overly restrictive or punish minor accidents, when they emphasize threats and punishments, when they smother their children with help,[110] children develop a sense of **shame at their own failures** and begin to **doubt their capabilities.**[111] They do not develop a sense of personal autonomy and self-control, but feel completely dependent on the parents who control them. They **lack confidence** in their own power to deal with the world.[112] As adults they may experience difficulties in self-concept and impulse control.[113] They may exhibit frequent procrastination, the need for direction and structure, embarrassment when complimented, and a tendency to be easily influenced by others.[114]

The goal of Stage 2 is for toddlers to grow in self-reliance and their ability to deal with setbacks. The basis for attaining this goal is **setting limits without blame or rejection.**[115] Toddlers will either satisfy some of their own needs—feeding, washing, and dressing themselves, using the bathroom[116]—with parental guidance and encouragement,[117] or they will shrink back from doing things on their own due to parental impatience,[118] excessive demands, or ridicule.[119] The former leads to autonomy, while the latter leads to shame and doubt.

How, then, do we help children engage the many learning tasks that confront them as they enter school? How do we stimulate their initiative so that they will attempt new assignments with optimism? Choices made in Stage 1 have a major impact on a positive resolution of Stage 2.

Stage 1: Trust-Mistrust

Infancy, from birth to one year of age, forms Erikson's first stage. During this time infants are totally dependent on adults for their care. The focus of this stage is learning that the world, as defined by caregivers, is dependable and reliable.[120] The kind of care they receive determines their fundamental dispositions toward others.[121]

The positive resolution of this stage is trust, a result of consistent, regular care for the infant's basic needs,[122] primarily by the mother.[123] Infants who are touched, held, loved, fed and kept dry develop feelings of contentment and trust in those who care for them. Such a caring environment permits children to think of their world as safe and dependable.[124] Adults who trust others are happier, better adjusted, and better liked than those who lack trust in others.[125]

The negative resolution of this stage is mistrust, the result of inadequate care, neglect or abuse. Children who are not cared for adequately during the first year of life[126] develop deep-seated feelings of fear and suspicion[127] concerning the world around them.[128] These feelings follow the child into adulthood as paranoia and insecurity.[129]

The goal of Stage 1 is for infants to achieve a sense of optimism, security, and trust in others. The basis for attaining this goal is the satisfaction of basic needs.[130] Infants will either be lovingly cared for and protected, or they will be ignored, neglected, or abused. The former leads to trust, while the latter leads to mistrust.

The table below summarizes senior adult characteristics resulting from positive and negative resolutions through all eight stages of life.

Characteristics of Senior Adults
Resulting from Positive and Negative Resolutions of Erikson's Stages

Stage	Negative Resolution	Positive Resolution
1	• Paranoia • Insecurity	• feelings of contentment and trust in others
2	• difficulties in impulse control • frequent procrastination • need for direction and structure • embarrassment when complimented • easily influenced by others	• can adjust to changing external demands without losing their sense of self-control
3	• easily depressed • self-abrasive • tend to have a low energy level	• take the initiative to learn new things • meet life's challenges with confidence

4	• timid and overly obedient • observers more than producers • frequently question their own abilities	• continue to develop new skills as they engage their world
5	• lack confidence • tend to reject authority	• know who they are • confident interdependence with others
6	• emotionally isolated • have difficulty giving or receiving love	• able to establish personal relationships based on openness and mutual confidence
7	• find little meaning or purpose in life other than self-indulgence • apathetic • bored	• creative • productive • engaged in teaching the next generation
8	• self-contempt and desperation • regret things still undone • worry that time is running out • harbor bitterness in the shortness of life and inability to start over	• general feeling of well-being • satisfaction with life • acceptance of what they have done and who they are, including failures • sense of dignity and wholeness

Erikson's Adaptation: Maladaptions, Malignancies, and Adaptive Strengths

Erikson's early work (1950) left the impression that the positive resolution of each stage leads to healthy personalities. Trust, autonomy, and generativity, for example, lead to a positive end. In fact, this is the obvious conclusion one reaches when looking at the summary table above. And yet we know that *too much* trust leads to naiveté and potential danger. Young children need a measure of "appropriate mistrust": "Do not talk with strangers." Too much autonomy leads to shameful behavior. Children need limits: "We do not remove our clothes in public." Too much generativity leads to exhaustion and burnout as we give more than we are able: "Learn to say no."

Each stage possesses unhealthy extremes and a healthy balance. Erikson called imbalance toward the positive pole **maladaptive** ("too much of a good thing"), and imbalance toward the negative pole **malignant** ("too little of a good thing").[131] Clinicians suggest that maladaptive behaviors tend toward neurotic disturbances, while malignant behaviors tend toward psychotic disturbances, requiring more radical intervention.[132]

The balance between positive (*syntonic*) and negative (*dystonic*) dispositions produces a healthy resolution, or **adaptive strength**,[133] of each of the eight developmental crises. We will investigate each of these in chronological order.[134] A table for each stage will summarize essential ideas for each stage.

Stage	Maladaptive	Adaptive Strength	Malignant
1	**Sensory Maladjustment**	**HOPE**	**Withdrawal**
	Unrealistic, overly dependent, gullible	**Realistic Trust in others**	Suspicious, paranoid, avoidance of others
		Trust	Mistrust	
	Trusting significant others in light of life's realities		

1. Trust, taken to an extreme by overprotective parents, leads to over-compliance in older infants.[135] In other words, over-care can produce an unhealthy dependency in children. Infants may become "unrealistic, spoilt, and deluded."[136] Erikson used the term "sensory maladjustment" to describe this condition. These children may grow into adults who exhibit characteristics of naiveté and gullibility, who seek others whom they can depend on to care for them.

Mistrust, taken to the extreme by neglect and abuse, leads to withdrawal. Long-term neglect and physical or verbal abuse can produce a "pathological impact"[137] that moves the infant beyond mistrust into withdrawal, which is a malignant avoidance of others.[138] These children may grow into adults who exhibit characteristics of suspicion and paranoia of others. They enjoy provoking conflict because it both bolsters their own sense of power and drives others away.

The healthy resolution of trust-mistrust is HOPE, defined by Erikson as "the enduring belief in the benevolence of fate, in spite of dark urges and rages that also mark the beginning of existence." As such, hope is the "basis of faith" brought about by the initial patterns of maternal care.[139] I use the phrase *realistic trust in others* to reflect the synthesis of trust and mistrust—trust that acknowledges dangers in the real world.

Stage	Maladaptive	Adaptive Strength	Malignant
2	**Shamelessness**	**WILL**	Compulsive
	Willful, demanding. Lacks propriety. Little or no self-restraint	**Free choice with self-restraint**	Self-doubt. Self-doubting. Self-assertion dies
		Autonomy	Shame & Doubt	
	Making autonomous choices in light of the rights and rules of others		

2. Autonomy taken to an extreme leads to shamelessness and willfulness. Parents may overde-velop autonomy in an attempt to avoid shaming their toddlers with rules and restrictions. Such chil-dren may assert their own wants in a willful manner, without an appropriate sense of propriety. There is little self-restraint, and toddlers can become reckless, inconsiderate, and thoughtless.[140]

Shame and doubt taken to an extreme leads to compulsive self-doubt. When parents consistently and severely punish toddlers for minor infractions, when they personally shame and belittle them, they move them beyond mere shame and doubt to the place of malignant and compulsive self-doubt.[141] Such children lack any sense of determination to assert themselves. They are constrained and self-limiting.[142]

The healthy resolution of autonomy-shame and doubt is WILL, defined by Erikson as "the unbroken determination to exercise free choice as well as self-restraint." A maturing will forms the basis for the "eventual acceptance of law and necessity."[143] I use the phrase *self-regulated free choice* to reflect the synthesis of autonomy (free-choice) and shame and doubt (self-doubting)—an autonomy restrained by proper boundaries, which form the "beginnings of a sense of identity."[144]

Stage	Maladaptive	Adaptive Strength	Malignant
3	**Ruthlessness**	**PURPOSE**	Inhibition
	Confronts authorities. Combative. Exploitive.	**Self-controlled Pursuit**	False guilt. Risk-aversive. Unadventurous.
		Initiative	Guilt	
	Aggressive pursuit of goals, constrained by appropriate boundaries		

3. Initiative leads to ruthlessness when permissive parents set few boundaries to guide preschooler exploration. Preschoolers will naturally extend themselves beyond the bounds of acceptable social behavior unless boundaries are set and maintained. Violation of these boundaries leads to a sense of guilt, which restrains confrontation and exploitation. Healthy guilt guides preschoolers away from excessive or offending behavior. Without appropriate restraint cause by a healthy sense of guilt, children can become ruthless in their actions toward parents, siblings, and other children.

Too much guilt—especially *false* guilt—can lead children to develop a malignant sense of self-inhibition. The fear of excessive punishment from parents or false guilt imposed by adults can cause children to withdraw into their own internal world.

The healthy resolution of initiative-guilt is PURPOSE, defined by Erikson as "the courage to envisage and pursue valued goals uninhibited by the defeat of infantile phantasies, by an imposed sense of guilt, and by the fear of punishment." Purpose is the basis for later ideals of action.[145] I use the phrase *self-controlled pursuit* to reflect the synthesis of initiative (active pursuit) and guilt (self-controlled)—initiative that is taken within appropriate family and social guidelines.

Stage	Maladaptive	Adaptive Strength		Malignant
4	**Narrow Virtuosity**	**COMPETENCE**		Inertia
	Obsessive specialist. Workaholic. Limited skill set.	**Wholesome Mastery**		Apathetic. Lazy. Failure to Complete Tasks.
		Industry	Inferiority	
	Mastering skills free of unwholesome obsession			

4. Industry taken to an extreme leads to narrow virtuosity. Narrow virtuosity results when "the whole child" is channeled into an obsessive practice of a limited set of skills.[146] Children become obsessive specialists as they focus more of themselves on increasingly narrow interests. Dreams of Olympic Gold can change a healthy involvement with sports into an obsessive drive to be the very best in the world. The maladaption grows as balanced industry gives way to obsession.

Inferiority taken to an extreme leads to inertia. Repeated failure to complete tasks, the perceived inability to develop required skills over time may lead to the malignant state of inertia, the "habitual inclination toward a sense of inferiority."[147] The healthy resolution of industry-inferiority is

COMPETENCE, defined by Erikson as "the free exercise of dexterity and intelligence in the completion of tasks, unimpaired by a forever threatening sense of inferiority." Competence becomes the basis for "cooperative participation in technologies and relies, in turn, on the logic of tools and skills."[148] This sense of competence might be described as the mastering new skills with confidence. I use the phrase *wholesome mastery* to reflect the synthesis of industry (mastery) and inferiority (recognition of limitations)—industry that acknowledges the dangers of workaholic obsession.

Stage	Maladaptive	Adaptive Strength		Malignant
5	Fanaticism	FIDELITY		Repudiation
	Extremist ideology. Excessive zeal. Self-seeking sycophant.	True to Self - True to Others		Socially disconnected. Rejection of others. Refusal to follow others.
		Identity	Role Confusion	
	Remaining true to oneself and one's belief system within the context of other belief systems			

5. Identity taken to an extreme leads to fanaticism. In the search for self, the central crisis for Erikson, adolescents are influenced by adult role models, "whether present and active among the young person's mentors or apparent on the horizon as heroes and leaders."[149] If adolescents fixate on a role model, or an ideology, they may be unable to separate their own identity from the ideology. This is fanaticism, a state of being motivated by "excessive, irrational zeal."[150]

Role confusion taken to an extreme leads to the repudiation of others as models. When adolescents confront too much confusion and contradiction in potential role models or ideologies, they may decide to follow no one, to reject all role models, and become socially disconnected.[151] Erikson called this a "repudiation of otherness."[152]

The healthy resolution of identity-role confusion is FIDELITY, defined by Erikson as "the ability to sustain loyalties freely pledged in spite of the inevitable contradictions of value systems." Fidelity is the "cornerstone of identity."[153] I use the phrase *true to self—true to others* to reflect the synthesis of identity and role confusion—personal identity that embraces healthy role models but is not enslaved by them.

Stage	Maladaptive	Adaptive Strength		Malignant
6	**Promiscuity**	**LOVE**		**Exclusivity**
	Trial sexual relationships. Sexually needy. Emotionally vulnerable.	**Committed Intimacy**		Unable to relate to others. Detached and lonely. Self-contained hater.
		Intimacy	Isolation	
	Capacity for personal commitment to one, in marriage, and to others, as [non-sexual] devoted friends			

6. Intimacy taken to an extreme leads to promiscuity. Young adults entering the military or college may experiment with trial friendships and short-term sexual relationships as their world expands and parental boundaries weaken. The self-serving nature of these alliances, coupled with a lack of long-term commitment, leads to the maladaption of promiscuity, leaving young adults emotionally vulnerable.[154]

Isolation taken to an extreme leads to exclusivity. Young adults may fail to establish meaningful relationships. Perhaps imbalances in earlier stages—inability to trust, lack of initiative, incompetence, self-doubt—sabotage these efforts. Whatever the cause, young adults may move beyond isolation into the malignancy of "hate-filled exclusivity."[155]

The healthy resolution of intimacy-isolation is LOVE, defined by Erikson as "the mutuality of devotion forever subduing the antagonisms inherent in divided function." Love is the "capacity for eventual commitment to lasting friendships and companionship in general, and [a long-term sexual relationship in particular]. Love is the basis for ethical concern."[156] I use the phrase *committed intimacy* to reflect the synthesis of intimacy and isolation—intimacy that lives within the boundaries of personal commitment to another, as in marriage, and to others, as in devoted friendships.

Stage	Maladaptive	Adaptive Strength		Malignant
7	**Overextension**	**CARE**		**Rejectivity**
	Overly involved do-gooder. Busy-body. Burned-out meddler.	**Self-Managed Nurture of others**		Disinterested in others. Cynical. Obsessed with self.
		Generativity	Stagnation	
	Nurturing others in family, church, community, and society-at-large while acknowledging the need to care appropriately for self as well			

7. Generativity taken to an extreme leads to overextension. The desire to "take care of what one truly cares for"[157] can become maladaptive when caring becomes more intrusive than helpful. When adults "help others" in order to satisfy their need to be needed, they find it difficult to refrain. They busy themselves in the affairs of others, "doing good" for them.[158] Overextension results from being overly involved with family, church, school, community, and society needs.

Stagnation taken to an extreme leads to an overt, cynical disinterest in others,[159] which Erikson calls rejectivity. Adults who are obsessed with themselves—choosing repeatedly to care for themselves and their own desires rather than others—can move beyond stagnation to rejectivity where they "do not care to care—for anybody."[160]

The healthy resolution of generativity-stagnation is CARE, defined by Erikson as "the widening concern for what has been generated by love, necessity, or accident; it overcomes the ambivalence arising with irreversible obligation." Care is the responsible nurturing of children and youth, as well as appropriate and constructive involvement with friends, community, and society. I use the phrase *self-managed nurture of others* to reflect the synthesis of generativity and stagnation—generativity that acknowledges the need to care for self as well.

Stage	Maladaptive	Adaptive Strength		Malignant
8	Presumption	WISDOM		Disdain
	Pompous arrogance. Lack of humility and humor. Conceit.	Satisfied Reflection		Blaming others. Miserable cynicism. Life is worthless.
		Integrity	Despair	
	"The detached concern for life itself, in the face of death itself." Erikson, 1986			

8. Integrity, taken to an extreme, leads to presumption. The last stage of life is reflective, providing a time for integrating the seven preceding stages of life. When senior adults ignore the negatives of life—past failures, regrettable decisions, and the inescapable fact of death[161]—they may develop a presumption of superiority over others. Presuming to be larger than life, adults can become arrogant and pompous.[162] Prejudice[163] and lack of humility and humor[164] characterize adults who presume to know more than they do.

Despair, taken to an extreme, leads to disdain. The world closes in on senior adults as they grow older and lose friends, freedom and mobility, and physical abilities.

Those who are unable to maintain involvement with the world due to natural limitations move toward a malignant disdain for life itself.[165] Disdain generates a miserable cynicism towards life, which is increasingly seen as worthless.[166]

The healthy resolution of integrity-despair is WISDOM, defined by Erikson as "the detached concern with life itself, in the face of death itself. It maintains and learns to convey the integrity of experience, in spite of the decline of bodily and mental functions."[167] I use the phrase *satisfied reflection* to refer the synthesis of integrity and despair—integrity as the integration of all elements of a life fitly lived.

Erikson's Ninth Stage: Gerotranscendence

Erik Erikson lived to the age of 91. He "personified his own theory of development in his achievement of personal and professional integrity" and passed away in 1994.[168] In 1997 his wife, Joan, revised *The Life Cycle Completed* (1982) and included a new last chapter devoted entirely to the theme of gerotranscendence, drawing on ideas developed by Lars Tornstam.

Tornstam defines gerotranscendence as "a shift in meta-perspective, from a material and rational vision to a more cosmic and transcendent one, normally followed by an increase in life satisfaction."[169] The phrase "shift in meta-perspective" implies a radical change of one's outlook on life from a concern with mundane issues to a **concern with universal values.**[170] This shift involves three levels of age-related ontological change.[171]

First, there is the **cosmic dimension** of life, or the feeling of being part of and at one with the universe. While gerotranscendent adults begin to feel part of the larger universe, their concept of personal space would decrease to, perhaps, the size of their hospital room.[172] This shift in perspective **lessens concerns with one's impending physical death** because there is **an increasing sense of continuity with the universe.**[173]

The second level of ontological change is the **perception of one's self.** While the cosmic dimension of life concerns the wider perspective of life and the world, the dimension of self-perception concerns **how persons perceive themselves** and the world around them.

The third level of ontological change experienced in gerotranscendence is an increase in **interrelatedness with others.** Gerotranscendent persons re-evaluate the meaning behind the ties they have established with family, friends, and others. This results in an increased sense of connection with past and future generations. "One becomes less self-centered and the sense of oneself expands to include **a wider range of interrelated others.**"[174] Gerotranscendent persons become **more open**

and responsive to others while at the same time becoming more selective in their use of such openness.[175]

Erikson's eighth stage **reflects backward** to the life that has been lived. Integrity, or wholeness, results from reflection that discovers well-being, acceptance, and satisfaction. Tornstam postulates a **future focus**, in that personal purpose and meaning come from a process of continued becoming.[176] This on-going process of becoming forms a connection with something beyond one's self.[177]

Some of the characteristics of gerotranscendence include the *increase* in tolerance for ambiguity, the quality of social contacts, altruism, self-confrontation, the acceptance of life's mysteries, and ego integrity. Further, there is a *decrease* in fears about life and death, self-centeredness, ego-centrism, and interest in material things. Tornstam gives us little help in constructing ways to assist seniors in achieving gerotranscendence. Still, from an Evangelical point of view, **it is interesting to watch secular theorists struggle with dimensions of human life beyond the self,** which for decades has been held to be supreme reality.

Life expectancy has increased substantially since Erikson first theorized his eighth stage of ego-integrity in the 1950's. Since Erikson believed personality continues to develop throughout life, one wonders what he would propose today with the additional fifteen to twenty years of life one has, on average, after achieving ego-integrity.

Criticisms of Erikson's Theory

Although Erikson's theory has been generally supported by research, several aspects have been criticized through the years. These criticisms view the theory as subjective, culturally narrow, male-oriented, and repetitious.

Most of Erikson's conclusions were drawn from personal and subjective observations that have only been partly substantiated by the kind of controlled experimentation and observation discussed in Chapter Two. There have been limited checks on Erikson's tendency to generalize from limited personal experiences.[178]

Erikson's views on identity formation require a child who actively explores over time and makes personal choices. Some cultures, however, do not provide the long-term parental support, individual freedom, and wealth needed to sustain a long period of moratorium. In these cultures, decisions are often made by parents and imposed on adolescents.[179]

Erikson's theory is seen by some as a male-oriented theory. Research conducted by Carol Gilligan (1982, 1988) and others indicated that males and females achieve identity differently. Males tend to look within themselves, to their own skills and competencies, to define who they are. Females tend to be more interpersonal in forming their identity. They find "themselves" in the context of "others." Men tend to form their identity before moving into the intimacy, following Erikson's order of Stage 5 and then 6. Women tend to form deep personal relationships, out of which they form their personal identity, reversing the sequence.[180]

More recent research, however, shows a narrowing of gender differences. Archer (1992a, 1992b, 1994) found no differences in identity across gender by vocation, religion, sex roles, values, and dating. Skoe (1991) confirmed the lack of gender differences on identity status, moral judgment, and a specially constructed *care interview*.[181] Sprinthall explains Erikson's male orientation as a natural extension of the male-oriented culture in which Erikson developed his theory.[182] More recent research shows that gender differences have diminished over the years.

The criticism of male-orientation presents another concern. Erikson focuses on "competence," for example, as the important outcome of the industry-inferiority stage. Research shows this is true for boys, who tend to focus on skills. It is less true for girls, who focus on relationships as well as competence.

Finally, some point to the repetitious similarity of stages. Autonomy, initiative, and industry all focus on "doing things on your own." Doubt, guilt, and inferiority all focus on "the need for sympathetic parental support." Despite these criticisms, Erikson's theory clarifies important aspects of human development.[183]

Implications for Christian Teachers

Paul wrote to the Corinthians, "Therefore, if anyone is in Christ, he is a new creation; the old has gone, the new has come!" (2 Cor 5:17). Since we are a "new creation" in Christ, and since "the old" is gone, why bother with human conceptions of personality development? Why should Christians be concerned about human growth and development?

The answer is found, first, in the thrust of Paul's message. Paul is referring to the spiritual truth that one who has come into vital union with Christ has been radically transformed. Believers see the world differently. Their outlook is changed from "the old" self-centeredness and perversion of the past. Paul does not imply that believers are instantaneously transformed into healthy, whole human personalities. His letters contain explicit testimonies of his concern for Christian growth and maturing as believers take off the "old garments" and put on the "new" (Col 3:8–12) in the social context of the Church. We saw this in the Center Pillar and Capstone of the Disciplers' Model in Chapter One.

The answer is found, secondly, in practical experience. Not all bad habits are defeated upon conversion. There is faith. And then there is growth. Self-denial and discipline, hated by the self-centered, are words of freedom and release to the faithful. Within this context of growth, there is ample room for Erikson's insights. Do we have difficulty trusting others? Are we shackled by shame or doubt? Do we possess a "natural" feeling of inferiority? Have we been fractured by unhealthy role models? Do we find ourselves seeking isolation rather than fellowship? Are we afraid to give ourselves away to others? Erikson provides a way of perceiving these difficulties in the context of life experiences.

It is never God's desire that children be abused. Jesus made that clear when He defined kingdom greatness in terms of childlike humility. And then He issued a warning. "Whoever causes the downfall of one of these little ones who believe in Me—it would be better for him if a heavy millstone were hung around his neck and he were drowned in the depths of the sea! Woe to the world because of offenses. For offenses must come, but woe to that man by whom the offense comes" (Matt 18:6–8).

When abuse occurs—the result of living in a sinful world—children carry emotional, psychological and relational scars through life. Mistrust, shame, guilt, inferiority, role confusion, isolation, stagnation, despair—all of these hinder the growth of individuals toward wholeness. Can Christ overcome these experiences? Can He heal the wounds? Yes, He can, and He does. We can help by being friends, helpers, and counselors in the process of healing. Erik Erikson helps us understand the mechanisms by which identity and relationships are healed.

Implications for Teaching in the Church

Space does not permit an extensive list of age-specific teaching suggestions.[184] But we can offer some suggestions for fostering healthy personality growth in the local church or church school. We will deal with instructional issues in later chapters.

1. Infants and Ones: "Realistic trust."

We teach infants that church is a safe place by promptly caring for their basic needs. Teachers provide comfort by holding and rocking them. They feed them when they are hungry. They change diapers when needed. Such actions, when carried out consistently and cheerfully, nurture a sense of trust in infants.

Long before children can express feelings with words, they experience the world around them in a deeply emotional way. The experiences of infants in church set the emotional stage for future church experiences.

2. Twos and Threes: "Free choice within limits."

Learning centers provide toddlers a safe environment to explore. Toddlers enjoy a variety of activities, including puzzles and art and playing with toys. Teachers balance freedom of toddlers to explore with guided supervision[185] by firmly imposing rules and restraints.[186] Toddlers need opportunities to do things for themselves, including eating, dressing, and toilet use.

Toddlers engage in constructive play—creating or constructing things, such as building a house out of toy blocks, drawing a picture, or putting together a puzzle.[187] When teachers reward toddlers' attempts and successes, and refrain from humiliating them when they have difficulties,[188] toddlers develop both self-control and self-confidence.

3. Fours and Fives: "Self-controlled pursuit."

Stage 3 revolves around the child's growth of power—that is, the ability to make things happen.[189] Preschoolers want to expand their world of experiences, to try new things. Language is rapidly developing, and they ask many questions.[190] Teachers help preschoolers develop a sense of accomplishment[191] by teaching new activities in small steps.

Preschoolers engage in make-believe play in which they act out roles, such as playing house, school, or doctor, or acting as a television character.[192] They encourage preschoolers to act out the stories using costumes and props that have been provided. They recognize the attempts of children, even if what they produce is unsatisfactory. If mistakes are made, teachers help preschoolers clean up, repair, or redo.[193] In these ways, preschoolers learn how to explore new things and attack new tasks within the bounds of appropriate behavior toward teachers and classmates.

4. Elementary Children: "Wholesome mastery."

Stage 4 emphasizes competence. Learning should be activity-centered, engaging as many of the senses as possible. Teachers develop a sense of competence in children by helping them set, and then work toward, realistic goals—monitoring their progress, and having them complete their learning tasks successfully.

Teachers provide opportunities for growth in responsibility by delegating tasks such as watering plants and distributing materials. Teachers help children avoid a sense on inferiority by focusing their attention on their own improvements, and by awarding those who are "most helpful" or "most hardworking."[194]

Children's play includes games with specific rules—they are able to understand and follow rules.[195] In these ways, children experience personal success as they tackle a variety of tasks and skill sets—emotional, social, academic, spiritual—in the context of Bible study.

5. Youth: "True to self—true to others."

Adolescents struggle to form a unified self-identity from 1) a complex array of changes and choices from prior stages, 2) parental expectations, and 3) a variety of role models. Physical abilities and appearance, friendships, academic skills, and teacher relationships confront teenagers with a confusing, at times overwhelming, array of influences.[196]

Churches can help teens deal with identity issues by providing a variety of positive, mature role models for them.[197] These role models can be biblical characters, historical figures, college students, young adults in the church, parents, and senior adults. Teachers work with parents to help students find resources for working out their personal problems,[198] including the pastor, youth minister, or a professional counselor.

Adolescents are susceptible to fads, trying out one role and then another, rebelling against church and family values, acting out their exaggerated desire for independence and freedom. Such behavior calls for the teacher's highest commitment of self-giving love, listening heart, flexibility of approach, and eagerness to help. Teachers provide strong support for personal experimentation as they tolerate teenage fads, so long as they are not offensive or disruptive. They can discuss fads of earlier eras. Teachers can help teenagers realistically evaluate their behaviors as they give feedback and focus on the consequences of their choices. Since teens are trying on various roles, teachers help them establish a sense of stability by separating *roles* from *person.*[199] In these ways, teachers provide teenagers reassurance in their search for their identity as a Christian in the face of conflicting role models and ideologies.

6. Young Adults: "Committed intimacy."

Erikson's priority for Stage 6 is giving "self" to "significant other" in marriage, to establish an intimate relationship for sharing life's joys and sorrows, for better or worse. A secondary issue for this stage is establishing intimate (non-sexual) social relationships in general. Churches can help young adults interact in Bible studies through discussing issues, sharing experiences, asking and answering questions, and solving problems. Smaller classes of ten to fifteen members permit better interaction than larger, lecture-type classes. Social events and team-based ministry projects outside of class deepen meaningful relationships among class members.

7. Median Adults: "Self-managed Nurture."

The Church provides abundant opportunities for median adults to give to others through ministry, for applying spiritual gifts to earthly needs, for participation and usefulness in God's kingdom. Church leaders bless members when they "call out the called," helping them match personal gifts with church ministries. This is the New Testament Church, where every believer is a gifted minister, a king, a priest before God, called to service in Jesus' name.

Generativity is at the heart of the teaching ministry of the Church where adults pass on to preschoolers, children, youth, and younger adults the principles of living in Christ. Jesus possessed integrity at the end of His life, humanly speaking, because He spent His active ministry in generativity: giving Himself away to others. Paul spent his later life not only as a "servant of Christ" (Rom 1:1), but as a "slave to everyone, to win as many as possible" (1 Cor 9:19). He gave himself away to others through teaching and preaching, through nurturing churches and training pastors. This is generativity.

As a minister of education in six churches, my work focused on the "training of the saints in the work of ministry" (Eph 4:12). I saw firsthand how adults who accepted God's call to lead, teach, and serve others grew spiritually. I witnessed the transformation of those who obeyed the Lord to "Take up My yoke and learn from Me" (Matt 11:29). Nevertheless, it was encouraging to find in Erik Erikson a secular scientist who pointed directly to psychological, social, and human growth benefits that come from self-giving ministry. Engaging median adults in self-disciplined and self-sacrificing service to others is the essential means by which they develop generativity, the only way to prepare against the debilitating effects of despair in old age.

8. Senior Adults: "Satisfied Reflection."

Churches help senior adults by using their gifts in ministry programs wherever possible. These seniors possess a lifetime of experience, a lifetime of spiritual growth. They are living longer, better, and more productively than any other time in history.

Churches help senior adults when they remember and acknowledge the leaders of the past, the committed saints of God who gave their lives and substance to build the work thirty, or forty, or fifty years before.

9. Transcendent Adults.

Joan Erikson embraced Torstam's concept of gerotranscendence. I cannot help but question the point of encouraging *formation of spirit* just prior to death, which, for secularists, means the end of existence. Why bother about moving seniors beyond a sense of well-being, satisfaction with life, acceptance of what they have done and who they are, all found in Erikson's eighth stage, to a poorly defined ninth stage of existence, when that very existence will soon be snuffed out?

Verbraak attempts an answer. Gerotranscendent persons seem to be in a transition period between a productive life and impending death. Because they are oriented towards facing death, there is "no longer a need or the time to pretend, or impress the outside world." Therefore, they have the freedom to focus on fundamental questions regarding their own lives: "one's place in the universe, one's perception of one's self and one's relationship with the rest of society."[200] Given an a priori viewpoint that death extinguishes the person one has become, I suppose this is the best that can be said, as empty as it is. **There comes a time in the natural span of life that reality mocks the theoretically positive outcomes of such developmental theories.** To add an abstract "cosmic" level to this secular reality merely twists the mockery into something quite ugly.

Fortunately, this depressing dilemma does not plague evangelical Christians or Christian educators and social workers. Spiritual formation among the elderly has as its goal the preparation of persons for life after physical death. Jesus said, "I am going away to prepare a place for you. If I go away and prepare a place for you, I will come back and receive you to Myself, so that where I am you may be also" (John 14:2–3). There is work to be done. "Well done, good and faithful slave! You were faithful over a few things; I will put you in charge of many things. Share your master's joy!" (Matt 25:23). The persons we become do not cease to exist at death, but continue in a truly transcendent reality. Such a view transforms the concept of spiritual formation in senior adults from preparation for death to preparation for a new way of living.

In Summary

We began the chapter with Erikson's fundamental precept: the prenatal interactive stimulation between infant and womb forms the basis for human personality development. We have seen how each stage of development, each crisis, revolves around personal interaction with an ever-widening environment: from womb to mother, to father and siblings, to playmates, to schoolmates, to significant role models, to spouse and intimate friends, and finally to community, society and the world at large. The final stage centers on positive healthy interaction with others within a collapsing environment.

Erikson's theory provides a structured model that demonstrates the relationship between human personality and life experiences. In general, we help individuals grow a healthy personality when we focus on success rather than failure, balance security and freedom, meet emotional needs and provide competent role models.

Church leaders and lay teachers will teach and preach more effectively if they use these insights to direct their efforts to heal past neglect and prepare for future success in their learners—whatever age they teach. It is God's good will, says Paul, that we become mature (Eph 4:13). This maturity is not merely a disembodied spiritual entity, but exists as a physical, emotional, relational, spiritual whole. "And Jesus increased in wisdom and stature, and in favor with God and with people" (Luke 2:52).

The process of becoming mature means getting rid of the fractured characteristics of the past and "clothing ourselves" with His characteristics (see Col 3:8–17). By His grace, and through His power, we grow as we give Him freedom to heal our fractured selves. May He bless us as we help others do the same, even as we teach!

Chapter Concepts

Adaptive strength	Healthy resolution between maladaptive and malignant personality poles
Autonomy	The positive ability to do things independently, within limits
Despair	The negative realization that goals are unachieved and time is short
Foreclosure	Identity commitment adopted from others without a personal crisis (Marcia)
Generativity	The positive caring for the next generation by giving of self
Guilt	The negative inhibition and fear to try new things on their own
Identity	The positive sense of knowing who one is and what one will do in life
Identity achievement	Identity commitment achieved through personal search and choice (Marcia)
Identity diffusion	Identity commitment not important. No serious search for self-definition (Marcia)
Industry	The positive drive to succeed, to persist, and to excel in mastering skills
Inferiority	The negative sense that one cannot succeed at anything
Initiative	The positive attacking new tasks and using freedom in socially appropriate ways
Integrity	The positive sense of dignity and wholeness in life, reflecting on life with satisfaction

Intimacy	The positive ability to form an intimate relationship with another
Isolation	The negative inability to establish reciprocal relationships with others
Maladaption	Excess toward the positive: "Too much of a good thing" leading to personality problems
Malignancy	Excess toward the negative: "Too little of a good thing" leading to personality problems
Mistrust	The negative sense that the world cannot be trusted
Moratorium	Identity commitment postponed, though the search for meaning continues (Marcia)
Psychosexual theory	Sigmund Freud's theory of personality which is anchored in human sexuality
Psychosocial theory	Erik Erikson's theory of personality that is anchored in human relationships
Role confusion	The negative sense of uncertainty about who one is and what one will do in the future
Shame and doubt	The negative sense of shame from failures and doubt about capabilities
Stagnation	The negative self-centeredness which has little interest in helping others
Trust	The positive sense that the world is dependable and trustworthy

Chapter Objectives

Learners will demonstrate understanding of Erik Erikson's original Stages of development by doing such things as. . .

- matching stages with life situations.
- explaining selected terms in their own words.
- creating church-related case studies reflecting a given stage.

Learners will demonstrate understanding of Joan Erikson's ninth stage of "transcendance" by comparing and contrasting it with biblical transcendence.

Learners will demonstrate an appreciation for the relational aspect of spiritual growth by sharing how Christ has strengthened a specific "fractured stage" through others.

Discussion Questions

1 Think of a member of your family or a close friend who reflects one of the poles of Erikson's eight stages. As you think over the lifespan of this individual, how does Erikson's theory fit their life experiences?

2 Which stage has caused you the greatest difficulty? Toward which pole in that stage did you move? Who helped you negotiate your way to resolution? What influence has this had on your later development?

3 Describe your greatest discovery in reading this chapter. It may be related to your own development or your future ministry. What implication does this discovery hold for your future development?

4 James Marcia describes four identity statuses. Think back to when you were sixteen to eighteen years of age, and decide which of the four statuses best describes you at that time.

HOW WE DEVELOP AS THINKERS

Jean Piaget and Lev Vygotsky: Theories of Cognitive Development

*"We are asking that you may be filled with the knowledge of His will in
all wisdom and spiritual understanding."*

Colossians 1:9

"The best candle is understanding."

—**Welsh Proverb**[1]

Chapter Rationale

Cognitive development is the gradual, orderly process by which mental processes become more complex and sophisticated.[2] Jean Piaget described the process by which minds are developed and organized to understand the world. Lev Vygotsky described the social component of cognitive development. The proper understanding of God's Word and world—the left pillar of the Disciplers' Model—is essential to Christian growth. The insights of Piaget and Vygotsky help Christian teachers in their efforts to guide learners into subject mastery and a biblical worldview.

Chapter Overview

➤ Historical Roots: Arnold Gesell
➤ The Essential Vocabulary of Jean Piaget
➤ Piaget's Four Stages of Cognitive Development

- ➤ Criticisms of Piaget's Theory
- ➤ Implications of Piaget's Theory for Teaching
- ➤ Contributions of Lev Vygotsky
- ➤ The Ultimate Goal of Lev Vygotsky
- ➤ Implications of Vygotsky's Theory for Teaching
- ➤ The Church as Social Context—The Kingdom as Culture
- ➤ *Chapter Concepts, Chapter Objectives, Discussion Questions*

Historical Roots: Arnold Gesell

At the turn of the twentieth century, psychologists believed that intelligence was genetically determined prior to birth. Differences in intelligence were quantitative.[3] The nature of intelligence was defined in terms of how fast one could learn. That is, fast learners were more intelligent than slow learners.

Arnold Gesell was the first to postulate that intelligence was developed after birth, in an unvarying sequence of steps. As head of the Institute of Child Development at Yale University, he developed many ideas regarding cognitive development in children. Most of Gesell's ideas were later discarded as oversimplifications, but one concept lasted. The growth in cognitive abilities follows a cycle of rapid change, or reorganization, and integration, when changes are organized into the thinking process.[4] Gesell showed that differences in intelligence were actually qualitative differences, not merely quantitative. Children of different ages think differently.

Jean Piaget, a biologist and philosopher by training,[5] provided a more robust picture of cognitive development. Piaget's cognitive theory, much like Erikson's personality theory, is anchored in the observation that individuals function within their environment in an interactive fashion. We know what we know as a result of the interaction between ourselves and our environment.[6] Piaget focuses on **individuals** interacting within a social context.

Lev Vygotsky, a Soviet psychologist and early contemporary of Piaget, focuses on **social context** more than individuals. Cognitive development, for Vygotsky, is the internalization of social and cultural experiences. Both Piaget and Vygotsky agree, however, that intelligence is "not simply poured into children."[7] Rather children actively construct their understanding of the world, creating it through their own activity.[8]

The Life of Jean Piaget

Jean Piaget was born in Neuchatel, Switzerland, in 1896. As his father was a history professor, he was raised in a scholarly atmosphere.

As a boy, he was curious about nature. He spent a great deal of time observing animals. He published his first professional paper on his observations of an albino sparrow. He was ten years old. He observed changes in the structure of shellfish as their environment (rough or calm water) changed.

Between the ages of eleven and fifteen he worked as a laboratory assistant to the director of the natural history museum in Neuchatel. At the age of fifteen, he published a series of articles on shellfish, which won him the position of Curator of Mollusk Collection at the Natural History Museum in Geneva. He turned down the position in order to finish school.

His godfather was a philosophy scholar and urged Jean to broaden his horizons through a study of philosophy and logic. Piaget earned his undergraduate degree in Natural Science from the University of Neuchatel in 1914 at age eighteen, and a Ph.D. in Biology in 1917 at age twenty-one.

Psychology captured his attention, and in 1918 he went to Zurich, where he was introduced to Freudian theory. The next year he went to Paris to study Abnormal Psychology. It was during this time that he worked with Alfred Binet, the developer of intelligence testing, to develop intelligence tests for children. He asked questions relating to time, space, numbers, causality, and moral judgment. He was fascinated by the differences in the answers given by younger and older children. In fact, he focused more on their wrong answers, finding that the same wrong answers were frequently given by children of the same age. He found that older children are not simply more intelligent, did not simply know more, but differed qualitatively in their thinking processes.

In 1921 he was named Director of Research at the Jean-Jacques Rousseau Institute in Geneva. This allowed him to study the cognitive behavior of children full time. For the next thirty years he quietly continued his research. His regular schedule was to spend the morning with friends, take a long walk to collect his thoughts, and then spend the afternoon writing.

Piaget received honorary degrees from Harvard (1936), the Sorbonne (1946), and the University of Brussels (1949). Yet he received little recognition for his theory in America until the 1960s. Sprinthall suggests two reasons for this. First, Piaget opposed Edward L. Thorndike's emphasis on Laws of Learning, preferring to study the child's thinking ability. Second, he wrote only in French and then in obscure language that was difficult to translate. A third reason may be the fact Piaget was not interested in formal educational practice but was fascinated with genetic epistemology, the biological basis for the growth of knowledge in a person.

Piaget's work eventually overcame these obstacles, and catapulted him to fame. Slavin calls him the "best known child psychologist who ever lived." Good ranks him with Sigmund Freud and B. F. Skinner as "the most influential psychologists of all times."

In 1969 Piaget received the Distinguished Scientific Award from the American Psychological Association. In 1975 he retired from his position at the Rousseau Institute but continued his study until his death in 1980.[9]

The Essential Vocabulary of Jean Piaget

Piaget developed a technical vocabulary to describe the processes by which humans construct mental representations of the world. In this section, we define twelve essential concepts Piaget used as building blocks in his theory.

Organization

Organization is the natural tendency to make sense of experiences by integrating them into logically related cognitive structures.[10] These cognitive structures are quite simple at first, but are built up—by combining, arranging, recombining, and rearranging behaviors and thoughts[11]—into ever more complex, coherent systems.[12] For example, infants can *look* at objects, and they can *grasp objects* when they happen to touch them. But they cannot coordinate the two. In time, however, infants organize these two behaviors into a higher level ability, which allows them to look at, reach for, and grasp an object.[13] This networking of behaviors and thoughts creates a complex cognitive network by which we perceive the world. Organization is the natural tendency to make sense of the world as we experience it.[14]

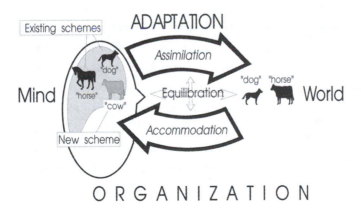

Schemes

Schemes are the cognitive structures produced as a result of the development process.[15] They are organized patterns of behavior or thought, produced through interaction with the environment,[16] which represent the world as we know it.[17] The terms *concept* and *idea* convey a layman's sense of Piaget's *scheme*.[18] Three schemes—"dog," "horse," and "cow"—are shown in the diagram above.

Schemes change as children develop cognitive networks. Schemes grow in number, allowing us to differentiate among similar objects, and they grow more complex, allowing us to see similarities among different objects. Since perception of the world depends on the level of development in the cognitive network, it is easy to see that adult concepts differ from children's. The mental processes used by children and adults also differ. The higher-level cognitive abilities of problem-solving and abstraction require a complex network of schemes, and this takes time and experience to create.[19]

Adaptation is the process by which schemes grow and change. Adaptation consists of two inter-related parts called **assimilation** and **accommodation.** The natural tendency on the mind to maintain balance between the two is called **equilibration.** The imbalance between what is known and what is experienced is called **disequilibrium.** We look at these related terms next.

Equilibration and Disequilibrium

Equilibration is the *natural tendency to maintain balance* between what one already knows, the cognitive network, and what one experiences in the world.[20] When this balance is disturbed—that is, when we experience something that does not fit what we know—we experience anxiety, discomfort, or confusion. This confusion is called *disequilibrium*.[21] Equilibration compels us to reduce the disequilibrium by restoring the balance, or *equilibrium*, between our understanding of the world and experiences in the world. Think of a rowboat on a calm lake. It is in a state of equilibrium. Now a speedboat rushes past, causing large waves that toss the rowboat up and down. In terms of cognitive functioning, the speedboat is an unfamiliar idea or experience. The rocking of the boat is the mental discomfort produced by the new experience. This disquiet sensation is disequilibrium. The desire of the fishermen in the boat is for equilibrium, the return of calm water. The desire of the learner is to eliminate the mental discomfort.

Equilibration is represented in the diagram at left as arrows between Mind and the World (representing mental correspondence with the world), as well as assimilation and accommodation (representing the balance between adaptation processes). We discuss these three concepts next.

Adaptation

Adaptation is the natural process of adjusting what is known, or what is experienced, or both, so that balance (equilibrium) exists between the mind and the world. Adaptation creates a good fit, though not always a correct fit, between one's concept of reality (network of schemes) and real-life experiences.[22] Adaptation consists of two parts. **Assimilation** refers to the process of *interpreting external experiences* so they fit what is already known. **Accommodation** refers to the process of *adjusting internal schemes* so they fit real-world experiences. Adaptation combines these two processes so that a state of equilibrium is maintained between our thinking and the world as we experience it.[23]

Assimilation

Assimilation is the process of interpreting external experiences so that they fit what is known. It is the first, *reactive*, component of adaptation. When an experience does not fit an existing scheme, we interpret the experience[24] or relate the information[25] to the scheme that provides the closest fit. In doing so, we often modify or distort what we have experienced. A child has a scheme of "fish." She calls minnows "little fish" and whales "big fish." Another child calls a skunk a "kitty."[26] In each case, experiences in the world are (mis)interpreted by established schemes that were inadequate to perceive the world—whales and skunks—correctly.

Writers define the term *assimilation* in a variety of ways. Some use terms very similar to my description above: "changing what is perceived so that it fits present structures,"[27] "to respond in terms of preexisting information [which] often involves ignoring some aspects to make it conform,"[28] "interpreting [an experience] in light of present schemes,"[29] or to "change the nature of reality to make it fit our cognitive structures."[30] This is the primary meaning of Piaget's term and results from disequilibrium.

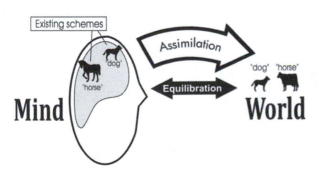

Others define assimilation as "relating new information to existing schemes,"[31] "experience incorporated into existing schemes,"[32] "simply taking in familiar experiences,"[33] or "using existing schemes to make sense of [the] world."[34] This second group of definitions emphasizes the *reinforcing* function of assimilation and reflects a *secondary meaning of the term* since it can occur without disequilibrium. While assimilation does not change the structure of schemes, it can affect the growth of schemes through processing familiar experiences. Assimilation in this sense is like putting more air in a balloon. The balloon gets larger, but it does not change shape.[35]

In the diagram on the previous page, we see a child who experiences both types of assimilation. He sees a cow and does not recognize it. Disequilibrium prompts him to search his memory for the closest match. He finds a "match," and incorrectly calls the cow "a horse." He sees a dog, recognizes it, and calls it "a dog."

Incorrectly calling a cow "horse" is an example of the first, and most important, type of assimilation, because it is prompted by disequilibrium. Though assimilation produced an incorrect match, it created equilibrium (horse-horse) and relieved the tension between known and unknown. *Correctly* calling a dog "dog" is an example of the secondary (reinforcing) type of assimilation.

Accommodation

Accommodation is the process of adjusting or creating schemes to fit what we experience. It is the second, reciprocal, component of adaptation. When an experience does not fit an existing scheme, we can accommodate ourselves to it by adjusting an existing scheme—so that it does fit—or we can create a new scheme. The girl who called minnows "little fish" and whales "big fish" creates a new scheme for whales: "mammals that live in water." The unfortunate child who thought skunks were kitties now has a scheme called "skunk" which he'll never again confuse with kitties.

Writers define accommodation as follows. "Modifying schemes in order to relate to new information,"[36] "to change schemes to incorporate experience,"[37] "to adjust our own ideas to make sense of reality,"[38] "reorganization of existing cognitive structures to deal with environmental demands,"[39] "development of new structures and restructuring old ones,"[40] "to respond to external characteristics by changing existing structures,"[41] and "changing existing structures to respond to new situations."[42]

In the diagram below, the child has created a new scheme "cow" to fit the new animal he has

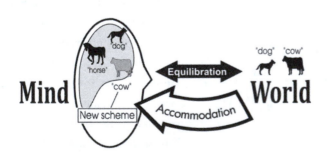

seen. Not only did he achieve equilibrium between his knowledge and new experience, he has changed the cognitive structure of his mind. He can now distinguish between horses and cows.

One final example underscores the process of adaptation. Little

Billy has a developing scheme of "dogness" by which he properly identifies Cocker Spaniels and German Shepherds as dogs. One day, walking along with his father, he sees a Chihuahua for the first time. He does not have a "Chihuahua" scheme, nor does his "dog" scheme include Chihuahua characteristics. He makes the best fit he can, but asks a question because he is unsure of his conclusion. "Dad, why does that lady have a rat on a leash?" While he reduces disequilibrium through assimilation (rat-rat), his best fit seems strange.

Billy's Dad explains that the animal is a Chihuahua, a kind of dog. He is surprised, "That's a *dog*?!" Since Billy trusts his Dad and accepts his explanation, he reconfigures his scheme of "dogness" to include Chihuahuas. Disequilibrium is reduced through accommodation. Billy's understanding of dogs is a little more complex.

Both accommodation and assimilation are necessary

Both accommodation and assimilation are necessary.[43] *Assimilation (without accommodation)* results in **remaking the world according to our own ideas**, never learning from others, and filtering every conversation through our own preconceived notions.[44] This self-centered distortion has become accepted educational practice in recent years, and even carries a label: "radical constructivism" (see Chapter Eight for an analysis). A person develops a few large schemes and would be unable to differentiate well.[45] However, assimilation with accommodation allows learners to understand the world as it really is.[46]

Accommodation (without assimilation) **remakes us into whatever we discover in the world,** creating new schemes for every new experience, always accepting at face value what others say, having no filters by which to test experiences or information. A person develops many small schemes and would be unable to generalize well.[47] Accommodation *with assimilation* provides a standard, or a pattern, by which we evaluate experience.

We need both processes to create equilibrium between *what we know* and *what really is*. Fortunately both occur continuously as we interact with our world.[48]

One last point should be noted before leaving the discussion of adaptation. The correspondence between "mental construction" and "real world" exists in Piaget's theory. Some contemporary textbooks redefine Piaget as having a more Postmodern frame of reference—"what really is" can never be known—than he had. Certainly learners construct their own understanding of the world (no one can learn for another), and that understanding never replicates the world exactly "as it is," being a replication. Yet Piaget did not espouse a subjective reality. The very concept of accommodation assumes a "something" to replicate in the mind. The closer the mental replication corresponds to that "something," the better the accommodation. We will discuss this more in Chapter Eight.

The Distinction Between Understanding and Believing

The apostle Paul commands, "Do not be conformed to this age" (Rom 12:2), and yet "in this age" we are being pressed by strong proponents and shifting cultural norms to embrace evolutionary theory, abortion-on-demand, and gay marriage. Some reject Piaget's accommodation because it seems to imply acceptance of every new idea. "We cannot accommodate ourselves to these things without compromising our Christian worldview." Piaget's accommodation does not mean acceptance of every new idea we experience. The focus of Piaget's theory is understanding, not belief.

When we share the gospel with new age devotees, we will do better if we understand what New Agers think. As we study their views, our thinking accommodates—that is, we create appropriate schemes that reflect—new age teachings. This does not require, or even suggest, that we believe new age teachings. We can study (and understand) evolution, but this does not make us evolutionists. Christians can study *Das Kapital* without becoming Communists, even as scholars can study the Gospels and not become Christians! Accommodation to a new idea (that is, understanding it) is not the same as heart commitment to that idea (that is, believing it).

Paul wrote, "Though I am free and belong to no man, I make myself a slave to everyone, to win as many as possible. To the Jews I became like a Jew, to win the Jews. To those under the law I became like one under the law (though I myself am not under the law), so as to win those under the law. To those not having the law I became like one not having the law (though I am not free from God's law but am under Christ's law), so as to win those not having the law. To the weak I became weak, to win the weak. I have become all things to all men so that by all possible means I might save some" (1 Cor 9:19–22).

Paul accommodated himself to the worldviews of various cultures in order to present the gospel to them effectively. He helped others accommodate their thinking to the gospel, one of the first steps toward faith. But New Testament faith—believing in Christ, committing to Christ—is another matter entirely. There is a difference between understanding and believing.

Operation

The term **operation** refers to an "action that can be carried out mentally." This mental capability frees us from having to literally perform the action.[49] An operation can be mentally undone, or reversed.[50] You will find the term "operation" embedded in three of Piaget's four stages of development—pre**operation**al, concrete **operation**al, and formal **operation**al—which we discuss a little later.

Conservation

The term **conservation** refers to the ability to recognize that properties stay the same despite changes in appearance or position.[51] Picture two tall glass beakers filled equally with water and an empty glass baking dish. It is obvious that the two beakers hold equal amounts of water. Pour the water from one beaker into the dish. Which has more water, the beaker, or the dish? Teenagers and adults immediately respond, "They are the same." A young child, age 2 to 5,[52] will point to the beaker. "Why?" you ask. The child will say, "Because it is taller." Younger children are not yet able to understand that water volume does not change just because it "looks" different (conservation of volume). In Piaget's terms, younger children are not able to "conserve volume."[53]

Roll clay into two equally sized balls. Ask, "Which is more clay?" The child will say they are the same. Then roll one of the balls into a clay rope. Ask, "Which is more clay?" (Conservation of mass). Ask, "Which weighs more?" (Conservation of weight). Younger children will say the clay rope "is more clay" and "weighs more" than the ball. Take two candy bars and break one of them into eight pieces (conservation of volume). A younger child will say the eight pieces is "more candy" than the larger whole (because there are more pieces). Show a child two equally spaced rows of five coins. Then spread out one row of coins and ask, "Which row has more coins?" (conservation of number). The younger child will respond that the longer row of five coins "has more coins" than the shorter row of five coins.[54] Conservation is the ability to recognize that properties stay the same despite changes in appearance or position.

Decentration

The term **decentration** refers to the ability to focus on more than one aspect of a situation at a time.[55] The opposite of decentration is **perceptual centration**, or **centering**, which refers to the tendency to focus on one aspect of a situation to the exclusion of all others.[56] Younger children focus, or *center*, on the height of the water in beaker and dish, the number of pieces of candy, and the length of the clay rope. They are not yet able to decenter from height, number, or length to correctly perceive volume (height, breadth, and depth combined). Higher water level equals more water. Longer rope means more clay. More pieces mean more candy. They are unable to "see" that volume remains constant.

A slightly different example involves monetary value. Ask a younger child whether they would rather have one quarter or ten pennies (show them the coins). They will choose the ten pennies because it is "more money." They do not understand the abstract concept of monetary value, and therefore center on the number of coins. More coins mean more money.

Reversibility

The term **reversibility** refers to the ability to mentally undo an action. Older children can mentally pour the water from dish back into beaker and reason that the amount of water is unchanged. Younger children cannot do this.[57] The inability to mentally reverse actions is called **irreversibility.** Younger children do not understand that superficial changes can be undone, or reversed, to return a situation to its former state.[58]

Egocentrism

The term **egocentrism** refers to the tendency to believe that other people see the world as we do.[59] Young children are not yet able to see things in any way other than their own perception.[60] Piaget and Inhedler (1956) conducted a famous experiment in which they seated children before a model of three mountains, two smaller cones placed side by side in front of a larger cone. They asked them to describe how the mountains would look to dolls seated at other places. Younger children described the other views as the same as their own[61] (see left diagram below). Older children were able to mentally "move around the table" and correctly express in words or drawings the views of the others (right diagram).

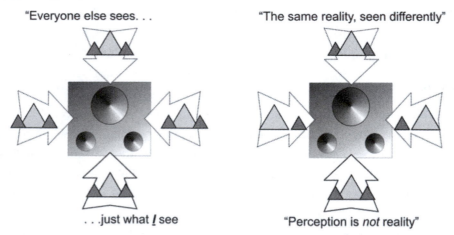

Young children *cannot* see things from other points of view, and cannot therefore see the cones as a three-dimensional reality. Adults have the ability to see various points of view, but often choose not to. For these adults, what they see *is* reality.[62] What we perceive of reality is a partial picture. As we learn more, listen more, experience more, and discuss more, what we perceive produces a mental structure closer to the reality we observe.

We have seen how "what we know" controls what we perceive (assimilation) and how we accommodate new experiences.[63] Since knowledge grows from birth to adulthood, it follows that "how we learn" differs with age. Piaget categorized these differences in four stages.

Piaget's Four Stages of Cognitive Development

Piaget suggested that human intelligence develops—from innate reflexes of infants to abstract logical reasoning of adults[64]—through an unchanging sequence of four stages.[65] Each stage represents a measurable difference in the quality of thinking from the stage that precedes it. Though each stage has an age range associated with it, determining the specific stage learners have attained depends on what mental capabilities they have, not how old they are.[66] In other words, all people pass through the same four stages, but not necessarily at the same age.[67] Each given stage is seen as an advance over the former stage and a limitation in relation to the succeeding one. Abilities in a lower stage do not disappear in later stages.[68] Rather new abilities are added to the old ones to complete, correct, or combine with them.[69] Given these general features of stages of development, we turn our attention to analyze each of the four. They are the sensorimotor, preoperational, concrete operational, and formal operational stages of cognitive development.

The Sensorimotor Stage (Ages Birth to Two)

Newborn infants possess innate reflexes[70] such as sucking, grasping, and the like. Their cognitive activity is limited to immediate experience through the senses. They have no language by which to label experiences or symbolize events and ideas. Therefore, they cannot remember.[71] The saying "out of sight, out of mind" is literally true for them.[72] They are bound to immediate experience.[73] Their thinking is limited to how the world responds to their physical actions.[74] Their responses are determined by the immediate situation: when they are hungry, they cry. Telling an infant, "Just a minute, I'm warming your bottle" has no meaning to her. She does not understand the words, does not understand time, and does not understand that she will soon receive the answer to her problem.[75] Learning **equals** immediate experience, vivid experience. Every new discovery is exciting, because it is a first. The sensorimotor period is a continuous peak experience.[76]

Sensorimotor learning is a slow, step-by-step process because the infant has little experience in the world, little by which to attach meaning to immediate experiences. Because infants possess no language skills beyond various kinds of cries,[77] learning is private and uncommunicative.[78] Still, the gradually developing ability to mentally represent objects and people prepares sensorimotor children for the next stage, where thinking shifts away from physical action to symbolic learning.[79]

Sensorimotor children should be taught, not merely "sat." Teachers help cognitive development by providing sensorimotor children a safe environment filled with a variety of toys. The process of teaching emphasizes basic motor skill experiences tied to God through nature, home and family, and friends at church. Activities include such things as painting with water, touching pine cones, playing with sand, helping bake bread, learning Scripture songs and thoughts, and the like.

Sensorimotor thinking does not end when children move to higher levels of thought. In fact, even seminary professors may demonstrate characteristics of sensorimotor thinking when confronted with an unfamiliar problem. Examples include such things as banging on a television when the reception is bad, or randomly jiggling wires under the hood of a car that won't start.

The Preoperational Stage (Ages Two to Seven)

While sensorimotor learning is gradual and tied to immediate experience, preoperational learning is lightning fast and mobile. Symbolic thinking begins as the immediate experience of the sensorimotor stage is replaced by concrete symbols—the word "tree" connected to actual trees. The stage is called **pre**operational in that thinking is limited by egocentrism, centration, irreversibility, and an inability to conserve.[80]

Preoperational thinking is egocentric. Ask why the sun is shining, and the child might say "Because I like to play outside."[81] Preoperational thinking cannot decenter. Shown two candy bars, one whole and the other broken into eight pieces, and asked "Which is more candy?", the child points to the eight pieces, unable to decenter from number of pieces. Preoperational thinking cannot be reversed. Ask a child, "Who is your brother?" and he will point to his brother. Ask, "Who is *his* brother?" and the child will likely say, "He doesn't have one."

The growth of language is central to this stage.[82] Vocabulary and grammar increase dramatically. The average two-year-old possesses two hundred to three hundred words. But by the age of five, this has expanded to more than two thousand words.[83] These words have concrete identifications, such as "horse," "tree," and "truck." Abstract concepts such as "fairness," "truth," or "democracy" have little or no meaning.[84] The development of language permits preoperational children to share ideas socially.[85]

Thinking during this stage is characterized by perceptual dominance.[86] The water in the beaker is "taller" than the water in the dish, so there is "obviously" more water in the beaker. To explain to a preoperational child *why the water is the same* accomplishes nothing more than to get the child to parrot back what you say, without any real understanding.[87] Since the words have no logical or objective meaning to preoperational children, they can make wonderfully humorous mistakes in recalling what they have "learned." A six-year-old, reciting the Pledge of Allegiance, says "the republic of Richard Stands and one naked individual." Another recalls what she learned in Sunday school: "Pontius was the pilot on the flight to Egypt." Still another recalled part of a worship service, in which God was addressed as "Father, Son and Holy Smoke."[88]

Preoperational children are intuitive, free-wheeling, and highly imaginative.[89] Their minds are filled with fantasy: talking animals, imaginary friends, wild stories, conversations with self and toys. They do not see things objectively.[90] There is no appreciation for the logical consequences of language: preoperational children talk to, rather than with, others.[91] "Hey, Daddy, look at that fat man standing next to you!"[92]

Preoperational children focus on states rather than transformations.[93] In the beaker and dish problem, they focus on the states of the water before and after pouring. Before, the water is the same in both beakers. After, the water in the beaker is taller than the water in the dish (therefore, there is more water in the beaker). They ignore the act of pouring, the transformation from one state to another. If preoperational children are asked to draw a picture of an upright stick falling, they will draw an upright stick, and another stick lying flat. Older children will include intermediate positions of the stick, showing the process of falling.[94]

We might try to "prove" to preoperational children that the water remains unchanged by pouring the water from the dish back into the beaker (so it "once again" equals the amount of water in the other beaker). It will not help. Repeating the process will bring the same results. If we were to ask "Why is the amount of water the same in the two beakers and different in the beaker and dish?" They may well respond, "It's magic."

One other major characteristic of preoperational thought is called **transductive** reasoning.[95] While **deductive reasoning** flows from a general statement to particular examples, and **inductive reasoning** flows from specific examples to a general statement, **transductive reasoning** merely focuses on particulars, without touching the general. Piaget's daughter missed her nap one afternoon. She remarked, "I haven't had my nap, so it isn't afternoon."[96]

We have made much of what preoperational children *cannot* do, at least when compared to the thinking of adults. And yet cognitive development makes great strides during this stage. Language acquisition, symbolic thought, and a wide range of conceptual abilities[97] make this an explosive time for learning. Preoperational thinking is illogical but not necessarily inferior. The intuitive, free-wheeling, and highly imaginative nature of preoperational thought forms the basis for creativity.[98]

Effective teachers of preoperational children focus on what children know, and ask questions to insure their explanations are connecting with their understanding. For example, if a preoperational child asks "Why are clouds white?" a lecture on reflection and absorption of various wavelengths of light will be lost on him. Ask him, "What white things do you know about?" After he names some things, ask "What is the same about them?" Then say, "See, clouds are like clean, fluffy balls of cotton. They look white because of the way light shines on them and because they don't have much dust or rain in them."[99]

Preoperational children normally want to please their teachers and will respond with answers they perceive their teachers want to hear. Just because children say the right thing does not mean they understand what that right thing means. Effective teachers of preoperational children build bridges to *their* cognitive abilities and instruct them in ways *they* can learn best.

Dr. Marcia McQuitty, Professor of Childhood Education at Southwestern Seminary, provides **general guidelines for teaching three-, four-, and five-year-olds** in Sunday school:

Three, four and five year olds will learn best in a room which provides *learning centers* and a corner of the room set up for *large group time. Learning centers* are designated portions of a room set up for home living activities, puzzles, books, music, art, blocks and nature. . . . In advance of the session, preschool teachers gather the materials to be used in each of the centers. Usually the director of the department prepares to tell the Bible story in the large group time. Preschoolers learn best when they have the same teachers in the room Sunday after Sunday. Preschoolers are curious, active, creative, self-focused and have short attention spans. They learn best when they can have hands-on experiences. Therefore, preparing the learning centers for preschoolers will enhance their learning experiences.

When older preschoolers enter the room, they should be directed to one of the centers and do the activity set up for the session. In some centers teachers will be available to give instructions if needed, talk about the Bible story, sing songs, and share Bible thoughts. Other centers, such as the block center, may not have a teacher available to guide the child's learning. If preschoolers hear the Bible story told in several of the centers, they will be better prepared to participate in the large group time. Preschoolers learn through repetition. Preschoolers, after working for a while in one center, may choose to move to another center.

Towards the end of the time spent in the learning centers, the teacher preparing for large group time will ask the preschoolers to put away all of the materials presently being used. Blocks are placed on the shelves and books are returned to the book rack. Puzzles are completed and placed in the puzzle rack. Art materials are put away and/or cleaned. Preschoolers learn to work together, finish a task and prepare for the large group Bible story time as they help clean up the learning centers. . . .

Teachers preparing for large group learning should consider the age and attention span of the children involved. Use the following suggestions as guidelines for the length of group time:

Three-year-olds	five to ten minutes
Four-year-olds	ten to fifteen minutes
Five-year-olds	fifteen to twenty minutes

A variety of activities should be planned for this Bible story time in a group setting. Learning activities include singing, praying, and sharing experiences, playing games, looking at Bible pictures, reading Bible thoughts, and hearing the Bible story. When actually telling the Bible story, teachers hold the Bible in their hands. Teachers can ask older preschoolers to pray in the large group. Sometimes we will be amazed at what preschoolers can learn!"[100]

Preoperational thinking is often found in adults. Three of the most common adult preoperational characteristics are egocentrism, centration, and creativity. Human beings are naturally **egocentric.** Insufferably self-centered adults—professional athletes, film and television stars, politicians, perhaps a next door neighbor—did not develop this way. Rather, they failed to grow out of their self-centeredness.[101] Teaching egocentric adults requires that we begin with their point of view and then help them to see another. Otherwise, we will be dismissed, and our ideas will be considered irrelevant or, worse, dangerous.

Adult centration is demonstrated by those who make an argument based on isolated and selective information while ignoring information that conflicts with their view. Years ago a woman sued a Board of Education in her state because textbooks they had approved "promoted the religion of secular humanism." She was featured on a prominent television morning program and asked to give an example of how the textbooks promoted secular humanism. She opened one of the books and smugly pointed to a large picture of a boy and girl standing at a stove. The boy held a spatula in one hand and a frying pan, on the burner, in the other. The girl stood beside him, watching. The caption under the picture read, "Jim cooks."

"How does this promote secular humanism?" the interviewer asked. "Well, everyone knows that the Bible says that women are supposed to cook! This picture teaches little boys that they are supposed to cook. That's secular humanism!" I was dumbfounded. First, many men are single and cook for themselves. Second, married men—particularly in today's hectic world—may need to pitch in and help cook. Third, cooking is enjoyable. Why shouldn't men be encouraged to do it? Fourth, where in the Bible does the Lord lay down the theological truth "And the man shall not cook, for this is woman's work"? Fifth, the picture of a boy holding a spatula does not promote "the religion of secular humanism." And finally, who was home cooking for this woman's five children while she was in New York taping the program? Who cooked for the family while she spent weeks at the state capitol? Her husband did the cooking. Her argument was based on highly selective information, and, more, it ignored the ways she violated her principle of "(only) women cook." This is adult centration.

On the positive side, the intuitive, free-wheeling and highly imaginative nature of preoperational thought forms the basis for **creativity.**[102] Highly creative adults step outside "what is logically known" to produce new ideas, designs, and perspectives—even new worlds in the form of fiction.

In summary, preoperational children are dreamers, explorers, and (innocent) magicians, dealing with illogical fantasies while they experiment with their world and their own thinking. As they experiment, they prepare the way for the next stage, in which they become logical manipulators of concrete experiences. They become literal-minded in the extreme, can deal with functional relationships (because they are specific), and learn to test problems systematically.[103]

The Concrete Operational Stage (Ages Seven to Eleven)

Stage Three produces the beginning of operational thought.[104] Thinking is characterized by two key developments. First, children overcome the deficiencies of preoperational thought (egocentrism, centration, irreversibility, and lack of conservation[105]) and second, they begin to think logically about concrete objects.[106]

The term "concrete" refers to the actual presence of objects or events.[107] Conservation and reversibility develop in the presence of tangible objects.[108] Concrete operational children can **mentally** pour the water back into the original beaker and recognize that the amount has not changed despite changes in appearance. They can **mentally** put the eight pieces of candy bar back together and recognize that the amount of candy is unchanged despite changes in appearance. Thinking is less egocentric, and more socio-centric. That is, children are more open to the views of others than before.[109]

Operations are tied to personal concrete experiences.[110] Children in this stage remain stymied by abstract experiences or hypothetical situations, which inhabit Piaget's fourth stage. For example, concrete operational children can solve visual problems, using (concrete) pictures or props more easily than (abstract) word problems, involving explanations. Children can analyze real conditions (concrete) much better than (abstract) hypothetical situations. Asking a class of concrete operational children a hypothetical question like "Suppose the sky were green?" would most likely produce a chorus of responses: "No, it isn't!"[111]

Concrete thinking is capable of seriation: the ordering of a group of objects according to increasing or decreasing length, weight, or volume.[112] This ability is required to solve problems like this: If A is greater than B, and B is greater than C, then what is the relationship of A and C? Preoperational children are stymied. Concrete operational children understand these relationships and that, under these conditions, A is greater than C.[113]

Concrete thinking is also capable of classification: categorizing objects according to common characteristics.[114] Suppose we have fifteen wooden beads. Ten of the beads are brown, and five are yellow. Ask preoperational children, "Are there more brown beads, or wooden beads?" and they will likely answer that there are more brown beads than wooden beads—even though they can acknowledge that all the beads are wooden! Concrete operational children have no problem seeing that there are more wooden beads than brown beads.[115] They can properly classify the fifteen beads as "wooden," and then "brown" and "yellow." Children in the concrete operational stage are not "brighter" than preoperational children. But they have acquired abilities for solving problems that they could not solve before.[116]

Teachers are effective in teaching concrete operational thinkers by using visual aids and props, particularly when discussing complex material. They let children test out what they're learning through hands-on projects. They keep verbal instructions brief and well organized. They use what children already know to bridge to new material. They confront children with logical problems.

Dr. Norma Hedin provides insight into teaching concrete operational children in Sunday school:[117]

- Use Bible stories that have one clear concept. Use visual aids to reinforce learning. Give concrete examples of concepts, such as how to show love for your neighbor or times when you can trust God.
- Provide opportunities for students to classify, categorize, and memorize. Utilize their strengthening mental abilities in their learning activities.
- Use frequent questions to clarify their thinking. Do not assume that the right answer equals right understanding. Ask "why" questions.
- Use prayer even though its meaning may be vague. The ritual of prayer becomes important along with other rituals like the celebration of holidays. Each exposure to these rituals deepens the child's understanding of their meaning.
- Make sure that teachers are comfortable living out their faith. Children are imitating adults and need teachers who model godly attitudes and actions.
- Use self-competition to encourage successful completion of learning activities without comparison to other children, which leads to feelings of inferiority.

Dr. Karen Kennemur, Assistant Professor in Childhood Education, Southwestern Seminary, describes the use of art, drama, edutainment—the use of media messages that both educate and entertain—music, creative writing, Bible games, storytelling, research, and ministry experiences[118] in teaching concrete operational children. These approaches to teaching are effective because they are activity-oriented, Bible-based, child-centered, and hands-on concrete learning experiences.

It may appear that stage three thinking is inferior because it reflects the thought of elementary children. Research has shown, however, that most thinking of middle school, junior high, and high school students is concrete operational. Research also shows that many adults never reach the fourth stage.[119] Over the years of local church ministry, it has been my experience that adults prefer defending familiar perspectives (stage 3) to considering problems in new ways (stage 4). Jesus' use of parables—concrete objects illustrating spiritual truths—suggests He recognized the need to teach adults in concrete ways in order to help them understand the abstract realities of God's kingdom. Abstract thought becomes possible, according to Piaget, about the age of eleven.

The Formal Operational Stage (Ages Eleven and Above)

Stage Four, the Formal Operational, is characterized by abstraction. Learners can examine abstract problems systematically and generalize the results.[120] They can operate with formal logic, constructing hypotheses—"what if" statements—and then testing them.[121] They can apply research tools to isolate and control variables,[122] as well as evaluate their own reasoning and engage in introspection. They develop concerns about society.[123] They can think logically about the possible as well as the impossible.[124] Formal thinkers no longer need props or equipment to work out solutions to problems. They can manipulate objects in their minds.

Examples of school subjects that require formal thinking include history (relationships among trends vs. the concrete study of events and dates), algebra (mathematical symbols vs. the concrete manipulation of numbers), biology (DNA structure vs. hands-on dissection), chemistry (atomic structure vs. hands-on chemical reactions) and literature (metaphor and symbolism vs. reading stories for their own sake). Without the ability to think abstractly, students must revert to memorizing what the teacher gives them.[125]

The Formal Operational stage is qualitatively different from the other three. The first three stages are tied to physical realities. Objects really are permanent. The amount of water does not change when poured from one container to another. Formal operations are less closely related to the physical environment. Practice in solving hypothetical problems and engaging in scientific reasoning may be the catalysts for formal operational thinking. These tend to be highly valued and taught in literate cultures, particularly in universities and colleges.[126]

Sprinthall makes the following comparisons between concrete and formal operational thinking. While the former is limited to the here and now, the latter extends thinking to possibilities. In the former, problem-solving is dictated by details of the problem; in the latter, problem-solving is governed by planned hypothesis testing. In the former, thought is limited to concrete objects and situations; in the latter, thought is expanded from concrete symbols to abstract ideas. In the former, thought is focused on one's own perspective; in the latter, thought is enlarged to the perspective of others.[127]

However, formal thinking is not all positive. Without a concrete foundation, abstract thinking can lead to idealistic solutions that are disconnected from reality. "Having just discovered this boundless freedom of the mind to envisage the ideal, adolescents create their Utopias and rebel against the generation that has yet been unable to make its Utopias realities."[128]

The disconnection between abstract perspective and concrete lifestyle causes no end of hypocrisy. A television evangelist preaches (abstract thoughts) against every kind of moral evil, and then cruises the red light district of his city, paying call girls for pornographic poses (concrete acts). A pastor preaches a Salt and Light sermon exhorting members to send their children to public schools, while he sends his own children to a private Christian school. A missionary preaches honesty and truthfulness, but trades in the Black Market illegally in order "to stretch the Lord's money." A men's organization studies missions around the world, but few engage in mission action in their own neighborhood. We sing "I Surrender All" with heart-felt emotion, but live for the Lord as it is convenient during the week. "We speak of the Ideal, but we live in the Ordeal."[129]

Jesus, the "Christ of the Book," was not as concerned with abstract theologizing as He was (and is) with concrete commitment to the Heavenly Father in the realities of day-to-day experiences. "If anyone wants to come with Me, he must deny himself, take up his cross daily, and follow Me" (Luke 9:23). He lived this reality even as He was dying on the cross in our place. We do His work His way. We connect solid theological abstractions with tangible concrete lifestyle choices. No red light districts. No hypocritical preaching. No Black Market. Mission Action more than Mission Talk. Living what we Sing.

Formal thinking skills help us understand the un-concrete world of spiritual things. Concrete thinking skills help us tie spiritual truths into solving real problems in a real world. Jesus specifically connected the concrete realities of His listeners to the abstract realities of God's kingdom by using parables.

"The kingdom of heaven is like **treasure, buried in a field,** that a man found and reburied. Then in his joy he goes and sells everything he has and buys that field. Again, the kingdom of heaven is like a **merchant in search of fine pearls.** When he found one priceless pearl, he went and sold everything he had, and bought it. Again, the kingdom of heaven is like a **large net thrown into the sea.** It collected every kind of fish, and when it was full, they dragged it ashore, sat down, and gathered the good fish into containers, but threw out the worthless ones. So it will be at the end of the age. The angels will go out, separate the evil people from the righteous, and throw them into the blazing furnace. In that place there will be weeping and gnashing of teeth" (Matt 13:44–50).

Summary of Piaget's Stages of Cognitive Development		
Stage	**Age**	**Intellectual Characteristics**
Sensorimotor	0-2	thinking limited to immediate experience pretending, miming memory visual pursuit, object permanence simple reflex to goal-directed behavior
Preoperational	2-7	thinking becomes intuitive and symbolic language begin to use symbols logical thought in one direction thinking remains egocentric and centered
Concrete Operational	7-11	thinking becomes literal and personal decentration reversibility conservation classification can solve hands-on problems logically cannot solve abstract problems
Formal Operational	11+	thinking becomes abstract and global can solve abstract problems scientific thinking systematic experimentation complex verbal skills concerns for societal problems

Based on Dembo, p. 357, Slavin, pp. 34-35, and Woolfolk (1993), p. 32

Again and again, Jesus began with realities familiar to His listeners, then used those concrete realities to express truths about the kingdom of heaven. We should do the same in our own teaching and preaching, so that adult learners will connect the realities of their own lives with the abstract potentials of a kingdom lifestyle.

Dr. Johnny Derouen, Assistant Professor of Student Ministry at Southwestern, provides the following **suggestions for teaching teenagers** who are moving into formal operational thought.

- Youth learn best from mature adults who provide them "living videos" for modeling. Effective adult models have a positive attitude toward youth, are willing to develop relationships with them, listen well, and reflect a vibrant walk with God.
- Youth learn best when truth meets their needs.
- Youth learn best when specific objectives are set.
- Youth learn best with they are properly prepared through learning readiness activities.
- Youth learn best in an atmosphere of love, trust, and acceptance.
- Youth learn best when they are actively involved with questions, discussion, and analysis.
- Youth learn best when a variety of learning activities are employed.
- Youth learn best when their minds are engaged in higher level thinking.

Dr. Margaret Lawson, Associate Professor of Foundations of Education at Southwestern, provides the following **observations on adult learning,** adapted from Malcolm Knowles:[130]

- *The Need to Know.* Adults need to know why they need to learn something before undertaking to learn it.
- *Learner Self-Concept.* Adults need to be responsible for their own decisions and to be treated as capable of self-direction.
- *Role of Learners.* Experience. Adult learners have a variety of experiences of life, which represent the richest resource for learning.
- *Readiness to Learn.* Adult learners are ready to learn those things they need to know in order to cope effectively with life situations.
- *Orientation to Learning.* Adults are motivated to learn to the extent that they perceive that it will help them perform tasks they confront in their life situations.

Criticisms of Piaget's Theory

Though Jean Piaget has had an enormous influence on educational practice, his ideas have been criticized through the years. By analyzing these criticisms, we can better understand the scope of his work. Here are some of the most common complaints.

Thinking of Children Underestimated

Piaget underestimated the thinking abilities of young children.[131] By requiring specific criteria for inferring a specific mental ability, and by using tests that were complex and removed from real life experience, younger children were generally rated as less capable than they really are.

Children's Thinking Cast in Negative Terms

Piaget describes lower stages in negative terms, emphasizing what children cannot do rather than what they can.[132] The very name "pre-operational" reflects this negativism: "before-operations." Pre-operational children *cannot* decenter, *cannot* conserve, *cannot* reverse, and they *cannot* see things from another's point of view. All of this is true, of course. Piaget was comparing qualitative differences in mental capabilities between children and adults. If adult thinking is taken as the standard of measure, then inabilities to function in adult ways will be expressed as negatives. Even so, research in the 1990s began to emphasize what younger children *can* do.

Adolescent Thinking Overestimated

Piaget overestimated Formal Thinking in adolescents.[133] Piaget proposed that from age eleven on, children developed formal thinking skills. Research in the 1980s reveals this is too optimistic. One study (1980) found that only 9 percent of ninth graders, 15 years of age, were mature formal thinkers. Thirty-two percent were just entering the concrete operational stage, 43 percent were in the concrete operational stage, and 15 percent were just entering the formal operational stage.[134] Another study (1984) found that 20 to 25 percent of college freshmen are consistently able to use formal operational reasoning.[135] A third study (1987) found that only 33 percent of high school seniors could apply formal operational reasoning.[136] A fourth study (1997) indicates that only 20 percent of children exhibit well-developed formal skills by the end of adolescence. A fifth study (1999) found that among 13- to-15-year-olds, 40 percent were early formal operators and 15 percent were mature formal operators. The researchers attributed this better result to specific teaching practices—"creating tables to display information and using tree diagrams to clarify grammatical structures"—designed to enhance formal skills.[137]

Piaget's Theory Universal?

Studies have shown that the sequence of stages proposed by Piaget is universal, but the rate of development differs from culture to culture. Formal operational thinking may not occur in every culture.[138]

Mental Abilities Really Develop in Four Distinct Stages?

Research has shown that the distinctness of each stage is not as clear-cut as Piaget originally proposed. Some aspects of "conservation of number" can be achieved by two-and-a-half years of age, even though children this age cannot perform Piaget's conservation task.[139] Research has provided mounting evidence that cognitive growth occurs as a continuous, gradual progression, with periodic jumps in abilities. To be fair, Piaget himself in his later work placed more emphasis on how thinking changes through equilibration, and less on the specific stages of development.

On the other hand, Woolfolk (2004) reports that brain research has found growth spurts in synaptic (nerve) connections throughout the brain cortex that correspond to Piaget's stages.[140] One might consider the stages as illustrative of macro changes in thinking, while micro-changes occur continuously as we interact with the world.

Biological Foundation?

Piaget believed that the sequence of development was determined by fixed biological processes. Researchers have questioned whether biological processes are relevant to cognitive development.[141] More recent brain research, cited just above, reenergizes the debate, demonstrating a definite link between physical changes in the brain and cognitive functioning. Cross-cultural studies re-affirming the sequence of stages[142] lends support to a biological case.

Key Role of Motor Activities?

Piaget connected cognitive growth to early motor experiences. Yet handicapped children, who have little motor experience, show normal cognitive growth.[143]

Despite these criticisms over the years, Piaget's theory is still held in high regard by contemporary educational psychologists (2002–2009).[144] Piaget's theory is a metaphor, based in philosophy and biology and intended to explain the development of mental capacities and functions. The explanatory strength of the theory, and its practical utility in teaching,[145] overcomes any problems caused by minor criticisms.

Implications of Piaget's Theory for Teaching

Piaget's view of education in general, and teaching in particular, is extreme in its emphasis on self-paced discovery by the learner and de-emphasis on instruction by the teacher.[146] He saw the goal of education as creating opportunities for learners to create or discover knowledge, not simply to increase the amount of knowledge in learners. When teachers overemphasize explanation of content to learners, they keep learners *from* "inventing and discovering" understanding on their own. Piaget's concept of effective teaching is not transmitting content. Learners merely learn the material by rote at a superficial (verbal) level and do not truly understand it. Rather, Piaget encouraged teachers to create situations in which meaning can be discovered by learners.[147] Early followers of Piaget called for a de-emphasis on transmitting knowledge by lectures and teacher-led discussions, replacing these with small group projects and problem-solving activities in which students do their own learning.[148]

The methodology of **pure** discovery, espoused by Piaget and developed into a full-scale approach to teaching by Jerome Bruner, evolved into the methodology of **directed** discovery, which encourages greater involvement of teachers in questioning, probing, directing, and encouraging learning. The impact of Postmodernism and more subjective forms of Constructivism has re-emphasized Piaget's discovery methodology. We'll discuss these issues in Chapter Eight.

In Christian circles, terms like "self-directed learning" and "inventing knowledge" cause quite a lot of anxiety, or, as Piaget might say, "disequilibrium." After all, we expect pastors to explain the Bible to their congregations. We expect Bible teachers to "teach the Bible"—that is, explain to learners what the Bible says (and means). We expect professors in Christian colleges to "teach the truth" so that students "get it right." Since this is so, what has Piaget to say to us? Quite a bit, actually. We'll look at general implications, and then several specific guidelines.

General Implications

Piaget underscores the fact that teaching must be more than talking at students. Teaching requires more than presenting a lesson to students if we hope to change the structure of thinking of students.

A line from the hymn "People to People" expresses the problem Piaget addresses in teaching. The line reads, "How do you tell an orphan child about the Father's love?"[149] The orphan has a scheme called "father," the content of which depends on his particular experiences in being orphaned. Whatever the scheme, it is different from the biblical image of God as Father, which is one of closeness, protection, guidance, strength, and discipline. The one who teaches this orphan about God as

"Father" must deal with the child's misconception of the term if the child is ever to understand what the *Bible* means by the term.

Piaget would tell us that teaching to establish biblical understanding is hampered by one-way communication. The better approach is for teacher and learners to enter into interactive conversations in which new material is related in meaningful ways to established ideas. In these interactions, Bible truths collide with learner (mis)perceptions and produce disequilibrium. How learners deal with disequilibrium determines whether the outcome is positive or negative. A positive outcome is (appropriate) accommodation to biblical truth (that is, learners change personal perceptions to correspond to God's Word). We read *out* of the text—we *exegete*—God's Truth, and then order our lives by it. A negative outcome is (inappropriate) assimilation of biblical truth (that is, interpreting Scripture so that it fits our own pre-conceived ideas). That is, we read *into* God's Word—we *eisegete*—our own truths. This "adding to" or "taking away from" God's Word is heresy (Rev 22:18–19).

Jesus said, "The scribes and the Pharisees are seated in the chair of Moses. Therefore do whatever they tell you and observe it. But don't do what they do, because they don't practice what they teach" (Matt 23:2–3). The religious leaders worshipped "the Law" but they did not live it. Teachers and preachers who make the Bible fit their own man-made ideologies may well worship what they have created. In so doing, they distort God's Word, and their worship is idolatry.

Piaget could well tell us to let the Bible speak to our students, to help them interact with its precepts, and accommodate their thinking to its message, so that they form a rational basis upon which God can grow them spiritually. Piaget might well agree with the apostle Paul that mere head knowledge (*gnosis*) about God "inflates with pride" (1 Cor 8:1). And yet Paul prays that believers would be filled with a personal, interactive, living, relational knowledge (*epignosis*) of God's will, along with spiritual understanding and wisdom, resulting in a life worthy of the Lord and pleasing to God, fruitful, powerful, persistent, joyful, and thankful (Col 1:9–12). As the minds of learners interact with the Mind of God through Scripture and is illuminated by the Spirit of God, a transformation of thinking takes place, a renewing of mind (Rom 12:2), a providing of Light to rescue us from darkness (Col 1:13). This Light leads bigots and racists to learn to be like God, Who "doesn't show favoritism" (Acts 10:34ff); it teaches materialists to put their trust in the Lord rather than possessions (Hab 3:17–19); it provokes the power-hungry to be a servant (Mark 9:35); it draws adulterers to faithfulness (Matt 5:27–28); persuades thieves and liars to be honest (Hos 4:2, Acts 6:3, 1 Pet 2:12); and on and on in a never-ending story, as we grow toward the spiritual maturity of the Lord Himself (Eph 4:11–13).

Make no mistake about it. Jean Piaget was a secular philosopher and biologist. He gave little if any thought to spiritual matters. And yet his observations and discoveries about human learning help us plan teaching approaches to infants, preschoolers, children, youth, and adults. My own goal as a Christian teacher is to provide situations in which learners intersect their thinking with the subject at hand, with the Lord and His Word, and with other learners so that they grow spiritually as well as academically through their studies. Here are several specific implications from Piaget's theory for doing this.

Specific Implications

1. Optimal discrepancy. The term *optimal* means "best or most effective." The term *discrepancy* means "difference." Piaget's term *optimal discrepancy* reflects a call for moderate levels of difficulty in teaching.[150] When teachers repeat ideas that learners already know, there is no disequilibrium. Established schemes may be reinforced, but thinking is not changed. Little learning, if any, will happen. Interest declines. Boredom grows.

When teachers present ideas that are foreign or frightening to learners, there will be too much disequilibrium. Some learners will be threatened, others angry. Still others may dismiss the ideas, and the teachers who espouse them, as dangerous. When teachers present ideas that both challenge learners and build on their previous knowledge, learners are neither bored nor threatened.

Optimal discrepancy is different for a preschooler and a teenager, for a day laborer and a professor. Knowing one's learners allows teachers to apply the principle of optimal discrepancy more effectively. They frame questions and explanations in a way that challenges the thinking of learners without provoking a riot among them. When dealing with controversial issues, effective teachers present various viewpoints or lead discussions of viewpoints with grace and sensitivity. They rock learner boats, but refrain from sinking them. Ignoring the balance of optimal discrepancy can lead to losing the opportunity to teach learners at all.

2. Direct Experience. "Interaction with the environment" leads to discovery.[151] Therefore, learning proceeds best through direct experiences with objects and events—experiences which are appropriate for the age of the learners. Direct experiences include activities[152] such as structured play, arts and music, and nature experiences for preschoolers; the use of visual aids and concrete props, projects and learning centers for children; drama and role play, hypothetical situations, and small group studies for youth; and real life experiences and testimonies for adults. Much of what we do in Christian teaching is verbal—teachers telling learners about the Bible. But *changing the understanding of learners* occurs best when learners are engaged as active thinkers rather than passive listeners.[153]

3. Social Interaction. Learners may have egocentric thought patterns. They may think that things *really are* the way *they see them*. Social interaction helps them become aware of the ideas and opinions of others. This process reduces egocentrism and helps thinking become more objective.[154]

Provide age-appropriate experiences that encourage learner-to-learner interaction (small group work) as well as teacher-learner (Q&A) interaction.

Learners in small groups (4 to 6 students) overcome individual differences in thinking better than learners in large classes (15+) where individual differences are easily hidden. Learners will more likely admit their confusion and lack of understanding in a small group than in a large class. More knowledgeable learners are better able to explain ideas in small groups than in large classes. This interaction helps both knowledgeable and unknowledgeable in ways that a large lecture class would not.

4. Thought-Provoking Questions. A thought-provoking question requires learners to consider what they know, decide what is relevant to the question, and then frame an answer based on that knowledge. A learner's answer is a window into their thinking. Incorrect answers should receive as much attention as correct ones,[155] because their correction helps learners understand where they went wrong in their thinking.[156]

Parroting back memorized answers to set questions does not reflect how deeply learners understand the subject, or whether they understand at all. Memorized answers may hold no meaning for learners at all, which leads to distorted memory: "and to the republic of Richard Stands."[157]

5. Learner Responses. A correct answer does not necessarily mean correct understanding. Effective teachers focus on the process of thinking, not just the product.[158] Ask the learner to explain how she arrived at her answer. Ask him why he answered the way he did? Focus on word meanings[159] by asking learners what they mean by the words they have chosen.[160] Consider the common mistakes your learners make in answering questions. Anticipate them and prepare explanations that emphasize these problem areas.[161]

6. Problem-Solving. Piaget defines teaching as creating situations where learners can make discoveries.[162] Problem-solving activities, such as discussing case studies or analyzing life situations, provide a rich discovery environment. Problems create disequilibrium. Problem solutions, based on available resources, bring about equilibration and a higher level of understanding. The methodology of problem-solving encourages interaction among learners and with the teacher: discussion, questions, hypotheses, opinions, research, and teamwork. Teachers and learners evaluate the solutions together to determine how well learners understand the fundamental principles involved.

7. Subsume New Material. Connecting new ideas to established ideas (schemes) through the use of active review makes the new material more meaningful and easier to master. The process of making these connections is called subsumption. It is difficult for learners to process new material when it is presented alone, absent links to past or future learning. Help *learners recall* principles and ideas they have already mastered (*active* review) that is relevant to the new material. Then build the new material on the base of this previous learning.

8. The Teaching Environment. The classroom is a "learning world." When teachers create a learning world that is safe and open, yet challenging, accommodation leads to a higher quality of learning. A positive learning world is one in which students can ask questions without fear of being rejected or humiliated. Where teachers listen as well as talk. Where ideas can be challenged, defended, or refuted without harsh words or flaring tempers. Where misconceptions can be aired without condemnation. Where teacher and learners interact, sharing questions and answers drawn from the material, but anchored in real life issues. The teaching environment is sometimes called "classroom climate." We devote Chapter Fourteen to a deeper discussion of this topic.

9. The Holy Spirit as Teacher. The biological mechanisms of equilibration and adaptation are not adequate to explain spiritual understanding or produce biblical results in renewing minds. Piaget's mechanisms help us understand a particular doctrine, or master ancient Middle East culture, or categorize the books of the Bible, or differentiate between similar biblical terms. But until our thinking interacts with the Lord Himself, until we learn *from Him* (Matt 11:29), we produce nothing more than biblical intellectualism and the pride it produces.

"Who do you say that I am?" Jesus asked. Peter responded, "You are the Christ, the Son of the living God" (Matt 16:16). Jesus replied, "You are blessed because flesh and blood did not reveal this to you, but My Father in heaven" (16:15–17). Spiritual truth is revealed, not "discovered."

In the hours before His death and subsequent resurrection, Jesus promised the disciples spiritual help by way of the Holy Spirit. "I will ask the Father, and He will give you another Counselor to be with you forever. He is the Spirit of truth. The world is unable to receive Him because it doesn't see Him or know Him. But you do know Him, because He remains with you and will be in you." (John 14:16–17). To do what? "But the Counselor, the Holy Spirit—the Father will send Him in My name—will teach you all things and remind you of everything I have told you" (14:26–27). "When the Spirit of truth comes, He will guide you into all the truth" (16:13).

The Holy Spirit provides *a spiritual environment* in which we may accommodate and assimilate the teachings of Jesus and grow spiritually. And *Who* is this Counselor, this Holy Spirit? Jesus identifies Himself with the Holy Spirit, His Divine Personal Presence in the lives of His disciples. "I will not leave you as orphans; *I am coming to you*" (John 14:18). Apostles Peter and Paul use the terms "Spirit of Christ" or "Spirit of Jesus" and "Holy Spirit" interchangeably.[163] However we handle the difficulties of the Trinitarian nature of God, the point is clear: *Spiritual understanding requires a Spiritual Teacher. No purely biological process can explain spiritual concepts to the satisfaction of the One Who made us to be like Him.*

Anyone can understand the religious meaning of the cross in Christianity through human teaching. But the spiritual meaning of the cross—of sacrifice, grace, and personal atonement—comes from heaven by means of the Spiritual Teacher. The Holy Spirit, the Spirit of Christ, is part of the immaterial environment in which we operate. Interaction with Him injects a spiritual underpinning to biblical studies, which leads to biblical thinking, which leads to biblical lifestyle.

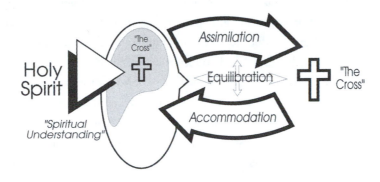

Jesus taught His disciples for three years. They lived together, ate together, shared ministry and miracles together. And yet, when the soldiers came to the garden of Gethsemane, they ran away. They understood a great deal from their experiences with Jesus. After all, Jesus was the greatest Teacher Who ever lived. But it wasn't until after the Resurrection, when Jesus appeared to them, and after Pentecost, when they were filled and empowered by the Holy Spirit, that they understood from a spiritual perspective what had happened. It was then they became courageous concerning the truths of the kingdom, and by His power, turned the world upside-down (Acts 17:6).

When we teach in a church context—sermons, Bible studies, discipleship classes—we may teach for a long time without visible results. Then, without any apparent reason, we see lives transformed, attitudes changed, and behaviors improved. This is the work of the Spirit of the Lord, Who moves, not in the constrained forces of biological processes, but freely like the wind: "The wind blows where it pleases, and you hear its sound, but you don't know where it comes from or where it is going. So it is with everyone born of the Spirit" (John 3:8).

Teachers do well to use Piaget's suggestions to provide the rational raw material for spiritual growth. Simply "depending on the Lord" in Christian teaching does not excuse poor methodology. But the spiritual transformation of learners happens as the Holy Spirit infuses the thinking of those who know Him with His own power, His own teaching. Spiritual teachers open their classrooms to "the Circle of the Model" by inviting Him, submitting to Him, and serving kingdom goals rather than their own.

Concluding Thoughts on Piaget

Jean Piaget described his goals for the educational process as follows:

The principle goal of education is to create men who are capable of doing new things, not simply of repeating what other generations have done—men who are creative, inventive, and discoverers. The second goal of education is to form minds which can be critical, can verify, and not accept everything they are offered. The great danger today is of slogans, collective opinions, ready-made trends of thoughts. We have to be able to resist, individually, to criticize, to distinguish between what is proven and what is not. So we need pupils who are active, who learn early to find out by themselves, partly by their own spontaneous activity and partly through material we set up for them; who learn early to tell what is verifiable and what is simply the first idea to come to them.[164]

Piaget's language disquiets some Christians because it is so open-ended, so man-centered, so oblivious to Scriptures' absolutes, even rebellious to the established order. All I need do is think of the Lord Who authored Scripture, and Who was best known on earth as Teacher. The Lord loved people and met their needs. He began with concrete experiences of their day and led them to consider the (abstract) spiritual reality of the kingdom. He asked questions and posed problems. He used concrete demonstrations, parables, and stories. He chose twelve men to "be with Him," to learn intimately, to observe closely, to experience firsthand the kingdom of God. He sent the disciples on mission trips for hands-on ministry experience. He demonstrated repeatedly that the Religious Establishment had missed God's Truth, and had gone after their own rituals, for the sake of their own power. Jesus established the Church as the base for teaching ministry (Matt 28:19–20). What Jesus did reflects Piaget's discoveries.

Or I think of the apostle Paul, who, as a Pharisee's Pharisee (Acts 23:6), assimilated the idea of "The Way" by condemning its early followers, hunting them down and putting them in prison. When Paul met the Lord on the road to Damascus, he was struck down by Truth. He immediately accommodated his thinking to the reality of the resurrection, because he had seen the Resurrected One. He spent three years in an Arabian desert re-thinking all of his Pharisaical training and Old Testament study. As a missionary teacher, he re-interpreted the Old Testament in light of the Cross and the Empty Tomb. He understood the Pharisees in particular and the Jews in general, having been trained in their schools. He understood the Greeks and the Romans, because he grew up in Tarsus and attended the university there. He taught in a variety of ways so people of all kinds could under-stand and come to faith in the Risen Lord. "I have become all things to all people, so that I may by all means save some" (1 Cor 9:22). Paul believed in the Church as a Learning Environment in which the lost could find salvation and the saved grow in the Lord. In all these ways, Paul reflected Piaget's discoveries.

We would do well to reflect Piaget's discoveries in our teaching, doing all we can in a human context to open minds to the unshakable Truths of God's Word and world.

Contributions of Lev Vygotsky

Lev Vygotsky has become widely known for emphasizing the social, cultural, and linguistic dimensions of cognitive development. Piaget viewed children as "busy and self-controlled individuals who, on their own, explore, form ideas, and test these ideas with their experiences."[165] Social interaction is a mechanism for adaptation,[166] a process involving individuals and their worlds. Vygotsky saw children as an integral part of the social fabric of parents, teachers, and community ("It takes a village"). Social interaction, not adaptation, is the origin of higher mental processes.[167] Piaget considered language a reflection of mental maturity[168] and an aid to developing symbolic thought, but not central to cognitive development.[169] Vygotsky considered language, the means of creating socially shared activities, essential to cognitive development. Piaget proposed a universal theory, based on biology, in which culture has little role. Vygotsky believed that culture provides the essential context for language and social interaction.[170]

The Life of Lev Vygotsky

Lev Semenovich Vygotsky (1896–1934) was a Soviet educational psychologist and a contemporary with Jean Piaget.[171] As a young boy, he had tutors who used the Socratic method primarily—a question and answer process that challenges current ideas to promote higher levels of understanding. These early experiences in learning, and his later experiences as a teacher, led him to the conclusion that cognitive development comes as a result of social interaction, language, and cultural context.[172]

He died at the age of 38 of tuberculosis and yet wrote a hundred books and articles on the subject of psychology and education. His writings were banned in the Soviet Union because he referenced Western psychologists[173] such as William James and Jean Piaget. Repressed by Josef Stalin, who was no friend to developmental psychology, his work did not appear in psychological literature until the 1980s.[174]

Social Interaction

The core of cognitive development is social interaction with a "more knowledgeable other." Group activities drive conversations, ideas are exchanged, and development occurs.[175] Social interactions begin with parents and siblings and later expand to teachers and classmates. These socially shared activities are internalized as cognitive processes and develop to the point where they can be "autonomously invoked"—that is, used independently. For Piaget, cognitive development makes social interaction possible. The *individual* precedes the *social.* For Vygotsky, social interaction is the primary source of cognitive development.[176] The *social* precedes the *individual.* Cognitive development results from the internalization of social experiences.[177]

Language

According to Vygotsky, language is the means by which we gain access to the knowledge of others. Language provides the tools for thinking about the world and solving problems. Language allows us to reflect on our own thinking[178]—a point demonstrated quite tangibly in "self-talk."[179]

Self-talk is free-floating external private speech that is a precursor to internalized private speech.[180] For example, a child may talk himself through an addition problem—"let's see, three plus two equals, ah, five"—he writes five on his paper. The words come from former interactions with the teacher who has worked through a similar problem and explained each step. Private speech is an intermediary step in the process of internalizing an external dialogue.

Woolfolk suggests that private speech is an indication that children need help with the task before them. She further suggests that teachers who require total silence in the classroom may hinder the work of children on difficult tasks.[181] Eventually, the internalization of self-talk will be complete, and children will be able to work problems "in their heads" without talking out loud.[182] Language is the medium for social discourse and is an essential precursor to cognitive development.

Piaget called private speech "egocentric speech" and considered it a reflection of the child's inability to consider the perspectives of others.[183] Language is an indicator of mental maturity already established. Vygotsky viewed language as essential to social interaction, which in turn produces mental maturity.

Culture

Culture provides the context for social interaction and language. Cultures pass on to successive generations the "psychological tools" used to interact with the world. These tools include such things as speech, writing, gestures, diagrams, numbers, chemical formulas, musical notation, rules, memory techniques and the like.[184]

Cultures differ in the fundamental ways. Some cultures are past-oriented, focusing on traditions and ancestors. Some are future-oriented, sacrificing present comfort for future benefits. Still others are present-oriented, living for today. Some cultures are group-oriented, forcing individuals into cultural modes; others are individually oriented, championing individual effort and creativity to transform. Some are active, engaging the world and solving problems; others are passive, accepting the world as it is, unable or unwilling to change it.[185]

Cultural differences extend even to the incidental use of words. Snowman lists the following words: "plate, box, peach, knife, apple, cup, potato" and asks readers to group them. He predicts we will group *plate, knife, and cup* (utensils), and *peach, apple, potato* (edibles). Those who do so use a taxonomic, or conceptual, framework for the grouping. But others might group *plate, knife, and apple*. It is a functional grouping in which two items permits the eating of the third. The rules by which we consider problems are cultural. As cultures differ, so does the cognitive development of members of that culture.

For Piaget, cognitive development is universal and biological, with little role played by culture. For Vygotsky, cognitive development is dependent on a particular cultural context, which provides the basis for language and social interaction.

Contrast of Piaget and Vygotsky on Cognitive Development

Component	Piaget	Vygotsky
Social Interaction	Cognitive development makes social interaction possible. The *individual* precedes the *social*.	Social interaction makes cognitive development possible. The *social* precedes the *individual*.
Language	Language is an indicator of mental maturity already established. *Development* precedes *language*.	Language is essential to the development of mental maturity. *Language* precedes *development*.
Culture	Development is universal and biological. Culture plays *little role*.	Development is dependent on cultural context. Culture plays *essential role*.

Nature of Development

Piaget saw cognitive development as proceeding from stage to stage as biological forces provide for increasing mental maturity. One example of this is the inability of infants to remember an object they can no longer see. He observed infant reactions when they are shown a toy which is then hidden under a hat. He discovered that younger infants do not remember the toy; older infants do and begin looking for it. His explanation was that "infants who had not reached the sensorimotor stage and, thus, had not achieved the ability to retain memory of a non-visible object, operated on the out-of-sight, out-of-mind principle."[186]

Vygotsky saw development as a continuous process of internalization of socially shared activities. His view of Piaget's task was that infants begin to realize that a toy is still present even when covered by a hat, *not* because they acquire some new mental operations, but because repeated social interactions stimulate such a response. The fact that children appear more capable in more supportive contexts argues against stages.[187]

The reality lies somewhere between brittle stages and smooth continuity. It is overly simplistic to think that preoperational children suddenly become concrete operational at age seven. Piaget himself wrote that the ages were suggestive. On the other hand, neuroscience has discovered spurts in brain growth that coincide with Piaget's age breaks in development.[188] Perhaps the best we can say is that human cognitive development is a highly complex process that proceeds in an uneven yet continuous direction toward mature thinking.

Parents provide the first social environment for the child. Therefore, says Vygotsky, developing concepts are "spontaneous by-products" of interactions with parents and are therefore unsystematic and unconscious. Language is limited to classifications of objects at home.[189] "Scientific concepts," however, are developed by schooling, in which psychological tools are learned through explicit and clear definitions.[190]

One should not read Western educational practice into Vygotsky's words. He had nothing but contempt for "instructors" in Tsarist schools who "know their subjects and curriculum and how to raise one's voice at the class in a difficult situation."[191] The "real secret of education," writes Vygotsky, "lies in *not* teaching." Vygotsky's ideal system is one where "the student educates himself" according to the "exact knowledge of the laws of education" where the teacher is "director of the social environment, which is the only educational factor."[192]

How do self-educating students and teacher-directors function in such a system? Vygotsky defined two essential concepts that integrate his view of learning and the role of the teacher. These are the "zone of proximal development" (ZPD) and "scaffolding."

Zone of Proximal Development

One of the more esoteric ideas of Vygotsky is his "zone of proximal development." At least two descriptions of ZPD can be found in current literature. I call these "snapshot" and "process" views (see the illustration on page 123). Learners fall into one of three areas regarding cognitive development and tasks. These are labeled A, B, and C in the diagram, and are the same for both views.

"**A**"—learners *can* solve problems or complete tasks **below their ZPD** with personal skills and *without help* from others.

"**B**"—learners *can* solve problems **within their ZPD** with personal skills and ***with help*** from others, and

"**C**"—learners *cannot* solve problems or complete tasks **above their ZPD** *even with help* from others.

Required tasks must fall within a learner's ZPD in order for that learner to benefit from assistance. This is reasonable since tasks below the ZPD provide no developmental benefit—they are easily done—and tasks above the ZPD merely stymie learners—they cannot be done even with help. In this sense, Vygotsky's ZPD is analogous to Piaget's concept of "optimal discrepancy." But what does this zone of development actually represent? It is here the two view differ.

The Snapshot View. In the snapshot view on the next page, ZPD reflects the difference between present (in)abilities[193] and potential abilities to accomplish tasks. The lower end of the zone ("B" left) represents the learner's present level of ability,[194] actual developmental level[195], or "what that learner can do alone, *without guidance*."[196] The upper end of the zone ("B" right) represents the learners' level of "ability [to complete a task] in collaboration with peers and under expert guidance,"[197] or "**what more** that learner can do *with assistance*."[198]

A new task falls within a learner's ZPD if it can be accomplished with help. When new tasks are beyond present skills (challenging), but not beyond potential skills (doable with help), they promote cognitive growth.

Students enter my research and statistics class with a wide range of skills and experiences. Let's let "Ben" represent students who enjoyed mathematics in high school and had a statistics class or two in college. Let's let "Brenda" represent students who were average math students in high school but took only required classes in math in college. Let's let "Brad" represent students who dislike math in general and made low grades in every math class they were forced to take in high school and college. These three have different ZPDs for the required tasks in my class.

Ben's ZPD is above many of the class assignments. He is able to do most of the assignments without assistance. Not only will he earn a high mark in the class, but he will most likely tutor others in the class.

Brenda's ZPD matches class assignments. She is able to apply herself and do every assignment, but she will require assistance along the way. She will ask questions in class or by e-mail, discuss assignments with classmates, and study sample problems in the textbook. As she uses these sources of help to work the assignments, her understanding of the material will deepen until she can work them without assistance.

Brad's ZPD falls below most of the assignments in the class. He will struggle to complete the assignments, even with assistance. Perhaps there are basic concepts Brad doesn't clearly understand. Perhaps he needs to develop calculator skills. Perhaps he looks at formulas globally—seeing formulas "all at once"—as confusing jumbles of letters. We need to clarify the meaning of processes and concepts, to demonstrate calculator skills, and to help him see formulas *sequentially*, as step-by-step of related calculations. By providing targeted remedial help, Brad can raise his ZPD sufficiently to do the assignments with the same assistance given to others. When Brad's ZPD matches course assignments, he is able to develop content mastery.

While we see growth in these students' abilities, their "snapshot ZPDs" represent the *stretch* between *what they cannot yet do and what they can do with help* "now." Woolfolk, on the other hand, focuses on a process view of ZPD.

The Process View. Rather than a snapshot of present/potential abilities, Woolfolk emphasizes what can be called a process view of ZPD. In this view, learners grow from "unable to do alone (with present skills)" to "able to do alone with newly achieved skills"[199] (see "process view" in illustration). New tasks require assistance, but as skills grow, less assistance is needed over time until learners can do them on their own. Woolfolk challenges teachers to put students in "situations where they have to reach to understand, but where support from other students or from the teacher is also available." As students work on difficult tasks they cannot do alone, they generally welcome assistance. **"As they progress, their thinking becomes smoother, more internalized, and more autonomous."**[200] Self-talk decreases. Toward the end of the development cycle, learners can perform the task alone and may view help from others as an irritating disruption.[201] Often the best help for students struggling with a task comes from classmates who have just solved the problem—those who are "just a bit better" at the task. By discussing the problems and their solutions, learners can organize their thinking about the tasks.[202] This internalized development prepares them for the next challenging task.

Regardless of these contemporary views of ZPD, Vygotsky's focus may not have been on specific tasks or skills, but rather the role of "others" in learning. He observed, "Children rarely did as well solving problems or completing tasks as when they were working in collaboration with an adult." Adults did not always teach them how to perform the task, but the "process of engagement with adults enabled them to refine their thinking or their performance to make it more effective." Tasks requiring guidance from (older) others underscore the important role of language and social interaction, central to Vygotsky's theory of learning and development.[203]

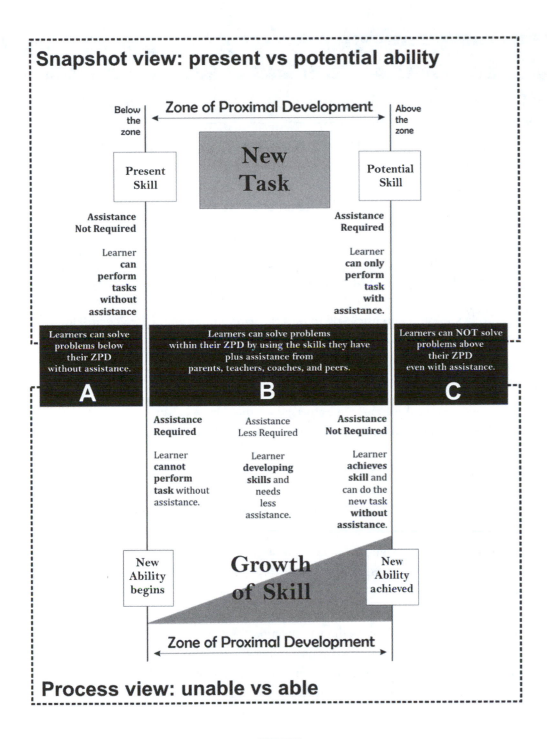

Zone of Proximal Development		
Elements	**Snapshot View**	**Process View**
Emphasis	*Readiness* for a Given Task	*Development* of skill
Range of Zone	Present Skill – Potential Skill *"In the moment"*	No Skill – Skill Achieved *"Over time"*
Lower End	**Unable** to do task alone Assistance Needed	
Higher End	Able to do task **with help** Assistance *Needed*	Able to do task **without help** Assistance *Not Needed*
Nature of Skill	*Potential* Skill to be Achieved	*Achieved* Skill

Scaffolding

Providing intentional assistance to learners who cannot learn on their own is called scaffolding. Just as builders raise physical scaffolding to support the initially weak walls of a building, so teachers provide psychological scaffolding to support new thinking until it can be processed and internalized. When the building is completed, the scaffolding can be safely removed and the building will stand. Similarly, teachers can remove the psychological supports that were necessary to establish understanding, and learners will continue to understand on their own. Let's look at some practical types of scaffolding[204] teachers use to support learning.

Modeling. Teachers demonstrate an example of an assigned task before assigning a task for learners to do on their own. Imitation precedes individual capability.[205] For example, after describing a procedure to determine whether two groups differ on some measurement (e.g., test score), display two sets of scores and walk students through the process of using it. Display the steps on an overhead screen. Enter the numbers and move through the process step-by-step to a successful conclusion.

After describing the role of an instructional taxonomy in setting up measurable targets for teaching, have students open their Bibles to a verse of Scripture, announce a level of learning, and then walk them step-by-step through the process of writing a measurable, meaningful instructional objective.

Thinking Aloud. While demonstrating a mathematical procedure, "think out loud" so students can hear your thoughts. Verbalize the internal discussion that goes on in solving problems. "Wait . . . is that what I want to do? . . . Now, what is the next step? . . . Okay, we have this part, now what do I need next?"

In considering the appropriate approach to writing an instructional objective, verbalize the internal discussion. "What is the focus of this verse? . . . What do we most want learners to draw from it? . . . We could do this. . . . Or, we could go this way. . . . So, that means we need to . . ." and so forth. Thinking aloud not only reinforces the visual demonstration with sound, but explicitly demonstrates the thinking process—the decision-making process—required in moving from verse and level to instructional objective.

Questions. While computing a procedure or writing an instructional objective, ask questions of the class. "What should we do next?" "What does this number represent?" "Am I forgetting something here?" "If you were teaching this verse, what would be your major focus?"

Questions engage learners who might otherwise lose focus in a one-way presentation. Questions cause learners to sort through the information they have learned as they deal with the confusion that remains.

Finally, encourage learners to ask questions. The explanations, feedback, and support given in response to student questions reduce their confusion.

The Ultimate Goal of Lev Vygotsky

Contemporary textbooks filter out Vygotsky's (1920s) Communistic idealism, re-making his theory into a type of student-friendly, group-oriented educational humanism. This is misleading. Vygotsky wrote, "The primitive ideal of the educator *qua* nursemaid, which demanded of the teacher warmth, tenderness, and concern, is not quite to our taste."[206]

Vygotsky's writings are filled with loathing for the traditional Tsarist "instructors," and glorious praise for the new Soviet era. He held a passionate faith in science to determine the appropriate "laws" of education. Наука есть вернейший путь к овладению жизнью (*Science is the truest pathway to the mastery of life*).[207]

Scientific technology had, for Vygotsky, replaced the "brutish routine" in industry. The "dark elements of ideology" (i.e., *religion*) had been replaced with science. And now, ever onward and upward, science would continue to perfect the true nature of Man. Parents would be replaced by teachers—the unsystematic, spontaneous home-based concepts replaced by "scientific concepts" learned at school. Even in school, the educational process would no longer be left to individual instructors, teaching individual subjects, and specified curricula. A "new system would soon be in place," (1926) in which the "laws of education," defined by scientific discovery, would be applied in socially-sensitive schools. "The future teacher would no longer be an instructor, but rather an engineer, a seaman, a political worker, journalist, scholar, judge, and doctor" drawing "self-educated students" into "close interaction with each other and life itself."[208]

The **"re-creation of Man through socialist reorganization"**—Vygotsky's goal of education— would soon be an established reality under the rule of the "transparent Soviet dictatorship," in order to produce a "higher sociobiological type,"[209] a Soviet "super-man."[210] Vygotsky's views of culture, social interaction, language, and school were all anchored in this goal.

It is little wonder that Vygotsky rejected Piaget's call to "view children as . . . self-motivated *individuals*, who, <u>on their own</u>, *explore, form ideas, and test these ideas with their own experiences.*" Such freedom of thought would not allow the "transparent dictatorship" to properly mold its children into the prescribed "higher type" of Man. According to Vygotsky, there was no need for children to reinvent culture on their own. Through properly managed "social interaction with a more knowledgeable other,"[211] children would internalize all the "psychological tools" and "scientific concepts" they need for growth.[212]

Implications of Vygotsky's Theory for Teaching

Putting aside Vygotsky's failed worldview, defined by science-as-religion and Soviet Communism, we can say without doubt that his sociocultural theory bears study by Christian teachers. We have provided an overview of learning characteristics as well as numerous classroom examples to illustrate the process of cognitive development from Vygotsky's point of view. Here are the most important implications for today's classrooms.

1. Organize classroom instruction around meaningful activities and authentic tasks.[213] *Meaningful* and *authentic* refer to activities that are relevant to the life situations of learners in the class. Vygotsky wrote, "Only life educates."[214]

2. Use scaffolding to help students progress through their zones of proximal development.[215] Provide models, prompts, coaching, and feedback. As students grow in their competence, reduce these supports[216] until they are no longer needed.

3. Structure classroom tasks to encourage student interaction.[217] Experiment with peer tutoring—students who have completed tasks help those who have not.[218] Have students work in small groups to do complex tasks.[219]

4. Teach students how to use tools and learning strategies in completing their tasks—dictionaries, computer searches, spreadsheets, outlining, and the like.

5. Model the use of tools in demonstrations. Think aloud as you use them.

6. Teach students how to ask good questions and give helpful explanations.[220]

7. Encourage students to talk themselves quietly through difficult tasks.

8. Present students with some tasks that will require help.[221]

The Church as Social Context—The Kingdom as Culture

As we saw in Chapter One, the Central Pillar of the Disciplers' Model is "Building Relationships." The Church is God's Family. We pray "*Our* Father in heaven." We are spiritual Brothers and Sisters. We teach one another in a Church-social and kingdom-cultural context. While our goal—"to grow up into Him Who is the Head, that is, Christ"—is vastly different from Vygotsky's Soviet super-Man, the processes he discovered in his short life provide insights, especially for highly individualistic Americans, into the importance of us-ness in learning and growing as citizens of the kingdom of God.

We come together in local churches, drawn from different regions, socioeconomic levels, backgrounds, and experiences. The only thing that binds us together is our common experience of salvation through faith in Jesus Christ. The Church is a sociocultural context in which we worship and learn together—praying, singing, ministering, giving, and receiving. With Christ as our Head, we grow together as various parts of the Body, separate, yet one, a social re-organization. Under the direction of the Holy Spirit, individuals move from pagan to believer, believer to disciple, disciple to teacher, teacher to leader, and leader to missionary. Individuals, engaged in God's Family, Christ's Body, form an us-ness that extends to every corner of the earth.[222]

In Conclusion

The Great Commission—reaching people where they are and teaching them all things after they are reached—requires the flexibility of thinking, the age-appropriateness of activities, and the problem-solving skills Piaget so ably suggested. Part of God's wonderful design was discovered and systematized by Piaget's life-long observations, and he helps us in ways he never dreamed.

Soviet Communism was Satan's counterfeit to the kingdom of God. Lenin was Father. Stalin the Savior-Son. The school system was the Church. Teachers were pastor-priests. Party members were true believers. Heroes of the Soviet Union were saints, rewarded and worshipped for their dedication. Within this context, Lev Vygotsky analyzed (1920s–1930s) how human beings learn *together*. The system, and those who killed millions of their own people defending it, are dead now, thoroughly discredited. And yet Vygotsky speaks across a gulf of 75 years and helps us in ways he never dreamed.

Chapter Concepts

JEAN PIAGET	
Abstract thinking	Theoretical thinking, expressing meaning apart from specific objects
Accommodation	Modifying or creating schemes to fit experience in the world
Adaptation	Mechanism of cognitive change involving assimilation and accommodation
Assimilation	Modifying (interpreting) experience in the world to fit existing schemes
Classification	Assigning objects to groups on the basis of common characteristics
Cognitive development	Intellectual growth that permits the creation of new ideas from existing information
Concrete operational	Stage three: ability to think operationally with objects
Concrete thinking	Practical thinking, expressing meaning applied to actual objects
Conservation	Recognizing that a quantity does not change despite changes in appearance
Decentration	The ability to focus on more than the most prominent element of a problem
Disequilibrium	Confusion caused by a difference between what is known and what is experienced
Egocentrism	The belief that other people see a situation the way "I" do
Equilibration	The process of re-establishing balance between what is known and what is experienced
Formal operational	Stage four: ability to think operationally with abstract ideas
Language	An indicator of cognitive development but does not raise intellectual functioning
Operation	An action which can be carried out mentally

Optimal discrepancy	Difference between "known" and "experienced" that allows best learning to occur
Organization	The natural tendency of the mind to organize the world of experience
Preoperational stage	Stage two: characterized by language acquisition and fantasy; unable to think operationally
Reversibility	The ability to mentally undo an action
Scheme	Mental representation of experience or behavior
Sensorimotor stage	Stage one: cognitive development characterized by the five senses and movement
Social interaction	Mechanism for engaging adaptation
LEV VYGOTSKY	
Cognitive development	Internalization of social experiences
Culture	Provides the context for social interaction and language
Language	Essential to social interaction and a precursor of cognitive development
Scaffolding	Initial support for learning tasks which is removed as competence grows
Self-talk	External (audible) or internal conversation with ourselves. Private speech
Social interaction	Socially-shared activities that form the primary source of cognitive development
ZPD	Zone of proximal development. Frame of development for tasks.

Chapter Objectives

Learners will demonstrate knowledge of Piaget's theory by matching definitions with the terms organization, adaptation, assimilation, accommodation, equilibration, conservation, reversibility and egocentrism.

Learners will demonstrate understanding of Piaget's theory by explaining the role of organization, disequilibrium, assimilation, accommodation, and equilibration in cognitive development.

Learners will demonstrate understanding of Vygotsky's theory by explaining the role of the zone of proximal development and scaffolding in cognitive development.

Learners will demonstrate understanding of cognitive development by comparing and contrasting Piaget and Vygotsky on the concepts of cognitive development, social interaction, stages of development, language, and culture.

Discussion Questions

1 Read the following quotes, and paraphrase them as you might do in explaining them to someone who has not studied Piaget's theory.

 a. "Adaptation is the process of adjusting schemes and experiences so that we maintain a state of equilibrium."[223]

 b. "It is difficult to assimilate experiences beyond the level of mental development. Thus, as teachers, we can get children to say they know, or force them to memorize, but we should not be fooled into believing that they really understand. Piaget might say, 'To know by heart is not to know.'"[224]

 c. "Accommodation is changing existing schemes in order to incorporate experience."[225]

 d. "Equilibration maintains the balance between assimilation and accommodation."[226]

 e. "The ability to conserve requires reversibility."[227]

 f. "An operation is a scheme whose major characteristic is that it can be reversed."[228]

2 Consider a current situation in national politics or religious news. What are the major viewpoints to this situation? How do these viewpoints reflect assimilation and accommodation?

3 Develop an example which includes "scheme," "disequilibrium," "assimilation," "accommodation," and "equilibration" using a biblical concept such as "love," "believe," or "submission."

4 Choose one of the four major age groups—preschoolers, children, youth, or adults—and develop guidelines for teaching that group. Include common mistakes you've experienced in teaching this group.

5 Consider experiences you have had in small group Bible studies in light of Vygotsky's ideas of social interaction. How did the group's discussion affect your thinking on Bible passages or themes? In what ways did you internalize the group discussion?

6 According to Piaget, would better learning occur in a single large adult Bible study class or several small groups?

7 An associate pastor uses repetition to teach a group of first- and second-grade children in Vacation Bible School on "what to say to the pastor when they walk down the aisle on Sunday to make their profession of faith." Based on this chapter, is this a good thing to do? Why or why not?

8 Compare and contrast the snapshot and process views of ZPD.

9 Think back to a school experience in which you were given a task beyond your capability. How did the teacher use scaffolding to help you master the task?

How We Develop Moral Decision Makers

Lawrence Kohlberg: Moral Reasoning Development Theory

"There is a way that seems right to a man, but its end is the way to death."

Proverbs 14:12

"A man is not honest simply because he never had a chance to steal."

—Yiddish Proverb[1]

Chapter Rationale

Teaching and learning are dynamic moral processes. At a basic level, rules are necessary to govern classroom discipline and order, fairness, equal opportunities to succeed or fail, and honest measures of evaluation. Personal life issues such as parental support, nutrition, drug or alcohol use, promiscuity, violence, abortion, and racism affect learning, achievement, and growth.

One might think that teaching in a Christian context is, in itself, moral. But faith in Christ and morality are two different issues. If we do not make a conscious effort to teach our children principles of moral decision-making—principles that reflect our biblical faith—then whose principles will they learn?

Lawrence Kohlberg extended the work of Jean Piaget into the area of moral reasoning. Kohlberg's stages provide a framework by which we can help learners analyze their own approaches to moral dilemmas.

Chapter Overview

Moral Dilemma One: The Boy and the Tavern

One warm summer Sunday afternoon in 1964, a fourteen-year-old was walking from house to house in his church's neighborhood distributing booklets. He was part of a youth evangelism project planned and directed by his church. They had washed cars and cleaned yards, collecting money to purchase Gospel booklets of Mark. Now they were out in the neighborhood distributing them.

As he walked along, he came to a quiet neighborhood tavern. He began to walk on by, but a question stopped him. "Should I go in and give Gospels to the people inside?" He was alone on the street. He had no instructions from his youth minister regarding taverns. If you had been this teenage boy, would you have entered the tavern and distributed booklets to the people? Why or why not?

(Consider what you would do, and why, and write it out. You will use this a little later.)

> ### Moral Dilemma Two: The Document and the Lord's Supper
>
> You are invited by a missions agency to help with a project in a foreign country. As part of your preparation to travel overseas, you sign a document in which you agree "not to use alcohol or tobacco products" while on the trip. You arrive early on Sunday morning and spend the day with national hosts before joining your team on Monday. Your Baptist hosts take you to the worship service at their church, where they celebrate the Lord's Supper. You know that Baptists in this country use wine in their Lord's Supper observance. As the cup of communal wine is passed to you, do you sip the wine? Or do you refuse? Why or why not?

Historical Roots: Jean Piaget and Moral Development

A moral dilemma is a problem that has no clear course of action because any decision one makes presents both positive and negative consequences.[2] Just as children differ from adults in personality (Erikson) and cognitive development (Piaget and Vygotsky), so they differ in their approaches to solving moral dilemmas.

Although Jean Piaget is best known for his theory of cognitive development, he did not limit his studies to cognitive issues. Using the same methodology established in cognitive studies, he studied moral development as well.

He began by observing children play the game of marbles.[3] How did they play? What rules did they follow? How consistently did they follow them? He found that children interpreted rules differently according to their age.[4] Below the age of two, children simply play with the marbles without regard for rules. Between the ages of two and six,[5] children show an awareness of rules—and try to go along with them[6]—but do not understand their purpose or need to follow them.[7] Between six and ten,[8] children are moving into the concrete operational stage of thinking. They begin to view rules as "sacred pronouncements" handed down by authorities—usually older children and parents.[9] Rules are fixed, unchangeable edicts.[10] After the age of "eleven or so,"[11] children move into the formal operational stage of thinking. They begin to understand that rules are agreements reached by mutual consent.[12] Rules exist to give direction, but they can be changed.[13]

In addition to observing children play marbles, Piaget presented moral problems to children in the form of stories. He would listen to their reactions and then ask questions to analyze their thinking.[14] Here is the story of Augustus and Julian:

> There was a little boy called Julian. His father had gone out and Julian thought it would be fun to play with father's ink-pot. First, he played with the pen, and then he made a little blot on the

table cloth. Another little boy who was called Augustus once noticed that his father's ink-pot was empty. One day when his father was away, he thought of filling the ink-pot so as to help his father, and so he should find it full when he came home. But while he was opening the ink-pot, he made a big blot on the table cloth.[15]

Another story reads like this:

A boy named John is called to dinner. As John opens the dining room door, it hits a tray holding fifteen cups, all of which break upon hitting the floor. A boy named Henry tries to get some jam from a cupboard while his mother is out of the house. Balanced precariously on a chair, in the process of reaching for the jam, he knocks over a cup and breaks it.[16]

Piaget would ask, "Are these children equally guilty? Which of the two is naughtiest and why?" Piaget found that younger children reacted differently to the stories than older children. On the basis of their interpretation of rules and reactions to his stories, Piaget concluded that six-year-olds deal with moral issues differently than twelve-year-olds.

Morality of Constraint, Morality of Cooperation

Piaget eventually proposed three stages of moral reasoning based on his observations. The first, reflected in children below age five, he called **premoral**. In this stage, children are not concerned with rules. They simply want to have fun and rules shouldn't get in the way of that.[17] Moral development begins about age six[18] or seven[19] in Piaget's second stage. This stage is called **moral realism**[20] or the **morality of constraint**.[21] Rules simply exist. They are absolute and cannot be broken. If a rule is broken, punishment is determined by the damage done. Intentions or motivations should not be considered.[22] So, children in Stage two will say that Augustus and John are more guilty than Julian and Henry because Augustus made the larger blot and John broke more cups. The fact that Augustus was trying to help while Julian was misbehaving, or that John had an accident while Henry was misbehaving, does not change the damage that was done. Piaget used the term *heteronomy* to refer to this stage because rules are handed down by an outside [*hetero-*, other] authority [*-nomy*].[23]

At about the age of ten[24] or eleven,[25] children move into Piaget's third stage, that of **moral relativism**[26] or the **morality of cooperation**.[27] Rules are flexible.[28] They were made by mutual agreement and can be changed. If a rule is broken, punishment is determined by both damage and intention.[29] Piaget used the term *autonomy* to refer to this stage because rules are internalized principles and ideals [*auto-*, self].[30] Rules are what we make them to be.[31]

Example from a School Fair

One day I was helping my wife at a school fair. The booth next to hers was a Ring Toss booth. The teacher in charge had her two children helping her, a seven-year-old daughter and a fourteen-year-old son. The son had built the booth and provided the muscle for the day-long event. The daughter served as ticket collector. It was late in the day. The fair was over and folks were packing up their things. The teenager walked around to the front of the booth and said to his sister, "Give me a ring." His sister looked up at him and replied, "Where's your ticket?" "I don't need a ticket—just give me a ring!" The fact that tickets were no longer being sold, that the fair was over, and that people were leaving made no difference to the sister. "If you don't have a ticket, you don't get three rings."

The teenager was too tired to argue, and so took another approach. He walked around to the back of the booth where they kept the coffee can bulging with the now worthless tickets they had collected. He picked up a ticket, walked back to the front of the booth, and gave it to his sister. She beamed as she handed him three rings and said, "That's better!" "I only want one ring, not three." "You paid your ticket, you get three rings—*that's the rule*." So he gave up and took the three rings. He tossed them at the coke bottles and made ringers with all three. "Here's your flag," said the sister, as she handed her big brother a cheap plastic flag. "I don't want it—keep it." "You made a ringer, so you get a flag." He took the flag, stuffed it in his back pocket, started to walk away, and then stopped and said, "Give me another ring." Without hesitation, she asked, "Where's your ticket?" This time, as he walked around the booth, his sister watched him. When she saw him reach into the can, she began to scream, "Momma, Momma, Johnny's stealing a ticket!"

Did Johnny's behavior constitute stealing? Did he steal the tickets?

The sister reflected a **morality of constraint** as she followed the rules her mother had given her. Ticket, three rings, a flag. She certainly believed her big brother was stealing.

The teenager reflected a **morality of cooperation** as he perceived the situation in its larger context. He had worked all afternoon in this booth. All he wanted to do was toss a ring or two before they took the booth apart. He took the worthless ticket from the can only because his sister demanded a ticket. Tickets were no longer being sold—he could not buy one if he wanted to. The money from the ticket he used was already counted and rolled, ready to be deposited in the school's account in the morning. He was not stealing.

The final word in the conflict came from the mother, who, worn out from a long, hot day, turned to her accusing daughter and said, "Oh Janie, be quiet—and help your brother pack this stuff in the car."

The chart on the next page helps contrast the morality of constraint and the morality of cooperation. It was upon this foundation that Lawrence Kohlberg built his own theory.

Sources of control for thoughts and actions

External Control	Internal Control
Heteronomous Morality *Moral Realism* *Morality of Constraint* (Typical of 6-year-olds)	*Autonomous Morality* *Moral Relativism* *Morality of Cooperation* (Typical of 12-year-olds)
Holds a single, absolute moral view of rules. Behavior is right or wrong	Aware of different viewpoints regarding rules
Rules are fixed and unchangeable	Believes rules are flexible
Guilt is determined by the amount of damage that results	Considers wrong-doers' intentions in evaluating guilt
Rules are imposed by higher authority and must be obeyed	Obey rules out of concern for the rights of others
Letter of the law: no exceptions are allowed	Spirit of the law: exceptions possible
Rules are literal and absolute, and not open for negotiation	Rules are abstract and relative, and open to negotiation
Punishment is required if a rule is broken	Punishment is not automatic*

*Snowman, 56 and Slavin, 60

Kohlberg's Theory of Moral Reasoning Development

Lawrence Kohlberg was changed forever by the systematic slaughter of six million Jews, the Holocaust, in the 1930s and 1940s. At the Nuremburg trials, leader after leader proclaimed personal innocence by saying, "I was only following orders." *Following orders* to machine gun women, children, and old men. *Following orders* to lead innocent people into "showers," where they were gassed. *Following orders* to work men and boys until they died of starvation. How could a moral nation, a moral people, as the Germans were, Lutherans and Catholics, so quickly become the executioners of a people, the Jews? Is there a higher law than society? These thoughts focused Kohlberg's life's work.[32]

The Life of Lawrence Kohlberg

Lawrence Kohlberg was born in 1927 in Bronxville, New York, the youngest of four children.[33] His well-to-do parents provided a comfortable and academic life in elite private schools.[34] Kohlberg recalled that his high school years frequently found him on probation for smoking, drinking, and visiting girls in a nearby school.[35]

In 1945 he enlisted in the Merchant Marines and volunteered to bring a ship of two thousand Jewish refugees through a British blockade of Palestine. The ship was rammed and boarded by British forces, and, in the confusion, several were killed, including women and children.

Kohlberg was sent to an internment camp in Cyprus, where he began to question the rules of justice and concern for people against the legal rules of society.[36] He escaped from the camp and later made his way to the University of Chicago, where he completed his undergraduate degree in two years. He enrolled in the Ph.D. program in 1949. His primary interest, prompted by the Holocaust and his internment, was moral reasoning. He studied psychoanalysis under Brune Bettelhiem, humanism under Carl Rogers, and behaviorism under Jacob Gewirtz, but rejected these socialization theories as inadequate to deal with the moral problems people face. He then turned to Piaget's studies of cognitive development.[37] His Ph.D. thesis developed an original framework of stages of moral development.[38]

In 1962 he became assistant professor at the University of Chicago and instituted the Child Psychology Training Program.[39] In 1968 he became a full professor at Harvard, where he established the Center for Moral Development and Education.

He spent the next two decades researching moral development in children and adults[40] in nine countries,[41] including Great Britain, Malaysia, Mexico, Taiwan, and Turkey.[42] Kohlberg was not interested so much in whether his subjects made the "right" or "wrong" responses, but in how they explained their judgments.[43]

In 1972 while conducting studies in Central America, he contracted a parasitic disease that left him continuously nauseated. No cure was available and Kohlberg quickly went from a vibrant young man to a man racked with pain and depression. Though his fame spread and he was surrounded by scholars wanting to learn from him, his depression became steadily worse.[44] On January 17, 1987, he mysteriously died[45] by drowning in Boston Harbor[46] at the age of fifty-nine.

The basic principle Kohlberg espoused throughout his adult life was "to treat every person as an end in himself or herself, not as a means to some other end. Respect for every human being is the essence of justice."[47]

Kohlberg followed Piaget's methodology by using stories to study the moral thinking of children of various ages. Each story posed a moral dilemma. Subjects were asked **what** the main character in the story should do, and **why**. The most popular Kohlberg story goes like this:

> In Europe, a woman was near death from cancer. One drug might save her, a form of radium that a druggist in the same town had recently discovered. The druggist was charging $2,000 for the drug, ten times what the drug cost him to make. The sick woman's husband, Heinz, went to everyone he knew to borrow the money, but he could only get together about half of what it cost. He told the druggist that his wife was dying and asked him to sell it cheaper or let him pay later, but the druggist said "No." The husband became desperate and broke into the man's store to steal the drug for his wife. *Should the husband have done that? Why or why not?*[48]

Kohlberg used the responses of children to these questions to establish his theory of moral reasoning development. Kohlberg's theory consists of three levels. He called these preconventional, conventional, and postconventional. Each level contains two stages of development, six stages in all. We define each level and each stage within the levels and provide likely responses to Heinz's dilemma.

Preconventional Morality

People make moral decisions at this lowest level of reasoning based on what is best for themselves, with little or no regard for others' needs or feelings.[49] Moral judgments are made in order to avoid punishment from those in authority[50] and to further one's own interests.[51]

Stage I: Punishment—Obedience: "You Might Get Caught"[52]

In Stage I, an act is considered right or wrong in terms of the personal consequences to the actor. People at this stage of reasoning simply obey authority figures to avoid being punished.[53] Children are egocentric and cannot see situations from another's point of view.[54] Obedience is good in and of itself.[55] A behavior is moral if it doesn't get punished.[56] Wrong behaviors are those that are punished.[57]

While educational texts tend to focus on positive implications of this stage,[58] there are dark implications as well. We might state this dark side as "All things are lawful to me so long as I do not get caught." Such reasoning is found in future ministers who plagiarize seminary papers. Or cheat on exams. Such reasoning is found in church staff ministers who use church funds for personal purchases. Such reasoning is found in Christian businessmen who file dishonest tax returns, and "saintly" teens who get high with a little help from friends. *A behavior is moral if it doesn't get punished.*

**Consequences
to *me***

———————

Avoid
Punishment

On the other hand, seminary students who do not plagiarize papers or cheat on exams, and ministers who scrupulously avoid personal purchases with church funds, and businessmen who file honest returns, and teens who avoid drugs **because they might get caught** also reflect this stage.

People at this stage of reasoning will most likely say that Heinz should not steal the drug because if he is caught, he will go to jail.[59] On the other hand, some might reason "he'll be in big trouble" if he lets his wife die,[60] or that it is all right for him to steal the drug, if he can do so without being caught.

Stage II: Instrumental—Relativist: "Let's Make a Deal"[61]

In Stage II, people recognize that others also have needs and these should be taken into consideration as they satisfy their own personal needs.[62] Fairness and reciprocity with others[63] modify self-centeredness, and yet people remain hedonistic at Stage II[64]—still looking out for themselves[65] and what makes them happiest.[66] There is recognition of others' needs, but only to the extent that you can use their needs to get what you want from them.[67] The primary motivation of Stage II thinking is the desire for benefit. There is no genuine concern for the welfare of others, apart from a kind of temporary mutual satisfaction.[68]

Statements like the following reflect Stage II thinking: "You scratch my back and I'll scratch yours."[69] "Do for me and I will do for you."[70] "An eye for an eye, and a tooth for a tooth."[71] "Nice guys finish last."[72] "Don't bite the hand that feeds you."[73] Rules are followed "if it is in my best inter-

**You and I
are both
important**
but I come first

———————

"Even"
Trades

est."[74] Put another way, obeying rules should bring some sort of benefit.[75] Perhaps the clearest continuous illustration of Stage II thinking is found in congressional politics: "If you will vote for my bill, I'll vote for yours (even though I do not agree with it)."

Stage II emphasizes "even" exchanges,[76] "fair" deals, and "equal" trades.[77] I put quotes around these terms because the *best* deals in Stage II benefit the initiators, reflecting a form of manipulation.[78] Con artists earn their living by convincing others that the fraudulent services and products they offer have real value, and yet they have little regard for others. In fact, they lack genuine empathy.[79]

People at Stage II would most likely say Heinz should steal the drug since the druggist "refuses to make a deal"[80] that would benefit both people. The overcharging of the druggist makes him a robber, and so, "in fairness," Heinz is justified in stealing from him.[81] Had the druggist been willing to make a deal, Heinz would not have had to steal the drug.

In summary, preconventional moral reasoning acts on the basis of what is "best for me," or what will "satisfy my needs."[82] This level of reasoning develops in children four to ten years of age.[83]

Conventional Morality

Conventional morality develops as children move from egocentric to socio-centric thinking. They begin to see the world from others' points of view.[84] They begin to internalize the socialization they receive from parents and peers.[85] Moral decisions are increasingly based on the approval of others, and spring from family expectations, traditional values, the rules of one's social group (club, church, subculture), the laws of society, and loyalty to country,[86] regardless of the immediate and obvious consequences.[87] Conventional morality is a morality of conformity, designed to maintain the social order.[88]

Stage III: Good Boy—Nice Girl: "Right Actions Impress Others"[89]

In Stage III, approval from others—especially those in authority such as parents and teachers—is all important.[90] Right actions are defined as those that reflect loyalty and living up to the expectations of others. Good behavior is whatever pleases or helps others and is approved by them,[91] and reflects a sense of social conformity.[92] A teenage girl who keeps curfew—because she knows her parents will worry if she doesn't—is reasoning at Stage III,[93] where mutual trust and loyalty are evident.[94] Statements like the following reflect Stage III reasoning: "Your parents will be proud of you if you are honest"[95]—*We're honest, not because honesty is right, but because they'll be proud.* "Be considerate of others and you'll get along just fine"[96]—*We're considerate of others, not because politeness is innately good, but because we'll be treated better if we're nice.* "No man is an island"[97]—*We live in a social context that requires us to take the perspectives of others into account when making decisions.*

What do you value?
I'll do it to impress you

_____

Be "good"

The basic motivation for right action in Stage III is the anticipation of the disapproval of others.[98] This evokes negative examples as well. A Christian secretary is required to attend her office Christmas party, where alcohol is served. While she does not normally drink socially, she participates in several toasts because she wants her boss to see her as a "team player," which she knows is very important to him, and to her future advancement.

Stage III reasoning is not simple compliance, however. One of my Russian students did poorly on an exam. As I talked with him about it, I learned that he had not followed my instructions in how to prepare. When I asked him why, he said "I did not want to be guilty of Stage III thinking." By following my guidelines for study, he assumed he was showing poor moral reasoning. But there was no moral dilemma for him in following my advice. I was helping him. Had he followed by advice, he would have earned a better grade on the exam. When parents, teachers, and pastors expect the best for us, it does not reflect poor moral reasoning for us to act on their advice. It is helpful to remember the holocaust context of Kohlberg's theory. "I was only following orders" is Stage III reasoning. Soldiers did not want to kill innocent people, but their superior officers ordered them to. The essential quality of Stage III is how to solve moral dilemmas presented when those in power over us expect us to do things we would not normally do.

People at Stage III look to others for direction.[99] Some suggest that Heinz should steal the drug because "good husbands care about their wives" and "people would disapprove if he let her die,"[100] especially if his close friends hold to these positions. Others might say he should not steal the drug because people—especially community leaders and officials—know that stealing is wrong and would strongly disapprove.

Stage IV: Law and Order: "Know the Rules and Obey"[101]

In Stage IV, the approval of others of Stage III is translated into rules and laws—codified wisdom—which hold society together.[102] In a pluralistic society, laws must take precedence over personal wishes.[103] Moral decisions, then, are based on meeting social and religious responsibilities, upholding the law, and contributing to society and its institutions.[104] "Good" acts come from knowing the rules

What are
society's laws and
expectations?
_____

Obey the
law

and obeying them without question. Legal acts are good acts.[105] Right is doing one's duty, showing respect for authority, and maintaining the social order for its own sake.[106] Concern for others is still the focus, but rules, order, and the greater good of society for its own sake are key criteria.[107]

Statements like the following reflect Stage IV thinking. "It's against the law, and if we don't obey laws, our whole society might fall apart."[108] "Don't tear off the tags on pillows because it says not to." "We check out of the hotel at twelve noon because that is the stated check out time." "Pay taxes even if the rest of the world cheats."[109] Conventional reasoning emphasizes rules that reflect the expectations of family, church, community, or nation. These rules are valuable in their own right[110] and should be obeyed. Just as the majority of adults think at Piaget's third stage, so the majority live at Kohlberg's conventional level of moral reasoning.[111]

The Holocaust was not simply a matter of rogue military leaders privately committing genocide in Hitler's name. The whole of German society became enmeshed in the killing by conforming to social conventions, obeying legal commands, and carrying out the directives of government leaders. Judges, police officers, teachers, religious leaders, railway workers, telecommunications workers, neighbors—everyone in the society knew what was happening and quietly acquiesced. The relatively few who did not, died in the camps. This "lawful" conventional thinking led to the enslavement of Europe and the horrible deaths of millions of innocent men, women, and children. Conventional, societal morality was insufficient to prevent the horror. Surely, thought Kohlberg, there had to be a higher level of moral reasoning.

Motivation for right action at Stage IV is the anticipation of dishonor[112] that results from breaking societal rules. People at Stage IV would probably say Heinz should not steal the drug because "stealing is wrong for everybody; he should find another way of getting the drug."[113] After all, if "everyone disobeyed laws against theft, our society would be in chaos."[114] Others might reason that Heinz should steal the drug, but realize that "he must eventually pay the druggist back or accept the penalty for breaking the law."[115] This level of reasoning develops in children ten to thirteen years of age.[116]

Difficulties arise with a rigid law-and-order orientation. What do we do when laws conflict with each other, or are unclear? In Heinz's case, the law protects the druggist against theft. But what defends the right of Heinz's wife to live?[117] My wife and I led a mission group of teenagers into the mountains of Virginia to cut wood for a "firewood ministry." The ministry was begun when two elderly women died from the winter cold after the electric company cut off their power. The company was well within their legal rights to stop providing electrical power, but extreme situations such as these beg for a higher stage of reasoning.

Postconventional Reasoning

Postconventional reasoning develops as adolescents move into the formal operational stage of thinking. Moral judgments are made according to abstract principles[118] of social convention and universal ethics. Decisions are complex and comprehensive, based on diverse points of view and general principles.[119] There is a deliberate effort to clarify moral rules and principles to arrive at self-defined notions of good and evil.[120] That is, people define their own values in terms of ethical principles they have chosen to follow.[121] Beyond personal wants or needs, beyond deals and loyalty, beyond legal prescriptions, "*principled* morality"[122] is based on such overarching ideals as justice, love, equality, and the dignity of all human life.[123]

Stage V: Social Contract: "Rules Are What the Group Decides"[124]

At Stage V, people recognize that rules represent agreements among individuals about behavior. Rules are seen as "useful mechanisms to maintain order rather than absolute dictates that must be obeyed."[125] A social contract is an implied agreement among members of a group—society, church, club, or gang—which is evaluated on the basis of "the greatest good for the greatest number."[126] At Stage V, there is democratic agreement on rights, standards, and the need for change. There are no

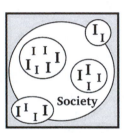

Agreed-Upon Community Rules

Do what is best for *our* community

legal absolutes[127] as in Stage IV. Rather, individuals evaluate laws in terms of justice and human rights, and reinterpret or change them as needed.[128] People at Stage V conform to society's laws so long as they guarantee and protect the rights of individuals in the society. Under certain circumstances, laws may have to be disregarded, such as when a person's life depends on breaking a law.[129] Laws are not followed blindly for their own sake, but to the extent they protect life, liberty, and the dignity of individuals.[130] In short, concrete laws give way to the formal principles that undergird them. Individuals live by the mutually-accepted rules of the group to which they belong.

Most writers identify "the group" as society-at-large, as we can see in the quotes above. But Clouse refers specifically to alternate systems where social contracts flow out of a concern for the welfare of smaller communities.[131] Examples include religious sects like the Amish or Quakers. We can also include civic organizations such as Kiwanis or Lions. Members of these smaller communities take on the codes and rules of their communities. Churches are social communities that set guidelines for behavior. Members of various denominations live by differing sets of rules. Colleges set varying sets of standards for their students. Students freely choose to follow the rules by their decision to enroll in a particular school.

One of the greatest moral dilemmas of American society is found in the abortion debate. The 1973 *Roe v. Wade* Supreme Court decision rendered all laws restricting abortions unconstitutional. Essentially, abortion rights became the law of the land. Since abortion is legal, many consider it "the right thing to do" in cases of rape, incest, disability, poverty, and in some cases, mere inconvenience or the gender of the child. Many others oppose abortion-on-demand on the basis that human life begins at conception, and abortion is the destruction of human life. Pro-choice advocates hold to a social system based on a woman's "right to choose." Pro-life advocates hold to a system based on a developing child's right to live. Though "the law" has been established by a ruling of the Supreme Court, the real-life battle over principles of love, justice, and compassion continues—for the mother on one side, for the defenseless child on the other. These debates proceed at Stage V, but they are fueled by passions for and against an individual woman's right to choose death for her own child.

In the Preface, I shared a story from Richard Wurmbrand's newsletter *Voice of the Martyrs* depicting an icy baptism of evangelical Christians in Russia. One of Wurmbrand's ministries was smuggling Bibles into the Soviet Union. I remember sending some of my allowance to the organization to help that effort. It seemed to me the Soviet law banning the import of Bibles was a bad law, and that I should support people who risked imprisonment to get God's Word to people behind the Iron Curtain. A few years later (1972), I discovered that my pastor, whom I love to this day, strongly opposed the smuggling. "If we do not respect the laws of the Soviet Union, and violate those laws, even to get the Bible into the hands of people who need them, then we destroy any basis for establishing trust for future agreements."

On my first trip to Odessa, Ukraine (1996), I met Alexander Karnayk, the academic dean at the time, and a good friend to this day. I asked him if he had ever heard of Wurmbrand. His face brightened. "The very first Bible I ever owned was a Wurmbrand Bible. In fact, I carefully copied it by hand and presented the copy to my wife as a wedding present." I asked him if Wurmbrand did the right thing in breaking Soviet law to smuggle Bibles. Without a pause, he said, "I thank God every day of my life for the work of Richard Wurmbrand. There are many in God's kingdom today because he and his organization risked prison and worse to bring us Bibles." My pastor was thinking Stage IV. Obey the law. Wurmbrand's ministry was living Stage V. Break the (bad) law and provide God's Word to people who need it.

It is interesting that Stages I and V both address breaking the law. But the nature of law-breaking is very different in the two stages. **First**, Stage I law-breakers view laws as unwanted restrictions to personal desires. When caught, Stage I law-breakers deny their guilt in order to escape punishment. Stage V law-breakers view law as important and, in most cases, believe that laws should be respected. If a law must be broken in order to serve a higher good, then law-breakers are willing to face the consequences of their actions. **Second**, Stage I law-breakers experience little or no anxiety over breaking laws. Stage V law-breakers take their actions very seriously and experience great anxiety over breaking laws. **Third**, Stage I law-breakers show little concern whether a law is just or unjust. They do as they please and make every effort to escape punishment. Stage V law-breakers ponder underlying principles and break only those laws that they determine to be unjust.[132]

At Stage V, people will most likely say that Heinz should steal the drug because "the value of human life outweighs the druggist's individual right to own property,"[133] or "make a large profit."[134] Or, perhaps, he should steal it because it would be wrong for Heinz to refrain from stealing and let his wife die.[135] Others might argue that Heinz should not steal the drug. Rather he should work with others to change laws that allow people to die while protecting large profits for those who make medicines, or at least provide humane directives for judges who preside over such cases.[136] One writer suggests Heinz should not steal because in stealing he "deprives the druggist of his right to make a living and, therefore, his dignity."[137]

Stage VI: Universal Ethical Principle: "Right Action Based on Self-Chosen Principles"[138]

The language used to describe Stage VI is very similar to Stage V. "Philosophers themselves are unclear on the distinctions."[139] One clear distinction for me is that Stage V thinking tends to be focused on groups—mutually-agreed principles—while Stage VI thinking tends to be focused on individuals. William Wallace (*Braveheart*) led Scottish clans to band together to throw off English rule. He was betrayed by his own countrymen and handed over to King Edward I. He refused to recant his call for Scottish freedom and was tortured and executed in August 1305. He is considered a hero of Scotland to this day. Others might see Wallace as an outlaw who killed an Englishman and then fought English soldiers sent to capture him. He led with passion and built an army to drive English forces from Scotland. He then invaded England itself. After his defeat at Falkirk, he continued to fight English forces until he was captured and executed for treason. Stage I rebel, or Stage VI hero? Avoiding punishment for crimes or freeing Scotland from oppression? One is hard-pressed to see his life of violence, war, and conquest as comparable to others who gave their lives helping others achieve justice and love.[140]

William Wilberforce became an evangelical Christian in 1785, five years after his election to the British Parliament. He joined a group of abolitionists in 1787 and began to speak out against the evils of the British slave trade, fighting against powerful financiers who made fortunes providing ships to the slave traders. He fought for abolition for years, often being attacked and ridiculed, but in 1807 Parliament passed the Slave Trade Act.

Agnes Bojaxhiu, a Roman Catholic missionary, literally spent her life "battling conditions of extreme poverty because she felt a moral imperative to do so."[141] She did so because she was a Christian who knew the Lord and surrendered her life to Him. She served Him by building a ministry that continues to help the poorest of the poor around the world with schooling, medical care, and the grace of dying with dignity. She wrote, "Words which do not give the light of Christ increase the

**Self-Chosen
Universal
Principles**

**Do what is
best for
everyone
everywhere**

darkness." And again, "I am a little pencil in the hand of a writing God Who is sending a love letter to the world."[142] She is a prime example of Stage VI living. She is better known by the name Mother Theresa of Calcutta.[143] Let's identify principles that recommend King, Wilberforce, and Bojaxhiu as representatives of Stage VI.

Reasoning at Stage VI is based on principles that are abstract, ethical, universal, and consistent. These principles include justice, reciprocity, equality of human rights, and respect for the dignity of individuals.[144] Stage VI reasoning weighs all related factors, and then makes the most appropriate decision for a given situation. Moral decisions are based on consistent applications of self-chosen ethical principles.[145] They answer to a strong inner conscience and willingly disobey laws that violate their own inner principles.[146] These Stage VI principles move beyond concrete laws,[147] like the Ten Commandments (Exod 20), to the abstract, like the Golden Rule: "Therefore, whatever you want others to do for you, do also the same for them" (Matt 7:12).[148] Kant's maxim, which states "Act only as you would be willing that everyone should act in the same situation," is another Stage VI principle. Yet another is "Love your neighbor as yourself" (Lev 19:18b; Matt 22:39).

Researchers who studied Kohlberg's ideas found so few subjects reaching Stage VI that the stage itself came to be considered little more than a theoretical possibility.[149] None of the empirical studies conducted in three countries provided evidence for Stage VI. As a result, Kohlberg (1984) revised his stages by collapsing Stage VI back into Stage V. The most recent texts used as the research base for this text (1998–2009) all report the six stages as proposed by Kohlberg, though most acknowledge the *theoretical* nature of Stage VI.[150]

Yet there is ample evidence of moral reasoning beyond social contract. In the 1980s, Roman Catholics along the U. S. southern border sheltered El Salvadorans, violating U. S. law, because the Catholic nationals had escaped death by execution squads. Several priests and nuns were sent to prison for their individual participation in the pro-life action. One might make a case that American Catholics protecting El Salvadoran Catholics is Stage V due to group-consensus. But the majority of Catholics did not participate in these law-breaking actions. Individual priests and nuns chose to break U.S. law and go to prison for protecting others. These individual, self-chosen actions, based on universal principles of justice and love, reflect Stage VI thinking. By standing by their convictions, despite prosecution, these individuals publicized a bad situation. Soon after the situation came to light, the law was changed.

Yet another example is found in a letter by Martin Luther King, written from a Birmingham jail cell:

You express a great deal of anxiety over our willingness to break laws. This is certainly a legitimate concern. Since we do diligently urge people to obey the Supreme Court's decision of 1954 outlawing segregation in the public schools, at first glance it may seem rather paradoxical for us consciously to break laws. One may well ask: "How can you advocate breaking some laws and obeying others?" The answer lies in the fact that there are two types of laws: just and unjust. One has not only a legal but a moral responsibility to obey just laws. Conversely, one has a moral responsibility to disobey unjust laws. I would agree with Saint Augustine that "an unjust law is no law at all."[151]

Dr. King's postconventional perspective raises an important question: How does one determine when a law is just or unjust? A just law is a man-made code that squares with moral law or the law of God. An unjust law is a code that is out of harmony with the moral law. To put it in terms of Saint Thomas Aquinas: An unjust law is a human law that is not rooted in eternal law and natural law. Any law that uplifts human personality is just. Any law that degrades human personality is unjust."[152]

At Stage III, people may apply the Golden Rule to their family and close friends. But at Stage VI, the Golden Rule is applied to everyone everywhere: to the criminal as well as his victim,[153] to the pregnant woman as well as her unborn child, to the rich and the poor, to the young and the old, to the male and the female, to Americans and to foreigners.[154]

At Stage IV, people obey fixed rules and laws. But at Stage VI they live out principles that are better than laws. Principles expose unjust laws and insure that just laws are obeyed. Principles have no loopholes, nor do they provide immoral, legal slack.

At Stage V, people make principled decisions as part of a group consensus. But at Stage VI, they consistently hold to principled decisions, even if they must stand alone. In summary, postconventional reasoning emphasizes self-chosen abstract principles, such as justice and love, which people apply consistently in every situation. This level of reasoning develops in children from age thirteen on.[155]

Christians and "Self-chosen"

It should be noted that some Christians baulk at the term "self-chosen." It is true that Kohlberg was a secular humanist and believed that individuals are responsible for constructing their own moral framework. But there is another perspective on "self-chosen" that is essential for evangelicals to understand. Earlier in the chapter, I mentioned "future ministers who plagiarize seminary research papers." Ask any of these seminary plagiarists, "Is plagiarism acceptable behavior for Christians?" and all will respond, without hesitation and unanimously, "No." And yet they plagiarize their papers. Why?

Some report time pressure due to "church work," or illness, or even personal irresponsibility in putting off the assignment. Some claim their work was finished "well," but then lost in some way. Some fault professors for expecting too much. While these students intellectually accept the idea of honesty, they personally choose to plagiarize. Honesty is not a "self-chosen value" for them. Truly honest students would have admitted the problem, asked for more time to complete the assignment correctly, and accepted (graciously) whatever penalty was deemed appropriate. Instead, they lied in attempting to present another's ideas as their own. "Self-chosen" refers to the principles we reflect in the actual decisions we make, the actual actions we take. We defined a just law as a "man-made code that squares with the law of God." Secularists focus on "man-made code." Evangelicals on "the law of God." But Stage VI reasoning requires that self-chosen values form the basis, consistently, for the actual choices we make. If they do not, personal values are nothing more than cheap platitudes.

At Stage VI, people will most likely say that Heinz should steal the drug because "the value of human life outweighs any other considerations."[156] Others might argue that Heinz should not steal the drug but work with others to change laws that allow people to die while protecting large profits for those who make medicines.[157] If these answers seem vaguely familiar, it is probably because they are very similar to responses we reported for Stage V. Sprinthall makes the distinction this way: at Stage V we judge the entire system of laws (rather than a specific law at Stage IV) on the basis of *common good and social utility*. At Stage VI, *an individual challenges a law by committing an act of civil disobedience* (stealing) and is willing to accept society's punishment for it.[158] Stage V emphasizes group consensus; Stage VI—individual conscience.

We come to the end of Kohlberg Six Stages, first presented in 1963. He later revised descriptions of these stages, and others modified them as more research was conducted over the years. You find nuances of researchers and writers pushing in one direction or another even in my synthesis here. However, I have attempted to point you to the core action, the essential meaning, of each stage. Just be aware that when reading other sources, you will surely find descriptions and explanations that differ from the condensations found here.

Kohlberg from a Christian Perspective

Ronald Duska and Mariellen Whelan suggest that Kohlberg's theory fits well with Christian doctrine and that his six stages provide a helpful filter for various levels of Christian practice.[159] At Stage I, people see God as the Determiner of Good and Bad and primarily as a **Punisher**.[160] People choose to do right in order to **avoid punishment from God**. Nehemiah chastised the Jewish nobles of Jerusalem for oppressing their own people through interest and enslavement of children, both forbidden by the Law, by invoking the fear of God: "What you are doing isn't right. Shouldn't you walk in the fear of our God?" (Neh 5:9). Nehemiah's Stage I rebuke reflected how far the nobles had fallen in disregarding the Law of God given through Moses.

At Stage II, God is seen as One Who cares for people's needs, as One Who **wants to make us happy**. Therefore, presenting the Lord as the One Who came to save us, and the kind of behavior He recommends to make us happy, would be most effective at this stage.[161] Put another way, people seek to receive God's blessings by giving God what they believe He wants, literally **making deals with God**.

At Stage III, according to Duska and Whelan, people desire group identification. People expand their family circle to include church membership and begin to take on the roles and duties defined by that community. The "church family" helps define good and bad behavior in terms of what they approve. That is, the good thing to do is what the church approves. People are not self-interested in this stage, except that they would like the approval of their church.[162]

I personally find this description more closely related to Stage V, where group consensus is so important. For me, Stage III would focus on **impressing Christian parents or the pastor** (on a human level) or **impressing God** (on a spiritual level) by our good behavior—that is, behaving in ways we know they approve. The danger at Stage III is blindly following a charismatic leader.

Stage IV emphasizes authority, fixed rules, and maintenance of the social order. Church members at Stage IV show little or no egotism. Rather they demonstrate a selfless and passionate defense of the church and its authorities as the defenders of the correct order of things.[163] People choose to **behave in accordance with the laws of their church**, accepting them as valid simply because the church holds them.

At Stage V, right action requires **knowing and free choice** more than mere acceptance of laws that one has always obeyed. In order for a choice to be made, one has to have at least two options. A knowing and free choice permits individuals the opportunity to **step out of a system of values and beliefs once blindly followed, in order to compare that system with others**.[164]

A college freshman grows up in church—faithful to the Lord and his youth group, a dedicated church member. He heads off to college and finds a very different world of parties and priorities. He may well *crash and burn* as he tries new experiences and suffers the consequences. If his former faith is real, he will one day "come to himself," like the prodigal, and freely choose to embrace the Lord in a whole new way. His faith will no longer be a copy, handed down by loving parents, but will be his own.

At Stage VI, individuals **evaluate systems of beliefs and values from an ideal perspective**. Christ came to fulfill the Law, not to do away with it (Matt 5:17). Time and again, Jesus challenged the [Stage IV] legalism of the Pharisees that destroyed the spirit of the Law. Time and again, He appealed to a higher order, the kingdom of God, which gave us an ideal by which to judge the real. He appealed to the highest principles of all, justice and love, which are based on the belief that we are all God's children,[165] all beloved of God,[166] and the insistence that even the highest authority should be the humblest servant.[167] **One is hard pressed to find a more consistent pattern for Stage VI living than in the example and teachings of Jesus.** As His disciples, we should endeavor to grow, in our day-to-day behavior, as well as our thinking, toward the Master, toward Stage VI.

Criticisms of Kohlberg's Theory

Despite the wide-ranging influence of Kohlberg's theory, there are several criticisms of his views that need consideration as we develop our approach to moral issues.

1. Are the Stages Sequentially Fixed?

Some research suggests that Kohlberg's stages are neither sequenced nor consistent. "People reason out of several stages simultaneously, depending on the nature of the moral issue."[168] Other studies found that their "subjects reverted randomly to an earlier stage. There was generally a lack of consistent response from a given stage."[169] These findings, however, target moral *choices*, which involve more than a level of reasoning.

Research has consistently shown that the sequence of Kohlberg's stages of reasoning is fixed, just as the sequence of Piaget's cognitive stages is fixed. "Trends of stage and sequence without reversals/regressions have been documented by substantial research in other countries and cultures."[170] We might say in summary that moral *reasoning* proceeds in a fixed sequence,[171] but moral choices—specific responses and behaviors—are more random, depending on the situation. This is intuitively obvious when given an example like "future ministers who (choose to) plagiarize on a given research paper." Obviously, seminary students have developed moral reasoning beyond Stage I. And yet, even in making this *choice*, the plagiarist *reasoned* at Stage I (just as an adult writer "thinks at a preoperational level" while writing fiction). Adults who have achieved formal operational thought do not always think at this level. In the same way, adults who achieve Stage VI moral reasoning do not always reason at this level.

2. Decisions or Behavior?

Kohlberg focused on how people consider moral dilemmas. He did not focus on what they actually did.[172] Studies have shown that individuals at different stages behave the same way. Individuals at the same stage behave in different ways.[173] Emotions, competing goals, relationships, and moral maturity (character) all operate in the choices we make. The ability to *reason* at a given level does not insure *action* at that level.[174] Kohlberg acknowledged this criticism and called for more research on predicting behavior from stage.

One such study provided an opportunity for students to cheat without being caught. Seventy percent (70%) of preconventional thinkers cheated. Fifty-five percent (55%) of conventional thinkers cheated. Fifteen percent (15%) of postconventional thinkers cheated. While members of all three groups cheated, the percentages *demonstrate a tendency* to act according to one's beliefs.[175] One's level of moral reasoning **describes how one might behave**, but it does not prescribe **how one will act in any given situation**.

3. Morals or Social Conventions?

Kohlberg is criticized for not differentiating between moral issues and social conventions.[176] Social conventions are arbitrary rules determined by a particular social group. Rules like "It's rude to eat with your hands" or "Men don't wear dresses" are not morally right or wrong.[177] Moral issues deal with fundamental rights of individuals, the general welfare of the group, and the avoidance of harm. Even children as young as three can differentiate between social conventions ("Being noisy would be okay, if there were no rule against it") and morals ("Hitting another child is wrong, even if there is no rule against it)."[178]

4. Counter-Culture Values at Stage V?

Since Stage V emphasizes *group consensus* and defines the right act as one that the *group approves*, then some might suggest that counter-culture groups like street gangs, organized crime "families," or cultic groups can achieve Stage V thinking. But Stage V also emphasizes *principled thinking* and emphasizes such qualities as equality, justice, and human rights. It is hard to make a case for gang behaviors—theft, vandalism, murder—resulting from principled thinking. Terms such as "enlightened conscience,"[179] "greatest good for the greatest number,"[180] and "abstract concepts,"[181] point to a level of reasoning beyond mere group consensus.

Clouse emphasizes that Stage V thinking stands upon Stage III (society needs leaders) and Stage IV (those who disobey the law will have to face the consequences). People at Stage V know there is a higher law of human justice, which should be followed despite what is "legislated by the courts."[182] Given these values, group consensus among counter-culture groups rightly belongs to Stages I (avoid rejection, ridicule, and punishment from others in the group), Stage II (give loyalty to others, gain "safety" from others), and Stage III (obedience to leader, acceptance from leader), rather than the principled Stage V.

5. Biased in Favor of Males?

Critics point to the fact that Kohlberg validated his theory on a "relatively small sample of white, middle-class American males under 17 years of age."[183] Based on this sample, Kohlberg anchored his theory around principles of justice and fairness. Reasoning based on caring for others and maintaining relationships scores lower in Kohlberg's theory.[184] Since men tend to focus more on rights, and women tend to focus more on responsibilities,[185] men tend to score higher in Kohlberg's hierarchy than women—Stage III for women and Stage IV for men at the same age.[186]

Carol Gilligan, mentioned in connection with Erikson's view of identity in Chapter Three, challenged Kohlberg's male bias with her own "ethic of care" (1982, 1984, 1989).[187] Moral reasoning in women, according to Gilligan, follows a three stage process from "self-interest" to "commitment to individuals" to "responsibility and care for all people."[188] Kohlberg responded by admitting that the study of the moral domain could be enlarged to include affective elements of caring, love, and responsibility, but that these should not be considered a morality separate from rational justice reasoning.[189] To assign justice solely to men and caring solely to women is to do injustice to the capacities of both sexes.[190] While caring and justice are important to both men and women,[191] and both men and women use caring and justice orientations to think about moral issues, research continues to suggest that females as a group tend to use a caring orientation slightly more than males, and males use a justice orientation slightly more than females.[192] Gilligan does not argue superiority for either orientation, but urges the recognition of a difference between the two.[193] In spite of this, Ormrod (2006) reports "most research studies do not find major gender differences in moral reasoning."[194]

Snowman (2009) summarizes the most recent research on gender differences in moral reasoning, citing these major findings. 1) "Females are just as likely as males to use justice and fairness concepts in their reasoning about hypothetical moral dilemmas." 2) "When females are faced with their own real-life moral dilemmas (abortion, civil rights, environmental pollution) rather than hypothetical ones, they are more likely to favor a caring-helping-cooperation orientation than a justice-fairness-individual rights orientation."[195] Christian teachers would do well to emphasize both justice (Exod 23:6; Matt 12:18) and caring (Rom 12; 1 Cor 13) perspectives when dealing with moral issues.

6. Western Bias?

Critics of Kohlberg's theory contend that postconventional reasoning may be biased in favor of Western cultures where individuality is prized. Amish and Native Americans deemphasize individuality and place more value on cooperation, collaboration, and group orientation.[196] Individuals in these cultures would rate lower on Kohlberg's hierarchy because of their more conventional orientation. As we have already discussed, researchers have found that Kohlberg's stages exist—and in the same sequence as he theorized—in many cultures. What varies from culture to culture is the *rate* of development and the *end point* of development.[197] While the first four stages appear in most cultures, postconventional reasoning does not. This suggests a Western bias in the theory.[198]

Implications for Teaching

What are the implications of Kohlberg's theory for teachers? Here are nine for your consideration.

1. Create an Open Class Atmosphere

Teachers encourage authentic discussions of moral dilemmas when they create a learning environment that is emotionally safe. Learners are more likely to share personal views of right and wrong when their opinions are valued, and they are respected. Teachers foster an atmosphere of openness in the classroom by being fair in their relationships with students.[199] They model the role of an accepting, open person.[200] Teachers help students engage each other positively by practicing listening and communication skills. Creating an accepting, open atmosphere in a classroom takes time since learners need to be confident that teachers will not ridicule or humiliate them.[201]

2. Embrace the Role of Model

Teachers are **role models** for their students. They model prosocial behaviors as they interact with students with trust, empathy, and attention. They model prosocial behaviors by sharing community projects with the students and inviting them to join the efforts.[202] "I will be working at the community Food Bank this Saturday from nine in the morning until noon. You are certainly welcome to join me in packing groceries for the poor." Teachers model ethical thinking as they lead discussions of moral issues from a variety of points of view.[203]

Teachers fill the role of **masters** of morality by advocating good behavior and demonstrating a strong conscience. They teach proper values and principles, serving as the source of values for their classes.

Teachers serve as **facilitators**, helping students develop and understand their own values. In this approach, the students are the source of values.

Teachers function as **mentors**, relating to their students as guide, friend, or enlightened leader from whom students can gain moral guidance.[204]

3. Increase Awareness of Moral Issues.

Discuss real and hypothetical moral dilemmas in class. Use experiences in the classroom as opportunities to heighten moral awareness.[205] It is more effective to integrate moral issues into the regular curriculum than to provide a separate "moral education" lesson.[206]

4. Expect a Variety of Responses to Dilemmas.

Expect a variety of responses regarding the age of learners.[207] Younger children respond to moral dilemmas differently than older children.[208] Stress concrete actions rather than abstract principles when teaching younger children. Stating a general principle ("You shouldn't play with toys that belong to other children") is less effective than emphasizing concrete actions ("Be careful with that toy or it might break").[209]

Further, expect a variety of responses from students of the same age. Learners may operate on different levels of moral reasoning[210] and will respond to moral issues differently. Do not assume that all students in a given grade level will respond the same way.

5. Ask "Why?"

Student answers to the "*Why?*" question provide the best measure of their present stage of reasoning.[211] Subject responses to the Heinz problem were simple yeses and nos. But it was their explanations of *why they answered yes or no* that revealed their level of thinking.

When I tell the story of the teenage boy and the tavern, and ask if they would have entered the tavern, I have students move to one side of the room for "Yes" and the opposite side for "No." Most of them move quickly and without hesitation. And most of them move to the "no" side. I move in between the groups and pick a "no" member at random. "Why did you move to this side?" I turn to the "yes" group and pick a student at random. "Why did you move to this side?" I alternate from side to side until a dozen students have responded. Their answers vary, reflecting differing stages of thinking. You can see sample responses in the text box at the end of the chapter. By this exercise, students see for themselves how differently they consider the dilemma. Remember that these responses come from a group most would consider quite narrow: graduate school, evangelical Christian, mostly Caucasian, mostly middle class, mostly Southern Baptist, mostly future ministers of the gospel. It is not enough to know *what* learners would do. It is essential to know *why* they choose that action in order to determine their stage of thinking.

6. Personal Choice.

Encourage students to make a personal choice in the dilemma, and then ask them to justify their response.[212] In my experience, students prefer to make general—*non-committal*—responses like "Fourteen-year-olds shouldn't go into taverns" or "I would never let *my* teenager go into a tavern!" Redirect attention to the correct question: "Would *you* go in? Why or why not?" This redirection makes the discussion of moral issues more real than hypothetical.

7. Alternatives.

Just as we find a variety of responses to a given moral dilemma, so there are a variety of alternatives for how to solve it. Lead students to analyze the advantages and disadvantages of various actions by discussing the pros and cons of each choice. Following Piaget's views of social interaction as a reinforcement of cognitive development, teach students to "understand and respect the perspectives of others."[213] Even when we do not agree with others' perspectives, understanding them provides a richer sense of the problem.

8. Present Stage Plus One.

Research has consistently shown that stage development proceeds sequentially, without skipping steps.[214] Therefore, the most effective strategy in developing moral reasoning skills is to discuss alternative responses *one stage above* the student's level of reasoning.[215]

One day I was teaching a group of college students in Donetsk, Ukraine. We were discussing Kohlberg's stages. One student raised his hand and asked to speak. He came to the front of the room, struck an academic pose, and proceeded to explain to all of us the superiority of morality in the former Soviet Union. "Perhaps in America, children need to progress step by step toward the highest level of morality, but children in the Soviet Union have already achieved this." He was deadly serious. There was a pause for a few seconds, and then the class of forty burst out laughing. He sat down rather sheepishly, but soon joined the discussion of morality in Ukraine. He was espousing a dated political correctness. Most of the class saw his statement as empty and meaningless. Certainly it was not true—there, or anywhere. They recognized that moral development is a human process, not an American one. "Even children in Ukraine" develop the capacity to reason one step at a time.

Piaget believed learning by heart was not true learning. Students need to accommodate their thinking to new ideas and experiences for learning to be their own. In the same way, students must work their way through the stages of moral reasoning for themselves if their moral code is to be truly their own. Teachers provide guidance, but ultimately, learners make the life-changing choices.

Moral Reasoning, Jesus, and the Pharisees

We close this discussion of moral reasoning with two instances from the life of Jesus that illustrate His conflict with the religious thinking of His day. The first regards a woman caught in the act of adultery. Jesus was teaching in the temple court one day when . . .

> The scribes and the Pharisees brought a woman caught in adultery, making her stand in the center. "Teacher," they said to Him, "this woman was caught in the act of committing adultery. In the law Moses commanded us to stone such women. So what do You say?"
>
> When they kept on questioning Him, He straightened up and said to them, "The one without sin among you should be the first to throw a stone at her" (John 8:3–7).

The Law of Moses declares "if a man commits adultery with a married woman—if he commits adultery with his neighbor's wife—both the adulterer and the adulteress must be put to death" (Lev 20:10). There is no gray area here. No nuance. This is straightforward Stage IV Law. God's Law. Notice, however, that the religious leaders did not follow the Law completely. They did not bring the man to Jesus—the man who, by definition, must have also been "caught in the act." The Law is clear: *both* are to be killed. Since they set up this situation to trap Jesus, they were not fully committed to following the whole Law. In my darker moments, I can't help but wonder whether the man was one of the "scribes or Pharisees." After all, by volunteering to commit adultery, he provided the situation by which they would trap Jesus, for the "good of Israel."[216]

The trap was indeed set. If Jesus said, *Stone her, according to the Law*, His popularity among the people would suffer. Worse than this, He would have reinforced the misuse of the Law, as well as the sin of the leaders. If He said, *Do not stone her!*, then He would be seen as violating Mosaic Law, and be branded a false prophet. The Pharisees believed He would lose either way.

But Jesus moved beyond their conventional thinking to postconventional and established a principle: "The one without sin among you should be the first to throw a stone at her" (John 8:7). The moral test at Stage VI is whether we are willing to apply the principle to self as well as others.[217] Jesus was without sin and threw no stones. The mob hesitated and then began to drop the stones in their hands and walk away. The older, presumably wiser (*or more sinful*), dispersed first, followed by the younger, more militant ones.

Did Jesus break the Law? Did He demonstrate a casual regard for Scripture, changing it to fit the immediate situation? No, He did not come to destroy, but to fulfill the Law (Matt 5:17). Forgiveness based on faith supersedes arbitrary punishment, because all of us have sinned. Paul wrote that the **Law was a pedagogue** [a household slave, charged with accompanying a child to school][218] put in charge to lead us to Christ. Now that we have been justified by faith, we no longer need the Law (Gal 3:25). Jesus fulfilled the Law and made it complete. Jesus was not breaking the Law because He told the woman, "Go, and from now on do not sin anymore" (John 8:11). Jesus recognized adultery as sin and told her never to do it again. But He lifted her by grace to a new place, a kingdom place, where a different morality exists, one centered in the Ruler's love and justice rather than blind obedience to or dishonest manipulation of rigid rules.

The second example is found in the confrontation between the Pharisees and Jesus over the Sabbath. "There [in the synagogue] He saw a man who had a paralyzed hand. And in order to accuse Him they asked Him, 'Is it lawful to heal on the Sabbath?' But He said to them, 'What man among you, if he had a sheep that fell into a pit on the Sabbath, wouldn't take hold of it and lift it out? A man is worth far more than a sheep, **so it is lawful to do good on the Sabbath**.' Then He told the man, "Stretch out your hand." So he stretched it out, and it was restored, as good as the other. But the Pharisees went out and plotted against Him, how they might destroy Him" (Matt 12:10–14).

The Sixth Commandment states, "Remember the Sabbath day by keeping it holy" (Exod 20:8 NIV). The Pharisees interpreted this rule to mean more than Scripture said. They used it as a way to control the people. Jesus taught that, "The Sabbath was made for man, not man for the Sabbath" (Mark 2:27). And He laid down a new kingdom principle: "It is lawful to do good on the Sabbath."

In fact, Jesus taught that if His followers would simply live at the principled level by loving God with all their hearts and loving their neighbors as they love themselves, they would fulfill every rule and commandment of Scripture (Matt 22:37–39). May God bless you as you challenge your students not only with alternative approaches to contemporary moral issues, but lead them to see life from the perspective of the King and His kingdom.

Moral Relativism and Our Relationship with Jesus

Pluralistic society and existential philosophy have moved our culture increasingly toward moral relativism. Moral relativism emphasizes the individual's own perspective as the center of truth-seeking, the standard for decision-making.

There is a sense in which this is true. Evangelical Christians believe firmly in biblical authority, embracing the Bible as God's Truth. Yet the Bible will not change a person's life until Scripture becomes "Truth that matters to me." This is an existential event. No one can make a faith commitment for Christ by proxy. Believers must make that choice for themselves. That is an existential event. One may give intellectual assent to the ideas that Christians love their enemies, and pray for those who persecute them (Matt 5:44), but until we live according to this standard, it is not Truth-that-matters-to-me. Each one of us stands at the center of our own existential moments, at the center of this truth-seeking.

On the other hand, Charles Sell reminds us that relativism undermines Christian growth when it challenges "every source of authority to which theology can appeal . . . our evangelical faith contends that absolute truth lies in Scripture, not in our experience."[219] This is why evangelical Christians wince at terms such as "internal authority" and "self-reflection." These terms are often used by secularists to demean Scripture and Church, while worshipping an individual's freedom to choose. Existential excess has been the rule in America since the early 1960s. The social agenda of Existentialism is "Revolt from the Norm." The anarchy and chaos we have experienced since the 1960s Revolution is the result of a society obsessed by individual freedom. It is the sin of the Garden of Eden: "Did God really say?" (Gen 3:1). Break free from artificial boundaries. Break free from community. Break free to Self and Self-chosen principles. And our nation has. The schools followed through intentional Self-focused teaching methodologies and continue to emphasize relativistic views (see Chapters Eight and Ten).

Where we find individuals determining for themselves what is good, there we find murder, rape, divorce, and robbery. We have become violent America, one individual at a time. So how does the Christian balance Truth and personal choice? How do boundaries and freedom coexist?

The best analogy for me is the tension found in flying a kite. In order for the kite to fly, there must be a string anchoring the kite to the ground, and there must be a steady wind. The string is analogous to Scripture, the wind to personal experiences. Scripture anchors personal experiences, setting God's boundaries within which we are free to live. Without this anchor, individual experiences carry us away into any number of conflicting views.

The wind lifts the kite into the sky. Without personal experiences with God, the Scripture remains objectively cold and distant.

If the wind stops blowing, the kite falls. If we let go of the string, the kite falls. Both anchor and wind are needed.

Oppression results from having boundaries without freedom. Chaos results from freedom without boundaries. God's **eternal** Truth in Scripture becomes **experiential** "Truth-that-matters-to-me" as we anchor experiences-with-Christ in Scripture, and quicken Scripture through experiences-with-Christ.

In this context, Piaget and Kohlberg help us understand the natural side of human growth, and provide insight into some of the hindrances to healthy development. They help us conceptualize our own experiences, and then differentiate among those who live at different levels of socialization, thinking, and moral reasoning. More subjectively, Piaget and Kohlberg help us identify and evaluate our own thinking processes, our own position in their stages, and in so doing, help us far more than they ever dreamed.

The Teen and the Tavern Revisited

If you have not yet done so, check your written response to the Tavern dilemma against the list at the end of the chapter (See "Dilemma One"). The responses listed there, by stage, reflect typical answers that I receive from seminary students. If you have read *Called to Teach* (1999), you are familiar with the story about the teenager and the tavern. If not, read on.

The teenager in the story is me. The situation is true. I stood before the quiet neighborhood tavern for several minutes, weighing whether I should go in and distribute Gospels of Mark to the patrons. As I prayed about the situation, I wrestled with different thoughts. What would my pastor think? What would Mom say? What if someone from the church saw me coming out of the tavern? Finally, however, one thought captured me: these people needed God's Word as much or more as the people who lived in the neat row houses I'd been visiting. I decided to go into the tavern.

I climbed a steep set of concrete steps, took a breath, and pushed through the double doors. Much to my surprise, I found myself facing a second set of double doors as the first doors closed behind me. Standing in darkness, I paused to consider what I might find on the other side. But I had already determined to go in, so I pushed on through. When the second set of doors closed behind me, I found myself in a very dark room. I couldn't see a thing except for a small red neon *Schlitz* sign hanging on the back wall. By the sign's dim reflection on the tavern floor, I saw that the space between the back wall and me was clear, so I headed for the sign.

My eyes were straining for enough light to get my bearings, but all I could see was the sign. By the time I reached the sign, the pupils of my eyes were fully open, so that—as I turned around to face the entrance—I was able to see, on my left, a row of booths containing ten or twelve people. And on my right I saw a long bar, with high stools, several occupied, and on the wall behind the bar, row upon row of bottles of every shape and color. Part of me knew I was where I shouldn't be, and I wanted to leave as soon as possible.

But another part knew why I was there, so I began walking, handing Gospels of Mark to people, first to those in the booths on the left, and then to those at the bar on the right. I could see in front of me a tiny line of light squeezing between the doors I'd just come through. The closer I moved toward that light, the more I wanted to be done with the task and out of the place. I handed a Gospel of Mark to the last patron at the bar and made for the door. Panic was beginning to set in. Time slowed, so that I felt as if I was walking through molasses.

Suddenly, a sharp, deep voice struck out at me, *"Hey!—You!"* It was the bartender, and I was terrified. I was caught! Would he call the police? Would he yell at me? Curse me? Physically throw me out of the place? I turned toward him, and swallowed hard. "Yes, sir?"

"Well, now, where's *mine?*" I walked over to him and handed him a booklet. "Here you are, sir. It's the Gospel of Mark. God bless you!"

I turned and headed back to the doors. He spoke to my back, in the same deep, but softer, voice. "And you too, son!" Out through the doors I went, out into the blazing afternoon sun, and down the steps. It took several minutes for my eyes and soul to adjust to the bright sunlight. But I still wonder, now nearly fifty years later, what God did with His Word, delivered by a small boy, to a dozen folks in that little tavern. Perhaps one day I'll find out, but for now, it's enough to know that I did the right thing.

Chapter Concepts

Autonomy	Rules are internalized principles and ideals [auto-, *self*; -nomy, *authority*]
Christlikeness	Conforming to Christ's Example and Word. Becoming like Christ.
Conventional reasoning	Kohlberg's second level, consisting of Stage III and Stage IV reasoning
Good boy/nice girl	Stage III: "Right actions impress others."
Heteronomy	Rules are handed down from an outside authority [hetero-, *other*]

Instrumental/relativist	Stage II: "Let's make a deal!" Reciprocity. Exchanges and trades.
Law and order	Stage IV: "Know the rules and obey."
Moral dilemma	A problem which presents both positive and negative consequences
Moral reasoning	The act or process of forming judgments or conclusions concerning moral dilemmas
Moral realism	Position that morals are absolute, fixed, and unchanging. Rules simply exist.
Moral relativism	Position that morals exist relative to those who hold them and can be changed
Morality	An established system of morals. The general level of moral functioning of a group
Morality of constraint	Piaget's term for moral realism: rules are fixed
Morality of cooperation	Piaget's term for moral relativism: rules are flexible
Postconventional reasoning	Kohlberg's third level, consisting of Stage V and Stage VI reasoning
Preconventional reasoning	Kohlberg's first level, consisting of Stage I and Stage II reasoning
Punishment/obedience	Stage I: "You might get caught." Avoid Punishment.
Social contract	Stage V: "Rules are what the group decides." Cooperate with the Group
Universal ethical principle	Stage VI: "Right action based on self-chosen principles." Act on love and justice for all

Chapter Objectives

Learners will demonstrate knowledge of Kohlberg's six stages of moral development by matching stages with definitions.

Learners will demonstrate understanding of Kohlberg's theory by doing such things as . . .

- explaining selected terms in their own words.
- matching stages to given scenarios
- creating church-related case studies that reflect a given stage.

Learners will demonstrate appreciation for Kohlberg's theory by sharing a moral dilemma they recently faced, explaining how they resolved it, and giving reasons why they took the action they did.

Discussion Questions

1 Describe an experience from your childhood in which you played with children several years older than you. What do you remember from that experience related to morality of constraint and morality of cooperation?

2 How did you react to the story of the teenager and the tavern? After reading the chapter, did you change your view on what you might have done in that situation?

3 Choose two of Kohlberg's six stages. 1) Explain the meaning of the stage. 2) Relate a personal experience you have had to each selected stage. What was the conflict? How did you resolve it? How does your struggle in this situation reflect the stage?

4 How are "morality," "moral reasoning," and "Christlikeness" different?

Answer to Dilemmas at the Beginning of the Chapter

Dilemma One

Sample responses to Dilemma One can be divided into the following stages. Kohlberg does not tell us what to do. He only frames the type of thinking that precedes the behavior. These statements reflect some of the responses I hear from seminary students. **Should I go into the bar?**

Stage I: Avoid Punishment

__No, because I might get caught and get into trouble

__Yes, because the chances of being seen by someone from church are small.

Stage II: Make a Deal

__No, because I get nothing extra for the extra risk.

__Yes, because I may be rewarded for my extra risk.

Stage III: Please Superiors

__Yes, because my parents (pastor) would be proud of my faithfulness.

__No, because my parents (pastor) would be very unhappy with me.

Stage IV: Obey the Law

__No, because I am underage. It is against the law for me to enter the tavern.

__Yes, because it is my duty. The Church expects us to carry out the evangelism task.

Stage V: Cooperate with the Group

__No, because our youth group did not agree to go into taverns, only to houses.

__Yes, because our youth group agreed to cover the whole area. I agreed to help.

Stage VI: Act on Love and Justice for Others

__No, because love and justice tell me to pass them by and go to the houses.

__Yes, because the people inside need God's Word. Love and justice tell me to go in.

Dilemma Two

I chose to participate with my Ukrainian Baptist brothers and sisters in the Lord's Supper. I took a sip of wine when the common cup was passed. Here was my reasoning. 1) I was not "using alcohol" in the sense of social drinking. 2) Ukrainian Baptists do not consider a sip of wine in the Lord's Supper as "using alcohol." In fact, they laugh when I present this "dilemma" to them. 3) Ukrainian Baptists use wine in the Lord's Supper, but they do not drink socially. 4) Southern Baptist missionaries who serve where Baptists use wine in the Lord's Supper regularly participate in the worship services and "sip wine." 5) The intent of the International Mission Board document is to provide guidelines to volunteers who might do harm to a mission project through the casual use of alcohol and tobacco. 6) It would have been offensive to my hosts to refuse to participate. 7) I prayed, and felt the Lord's freedom to participate. I did this with full knowledge that I will be held accountable by God for my decision.

In May 2008, I was invited to the dacha (a small cabin in the country) of my Russian tutor and his wife outside Kiev, Ukraine. Several times, a dinner guest, a neighbor, offered me—strongly!—various kinds of alcoholic beverages: beer, wine, vodka. I refused, almost to the point of rudeness. I prayed about this, because—though I do not "drink"—I did not want to be overly rude. Did not Jesus say, "It's not what goes into the mouth that defiles a man, but what comes out of the mouth, this defiles a man" (Matt 15:11). But as I prayed, I sensed that I should resist. Vladimir, my tutor, is not a believer, but he was gracious and softened the tension by offers of fruit juice, which I gladly accepted.

A few days later, during a language lesson, Vladimir asked me whether I *ever* drank beer or wine. I told him that I did not. He had difficulty understanding abstinence though he was well aware of, and opposed to, the destructive effects of student drunkenness on his own campus.

The next day he told me about Muslims he knew in Yemen and Dubai who gave him money to buy whiskey for them. I was surprised. "But I thought Muslims are forbidden to drink alcohol!" He looked at me, smiling, and softly said, "So they say. So they say." I thanked the Lord for helping me make the right decision in that particular situation. My abstinence formed a part of a consistent witness to this man, whom the Lord is drawing to Himself.

UNIT 3
Educational Psychology and Learning

"The learner is central in the teaching-learning process."

In Unit 2, we focused on *the learner* by analyzing stage-differences in personality, mental maturity, and moral reasoning. Now in Unit 3 we focus on the *teaching-learning process* itself.

Common views of teaching and learning can be quite simplistic. For nearly thirty years here at home, and more than twelve years abroad, I have asked students to write out definitions for teaching and learning at the beginning of our courses. The most common description of teaching is "giving information." The most common description of learning is "receiving information."

But learning is far more than receiving information. Learning is an "enduring . . . change in behavior or capacity acquired through experience."[1] A **change in behavior** refers to enhancing abilities and mastering skills. A **change in cognitive capacity** refers to establishing a useful knowledge base and creating a meaningful synthesis of concepts, principles, and perspectives. A **change in affective capacity** refers to increasing the number of positive values, strengthening those values, and organizing them into a coherent value system.

These changes are acquired through learning experiences—repetition, direct instruction, group interaction, personal discovery and reflection, project participation, examination—that leave enduring marks on learners. Each of the perceived changes in motor skills and mental functioning is mirrored in the warp and woof of neurons and synapses in the deepest parts of the brain for as long as we live. All of these elements are subsumed under the umbrella of learning.

Unit 1 underscored this complexity of learning. The Disciplers' Model points to changes in thinking, valuing, and relating with others as learners grow in response to intentional experiences. Philosophy defines human knowing in many ways, each with its own perspective, process, and outcome. In response to this complexity, educational psychologists have proposed a variety of theories to make intentional learning more efficient and effective.

Therefore, teaching is the systematic planning and effectual execution of educational experiences that result in enduring changes. This entails far more than "giving information." What, then, *do* we

---

do when we walk into a classroom? How do we help students make enduring changes—head, heart, and hand—as we meet with them session by session? Unit 3 embraces these questions.

Chapter 6: Traditional Behavioral Learning

Behavioral learning theory is the oldest educational system of the three systems addressed in Unit 3. As implied by its name, the focus of Behaviorism in education is the behavior of students, which includes both academic and social skills. What can we do as teachers to change the behavior of learners to support educational processes and goals? How do we help learners develop academic and interpersonal skills that form the basis for future learning?

We consider the ideas of John Watson, Ivan Pavlov, E. L. Thorndike, and B. F. Skinner for changing behavior through reinforcement. Chapter Six describes the present state of Traditional Behavioral Learning Theory.

Chapter 7: Social Behavioral Learning

In the 1960's, Behaviorists began to realize that operant conditioning provided too limited an explanation for learning. While behavioral purists have held to traditional views, most have integrated cognitive processes that cannot be directly observed, such as expectations, thoughts, and beliefs. In a sense, these theorists returned to John Locke, who focused on experience as the source of all knowledge, but also spoke of the innate capacities of the intellect.

We consider the ideas of Albert Bandura for changing behavior through observation and imitation of behavioral models. Chapter Seven describes the present state of Social Learning Theory, as well as Social Cognitive Theory, which reflects Bandura's most recent work.

Chapter 8: Cognitive Learning I

Cognitive learning theory emphasizes the thinking of students, rather than behavior or attitudes. The apostle Paul wrote, "Do not conform any longer to the pattern of the world, but be transformed by the renewing of your mind" (Rom 12:2a). Paul saw the mind as the center of activity both for conforming to worldly patterns and for being transformed according to God's will.

Building on the ideas of Jean Piaget, we consider the ideas of Ernst Mach, Max Wertheimer, Wolfgang Kohler, and Jerome Bruner for constructing meaning. How do we learn from the world around us? What role does perception play in the learning process? Chapter Eight presents the historical development of cognitive theory, from the early 1900s to the present state of Cognitive, Social, and Radical Constructivism.

Chapter 9: Cognitive Learning II

Despite the advances of Constructivism over the last dozen years, Information Processing Theory continues to provide important insights into how the mind makes sense of the world. Where Behaviorists emphasize external behavior, and Constructivists emphasize the use of what we know to solve problems, Information Processing Theory emphasizes the mechanisms by which we attend to, recognize, transform, store, and retrieve information.

The key term in this list is *transform*, which refers to the way the mind encodes sense data into mental structures. Using the personal computer as an analogy for sensory input and processing, Chapter Nine presents IPT and its explanations of how we learn, why we forget, how we can we improve our ability to remember, and how cognitive structure is actually created.

Chapter 10: Humanistic Learning

Humanistic learning theories, the "new wave" of learning in the 1970s, emphasized the values and attitudes of students rather than their behavior or thinking. Today, one is hard-pressed to find any reference to Humanistic Learning Theory in contemporary educational psychology textbooks. But make no mistake: the tenets of humanistic learning have not disappeared. Rather they have been absorbed into the ever-growing Constructivist camps, especially Radical Constructivism, as well as broader-based, hybrid learning approaches, such as Cooperative Learning.

The self-centeredness of humanistic learning has become the water through which our society swims. The idealistic and self-centered foundations, laid for "future Man" in the 1960s and 1970s, have crumbled. Humanistic learning theories have been discarded by educational thinkers as ineffective *instructional* approaches. Yet Humanism itself lives on in Postmodernism, radical libertarianism, and the educational traditions of Summerhill.

The best values of humanitarian education live on in the local churches as well. People gather freely and enthusiastically, learning together, ministering to each other, giving freely to support churches and their ministries, volunteering time and energy, growing as citizens of the kingdom (or, freely choosing not to). For all these reasons, I have retained a separate chapter for these theories. We consider the ideas of founders Abraham Maslow, Carl Rogers, and Arthur Combs for helping students clarify personal values and strengthen personal value systems. Chapter Ten describes the present state of Humanistic approaches to teaching.

Chapter 11: The Christian Teacher's Triad

When we study the life and work of the greatest Teacher Who ever walked this earth, we do not find a Behaviorist, or a Cognitivist, or a Humanist. But we do find the Master Teacher Who engaged His learners personally and met their discipling needs **head, heart, and hand**.

Educational problems do not fall neatly into any one system: some are behavioral, some cognitive, and others affective. Effective teachers move freely from system to system, engaging learners where they are, helping them master the subject, and grow as a result.

The Christian Teachers' Triad helps provide flexibility in our responses to student needs—head, heart, and hand. Chapter Eleven describes how to weave elements of all three systems of learning into a single, coordinated whole. We consider the Triad as a means to evaluate our own preferences in teaching, giving us a greater opportunity to engage *every learner* in our classrooms and congregations.

Chapter 12: Instructional Taxonomies

We convert educational theory into classroom practice by means of instructional taxonomies and the objectives that flow from them. Learners expect their teachers to lead them somewhere. We give them a clearer destination, as well as a better impression of the journey, when we show them in tangible terms what we expect of them. How do we select our approaches to learning from the variety that exists? What kinds of activities will we develop, and what results from them? How will we measure the learning that takes place? What implications do these questions have for long-range and short-range planning?

Chapter 12 provides a rationale for how instructional objectives strengthen the teaching-learning process. We overview the historical development of objectives, define the most popular taxonomies in education, and provide specific guidelines for writing real-world learning targets. Finally, two new taxonomy systems (2001, 2006) are introduced and explained.

TRADITIONAL BEHAVIORAL LEARNING

B. F. Skinner: Operant Conditioning Theory

*"Look! I am coming quickly, and My reward is with Me
to repay each person according to what he has done."*

Revelation 22:12

"Praise the young and they will blossom."

—Irish Proverb[1]

Chapter Rationale

Behavioral learning theory is the oldest educational system of the three systems addressed in Unit 3.[2] As implied by its name, the focus of Behaviorism in education is the behavior of students, which includes both academic and social skills. What can we do as teachers to change the behavior of learners to support educational processes and goals? How do we help them develop academic and interpersonal skills that form the basis for future learning?

Jesus said, "Everyone who hears these words of Mine **and acts on them** will be like a sensible man who built his house on the rock" (Matt 7:24). How do we help students practice in life what they learn in class? What can we do to reinforce biblically based, Christ-centered behaviors? Chapter Six highlights key behavioral ideas from history, emphasizes B. F. Skinner's Operant Conditioning, and concludes with a contemporary look at behavioral learning.

Chapter Overview

- ➤ Historical Roots
- ➤ B. F. Skinner and Operant Conditioning
- ➤ Educational Operant Conditioning: Programmed Instruction
- ➤ Computers and Education
- ➤ Suggestions for Using Operant Conditioning Principles
- ➤ Implications for Christian Teaching
- ➤ Traditional Behaviorism in the 2000s
- ➤ A Concluding Word on Traditional Behaviorism
- ➤ *Chapter Concepts, Chapter Objectives, and Discussion Questions*

Historical Roots

While learning is as old as humanity, theoretical formulations about how we learn date back to the Greeks. **Aristotle** (384–322 BC) established the foundation for contemporary behavioral learning theory in his Laws of Association. Learning proceeds, thought Aristotle, from mental associations between events. For example, if one sees a boy standing on a bridge, these two elements are associated in the mind. Later, if the observer thinks of the bridge, he will also think of the boy. The two elements have been associated. Other examples are "cup and saucer," or the "smell, texture, and taste of an apple." Aristotle called this tendency toward association of elements *contiguity*, referring to closeness in time or space ("this with that"). Observers also tend to associate elements that are alike ("this like that"), the law of *similarity*. Observers tend to associate elements that are different ("this unlike that"), the law of *contrast*.[3] Aristotle saw this process as a common sense approach to learning about the real world—that is, the physical world.[4] For that very reason, philosophers through the ages have accepted the Laws of Association as "commonplace . . . the activity of passive reason." They did not, however, consider them important since the Laws of Association did not lend themselves to abstraction of principles, the "domain of active reason."[5]

In the eighteenth and nineteenth centuries, English philosophers regarded association as the basis of mental life. They used it to explain memory, perception, and reasoning.[6] Philosophers David Hume (1711–1776), David Hartley (1705–1757), James Mill (1773–1836), and John Stuart Mill (1806–1873), provided a strong philosophical base for an associationist view of thought. One of the best known of this group of philosophers is John Locke.

John Locke (1632–1704)[7]

Like Aristotle, British philosopher John Locke rejected the Platonic idea that human beings are born with existing innate ideas. Rather he held that human beings are born with minds able to process sense data from the world, yet devoid of content, like a blank slate. Experience with the world writes on this slate, this "tabula rasa," to create understanding and personality.[8]

Circumstances, not heredity, temperament or choice, determine what is written on the slate.[9] Locke wrote that it was "In [experience that] all our knowledge is founded,"[10] and that there is "nothing in the intellect [which is] not first in the senses."[11] Locke made his entire system dependent on the association of sensations into simple ideas. He combined these simple ideas, drawn from sensations, with ideas of reflection, the result of active reason to derive complex ideas.[12]

More apropos than the blank writing slate of the seventeenth century, we might say that Locke's view of the mind is analogous to a contemporary calculator. This instrument has many built-in functions, but nothing in its memory stores when it is turned on. We enter data, press the appropriate keys, and the calculator processes the data in fixed ways. Such is the mind, according to Locke, when we are born. We are devoid of data, but possess the innate capacities to process experiences.[13] While behavioral purists would later reject his use of terms like "mind" and "intellect,"[14] he did provide a philosophical basis for a behavioral view of learning.

Wilhelm Wundt (1832–1920)[15]

The field of modern psychology grew out of the work of Wilhelm Wundt, who established the first experimental laboratory in Europe in 1879.[16] Psychology is the offspring from the marriage of philosophy and physiology and focuses on conscious experience. Wundt's goal was to discover the basic physical element, the "building block" of human experience, akin to the atomic elements in physics.[17] These basic elements he believed were connected through association to produce all personality and learning. He was hailed by behaviorists for this emphasis on basic elements and association, but soundly criticized by early cognitivists (see Chapter Eight). By this time, the simple notion that associations were "mysterious links between discrete mental entities" had been rejected. In its place was the idea that associative tendencies were established in the nervous system as a result of previous experience.[18]

His procedure for discovering this element, which he called *introspection*, called for subjects to look within themselves to discover their feelings and sensations. Behaviorists soundly criticized Wundt for this emphasis of self-reflection on internal states (though he was hailed by cognitivists), since behaviorists insist on defining human personality in terms of overt behavior. Still, Wilhelm

Wundt underscored the existence of a basic element of human experience, fundamental to behavioral thinking. Ivan Pavlov provided evidence of what that basic element might be.

Ivan Pavlov (1849–1936[19]): Classical Conditioning

Ivan Pavlov was a Russian physiologist. He won the Nobel Prize in 1904 for his work on digestion in dogs.[20] His experiments involved measuring dog salivation rates under differing conditions.[21] In the process of conducting his experiments, he discovered that the salivation rates changed for unexplained reasons. Dogs would begin to salivate at the mere sight of food, or, strangely enough, at the mere sight of his research assistants, *even if they carried no food.*[22] Pavlov began a series of experiments to discover the reasons for the spontaneous changes in salivation. What resulted from these investigations was a theory of learning called classical conditioning,[23] which focused on an association, or bond, between a stimulus and given response.

A **stimulus** (S) is a perceivable unit of the environment that may affect behavior.[24] A stimulus can be a sound (bell), a smell (fresh bread), a touch (hand on shoulder), a taste (hot buttered popcorn), or a sight (sunset). A stimulus may be **unconditioned** (UCs) in that it affects behavior without being learned. Food causes salivation as a reflex action. A puff of air in one's eye causes it to blink. A loud sound causes one to jump. Food, puff of air, and loud sound are all unconditioned stimuli. A response is any reaction to stimuli.[25] A **response** (R) may be **unconditioned** (Ur) in that is a reflex action to a stimulus and is not learned. Salivation in the presence of food is an **unconditioned response**. An eye blink in response to the puff of air and the physical jump from a sudden loud sound, are unconditioned responses.

Classical Conditioning

Before	During	After
UCs Ur	+	Cs Cr
Ns No response		

A **neutral stimulus** (Ns) does not result in any specific behavior because it has no association, no link, no bond with that behavior. A neutral stimulus becomes a **conditioned stimulus (Cs)** through the process of conditioning. When Pavlov's dogs first met his assistants, the assistants were neutral stimuli, unassociated with any behavior. One of the responsibilities of the assistants was to feed the dogs. As "food" and "assistant" were paired together over time, an association was created. The *unconditioned stimulus* of food was paired with the *neutral stimulus* of assistant until, in time, "assistant" became a *conditioned stimulus* for the *conditioned response* of salivation. Dogs salivated at the mere sight of the assistants, even though they carried no food. Pavlov's experiments focused on transforming a neutral stimulus (Ns) into a conditioned stimulus (Cs), which, in turn, produces a conditioned response (Cr). Let's see how he did this.

Pavlov presented dogs with food (UCs) along with a bell[26] or buzzer (Ns).[27] After several feedings, the dogs would salivate at hearing the bell or buzzer alone. The bell became a conditioned stimulus (Cs) and salivation became a conditioned response (Cr) to the bell. An association had been created between a neutral stimulus (bell) and a given behavior (salivation). Pavlov called the mental association, created by conditioning, a stimulus-response (S-R) bond. John Watson (see below), the father of behaviorism, saw in Pavlov's S-R bond the "basic element" Wundt had been looking for.

Processes of Classical Conditioning. The four basic processes of classical conditioning are extinction, spontaneous recovery, generalization, and discrimination.

Extinction. If the conditioned stimulus is presented without the unconditioned stimulus (if the bell is rung in the absence of food), the conditioned response will decay (salivation will decrease over time). The association between Cs and Cr weakens when Cs is presented without UCs.[28] A child who is afraid of all furry animals because he was once painfully bitten by a squirrel can disassociate pain and furry animals by playing with a well-behaved kitten.

Spontaneous Recovery. Extinguished responses are not lost permanently. After a time of extinction, presentation of the conditioned stimulus will provoke the conditioned response.[29]

Generalization. Once an association between the Cs and Cr is established, responses will generalize to other similar stimuli.[30] The child mentioned above was afraid of "all furry animals," and yet he was bitten by a particular squirrel, not all furry animals. Because the squirrel had fur, the child's response to the squirrel (fear) spread, that is, generalized, to other furry animals, and ultimately, *all* furry animals.

Discrimination. Organisms[31] can learn to discriminate among similar stimuli. When one tone of bell was linked with food and another tone was not, Pavlov's dogs learned to discriminate between them. They would salivate upon hearing one bell but not the other.[32]

Classroom Implications of Classical Conditioning. Classical conditioning focuses on *involuntary behaviors* that are outside our conscious control.[33] We can do little to strengthen, or weaken, specific classroom behaviors using principles of classical conditioning. How we conduct the class, however, creates an environment in which positive and negative associations can be formed.

Students who suffer from test anxiety did not consciously choose to fear examinations. No teacher set "fear of taking tests" as a course goal. Anxiety is associated with testing because of painful experiences—failure, humiliation, poor test questions, or inability to prepare—in the past.

Classroom climate (Chapter Fifteen) provides a veritable ocean of possibilities for positive or negative associations. Whether the sea is stormy or calm depends on our teaching style. Is the classroom a warm inviting place? Do students feel free to ask questions or share their thinking? Is the classroom a safe place to be? Are students able to share concerns? Does the teacher take time to answer questions or explain misunderstandings in class, or remain after class to help as needed? If so, then positive associations will result. If these positive associations are sufficiently nurturing, they will generalize to the teacher (students will *pursue* future classes with this teacher regardless of course taught). They will generalize (students will *pursue* future classes with this teacher regardless of who is teaching the course). They will generalize to the school (students will *encourage* others to attend). They will generalize to learning at large (students will do additional *study on their own*).

Or, is the classroom tense? Are student questions treated as interruptions? Is the teacher's demeanor gruff or cold? Does the teacher verbally abuse students, or humiliate them for perceived failures? If so, negative associations will result from the class. If these are sufficiently abusive, they will likewise generalize to the teacher (students will *avoid this teacher* regardless of course taught). They will generalize to the subject (students will *avoid the subject* regardless of who is teaching the course). They will generalize to the school (students will *transfer* to another school). They will generalize even to learning at large (students will *drop out* of college and go to work).

Effective teachers understand that "conveying content" is not enough. The *manner* in which teaching is conducted[34] and the environment that one constructs for learning to take place, is as important as lecture notes, PowerPoints, and assignments. Through classical conditioning, for better or worse, we teach far more than what we list in our course overviews.

John B. Watson (1878–1958[35]): The Father of Behaviorism

John Watson believed that Wundt's theorizing about thoughts, intentions, or other subjective experiences was unscientific.[36] Watson insisted that psychology focus on overt measureable behaviors, and, from this conviction, he fathered the doctrine of Behaviorism. While he criticized introspection and internal states, he did embrace Wundt's thinking on basic elements of human experience.

Watson wanted to create a science of psychology on par with the hard sciences. How do physicists, for example, study the solar system? They observe how it behaves. If psychology were to ever gain the status of a scientific discipline like physics, Watson believed, it would have to focus on how humans behave.

Watson was greatly influenced by Pavlov's work[37] and was the first to use it as the basis for learning theory.[38] Watson discovered in Pavlov's S-R bond the basic element in human learning and personality development, and he used this element to replace Wundt's internal states.

Watson, however, was an extremist. He made unsubstantiated boasts in his writing and was ethically questionable in his research on young children.[39] His best-known experiment involved a young boy named Albert. Albert was given a small rat to handle. As Albert played with the rat, Watson quietly moved behind the boy and, without warning, banged a metal bowl with a rod. From this sudden shock, Albert developed a fear of rats. Watson further showed that this induced fear could be generalized to a rabbit, a dog, a sealskin coat, and, for a time, Santa Claus's beard.[40]

Watson's contribution to the developing field of psychology was demonstrating the role conditioning played in developing emotional responses such as fears, phobias, and prejudices.[41] He believed that humans were born with a few reflexes and the emotional reactions of fear, love, and rage. All other behavior is established, he believed, by building new S-R associations through conditioning.[42] But how are S-R bonds intentionally created in an educational process? The answer to that question came from E. L. Thorndike.

Edward L. Thorndike (1874–1949[43]): Father of Educational Psychology

E. L. Thorndike has been called the father of educational psychology because his work was instrumental in bridging the conceptual gap between theoretical S-R associations and practical classroom teaching. Thorndike's theory has been variously called "instrumental conditioning"[44] because the learned behavior is instrumental in achieving goals, "trial and error learning"[45] because problems are solved by trying different behaviors until the correct one is found, and "connectionism"[46] because of its emphasis on connecting new responses with novel stimuli.

Thorndike placed animals in problem-solving situations and observed how they behaved. For example, a hungry cat would be placed in a cage with a latch. A bowl of food would be placed outside. As the cat clawed at the cage attempting to get to the food, it would accidently trip the latch. The door would open, and the cat would rush to the bowl and eat the food.

After a few trials, the cat became more purposeful in its behavior. Rather than clawing at the cage randomly, the cat would move more directly to the latch, and with increasing proficiency, open the cage. Practice increased proficiency. Thorndike extended Pavlov's work beyond mere reflex actions, showing how new responses to novel situations were formed.[47] Further, he demonstrated that stimuli occurring *after* a behavior had an influence on future behaviors.[48] This key discovery formed the basis for the later work of B. F. Skinner. Thorndike's experimental findings resulted in three fundamental laws of learning. These laws of learning have influenced educational practice to this very day.

The Law of Readiness states that learning proceeds best when learners are properly prepared to respond. If learners are ready to respond, there is satisfaction (which is rewarding) in being allowed to respond. There is frustration (punishment) in being forbidden to respond. If the learner is not ready to respond, there is frustration in being forced to respond.[49]

We see this law at work every day. We sit down to a wonderful dinner, tantalized by sights and smells. We are rewarded by the tastes and textures of the various foods, satisfied as we eat our fill. Or, perhaps, the phone rings and calls us away from the table, frustrated. A teenager walks his date to the front door and hopes the time is right for a good-night kiss. The kiss is satisfying. A "no" is frustrating.

In the classroom, learning proceeds best when learners are made "ready"—when they are engaged in the subject—at the beginning of the session. Educators still refer to the opening moments of a session as "learning readiness." The term refers to more than mere interest. It refers to intentional experiences that prepare learners psychologically for what is to follow. We might ask a question, or pose a problem, suggest a conflict between views, or raise a dilemma. The law of readiness goes further, however, than learning readiness activities. An examination is announced for a given day. Students come to class at the appointed hour with varying degrees of readiness. Those who have studied will be psychologically satisfied in proceeding with the exam; they will be highly frustrated if the exam is postponed. Learning proceeds best when learners are properly prepared to respond.

The Law of Exercise states that repetition strengthens S-R bonds, or practice makes perfect.[50] This law, sometimes called the law of use and disuse,[51] led to an emphasis on drill and practice in the classroom.[52] The more times Thorndike's cats freed themselves from the cage, the more proficient they became at the task. "Repetition is the mother of learning" is a common phrase in English and in Russian![53] Thorndike later modified this law to require *feedback* on the quality of responses that were being made,[54] because blind practice—practice done without feedback—has no effect on learning.[55]

On the first day of my research course, I write a string of Greek and English letters across the top of the blackboard. These letters refer to an extensive set of inter-related statistical concepts that form the basis for statistical analysis. On that first day, as I go over the roll and introduce the syllabus, I work my way through the string. We pronounce the terms (μ, "myoo") and give short definitions for them. Every day we begin the session by working through the string, adding a little each time.

I ask questions of the students and ask if they have questions. Over time I increase difficulty by writing subsets on some days or randomly writing a few letters around the large blackboard. By the time we arrive at Chapter Sixteen where these terms—building blocks for the statistics portion of the course—are used, most of the students easily call their names, explain their referents, and understand their relationships with the other terms. This application of the law of exercise creates within students a complex network of associations that forms the conceptual foundation upon which we build many statistical procedures.

The Law of Effect states that any response that is followed by pleasure or reward strengthens the association between that response and its stimulus. Similarly, any response that is followed by frustration or pain weakens the association. The law of effect goes beyond Aristotle's law of contiguity[56] to declare that learning is a function of the "consequences of the act."[57] The taste of the food at the meal, the satisfaction of hunger, the pleasantness of a goodnight kiss, the sense of accomplishment that comes from doing well on an exam for which one studied—these rewards strengthen the associations between stimuli and responses. The use of rewards in the classroom such as gold stars on charts, peppermints tossed to students who answer questions, and words of praise from the teacher all reflect the power of the law of effect.[58] In fact, the law of effect is the most important law of the three.[59]

Thorndike defined learning as the mechanical process of stamping S-R bonds[60] into the nervous system through repetition.[61] His theory describes how bonds are strengthened or weakened.

Thorndike saw little difference between animal learning and human learning, and therefore had a decidedly dehumanizing effect on American education. Thorndike's theory sees human learners as little more than organic robots, which are mechanically programmed through conditioning.

Despite this mechanical focus in learning, Thorndike's contribution was profound. His Law of Effect underscored the importance of motivation in education,[62] and provided the basis for operant conditioning,[63] the dawn of modern behaviorism, and the revolution of programmed instruction.

$$X \quad n \quad \Sigma \quad \Sigma X \quad \overline{X} \quad x \quad \Sigma x \quad \Sigma x^2 \quad s^2 \quad s \quad z \quad t \quad F$$
$$N \qquad\qquad\quad \mu \qquad\qquad\qquad \sigma^2 \quad \sigma$$

B. F. Skinner (1904–1990[64]): Operant Conditioning Theory

Thorndike's Law of Effect states that the consequences of an act increase the probability of that act.[65] This principle became the foundation of B. F. Skinner's Operant Conditioning theory, which he developed in the 1930s. By the 1950s his views dominated psychology and learning.[66]

The Life of B. F. Skinner

Burrus Frederick Skinner was born in Pennsylvania in 1904. He majored in English at Hamilton College in New York. He wrote poetry but was not satisfied with this result, so he entered Harvard University's graduate school in 1928 to study psychology. He earned his Ph.D. in experimental psychology in 1931. In 1936 he joined the faculty of the University of Minnesota, and during World War II he trained pigeons to guide missiles to their targets. In 1945 he went to the University of Indiana as Chairman of the Psychology Department. It was during this time he invented the "air-crib," a soundproof, air-conditioned, germ-free, glass-encased box for infants. His daughter Deborah spent most of the first two years of her life in it. Skinner tried to market it as the "Heir-Crib," but it was not widely accepted. In 1948 Skinner joined the faculty of Harvard University where he remained until his death in 1990.

His interest in educational applications of operant conditioning grew out of a visit he made to his daughter's elementary school class. He saw the activities disorganized and a waste of time. He believed that children could be taught much more efficiently if their behaviors were shaped in the same way as his experimental pigeons or rats. By the 1950s, he had developed "teaching machines" to lead children through their learning step-by-step with reinforcement.

His best known writings include *The Behavior of Organisms* (1938), *Walden Two* (1948), *Science and Human Behavior* (1953), *Verbal Behavior* (1957), *The Technology of Teaching* (1968) and *Beyond Freedom and Dignity* (1971).

Skinner was adamant in his defense of traditional behaviorism to the end of his life. Speaking to the American Psychological Association in August 1990 he said, "[Cognitive science] is an effort to reinstate that inner initiating-originating-creative self or mind which, in scientific analysis, simply does not exist. . . . I think it is time for psychology as a profession and as a science to realize that the science which will be most helpful is not cognitive science searching for the inner mind or self, but selection by consequences represented by behavioral analysis."

On August 10, the American Psychological Association presented Skinner with a citation for his outstanding lifelong contribution to the field. A few days later he died of leukemia at the age of 86.[67]

Operant Conditioning Theory

Contiguity (Aristotle) and classical conditioning (Pavlov) account for only a small percentage of learned behaviors. They describe how existing behaviors are paired with new stimuli, but do not explain how new behaviors are acquired.[68] They are inadequate explanations of most human learning because people do more than merely respond to stimuli. They consciously generate behaviors.[69] In classical conditioning, responses are *involuntary*[70] and *elicited*—drawn out—by specific stimuli.[71]

Operant conditioning, on the other hand, emphasizes the acquisition of new behaviors as organisms *operate* on their environment in order to reach goals.[72] The responses are *voluntary* and *emitted* by people or animals. These voluntary, emitted responses are called operants.[73]

Skinner did much of his research with rats or pigeons in a controlled environment, an enclosure, called a "Skinner box."[74] The boxes used with rats had a metal lever and a food dispenser. With each press of the lever, a rat received a food pellet. The boxes used with pigeons had a disk, which the birds pecked for the same result.

In moving about the box, the rat would accidently press the lever. The press of the lever was a voluntary, emitted behavior, a response (eR) to the environment. The bar-press resulted in the rat getting a food pellet. This pellet was a reinforcing stimulus (rS). Former associationists such as Pavlov, Watson, and Thorndike had emphasized the *S-R* bond, an association between a stimulus and an elicited response. Skinner reversed this order, suggesting an R-S association. When a voluntary response receives a reinforcing stimulus, the probability of that response increases.[75] This reinforcing stimulus, which Thorndike called a "satisfier," is the most important component in Skinner's theory.[76] In fact, Skinner did little more than repackage Thorndike's Law of Effect, replacing the satisfaction which comes from responding to a stimulus (stimulus elicits a response which is satisfying: S—eR$^+$) with the "reinforcing stimulus" (a voluntary response receives a reinforcing stimulus, which is satisfying: eR—rS$^+$). While Skinner's ideas were not new, his ability to popularize his research findings brought his ideas to the forefront of psychology.[77] Let's turn to the essential concepts of operant conditioning to see how Skinner's ideas have transformed educational thinking since the 1940s.

Strengthening Good Behavior through Reinforcement

Reinforcement is the process of using "satisfiers," or reinforcers, to strengthen behavior. A reinforcer is any event that follows a behavior and increases the likelihood that the behavior will occur again.[78] Put another way, a reinforcer is any consequence that strengthens the behavior it follows.[79] The food Thorndike placed outside the cage was a stimulus for the cat's attempts to open the door, but once eaten, the food became a reinforcer for door-opening behavior. The food pellets that dropped into Skinner's boxes were reinforcers. Stars placed on charts for work done well. A kind word. A pat on the back. A smile. These events or behaviors satisfy, and therefore strengthen behaviors that are associated with them.

Primary reinforcers. A primary reinforcer is a stimulus that reinforces without being learned. It is a satisfier linked to human needs or drives. Primary reinforcers include food, water, warmth, security, sleep, and sex.[80]

Secondary reinforcers. A secondary reinforcer, sometimes called a generalized[81] reinforcer, is a stimulus that was previously neutral but has, through conditioning, been associated with other reinforcers.[82] Secondary reinforcers include prestige, money, and success.[83] There are three basic classes of secondary reinforcers. *Social reinforcers* include behaviors like acceptance, hugs, personal attention, and smiles. *Token reinforcers*, sometimes called symbolic reinforcers, include money, grades, prizes, and points. *Activity reinforcers* include free play, games, music, or trips.[84]

Positive and Negative Reinforcement[85]

The examples cited above reflect pleasant consequences given to reinforce desired behaviors. LeFrancois joins many others to use the word *reward* to describe this type of reinforcement,[86] though Skinner would disapprove. He wrote in 1986, "We reward people, but reinforce behavior."[87] Skinner called this condition—providing pleasant consequences for specific behavior—**positive reinforcement**, because giving the positive reinforcer *increases the probability of the behavior it follows*.[88] Examples of positive reinforcement include the following:

	Pleasant	Unpleasant
Give	**Positive Reinforcement** *"Extra credit"*	**Presentation Punishment** *"Three swats"*
Take	**Removal Punishment** *"No internet"*	**Negative Reinforcement** *"No homework"*

"Anyone who answers questions correctly today will get a **package of Smarties candy**." (The teacher tosses the candies as students answer correctly. If a student answers incorrectly, the teacher helps them work through the answer until they get it right, and then tosses them the candy.)

"**Extra credit** will be given on your term paper if more than ten references are used."

Notice that the choice to answer in the first instance, or use more than ten references in the second, belongs to the students. Candy and extra credit do not insure compliance but increases the probability that students will choose to act in these educationally appropriate ways.

If an unpleasant stimulus is removed, then the probability of the desired behavior increases. This is called **negative reinforcement**.[89] The condition is called *negative* because something (unpleasant) is taken away, which is a positive condition. Some writers use the word *relief* to describe this situation.[90] Examples of negative reinforcement include the following:

- "If you complete all five problems in class today, there will be no homework tonight."
- "Anyone who maintains an average of 90 or better will not have to take the final exam."

The terms positive and negative in this context do not refer to good and bad effects. In positive reinforcement, we give some desirable thing. In negative reinforcement, we take away some undesirable thing. Both of these actions increase the probability of the desired (positive) behavior.

Weakening Bad Behavior through Punishment

Reinforcement, both positive and negative, strengthens good behaviors. We can also discourage improper behavior in the classroom. The use of a stimulus that decreases the probability of a response is called punishment. In some situations, teachers cannot avoid using punishment. For example, if children do something that places themselves or others in danger, punishment may be called for. Further, when attempts to use reinforcement have failed, punishment may be advisable.[91]

First, we can punish learners—that is, discourage improper behavior—by taking away a desirable consequence. This is called removal punishment,[92] because it removes privileges.[93] LeFrancois calls this condition "penalty."[94] It is also called Punishment II.[95] Examples of removal punishment include:

- "Since you did not clean your room, you may not use the Internet tonight."[96]
- "Since you grabbed the face mask of an opposing player, your team loses ten yards."
- "If your paper is submitted late, 25 points will be subtracted from your grade."

Second, we can punish learners by giving an undesirable consequence, which is an unpleasant reinforcing stimulus. This is called presentation punishment,[97] or Punishment I.[98] Examples of presentation punishment include:

- "If you run into the street again, you will get three swats."
- "If you are late for practice, you will have to run ten extra laps at the end."
- "If you talk during study hour, you will remain after class and pick up the trash."

The fundamental problem with punishment is that it does not teach *new* (appropriate) ways to behave. Punishment simply suppresses *old* (inappropriate) behaviors.[99] Thorndike found that pleasure was more effective in stamping new S-R bonds into the nervous system than pain was in stamping old bonds out.[100] Skinner found the same in his experiments: reinforcement teaches new behavior better than punishment un-teaches old behavior.

Skinner ranked the four possibilities of conditioning from most effective to least effective as follows: The best approach is reinforcement, either positive or negative. Both are equally effective in increasing positive behavior.[101] If there are undesirable behaviors to be weakened, use removal punishment: time out, separation of disruptive students, loss of free time.

Presentation punishment—verbal intimidation, corporeal punishment, and the like—should not be used within a classroom context. I remember one particularly dramatic experiment from my days of doctoral studies. Skinner used a metal grid floor for his mazes in one series of studies. This allowed him to administer an electric shock to rats as they learned to run mazes. His goal was to measure the difference in the amount of time it took a rat to learn to run a maze under two conditions: positive reinforcement (food) and presentation punishment (shock).

What he found was that electric shock produced faster learning times than food. Although rats learned the maze faster with shock than food, it also created fear of the cage itself, and they refused to run the maze at all. Even when Skinner increased the level of shock to the point of death and beyond, rats simply huddled in a corner and died.

Guilt is to human learners what shock is to rats. While research is mixed on the effects of spanking,[102] it is clear that producing fear in learners creates an environment where learning suffers and dies. As we just said, Thorndike found that *pleasure was more effective in stamping new S-R bonds into the nervous system than pain was in stamping old bonds out*. Loving parents use spanking in the context of care and protection in order to stop behaviors that are dangerous to their own children—running into the street, inserting a knife into an electric socket, jumping off a wall. The follow-up to the spanking is love and concern, as well as an explanation about why the spanking was necessary. Teachers are not the parents of their students and should not, in my opinion, ever use the stronger forms of presentation punishment—spanking, verbal abuse, humiliation—in educational contexts.

When it is necessary to use mild forms of punishment—such as reprimands or physical separation—consider the following suggestions.

1. Ignore the misbehavior if possible but when the learning environment is disrupted, misbehavior must be corrected.
2. Provide warning cues—making eye contact, slightly shaking the head "no," walking toward misbehaving students—before applying punishments.

3. Explain the problem. Learners need to know specifically what they are doing to earn the punishment.
4. Punish immediately. Punishments do not lessen infractions when applied some time after the infraction. Punishment and misbehavior must be closely linked to be effective.
5. Use appropriate intensity. Too much or too little punishment is ineffective in lessening misbehavior.
6. Apply punishments consistently.
7. Consider what changes in the learning environment may be made to reduce misbehaviors.[103]

Having said this, it is important to remember that punishment can lessen the frequency, duration, and intensity of inappropriate behavior, but the learner's behavior has not been changed.[104] Positive behavior change happens through reinforcement, not punishment.

Lack of Training Increases Classroom Misapplication

One difficulty in employing operant principles correctly is the fact that many teachers seldom have the opportunity to learn how to manage behavior correctly. Since the advent of cognitive and humanistic theories of learning in the late 1960s, behavioral learning has declined in popularity and focus, and consequently receives, less time in training. Teachers are unaware of how their well-intentioned actions can strengthen bad behavior. Two examples will illustrate.

John is teaching a sixth grade math class. He has asked several questions, which students have answered correctly. In the press of the class, he does not acknowledge Jane's correct answer as he did several other students. Jane feels hurt at the slight and begins to pout. John sees Jane pouting and remembers that he did not respond to her answer. So he says, "Very good, Jane. You are doing so well!" In an attempt to correct an earlier mistake, he has now reinforced the wrong behavior, praising Jane while she is pouting. Reinforcers need to be applied immediately after the performance (Aristotle's law of contiguity). John unintentionally strengthened Jane's tendency to pout.

Tim is talking to himself in the classroom and disturbing the children around him. He is doing this because he is bored with the class and does not want to be there. Rita, the teacher, ignores his talking for a while, but suddenly decides Tim is talking too much and too loudly. "Tim, be quiet!" she shouts (presentation punishment). Tim immediately stops talking, and the problem seems to be solved. But his boredom has now turned to frustration at being scolded. So he begins talking aloud to himself again, and this time, more loudly. Rita, unable to keep him from talking, sends him to the principal's office. She has just taken him away from what was boring him (her class). This is negative reinforcement and strengthens his talking behavior. In the future he will more likely talk aloud when bored so that he will be dismissed from the class.

Applying reinforcers appropriately is a complex classroom management skill. It is helpful to understand some specifics of how to arrange reinforcers for the greatest effect.

Reinforcement Schedules

The *way* that reinforcers are given has a direct impact on the *nature* of the behavior that is strengthened. The particular pattern of frequency and predictability of reinforcers is called a reinforcement schedule.[105] First, we will differentiate between continuous and intermittent reinforcement. Then we will distinguish among four types of intermittent reinforcement.

Continuous reinforcement refers to the practice of reinforcing *every occurrence* of a desired behavior.[106] When I am demonstrating a statistical procedure for the first time, I walk the class through the steps of solving a statistical problem. I explain each step, and then ask a question to see if the students understand. When the correct answer is given, I reinforce it, every time, with appropriate praise.[107] Continuous reinforcement is the most effective schedule type for learning new behavior.[108]

Intermittent reinforcement refers to the practice of reinforcing a desired behavior *periodically*.[109] This approach is "most effective in *maintaining* behavior that has already been learned."[110] Or, said another way, intermittent reinforcement makes learned behaviors more persistent, more resistant to decay. Intermittent reinforcement can be based on time interval (how much time passes between reinforcement events) or response frequency (how many responses occur between reinforcement events). Time interval and response frequency can be fixed or variable. This provides four possibilities.

A fixed (time) interval schedule is one in which a *fixed amount of time* lapses between reinforcers.[111] Examples of fixed interval reinforcement include such things as a teacher checking on small group discussions every ten minutes (positive feedback on good discussion), or scheduling a quiz every Friday (positive feedback on test performance). Because the reinforcement is *predictable*, target behavior *increases just before* the reinforcer.[112] As time approaches for the teacher to check on the group's progress, the group becomes more focused in their discussions. Students put off studying for the quiz until Thursday night, and then they study very hard.

Unfortunately, the target behavior *decreases right after* the fixed interval reinforcer has been applied.[113] When the teacher leaves to check on other groups, the students take a break. After the quiz on Friday, students relax until the next quiz approaches.

If the reinforcers stop, target behaviors weaken. If the teacher misses a check or two, students become less intense in their discussions. If a few quizzes are skipped, then Thursday night cramming declines.[114] I administer a comprehensive final in two of my classes. Every semester I have students who wait until a few days before the exam to study a semester's worth of material. When I assign semester-long research papers, there are always students who wait until the last week before the due date to begin writing.

Fixed interval reinforcement can provide the *fastest initial learning* of any of the intermittent types, but the behavior is also *less persistent*.[115] Shorter, more frequent quizzes may be better than major, infrequent exams for encouraging effort that is more consistent.[116] A year ago I changed my examination schedule from two to four examinations prior to the final comprehensive. This cost the course two full class sessions of explanation, demonstration, and discussion. But it focused student attention on half as much material for a given examination and provided twice the feedback on their personal performance. It provided twice as many opportunities for them to check their own study habits in light of test results. This has proven an effective improvement in the course, as measured by student grades on the final comprehensive exam.

A fixed ratio reinforcement schedule is one in which a *fixed number of responses* occur between reinforcers. Examples of fixed ratio reinforcement include such things as a teacher allowing students to start on their homework once they have worked three math problems correctly in a row. Or, for every ten assigned Scripture passages that are correctly translated from the Greek, students earn one extra point on their semester grade. Or, for every five verses of the Bible that children commit to memory, they receive a gold star on a wall chart. Behavior (memorizing Bible verses) is *persistent until the break point is reached* (five verses memorized) and the reinforcer (gold star on chart) is received. Then behavior (Bible verse memorization) declines.[117]

	Time Interval	Response Frequency
Fixed (predictable)	**Fixed Interval** **Fixed amount of time** *Every 30 minutes*	**Fixed Ratio** **Fixed number of responses** *Every 5 responses*
Variable (unpredictable)	**Variable Interval** **Random units of time** *Every x minutes*	**Variable Ratio** **Random number of responses** *"Slot machine"*

A variable (time) interval schedule is one in which a *random amount of time* passes between reinforcers.[118] Examples of variable interval reinforcement include such things as a teacher making checks on small group discussion after a random amount of time and administering unannounced quizzes. Since reinforcement events are *unpredictable*, student work is more consistent and students pause less often. Even if the teacher misses a check on the groups or skips a quiz every now and then, study behavior continues high.[119] *Persistence of behavior is greater* with variable interval reinforcement than with fixed interval, and behaviors are highly resistant to extinction.[120]

A variable ratio reinforcement schedule is one in which a *random number of responses* occur between reinforcers.[121] The most common example of variable ratio reinforcement is the slot machine.[122] A player deposits a coin into the machine and pulls the handle. Wheels spin, but there is no pay out. The cycle is repeated. Over and over. After a random number of coins and pulls, a random number of coins clink into the tray. With each pull of the handle, there is a possibility that hundreds, thousands or tens of thousands of dollars could be won. People sit at the machines for hours, depositing coins and pulling handles. Small winnings are deposited, one coin at a time, for the possibility of winning more. When I was in Las Vegas for the Southern Baptist Convention meeting a number of years ago, a friend told me of meeting an elderly lady who came to a particular casino one day a month, the day she received her Social Security check. She cashed her check and received a bucket of coins. Then she went to "feed Sally." Sally was a particular slot machine in the casino. She fed Sally by depositing her coins into the machine and pulling the handle. She did this until all her money was gone, and then she went home until the next check arrives.

Variable ratio reinforcement produces the *greatest degree of persistence*, and target behavior proceeds in a quick and steady manner.[123] I saw many people sitting at slot machines that week, pulling the handle "one more time." Unlike the casino commercials, I rarely saw anyone laughing.

In a classroom, variable ratio reinforcement occurs as teachers ask questions and call on students at random to answer.[124] Not only is this schedule effective in achieving persistence, but it is also practical to use in actual classroom discussions and question-answer sessions.

Superstitious Reinforcement. There is one other type of reinforcement worth mentioning before moving on to other concepts. Skinner noticed that pigeons often exhibited what he called superstitious behavior. One would turn in circles, another swing its head in a pendulum fashion. It seemed as if the pigeons were behaving ritualistically in an attempt to get food from the dispenser, even when the dispenser was programmed to dispense pellets on fixed intervals, regardless of behavior.[125] Superstitious reinforcement can also occur when reinforcers are *accidently* given, regardless of what behavior is taking place. Such a schedule results in erroneous connections between results and behaviors.[126] Black cats, broken mirrors, walking under ladders, and wearing a lucky shirt when competing in sports all reflect this kind of erroneous association. In a religious context, we could include idol worship under such superstitious reinforcement.

Extinction

Extinction is the weakening and eventual elimination of a response as a result of non-reinforcement.[127] When animals press a lever repeatedly, without receiving a food pellet, lever pressing decreases. If animals are removed from the Skinner box altogether, preventing them from responding at all, conditioning is retained.[128]

Some children misbehave in order to gain the attention of parents and teachers, because negative attention is better than no attention at all. If the misbehavior is not disruptive to class activities, it is best to ignore it. Why? Because giving attention to the student who is misbehaving is, in itself, a positive reinforcer for misbehavior. Ignoring the misbehavior weakens it and, in time, extinguishes it.

Since it is difficult to ignore misbehavior completely, particularly if it is disruptive of others in the class, teachers occasionally reprimand offenders. When this happens, variable ratio reinforcement is being applied, and the misbehavior is strengthened rather than weakened. Worse, it is strengthened by the kind of reinforcement that produces the greatest persistence.[129]

How are we to understand the use of extinction in the classroom? Teachers need to take some misbehavior in stride and simply let it go unchallenged. Avoid a hair-trigger response to every instance of misbehavior. When students fail to trigger a reaction from teachers, which is the pay off they were seeking, they may misbehave less.[130] If the misbehavior continues, it will need to be addressed in a systematic way. I share two examples to illustrate the concept.

One afternoon I was lecturing in a Moscow classroom and noticed two students in the far corner talking with each other. Both were writing in their notebooks. They pointed to what they had written and talked back and forth with each other. The students around them did not seem to mind. I was frustrated by their behavior because I did not know if they were paying attention or not, but I decided to ignore their huddle for a while. After about ten minutes, they stopped talking with each other, turned their faces toward me, and paid attention for the remainder of the day. At our first break time, I asked them why they had been talking. One of the students had been confused early in the session, and the other student was explaining the material so he could understand what I was saying. I was glad I had simply ignored their "misbehavior."

On another day here in the States, I was presenting introductory material at the beginning of a course. A young couple sat at the front row of tables, obviously happy to be together. They looked at each other, smiled, whispered, wrote notes in each other's notebooks, and generally flirted their way through the 75-minute session. Though they were bothering me, it seemed to me that no one else in the class was bothered by their exchanges, so I said nothing. But the behavior continued through the whole session—they were enjoying each other's company much more than my overview of science as a way of knowing! "Ignoring their behavior" did not cause the behavior to be extinguished. When I dismissed the class, I quickly moved around behind the couple and knelt down between them. I explained how distracting their behavior had been to me that day. They were completely surprised that I had noticed them at all. I asked them not to behave this way again, but if they did, I would have to separate them. From that point on, they sat together on the back row of tables, but their behavior was much more fitting for masters' students. While some are skeptical about the use of extinction as a non-reinforcement technique, it can be effective for reducing and eventually eliminating previously reinforced, undesirable behavior.[131]

Generalization and Discrimination

Stimulus *generalization* occurs when subjects give the *same response* to similar, but not identical, stimuli.[132] Rats trained to respond to a one bell tone will also respond to a different bell tone.[133] Stimulus *discrimination* occurs when subjects give *different responses* to similar, but not identical, stimuli.[134] Such discrimination is essential for learning how to respond in different situations. We use cues, signals, or information in the environment to know when a given behavior is likely to be reinforced.[135]

In a classroom situation, discrimination learning requires that feedback—information about the accuracy or appropriateness of a response[136]—be given for both correct and incorrect responses.[137] In order for feedback to be effective, it must be specific, immediate, based on the performance made, and contain corrective information.[138]

Statistics students employ generalization as they learn how Pearson's r, linear regression, multiple regression, chi-square, Spearman rho and the Phi coefficient are alike. (All are statistical procedures that measure relationships among two or more variables). Students employ discrimination learning as they differentiate among these statistics of relationship by data type and desired outcome.

The mean, median, and mode are all measures of central tendency (generalization). The mean is the average of a set of scores, the median is the "middlemost" score in a set, and the mode is the most frequently occurring score in a set (discrimination learning).

Controlling Antecedents

One of the questions I hear frequently from students addresses the link between pigeons pecking disks and students sitting in classrooms. It is obvious that teachers cannot wait for students to randomly hit on an appropriate behavior so they can reinforce it. How do we establish a new behavior?

The answer is to provide a stimulus to encourage the proper behavior, which can then be reinforced. This prior stimulus is called an antecedent.[139] By doing this we modify the basic R-S association to an A:R-S association: the antecedent (A) leads to a voluntary response (R) which receives a reinforcing stimulus (S). The reinforcing stimulus increases the probability that the response will occur in the future.[140]

After Skinner had programmed pigeons to peck a disk to get a food pellet, he introduced a light. If the pigeon pecked the disk when the light was on, it received a food pellet. If it pecked the disk when the light was off, no food pellet was given. The light was an antecedent. "Peck when the light is on and get a pellet. Peck when the light is off, and there will be no pellet." In working with human learners, we use two types of antecedents, the cue and the prompt. A *cue* is a behavioral signal for what behaviors will be reinforced or punished.[141] A *prompt* provides information so that learners can respond to cues correctly.[142]

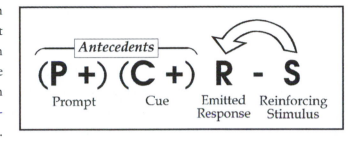

Cueing Behavior. Cueing is providing an antecedent stimulus just before a particular behavior is to take place.[143] Without cues, students make mistakes, which require correction. This leads to frustration. When teachers provide appropriate cues, students respond correctly, and receive reinforcement. This leads to satisfaction. For Skinner, the satisfaction—the consequence, the reinforcing stimulus— is the most important element in the chain. Cueing provides a proactive way to lead students to emit desirable behavior, which leads to satisfaction. Examples of cuing include the following:

- The teacher asks probing questions until students correctly solve a problem. (Questions provide cues to the solution)
- The teacher stands up at her desk in the front of the room. (The class focuses their attention on the teacher)
- The teacher asks a question of the class. (Students begin thinking of an answer)
- The teacher looks over the class after asking a question. (Students know he wants them to respond).[144]

Prompting. Prompts are verbal explanations of what cues mean. Prompts help students respond to cues appropriately. One of my students was a teacher of ninth graders who found it very difficult to quiet down when it is time to begin their Bible study. She was frustrated every Sunday because it took several minutes of pleading for the group to finally stop talking and give her their attention. By that time, they were disgruntled because they "had to study the Bible instead of talking with each other." She was upset because she had to fuss with them just to begin their study. She decided to experiment with Skinner's principles to see whether she could change this disruptive behavior. She explained the problem to them (difficulty in quieting the class) and suggested a solution. She recognized their need to talk with each other at the beginning of the Bible study hour. "But when it is time to begin, I will walk to the podium and open my Bible. When I do that, I am signaling that it is time to begin our study for the morning, and I'd like you to give me your attention." The prompt is her explanation. The cue is walking to the podium and opening her Bible. The target behaviors are to stop talking and turn their attention to the teacher.

The following Sunday, the ninth graders were talking excitedly with each other. At the appropriate time, the teacher walked from the back of the room to the podium, paused, placed her Bible on the podium, paused, and then opened it. Some grew quiet as she walked forward. More grew quiet as she stepped up to the podium. Most of the class grew quiet as she opened her Bible. There were small groups here and there still talking. She did not berate them nor speak to them. She spoke to the "most" who grew quiet. "Thank you all for remembering how we begin our class sessions. We have a very interesting passage to look into today, but let me start with a question." A few weeks later the teacher noticed that the class "naturally" grew quiet as she walked to the podium. She no longer needed to raise her voice. Indeed, she no longer needed to say a word at all.

Woolfolk gives a more complex example of students working in pairs in order to tutor each other. Working in pairs is the cue. The teacher prompts good peer tutoring behavior by providing a checklist of peer tutoring steps. As students learn the steps, the teacher extinguishes the list by having students no longer use it, though he reminds the students of the steps. He continues the process until no prompt for good peer tutoring is needed. The process of gradually removing prompts is called fading.[145] The teacher monitors progress, recognizes the good work of the pairs, and corrects mistakes.[146]

Encouraging Positive Behaviors through Behavior Modification

We have described principles of positive and negative reinforcement. We have presented ways to schedule reinforcement events to strengthen positive behavior. We have added to these corollary concepts to expand the scope of behavioral learning, and suggested ways to establish new behaviors with antecedents. There are six general approaches, which stand on this behavioral foundation, that are effective in initiating, establishing, and sustaining positive behavior. These are shaping, teacher praise, the Premack principle, token economies, self-reinforcement, and engaging parents as reinforcers.

Shaping. Most classroom behaviors—academic skills, social skills, language skills—are complex clusters of simpler behaviors. In these cases, teachers apply principles of behavioral learning step by step, moving learners ever closer to complex skill mastery. Shaping is a process of reinforcing a series of responses that increasingly resemble the desired terminal (complex) behavior.[147] The process of shaping moves from 1) reinforcing any response that in some way resembles the terminal behavior, to 2) reinforcing responses that more closely approximates the terminal behavior (while no longer reinforcing previous responses), to 3) finally reinforcing only the terminal behavior.[148] In training doctoral students to evaluate the doctoral proposals of fellow students, I provide a detailed checklist. As we move through the seminar, students use portions of the checklist to guide their evaluation of portions of proposals. By the end of the seminar, students are far more proficient in analyzing dissertation proposals. By this shaping process, they have also learned how to analyze their own proposal objectively, revising portions as needed.

In recent years, approaches for analyzing complex behavior systems have been created to guide application of behavioral principles. Three of these systems are Applied Behavioral Analysis (ABA), Functional Analysis, and Positive Behavioral Support, which we will describe at the end of the chapter.

Teacher Praise. When teachers acknowledge specific achievements with a sincere compliment, they reinforce the behaviors that made that achievement possible. Praise is feedback with an added affective (emotional) component. There is no reward a respected teacher can give—stars, candy, extra points—that has the reinforcing power of a sincere, targeted expression of praise. When learners move on to higher grades and different teachers, when stars, candy, and extra points are no longer given, the behaviors they reinforced often weaken (extinction). But heartfelt teacher praise continues to reinforce, even after teachers have passed away. Mrs. Nolan was my fifth grade teacher. Fifty years after being in her class, I find myself thinking, "Mrs. Nolan would have been proud of me for achieving this." She is still influencing my work.

After forty years of incessant humanistic emphases in education (see Chapter Thirteen), however, teacher praise has been reduced to handing out compliments to bolster self-esteem. This does not help change behavior.[149] To be effective in strengthening behaviors, praise must

- be genuine (flattery is obvious and de-motivating).
- be proportional to the level of performance (since excessive praise is flattery).
- focus on specific behaviors (rather than generally applied to all).
- come immediately after the behavior (delayed praise may reinforce wrong behaviors).

- award attainment of behavioral goals (not just participation in the process).
- not reward uninvolved students just for being quiet.[150]

Earlier in the text, we discussed "obvious truths" in teaching that research had shown to be wrong. Common sense tells us that praise is positive and should be used often, while criticism is negative and should be used rarely, if ever. Reality is more complicated. Students can perceive praise given for *effort* (rather than accomplishment), or for performance on *easy tasks*, as an indication that the teacher believes they have low ability (which is demoralizing). On the other hand, a critical statement such as, "Come on—you can do better work than this," communicates that the teacher really believes the student can master the task (which is highly motivating). In these cases, inappropriate praise hinders learning, and timely criticism enhances it.

Finally, teachers need to be sure that praise is focused on the better answers rather than the better students. When the best answers are praised consistently and appropriately, learners are encouraged to give better answers. When the best students are praised consistently, despite the quality of their answers, it conveys a sense of favoritism on the part of the teacher, and learning in the classroom suffers.[151]

Premack Principle. The Premack Principle is named for educational psychologist David Premack, who suggested (1965) using what *learners want to do* to reinforce what the teacher wants them to do.[152] Our four-year-old granddaughter loves to watch DVD videos. When Madi asks Gramma to watch a video with her, she may say, "Madi, let's pick up your toys (what Grandmother wants) and then we can watch a video (what Madi wants)."[153] When eating supper, Madi is often in a hurry to skip the meat and vegetables in order to get to dessert. "Madi, eat what's on your plate, and then we'll have a little dessert." The Premack principle is sometimes called "Grandma's Rule" for this very reason.[154] Our daughter Bonnie and her husband Robert use Premack's principle continuously to establish a "work first, play later" perspective. Madi's behavior demonstrates the power of the principle.

Speaking more generally, behaviors that naturally occur more frequently can be used as positive reinforcers for low probability responses.[155] Classroom examples include such things as these:

- Allow students to talk quietly with friends *after* they complete an individual worksheet.
- Exempt students from a homework assignment *after* they successfully complete a self-test.
- Exempt students from an exam *if* their daily average is above 90.

Teachers who say, "We'll go to recess first so that you'll be ready to settle down to your math lessons" miss Premack's point.[156]

Token economies. Teachers can strengthen positive behaviors in the classroom using a "token economy." A token is something that has little or no inherent value, but that can be used to purchase things that do have inherent value to learners. In society, money is our most common token. The paper and metal slugs have little value in themselves but have great value in what they can purchase.

One reason for the development of the token economy approach was the limited flexibility of more commonly used reinforcers. Candies and cookies, for instance, tend to lose their reinforcing value quickly when they are supplied continually. It is not always convenient to award free time for the opportunity to engage in a preferred activity immediately after a desired response. Social rewards (e.g., talking with friends) may not sufficiently reinforce some individuals. Tokens, however, can always be given immediately after desirable behavior, can be awarded according to one of the five schedules mentioned earlier, and can be redeemed for items or activities that have high reinforcing value to individual learners.[157]

In educational settings, students can accumulate checkmarks, gold stars, and happy faces, which they cash in later for any one of several reinforcers. A 2001 research study found that instructional activities such as doing math worksheets, working at the computer, engaging in leisure reading, and playing academic games are effective as educational reinforcers in token economies.[158]

Woolfolk cautions teachers that token reinforcement systems are complicated and time-consuming. Generally, they should be used only in three situations. First, token economies can motivate students who are *completely uninterested* in their work and have not responded to other approaches. Second, token economies can encourage students who have *consistently failed* to make academic progress. And third, token economies can be used to handle the class that is *out of control.*

In such situations, analyze the class environment to determine what might be triggering misbehavior. Are teaching methods and materials appropriate for the learners? Are class rules unclear or enforced inconsistently? Is the textbook too easy or difficult? Is the course pace too fast or slow? If these problems exist, the token system may improve the situation temporarily, but the students will still have trouble learning the academic material.

Some groups of students seem to benefit from token economies more than others do. Students with mental retardation, children who have failed often, students with few academic skills, and students with behavioral problems all seem to respond well to the concrete direct nature of token reinforcement.[159]

And yet evidence from a 2003 study showed that token economies have proven effective in getting college students to increase their degree of class participation.[160] Token economies, especially when combined with classroom rules and an appropriate delivery of reinforcers, are effective in reducing such disruptive classroom behaviors as talking out of turn, being out of one's seat, fighting, and being off task. "Reductions of 50% or more in such behaviors are not uncommon." Studies in 2000 and 2001 found that token economies are also effective in improving academic performance in a variety of subject areas. Token economies have been used successfully with individual students, groups of students, entire classrooms, and even entire schools.[161]

Self-reinforcement. Lev Vygotsky's cognitive views have been influential in recent years in modifying behavioral views. Sternberg lays out the process of self-reinforcement.[162] First, the learner receives a demonstration of the target behavior. Second, the adult models the behavior while providing guidance, talking aloud through each step. Third, the learner attempts the behavior without adult guidance, talking aloud to himself. Fourth, the learner attempts the behavior with faded self-guidance by whispering self-instructions. Finally, the learner practices the behavior with "covert self-guidance," speaking silently to himself.[163]

Involving parents. Three studies in 2001 found that home-based reinforcement programs are readily learned by parents and are effective in reducing undesired behaviors. Overall, this procedure has been successful in both reducing disruptive classroom behavior and increasing academic performance—for example, students spend more time on tasks and higher test scores.

The first step in a home-based reinforcement program is obtaining a formal agreement from parents and students to participate. Then a brief note or form is sent on a regular basis (daily or weekly) indicating whether the student exhibits the desired behaviors. For example, in response to the items "Was prepared for class" and "Handed in homework," teachers would circle "Yes" or "No." In response to a homework or test grade, the appropriate letter or percentage-correct designation is circled. The parents are then responsible for providing the appropriate reinforcement or punishment— for example, a temporary loss of privilege.[164]

Educational Operant Conditioning: Programmed Instruction

Designing a learning sequence that helps students attain competence requires three global steps. First, define the skill or competency to be learned. Second, determine what steps need to be taken to develop the defined skill or competency. Third, develop an instructional process that moves students through these steps to the defined skill or competency.

The finished product is a programmed instruction sequence, a "program,"[165] consisting of a series of instructional frames.[166] Each frame presents a small amount of material and a prompt of some kind—usually an objective question about the material presented in the frame. If the program is printed in a textbook format, options for answers will send them to various pages in the text. When students turn to the page associated with their answer, they are immediately told if their answer is right or wrong, and why. If they answered correctly, they are congratulated appropriately and given the page number for the next step in the sequence. If they answer incorrectly, they are given additional information and sent back to the original page to read the material and try again. Since the pages of the book do not follow each other sequentially, the reader-learner must answer each prompt correctly in order to discover the next instructional step in the sequence.

Computers have provided a more transparent way of sequencing frames, so that learners simply read the frame of material (less than a single screen), enter an answer on the keyboard, and receive immediate feedback, stepping their way to whatever competency the program has been written to provide. While computers are better able to present programmed materials, programmed instruction books can be used in areas where there are no computers or electricity.

By dividing the material into small portions and linking this with a required response from the learner, programmed instruction materials produce *maximum interaction* with the material, maximum individual feedback for answers given, and *maximum personal reinforcement*. Since programs are designed to provide what every learner needs to step through the frames successfully, *failure is minimized*. There is much less wasted time in stepping through the sequences, as compared to traditional classrooms, because each student proceeds according to their own abilities to learn.[167] Learners who finish sequences early can start another sequence, or, more likely in classroom situations, study additional materials, or work on other assignments.

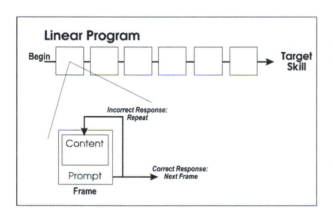

Instructional programs fall into two basic types. The *linear* program, developed by Skinner,[168] guides every student through every step of the program from beginning to end.[169] The major problem with linear programs is their inflexibility. The slower or less experienced student may not get enough help, and the faster or more experienced student may be bored.

The *branching* program, developed by N. A. Crowder (1961),[170]

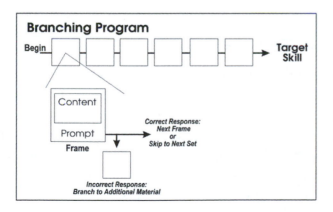

eliminates these deficiencies. Branching programs permit students to take different paths to the competency goal. If students answer a prompt incorrectly, they are directed to a sub-program that provides a more extensive learning experience before returning them to the original frame. If students demonstrate that they understand a series of steps in the program by answering initial questions correctly, the program may move them to the next series, skipping a number of repetitious frames.[171] Branching programs simulate the ability to adapt to the needs and abilities of individuals as learners travel along different branches, depending on responses. The degree to which this adaptation occurs depends on the sophistication of the program.

Skinner saw public education as disorganized and inefficient. Skinner's goal of education was to make students competent. Skinner's teaching machine approach provides several advantages. First, students must pay attention. Since responses must be given for the program to continue, students are actively involved in the learning process and not merely passive observers. Second, each student proceeds at his or her own rate. Learners are not held back by slower classmates or left behind by faster classmates. Third, reinforcement is immediate. There are no delays between the learner's response and the machine's feedback. Fourth, an educational program always uses positive reinforcement. Aversive techniques are never used. "Machines don't shout, hit, or tell parents." Fifth, machines can be set to keep track of errors automatically. These can be discussed later with the student, and in this important student-teacher dialogue, any misconceptions about the subject matter can be eliminated.[172]

Computers and Education

In the early years of computing, simple computer languages and primitive technology limited the sophistication of educational materials. In recent years, high definition graphics, multi-core processors, mass storage, and Internet connectivity has provided a rich resource for programming learning.

Computers as tools, teachers, and simulators

There are several ways computers impact the educational world. Computer literacy is the study of computers themselves, as well as computer use and programming. Computers are used as *learning tools* by providing assistance in word processing, data analysis, and communication. Computers serve as *teaching machines*, providing drill and practice exercises—sets of relatively simple exercises and problems that allow practice[173]—sophisticated multi-media resources, and tutorials—programs that mimic what the teacher does in class by teaching students new information and skills[174]—in a multitude of subjects. Computers permit *simulations* of activities that are either too costly or dangerous to actually do—flying a plane, conducting experiments with toxic chemicals, leading a squad in battle. Simulations can also demonstrate realities that cannot be observed directly, like human blood circulation, or 4-cycle engine operation.[175]

Integrated learning systems provide computer-based content, objectives, activities, and evaluations.[176] With the advent of artificial intelligence—programming which allows computers to simulate the learning process—*intelligent tutor systems* are being developed that modify their presentations according to learner strengths and weaknesses. The cutting edge of computer technology as I wrote in the original edition (1995) was *virtual reality simulation* environments.[177] Three-dimensional graphics, projected inside a helmet, surround the learner with a computer-generated world: a library, a plane's cockpit, a boxing ring, a battle zone. Virtual reality extends the simulation metaphor to integrate the learner inside the simulation.

Examples of simulation programs in 2009 include the following.[178] The program *Operation: Frog* (Scholastic) allows students to simulate the dissection of a frog. The program, complete with full graphics and video, allows students to rebuild the frog, providing practice in relocating its organs. The program *Great Solar System Rescue* (Scholastic) allows groups of students to role-play scientific experts who must collaborate with one another to find and rescue probes lost in the solar system. *Where in the World is Carmen Sandiego?* (The Learning Company) requires students to interpret clues, put new or known facts (such as the location of cities) to use, and to solve problems creatively.[179] Snowman (2009) suggests several Web sites to help teachers evaluate instructional software products.

- The Educational Software Selector (TESS): www.epie.org/epie_tess.htm
- Learning Resources and Technology Resources: lrt.ednet.ns.ca
- Software Evaluation Tool and Resources: kathyschrock.net/lcomputer
- World Village Educational Reviews: www.worldvillage.com/softwarereviews/educational.html[180]

Since Web addresses are volatile, I suggest you simply google "educational software" or "computer simulations" to find Web sites that provide the help you need.

Do Computers Enhance Learning?

While there is a wide range of possibilities in computer assisted instruction, computers are used primarily as learning tools and drill and practice teaching machines. Research has shown that programmed instruction allows for *faster acquisition* of material than more traditional classroom practices, but *not necessarily better* acquisition. As we stated earlier, learners who are already motivated to learn, and who already have a base of experience on which to build, are *de-motivated by the tangible rewards* of behavioral learning. Successful students find many computerized tutorials *boring*. They resent the overly repetitious frames.[181] Behavioral approaches are most effective for learners who have *little or no intrinsic interest* in the subject and *little experience* on which to build. Computerized materials, particularly the drill and practice type, are *best for disadvantaged learners*.[182]

Do computers enhance learning? This is like asking, "Do chalkboards enhance learning?" Or "Do PowerPoint presentations enhance learning?" The answer is, "It depends"—on how these tools are used. It is the same with computerized instruction.[183] There is nothing magic about computers. Technology cannot replace good educational practice.

A Bright Future for Computers in Education?

LeFrancois, writing in 1994 and quoted in the 1996 edition, presented predictions from computer-based proponents. I have taken the liberty to reflect on his words in 2009.

"Proponents of computerized education see a bright future in which students will have world-wide access to libraries, universities, research centers, and government agencies."

The Internet has indeed become a worldwide network, but unsavory elements make it a dangerous place for positive learning. Pornography, photo-shopped pictures, and commercial ready-made term papers distract, mislead, and offer short-cuts in ways unimaginable just a decade ago.

"They see students developing better skills in reading, writing, and arithmetic."

A good case can be made that just the opposite has happened. McDonald's now has cash registers with pictures on the keys so that high school students can press "cheeseburger" rather than remember its price and enter a number. The cash register also calculates the amount due and the correct change. Why learn arithmetic skills when a picture-based calculator gives the quick answer? Why pay attention to spelling when word processors spell-check? I find far more simple spelling mistakes in term papers now than twenty years ago: "too" rather than "two," or "are" rather than "our." These correct spellings remain unmarked by spell-check. Obviously, a *human* has not checked the writing.

Hand-held texting phones have generated a new language in which speed, not spelling, is important. Examples I picked up recently include "rufree@4?" ("Are you free at four?") and "lol cul8r" ("I am laughing out loud at what you said. I'll see you later.") After I wrote this section, I flew to a conference and texted my wife at work, "@g8" (at the gate). She was so proud! But these snippets of thought do little to enhance reasoning or proper language use.

"They envision stronger families as more people work on computers from their homes."

These idealistic dreamers assumed that being at home at the same time would mean the family would be "together." I am writing these words by computer, sitting at a large desk in our den.

My wife, nephew, and brother-in-law are sitting here in the den "with me." Each of them is working on their own laptop computer. The four of us are connected to programs, games, e-mail, and the Internet, but not to each other. At a recent "silent evening" event, eight of my wife's sign language students sat around the restaurant table. Every one of them was texting a friend that was someplace else. They were more connected by phone to others than they were to each other around the table.

To be fair, LeFrancois also referenced computer skeptics who had their doubts in the 1990s. They predicted **less developed academic skills as entertainment replaced reading and writing**. They saw **more violence in the schools** as students would act out the simulated computer violence they experienced in games. They saw, due to the cost of computers and software, a **greater academic gap between the haves and have-nots**. And finally, they saw **greater emphasis being placed on computer information than human advice**.[184] I think we would have to say the skeptics were more accurate than the dreamers were.

On the other hand, a 2005 research study analyzed data collected from tens of thousands of students in 31 countries and found that **performance in school was positively related to the use of a computer *at home*** for accessing the Web, to the availability of educational software *at home*, and to *moderate* computer use at school. Both low and high levels of use at school were associated with lower levels of achievement.[185]

A 2007 meta-analysis[186] of 52 studies published between 1983 and 2003 found a *moderate positive effect* for Computer-Based Instruction. Students who received CBI outscored those who received traditional instruction by an average of 21 percentile ranks.[187] Another 2007 study found that many teachers feel that being able to give their students meaningful access to "such a powerful learning tool" is, in itself, a significant reward.[188]

Despite positive findings, most education specialists agree that CBI cannot substitute for high-quality classroom teaching. "Successful teaching often depends on the ability of a live teacher to establish a positive emotional climate (by communicating interest, excitement, expectations, and caring), to monitor student actions and reactions (by reading students' verbal and nonverbal communications), and to orchestrate the sequence and pace of instructional events (by making additions, solutions, and modifications in lesson plans)."[189]

For this reason, Cuban (2001) concludes, "**Computers have been oversold** as a means to raise teacher and student productivity." Each type of computer program—drills, tutorials, simulations, integrated learning systems—"requires teachers to plan learning activities, interact with students, provide encouragement and feedback, and design assessments."[190]

Suggestions for Using Operant Conditioning Principles

Having looked at foundations and principles of traditional behavioral learning, we now summarize the significant ways teachers can promote positive behavior and lessen misbehavior in a classroom setting. The following 15 suggestions provide a teaching focus for the chapter.

1. Use cues (behaviors) and prompts (explanations of cues).

Use cues (behaviors) and prompts (explanations of cues) to help establish new behaviors[191] or warn of impending punishment.[192]

- "It is fine to talk with your friends as you come into class, but when I stand with my Bible open, I need to have your attention so we can begin." Standing with an open Bible is the cue. Explaining what the cue means is the prompt.
- "If you two boys continue to disrupt the class with your talking, and I have to speak with you about it again, I will speak to your parents."

2. Use an appropriate reinforcement schedule.

When introducing new material, give plenty of reinforcement by asking questions frequently.[193] After the new material has been learned, use an intermittent schedule to encourage persistence.[194]

3. Praise learner behaviors judiciously.

Insure that all learners receive some praise,[195] but praise learner behaviors judiciously.[196]

4. Use the Premack Principle.

Use the Premack Principle to identify reinforcers for your students.[197] This is done by observing the kinds of activities learners choose during free time, and then using those activities as reinforcers for instructional activities.

5. Provide feedback.

Provide clear, informative feedback on student work.[198] Remember that feedback is most effective when it involves both praise for correct answers and corrective information for wrong answers.[199]

6. Promote generalization.

Promote generalization by encouraging students to make comparisons and look for relationships among examples.[200]

- "In what ways did the actions of Barnabas reflect values taught by Jesus?"

7. Promote discrimination learning.

Promote discrimination learning by encouraging students to look for distinctives and contrasts among examples.

- "How did Peter and Judas, both disciples, differ in their reactions to their own betrayal of Jesus?"

8. Use negative reinforcement rather than punishment.

Use negative reinforcement ("relief") rather than punishment to curb inappropriate behaviors.[201]

- "Johnny, if you will work cooperatively with your project group for these last fifteen minutes, I won't tell your parents about your behavior today."

9. Use removal punishment ("penalty") rather than presentation punishment.[202]

- "Johnny, since you chose not to cooperate with your project group, please take your seat in the time-out corner."

10. Avoid reinforcing the behavior you're trying to punish.[203]

A reprimand is a positive reinforcer to one who is ignored most of the time. By giving attention to misbehavior, you reinforce it. Ignore minor behavior problems. Use cues and prompts to solve behavior problems before they occur.

11. Focus on student actions.

Focus on student actions, not personal qualities.[204] A common problem with teacher praise is that it goes to the best *students* rather than the best *answers*.

12. *Praise liberally, then require more.*

At the beginning of a school year or semester, praise appropriate behavior liberally and reward frequently. As student capabilities increase, require more effort for similar praise.[205]

13. *Avoid inadvertently rewarding misbehavior.*

Classroom behavior is far more haphazard than the controlled environment of a Skinner box. Check periodically whether you are inadvertently rewarding students simply by giving them attention for misbehavior.[206]

14. *Require responses.*

Require students to make frequent, overt, and relevant responses and provide prompt feedback.[207] My wife Barb does this in her American Sign Language classes by using her "vase of sticks." She writes students' names on Popsicle sticks, and keeps them in a pretty vase. During Q&A time, she asks a question, pulls a stick at random from the vase, and asks that student the question.

She lays the stick aside. When all students have answered a question, she returns the sticks to the vase and begins again. While it is true that students who have been selected can relax for the rest of the cycle, she asks enough questions that she goes through several rotations each week.

15. *Allow students to assist you in selecting a variety of reinforcers.*[208]

The best reinforcers are individualized for each student. It is difficult for teachers to discover what those reinforcers are. Student assistance helps supply meaningful reinforcers for teachers to use in applying the Premack principle.

Key Emphases from Traditional Behaviorism

The following twelve statements summarize essential distinctive of traditional behavioral learning. Use these terms to compare and contrast learning as defined in chapters 9 and 10.

1. The learner is a . . .	**MACHINE** Learning is programmed into the nervous system
2. The focus is on the . . .	**ENVIRONMENT** Environment determines behavior
3. Relationship of learning "whole" to its parts. . .	**WHOLE *EQUALS* SUM OF PARTS** The sum of the frames in a program equals the whole experience
4. Learning is . . .	**MECHANICAL** S-R bonds are stamped into the nervous system
5. The target learning domain is . . .	**PSYCHOMOTOR AND LOWER COGNITIVE** Drill and repetition best suited for knowledge and skills
6. The goal of learning is . . .	**BEHAVIOR CHANGE** Knowledge, understanding, and attitude are behaviors
7. Learning is strengthened by . . .	**REPETITION** The Law of Exercise
8. Learning is guided by . . .	**REINFORCEMENT** External rewards guide the direction of behavior change
9. Motivation keys on . . .	**DRIVES** Physical (primary) and psychological (secondary) drives
10. Feedback should be . . .	**IMMEDIATE, ON PERFORMANCE** Association of response and reinforcer requires contiguity
11. Best curriculum is . . .	**SIMPLE, SEQUENTIAL** Sequences of simple to complex, concrete to abstract frames
12. The Theory in Practice is . . .	**PROGRAMMED INSTRUCTION** Programs maximize reinforcement and minimize failure

Implications for Christian Teaching

What has been your reaction to this chapter on behavioral learning? What statements or positions caused you the greatest discomfort? What questions were raised concerning the role of the learner in the learning process? Now that you understand the basic positions of contiguity learning, classical conditioning, and operant conditioning, let's consider them from a Christian perspective.

Behaviorism as a philosophy

Issler and Habermas make a clear distinction between Behavioral learning theory and Behaviorism. *Behavioral learning theory* refers to explanations of how we act and why. *Behaviorism* is a "mechanistic, deterministic, metaphysical view about final causes of all human behaviors. As Christians, we can use principles from the former, but we must reject the latter."[209] Skinner believed that humans are as enslaved by their environments as his rats were by his experimental boxes. We are programmed, like a machine, by the environment in which we live. This is what Issler and Habermas mean by mechanistic. The environment controls behavior, and human ideals or emotions or will or profound ideas have little or nothing to do with it. And whoever controls the environment, controls people.[210] This is what Issler and Habermas mean by deterministic.

Jesus certainly did not agree with this mechanistic view of human behavior and personality. He said, "A good tree doesn't produce bad fruit; on the other hand, a bad tree doesn't produce good fruit. For *each tree is known by its own fruit*. Figs aren't gathered from thornbushes, or grapes picked from a bramble bush. A good man produces good out of the good *storeroom of his heart*. An evil man produces evil out of the evil storeroom, for his mouth speaks from the overflow of the heart" (Luke 6:43-45, italics mine). Behavior reveals the person within, but *there is a person within*. We are not helpless recipients of environmental stimuli, as Skinner suggests.

Jesus calls us to overcome the world (Rev 3:21) in His power, because He has already overcome the world (John 16:33). Paul reflects this same sentiment when he warns us, "Do not be conquered by evil, but conquer evil with good" (Rom 12:21). Paul believed we have power over our environment and demonstrated it in his own life. If we only had Skinner's ideas to guide us, we would predict that Paul stopped preaching the day he was stoned and left for dead outside Lystra (Acts 14:19). Instead, "he got up and went into the town" (14:20). He left the next day for nearby Derbe, but after leading many to faith in Christ there, he returned to Lystra again (14:21).

Behaviorism is appealingly simple,[211] an advantage in a scientific society that deems simplicity a virtue. Behavioral principles are relatively easy to master. And research has shown them to be effective.[212] But behaviorism is not universally accepted even among secular theorists.

Phillips and Soltis question Skinner's suspicion of non-observable internal states. Physics, the premier observational science, studies quarks (sub-atomic particles), which no one has seen.[213] Gravity is invisible, though its influence is not.[214] Why rule out the intellect?

Further, research has shown that behaviorism cannot explain how language develops. Young children can correctly understand sentences they've never heard before.[215] Sprinthall writes that traditional behaviorism should not be accepted at face value. There *are* differences between rats and children in the way they operate in the environment.

Further, research has shown that conditioning is not permanent or automatic, as Skinner believed.[216] We return, therefore, to Issler and Habermas: Christians can certainly use behavioral principles in strengthening positive behaviors without accepting the worldview of Behaviorism. We are not alone in rejecting the mechanistic, deterministic philosophy underlying conditioning theory.

Ethical considerations

We mentioned earlier that Ivan Pavlov was awarded the Nobel Prize in 1904 for his work in dog physiology. By the time of the Soviet October Revolution in 1917, he had become a world renowned scientist, having received an honorary doctorate from Cambridge University (1912) and the Order of the Legion of Honour from the Medical Academy of Paris (1915). On January 24, 1921, Pavlov received a special government decree, signed by Lenin, noting "the outstanding scientific services of Academician I. P. Pavlov, which are of enormous significance to the working class of the whole world."[217]

Pavlov had provided the Soviet State with behavioral tools by which its citizens could be shaped into the Soviet super-Man proclaimed, as we saw earlier, by Lev Vygotsky. Classical conditioning had an important place among the "scientific law of education" referenced by Vygotsky. American soldiers captured during the Korean War were confronted by these tools, which were known as brainwashing techniques. Classical conditioning and operant conditioning principles were used, along with brutal and relentless torture, to force POWs to make written and oral statements disloyal to the United States. It is estimated that one in three POWs committed treasonous acts while in captivity. As a result of the devastating effects on mind and morale of American forces captured in battle, President Eisenhower created the Uniform Code of Military Conduct, as well as special training, to combat the effects of physical torture and psychological conditioning.

When teachers use these same principles to quiet student talking, increase attention, improve homework efforts, and the like, are they *manipulating* behavior? Are they *brainwashing* their learners? Or, to ask the question more positively, "How do we use behavioral learning principles in an ethical way?"

Justified Purposes. Teachers are ethical in the use of behavioral techniques when they use them to help students succeed. Teachers manipulate learners when they shape them to teacher demands. For example, it is manipulative to threaten the loss of free time unless students talk quietly during small group discussion (because the teacher prefers quiet to murmuring).

Success in learning involves beliefs and rational thought and is more than conditioning that focuses on performance.[218] Teachers who use behavioral principles to enhance this larger perspective can do so ethically. Helping my students memorize a sequential string of related symbols and names through repetition prepares them to correctly use these symbols and names later in the course.

Student acceptance. If teachers use behavioral principles—reinforcers, and certainly punishments—to impose their own attitudes, beliefs, and values upon students, it is manipulation. Changes in learners should occur for reasons that learners accept.

There is a behavioral weight loss center in our city. Before treatment begins, counselors go through the various techniques used at the Center. Clients approve the treatment plan ahead of time. If at any time during the treatment plan, or during any session, a client chooses to stop a given technique, they are free to do so, simply by asking to stop. The goal is weight loss. The specific techniques applied to achieve that goal have the approval of the client. Given these conditions, no technique can be considered manipulative, even if it tends to be unpleasant,[219] because the client is in charge of its administration. When behavior changes have student cooperation, they are not manipulative.[220]

Honest rewards for honest behaviors. Some writers oppose the use of external reinforcers because the practice reflects a kind of bribery in the educational process. "Do this, and you will receive a reward." Such a view misunderstands bribery, which is paying someone to do something dishonest, illegal, or immoral. If the target behaviors are honest, and students are aware of the reinforcers being used, then reinforcement is not bribery.[221]

Justified purposes, student acceptance of techniques, and honest means toward honest ends provide helpful checks against the manipulative use of powerful behavioral tools.

Traditional Behaviorism in the 2000s

Recent textbooks[222] continue to cite research findings from the 1970s, 1980s, and 1990s, giving the impression that little work is being done in the area of traditional behaviorism. The work does continue, however. Recent developments in traditional behaviorism concern the complexity of student behavior in the classroom. Three new areas continue to address these complex behaviors.

Applied Behavioral Analysis (ABA)

Applied Behavioral Analysis (ABA) is the systematic application of behaviorist principles in educational and therapeutic settings. ABA is based on the assumptions that behavior problems result from past and present environmental circumstances. Those circumstances are studied in order to determine ways to modify a student's environment to promote responses that are more productive.[223]

Functional Analysis

Functional Analysis, or a Functional Behavioral Assessment, attempts to identify "significant, pupil-specific social, affective, cognitive, and/or environmental factors associated with the occurrence (and non-occurrence) of specific behaviors." This broader perspective offers a better understanding of the function or purpose behind student behavior. Behavioral intervention plans, based on an understanding of why a student misbehaves, are extremely useful in addressing a wide range of problem behaviors.[224]

Positive Behavioral Support

Positive Behavioral Support takes Functional Analysis a step further. After identifying the purposes that inappropriate behaviors may serve, a teacher (or team of teachers) develops and carries out a plan to encourage appropriate behaviors: alternative behaviors, modifying classroom environments, creating a predictable daily routine, providing opportunities to make choices, and adapting the curriculum.[225]

Ormrod suggests that the above procedures may be effective when other approaches have failed, but warns that these kinds of analyses are time-consuming.[226]

A Concluding Word on Traditional Behaviorism

We have updated many older citations with more recent texts, but not all. The essentials of behavioral learning have stood the test of time. Recent resources continue to provide both positive and negative views of behavioral learning. These sources cite the following negatives.

- Behaviorism suggests that information should be broken down into specific items that allows learners to display observable behaviors that can then be reinforced. Most of what is taught in schools cannot be effectively acquired through reinforcement of specific items of information.[227]
- Behaviorism cannot explain higher order functions such as language. For instance, a classic study by Chomsky and Miller (1958) demonstrated that even people with small vocabularies would have to learn sentences at a rate faster than one per second throughout their lifetimes if their learning was based on specific behaviors and reinforcers.
- Research suggests that offering reinforcers for engaging in intrinsically motivating activities—activities interesting for their own sake, such as playing a video game—can decrease interest in those activities.

- Some critics hold the philosophical position that schools should attempt to promote learning for its own sake rather than learning to gain rewards.
- Other critics argue that behaviorism is essentially a means of controlling people rather than a way to help students learn to control their own behavior.[228]

On the other hand, there are positives cited in contemporary literature.

- It is generally accepted that experience influences the ways we behave, and this idea at the core of behaviorism. For example, teachers understand that a timely, genuine compliment can increase both learner motivation and the way students feel about themselves.
- Supporters of behaviorism ask if we would continue working if we stopped receiving paychecks, and do we lose interest in our work merely because we get paid for it. The answer to their rhetorical questions is an obvious "no," a positive for reinforcement.
- Research indicates that reinforcing appropriate classroom behaviors such as paying attention and treating classmates well decreases misbehavior. Behaviorist classroom management techniques are often effective when others are not.[229]

In short, behavioral learning theory works well in situations for which it is well suited. But there are many other situations. We learn some behaviors simply by observing the behavior of others. We turn to this form of Behaviorism in the next chapter.

Chapter Concepts

Antecedent	Prompts and cues that creates new behavior that can be reinforced
Behaviorism	A mechanistic, deterministic view about final causes of all human behaviors
Branching program	Program that permits *different instructional paths* to the competency goal
Contiguity	Nearness in time or space
Continuous reinforcement	Reinforcing *every* occurrence of a desired behavior
Cue	A *behavior* that triggers a desired behavior (antecedent)
Discrimination	Subjects give *different responses* to similar, but not identical, stimuli
Elicited behavior	Behavior that is *drawn out* by a stimulus
Emitted behavior	Behavior that is made without a prior stimulus
Extinction	Weakening and eventual elimination of a response as a result of non-reinforcement
Feedback	Corrective information about the accuracy or appropriateness of a response
Fixed interval schedule	Reinforce behavior after a fixed amount of time ("Every Friday")
Fixed ratio schedule	Reinforce behavior after a fixed number of responses ("Every 5 problems")
Frame	A screen or page of material, and a prompt of some kind
Generalization	Occurs when subjects give the *same response* to similar, but not identical, stimuli
Intermittent reinforcement	The practice of reinforcing a desired behavior *periodically*.
Introspection	Looking within to discover feelings and sensations (Wilhelm Wundt).
Law of Readiness	When ready to respond, there is satisfaction in responding (Thorndike)
Law of Exercise	Repetition strengthens S-R bonds (Thorndike)
Law of Effect	Any response followed by pleasure strengthens the S-R bond (Thorndike)

Linear program	Guides every student through every step of the program from beginning to end
Negative reinforcement	Take away an undesirable activity or element (Positive effect)
Positive reinforcement	Provide a desirable activity or element (Positive effect)
Premack principle	Work first, then play. Use desired activities to promote needed activities
Presentation punishment	Provide an undesirable activity or element (Negative effect)
Primary reinforcer	Reinforcer linked to unlearned human drives (food, water, sleep)
Program	A sequence of instructional steps leading to a target competency
Programmed instruction	Educational method that uses programs to lead students to competencies
Prompt	An explanation of a cue (antecedent)
R-S bond	Association between an emitted response and a reinforcing stimulus (Skinner)
Reinforcer	Any element or activity that increases the probability of a particular behavior
Removal punishment	Take away a desirable activity or element (Negative effect)
Response	A behavior or action
S-R bond	Association between a stimulus and an elicited response (Pavlov, Thorndike)
Secondary reinforcer	Reinforcer linked to psychological needs (money, status)
Spontaneous recovery	After a time of extinction, a conditioned stimulus elicits a conditioned response
Stimulus	Perceivable unit of the environment that may affect behavior
Tabula rasa	Blank slate. Minds able to process sense data, yet devoid of content at birth
Variable ratio schedule	Reinforce behavior after a random number of responses ("Every x instances")
Variable interval schedule	Reinforce behavior after a random amount of time ("Every x minutes")

Chapter Objectives

Learners will demonstrate knowledge of the behavioral learning by. . .

- recalling the origins of Associationism-Connectionism, including contributions of Aristotle, Wundt, Watson, Pavlov, and Thorndike
- recalling distinctions among positive and negative reinforcement and two types of punishment

Learners will demonstrate understanding of behavioral learning by . . .

- differentiating between a conditioned stimulus and an unconditioned stimulus
- differentiating between S-R bonds and R-S bonds
- differentiating between primary and secondary reinforcers
- describing the effectiveness of programmed instruction in terms of reinforcement, failure, interaction, and individualization
- explaining how to initiate new behavior by using antecedents
- contrasting linear and branching programs

Learners will demonstrate appreciation for computers in education by sharing how the use of computers has personally enhanced their learning experiences.

Discussion Questions

1   Describe two specific instances of classical conditioning in your church or school. (Here's something to get you started: "The quickest way to quiet a church group is to say, 'Let's pray.'")

2   Compare and contrast S-R and R-S associations.

3   Explain the meaning of "P + C + R - S."

4   Give church-related examples of positive reinforcement, negative reinforcement, removal punishment, and presentation punishment.

5   What erroneous theology have you discovered that can be attributed to superstitious reinforcement? (Example: "I closed my eyes, opened the Bible at random, and pointed to a verse to get a word from the Lord.")

6   Differentiate between linear and branching programs. What experiences have you had with either type of program?

7   Compare and contrast learning experiences you have had in traditional versus on-line courses. Focus your comparisons on quality of learning, convenience, interaction with teacher, interaction with classmates, and overall experience. If you had the choice between these two forms of course in the future, which would you choose? Why?

7

SOCIAL BEHAVIORAL LEARNING

Albert Bandura: Social-Cognitive Learning Theory

"Shepherd God's flock among you . . . not lording it over those entrusted to you,
but being examples to the flock."

1 Peter 5:2–4

"Children have more need of models than critics."

—French Proverb[1]

Chapter Rationale

In the 1960s Behaviorists began to realize that operant conditioning provided too limited an explanation for learning.[2] While behavioral purists held on to traditional behaviorism, most have integrated cognitive processes[3] that cannot be directly observed, such as expectations, thoughts, and beliefs.[4] In a sense, these theorists returned to John Locke, who focused on experience as the source of all knowledge, but also spoke of the innate capacities of the intellect.

Albert Bandura led the way in this transition, beginning in the early 1960s, by observing that many of our most persistent habits and attitudes result from simply watching and thinking about the actions of others. Bandura's early work, which focused on social behaviors, was labeled Social Learning Theory.[5] He laid out his break with traditional behaviorism in his book *Social Learning Theory* (1977).[6] Social Learning Theory was considered a neo-behavioral approach to learning,[7] because it embraced cognitive elements, which Skinner opposed his entire life.[8]

In 1986 Bandura published *Social Foundations of Thought and Action: A Social Cognitive Theory*,[9] and Social Cognitive theory was born. Bandura continues (2008) to research and write, pushing his theory further into a cognitive perspective. In this chapter, we look at Bandura's original ground-breaking theory, the effects of modeling and imitation in learning, and the implications of both Social Learning theory and Social Cognitive theory in churches and Christian classrooms.

Chapter Overview

➤ Traditional Behaviorism and Social Learning Theory
➤ Albert Bandura: Social Learning Theory
➤ The Process of Social Learning
➤ Social Learning in Action: The Advertising Industry
➤ Observational Learning and Research
➤ Other Effects of Modeling and Imitation
➤ Using Social Learning Theory Principles
➤ Social Cognitive Learning Theory: The Role of Expectations
➤ Implications for Christian Teaching
➤ *Chapter Concepts, Chapter Objectives, Discussion Question*

Traditional Behaviorism and Social Learning Theory

Cognitive theorist Jean Piaget emphasized the interaction between mind and environment in his concepts of adaptation and equilibration, and proposed elemental cognitive structures called schemes to explain how we construct a mental representation of the world (see Chapter Four). These mental structures, and the mental processes that form them, are the very elements that Thorndike (S-R+) and Skinner (eR-rS+) denied in favor of bonds and reinforcement (see Chapter Six).

The problem that continues to plague traditional behaviorists, however, is that behaviorism simply cannot account for learning that occurs through modeling and imitation.[10] Many of our most persistent habits and attitudes[11] result from simply watching and thinking about the actions of others.[12] These rational behaviors simply cannot be explained as R-S bonds in the nervous system.

Albert Bandura proposed his Social Learning Theory to explain how behavior is changed through observation. The roots of Social Learning theory are found in 1940's research that disputed Skinner's assertion that all behavior change results from reinforcement.[13]

Albert Bandura: Social Learning Theory

Albert Bandura (1925–) became the acknowledged spokesman for social learning theory, writing the definitive work on the subject in *Social Learning Theory* (1977).[14] To explain some limitations of the behavioral model, Bandura distinguishes between the acquisition of knowledge (learning) and observable performance based on that knowledge (behavior). That is, Bandura suggests, "we all know more than we show."[15]

Social learning theory moved away from traditional behaviorism in three distinct ways. First, direct reinforcement of the observer is not necessary for learning to occur.[16] When an observer wants to be like the model, learning occurs simply by observing the model.[17] Learning is strengthened in the *observer* when the *model* is reinforced.[18] Bandura called this type of reinforcement *vicarious*[19]—a term that means, "in the place of another."

Second, social learning theory integrates cognitive processes into its behavioral view. Bandura includes in his theory rational encoding and mental representation of observed behaviors, which is a dramatic departure from traditional behaviorism. The fact that observers are selective in who they imitate, that imitated behavior may not occur until days after the observations, and that behavior occurs without direct reinforcement[20] indicates the working of rational processes.[21]

Third, Bandura sees behavioral learning as an interaction between learner and environment, in that the environment influences the learner, and the learner influences the environment.[22] Bandura's view is closely associated with Piaget's concept of adaptation and is called *reciprocal determinism*. This is a break from traditional behaviorists, who believe that all behavior is controlled by the environment—a view called *mechanistic* determinism.

Bandura is best known for his studies with Bobo dolls.[23] He made a film of one of his students, a young woman, essentially beating up a Bobo doll. The woman punched the clown, shouting "sockeroo!" She kicked it, sat on it, hit it with a little hammer, while shouting aggressive phrases. Bandura showed his film to preschoolers. They were then taken to a playroom where they found a brand new Bobo doll, along with a few little hammers. The children showed aggression toward the Bobo doll, punching it, kicking it, sitting on it, hitting it with the little hammers, and shouting "sockeroo," just as they had seen on the film.[24] Without reinforcement of any kind, these preschoolers showed they had learned aggressive behavior, which they acted out freely.

In another experiment, Bandura placed a child at a table with a toy. Nearby was a second table. In condition (1), no one was sitting at the other table. In condition (2), an adult sat at the second table playing with Tinker Toys. In condition (3), the adult played with Tinker Toys for one minute, then moved to a Bobo doll and began hitting, kicking, and shouting at it. Ten minutes after the experimental treatment, the child's toy was taken away, producing mild frustration. The child was placed in a second room, alone, and furnished with toys, including the toys in the first room. Under conditions (1) and (2), children showed little aggression. Under condition (3), children showed considerably more aggression.[25] Though the child was not directly reinforced for any behavior, the child's behavior changed in the direction of the aggressive model.

In yet another experiment, Bandura showed children a film of adults interacting with the Bobo doll. Children who saw an adult rewarded for aggressive behavior were more likely to behave aggressively toward the doll than children who saw the adult punished for the aggressive behavior.[26]

Bandura conducted many variations of the Bobo doll experiments. Models were rewarded or punished in a variety of ways, and the young observers were rewarded for their imitated behaviors. Models were made less attractive or less prestigious. When Bandura was criticized for using Bobo dolls to study aggression—a toy that is *supposed* to be hit—Bandura made a film in which a young woman beat up a *live clown*. When the children were taken to another room where they found a live clown, they proceeded to punch him, kick him, hit him with little hammers.[27]

The Process of Social Learning

Just how does social learning occur? Bandura describes four components of the process: paying attention, retaining information or impressions, producing behaviors, and being motivated to repeat the behaviors.[28] More simply, these stages are called attention, retention, production, and motivation.[29]

Attention

Learning begins when an observer pays attention to a model, or, put another way, learning begins when a model gains the attention of an observer.[30] Teachers secure the attention of learners, parents secure the attention of children, and pastors secure the attention of church members. Without

Social Learning Stages	
Attention	Observer **attends to the behavior** of a respected model
Retention	Observer **encodes behavior**, allowing for recall and mental rehearsal
Production	Observer **practices behavior** on his own, moving it from mind to body
Motivation	Observer may be **reinforced** directly or vicariously, or reinforce self

attention to the model's behaviors, learning will not occur. How do models secure the attention of learners?

Attention is attracted, *intentionally or not,*[31] by the perception that models possess high status, competence, popularity,[32] success,[33] or similarity.[34] Leaders, teachers, parents, and older children all possess a higher status than observers possess, and attract attention from them. Models who demonstrate desired expertise—whether it is in school subjects, sports, or hobbies—attract attention. Models possessing some form of popularity, celebrity, or fame—the "star" quarterback at school, Hollywood stars or professional sports' heroes, great leaders in history—attract attention. Finally, models who are similar to observers in some way—successful classmates, or persons of the same ethnicity, language, life condition, or interests—are generally more effective in attracting attention than models who are different.

There are some important exceptions to these general rules. First, competent models are more effective than incompetent ones, regardless of similarity.[35] Second, gender differences do not influence the modeling of academic skills, but observers tend to behave more like their own gender.[36] Third, observers with a negative self-concept or learning disability do better with a coping model (one who struggles and overcomes difficulties) than with a mastery model (one who performs well without difficulty).[37] Parents are the most important models,[38] but teachers play a powerful modeling role as well.

Teachers are natural models for their students because they are have high status in the classroom, and are consistently accessible.[39] Teachers improve their influence as models by being competent: making clear presentations, highlighting key ideas, providing interesting cues, and using novelty and surprise.[40] Given the general principles of attention, we can also say that teachers improve their influence by identifying with students, connecting course material to the needs of students, and demonstrating concern for students' success.

Yet teachers must do more than simply gain attention.[41] Teachers secure better performance from students only when they focus student attention on the targeted classroom behaviors to be learned.[42] Beyond specific class tasks and skills, teachers model general academic skills, such as problem-solving and creative thinking. They model specific skills by step-by-step demonstration. They model personal traits such as values and beliefs.[43]

Models need not be positive to be effective.[44] Years ago, while ministering among the Deaf in Irving, Texas, I met two deaf men who were leaders of their respective social groups. One was a deacon of First Baptist Church, a devoted Christian, a loving father and husband, a caring man. The other was an unemployed alcoholic who used his wife's paycheck for his drunken binges. He lied any time it was to his advantage. He also happened to be a good bowler.

Both men enjoyed the status of "chief of the tribe" in their respective, and very different, groups. Both men were held in high regard by their groups, and both men influenced the behavior of individuals in their groups—the one to live for Christ, and the other to live for self. In short, behavioral learning occurs when a lower status observer *carefully watches* the behavior of a higher status model. "Higher status," whether observing an outstanding deacon or drunken bowler, is a relative term and emphasizes the desires and intents of the observer.

Over the years I've served six churches as minister of education. In every one of these churches, I found teachers who taught their classes poorly. And yet these same teachers refused (by their consistent absence) to attend training conferences or teachers' meetings. Where did they learn that the poor methods they used were acceptable? I believe these poor teachers merely taught the way their (respected) teachers taught them. Though these model-teachers used ineffective and even damaging teaching methods, they in some way shared themselves, their time, and their love with their student-observers. When the student-observers became teachers themselves, they taught as they observed their teacher-model teach, poor methods and all.

Changing behavior under such circumstances is very difficult because the mere suggestion of better approaches may well be taken as criticism of the teacher-model who loved them. The only way to overcome these deeply ingrained behaviors is to love teacher-observers, build relational bridges to them, and, over time, model better approaches for teaching. The first step in modeling new behavior is to gain attention through competence, status, success, and similarity.

Retention

Retention—"retaining information or impressions"—refers to the observer's encoding of the model's behavior into memory[45] so that it can be remembered and produced at a later time.[46] Retention is closely related to Piaget's concept of accommodation, in which behaviors are converted into schema. The encoding may result in mental images[47] that allow observers to "see" the behavior in action, or in verbal descriptions of the behavior[48] that observers can recall.

Once behavior is encoded in memory, learners can mentally rehearse behaviors.[49] Mental rehearsal calls to mind Piaget's concept of "operation" by which learners mentally manipulate objects. Perhaps the most common expression of mental rehearsal is found in athletes. Downhill skiers stand in the starting gate and, with closed eyes, bob their heads and shift their bodies as if clearing the gates on the course. Gymnasts, as they wait their turn on the balance beam, walk through their routine in their minds, moving arms and taking steps in representations of the actual movements. This is mental rehearsal. The effectiveness of mental rehearsal is verified by experience. Those who focus on specific skills find performance on those skills improved.

Beyond anecdotal improvement reported by these athletes, brain research in the past decade shows that merely *thinking about an action* lights up[50] the same brain regions that *performing the action* lights up. The brain knows no difference between thinking about an act and performing the act.[51] Perhaps this is why Jesus warned about protecting one's thought life.

"You have heard that it was said to our ancestors, 'Do not murder, and whoever murders will be subject to judgment.' But I tell you, everyone who is angry with his brother will be subject to judgment" (Matt 5:21–22). "You have heard that it was said, 'Do not commit adultery.' But I tell you, everyone who looks at a woman to lust for her has already committed adultery with her in his heart" (5:27–29). Mental rehearsal changes brain states in the same way that actual performance does, for good or ill, preparing the way for acting out the observed behaviors.

Production

Attending to model behavior, encoding model behavior, and engaging mental rehearsal is not enough to produce skillful action. Production, or reproduction,[52] refers to the cycle of selecting and organizing the behavioral elements stored in memory, performing the behavior, and then refining performance on the basis of feedback.[53] Observers work the mental images out of their minds and into their bodies, developing encoded skills, by practicing the behaviors on their own.[54] Learners may need "practice, feedback, and coaching about subtle points" before they can reproduce the observed behavior, especially in instances where new behavior is being established. Practice *with feedback* makes the behaviors "smoother and more expert."[55]

Motivation

Bandura originally used the term reinforcement for this fourth stage, but his definition is broader than the direct reinforcement of traditional behaviorism. Bandura later began to use the broader term "motivation."[56] Bandura agreed with Skinner that **direct reinforcement** is valid. Using his four stages, we can illustrate direct reinforcement like this: an observer watches a model, encodes the model's behavior, performs the behavior, and is reinforced or punished as a result of the behavior.[57] In direct reinforcement, *observers* are reinforced on the basis of *their own behaviors*.

While Bandura saw direct reinforcement as valid, he also believed it is limited in its explanation of human behavior.

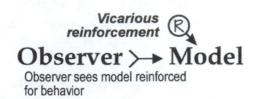

Observer sees model reinforced
for behavior

Bandura suggested a second type of reinforcement, the key to observational learning, which he called **vicarious reinforcement.**[58] Vicarious reinforcement describes how an observer is reinforced by how *the model* is reinforced or punished.[59] If the model is reinforced, the observer tends to imitate the behavior. If the model is punished, the observer tends to avoid that behavior. Vicarious reinforcement explains how we learn from the ways *others are affected.*[60]

While direct reinforcement can only be applied one learner at a time, vicarious reinforcement effectively reinforces entire classes or congregations simultaneously. Praising one student for his or her good question encourages everyone to ask good questions.[61] Asking the most talkative student to work quietly encourages all to work more quietly. Using the testimony of one member of the congregation as a sermon illustration encourages many to behave in a similar way. Much of the reinforcement experienced in classrooms is vicarious.[62]

Observer behaves according to own standards
and provides own reinforcement

Bandura suggested a third type of reinforcement, in which learners set personal performance standards[63] and control their own reinforcers.[64] He called this type of reinforcement **self-reinforcement**. Learners can observe their own behavior, judge it against their own standards, and reinforce or punish themselves for it.[65] Some students sit quietly, studying on their own, even when the class is allowed to talk quietly with each other. Some students go beyond research paper guidelines to use more references than required, or to write more pages than required. Some students study books beyond the reading assignments of a class. These are examples of self-reinforcement: students go beyond requirements for reasons valid for themselves. One writer suggests that the fact that young people tend to dress alike "illustrates the point. The similarity of dress reflects a sense of belonging, which is self-reinforcing."[66] Bandura's emphasis on rational encoding and self-reinforcement distanced his behavioral theory from Skinner, who opposed the influence of cognitive perspectives right up until his death in 1990.[67]

Social Learning in Action: The Advertising Industry

The advertising industry has long used social learning principles to sell products. Their goal is to garner attention and encode "use of their product" in memory so that, when confronted by a wide variety of products, consumers will choose their brand. I had to smile as I read over the examples I suggested in the first edition—*Pontiac* and excitement,[68] *Ultrabrite* and kissably-sweet breath, and *Virginia Slims* cigarettes' "You've come a long way Baby!" These examples, relevant in 1995, are so dated today that they seem like parodies. The truth is we experience high-tech examples of social learning every time we watch a commercial—beautiful, exciting, energetic people enjoying "the product," whether it is a beverage, a new car, or a wheelchair. The message is clear. *If you want excitement, passion, fun, or status, then you need our product.*

In summary, Bandura separated the acquisition of knowledge (learning) from the production of behavior (performance). Learning occurs through the rational encoding of observations. Behavior based on that knowledge occurs as a result of motivation. Perhaps the most telling distinction between Skinner and Bandura is this: while Skinner believed that emitted overt responses (eR) preceded reinforcement (rS⁺) and learning, Bandura showed that learning—*encoding behaviors*—occurs through observation before learners begin to make overt responses.[69]

Observational Learning and Research

Observational learning, an educational moniker for Social Learning Theory, has been found to be a powerful force. A 1996 study found that observational principles enabled learning-challenged preschoolers to learn basic first aid lessons. A 1998 study found observational learning helped children overcome their fear of water in a physical education swim class. Studies in 1997 and 1999 found videotaped models were effective in teaching instrumental music.[70]

Bandura is best-known, however, for his work on television violence, which began in the early 1960s and continues to the present. He demonstrated that exposure to television violence can produce at least four effects in viewers. First, it *teaches aggressive styles of conduct* by modeling violent reactions to life situations. Second, it *weakens restraints* against aggression by glamorizing violence. When good triumphs over evil violently, viewers are even more strongly influenced. Third, it habituates and *desensitizes reactions to cruelty*. And finally, it *shapes our images of reality*. As an example, only 10 percent of major crimes in American society are violent, but on television, *77 percent* of major crimes are violent. Excessive exposure to televised violence increases people's fear of becoming crime victims. Bandura noted (1997) that "children and adults today have unlimited opportunities to learn the whole gamut of homicidal conduct from TV within the comfort of their homes."[71] It has only gotten worse in the past ten years as cultural libertarians seek to televise, as entertainment, the breaking of every social taboo. This is doubly disturbing, given Bandura's experiments showing that television viewers learn behaviors as effectively from *televised* models as from models in real-life.[72]

Bandura's original research in the early 1960s—focusing on aggression and the Bobo doll—led television broadcasters and the Federal Communications Commission to set limits on the amount of violence that could be broadcast over television. Over the next three decades, these restrictions were relaxed. Not only did the amount of television violence increase, but the nature of the violence became more vivid and graphic. Video games have become more violent, and in their wake, violence is increasingly acted out in homes and schools, and on the streets.

One example of the renewed interest in television violence is a 1994 study on the effect of watching *Power Rangers*, a popular children's program. After watching Power Rangers, children were found to "harass, karate kick, and shove playmates." Parsons concludes his (2001) discussion of observational learning by saying the "potential power of observational learning in the subtle or not-so-subtle effects on children that may result from their observing television, movies, and real adult models, including teachers, are things that need to be considered, reviewed, and researched."[73]

Other Effects of Modeling and Imitation

Modeling and imitation produce new behaviors,[74] as we have seen. There are four other effects as well that can be induced through modeling. First, modeling can *strengthen inhibitions*. An inhibition is a "self-imposed restriction on one's behavior."[75] *Inhibitions* dampen behavior, causing one to refrain from a behavior because someone else refrains.[76] Observers know how to perform the act, but simply don't. "Should we begin eating our salads?" Meredith and Chris ask themselves at the posh banquet. They look at the head table to see if the hosts are eating. They aren't, so they wait.

Second, modeling can *weaken inhibitions*. Disinhibition encourages inappropriate behavior, causing one to behave in a certain (inappropriate) way because someone else does without being punished.[77] A youth group is having a Bible fellowship where pizza is served. The leader announces the ground rule is "two slices of pizza," so that there is enough for everyone. John notices that some take four or five slices but are not reprimanded for it. So he takes four slices as well.

Third, modeling can *facilitate existing behaviors*. *Facilitation* encourages appropriate behavior, causing one to do something (positive) that he normally does not do, because he lacks sufficient motivation—for example, beginning to applaud.[78] As another example, Jose sits quietly in class, mulling over a question. But he remains silent. Several students ask questions and receive both good answers and warm encouragement. Jose raises his hand and asks his question.

Fourth, modeling can *arouse emotions*. Natasha observes the uneasiness of a diver on a high board and becomes more fearful of diving herself. Zhenya sees the pride of accomplishment in a classmate successfully solving a difficult statistics problem, which causes him to attempt to solve similar problems in the future.[79] In these last four instances, existing behaviors are hindered or encouraged, but no new behaviors are learned. Yet we do see changes in affect (emotions) and cognition (thinking).

In all these examples, we see *direct* modeling at work, in which an observer imitates the behavior of a model. Social learning theorists, however, also see power in *symbolic* modeling, in which learners are presented models in books, plays, movies, or television.[80] Christian teachers employ symbolic modeling when we encourage learners to imitate selected behaviors of Bible characters, or great men and women of faith in history. Finally, we can use *synthesis* modeling, in which learners combine portions of observed acts.[81] Madi sees her father open a cupboard door and her mother climb a step-stool to get a book from a shelf. Later she climbs the step-stool and opens a cabinet door to get a cookie for herself.

In summary, modeling forms the heart of social learning theory. Children are better readers when parents read at home. Beginners master new athletic skills more effectively when shown specific techniques for improving performance. Children are less likely to use vulgar language when people around them refuse to use such terms. While one might make the case that such examples merely reflect Skinner's emphasis on the environment, there is a critical difference between Operant Conditioning and Social Learning theory. For Skinner, behaviors must be emitted and then reinforced in order to be learned. For Bandura, all that is necessary is for the behavior to be observed in a respected model.

Using Social Learning Theory Principles

Modeling and imitation happen whenever people are together. Those with perceived lower status observe how to behave from those who perceived higher status. Whether we're in a classroom, or church meeting, at a party, or formal dinner, observational principles are at work. We have suggested many ways to use Social Learning Theory as we have worked through it. Let's focus on what teachers can specifically do to enhance an intentional learning process in church and classroom.

Teaching New Behaviors

Teachers are effective models in teaching new behaviors as they demonstrate, clearly and systematically, the skills under study.[82] They do this by focusing attention on critical elements of the skill, thinking out loud as student questions are considered,[83] using step-by-step demonstrations with verbal explanations, and contrasting good and bad examples.[84] They improve modeling by showing enthusiasm for the subject they teach.[85] Behaviors are as wide-ranging as life—how to treat people, how to use a commentary or encyclopedia, how to pray, how to use a concordance, how to ask a question, how to share our faith, how to dress, how to speak, how to listen, how to be patient in the face of frustration. The *ways teachers behave* in the classroom teach far more than the *words they speak*.

Woolfolk cites an example of a preschool teacher getting into the sandbox with her students to show the difference between "playing with sand" and "throwing sand."[86] Actions definitely speak louder than words. Therefore, successful teacher-models live out before their students what they verbally explain to them.

Strengthening or Weakening Inhibitions

The contagious spread of behaviors in the class, whether good or bad, through imitation from student to student, is called the *ripple effect*.[87] Students who break rules, misbehave, turn work in late, or engage in other inappropriate behavior will encourage others to do the same if their behavior is not corrected. A warm, but firm, reprimand of those who misbehave will *strengthen the inhibition to misbehave* in other students in the class. Docking every paper that is turned in late will encourage others to submit their work on time (the word will get around without public announcements). Being "gracious"[88] in accepting work late without penalty will only encourage others to be late as well.

On the other hand, students may be inhibited in asking questions because they were humiliated by a former teacher for asking "dumb" questions. This is particularly true at the beginning of a semester as students look for clues about acceptable behaviors in the class. Teachers *weaken the inhibition to ask questions* by being open to student questions and praising student willingness to ask them. Gentle treatment and high praise for students who volunteer to participate early in the semester encourages others to participate as well.

Social Cognitive Learning Theory: The Role of Expectations

Bandura continued to push the cognitive envelope of his social learning theory. In 1986 he published *Social Foundations of Thought and Action: A Social Cognitive Theory*,[89] and Social Cognitive theory was born. Some textbooks use the newer label to describe Bandura's original theory.[90] But there are differences.

Social Learning Theory, as we have just seen, emphasizes vicarious reinforcement and observational learning. It is a behavioral theory with cognitive elements. Bandura's goal in Social Cognitive theory is to present a far more complex view, explaining how learning results from interactions among three elements: (1) personal characteristics, such as thought processes, self-perceptions, and emotional states; (2) behavioral patterns; and (3) the social environment, such as interactions with others. Growing out of this work are three related areas: **self-control** (controlling one's behaviors in the absence of reinforcement or punishment), **self-regulation** (consistently using self-control skills in new situations), and **self-efficacy** (how capable one feels to handle particular tasks).[91] Space does not permit detailed explanations of each of these branches,[92] but perhaps a look at the role of "expectations" would provide a helpful perspective into current research.

The manner in which learners (or their models) are reinforced in the present creates expectations—mental states of anticipation—for future behaviors. Expectations affect how people process new information and influence people's decisions about how to behave. When an expected consequence does *not* occur, this produces a reinforcing or punishing effect in and of itself.[93]

For example, students discover on the first exam that all of the questions come directly from the textbook. Not a single question comes from the class lectures. Students will read the textbook more carefully, but miss class more frequently. If, in another class, all the questions on the first exam come directly from class lectures, and none from the textbook, students will attend class consistently, but rarely open their textbooks.[94]

For years, Albert Bandura's Social Learning theory was presented as an alternative approach to behavioral learning. Social Cognitive theory moves Bandura's work far closer to Cognitive Constructionist (Piaget/Vygotsky), Discovery (Jerome Bruner), and Information Processing models of learning. We will look at these in Chapters Eight and Nine.

Despite the violence in contemporary television programming, and Bandura's warnings about the effects of viewing violence, the Academy of Television Arts & Sciences awarded him the 2007 Rogers Award for Achievement in Entertainment-Education. "The Rogers Award honors exceptional creativity in the practice of entertainment-education and excellence in research on the use of entertainment to deliver pro-social messages aimed at improving the quality of life of audiences in the United States and abroad." The award was given on September 19, 2007, in Los Angeles.[95] The citation continues:

> Importantly, Bandura's experiments showed that audience members learn models of behavior as effectively from televised models as from ones in real-life. These principles of role modeling, derived from the Bobo doll experiments and articulated in Bandura's social learning cognitive theory, were creatively employed by Miguel Sabido at Televisa, the Mexican national television network, to produce seven entertainment-education telenovelas between 1975 and 1982, including *Ven Conmigo*, which was about adult literacy. Data gathered by Mexico's Adult Education System showed that between November 1975 and December 1976 (the period during which *Ven Conmigo*, the telenovela promoting adult literacy was broadcast), 839,943 illiterates enrolled in adult literacy classes in Mexico.[96]

There was no mention in the citation about how prime-time televised models affect children's views on religious faith, homosexuality, honesty, racism, politics, or even violence, which formed the focus of Bandura's work for decades.

Implications for Christian Teaching

We addressed the social context of Christian growth and learning in Chapter One, when we presented the Central Pillar of "relationship building." Stones polished by the surf, or left rough in their isolation.

We addressed the social context of learning in Chapter Four, as we studied Piaget's "social interaction" of individuals, and Lev Vygotsky's socio-cultural views of education. "No man is an island" expresses a deeply human component of life, part of God's design.

The Church is a body of believers drawn from all walks of life and placed, intentionally together, in a social context for one valid reason, namely, their faith in Jesus Christ. The Church is a context for social learning, in which those who are mature—rationally, emotionally, relationally, spiritually—are models for converts and young Christians.[97] The apostle Paul underscores the importance of social learning in Colossians 3:8–17.

Social Context and Garment Change

Paul uses the image of clothing to address the need for changed lives in the Colossian Christians. He is writing to believers (3:12), spiritually clean because of their faith in Christ, but worldly in the ways they behave. His description of what they must "put away" or take off, on the one hand, and "put on" on the other, paints a vivid image of the **social dimension** of Christian learning.

A farmer works in the field all day. He comes in from the field, lays aside his dirty, sweat-stained clothes, and bathes. Now clean, he returns to his soiled work clothes and puts them on. This was the state of the Colossian Christians, "washed" (saved) and dressed in soiled clothing (lifestyle).

What *are* these sweat-stained filthy rags we are to take off? Paul lists the behaviors of "anger, wrath, malice, slander, and filthy language from your mouth" (Col 3:8). Take off *anger,* which is "an abiding, settled, and habitual anger that includes in its scope the purpose of revenge."

Take off *wrath*, which is "the boiling agitation of the feelings, a sudden violent anger."

Take off *malice*, which is ill will toward others, a state of "malignity, ill-will, desire to injure, wickedness, [and] depravity."

Take off *slander*, which is "vilification of others, slander, detraction, [and the use of] speech injurious to another's good name."

Take off *filthy language*, which is "foul speaking, [or] low and obscene speech."[98] Like the odorous clothes of a field hand, these behaviors—anger, rage, slander, and abusive language—need to be replaced with garments fit for a clean body.

Paul says the garments we need to put on are "heartfelt compassion, kindness, humility, gentleness, and patience" (Col 3:12). Put on, "clothe with, envelope yourself with,"[99] the pure garment of *heartfelt compassion*, which is soft-hearted concern, "tender mercies, affections" toward others.

Put on the soft garment of *kindness*, which is "a gentle, gracious disposition" toward others, springing from compassion. Those dressed in such garments see a need and respond, not only with tender feelings, but by tangible help.

Put on the linen garment of *humility*, which is "having a humble opinion of one's self, a deep sense of one's (moral) littleness, modesty, lowliness of mind." Humbleness of mind means thinking rightly about ourselves before God, and among others. Not too high, which is self-aggrandizement, and not too low, which is self-depreciation. True humility is recognizing our strengths and our weaknesses. We thank God for the strengths (for they are gifts given by Him), and then use those strengths to help others in their weakness. We ask God to help us in our weaknesses (we are powerless to overcome them alone), and allow others to minister to us as we need. Our strengths in the Lord allow us to be useful and have purpose. Our weaknesses keep us from becoming self-sufficient and arrogant.

This allows us to put on *gentleness*, or meekness, which is "an inwrought grace of the soul, that temper of spirit in which we accept God's dealings with us as good, and therefore without disputing or resisting. . . . This meekness, however, being first of all a meekness before God, is also such in the face of men, even of evil men, out of a sense that these, with the insults and injuries which they may inflict, are permitted and employed by God for the chastening and purifying of His elect (Trench)." Gentleness allows us to treat others, whether above us or below us, with respect.

Without humility, we cannot be gentle. Self-important people look down on others, or worse, keep them under their control and authority. Teachers and pastors often use their positions, not as humble servants, but as domineering kings. Self-depreciating people tend to criticize others, berate them, complain about what they do. Neither autocratic control nor whining criticism is gentle. With the appropriate mental attitude of humility, we help those weaker than us because in our strength we know that they are no threat. We can also praise those who do well what we cannot, because their success does not take away from our own.

Barnabas is my favorite example of Christian humility. Barnabas championed Saul before the fearful disciples (Acts 9:26–28), and later brought him to Antioch to teach with him (11:25–26). Barnabas is listed first among Antioch's teachers, while Saul is listed last (13:1). The Holy Spirit selects "Barnabas and Saul" for a mission trip (13:2). When Saul becomes Paul, and takes over the mission team in Cyprus ("Paul and his companions," 13:13), older Barnabas does not object. Later, after his famous break-up with Paul over the young quitter, John Mark (15:37–40), Barnabas takes his nephew with him to Cyprus, and disappears from history. But Paul, to his credit, eventually learns to appreciate John Mark, thanks, no doubt, to the continued influence of Barnabas. He asks Timothy in his last letter to bring John Mark to him in prison "for he is useful to me in the ministry" (2 Tim 4:11). Paul was martyred soon after this, and John Mark went on to write the first Gospel, the Gospel of Mark. Barnabas is a prime example of Christian humility.

Finally, Paul says we are to put on *patience,* which "speaks of the man, who, having to do with injurious persons, does not suffer himself easily to be provoked by them, or to blaze up in anger. The word expresses patience under the ill-treatment of others." Patience, or long-suffering, speaks of persistent emotional control even in the face of mistreatment by others. And "over all these . . . put on love" (Col 3:14). Paul completes the picture. The well-dressed first century man wore an inner tunic, an outer tunic, and a cloak, all held in place by a belt. In the same way, the well-dressed Christian wears spiritual garments, held in place by the belt of agape-love (Col 3:14).

What is striking to me is that these characteristics are **social** in nature: anger and wrath *toward others.* Slander and abusive talk *toward others.* Compassion and kindness *toward others.* Humility and gentleness *toward others.* Persistent patience *toward others.* We eliminate evil social behaviors and develop godly social behaviors as we interact with and relate to others. This social perspective of spiritual growth calls to mind *Jesus'* miraculous raising of His friend Lazarus from the dead. "'Lazarus, come out!' The dead man came out bound hand and foot with linen strips and with his face wrapped in a cloth" (John 11:43–44a). But He told the *people standing around him* to release him from his old grave clothes. "Jesus said to them, 'Loose him (from his grave clothes) and let him go'" (John 11:44b).

Jesus gave Lazarus new life. His friends and family changed his dead man's linens for clothes fit for one now alive. Jesus has given us new life by means of our faith in Him and His work. Our quickening from death to life happened in an instant, when we placed our faith in Him. Our spiritual development, however, is a Spirit-energized social learning process in which we interact with the Lord and with each other in His name. The Church is the social context, the Bible is the content, and the Spirit is the Enabler of supernatural change as we work together, live together, reason together, and overcome disagreements and differences together.

Social Context and Modeling

Finally, Paul challenged the hypocrisy of religious leaders who speak one thing and live another. He writes, "Now if you call yourself a Jew, and rest in the law, and boast in God, and know His will, and approve the things that are superior, being instructed from the law, and are convinced that you are a guide for the blind, a light to those in darkness, an instructor of the ignorant, a teacher of the immature, having in the law the full expression of knowledge and truth—**you then, who teach another, do you not teach yourself?** You who preach, 'You must not steal'—do you steal? You who say, 'You must not commit adultery'—do you commit adultery? You who detest idols, do you rob their temples? You who boast in the law, do you dishonor God by breaking the law? For, as it is written: 'The name of God is blasphemed among the Gentiles because of you'" (Rom 2:17–24).

Paul could easily ask us—seminary professors and students, pastors, missionaries, leaders, teachers—the same questions. Our lifestyles, the way we choose to behave every day, ripple outward to those around us, whether we are aware of our influence or not. As we grow and use our spiritual gifts, we become increasingly powerful models for others. This is why Paul warns us to "Let the word of Christ dwell in you richly as you teach and admonish one another with all wisdom, and as you sing psalms, hymns, and spiritual songs with gratitude in your hearts to God" (Col 3:16). It makes a difference! May God bless you as you become a model worthy of imitation, in Jesus' name.

"Shepherd God's flock among you . . . not lording it over those entrusted to you, but **being examples to the flock**" (1 Pet 5:2–4).

Chapter Concepts

Attention	Stage 1: The act of focusing the mind on the behavior of a (respected) model
Cognitive Social Theory	Learning is interaction of personal, behavioral, and environmental factors
Direct Reinforcement	Observers are reinforced for their own behavior
Model	A person of higher status, whose behavior is attractive to others
Modeling	The process of influencing the behavior of an observer
Motivation	Stage 4: Stimulating behaviors of observers
Observational learning	Learning behavior by observing and imitating models
Observer	A person of lower status who imitates the behavior of models
Production	Stage 3: Observers perform imitated behaviors on their own
Retention	Stage 2: Observers cognitively encode behaviors of models
Self-Reinforcement	Observers reinforce their own behaviors by personal standards
Social Learning Theory	Learning by observation and imitation without direct reinforcement
Vicarious Reinforcement	Observers are influenced by seeing models rewarded or punished

Chapter Objectives

Learners will demonstrate knowledge of the Social Learning theory by . . .

- recalling the four stages of social learning
- recalling the three types of reinforcement suggested by Bandura

Learners will demonstrate understanding of Social Learning theory by . . .

- explaining three basic ways the theory differs from traditional behaviorism
- differentiating between Skinnerian reinforcement and vicarious reinforcement
- explaining at least one Bobo doll experiment
- creating a fresh example for each stage of social learning
- contrasting vicarious reinforcement and self-reinforcement
- defining inhibition, disinhibition, and facilitation in their own words
- contrasting direct reinforcement and direct modeling
- contrasting direct, symbolic and synthesis modeling
- explaining the implications of the ripple effect for classroom teaching

Learners will demonstrate appreciation for Social Learning theory by . . .

- sharing a televised commercial which has been effective in causing them to try a product
- sharing an experience in which an expectation influenced their behavior
- testifying about behavior learned from an important model in their lives

Discussion Question

1 Early Christians were severely persecuted by the Romans for refusing to renounce Jesus as Lord. They were thrown to wild animals, set afire as torches for Nero's parties, and forced to fight as gladiators. It is very difficult to explain voluntary martyrdom using Skinnerian reinforcement and punishment. How would Social Learning theory explain their behavior?

COGNITIVE LEARNING I

Jerome Bruner and Discovery Learning
Cognitive, Social, and Radical Constructivism

"For as he thinks within himself, so he is."

Proverbs 23:7

"Do not conform any longer to the pattern of the world, but be transformed by the renewing of your mind."
Romans 12:2a

If you wish to know the mind of a man, listen to his words.

—Chinese Proverb[1]

Chapter Rationale

Cognitive learning theory emphasizes the *thinking* of students, rather than their behavior or attitudes.[2] The apostle Paul wrote, "Do not conform any longer to the pattern of the world, but be transformed by the renewing of your mind" (Rom 12:2a). Paul saw the mind as the center of activity both for conforming to worldly patterns and for being transformed according to God's will.

Building on the ideas of Jean Piaget, we consider the ideas of Ernst Mach, Max Wertheimer, Wolfgang Kohler, and Jerome Bruner for constructing meaning. How do we learn from the world around us? What role does perception play in the learning process? Chapter Seven presents the historical development of cognitive theory, from the early 1900s to the present state of Cognitive Constructivism.

Chapter Overview

- ➤ Historical Roots
- ➤ Jerome Bruner and Discovery Learning
- ➤ Cognitive Learning Theory in the 2000s
- ➤ Contemporary Constructivism in the 2000s
- ➤ The Teacher's Role in Constructivist Classrooms
- ➤ Constructivist Outcomes: The Nature of Reality and Knowledge
- ➤ Questioning Constructivist Claims
- ➤ Constructivism and Christian Teaching
- ➤ *Chapter Concepts, Chapter Objectives, Discussion Questions*

Historical Roots

Cognitive learning theories are explanations for learning that focus on the internal mental processes people use in their effort to make sense of the world.[3] Cognitive theorists believe, in contrast to behaviorists, that non-observable cognitive processes, based on human perception, can be studied in a scientific manner.[4]

Perception is the act of attaching meaning to information we receive from the world around us. Cognitivists view learning as a reorganization of perceptions. Learners develop a clear understanding of the world, or any subject in the world, through perceptual reorganization. Cognitive theories focus on the *mind* rather than the nervous system, *insight* rather than A-R-S bonds, and *understanding* rather than behavior. They see learners as conscious, perceiving thinkers, able to acquire meaning from the world.[5] Certainly, say cognitive theorists, one can condition children to associate bits and pieces of information. But without an underlying understanding of the information, the associated bits remain virtually useless.[6] This perspective of learning drives all of the cognitive theories.

Cognitive theories grew out of Gestalt psychology, which developed in Germany in the early 1900s and entered America in the 1920s. *Gestalt* is roughly translated as *configuration*[7] (or *pattern*[8]) and emphasizes "the whole"[9] of human experience. We will analyze several pioneers in cognitive learning—Ernst Mach, Max Wertheimer, Wolfgang Köhler, and Kurt Lewin. Then we'll focus on Jerome Bruner, who, more than any other, overcame Behaviorism's hold on educational psychology, and changed the direction of American education in the 1950s.[10] Finally, we'll focus on Constructivism, a present day revolution in educational psychology,[11] which is founded on the work of Jean Piaget, Lev Vygotsky (see Chapter Three), and Jerome Bruner.

Wilhelm Wundt (1832–1920)[12]

You will remember that early behaviorists readily embraced Wundt's concept of a "basic element" in human experience. Gestalt psychologists, on the other hand, opposed Wundt's idea of "basic element." They believed that Wundt led psychology away from a holistic view of human experience as he tried to develop a table of psychological elements[13] similar to the atomic table. The wholeness of experience is lost when we focus only on its smallest parts, much as the beauty of a rose is destroyed in its dissection into stamen, stem, and petals.

Or consider music, which may be defined as the *gestalt* of notes, rhythms, and time. Behaviorists may well succeed in studying the individual notes in a musical composition, but they lose the music in the process. Gestaltists believe the same is true in human learning.

Wundt therefore gave birth to two widely divergent views of learning. Behaviorists focus on the "basic element" of S-R bonds, while Gestaltists focus on Wundt's introspective approach to studying non-observable human mental processes.

Ernst Mach (1838–1916)[14]

Both Wilhelm Wundt and John Watson wanted to make psychology a credible scientific discipline. Their assumption was this would be accomplished if psychology used methods similar to other scientific disciplines—especially the hard sciences, like physics.

Mach rejected such thinking. Psychology is not physics. Humans *perceive* the world around them, planets do not. Sensations of relationship in the minds of humans do not necessarily correspond to the physical reality they see. Earlier in the text, I presented three dots on the page and asked you to label what you saw. Some of you saw the dots as the three points of a triangle. Nothing in the dots themselves suggested this. Their configuration prompted the relationship.[15] Mach rejected the behavioral view that human learning is defined by bonds mechanically stamped into the nervous system by repetition. Human learning is grounded in our interactive perception of the world.[16]

Max Wertheimer (1880–1943)[17]

Max Wertheimer is the father of Gestalt psychology. The basis for Wertheimer's work came from his study of perceived movement. One wintry day in 1910, Wertheimer was traveling across Germany by train. During a stop in Frankfurt, Wertheimer was absentmindedly looking down the row of shops facing the train, when his eyes fell upon the display window of a toy shop. There in the window was a child's toy that prompted a connection to a problem he was trying to solve. The *toy* was a stroboscope,[18] the precursor of motion pictures. The *problem* was explaining the perception of "apparent motion"—perceived movement when no movement actually takes place.[19]

Wertheimer went to the shop and purchased the toy. Picture a cylindrical lamp shade of sorts, constructed in such a way that it spins on a wooden handle. There are vertical viewing slits in the cylinder, and a series of stop-action photographs lining the inside. In Wertheimer's case, the stills featured a galloping horse. Spin the cylinder, look through the slits, and find there, not a series of individual photographs, but rather a galloping horse. The rapid succession of still images created a sense of movement, which Wertheimer called the "phi phenomenon."[20]

The psychological problem of the sensation of movement had proven a challenge for Wundt and other behaviorists. Wundt attributed apparent movement to "kinesthetic sensations produced by the movement of the eyes."[21] Wundt maintained his ideological focus on individual elements.

When Wertheimer arrived at the University of Frankfurt, he formed a group of psychologists to study this problem. He proposed an experiment in which subjects were shown "suitable pairs of lines as to require two simultaneous movements in opposite directions. Phi phenomenon still occurred. Since the eyes could hardly move out in both directions at the same time, Wundt's explanation fell to the ground."[22]

Returning to the illustration of the child's toy, the *perceived movement* of the horse produced by the stroboscope cannot be explained by analyzing *each picture*, but only as all the pictures are taken together. Wertheimer coined the term "Gestalt" to express this "all parts together" concept.[23] Just as it is useless to focus on any one picture in the stroboscope, it is useless, wrote Wertheimer, to focus on the smallest parts of learning or perception.[24] He was referring, of course, to Wundt's elements, what Ivan Pavlov called S-R bonds.

The *whole* of an experience gives meaning to the *individual parts* of the experience. "The whole is greater than the sum of its individual parts"[25] captures Wertheimer's use of the term "Gestalt."[26] Wertheimer held that the human mind gives organization to the world. The mind is not simply a *connecting* system, as in Thorndike's Connectionism, but a *transforming* system.[27]

Professor Wertheimer worked with assistants Wolfgang Köhler in 1912 and Kurt Lewin in 1916. Both became renowned cognitive theorists in their own right. In 1933 Wertheimer moved to the United States and established the New School for Social Research at New York University. He worked there until his death in 1943.[28] Throughout his work, he criticized the educational practices of repetition and rote memorization as blind and unproductive.[29]

Wertheimer and his followers formulated six laws of perception to explain how we attach meaning to information we receive from the world around us. These are the laws of Prägnanz [pr. prehg-*nah*nts], similarity, proximity, closure, good continuation, and membership character.

The **law of Prägnanz** states that people impose order on a disorganized perceptual field in a predictable way.[30] In other words, we naturally attempt to reduce confusion and make sense of what we see. Piaget's concept of *organization* refers to this same tendency, which may well have been derived from Wertheimer's law of Prägnanz. This first law states *that* we impose conceptual order on our perceptions. The remaining five laws flow from it, and state *how* conceptual order is imposed.

The **law of similarity** states that similar objects, in terms of form, shape, size, or color, tend to be perceived together.[31] How many squares do you see in the group of objects at left?

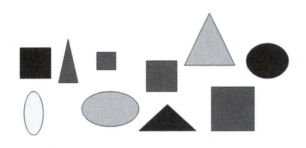

Four, you say?

Good. How many black objects?

Three? Good.

As you looked at the individual objects, you immediately recognized similarities among them. And you naturally grouped them by those similarities.

The **law of proximity** states that objects tend to be grouped according to their distance from other objects.[32] How many dots do you see here?

Twelve?

Correct. Did you count 1, 2, 3, 4, 5, . . . 12 dots? I suspect you did not. I'll wager you recognized three groups of four dots, and multiplied 4 x 3 = 12 dots. How many dots do you see here?

I suspect you looked at the first group of 5, recognized the other three groups were the same, and immediately thought (4x5=) "20 dots." Was I right?

How many dots do you see here?

Each cluster has five groups of five, which equal 25. Four clusters of 25 make 100 dots. When I do this exercise in class, someone will shout out "100!" less than a second after I display the pattern. Pattern recognition, a mental process, provides nearly instantaneous answers to these questions. The mind uses pattern recognition in far more complex ways, but even in these simplistic examples, you have responded correctly *without repetition, drill and practice, or overt reinforcement* on my part. The law of proximity makes pattern recognition possible.

The **law of closure** states that closed areas are more stable than open ones. Incomplete images tend to be perceived as complete. A 350° arc is perceived as a circle. Three dots are perceived as a triangle. Closure is the psychological equivalent of reward in association theory, in that it produces the "satisfying, tension-relieving end-state that terminates activity."[33] Closure may well be the psychological basis for gossip, as the mind naturally "fills in the gaps" of partial stories with the storyteller's own imagination!

The **law of good continuation** states that the repeated reproduction of images tends to change them from distorted forms (below left) to more symmetrical and balanced forms (below right).[34]

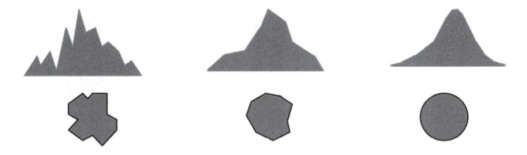

It is easier to see trends in monthly averages of Sunday school attendance figures than in individual attendance figures themselves. The circle above right is more stable conceptually than the irregular figure at left. The mind naturally simplifies complex information into simpler forms (loosing detail in the process).

The **law of membership character** states that a single part of the whole gets its characteristics from the whole.[35] Look at the picture at left. What is this? If you are familiar with these objects, you may answer right away. If you are not, you are searching your memory stores for matching patterns. The problem is that there is not enough information to allow for confident guesses. More context, a broader view, more relevant information would help. To see this additional context, look at the picture below—the cut-out at left is shown in the larger picture by a white rectangle—and you will have no trouble identifying what these are.

My wife and mother-in-law love to work jigsaw puzzles when we get together on holidays. They like the *5000 pieces* variety. They sit for hours, sorting through bits of colored cardboard, talking about whatever comes up. One of their recent challenges was a close-up picture of golden brown potato chips. Just potato chips. Another was a close-up of a single Oreo cookie. Each jigsaw puzzle piece was meaningless in itself, a mere smudge of color (potato chip yellow or Oreo blackish-brown), but taken together with all the other pieces, in their proper configuration, they formed a complete picture. Barb and Virginia successfully completed both puzzles, not by focusing on colors, but by finding edge patterns, beginning with the flat-sided outside pieces, and moving in from this frame.

Each piece takes on its special meaning as it is placed in the proper context. If just one piece out of 5000 is missing, the beautiful picture is ruined.

These six laws—Prägnanz, similarity, proximity, closure, good continuation, and membership character—form the basis of Gestalt psychology, and the foundation of cognitive learning. Wertheimer "never wrote a systematic statement of Gestalt psychology. It is probable that he had no desire to do so . . . . He had a restless, inquiring approach to many aspects of life and psychology, and he was prodigal with his carelessly tossed-off insights. [Yet] his spontaneity and brilliance made for his productive contribution to psychology."[36]

Wolfgang Köhler (1887–1967)[37]

Wolfgang Köhler was the first subject of Wertheimer's "perception of motion" studies at the University of Frankfurt in 1910. He and Kurt Koffka, Wertheimer's second subject, were destined to become second only to Wertheimer in their influence in Gestalt psychology. Köhler remained at the University until 1913, when he accepted an opportunity to do research with apes on the island of Tenerife, off the coast of Africa.[38] He remained there longer than planned because of World War I.[39]

In one experiment, an ape was placed in a cage—an outdoor playground without a top[40]—with a banana hanging over the cage beyond reach. Two boxes of different sizes were also in the cage. Reaching the banana required moving the larger box into position, placing the smaller box on top, and then climbing to the banana.[41] The apes were able to do this without trial and error, without stimulus-response bonding. They "sized up the situation," understood the problem, and "saw" the solution.[42]

A second experiment placed a banana outside the cage. Also outside the cage, but within reach, was a stick. The apes "studied" the situation for a moment, picked up the stick, and used it to drag the banana to them. Köhler's most famous chimpanzee, Sultan, was able to fasten two sticks together in order to retrieve the banana.[43]

In yet another experiment, Köhler placed a wooden stick in the rafters of the experimental cage in the presence of the chimps, but in a place where it could not be seen. The chimps were taken to their sleeping quarters. The next morning one of the chimps was brought into the experimental cage, and a bunch of bananas was placed outside the cage. The chimp looked for a "tool" with which to drag the bananas within reach. He did not find any sticks close by. But then he looked up toward the ceiling, remembered where the stick had been hidden, climbed into the rafters, retrieved the stick, and used it to get the bunch of bananas.

The problems of boxes and banana and the sticks and banana were perceived, reorganized and a solution devised. The problem was seen as a unified whole.[44] Köhler introduced the term *insight*—solving problems by grasping relations[45]—as an alternative to Thorndike's trial and error approach to problem solving. Learning does not require "stamping in correct responses through repetition."

Some chimps demonstrated better insight than others. One chimp in Köhler's group was deemed "relatively stupid." He was present when the others learned to use a box as a tool to reach the banana—many times. The others tried to show him how to use it, but his behavior imitated only parts of their behavior. "He would move the box, but, as often as not, away from the food. He would then climb on the box and jump, but not under the banana and, after climbing off the box, would then jump up under the banana." He was a never able to put all the various elements altogether. In the language of Köhler, he "never formed the Gestalt." For this chimp, there were two separate groups of actions, "climb-box-jump" and "jump-under-fruit." He did not relate the parts of the activity to the essential structure of the total situation. This consistent finding became an indication of intelligence.[46] Köhler formally presented his findings in the book *Mentality of Apes* published in 1925.[47]

Kurt Lewin (1890–1947)[48]

Kurt Lewin[49] earned his doctorate at the University of Berlin and later taught psychology and philosophy there. He was introduced to Gestalt psychology through Wertheimer's lectures in Berlin and Frankfurt.[50] He came to the United States in 1932 and taught at Stanford, Cornell, Iowa, and M.I.T.[51]

Lewin developed Field Theory based on the principles of Gestalt psychology. He viewed persons as existing within a psychological field of forces, a "life space," to which they reacted. This field of forces is much like the magnetic field surrounding a magnet, invisible but powerful. Life space is composed of persons and objects within our perceptional range. It also includes one's goals, wishes, aspirations, values, and attitudes.[52] If a student imagines a gunman in the hallway outside her classroom, that gunman influences the learning readiness of the student, even if he does not exist.

Lewin viewed learning as a reorganization of life space, a restructuring of the cognitive structures that produce better understanding and behavior.[53] Group discussion and small group learning became popular teaching methods because they were effective ways to intersect the life spaces of students.

Jerome Bruner (1915–)[54] and Discovery Learning

More than any other theorist, Jerome Bruner changed the direction of American psychology, overcoming the hold of Behaviorism with his insights into cognitive theory.[55] Bruner saw little value in studying rats, cats, or pigeons to understand how children learn in a classroom setting. He gathered his data from children in classroom settings.[56] He believed that the goal of teaching is to promote the general understanding of a subject to help *students*[57] form global concepts, *students* build clear generalizations, and *students* create cognitive networks of ideas.[58] His view is called Discovery Learning, which emphasizes students discovering solutions to presented problems—individually **or** in groups.[59] Bruner believed that the facts and relationships children discover through their own explorations are more usable and tend to be better retained than material they have merely committed to memory.[60] In fact, Bruner opposed Skinner's methodology of linear programmed instruction because he believed it promotes too much dependence on the program. Bruner found that discovery learning sharpens problem-solving skills and produces greater confidence in the ability to learn as students "learn how to learn."[61]

The Life of Jerome Bruner

Jerome Bruner was born in New York City in 1915. He received his undergraduate degree from Duke University in 1937 and his Ph.D. in psychology from Harvard in 1941. During World War II, he led efforts in psychological warfare out of General Eisenhower's headquarters. He studied propaganda techniques used by Germany. After the war he returned to Harvard as professor of psychology. In 1947 he published a paper on how values and needs affect human perception. This paper laid the groundwork for an American school of cognitive psychology.

Gestalt psychology and cognitive theories had flourished in Europe since 1910, but Behaviorism—guided by Thorndike and Skinner—held sway in America. The study of "thinking" was seen as subjective and unscientific. Bruner changed the direction of American psychology by his prolific research and writing. He conducted studies in perception (1951) and thinking (1956). His major works include *A Study of Thinking* (1956), *The Process of Education* (1962), *Toward a Theory of Instruction* (1966), *Learning about Learning* (1966), *Studies in Cognitive Growth* (1966), *The Relevance of Education* (1973), and *Beyond the Information Given: Studies in the Psychology of Knowing* (1973).

In the late 1950's, Bruner served as chairman of a series of conferences consisting of scientists and educators. The purpose of the conferences was to evaluate American education in light of the Soviet Union putting Sputnik I into orbit. The result was his book *Process of Education* (1962), which became a classic. Bruner established the Harvard Center for Cognitive Studies in 1960. The American Psychological Association presented Bruner with the Distinguished Scientific Award in 1963. His influence in the field of educational psychology came from his ability to speak intelligently about education to his fellow scholars as well as educators.[62]

Bruner promoted discovery learning as part of the larger picture of learning.[63] To rediscover basic facts and truths in all subjects would be time-consuming and wasteful,[64] so Bruner left room for direct instruction in subject foundations and terminology. Discovery learning builds upon direct instruction to help students see the relationships among principles and concepts. It leads to longer-lasting retention of the material, as well as higher self-esteem in learners. Discovery learning encourages the development and use of creative thinking skills, involving formal logic, but more, including beliefs, desires, expectations, emotions, and intentions of learners.

For the decades of the 1960s and 1970s, Jerome Bruner's Discovery Learning was to cognitive theory what B. F. Skinner's Operant Conditioning was to behavioral theory. Before moving into modifications of Bruner's views in later years, let's look at implications of Bruner's Discovery Learning theory that remain valid today.

Key Concepts in Discovery Learning

Bruner's concepts of structure and motivation reveal the depth of difference between his theory and that of Skinner.

Structure. Bruner held that any subject can be organized in a way that allows it to be taught to almost any student.[65] He did not mean that nuclear physics can be taught to a six-year-old, but he would say there are meaningful concepts in nuclear physics that could be taught in a way that a six-year-old would understand. The phrase "could be taught in a way" refers to the structure of the subject, that is, the fundamental ideas of the subject, and how the fundamental ideas relate to one another.[66] These fundamental ideas can be reduced to a diagram, or set of principles, or a formula,[67] simple in form, yet complex in substance. Consider for a moment the objectivity of Bruner's view. There *is* an objective structure. There *are* fundamental ideas that relate to each other. There *exists* a visual form for such objective ideas, which are arranged in a knowable structure. Keep this objectivity in mind as we move into more existential and postmodern forms of cognitive theory, which emphasize the *subjective* nature of knowledge and its *creation* by learners.

The Disciplers' Model is a simple diagram of seven components. Yet the inter-related meanings associated with each component, and with the Model as a whole, reflect a broad sweep of issues in Christian education, spiritual formation, and discipleship. I can share the Model in ten minutes but have also structured two-week intensive seminars around it.

Daryl Eldridge[68] and I were sharing a cup of coffee one afternoon—still a favorite pastime of mine when he is in town—when the Disciplers' Model came up. He was a budding new professor at the time, long before he became dean of our school. He laughed and said, "Your model is so broad that anything related to teaching and learning would fit into it." I thought at the time he was just having some good natured fun at my expense, but I now look back on that statement as a great compliment, and a good example of Bruner's meaning of structure. Structure is facilitated by three components: presentation, economy, and power.

Presentation. Unlike Piaget, who believed that cognitive differences are linked to biological age,[69] Bruner believed that people possess different *modes* of understanding, and that these modes were available to learners of any age. He called these modes the *enactive*, the *iconic*, and the *symbolic*.

Enactive understanding is based on actions, demonstrations, and hands-on experimentation. It is wordless. One learns to ride a bike, play the piano, or conduct brain surgery by an enactive process of hands-on experience—learning *physically*.

Iconic understanding is based on pictures, images, diagrams, models, and the like. Artists and engineers emphasize iconic understanding—learning *visually*.

Symbolic understanding is based on language, using words to express complex ideas.[70] Mathematicians and philosophers emphasize symbolic understanding—learning *intellectually*. Bruner suggested that presenting material in the sequence of enactive (hands-on experimentation), iconic (creating diagrams and illustrations), and symbolic (expressing fundamental concepts in words) modes helps students develop structural understanding of the subject.[71]

Economy. Teachers confuse students when they provide too much information at a time, or present information too quickly. The fewer the pieces of information students must keep in mind to continue learning, the greater the economy of learning. Teachers do well to present material in small doses. Give time for students to process the material between doses. Provide summaries of facts and concepts periodically to allow students to organize the material.[72]

Power. A powerful presentation is a simple presentation. Simple, but not simplistic. Reducing large quantities of facts to formulas, models, or diagrams helps students understand the essential relationships in the material. Albert Einstein revolutionized the world of energy with his simple yet profound formula **e=mc²** [the *amount of energy* released in a nuclear explosion is equal to the *mass of the nuclear material* multiplied by *the speed of light squared*].[73] The string of statistics symbols I mentioned earlier, while overwhelming to some students the first time they see it, actually provides a structure for five chapters of detailed text. The Statistical Flowchart in my research text reduces 13 chapters of statistical procedures to a single page, organizing them by research question, type of data, and number of variables/groups. The flowchart structures these chapters, doing so with iconic (pictorial) presentation, economy, and power.

Motivation. Bruner believed that external rewards—reinforcers like stars on charts, or candies—were an artificial means to encourage students to learn. All children, wrote Bruner, have an innate will to learn.[74] Intrinsic motivation sustains that will to learn; extrinsic motivation does not. Intrinsic motivation comes from the students' own curiosity, their drive to achieve competence, and reciprocity—the desire to work cooperatively with others. These are rewarding in themselves, and thus, self-sustaining.[75] The teachers' responsibility is to insure that these natural motivators are not impaired by irrelevant and dry presentations, frustrating expectations, and unwholesome competition among students.

In fact, reinforcement may well be an artificial means of motivation. Extinction of established bonds reflects the artificial nature of some forms of reinforcement. Yet, if teachers can engage disinterested learners[76] with stars, candies, or praise, focusing on performance, they may be able to move learners toward a sense of curiosity, a desire for competence, and even the risk of working with others. These latter forms of motivation, says Bruner, are self-sustaining.

Statistical Flowchart

Accompanies explanation on pages 5-4 to 5-7 in text

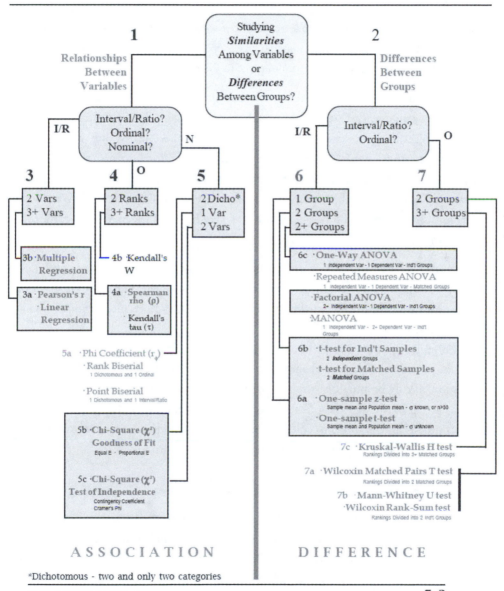

1
Relationships
Between
Variables

Studying *Similarities* Among Variables or *Differences* Between Groups?

2
Differences
Between
Groups

I/R — **Interval/Ratio? Ordinal? Nominal?** — N

3
2 Vars
3+ Vars

3b ·Multiple Regression

3a · Pearson's r · Linear Regression

O

4
2 Ranks
3+ Ranks

4b ·Kendall's W

4a · Spearman rho (ρ)
· Kendall's tau (τ)

5
2 Dicho*
1 Var
2 Vars

5a ·Phi Coefficient (r_φ)
·Rank Biserial
1 Dichotomous and 1 Ordinal

·Point Biserial
1 Dichotomous and 1 Interval/Ratio

5b ·Chi-Square (χ²)
Goodness of Fit
Equal E · Proportional E

5c ·Chi-Square (χ²)
Test of Independence
Contingency Coefficient
Cramer's Phi

I/R — **Interval/Ratio? Ordinal?** — O

6
1 Group
2 Groups
2+ Groups

6c ·One-Way ANOVA
1 Independent Var · 1 Dependent Var · Ind'l Groups

·Repeated Measures ANOVA
1 Independent Var · 1 Dependent Var · Matched Groups

·Factorial ANOVA
2+ Independent Var · 1 Dependent Var · Ind'l Groups

·MANOVA
1 Independent Var · 2+ Dependent Var · Ind'l Groups

6b ·t-test for Ind't Samples
2 *Independent* Groups

·t-test for Matched Samples
2 *Matched* Groups

6a ·One-sample z-test
Sample mean and Population mean · σ known, or n>30

·One-sample t-test
Sample mean and Population mean · σ unknown

7
2 Groups
3+ Groups

7c ·Kruskal-Wallis H test
Rankings Divided into 3+ Matched Groups

7a ·Wilcoxin Matched Pairs T test
Rankings Divided into 2 Matched Groups

7b ·Mann-Whitney U test
·Wilcoxin Rank-Sum test
Rankings Divided into 2 Ind't Groups

ASSOCIATION

DIFFERENCE

*Dichotomous - two and only two categories

© 4th ed. 2006 Dr. Rick Yount

5-3

The Discovery-Oriented Teacher

Bruner's initial ideas follow Jean Piaget and place great emphasis on *students discovering relation-ships* among the fundamental ideas of a subject. At the end of Chapter Four we quoted Piaget and repeat part of that quote here:

"So we need pupils who are *active*, who learn early to *find out by themselves*, partly by their *own spontaneous activity* and partly through material we set up for them; who learn early to *tell what is verifiable* and what is simply the first idea to come to them."[77]

Discovery learning emphasizes student activity, student initiative, and student solutions. Bruner knew that students would learn fewer facts through this approach but would gain a deeper under-standing of the subject that could well continue beyond the classroom. It is one thing to be able to answer a teacher's questions, but it is quite another—*better*—thing for students to learn to ask ques-tions of themselves, and then find the answers.

The focus on learner-centered problem-solving, Bruner's original theory, has become known as *pure discovery learning*. Teachers who are able to use discovery methods effectively reflect the following characteristics: They . . .

- prepare students for interactive activities by insuring they understand basic vocabulary and operations required for higher level thinking (accomplished through direct instruction).
- are well-versed in the subject, enabling them to move easily from inter-connected concept to concept.
- model high levels of thinking competence, weighing student questions before answering, reframing statements to make them more focused, pulling relevant examples into the class discussion, asking probing questions to further student understanding, and the like.
- serve as group facilitators and presenters of problems more than tellers of facts.
- serve as guides for the student-centered learning process and take care not to short-circuit the discovery process by giving students the answers prematurely.

Criticism of Discovery Learning

Pure discovery methods soon (late 1960s) came under attack as being too time-consuming. Teachers observed that waiting for students to discover concepts and principles for themselves was often a waste of precious class time. Students could certainly learn more quickly with teacher-struc-tured explanations. Skinner strongly opposed discovery learning as being *inefficient*. He wrote:

It is quite impossible for the student to discover for himself any substantial part of the wisdom of his culture, and no philosophy of education really proposes that he should. Great thinkers build on the past, they do not waste their time rediscovering it. . . . It is equally dangerous to forego teaching important facts and principles in order to give the student a chance to discover them for himself.[78]

There are also *interpersonal problems* with pure discovery. Students become frustrated with those who dominate much of the discussion time and who make most of the discoveries. Jealousy, resentment, and inferiority are often generated in highly social environments. In any educational setting, someone has to do the talking. With pure discovery, this someone is a fellow student. Yet most students would rather hear a teacher—an expert in the subject—explain it clearly rather than listen to a fellow learner who is struggling with the subject.

Finally, pure discovery methods are simply *inappropriate in some settings*. If the subject matter is difficult, or if students come from disadvantaged backgrounds, pure discovery is less effective than direct instruction. Discovery approaches are inappropriate if class time is limited since students may not have sufficient time to discover all the necessary links among concepts and principles.[79]

David Ausebel (1968) was one of the most vocal early critics of discovery learning.[80] Students often do not know what is important or relevant, and many students need external motivation to do the work required to master school subjects. He proposed an alternative model of instruction, called *reception learning*. Teachers provide students systematic, teacher-planned instruction on meaningful information. Teachers structure the learning situation, select the appropriate materials, and then present them in an organized manner—moving from general ideas to specifics.[81] In this way, the material is pre-processed for learners, *giving* them a conceptual framework rather than requiring them to build the framework themselves. Such a framework, said Ausebel, allows students to subsume new ideas.[82]

In response to these criticisms, *directed discovery methods*[83] were developed. In directed discovery, teachers control the learning process as they direct students to make discoveries. Teachers emphasize contrast among concepts and principles. They lead students to make educated guesses and then analyze which guess is most correct. They ask conceptual questions to help students integrate the subject into their thinking. Teachers have students consider the consequences of answers they give. Finally, they help students learn-by-doing by making assignments to be done outside of class.

Discovery Learning and Bible Teaching

My studies of Jerome Bruner and discovery learning during seminary forever changed my approach to teaching people the Bible. For several years I taught Sunday school classes the way I had been taught growing up. I presented lessons, taught ("told") facts, and shared stories. Rarely did I deal with concepts, ideas, and principles in Scripture. And I did not know enough to focus on the structure, the inter-connectedness, of Scriptural truth. Bible truths existed as discrete facts, not a network of Truth. I did most of the talking. As I studied Bruner's approach to learning and put his principles into practice in teaching deaf adults and teenagers, our Bible study sessions took on new life. If I had to choose one statement from all my seminary studies that did more to change my approach to teaching Scripture, it would be a quote from Jerome Bruner:

> We teach a subject not to produce little living libraries on that subject, but rather to get a
> student to think . . . for himself, to consider matters as an historian does, to take part in the
> process of knowledge-getting. Knowing is a process, not a product.[84]

In the context of Bible study, we might paraphrase Bruner to say that we teach not to create libraries of Bible facts, but to help students think biblically, to consider real-life problems from God's point of view. I watched as the lives of my learners were transformed by the integration of biblical truth into their everyday problems and decisions. The Disciplers' Model presented in Chapter One grew out of my experiences in teaching during seminary—and Jerome Bruner's ideas were a large part of that.

Cognitive Learning Theory in the 2000s

Contemporary cognitive theory can be described by five terms: Cognitive Constructivism, Social Constructivism, Radical Constructivism, Information Processing Theory, and Construct*ion*ism. In the former edition, I responded to various contemporary (1995) definitions of Constructivism by making a distinction between *objective* Constructivism, in which personal reality is *derived* from the world of experience, and *subjective* or *relativistic* Constructivism, in which personal reality is *created* from the world of experience.[85] What I termed *objective* Constructivism grew out of Piaget's theory and Bruner's Discovery Learning, and is now called **Cognitive Constructivism**.[86]

The second branch of cognitive theory is **Social Constructivism**, which integrated Discovery Learning with Vygotsky's insights into community and culture. Knowledge is constructed from social interactions and experience. Knowledge reflects the world "as it is filtered through and influenced by culture, language, beliefs, and interactions with others."[87] The distinction between *cognitive* and *social* constructivism is found in the role of social interaction, which mirrors the distinction made between Piaget and Vygotsky in Chapter Four. Piaget emphasized the personal, individual development of cognitive skills, which allowed learners to interact with one another. Vygotsky emphasized cognitive development as the internalization of socially-derived meaning. For Piaget, cognitive development precedes social interaction; for Vygotsky, social interaction precedes cognitive development. Cognitive (individual, psychological)[88] constructivism refers to the former, Social constructivism to the latter.

What I termed *subjective* Constructivism in the first edition has now developed into **Constructionism** and **Radical Constructivism.** Construct*ion*ism refers to the process of constructing public knowledge in the academic disciplines of science, history, and economics—that is, determining the content, structure, and purpose of the disciplines. Constructionism analyzes how common-sense ideas and everyday beliefs are communicated. Constructionism is concerned more with public policy than individual learning. Since this viewpoint considers all knowledge as socially constructed, it presents an extreme view of relativism, in which all knowledge and all beliefs are equal. This is held to be true, despite the fact that, even in secular classrooms, we know that not all beliefs are equal. There are some values, such as honesty and justice, which are clearly superior to others, such as bigotry and deception.[89] Constructionism, with its extreme relativistic viewpoint and lack of interest in individual learning, will not be pursued here.

Radical Constructivism is to educational psychology what Existentialism is to philosophy. While addressed under the general umbrella of constructivist theories, it is more an outgrowth of Bruner's Humanistic leanings. As we shall see in Chapter Ten, Humanistic Learning Theory has disappeared from educational psychology texts. Yet, its focus on Self and Choice continues under the banner of Radical Constructivism.

That which I warned against in 1995 has become stronger in secular education circles over the past dozen years. These radical views of reality and truth have influenced Constructivism as a whole, so that even general descriptions of Constructivism sound increasingly subjective.

Adding to the confusion is the fact that some writers use Constructivism to describe these various camps without distinction.[90] Woolfolk goes so far as to characterize Constructivism as a "vast and woolly area in contemporary psychology, epistemology, and education."[91]

The second major branch of cognitive theory, **Information Processing Theory**, well established in the 1990s, was included in the original text. Knowledge is acquired by constructing a "meaningful" representation of the outside world by means of direct teaching, feedback, and explanation. Bruner opposed this view, which uses computer processing as an analogy to mental processing, because he believed it focused too much on a logical, or computational,[92] mode of thinking.[93] We will consider this branch in the next chapter.

We will analyze Cognitive and Social Constructivism here, since these are rooted in Jerome Bruner's Discovery Learning, as well as Jean Piaget and Lev Vygotsky before him.

Contemporary Constructivism

Contemporary constructivism includes cognitive, social, and radical constructivist views. **Cognitive constructivism**, which is based largely on Piaget's work, focuses on individual, internal constructions of knowledge.[94] It stresses the personal search for meaning as learners interact with the environment and modify existing schemes. While *interaction with others* enhances the process, constructivists see its primary function as generating cognitive dissonance, or disequilibrium for the individual.

Cognitive constructivism emphasizes learning activities that are experience-based and discovery oriented. There is a built-in distrust of teacher attempts to instruct learners directly.[95] One reason for suspicion of direct instruction is the belief that the "essence of one person's knowledge can never be totally transferred to another person" because perceptions are individually constructed from personal experience. Since constructed perceptions are heavily influenced by age, gender, race, ethnicity, and prior learning, "one cannot duplicate what they've learned in another."[96] Further, while teacher-student interaction is important as a source of general social interaction, constructivists insist that teachers need to "guard against imposing their thoughts and values on developing learners."[97]

Cognitive constructivists focus on the knowledge, beliefs, self-concept, and identity of *individual* learners, emphasizing inner psychological representations of the world more than outer social connections. For this reason they are sometimes called *individual* constructivists. When asked about the role of the teacher in such a student-dependent, self-constructing system—other than providing materials and supporting the learning environment—Eggen and Kauchak (2007) respond, "This question hasn't been satisfactorily answered."[98]

Social constructivism, strongly influenced by Vygotsky's work, suggests that learners construct knowledge within the context of a social group, and then internalize it. According to social constructivists, the process of sharing individual perspectives results in learners *constructing understanding together* in ways that are not possible alone. Creating situations in which learners can exchange ideas and collaborate in solving problems is an essential teacher role. "Social constructivism has become the view that is most influential in guiding the thinking of educational leaders and teachers."[99]

Radical constructivism views learning as individually created and individually oriented. There is *no objective reality or truth* in the world to attain and internalize as knowledge. "The very concept of an objective reality or truth is an educational illusion. The only reality is what the individual mind can conjure."[100] Alexander recounts a case where Gloria, an elementary student, states that Judge Joe Brown and Judge Judy are members of the Supreme Court. A "radical constructionist would probably not [be] . . . concerned about Gloria's announcement . . . . Rather, these theorists would explore the students' ideas about judges *without attention to the correctness of the initial responses*. They would appreciate and build on whatever interpretations or constructions the students have made—constructions as unique as fingerprints [emphasis mine—RY]."[101]

The chart on the next page[102] summarizes major differences across the three views of Cognitive, Social, and Radical Constructivism just described. It is an oversimplification of the literature since writers take different perspectives in laying out the comparisons and contrasts of the various theories.

CONSTRUCTIVISM			
Elements	**Cognitive Constructivism**	**Social Constructivism**	**Radical Constructivism**
Major Theorists	Jean Piaget Jerome Bruner	Lev Vygotsky Jerome Bruner	Abraham Maslow Carl Rogers
Reality	Objective/Interactive	Interactive within culture/group	Subjective/Personal
Mental Representation	Individuals reconstruct reality	Individuals internalize social interactions	Individuals personally create reality
Definition of Meaning	Psychological constructs of objective reality	Negotiated meanings within communities	Subjective expression of Self
Methodology	Experience-based activities Discovery learning	Collaboration in problem-solving activities	Individually-oriented activities
Educational Philosophy	Realism	Pragmatism	Existentialism
Social Interaction	Cognitive skills permit social interaction	Social interaction creates cognitive skills	Personal choice

Five Major Characteristics of Constructivism

Taking **Cognitive** and **Social constructivism** together, we can list four general characteristics of this approach to teaching and learning.

Learners are not passive recipients, but active builders. Learners construct knowledge and understanding that makes sense to them. Learners are not merely recipients of information, but actively involve themselves in constructing understanding of subjects. "This is an accepted principle of all cognitive learning theories."[103]

New learning depends on prior learning. The ideas that learners construct depend directly on the knowledge they currently possess.[104] The developing structure of ideas is strongly influenced by students' prior knowledge. "A review of 183 studies in 1999 concluded that a strong relationship exists between prior knowledge and [present] performance."[105]

Engaging others in learning tasks facilitates personal learning. Cognitive (Individual) constructivism emphasizes interaction as a source of disequilibrium for individual learners. Social constructivism emphasizes shared or *negotiated* meaning,[106] which is then internalized by individual learners.

Meaningful learning occurs through real-world tasks. Rather than confront learners with abstract principles that are "often irrelevant to real-world conditions," constructivists process subjects in *authentic activities*. For example, have students use math skills to balance a checkbook, or apply writing skills to completing a job application.[107]

Softening objective truth. Educational texts reflect a continuing shift from objective to subjective truth. Existential and Postmodern influences have moved Constructivism as a whole toward the position of radical constructivists, for whom the personal constructions of learners are more important than correctness of those constructions.

The Teacher's Role in Constructivist Classrooms

While the question of teacher role in Constructivism "hasn't been satisfactorily answered,"[108] theorists make general observations about how Constructivist teachers manage their classrooms. Teachers using Constructivist principles engage in the same basic tasks as teachers in traditional classrooms. They specify learning objectives, prepare learning activities, and design assessments. "The primary change is a shift in emphasis away from teachers merely providing information and toward teachers promoting interaction that makes student thinking open and visible."

Teachers expand thinking by supplementing "existing knowledge" of learners with a variety of examples and other "representations"—visual aids and object lessons—of the content being taught.[109] Teachers make school subjects more relevant to learners by connecting content to the real world. Teachers are intentionally skeptical of their own ability to convey ideas clearly. *Explaining a concept correctly* does not insure that learners *understand it correctly*, because learner understanding is constructed within their own mental frames. Likewise, just because learners answer questions correctly—particularly if the questions are fact-based rather than concept-based—does not mean they understand the material correctly, because they can merely memorize right answers. As we saw in Chapter Four, Piaget believed "learning by heart" is not learning at all.

Constructivist teachers promote high levels of interaction among learners by encouraging the sharing of ideas, placing learners in situations where they learn from others, and prompting learners to articulate what they understand.[110] Constructivist teachers employ a spiral curriculum, in which they introduce the fundamental structure of subjects early in the school year, and then revisit them periodically in more and more complex forms over time.[111]

Snowman provides a list of specific characteristics of a Constructivist classroom. As I studied them, I found myself connecting his characteristics to my Christian Teacher's Triad conference. I present eight of Snowman's characteristics below, in italics, following it with how each applies to the context of the conference.

1. Determine what students know

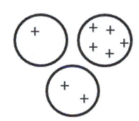

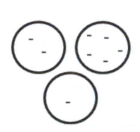

"The teacher's first task is to determine the completeness and accuracy of what students currently know about key topics." Since new learning is filtered through and constructed from established understanding, teachers need to know what learners already know.

At the beginning of the Triad conference, I ask teachers to reflect on their own teachers over the years, and select from all of them their best teacher. "Think about this 'best teacher' of yours. What made this individual your best teacher? Jot down several words or phrases that describe this person as a teacher." After a minute or so, I call for responses, and place plus signs, without comment, into one of three circles I've drawn on the board. Then I ask them to think about their *worst* teacher, and to jot down words or phrases that characterize this person as a teacher. After a minute or so, I call for responses, and categorize them by placing check marks in a second set of three circles. In doing this I have created two diagrams based on the participants' own experiences. The diagrams are defined later in the seminar, but they remain displayed throughout the sessions as a reminder of their own personal connections to what constitutes "good and bad teaching." You will notice the majority of pluses and minuses fall in the same sphere (upper right). This is always the case, regardless of how many answers participants give.

2. Help students restructure current knowledge

"Teachers help students create realistic learning experiences that will lead students to elaborate on and restructure current knowledge." The three circles are described by giving verbal definitions and practical examples, using words and phrases participants used in their own descriptions of "best teachers." Doing this creates conceptual connections between the new material and the real world teaching experiences of participants. In the first exercise, the three circles are displayed as separate circles, independent and without overlap. As the three circles are defined, they are placed in a Venn diagram form, creating a single, triadic diagram. Since the triadic diagram rings true in their own experiences, they are willing to consider new ideas (those that lie outside their own preferences) about "good teaching."

3. Engage students in problem-based activities

"Students frequently engage complex, meaningful, problem based activities."

I define the three spheres of learning as *thinking, feeling and valuing,* and *doing,* and provide specific and distinctive characteristics of each of the three spheres. I ask participants to divide themselves into three groups by physically standing up and moving to one of three designated areas in the room. This creates smaller groups of thinkers, feelers, and doers. If any group is too large for interaction, I divide it in half. When the groups are assembled, I ask them to discuss their preferences in *learning* among themselves, eventually creating a list of three most important characteristics they look for in a Bible study class. In the second phase, I ask groups to do the same with their *least* desired characteristics. In each phase, the groups have about ten minutes to discuss, interact, and decide on their "top three."

I do not *tell* them what they *should* find. Groups freely discuss their own perspectives and freely develop their "list of three." But these responses are always the same, no matter where in the world I am, or what group of people I am addressing. I have come to the confident opinion that *thinkers, feelers,* and *doers* give the same general responses because these responses are part of human Reality. These characteristics are part of God's human design, and they are—at least in my twelve years of experiences—universal.

My questions to the groups are not, in reality, open-ended. I know going into the exercise that *thinkers* will give certain responses: they prefer clear explanations, structure, depth, and new insights. "What does this passage *mean?*"

Feelers will always prefer freedom, spontaneity, personal stories, and personal relevance. "How does this passage relate *to me?*"

Doers will always prefer practicality, efficiency, and guidelines for competent Christian behavior and ministry. "*What do I do* in my life and work based on this passage?" The power of this exercise comes from the realization of participants that the "truths" displayed on my slides bubble up out of their own personal experiences. The correspondence between personal experiences and conference explanations infuses the discussions with Truth, Relevance, and Competence—and this generates enthusiasm in all three groups.

4. Provide opportunities for discussion

"*Students have frequent opportunities to debate and discuss substantive issues.*" Time is planned for students to talk with each other, in order to compare and contrast their own ideas. In constructivist settings, learner talk is more important than teacher talk.

At the end of the first phase of small group work in the conference, groups are called to share their list of three "preferred characteristics," one at a time. The unveiling of each group's list provokes animated reactions from the other two. When thinkers declare their preference for structure (verse by verse, concept by concept) and depth (profound meaning) in their studies, feelers and doers often respond with feigned groans and an occasional good-natured shout of "Boring!"

When feelers declare their preferences for spontaneity (freedom from lecture and strict lesson plans) and testimony (sharing life stories with each other), thinkers and doers often respond with groans and a resounding "Superficial!"[112]

When doers declare their preferences for practicality (How do I use this at home and at work?) and efficiency (Don't waste time with *paralysis of analysis* and *vacuous stories*), thinkers and feelers often respond with more groans and a cry of "Busy work!" These break-downs and responses have held true since I began doing this in the mid-1990s, whether I was working with seminary students in Fort Worth, African-American Sunday school teachers in Oklahoma City or Houston, teachers in Sao Paulo, Brazil, or Bible Institute students in the former Soviet Union. Debate across the three groups is always lively and makes my point: "These different viewpoints are part of God's design for human learning, and they sit, personified, in all our classes until we drive them away with one-dimensional teaching."

5. Help students think for themselves

"*The primary goal of instruction is for students to learn to think for themselves.*" This goal of students thinking for themselves is common to all cognitive theories of learning, and reflects the influence of John Dewey's pragmatic foundation[113] of constructivist views.

As the three groups discuss their lists of best three and worst three, each teacher-participant is left to consider whether their own approach to teaching is driving people away. "How am I reaching out to every member—thinker, feeler, doer—of my class?" The subjective dynamics are different for every teacher in the conference—their backgrounds, experiences, class situations, and preferences color how they process the information given. What each specifically learns is unique to them. Yet, the overall goal of the conference is always achieved: for teachers to consider, in real ways, their approaches to teaching in the context of three spheres of learning. While the actual outcome for each participant is unique and subjective, there is an objective reality to be mastered, and that reality is represented in the Christian Teachers' Triad (Chapter Twelve).

6. Engage students in high-level cognitive processes

"Students engage in such high level cognitive processes as explaining ideas, interpreting texts, predicting phenomenon, and constructing arguments based on evidence." Despite an emphasis on social interaction through discussions, small groups, and projects, cognitive theorists emphasize the mastery of conceptual networks (rather than competent behavior or values clarification, which cognitivists believe naturally flow from proper understanding).

Participants in the Triad conference defend their own preferences, contrast themselves with other groups, and compare the presentations of all three groups to the diagrams as defined in the seminar. In areas where conference principles confirm what good teacher-participants already understand, value, and do, their mental representations are strengthened. Where conference principles push the boundaries of mental representations, the processes of disequilibrium and accommodation expand them. Teachers often share predictions of what might happen in their own classes should they use the broader range of approaches presented in the conference.

7. Engage students in long-term projects

"Beyond giving written examinations, teachers require students to write research reports, deliver oral presentations, build models, and engage in problem solving activities." Clearly, the constructivist focus is to engage learners at higher levels of thinking than is possible with examinations—which, unfortunately, usually default to simple recall and comprehension-level questions (see Chapter Fifteen for the antidote).

While participants in the conference *establish a new framework* for expanding their personal model of teaching, the single three-hour conference does not lend itself to long-term cognitive processing. My prayer, of course, is that teachers will continue to use the Triad as a tool to analyze and evaluate their own teaching, as well as teaching approaches they encounter in the future. The conference provides teachers a snap-shot of triadic teaching, but teachers create the on-going motion picture of change on their own with the Lord.

In the late 1990s, Dr. Mike Barnett[114] and I developed a course for Columbia International Seminary. We married missions and discipleship through a problem-based, research-oriented approach. We divided the class into seven regional groups. Each regional group was assigned an element of the Disciplers' Model. Six three-hour sessions were given to introduction, instruction (discipleship and missiology), and exams. Two sessions were given to supervised group work in class, and seven sessions were given to group presentations. Groups studied culture, language, and barriers to the gospel prominent in their region, and "solved the problems" of crossing cultural barriers through their assigned Model element. The student-led presentations were divided into two hours for presentation and group interaction, thirty minutes of "fellowship" around culturally-appropriate foods, and thirty minutes of critique and comment from the two professors. Exams formed a small percentage of the semester grade, and yet students gave the course high ratings in terms of learning content, practicality, and helpfulness in preparing them for teaching and missions.

8. Assess student progress continually

"Student progress is assessed continually rather than just at the end of the unit or the end of the semester."[115] Constructivist teachers accomplish continual assessment by asking questions, posing problems, and debating positions. Even operant conditioning theory predicts that end-of-unit or end-of-semester examinations cannot motivate consistent learning (a disadvantage of fixed interval reinforcement). Frequent questions and interactions allow teachers to assess learning continuously.

Throughout the Triad conference, I ask questions of participants, and participants are encouraged to ask questions of their own, as each slide is shown. Each slide repeats the cycle of input-process-question, which builds an increasingly complex network of principles for "teaching *everyone* in the class." The cycle is repeated more than 60 times over the three-hour conference.

9. Revise course content and teaching approaches regularly

"Subject-matter disciplines and their knowledge bases are seen as continually undergoing revision." This principle addresses courses we teach repeatedly. Subject matter is not static. New discoveries are made on a regular basis. Learner characteristics—previous learning, expectations, and study skills—change from year to year. New approaches need to be used to engage "this class" of students. Teachers who teach from notebooks yellowed from age do their students a disservice. Teachers do well to analyze and, as necessary, revise every session in light of learner needs.

As I learn more and create better ways to explain the concepts and principles of the Triad, I adjust slides and slide sets. In fact, I have nearly *one hundred* different Triad slide sets dating from 1995 that reflect changes over time in the way I present these ideas.

In addition to these newer constructivist characteristics, Snowman includes older suggestions, drawn from Discovery Learning, that remain effective in the classroom despite the passage of time. Constructivist teachers help students expand their conceptual networks, says Snowman, by (1) emphasizing contrast among ideas, (2) stimulating informed guessing, (3) encouraging participation, and (4) stimulating [student] awareness [of subject structure].[116]

The Triad conference (1) emphasizes contrast among the three spheres of learning, while synthesizing all three into a single triadic view of learning and teaching; (2) stimulates informed guessing by asking how given learners and teachers—thinkers, feelers, and doers—might react to various teaching situations; (3) encourages participation by engaging willing volunteers to share their "favorite" and "worst" teacher stories, working within their own triadic group, and engaging participants in other spheres; and (4) stimulates awareness of the tendency teachers have to teach predominantly from their own sphere—and the (negative) impact that has on learners.

Constructivist Outcomes:
The Nature of Reality and Knowledge

As I have examined contemporary textbooks and Web sites, no aspect of the "vast and woolly area"[117] of Constructivism is as confusing as its desired outcome. The range of notions expressed in the 1990s that caused me to whisper a warning has only grown larger and more extreme. At one end of the range is a more objective view of Constructivism, illustrated by the Triad conference above, an approach to teaching I use every week in our Bible study class of Empty Nesters.[118] At the other end of the range is a radical re-socialization movement, which, through "authentic activities," converts reading, 'riting, and 'rithmetic into politically correct, often radically left, indoctrination exercises. What Vygotsky envisioned for the Soviet Union and the world, through "culturally relevant social interaction," is now practiced openly in some American schools. Even so, this should not cause us to reject Constructivism out of hand. A Chevy Malibu can be used for a family vacation or a drive-by shooting. It is not the make of the car, but those driving it that makes the difference. It is the same for Constructivism. So what is the desired outcome? I suggest three possibilities.

An objective mental representation of the world as it exists

Some proponents of Constructivism suggest that students should *discover for themselves* every fact, principle, or formula they need to know. This is not Jerome Bruner's position. Discovery, said Bruner, is "simply too inefficient a process to be used that widely." There should first be a mastery of facts, concepts, and terms that form the essentials of a subject. Discovery can then build on this foundation. Some Constructivists believe that "learning from others [direct instruction] can be as meaningful as personal discovery."[119] These statements suggest that *objective knowledge exists that does not need to be created by learners.* Using Piaget's language, learners accommodate their thinking by creating or modifying schemes to reflect what they experience in the world. Let me underscore the emphasis: "creating schemes to reflect objective knowledge."

When, for example, students master the chi-square formulas in statistics, they have constructed an *objective* mental representation—a network of inter-connected symbols and meanings—that allow them to analyze a particular kind of data in a particular research situation. Using this network of meanings, they can correctly apply the appropriate formula, correctly calculate the chi-square value, and correctly interpret its meaning in the context of the study.

By objective, I do not mean to imply that every student has the same network of meanings. Some students require more foundation, others require more elaboration, and still others require more examples. But all who have learned the formulas can remember, explain, and use them correctly. Students have not created their own formulas "based on personal backgrounds, language, ethnicity, or religious preference." The chi-square procedures are the same for all who wish to analyze data for which it was developed.

Russians and Ukrainians use samovars to brew tea. The samovar itself boils water. Atop the samovar is a pitcher that contains a very strong tea concentrate, called *zavarka.* Tea is made by pouring a small amount of *zavarka* into a cup—how much varies according to taste—and then diluting the *zavarka* with boiling water from the body of the samovar. The first time I saw a samovar, I took the "tea" pitcher and poured my cup full of *zavarka,* neglecting the boiling water altogether—and added two teaspoons of sugar. My reaction to tasting the sweet, undrinkable mess was "Ukrainians certainly like strong tea!" Piaget would call this assimilation: I made a cup of tea (incorrectly) according to what I knew about tea.

A student came into the dining room and made a cup of tea properly. I accommodated my thinking to the *real* world of Ukrainian tea and made myself a second, and very delicious, cup of tea. There is subjectivity here, of course, in how strong to make the tea. But the central concept is an objective one. Mix *zavarka* with boiling water to make tea. I've never made myself a cup of undiluted *zavarka* since.

This is how I read Piaget and Bruner in graduate school in the 1970s. There is an external world. There is a natural inclination of the mind, called organization, to make sense of the world. Snowman (2009) follows Piaget as he describes adaptation as "the tendency to adjust to the environment . . . the process of creating a good fit or match between one's conception of reality (one's schemes) and the real-life experiences one encounters."[120]

Woolfolk (2004) moves away from an objective focus when she suggests that "correct representations" of the world are not a concern for Constructivists. Rather, they are "more interested in meaning as constructed by the individual."[121] In her view, Constructivists are more concerned with subjective constructions than with the correspondence of those constructions with the real (objective) world. And yet, just five pages later, she describes a spiral curriculum as one that "introduces the fundamental structure" of a subject at the beginning of the semester, and then "revisits" the subject "in more and more complex forms over time."[122] This suggests a sharpening of understanding toward an objective network of ideas. If teachers are not concerned with correct representations, why spiral? Why revisit?

Let me use, again, the example of statistical symbols (fundamental structure) I display the first day of class. I return to them again and again during the semester (spiral curriculum) because my goal is for students to construct a mental representation of the inter-connectedness of all the symbols. Not *any* representation. Not a *personally relevant* representation, but a *conceptually correct* representation. The cluster of symbols and their referents are objectively true. They provide a real foundation upon which to build other, more complex, approaches to data analysis. To make my point crystal clear, I am not referring to rote memorization of the symbols, which is useless in problem-solving, but an interactive, flexible, conceptually correct network of meanings.

It is this objective constructivism that drives my study of the Bible with others. The prophet Isaiah declared, "The grass withers, the flowers fade, but the word of our God remains forever" (Isa 40:8). While each of us comes to God's Word differently—with various backgrounds, hurts, needs, experiences—our differences do not change God's message. It is that message we seek, for in that message is life (John 20:31). We begin with the essentials, but, in a spiral curriculum, we revisit His Word again and again, in increasingly complex forms over time, constructing a complex, yet meaningfully networked, representation of His will and His way in our minds. While this view has guided my thinking for four decades, it certainly is a minority view among educational theorists today who move toward views that are more subjective.

A subjective mental representation of the world

The philosophies of Existentialism and Postmodernism question the ability to objectively know anything. Woolfolk (2004) underscores this when she suggests that Constructivists are "more interested in *meaning as constructed by the individual*."[123] Alexander elaborates (2006): Knowledge of the world "cannot exist without human construction." Knowledge of reality is "individually formed." It exists as an "individual possession."[124]

Two sisters had a running argument for years over an orange sweater. The older sister would come home from college, find the sweater in her sister's closet, and take it. The sweater was hers. She had only loaned it to her younger sister. She distinctly remembered when and where she bought it. Her younger sister insisted the sweater belonged to her, that *she* had bought it, and the older sister had merely been with her at the store. The argument continued until the older sister simply gave the sweater to the younger.[125]

Despite the differences in recollection by the two sisters, there exists *one true* story here. One sister actually bought the sweater, and the other did not. While a true story exists, constructivists in this camp are more interested in the meanings constructed by the sisters than what really happened, even though the event was real.

A subjective creation of a world of our own

The most radical form of constructivism, briefly mentioned earlier, rejects the possibility of objective knowing altogether. "We cannot know an objective reality. Rather, we construct our own subjective understanding of our experiences, interpreting everything in light of what has already been experienced and learned."[126] Put another way, "No two people have the same experiences, physiologies, or environments; therefore, no two people will construct the same knowledge." However, even though this knowledge is personal, people often agree about what is true[127] to the extent that "their constructions seem to function in the same way in given situations."[128] In other words, reality, truth, and beauty are all a matter of personal choice, personal creation. If two should happen to agree, so much the better, *but there can be no contradiction*. People "actively construct their own knowledge, and that reality is determined by the experience of the knower, rather than existing as an objective truth distinct from the individual."

Which sister's recollection was right? The consensus in this camp is that it really does not matter in terms of the sisters' behavior or the outcome of the story.[129] "The truth" simply isn't important. In this strain of constructivism, "Truth is where it always is . . . in the mind of the beholder."[130]

Mental Representation of the Real?

You will find these last two explanations—subjective representation and subjective creation—difficult to keep separate as you read the literature. When theorists speak of "the mental representation" as more real than "the object represented," they lead us to a place of academic abstraction that has no tangible anchor or practical purpose in teaching. I sometimes get the feeling I am talking to Humpty Dumpty in Alice's Wonderland: "When I use a word . . . it means just what I choose it to mean—neither more nor less."[131]

In court cases, eye-witnesses provide testimony. Their (subjectively constructed) accounts of events differ in all sorts of ways. If I read subjective constructivists correctly, these variances do not matter, for all eyewitness accounts are equally valid, since all have been personally constructed. And yet the goal in giving testimony is to piece together, eventually, what really happened (the real). The truth, we assume, is important to the defendant, especially if he is innocent.

Let's say I take a class of ten doctoral students to a California beach at sunset. Each has a camera, and I ask them to take a picture of the waning sun. When I compare the ten pictures, I find that no two photographs are the same. One student zoomed in to emphasize the wispy clouds drifting across the orange face of the sun. Another zoomed out to frame the bright orange speck by palm trees and ocean surf. A novice used automatic settings, while a digital expert manually set her camera for dramatic effect. One opted for full color while another chose high contrast sepia. Ten photographs, no two alike, and yet there was but one sunset. Each photograph captured a part of the real, expressing *subjective choices* of the photographer as well as *the sun as it was* in the moment. The photographs cannot capture the richness of the Real, but neither do they render the Real unimportant.

Later, when I show the ten photographs to another student who was unable to go, he begins, photo by photo, to construct a mental representation of how that sunset looked. He will never experience the sunset as it was, but he will construct a better mental representation of it with the various (incomplete) photos than without them. Perhaps one day he will go to that beach and experience the Real Thing for himself.

That is my goal in teaching. The precious time we share in the classroom must be about realities that matter, otherwise, why teach? The procedures we use, the questions asked and answered, the problems posed and processed, and the ways we engage one another head, heart, and hand have meanings that stand above whatever personally created perceptions we each generate.

Despite this common sense approach to reality, we are confronted time and again by theorists who insist that the only "real" reality is what we conjure up in our own minds. *If this is true*, why can't I create my own understanding of Constructivism based on my background and experience. Why should I pay attention to what these authors say? Why do they write books at all? If all constructions of knowledge are equal, why read them? *Surely, they cannot believe that.*

Constructivism, like the Bible or biology, means "something," not "anything." That something may be complex and hard to clarify as it continues to evolve, but it possesses an objective reality. Whatever it is, I do not "create Constructivism" by constructing my own understanding of it. What I do create is a mental network, which I label Constructivism. This network of concepts, especially in the beginning of my study, based on a book or two, may or may not be correct. As I continue to study, I spiral back again and again, book after book, to essential themes and constant factors, deepening the network of inter-related concepts subsumed under the umbrella of Constructivism. At any point in time, I have a better understanding of it than I had before. In this sense, I create my own internal knowledge base of Constructivism, but I do not create Constructivism.

Perhaps this is what the writers mean after all. If it is, why do I continue to hear libertine echoes of "personal perception is the only reality there is"? This *perception as reality* is patent nonsense, created by clever people who fear, I suspect, the actual existence of Reality and Truth, for if they exist, it would have serious implications for them. Disdain for objective reality may be the result of a spiritual battle in which subjectivists prefer to say "What I know is all the reality that matters," and live in blissful ignorance of issues larger than self.

Questioning Constructivist Claims

As I read through various texts, attempting to clarify the use of terms, the various perspectives, and especially the common implications for teaching, I found myself having visceral reactions to one statement after another. I began noting these reactions in comments and lay them out for you here. In doing so, I am opening my mind to you, displaying the kinds of things that hooked me into responding. Some of the following may be redundant to earlier portions of the chapter. There, my purpose was to present a smooth narrative, describing three views. Here, my purpose is to react specifically to constructivist terms and phrases. Perhaps the open dialogue will help you as you reflect on this chapter.

1. "The five terms"

The five terms are Constructivist labels: **Cognitive** Constructivism, **Social** Constructivism, **Radical** Constructivism, **Information Processing Theory**, and **Construct*ion*ism**. There is a great deal of confusion in the literature about constructivism.

There are **philosophical** differences—how Realist or Existential are the authors? There are **social** differences in the authors—how much learning is achieved individually and how much in social context? There are **political** differences in the authors—is the goal to provide understanding of subjects or infuse politically correct values? Authors use the same terms to mean different things, and different terms to mean the same things. Some focus on recent research, while others reach back to research that is decades old, in order to make applications today. It is difficult to know, when reading any given textbook, what hidden meanings lie behind the words. All these factors add to the confusion.

2. "Objective Constructivism"

Is there such a thing as *objective* constructivism? Don't all forms of constructivism emphasize the personal creation of mental representations, which must, given human learning, be subjectively influenced? Suppose two students write a paper on Jerome Bruner. They select various sources and write very different papers. And yet, if there is "truth" in the papers, they will essentially report the same issues. If they do not, we can conclude the papers reveal more about the writers than they do about Jerome Bruner.

Contemporary writers emphasize the subjective nature of what is created more than the objective truth of what is represented. To put it in the context of the illustration above, they appear to be more interested in students *revealing themselves* in their papers on Bruner than in students describing Bruner. In this sense, a "research paper" is little more than an academic invitation to engage students in self-revelation.

I have used the term **objective Constructivism** to emphasize that mental representations, personally created by each learner, should correspond to real world events—such as the life and thought of Bruner as it was. We will discuss the proper place for self-revelation in Chapter Ten.

3. "Social interaction"

Some use the term *social interaction* to mean teachers and students talking *with* each other (as opposed to teachers talking *at* students). Most view social interaction as class discussions, or perhaps small groups of students working on projects (Piaget, Bruner). These expressions certainly fit a Christian view of teaching and learning (Relational Pillar).

Still others view social interaction as the means of re-socialization of students (the internalization of politically correct cultural views), or enculturation, at the level of classroom, school, community, or society (Vygotsky).

4. "Students' prior knowledge"

We reported a 1999 review of 183 studies that found a strong relationship between prior knowledge and performance. Isn't this association of variables obvious, given the fact that learning any material which is completely new, without any previous knowledge, would be far more difficult than learning material that is an extension of what is already known.

5. "Even listening to a lecture involves active attempts to construct new knowledge"

Here is the full quote: "Constructivists assume that all knowledge is constructed from previous knowledge, irrespective of how one is taught . . . even listening to a lecture involves active attempts to construct new knowledge." This mention of listening to lectures is not the thrust of most writers in the field, who suggest that all knowledge is constructed from personal experiences or group activities. At least this writer opens the door, as Jerome Bruner did himself, for direct instruction. But many do not.

6. "Authentic activities" . . . applying writing skills to completing a job application"

Here is the full quote: "Authentic activities," such as using "math skills to balance a checkbook, or apply writing skills to completing a job application." Doesn't mastery of mathematical symbols and concepts require more than balancing a checkbook, which is accomplished by simple addition and subtraction? Doesn't learning to write skillfully require more than filling in blanks on a job application? Perhaps these "authentic tasks" are relevant in alternative school programs and appropriate for students who do not plan to attend college. But balancing checkbooks and completing job applications will not provide the foundation for critical thinking, hypothesizing, and analyzing theoretical perspectives in college and beyond.

Do "authentic activities" and "real world tasks" focus on commonsensical behaviors that parents once taught? Or, perhaps these suggestions are oversimplifications. Perhaps the focus of authentic tasks is to create a learning environment inside the classroom that reflects realities outside the classroom, so that learners can more easily transfer what they learn to their lives outside of school. Is this more necessary now because contemporary parents are more self-absorbed and less engaged in teaching their own children than a generation or two ago? Are contemporary schools replacing civic-focused subjects with life-focused subjects? Are they intentionally replacing parent-driven social engineering (family) with teacher-driven social engineering (State)?

Writers that are more reasonable promote "authentic activities" as those that place academic subjects in the context of real world applications. They emphasize 1) prior mastery of academic skills and concepts in several relevant areas, which are then 2) used in out-of-class projects. In a church context, we could distinguish between a weekend "study of missions" (academic) with "participation in a weekend mission trip" (authentic).

The best learning experience would be created when both academic and authentic activities are used. The academic would be classroom study of age-group characteristics, principles of teaching and learning, crafts, recreation, and sharing the gospel. The authentic would be a two-week mission adventure in which teens move across cultural divides to organize, teach, lead, and witness to children different from themselves.

7. "From teachers merely providing information toward teachers promoting interaction"

"The primary change is a shift in emphasis away from teachers merely providing information and toward teachers promoting interaction that makes student thinking open and visible." What educational theorist, what professional educator, what educational philosopher ever defined teaching as merely providing information?

The goal of doing better than *merely providing information* is, of course, nothing new. It extends back to the earliest days of educational psychology, and perhaps back to Cain and Abel's lessons on acceptable sacrifices. This bromide continues to be repeated, in my opinion, because teachers naturally revert to *teaching as telling*, as it is easier than actually engaging students head, heart, or hand.

8. "Teachers need to guard against imposing their thoughts"

Teacher-student interaction is important but teachers need to guard against imposing their thoughts and values on developing learners. Does this writer use the word "imposing" to mean "forcing," or "influencing"? Who but a tyrant would enlist teachers for the purpose of re-socializing children according to government fiat? Then again, what teacher can prevent influencing children with whom he or she interacts? That is why good character in leaders is important. For even in selecting activities, creating open-ended questions, and providing "free choice" in the selection of group projects, teachers' values shine through. Does fairness mean "everyone succeeds equally" [lower the standards until everyone "succeeds"] or "everyone has equal opportunity to succeed" [even if some fail]? Can children choose from a variety of activities that require different skill sets (some will be left out of some activities), or must all children be limited to a few activities that everyone can handle? These basic human values will be communicated through teacher-student interaction because teachers are human beings and cannot be value-neutral.

Further, when teachers set up "authentic activities" for their students, it is difficult not to impose underlying political views. Taking a first grade class on a field trip to their teacher's lesbian wedding[132] changed these six-year-olds in ways no one can predict ("internalization of social interaction"— Vygotsky), and at a time before they can possibly comprehend what homosexual behavior is. Setting up "authentic activities" and then allowing students to "construct their own knowledge" from the events is dereliction of duty by those charged to prepare children to take their rightful place as a contributing member of society.

9. Teaching is "helping individuals create personal views"

Do these "personal views" need to correspond to any external reality or standard? Is it enough for my statistics students to explain their failure of an exam by saying "I thought chi square was used this way"? Certainly, this (incorrect) understanding was personally constructed. Or should I expect them to understand chi-square "correctly"? The answer is obvious in the real world. I want pilots who know how to control the jetliner that is carrying me across the Atlantic Ocean, especially during landings! I want a highly trained surgeon to operate on me—and I'd prefer one who has successfully completed a hundred operations before mine. Their personally constructed views are fine with me, so long as those personal views correspond with "best practices" in flight and surgery, respectively.

10. "Social constructivism has become the view that is most influential"

Here is the full quote: "Social constructivism has become the view that is most influential in guiding the thinking of educational leaders and teachers." This 2007 declaration is frightening, given Vygotsky's goals in the Soviet Union of the 1920s and 1930s, the increasing power of the political left in our own country today, and the subjective direction of American education over the past forty years. It is a matter Christian teachers need to take seriously as we struggle to maintain a free Church in a free State.

I hope these musings have been helpful to you in broadening the narrative. In every subject we teach, there are realities, essentials worth knowing, worth understanding, worth mastering. As we help students perceive those realities better, as we help them construct knowledge that correctly corresponds to those essentials, we lay a firm foundation for further learning. As we sift through the sands of clutter, contradiction, and confusion, what teaching nuggets can we find, polish, and preserve for the advancement of our students in kingdom life and citizenship? These concerns find spiritual meaning in the way we handle the Word of Truth.

Constructivism and Christian Teaching

Building on early discoveries in Piaget's Cognitive Theory, Bruner's Discovery Learning, and, more recently, Constructivism, we make the following suggestions for teaching in a Christian context. We anchor them in the fact that Reality exists, and Truth can be known.

Teaching out of the law of Prägnanz

Students come into our classrooms with an existing conceptual framework, unique to their culture, background, family, and previous experiences. No matter what we say, what questions we ask, or what illustrations we use, students process the session in the context of their own perceptual framework. This mental activity is continuous, and learners are usually unaware they are changing our words into forms that make sense to them. No matter what we do within the context of the class, learners will leave with an experience that is both unique to themselves (ten photographs) and shared by everyone in the room (the sunset).

Teachers do well to intentionally provide ways for learners to openly process their thinking. This can be done through objective questions ("How did David express his sorrow for the loss of King Saul and Jonathan?") and subjective questions ("How did you express sorrow when you lost a loved one?"). The questions provoke thinking in all learners. The answers we receive from selected learners are windows into their minds, revealing their conceptual frameworks.

Teaching out of the law of similarity

Familiar Bible verses, spiritual truths, theological concepts, and religious phrases will be readily recognized by learners and re-woven into cognitive structures, strengthening them. *Unfamiliar* viewpoints and ideas will be suspect. They will be resisted as disequilibrium causes increased anxiety. Learners may ask questions for clarification and reassurance. This is a normal part of the accommodation process. If meaningful answers are not received, unfamiliar ideas will be shelved for further consideration, and may simply be rejected outright. Teachers do well to begin explanations with well-established truths before addressing less familiar ideas.

When we began a recent study of 1 and 2 Samuel, we located its history in the general context of Old Testament chronology, and then the specific context of King Saul and King David. The first study from 1 Samuel set the context for the following sessions. Each successive session was anchored in the preceding one. Over the course of study, the cultural context of Israel in 1000 BC developed, but familiar spiritual truths—God's faithfulness, protection, and love; David's obedience, devotion, sin, and submission—shone through as eternal principles as valid today in Texas as they were then and there. As participants saw similarities of David's experiences with their own, individual testimonies added to the conceptual framework of everyone in the class.

In the study of statistics, basic concepts of mean and standard deviation lead to the one-sample z-test, which leads logically to the one-sample t-test, which leads logically to two types of the two-sample t-test, which leads logically to one-way analysis of variance. By connecting new material to old material, emphasizing similarities that new procedures have with prior ones, students are better able to process the differences they confront in the new procedures.

Teaching out of the law of closure

Learners want so much to understand what we teach, that they fill in the gaps in understanding from their own imaginations. They make sense of our words, reducing disequilibrium, even if they distort them in the process. This is assimilation: changing what they experience to fit what they already know. Teachers do well to provide complete explanations and illustrations. Asking questions and presenting problems provide ways to make learner thinking visible. It is rather easy to determine whether learner representations have been correctly constructed or distorted through closure.

One way distortion creeps into our thinking is to study, say, God's characteristics in isolation. One study may focus on the "love" of God without mention of His holiness or wrath. Learners can walk away with an unbalanced understanding that "God is *love*, therefore . . ." This can lead to all manner of heresy. If God is love, why does He send anyone to hell? Why did He let my Daddy die? Why did God command Israel to destroy the Canaanites?

Or we may study the "wrath" of God without mention of His love and care. Learners can walk away with an unbalanced perspective of a cold, distant, holy, angry God. The truth is that God is love-wrath. He loves us and wants to rescue, redeem, sanctify, and eventually glorify us. He hates sin and will not tolerate it. God's love-wrath is like fire. When in right relationship to fire, we are warmed. When in wrong relationship to fire, we are burned. The difference between Love and Wrath is not in the holy, loving fire, but in our relationship to Him.[133]

By providing this larger picture, there is less chance for distortion through closure. When we focus on sin, we also discuss salvation. When we focus on sanctification, we also discuss disobedience. When we discuss holiness, we also consider the profane. When we study grace, we balance it with some discussion of justice. When encouraging students to be strong in their convictions, we remind them that they are also to accept and love others. When prompting toward spiritual growth, we also emphasize the danger of becoming proud of our spiritual growth. We are not to speak lovingly without truth, or speak truthfully without love—we are to "speak the truth in love" (Eph 4:15). Without balancing related truths, biblical concepts can be seen as one-dimensional, disjointed, and rigid. I ask myself as I prepare, "What distorted extreme might learners carry away from this study?" and then I intentionally touch on those issues—"Now this *doesn't* mean that . . ." Teachers do well to paint the larger picture, even as they discuss the details, to help learners avoid misunderstanding through closure.

Teaching out of the law of good continuation

Learners naturally simplify concepts. In so doing, they lose important details, merging distinctions into confusion. For example, I am surprised how many Christians think "the God of the Old Testament" is holy and full of wrath, while "the God of the New Testament" (Jesus) is forgiving and loving, as if there are two different Gods in Scripture. This is, of course, not true. God is Love-Wrath in both Old and New Testaments. Didn't Jehovah God show His love and mercy to Israel, even in the face of sin and idolatry? Didn't Jesus express wrath as He cleansed the temple with a whip, overturning the money-changers' tables? We tend to reduce God to simplistic formulas. The result of this reduction, following the law of good continuation, is a god-created-in-our-own-image, and this is idolatry. Teachers do well to connect general principles to specific differences, helping learners to construct a more truthful representation of God, His Word, and His work.

Teaching with insight

Learners naturally seek consistency within their own mental networks and use insight to create answers to questions that arise. Teachers do well to provide opportunities for learners to "cogitate" over Bible-Life issues, to suggest discoveries they have already made in the context of the study, and to consider the insights of others. In a recent class session with our Empty Nesters, I asked what "Do's and Don'ts" they would suggest to people experiencing a tragic loss. Learners responded with many insights they had made over the years, and each response triggered new thoughts in others. Each suggestion strengthened, through multiple insights, a biblical response toward tragedy and loss.

Teaching in the context of life space

Each class of learners forms a living, dynamic, conceptual "life space," which provides a rich resource of ideas for constructing representations. Teachers do well to manage this Life Space, encouraging positive ideas ("How might we show respect, as David respected King Saul, for the leaders God chooses?") and keeping discussions peaceful ("Let's step back a moment and see how to find some common ground.") Before teaching the passage on Tamar (2 Sam 13), assume there may be members in the class who have been sexually abused. Unspoken hurts, unfulfilled dreams, and hidden attitudes are as much a part of the *life space* of a class as the words actually spoken. Teachers do well to consider the class as a living entity, made up of individual learners that learn to think within this social context (Vygotsky).

Teaching with direct instruction

While many contemporary constructivists minimize direct instruction methods, the father of Discovery Learning did not. Bruner considered basic facts and concepts the building blocks for higher-level thinking and emphasized the importance of insuring learners master these basics before engaging in tasks that are more creative. Teachers do well to set the context, raise a question, and explain conflicting views. Define essential terms. Compare and contrast two passages. And then move into more socially-interactive, open-ended, problem-solving activities.

Teaching with iconic presentation

Much of the teaching in Christian contexts is verbal, and therefore highly symbolic. Iconic presentation is based on pictures, diagrams, models, and the like. Teachers do well to include visual aids to support verbal explanations.

I find it helpful to place an incomplete diagram on the marker board before the class convenes. As learners enter, they see the diagram and naturally begin to wonder what it represents (curiosity). As we move through the session, I add to the diagram, labeling its parts as we go along. The visual reinforces the verbal, and the completed diagram provides an iconic image of the key ideas we discuss.

Teaching with power

Conceptual power refers to simplicity in presentation. Teachers do well to increase power in presentations by emphasizing a few essential concepts, with supporting details, more than many words in a continuous stream. The incomplete diagram mentioned above provides power in the lesson, as many words are reduced to an easy-to-remember diagram.

The 1974 *Teacher Guide* for our deaf adult Sunday school curriculum suggested five or six "central truths to cover" each week. When I attempted to cover *all* of the suggested central truths, I found that members remembered very little from one week to the next. Based on the principle of Brunerian power, I began to choose the most important of the central truths (in light of the needs of the learners in the class) and focused the entire session around establishing clear understanding of that one truth. Members remembered these focused truths from week to week far better, which allowed us to build more complex perspectives over time.

Teaching with economy

An abundance of Sunday school lesson materials and the limited time for interaction encourages many teachers to revert to talking through lessons. The frenetic drive to "cover the lesson" in the time allotted results in all sorts of poor teaching practices. Teachers do well to remember that more words do not necessarily produce better learning. Pacing the class—providing a small dose of information, explaining key ideas, asking questions, and then repeating the cycle—transmits fewer facts but establishes better understanding. Teachers do well to layer their preparation with essential concepts, supporting principles, and then supporting details. Engage learners with each layer as time allows.

This same planning approach is helpful in church school, college, and seminary classes as well. Use instructional objectives (see Chapter Twelve) to target essential course outcomes. Break these down into thematic units that build systematically toward course outcomes. Write unit objectives to target essential outcomes. Plan each session to support unit outcomes with relevant course details. While allotted time and learner needs vary from semester to semester, the sequential layers of essential concepts, supporting principles, and supporting details help learners construct clear mental representations of subjects.

Teaching with authentic motivation

Bruner rejected tangible reinforcers as an artificial way to encourage learning. Teachers do well to use curiosity to stimulate participation. I mentioned the use of an incomplete diagram above, which promotes natural curiosity before a word is spoken. A simple question written on a marker board can provoke the attention of learners. The innate desire in many learners to work cooperatively with others in the class is a self-sustaining form of motivation.

Teaching as modeling good thinking skills

Learners learn how to construct clearer mental representations when they observe teachers who model these skills. By listening carefully to student questions, weighing questions before answering, considering responses aloud (that is, engaging in public self talk), and reframing statements for clarity, teachers provide excellent role models for learners. "A disciple is not above his teacher, but everyone who is fully trained will be like his teacher" (Luke 6:40).

Teaching through directed discovery methods

Teachers do well to emphasize contrast among concepts and principles, to encourage learners to make informed guesses based on what they know, and to pose problems to solve, or ask conceptual questions for students to consider. Follow up by having learners evaluate their own guesses, and consider the consequences of answers they give.

Teaching by building on previous sessions

New learning depends on prior learning. Teachers do well to connect the present session with previous ones. By revisiting issues studied previously in the context of present material (spiral curriculum), teachers aid the understanding of the new while strengthening the structure that already exists. Connecting concepts in this chapter to Jean Piaget and Lev Vygotsky (Chapter Four) was intentional, since Constructivism stands on the foundation they laid.

Teaching by assigning real-world tasks

Teachers do well to assign a task to be done during the week that strengthens the learning begun in class. We can use ideas derived from Scripture to assign tasks at home ("Children, how can we help parents this week?") or at work ("What are specific actions we can take on the job to be a positive witness for Christ?"). By doing so, we release learners to construct mental representations of Reality and Truth based on Scripture, in their lives, under the tutelage of the Holy Spirit.

In my research class, I assign statistical problems that relate to ministry or Christian living themes. In my teaching class, I make assignments that connect course principles to student experiences in Bible study classes and worship services. Authentic tasks help dissolve the natural walls students tend to erect between "school," "home," and "church."

In Summary

Constructivists declare that learners need to be active rather than passive in the learning process, to be builders of knowledge and understanding rather than recipients of what teachers tell them. Learners construct cognitive representations of life and reality from the interaction between what they experience in the world and what they already know. Social interaction facilitates personal learning, whether it provides a source of disequilibrium for individual learners, or creates communal truth. Meaningful learning occurs through tasks that have real-world connections.

Christian constructivists certainly agree that learners construct cognitive structures—only learners can learn. But most Christians reject the Humpty Dumpty version of personally-created reality. While all human learning is incomplete, mainstream Christian teachers focus on the goal of understanding subjects as they are and creating cognitive structures that correspond with the world as it is.

The distance between Christian education and Constructivism continues to grow as Constructivism increasingly moves away from objective reality, toward group-think and self-revelation.

Information Processing Theory emphasizes cognitive processes by which learners transform sense perceptions into memories, concepts, and beliefs. IPT also describes the mechanisms of forgetting, which are often overlooked in other theories. We turn to this perspective of cognitive learning in the next chapter.

Chapter Concepts

Cognitive learning theory	Learning theory system that emphasizes rational thought over behavior or attitude
Constructivism	Focuses on individual, internal, rational constructions of knowledge (re: Piaget)
Directed discovery	Teachers control the learning process as they direct students to make discoveries
Discovery learning	Teachers help students form concepts, build generalizations, create cognitive networks
Economy	Present material in small doses. Give time for processing the material.
Enactive mode	Understanding based on *actions, demonstrations, and hands-on experimentation*
Gestalt	Gestalt: configuration (or pattern). Emphasizes "the whole" of human experience.
Iconic mode	Understanding based on *pictures, images, diagrams, and models*
Insight	Solving problems by grasping relationships among objects or events
Law of Closure	Incomplete images naturally perceived as complete (e.g., three dots and triangle)
Law of Good Continuation	Reproduction of images: mind changes them from distorted to symmetrical forms
Law of Membership Character	A single part of the whole gets its characteristics from the whole (e.g., puzzle piece)
Law of Prägnanz	Mind naturally tends to make sense of the environment (cf. Piaget: *organization*)

Law of Proximity	Objects tend to be grouped according to their distance from other objects
Law of Similarity	Objects similar in form, shape, size, or color, tend to be perceived together
Life Space	Psychological field of forces to which people react. Invisible but powerful.
Perception	Meaning we attach to information we receive from the world around us
Power	A powerful presentation is a simple (not simplistic) presentation (e.g., *Triad*)
Presentation modes	Enactive, iconic, symbolic modes of presenting information (Bruner)
Pure discovery	Jerome Bruner's original theory (vs. *directed* discovery)
Reception learning	Structure learning: select materials and present them in an organized manner
Structure	Fundamental ideas of subject, and how they relate to one another
Symbolic mode	Understanding based on *language*, using words to express complex ideas

Chapter Objectives

Learners will demonstrate knowledge of cognitive learning theory by describing the origins of Gestalt psychology, including contributions of Mach, Wertheimer, Köhler, and Lewin.

Learners will demonstrate understanding of cognitive learning by . . .

- Differentiating the views of Mach and Watson, Werthiemer and Pavlov, Köhler and Thorndike, and Bruner and Skinner.
- Giving at least two examples for each law of perception from their own experience.
- Explaining key elements in Bruner's discovery learning, including structure, motivation, student activity, and teacher role.
- Contrasting among Cognitive Constructivism, Social Constructivism, Radical Constructivism, and Constructionism.

Learners will demonstrate appreciation for Constructivism by sharing an experience in which an objective biblical concept was personally "constructed."

Discussion Questions

1 Discuss how Gestalt psychology differs from stimulus-response psychology. Include differences relating to the mind, the learning outcomes, and the methodology.

2 Compare and contrast the ideas of the following paired theorists: Watson and Mach, Pavlov and Wertheimer, Thorndike and Köhler, and Skinner and Bruner.

3 Choose three of the laws of perception. Define the law and give an example of it from your own experience.

4 How does Lewin's concept of life space apply to the teaching ministry of the Church. That is, how does "church community" promote growing in spiritual understanding.

5 Choose a favorite Bible passage, at least a chapter in length. Explain how Bruner's approach to teaching would differ from a verse-by-verse study of the passage. (Focus on structure.)

6 Differentiate among pure discovery, directed discovery, and reception learning methods.

7 Differentiate among Cognitive Constructivism, Social Constructivism, Radical Constructivism, and Constructionism.

8 Survey the suggestions for teaching. Select at least three that your teachers have used in past courses. What was your reaction to them?

COGNITIVE LEARNING II

Information Processing Theory

Listen closely, pay attention to the words of the wise, and apply your mind to my knowledge. For it is pleasing if you keep them within you and if they are constantly on your lips.

Proverbs 22:17–18

Unless we remember, we cannot understand.
—**Edward M. Forster 1879–1970, British Novelist**[1]

Memory is deceptive because it is colored by today's events.[2]
—**Albert Einstein**

Chapter Rationale

Despite the advances of Constructivism over the last dozen years, Information Processing Theory continues to provide important insights into how the mind makes sense of the world. Contemporary IPT is considered a Constructivist view by some, in the sense that it emphasizes "the use of existing knowledge[3] to interpret new information and build new knowledge structures."[4]

Where Behaviorists emphasize external behavior, and Constructivists emphasize the use of what we know to solve problems, Information Processing theory emphasizes the mechanisms by which we attend to, recognize, transform, store, and retrieve information. The key term in this list is *transform*, which refers to the way the mind encodes sense data into mental structures. Using the personal computer as an analogy for sensory input and processing, IPT explains how we learn, why we forget, how we can improve our ability to remember, and how cognitive structure is actually created.

IPT also functions as a cognitive framework for studies in brain-based learning (see Chapter Sixteen), in which cognitive structures are defined in physiological terms.[5] Though IPT is no longer the premier cognitive theory it was in the 1990s, it continues to offer clear guidelines that affect "how much we learn, how well we learn, and whether we learn at all."[6] IPT forms a conceptual bridge between the mental aspects of cognitive theory, and the neurological aspects of brain-based learning.

Chapter Overview

➤ Historical Roots
➤ The Computer as a Model of Learning
➤ The Information Processing Theory Model
➤ Information Processing Operations
➤ Information Processing Theory in the 2000s
➤ Implications of Information Processing Theory for Teaching
➤ *Chapter Concepts, Chapter Objectives, Discussion Questions*

Historical Roots

E. C. Tolman (1886–1959) is the "ancestral hero"[7] of Information Processing theory. His experiments with rats and mazes led him to the conclusion that the animals were creating an internal representation of the maze—a cognitive map of the environment. Though he considered himself a behaviorist, he studied under Kurt Koffka,[8] a colleague of cognitive researcher Max Wertheimer, and he broke ranks with behaviorism by discounting S-R bonds in favor of cognitive maps.[9] Tolman's ideas were not widely accepted because he was unable to translate his findings into a form that teachers could use in their classrooms.

Disenchantment grew with the learning theories of the 1940s and 1950s. Training programs for pilots in World War II demonstrated that pilots were complex information receivers and processors. Communication research in radio and television provided better models for human thought. The advent of the computer, however, provided the most powerful model for human symbol-manipulation.[10]

The growth of cognitive learning theory, Tolman's cognitive map theory, and the computer combined to provide a new way (1970s) of looking at learning. Information Processing theory emphasized *how* a pigeon learns to discriminate, *how* a rat learns to run a maze, and *how* a child learns to recognize words on a page.[11] Its focus on internal mental processes set it apart from traditional behaviorism, and established it firmly in the cognitive learning system of theories. IPT defines learning as the result of interaction between learners and their environment,[12] but emphasizes the objective reality of the world more than recent (2006) Constructivist approaches.[13]

Theorists describe two modes of information processing. The first is called *automatic*,[14] or incidental,[15] processing. This unconscious process records every experience and event in our lives without conscious intention or attention. The second is *intentional*[16] processing, which is the result of attention and study. We will focus the chapter on intentional processes since these have significance for teaching and learning in educational settings.

The Computer as a Model of Learning

Tolman's ideas lay dormant for years, waiting for a way to make his discoveries relevant to classroom learning. The advent of the personal computer (1970s) provided the metaphor that moved theoretical positions into a formal learning theory. Advances in computer technology, such as parallel processing,[17] continue to provide analogies for cognitive functions (parallel distributed processing, 2000).

Computers consist of four basic structures. These are input devices (keyboard, mouse), working memory (RAM, random access memory) where programs are executed, long-term memory (hard disk) where programs and data are stored, and output devices (monitor, printer). Computers process data by transforming input, storing results for later retrieval, and displaying output. As we can see in the diagram at left, INPUT enters the system from the left, passes through a memory structure called the keyboard BUFFER, then passes to the working memory where programs and data interact (word processing, spreadsheets, presentation programs). Results of the data manipulation (documents, calculations, slide shows) are

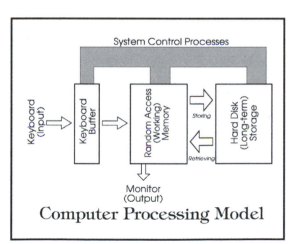

Computer Processing Model

stored "permanently" on the hard drive. The monitor provides a visual representation (output) of what the program is doing. The system control bus connects the various components of the computer so that they function together to accomplish the computational tasks for which it was designed. Information Processing Theory mirrors these elements in describing human learning.

The Information Processing Theory Model

A model is a representation that describes and visualizes what is impossible to observe directly.[18] The IPT model shown below reflects the interaction between cognitive *structures* and cognitive *processes* that control learning. The cognitive *structures*, or memory stores, are information storage units in the brain. The classic IPT model depicts three major types of memory stores: sensory registers, short-term memory, and long-term memory. Contemporary models, influenced by discoveries in brain research over the past fifteen years, reflect increasingly complex networks of overlapping memory stores. The

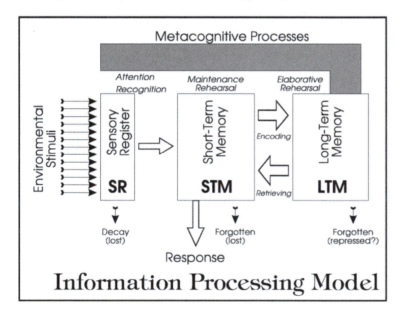

Three-Component model remains the most common depiction of IPT.

Cognitive *processes* are mental actions that transfer information from one unit to another, and transform information into various kinds of memory. These processes include attention, recognition, maintenance rehearsal, elaborative rehearsal, encoding, and retrieving.

Metacognitive processes are the executive control processes that govern the operation of the other cognitive processes.[19] IPT proposes a series of stages, or steps, in the processing of incoming sense data. These steps are 1) attending to a stimulus (sight, sound), 2) recognizing the stimulus, 3) transforming the stimulus into a mental representation, 4) comparing it to information already stored in memory, 5) assigning meaning to it, and 6) acting on it.[20] We will first define each major structure in the system, and then explain how the mind transforms perceptions to cognitive structure. We will finally suggest ways IPT can help students improve their ability to process, retain, recall, and understand the subjects we teach.

Sensory Registers (SR)

The environment bombards our senses with hundreds of stimuli—sights, sounds, smells, tastes, and touch.[21] In a classroom, learners are surrounded by the multi-media stimuli of lectures, Power-Points, videos, and group discussions. The learning process begins as physical sensations meet the physical receptors of the body. Light waves stimulate rods and cones in eyes. Sound waves stimulate ear drums. Heat (cold), humidity, and air movements stimulate skin receptors. These organic input devices are the "keyboards" by which the environment enters data into memory buffers for processing.

Human sensory data is transmitted through nerves to specialized regions of the brain called sensory registers.[22] Taken together, sensory registers form sensory memory. A sensory register might be thought of as a mental buffer between the sense organs and working memory.[23] Sensory memory is volatile and holds data for one to three seconds before it is either processed further, or lost forever. Sensory data exists in SR in the same form as it is perceived, in the form of video or sound clips. We'll discuss how this is done in the section on processing.

Short-Term Memory (STM)

We remember specific stimuli because we pay attention to them long enough to move them into short-term memory.[24] Short-term memory, sometimes called "working memory"[25] or "active memory"[26] retains new information as we consciously work on it. It contains everything that is in our immediate awareness.[27]

Short-term memory filters stimuli coming in from the sensory registers and decides what to do with them. The basic choices are to ignore them (or simply be unaware of them, like music playing in the background), retain them by repeating them, or process them for permanent storage in long-term memory.[28] STM is, in a very real way, our conscious mind, where thinking is done, and where details are held until a problem is solved.[29]

Data storage in STM is limited to *five to nine items for up to a minute* for adults.[30] Three-year-olds can hold about three items, seven-year-olds about five items and teenagers from five to nine items.[31] Suppose we look up a telephone number for a local repair shop. We read the number from the telephone book and repeat it aloud a few times. We turn to the phone and dial the ten-digit number correctly. The line is busy. A minute later we decide to try again. We will probably not remember the number and will have to look it up again. STM has discarded the number.

Television and radio advertisers use a process called chunking—packing several items together to be processed as a single unit—to help viewers remember what number to call to order their product. "Rather than present you with 11 separate numbers to dial in order to get your volume of *Art Treasures of the World*, you are told to dial 1-800 ART INFO, which is at most three separate units."[32] Most viewers already know that "1-800" is the toll-free prefix. Viewers only need to remember ART and INFO in order to dial the number correctly.

Using the strategy of chunking, the limited storage of STM can be increased by combining separate items into larger, more meaningful units. The letters "u n r" require three units of storage. Putting them together as "unr" makes them easier to remember but still requires three storage units. But putting them together as "run" makes them much easier to remember because the word has meaning for us and takes up only one storage unit.[33] If I asked you to memorize this list of letters—aceefiiighmnnnnooooprrrsstty—it could take quite a while. You might chunk them into ace-fiiig-hmnnn-oooo-prrr-sstty, which is easier to recall. But if I chunked them into "information processing theory," you could recall each letter effortlessly, because you know the term. The first list requires 27 memory units, and a lot of repetition. The last form requires only three.

Due to limited storage capacity, the STM is a bottleneck in processing information. If teachers overload students with detailed information, they have difficulty remembering the material, thinking about the material, and solving problems based on the material.[34] If teachers present unstructured information at a pace beyond which students can process it, much of it will be lost.[35]

In short, STM is the conscious part of the information processing system that handles a limited amount of new information for a brief period.[36] Without an intentional decision to rehearse or encode the information, it will be lost in a matter of seconds. If, during these seconds, we can make sense of the information, we encode it for long-term storage.[37]

Long-Term Memory (LTM)

Long-term memory is the mind's permanent information storage device.[38] It is virtually unlimited in capacity[39] and contains a permanent record of everything[40] an individual has experienced (automatic processing) or learned (intentional processing). LTM is capable of holding encoded information for a lifetime.[41] The various kinds of knowledge (see Table), interests, skills, and attitudes stored in LTM influence *what* we perceive, *how we interpret* our perceptions, and whether we *choose to process* information at all.[42]

Though encoded information remains in LTM forever,[43] it does not follow that we can retrieve or decode it all. While LTM stores every experience, many of these experiences are beyond our ability to remember them.[44] These irretrievable memories are known to researchers because direct electric

Five Kinds of Knowledge

Type	Description	Example
Facts	Elements of factual knowledge	How many sides does a square have?
Concepts	Categories, principles, and models	What is the difference between . . .?
Procedures	Rules, algorithms, lists of steps	Rule: to make a noun plural, add 's'
Strategies	General approaches for improving learning	Design a plan for composing an essay
Beliefs	Personal views of learning capability	"I have the ability to learn statistics."

Drawn from Mayer, 19-20, who also mentions other types of knowledge not represented by most educational research: affective, motoric, personal, and social knowledge. As you can see, this is an all-inclusive definition of knowledge, but fits the usage of the term in IPT.

stimulation of various parts of the brain causes specific memories to be recalled. In one such experiment, an adult remembers details of his third birthday party: the smells of food cooking in the house, the dress his mother wore, the presents he received, the names of his friends. Each of these memories was verified as accurate by others present at the party. Scientists were not able, however, to know where specific memories were stored, so the recalled events were randomly remembered. If we need to use encoded information later, on demand—when taking an exam or solving a problem—then information must be intentionally encoded ("learned").

The LTM contains both *explicit* (conscious, intentional) memory and *implicit* (unconscious[45], "tacit"[46]) memory. *Explicit* memories[47] are intentionally encoded (transformed, "learned") and can be deliberately recalled (retrieved). We are *aware* that we know and can remember this information.

Explicit memories can be *episodic* or *semantic*.[48] *Episodic memory* stores life events (episodes) just as they happen. These autobiographical images of life,[49] such as the third birthday party mentioned above, or our first day of school, or a trip overseas, are stored in a form similar to a video tape[50] that allows us to play them back in our minds. Episodic memory also "keeps track of things," such as "jokes, gossip, and plots from films."[51] Episodic memories are tied to a particular time and place, especially the memories of the events in our lives.[52]

Semantic memory, very important in school settings,[53] stores meanings—facts, concepts, principles, rules, problem solving strategies, thinking skills and the like.[54] These memories are not connected to any particular event and are stored as *propositional networks*, *images*, and *schemas.*

A *propositional network* is a set of interconnected concepts that are stored as meanings rather than exact words. Recalling one part of a network activates recall of another, since concepts exist in relationships with each other. We are not aware of these networks, because they do not exist in conscious, working memory,[55] but all mental action depends on them. When we ask someone his or her name, we simply ask, "What is your name?" We do this as English speakers *without any consideration of how to put those words together.* Deaf people sign (transliteration:), "Your name—what?"[56] Russians ask (transliteration:) "How you (they) call?" [«**Как Вас зовут**?»]. These three phrases mean "What is your name?"—though the words/signs and grammatical structures differ. Americans, deaf persons, and Russians automatically ask the question *without thinking how*, drawing on their respective semantic memories to supply the elements.[57]

Images refer to pictorial representations of encoded information. If I were to ask you to describe the Discipler's Model, you would "picture" the diagram in your mind, moving from element to element, recalling its name and focus. Researchers do not agree on how images are stored. Some suggest images are stored as literal pictures, while others believe they are stored as propositions that are converted to pictures upon recall.[58]

Long Term Memory				
Explicit Memory (conscious)		**Implicit Memory** (unconscious)		
Episodic Memory	**Semantic Memory**	**Classical Conditioning**	**Procedural Memory**	**Priming**
Personal experiences Specific times and places	*Meaning: Facts, Theories Concepts, Schemas* **Declarative Knowledge** ("knowing that")	*Unconscious fears "Test anxiety"*	*Bat a ball Compute a formula* **Procedural Knowledge** ("knowing how")	*Implicit activation of concepts in LTM through associations*

Summarizes data drawn from Woolfolk (2004), 247-252

Schemas (schemes) are *abstract* knowledge *structures* that organize "vast amounts of information . . . for representing an event, concept, or skill"[59]—a concept very similar to Piaget's term. A scheme is *abstract*, because it synthesizes information drawn from many cases. It is a *structure*, because it represents the interrelatedness of information components. When a new (external) experience matches an existing well-formed scheme, recognition and comprehension occur.[60] There is no disequilibrium. But if a new experience has no scheme to match, or if the scheme is faulty, then the new experience creates confusion, or disequilibrium. Some writers use the term *declarative* knowledge ("I know *xyz.*")[61] to refer to what is stored in semantic memory.[62]

The second type of LTM memory is called *implicit* memory, which refers to memories that lie below conscious awareness but have influence over behavior or thought. Implicit memory is further divided into *procedural memory*, *classical conditioning effects*, and *priming*.[63]

Procedural memory stores information concerned with knowing how to do something and includes skills like riding a bike, playing the piano, or writing a research paper.[64] Procedural information is stored in a sequence of stimulus-response pairings.[65] When students say, "I know the formula, but I can't use it," they demonstrate declarative knowledge ("knowing that") without procedural knowledge ("knowing how").

Another type of implicit, or out-of-awareness, memory contains *classical conditioning associations* (see Chapter Six). Examples include the anxiety that some students experience as they await the distribution of exams, or the increase in heart-rate upon hearing the sound of a dentist's drill.[66]

The third type of implicit memory is *priming*, which is the "implicit activation of concepts in LTM."[67] Earlier, we mentioned that we can activate the recall of one part of a network by recalling another since concepts exist in relationships with each other. A song fragment, or the way the sun shines through clouds, or a familiar tone in a stranger's voice, or a whiff of vanilla, or thousands of other random stimuli, can implicitly call up encoded memories, because associations spread through the memory system.[68] In a general sense, the LTM stores background knowledge, which includes all prior learnings and experiences. The richer and more varied one's background knowledge, the easier it is to relate new information to it.[69] The more one learns, the easier it is to learn.[70]

In summary, sense receptors transmit raw sensory data in the form of electrical impulses to sensory registers (SR) in the brain. Information is transferred to short-term memory and either automatically encoded into long-term memory, or, under the right conditions, intentionally encoded into LTM for later retrieval. Let's see now how data is transformed into long-term memories and conceptual networks.

Information Processing Operations

The cognitive processes of *attention* and *recognition* move data from sensory register (SR) to short-term memory (STM), *maintenance rehearsal* maintains data in STM, and elaborative rehearsal (with the associated characteristics of *meaningfulness, organization, activity, and mnemonics*) move encoded data from STM to LTM. We will also discuss hindrances to recalling encoded LTM data (otherwise known as "forgetting"). We discuss these processes sequentially, but the mind can encode and decode data simultaneously.[71]

Moving Data from Sensory Register to Short-Term Memory

Information is stored in sensory registers as a series of snapshots (visual data) or wave forms (auditory data), and retained there from one-half to four seconds before they decay and are lost. These registers hold an exact copy of the stimuli, just as they are perceived[72] by sense receptors. You can

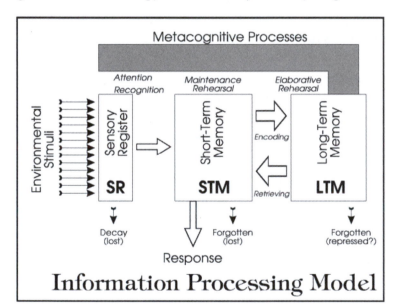

Information Processing Model

actually experience sensory decay with a couple of simple exercises.

Hold your right index finger in front of your face, pointing to the ceiling, palm facing left, and wiggle it back and forth rapidly ten times. As your finger moves left and right, you will notice a blur in the gap between the two extreme positions. This blur is the residual trace of visual data in the sensory register.[73] Pinch your arm for a few seconds, and then let go. You will continue to feel the pain of the pinch for a few seconds. The lingering pain is the residual trace of tactile data in the SR. In both cases, sensory registers hold on to the sensory information very briefly after the stimulus has stopped.[74]

Visual images fade more quickly than sounds. The faster fade time of visual memory prevents blurred vision. The slower fade time of auditory memory allows the "blurring" of notes together to make music, and of phonemes together to make spoken language. If the snapshots, sound bites, and touches are not recognized or attended to within that time, they quickly fade away and are lost. If they are attended to, then they are passed on to short-term memory.[75]

Paying *attention* to specific stimuli results in selective focusing. We process what we attend to and lose what we ignore.[76] *Recognition* refers to matching an incoming stimulus with stored information in LTM.[77] For example, let's say a boy is walking down the street and sees an animal. The event is transmitted from retinas to visual registers (SR), and into STM. If he ignores the animal, the glance will soon be forgotten. If he focuses his *attention* on the animal, images of various known animals are automatically retrieved from LTM until a match is found. "Look, Dad, it's a Cocker spaniel." This is *recognition*. *Attention* and *recognition* are two key elements in moving information from SR to STM.

As soon as stimuli are received by the senses, the mind begins working on some of them. The sensory images that we consciously process are not exactly the same as what we saw, heard, or felt. Sensory images are what our sense receptors perceived.[78] That is, STM contains perceived reality, not objective reality.[79] Further, what we attend to and what we recognize is a function of prior learnings, the network located in LTM.[80] Our mind acts as a filter, which tends to change what we receive in order to fit what we already know. Piaget called this natural tendency assimilation. As we process new information, build new networks of ideas, and restructure schemes according to new experiences, we learn. Piaget called this accommodation.

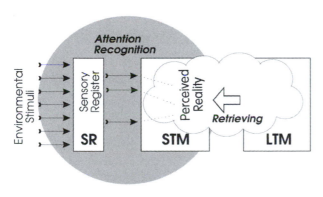

The fact that STM is limited to perceptions, filtered by what is known, does not mean objective truth is out of reach. Piaget, Vygotsky, and a host of Constructivist and IPT theorists emphasize the interactive nature of human learning. We not only perceive, but we also compare perceptions to what is known. Perceived realities accommodate, over time, to the world as it is. This is the IPT version of the spiral curriculum discussed in the last chapter.

STM Implications for Teaching

What implications can we draw from attention and recognition? First, what teachers do from the moment we step into the classroom is important. Having invested time and effort in preparation for the session, most teachers are eager to begin. They have a built-in motivation, even enthusiasm, for engaging learners with the topic of the day. It is a mistake, however, to assume our students share that enthusiasm. Teachers do well to consider specific ways to gain the (positive) attention of learners. Attention getters include demonstrations, displays, pictures, maps, graphs, thought-provoking questions, and relevant personal stories.[81]

Second, *bad classroom experiences* in the past create a barrier for the information we wish to present. Encoded bad experiences (LTM) create a negative filter that deselects incoming information, and simply dulls student attention. Teachers facilitate attention by emphasizing that the topic of the day is useful, enjoyable, informative, and meaningful.[82] When teachers successfully conduct a meaningful session, we weaken the effect of previous bad experiences.

Third, variety is important in the classroom.[83] If, for example, teachers begin class the same way every day, students become used to it, and attention suffers. Overuse of any methodology (lecture, group discussion, projects, Q&A, small group problem-solving) will cause monotony, and attention will suffer.

We have seen that it is easy to overload the STM with too much new information, which limits the ability of students to think and solve problems.[84] Teachers overcome this limitation in two ways. First, we help students *overlearn basic information and operations* so that they can be used with little difficulty. To overlearn means to continue studying or memorizing something past the point of proficiency. Many Christians have "overlearned" John 3:16. We can go for weeks, even months, without thinking of the verse. But when asked, we can quote it without hesitation or error. Overlearning simple math operations helps students calculate without much thought. Overlearning grammar rules helps students write better in language courses, because they can focus more on the content of writing than its form.

The ability to use explicit knowledge immediately and with little conscious effort is called *automaticity*.[85] The earlier example of asking "What is your name?"—without conscious thought of how to construct the sentence—illustrates automaticity. Overlearning is the means. Automaticity is the result. Since learners can handle overlearned details immediately and with little effort, STM processing can be focused elsewhere, and bottlenecks are reduced.

A second way teachers overcome STM bottlenecks is to *change the presentation style* in ways that help students to process information more efficiently. Teachers do well to present information in smaller doses, and to provide periodic summaries of key ideas. Using visual aids reinforces verbal explanations. When students are unable to answer our questions, or have difficulty framing a question, they are suffering from STM overload.[86]

Maintaining Information in Short-Term Memory

You may remember that STM can hold up from five to nine pieces of information for as long as a minute.[87] If learners do not do something to extend the life of the information in STM, it will decay and be lost.

The most common way to extend the time STM stores information is called *maintenance rehearsal*,[88] or *rote* rehearsal, or simply *repetition*.[89] By repeating information several times, without altering its form,[90] either aloud or mentally,[91] we can maintain it in STM longer than the one minute limit. However, such repetition has no direct effect on the memory structures in LTM. That might bear repeating. *Repetition has no direct effect on the memory structures in LTM.* Repetition simply increases the time students hold information in STM.

Earlier, we gave the example of looking up, and then forgetting, a telephone number, due to the limitation of STM. Repeating the number several times will maintain it in STM long enough to dial the number. Another example involves entering numbers into a calculator. One student might enter the numbers one at a time by looking at a number, entering it, and looking at the next. Another student might look at five numbers, repeat all five aloud once or twice (*maintenance rehearsal*), and enter all five at one time.[92]

Students often complain, "I read these chapters a hundred times, but I still answered too many exam questions wrong!" Assuming the test questions were well-written, and the "100 times" is an exaggeration, we can interpret the student's lament as repetition without transformation. Encoding meaningful information so that it can be retrieved and used correctly requires more than repetition: it requires *transformation* into meaningful, long-term forms. Let's see how this is done.

Moving Information from Short-Term Memory to Long-Term Memory

The longer learners hold information in STM, the more likely they will encode it for long-term storage.[93] Transferring information from STM to LTM[94] requires that the information in STM be encoded. Learners encode information by forming mental representations of the information, called schemes, based on its essential features.[95] Forming schemes requires relating the new information to concepts already stored in LTM.[96]

Earlier, we defined procedural memory as an implicit form of memory residing in LTM. Procedural knowledge ("knowing how") is encoded in a three-stage process: the declarative, associative, and automatic.

In the *declarative stage* of procedural knowledge development, students learn the facts about a procedure. For example, when students are introduced to the Eight Stages of Erikson, they learn the names of the stages, as well as facts about each stage. In the *associative stage* of procedural memory, students can perform the procedure, but "they must think carefully about what they are doing," and their "thoughts place a heavy cognitive load on their working memories." Students asked to name which stage of development best fits a given case study will think of several stages that seem to fit, concentrating on the case study, and comparing it with the various characteristics of stages in order to select the correct one. In the *automatic stage*, students perform the procedure with little conscious thought.[97] Students asked to name which stage of development best fits a given case study will immediately "know," without going over the list, or considering several stages, that the case study fits best in stage, say, three. In time, the rules and connections that make these comparisons become established as implicit memories, and work below the threshold of consciousness.

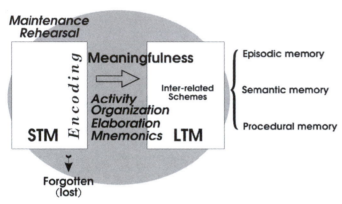

In order for information to be encoded, it must possess *meaningfulness*, which describes the complexity of connections between one idea and others already encoded in LTM.[98] The four classic ways to increase the meaningfulness of information to students are activity, organization, elaboration, and mnemonics.[99] We define each of these in turn.

Activity. Teachers facilitate meaningfulness by engaging students in activities that require correct understanding and by working with them until teacher explanations make sense.[100] After I explain "Levels of Learning" and demonstrate how to write instructional objectives (Chapter Twelve), I divide the class into two groups. I give both groups the same Scripture verse and a specific level of learning, and ask them to write an instructional objective that is correct in form and content. When both groups are satisfied with their statement, I have a volunteer from each group to write their objectives on the board. Statements are seldom correct on the first try. *Verbal explanations are not sufficient for encoding complex procedural skills.*

I ask each group, in turn, to evaluate the other's objective. We discuss why each statement falls short. I have them compare the model objective with their own and point out differences. We repeat the exercise with the same verse and a different level of learning.

Sometimes I have repeated this exercise five or six times, and each time the groups improve their statements. In the end, both groups can write clear instructional objectives, which helps them focus the elements of their sermons or lesson plans. The activity of working together, and evaluating each other,—*and finally evaluating the evaluations*—makes the material meaningful.

In my statistics class, I provide worksheets for each chapter on-line. Students can download them, work through the required analysis, and then compare their answers with the appropriate answer key that is posted a week later. I also provide sample test questions, which students can answer and, when finished, get feedback on why right answers are right, and wrong answers are wrong. Students who choose to engage these problem-solving activities always process the course material more effectively than those who merely read the text.

Organization. Organization refers to separating information into categories or patterns that reflect built-in connections. Well-organized content emphasizes the connections among its elements, making the content meaningful. Organized information is easier to encode, and more complete when retrieved.[101] Students learn better when they create their own structures (e.g., Bruner's pure discovery), but teachers who present information in pre-organized forms will accelerate meaningfulness [e.g., directed discovery and reception learning]. Examples of ways learners can organize information include charts, matrices,[102] hierarchies, tables, flowcharts, and chronologies. Older students organize better than younger students do. Skilled students organize better than unskilled students do. Familiar material is easier to organize than new or unfamiliar material.[103]

Elaboration. Elaboration, or elaborative rehearsal,[104] refers to the process of relating new information to encoded concepts already in LTM.[105] It is the process of increasing the number of associations among concepts, by either forming additional links, or adding new information.[106] Teachers prompt elaborative rehearsal when they have students paraphrase new definitions, create new examples, explain the material to a peer, or apply the material in solving problems.[107] The goal in elaboration is to create logically interconnected information, so that any part can be used to retrieve the other parts.

Mnemonics. Mnemonics (pronounced *neh-MA-nix*) are cognitive strategies that help learners form associations that don't naturally exist in the content.[108] Mnemonics provide an *artificial* basis for organization and meaningfulness[109] since they are, by nature, contrived aids. Mnemonic devices include the *loci* (pr. *LO-sigh*) method, rhymes, acronyms, acrostics, pegwords, and keywords.

Loci method. The loci method of association is the oldest known mnemonic, dating from classical Greek times.[110] It is also the most popular.[111] The word *loci* is the plural form of *locus,* which means place or locality,[112] and is sometimes called the place method.[113]

For example, a student might associate three rooms in his house with the three learning theory systems. The "library," for example, contains cognitive theories of learning. A "computer" in one corner of the library contains IPT information. A "bookshelf" that is under construction in the library contains Constructivist information. In order to recall essential information on cognitive theories of learning, "walk into the library" and retrieve the information that is stored there.

Rhymes. Simple rhymes can make recalling arbitrary rules simpler. Two of the most well-known are "i before e except after c" and "30 days hath September, April, June, and November. All the rest have 31—*except February.*"[114]

Acronym. An acronym (pronounced *AK-ra-nim*) is a first-letter mnemonic[115] that forms words from the first letter of each item. "HOMES" is an acronym for the five Great Lakes: **H**uron, **O**ntario, **M**ichigan, **E**rie, and **S**uperior. ROYGBIV (pronounced *ROY-gee-biv*) are the seven colors of the spectrum: **R**ed, **O**range, **Y**ellow, **G**reen, **B**lue, **I**ndigo, and **V**iolet. Acronyms are effective for recalling short lists.[116] Some acronyms have become words in their own right, such as SCUBA (**s**elf-**c**ontained **u**nderwater **b**reathing **a**pparatus), LASER (**l**ight **a**mplification by **s**timulated **e**mission of **r**adiation), and RADAR (**ra**dio **d**etecting **a**nd **r**anging).[117]

Acrostic. An acrostic (pronounced *a-CRAW-stik*) is a sentence mnemonic[118] that forms sentences from the items to be learned. An acrostic for ROYGBIV might be "**R**ichard **O**f **Y**ork **G**ave **B**attle **I**n **V**ain." In helping to recall the naval equivalents of left and right, one might use these sentences: "The ship **left port**" and "The **star board**er is always **right**."[119]

Pegword. A list of previously memorized pegs, usually based on rhymes (1=bun, 2=shoe, 3=tree, etc.), is used to compose interacting images with items to be remembered.[120] Let's say you need to go to the store for fish, roses, and a carton of cokes. Picture a bass—head, scales, and all—wrapped in a hamburger **bun**, roses growing out of a **shoe**, and the carton of cokes wedged up in a **tree**. By recalling the pegwords bun, shoe, and tree, you will remember the grocery list.

Keyword. The first step in creating a keyword is to isolate part of a foreign word that, when spoken, sounds like a real English word.[121] The Spanish word for a letter (as in mail) is *carta*. Isolate part of the word that sounds like an English word: *cart*. This is the keyword.[122] Second, form a connecting visual image between the keyword and the English translation.[123] Picture a shopping cart holding a giant letter. This forms an acoustic link between the keyword and the English translation. Research has shown this method to be effective for learners from preschool to college.[124]

Use Mnemonics with Caution in Teaching the Bible. While mnemonics can help learners memorize disjointed pieces of information, the Bible is filled with naturally interrelated pieces that make up the Whole. Focus on these meaningful relationships across writers and Testaments. Do not use mnemonic devices as a substitute for clarifying the actual inter-connectedness of Scripture.

Take care in choosing the images you use with mnemonic devices. While zany images are easier to remember (e.g., a bass wrapped in a hamburger bun), they will do more damage than good if the zany images mock the very truths we're attempting to teach.

LTM Implications for Teaching

In light of these discoveries of information transformation, we suggest the following implications for teaching.

Subsumption. Teachers do well to relate new material to established learning, since encoding requires new information in STM to be connected to schemes in LTM. This is a principle common to all cognitive theories.

Activity. Teachers do well to engage students in meaningful activities. Have them write out questions about the material. Have them paraphrase explanations from their notes or textbooks. Let students analyze examples, solve problems, write essays, engage in hands-on experimentation, or take practice application-oriented (rather than simple recall) tests.

Organization. Teachers do well to present information in pre-organized forms. Examples of ways information can be organized include charts, information matrices,[125] conceptual hierarchies, tables, flowcharts, and chronologies.

Elaboration. Teachers do well to provoke increasing complexity in concept networks. Begin with a simplified view, and then introduce contrasting ideas. Move from the simple to the complex. Move from concrete objects to abstract ideas. Move from definitions to principles. If you give students sample test questions for practice, have them manipulate each question to ask the same thing a different way.

Structure. Teachers do well to create a natural structure of the material to be learned. But when this is not possible, judicious use of mnemonic devices can provide an artificial network of associations that help learners retrieve information when needed.

Rote Memorization. While we have spent many words discussing encoding and retrieval of lists, charts, and tables, IPT theorists do not emphasize rote memorization. "Very few things need to be learned by rote."[126] The focus of IPT is the transformation of information into conceptual networks, yet, there are times when material needs to be learned by rote. When those times occur, teachers do well to help students with the task by using advance organizers,[127] active recall,[128] short drills,[129] distributed practice,[130] and knowledge of results.[131]

Forgetting as Inability to Retrieve Information from LTM

Information that has been properly encoded into LTM, whether intentionally or automatically, remains in LTM for life. Why, then, do we forget? IPT proponents answer this question by defining "forgetting" as being *unable to retrieve information* for use in STM. IPT theorists suggest four reasons we have difficulty retrieving encoded information. These are disuse, distortion, repression, and interference.

Disuse. If encoded information is seldom retrieved and used, then the ability to retrieve the information decays over time.[132] "Once they have learned it, students will forget an item unless they use it."[133] Most of us spent hours in high school classes diagramming sentences, proving geometric theorems, and dissecting frogs. Few of us need these skills in the daily course of events. While

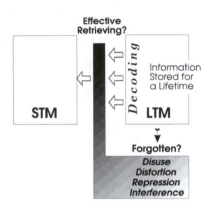

such school skills may have developed underlying critical thinking skills—Dr. Budd Smith[134] has long contended that the ability to diagram sentences is directly linked to the ability to write instructional objectives—the fact remains that most adults "have forgotten" much of what they learned in high school. All that remains are vague memories. Disuse takes away the ability to retrieve encoded information, even if that information was correctly encoded and well established in the past.

Distortion. When information is encoded incompletely, it will necessarily be retrieved incompletely. Incomplete encoding may be due to poorly organized presentations or confusion in the learner. Even when information is encoded completely, we may be able to retrieve only a part of it due to lack of elaboration or disuse. In trying to make sense of what we recall, the mind tends to fill in the memory gaps with other, sometimes unrelated, information (the cognitive law of closure). The result is distorted recall. Ormrod calls this a "reconstruction error."[135] Distortion produces memories that differ from the events that caused them.

Repression. Harsh criticism by a teacher, humiliation by classmates, or even personal shame over failure cause emotional pain in learners. Learners naturally repress these bad experiences, but also repress information from the courses that create these experiences. Elliot underscores the importance of repression and forgetting (2000), "If experiences are sufficiently severe, amnesia (the partial or total loss of memory) results." The degree to which students suffer from repression in the normal course of the school day has "never been established because of the lack of experimental control that can be introduced."[136]

Interference. Confusion can occur when similar concepts interfere with each other during retrieval. Information is lost as some retrieved data detracts from others,[137] or when data is mixed up with, or pushed aside by, other data.[138] There are two basic types of interference: proactive inhibition and retroactive inhibition.

Proactive inhibition occurs when "interference is caused by learning that occurs *before* the memory event" [*italics mine*]. When learning two verses of Scripture, the first verse, already learned, will interfere with learning the second verse.

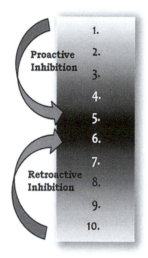

Retroactive inhibition occurs when "interference is caused by learning that occurs *after* the memory event"[139] [*italics mine*]. The process of learning verse two interferes with remembering verse one.

When learners commit a text—Bible passage, poem, or song—to memory, why is the *middle section* of the text the last to be mastered? The answer is found in the compound effects of interference. Memory of the middle section is hampered by both (proactive inhibition from the first, and retroactive inhibition from the third). Mastery of the middle portion requires continued effort to overcome both kinds of interference.

By contrast, memory of the first section is hampered only by retroactive inhibition (second and third sections interferes with recalling the first). Memorizing the last section is hampered only by proactive inhibition (first and second sections interfere with learning the third).

The compound effects of proactive and retroactive inhibition causes the middle portion to be "forgotten" first. The last section will be forgotten next, and eventually, the first section will be forgotten.

A popular approach to sermon construction is "conceptual introductory story," "Scriptural exegesis and explanation," and "emotional application story." Given the reality of interference, listeners will naturally *forget Scripture first* (middle section of sermon), the emotional conclusion second, and the introductory story last.

Implications for Teaching: Enhancing Retrieval

The antidote for disuse. Teachers help learners overcome disuse by prompting them to use what they have already learned in present sessions. Review prior learnings as new material is introduced.[140] Active review (students recall) is more effective than passive review (teacher reminds) in reinforcing established knowledge. Homework assignments prompt learners to use materials on their own. Each time class materials are used in completing tasks—answering questions, solving problems, writing essays, creating presentations—the retrieval paths are strengthened.

The antidote for distortion. Teachers help learners overcome distortion by emphasizing *meanings* inherent in the material. Undistorted retrieval requires more than intentional encoding—it requires *undistorted* intentional encoding. Elaboration reduces distortion as it reinforces natural relationships among concepts. Mnemonics reduce distortion as they create contrived relationships among concepts.

The antidote for repression. Teachers help learners overcome repression of encoded information by making the learning environment, and learning activities, as pleasant as possible. When learners feel safe in the classroom, when they feel they "belong" in the class and are accepted by teachers, repression is virtually eliminated.

The antidote for interference. Teachers help learners overcome interference by insuring presentations are properly organized[141] to clarify comparisons and contrasts of related concepts. Emphasizing distinctions between easily confused concepts reduces interference between them. Helping students overlearn essential elements[142] in course materials reduces confusion. Using active review and targeted comparisons[143] helps learners retrieve concepts correctly. Distributing explanations and illustrations throughout a session reduces the compound effects of proactive and retroactive inhibition on memory. For example, changing sermon structure from *story-exegesis-story* to <u>*repeating cycles*</u> of *story-(exegesis-illustration)-(exegesis-illustration)-(exegesis-illustration)-story* will help listeners remember Scriptural truths longer.

In summary, teachers help learners to correctly retrieve encoded course material by prompting learners to use course concepts in later sessions (overcoming disuse), by insuring completeness of meaning and structure in presentations (overcoming distortion), by creating a warm and open classroom atmosphere (overcoming repression), and by use of emphasis, review, and cycles of explanation-application (overcoming interference).

Levels and Types of Metacognition

Metacognition, defined by John Flavell in 1976,[144] refers to the ability to observe and control cognitive processes—attending, recognizing, rehearsing, encoding, and retrieving.[145] Metacognition allows us to think about how we think, through a series of levels.

Levels of Metacognition. Metacognitive processes differ in level of abstraction. Level one refers to information processing as we have described it: students *learning subjects*. Snowman refers to level one metacognition as "tactical learning." Level two metacognition refers to students *learning how to learn*. How are they functioning as information processors? What can they do to improve the processes? Snowman calls level two metacognition "strategic learning."[146] Level three metacognition refers to students *setting higher standards for learning*. Are personal standards high enough? Are students considering all the factors that go into successful learning? Level four metacognition evaluates the evaluation process. Are there elements affecting the learning process that have been overlooked?

A Practical Example of Metacognition

A student prepares "to the best of his ability" for an exam (level one: he studied) and does poorly. Upon reflection, he decides he waited too long to begin preparing and then stayed up too late in a last minute effort to get ready for the exam. He was tired when he took the exam (level two: he analyzed his study). He corrects these things—studies earlier, gets more sleep—takes the second exam, and does poorly. He now evaluates his analysis of his initial poor performance. Perhaps he looked at the wrong things. He rethinks his study habits in a broader context (level three: he evaluates his approach to analysis), asks questions of other students and the teacher for suggestions, and prepares differently for the third exam. If he still does poorly, he will evaluate the way he is evaluating his approach to analysis of study skills (level four: evaluating the approach to evaluating). Eventually he will find the problem in his study habits and develop study skills that will allow him to do well on future examinations.

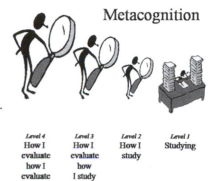

Metacognition

Level 4	Level 3	Level 2	Level 1
How I evaluate how I evaluate	How I evaluate how I study	How I study	Studying

Types of Metacognition. Metacognitive processes differ in type. *Meta-attention* is the conscious awareness and regulation of attention. What helps students maintain focus on learning in the classroom and at home?[147]

Do learners attend (that is, pay attention) better when seated in the front of the room? In the back? Do students attend to class activities better when they review assigned reading (or does the review create boredom?). Do they do better on homework assignments when listening to hip hop playing in their

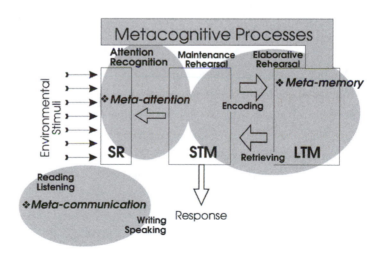

MP3 ear buds, or in a quiet room? Teachers do well to encourage students, regularly, to monitor their own study habits.

Meta-communication is the awareness and regulation of modes of communication: speaking, listening, writing, and reading. A student answers a question, pauses, and then says, "Wait, let me rephrase that." She listened to her own answer, judged it incomplete, and asked to try again. Another student misses part of a lecture and says, "I didn't quite hear that. Would you repeat it?" These examples reflect meta-communication.[148] Teachers who model good speaking and listening skills help focus student attention on them.[149]

Meta-memory is the awareness and regulation of memory strategies, of ways to remember better. Younger children rely on rote memorization and remain unaware of better strategies even when the strategies are suggested to them. By the age of ten, children are more effective in using efficient memory strategies.[150] Metacognitive processes permit learners to evaluate their own learning processes and improve them.

Information Processing Theory in the 2000s

The flow of sensory data from sense receptors to LTM continues to be investigated by cognitive theorists. The three-component model (SR—STM—LTM) presented here has been criticized for either being too simplistic, or too compartmentalized. It is seen as *overly simplistic* by those who point to the many sub-systems and interactive sub-processes that make up these components. The three-component model is seen as *overly compartmentalized* by those who consider the various memory functions—SR, STM and LTM—as nothing more than different activation states, or "various levels of processing,"[151] of a single memory. Three models attempt to address these concerns. These are the *Parallel Distributed Processing (PDP)* model, also called the Connectionist Model, the *Working-Memory (WM) model,* and the *Levels-of-Processing (LOP)* model.[152]

Parallel Distributed Processing Model. The PDP, or connectionist, model emphasizes *connections between* elements in memory more than the elements themselves. The concept "dog," for example, is stored as a network of various elements—"animal," "barks," "furry," "four-legged." The concept "dog" exists in the network of connections that link elements. Activation of one element in a network may prompt activation of other elements, also called *nodes*, echoing the discussion of elaboration earlier in the chapter. Activation of nodes occurs along many parallel connections in various networks, giving rise to the PDP label.

Essential to a connectionist model is the view that useful knowledge "resides in the connections among nodes"[153] rather than the nodes themselves. Without the connections, we would not be able to retrieve the concept "dog"—indeed, the concept would not even exist. The connectionist model is appealing in that it "seems to have a direct tie to the biology of the brain."[154] IPT (cognitive functioning) and neuroscience (bio-chemical functioning) have been converging in the literature for years, and the connectionist model supports this convergence.

The Working Memory Model. Explanations of the three-component model generally use the term "working memory" as a synonym for short-term memory, as we did earlier in the chapter. An alternative model uses the term "working memory" to identify an *active part of LTM that also includes STM*. Working memory (WM) holds the most recently activated portion of LTM and moves activated elements in and out of temporary memory stores. Whereas the classic STM is depicted as a passive receptacle of data, WM is active in integrating acoustic and visual data, organizing information into meaningful chunks, encoding concepts, and linking new information to existing forms of knowledge in LTM.[155] WM is the "workbench of memory" where active mental effort is applied to new and old information.[156] Theorists in the early 2000s describe WM as the component that does most of the work of the memory system.

WM consists of smaller components. A *central executive* "focuses attention, oversees the flow of information throughout the memory system, selects and controls complex voluntary behaviors, and inhibits inappropriate thoughts and actions." Other sub-components handle visual data, auditory information, and meanings.[157] WM manages many of the cognitive controls we discussed under metacognition.

Levels-of-Processing Model. Responding to the criticism of compartmentalization, LOP replaces the three distinct memory stores (SR, STM, LTM) with as many memory stores as is needed to encode items.[158] LOP rejects the idea of distinct boundaries between memory stores, suggesting instead that memory storage is allocated along a continuous dimension of *depth of encoding*.[159]

The goal in learning is to process meanings as deeply as possible. Simple repetition of words and definitions results in shallow processing. Providing synonyms for words requires deeper processing. Determining whether words describe learners themselves ("the self-reference effect") requires still deeper processing. Even when the words do not describe learners, they are recalled at higher levels, "merely because learners considered whether the words were self-descriptive."[160]

Impact of Alternative Models on the Classroom Practice. The increased complexity of suggested alternative IPT models reflects discoveries of how the human mind processes information. This increased complexity does little, however, for the classroom. The PDP model suggests that neural networks are strengthened when teachers provide learners with background information related to new topics, review information and concepts already studied, and provide intentional opportunities for repetition and practice.[161] The WM model suggests the use of active recall and the integration of new information with existing knowledge.[162] The LOP model emphasizes elaboration and meaningfulness. Suggestions for teachers repeat what has been suggested already in the three-component model.[163]

The Three-Component Model Revisited. Current educational psychology texts present IPT in its three-component form[164] as we have described here. Discussions of alternative models vary from text to text. The fact remains that, however writers classify and sub-divide the various components, the fundamental concepts found in IPT help us understand how the human mind processes information. IPT is the "most prominent cognitive learning theory of the twentieth century," and continues to provide "important implications for teaching today."[165]

Implications of Information Processing Theory for Teaching

Teaching suggestions have been made at each stage of the process. Here we provide some general IPT implications for planning and conducting classroom instruction.

Attract attention[166]

Secure attention by doing such things as posing a problem, asking a question, verbally painting a mental image, or presenting a diagram. Resist the temptation to gain attention by shock or surprise. Throwing firecrackers into the middle of the group, faking a fall to the floor, pretending to be upset and yelling at the class, or suggesting there might be a gunman in the hallway[167]—all of these "gain attention," but they do not promote learning. In the extreme, they create an unhealthy learning environment.

Maintain Attention[168]

Teachers maintain attention throughout the session by changing speech rhythms, pitches, and volume, asking a question, or moving to a chalk or marker board to write a word or draw a simple diagram. Facial expressions (smiles, frowns) and body language (eyes, nods, slump, leaning forward) suggest the level of attention of students. When attention wanes, re-engage (*re-attract*) students.

Engage students' thinking about their learning[169]

Ask questions about students' work, such as "How did you get your answer?" Or, "Why did you choose that process?" Or, "Why do you think <historical event> happened?" Such questions go beyond simple recall of answers and address how students process the information in the course.

Encourage student self-attention[170]

Help students control their own attention behaviors—to focus on course or examination objectives, to consider the rewards of good study habits, or to separate themselves from students who distract. Encourage students to ask themselves what prevents them from paying attention, and show them ways to overcome these problems.

Emphasize clear organization in presentations

Structure presentations[171] by the use of outlines, flowcharts,[172] or advance organizers[173] to provide students with pre-processed organization. Avoid irrelevant stories, "wanderings," and "rabbits."

Give feedback to students on the quality of their thinking

Help students evaluate current learning strategies in light of performance on examinations and projects. Learning effectiveness improves as students try alternative approaches to learning.[174]

Use elaboration to increase meaningfulness of the material[175]

Ask questions that require comparisons, relationships, and patterns. "How does <this> compare with <that>? How are they different? Give an example." Explain the relevance of present studies to life issues of students.[176] Ask students to think of connections between the present study and their own lives.[177] Allow time at the end of class for students to review their notes and ask clarifying questions.[178] Ask for and use a variety of examples. Have students summarize lectures.[179] Encourage students to develop concept maps[180]—translating text to diagrams[181]—of the material. Make assignments that require (older) students to organize a body of material on their own.[182] Minimize rote memorization of facts,[183] and build factual networks around clearly understood concepts.

Help students develop mnemonic devices[184]

Provide mnemonic devices to help younger students remember easily confused terms.[185] Teach students how to create various types of mnemonics for themselves.[186] Use mnemonics when the material does not lend itself to the natural organization of concepts inherent in the material. Use mnemonic images with care and sensitivity so that they do not undermine the seriousness of what is being learned.

Overcome interference

Present closely related ideas at the same time, stressing similarities and differences.[187] For example, when teaching youth or adults the meaning of *agape* love, also define *phileo* [friendship love] and *eros* [romantic or erotic love]. When teaching about the sovereignty of God, also discuss (briefly) the concept "free will of man." When teaching about God's holiness (wrath), mention God's grace and mercy (love). Take care not to teach single-dimension concepts but rather the multi-dimensioned truths of Scripture. Use active review to summarize distinctions among closely related ideas.

Enhance meaningfulness in your teaching

Use concrete analogies to make abstract information more tangible, more meaningful.[188] Analogies are more effective when students are familiar with them. It is less important that the analogy itself be closely related to the concept.[189] Jesus used sheep and goats to illustrate two kinds of character. His listeners readily understood what He was saying because they knew about sheep and goats. When we use these analogies, we have to teach most of our members about sheep and goats. Our teaching is more effective when we use analogies that our students have experienced.[190]

Help students know what they are expected to retrieve

Be specific in task assignments.[191] Focus attention on essentials in the course. Give students study questions to consider as the content is presented.[192] Provide a study guide, a list of objectives, or sample test questions to frame students' preparation for examinations.

Help students improve their recognition ability

Provide clear, complete, and explicit directions for younger learners. Younger children have less stored in LTM[193] and therefore less ability to logically relate what they know to assigned tasks. Identify basic terms students should memorize.[194]

Lead students to rehearse important concepts

Use *elaborative* rehearsal—emphasizing meaning and chunking[195]– to help students encode key ideas clearly. *Rote* rehearsal is one of the earliest tactics learned in school and is used by everyone occasionally.[196] By the age of eight, children can begin rehearsing *sets* of facts rather than lists of individual facts.

Guide students in metacognitive processes

Help students think about ways they learn and remember.[197] Help students set goals for themselves, or describe steps they take in solving problems, or keep a log of terms that are clear and unclear, or describe procedures they use in completing an assignment.[198]

Key Emphases from Cognitive Learning Theories

The following twelve statements summarize essential elements cognitive learning. Use these terms to compare and contrast behavioral learning (Chapter Six) and humanistic learning (Chapter Ten).

1. The learner is a. . .	**MIND** Learning is an interactive process between mind and world
2. The focus is on the. . .	**PERCEPTION** Learners construct knowledge systems based on perceptions
3. Relationship of learning "whole" to its parts	**WHOLE *IS GREATER THAN* SUM OF PARTS** Learners add to class learning experiences from their own
4. Learning is. . .	**RATIONAL and INTERACTIVE** The mind learns from interaction with concepts and other minds
5. The target learning domain is. . .	**COGNITIVE** Building knowledge systems: facts, concepts, principles, schemas
6. The goal of learning is. . .	**CHANGE IN UNDERSTANDING** Making sense of the world, problem-solving, analysis, synthesis
7. Learning is strengthened by. . .	**INSIGHT INTO CONCEPTUAL RELATIONSHIPS** Rehearsal, organization, activity, elaboration
8. Learning is guided by. . .	**APPLICATION TO LIFE** Meaningful learning prepares learners for future tasks
9. Motivation keys on. . .	**CURIOSITY, MEANINGFULNESS** Learners have an intrinsic desire to understand
10. Feedback should be. . .	**DELAYED, BASED ON PERFORMANCE** Allow time for concepts and principles to develop, then critique
11. Best curriculum is. . .	**PROBLEM-SOLVING** Sequence sessions to move from information to cognitive skills
12. The Theory in Practice is. . .	**DIRECTED DISCOVERY and CONSTRUCTIVISM** **INFORMATION PROCESSING THEORY**

Self-questioning

Have students write their own questions about the content under study. Writing conceptual questions—questions that focus on concepts rather than simple recall of facts—helps students process the material.[199] The effectiveness of this technique increases with 1) the clarity of instructions concerning types of questions, 2) the amount of practice students have in writing questions, 3) and the amount of time given to digest the material and write questions.[200]

Note-taking

Show students how to improve their skills in taking notes from lectures or assigned readings.[201] Research is unclear about *what makes* note-taking effective—should notes be brief or detailed? Should notes focus on facts or ideas? Should notes be kept in verbatim form, or reorganized? Yet, evidence suggests two basic benefits from taking notes. First, taking notes leads to **better retention and comprehension** of material than listening or reading alone. Second, reviewing notes provides **opportunities to recall and comprehend** the material.[202]

Provide skeletal outlines of lectures to students,[203] but take care to balance detail with structure. Giving students too much detail makes lectures predictable and boring. Giving too little structure may cause confusion. Skeletal outlines help pre-package the material so that students can more easily see the organization of lectures. Organization is essential for long-term learning because taking notes without making sense of them—without an elaboration process—does not aid the learning process.[204]

With the advent of Internet learning, many professors place their PowerPoint slide sets online so students can review them, and even download them to their personal computers. Certainly there are copyright issues, but the provision of slide sets help organize course material for those studying a subject for the first time.

In Summary

When the first edition of *Created to Learn* was written, contemporary educational psychology texts gave more attention to Information Processing Theory than any other learning theory. Fourteen years later, Constructivism has taken its place as the dominant learning theory system. However, IPT continues to offer a rich assortment of specific strategies to help students "make sense" of the subjects we teach. IPT also provides a conceptual bridge to brain research of the last fifteen years. We will discuss many of these discoveries in Chapter Sixteen.

We leave cognitive expressions of learning, and move into the third system of learning—a system that has all but disappeared from secular texts, and yet continues to influence educational thinking. That system is Humanistic Learning theory.

Chapter Concepts

Acronym	A first-letter mnemonic that forms words from the first letter of each item
Acrostic	A sentence mnemonic that forms sentences from the items to be learned
Activity	Engaging students in activities that require correct understanding (meaningfulness)
Attention	Giving conscious mental focus (sustained concentration) to a person or object
Automatic processing	Unconscious mental recordings of experiences without intention or attention
Automaticity	Spontaneous recall of material that has been overlearned (i.e., John 3:16)
Background knowledge	All prior learnings and experiences, which are stored in LTM.
Chunking	Packing several items together to be processed as a single unit ('unr' vs 'run')
Cognitive map	A mental representation of the environment, e.g., a maze
Cognitive process	Mental actions that transfer and transform information, e.g., recognition
Cognitive structure	Refers to information stores or data storage units in the brain, e.g., STM, LTM Declarative knowledge The knowledge of meaning: facts, theories, concepts, schemas
Distortion	Source of forgetting: filling in recall gaps with unrelated information
Disuse	Source of forgetting: the ability to retrieve the information decays over time
Elaborative rehearsal	Process of relating new information to encoded concepts already in LTM

Encoding	Process of transforming information (STM) into meaningful forms (LTM)
Episodic memory	Memory that stores life experiences as specific events with time and place
Intentional processing	Conscious mental recordings of experiences with intention and attention
Interference	Source of forgetting: new and established learning interfere with each other
Keyword	Mnemonic device that forms an acoustic link between words of two languages
Level-of-Processing (LOP)	Alternative model: Describes memories as depth of processing rather than stores
Loci, or place, method	Mnemonic device that places things to be remembered in familiar locations
Long-term memory (LTM)	The mind's permanent information storage device
Maintenance rehearsal	Repeating information (rote rehearsal, repetition) to extend memory time in STM
Meaningfulness	Complexity of connections between one idea and others already encoded in LTM.
Metacommunication	Awareness/regulation of communication: speaking, listening, writing, and reading.
Meta-memory	Awareness/regulation of memory strategies, of ways to remember better
Metacognitive process	Executive control processes that govern other cognitive processes
Mnemonics	Strategies to aid LTM encoding by forming associations not naturally in content
Objective reality	Reality "as it is," without distortion my subjective perception (vs. perceived reality)
Organization	Presenting information in pre-organized forms (meaningfulness)
Parallel Distributed Processing	Alternate Model: PDP describes simultaneous activation of parallel paths

Pegword	Mnemonic based on memorized pegs (e.g., 1=bun, 2=shoe, 3=tree, etc.)
Perceived reality	Subjective reality created as STM filters incoming sense data (vs. objective reality)
Perception	The synthesis of sense data with what is known to create perceived reality
Proactive inhibition	Having learned "A," it is more difficult to learn "B," because "A" interferes.
Procedural knowledge	Knowledge of procedures: how to do things (e.g., ride bike, play piano)
Procedural memory	Stores information concerned with knowing *how* rather than knowing *that*
Recognition	Matching an incoming stimulus (senses) with stored information in LTM.
Repression	Bad experiences cause emotional pain that inhibits decoding of learning
Retrieval	The intentional decoding of information stored in LTM.
Retroactive inhibition	While learning "B," memory of "A" is impaired because "B" interferes.
Rhymes	Used as mnemonic device, as in "i before e except after c"
Scheme	Abstract knowledge structures that represent events, concepts, or skills
Semantic memory	Stores declarative knowledge: meanings—facts, concepts, principles, rules
Sensory register	Memory store: stores sensory data received from physical receptors (eye, ear, skin)
Short-term memory (STM)	Retains information as we consciously work on it ("working" or "active" memory)
Working Memory (WM)	Alternative model: Active LTM component which possesses executive function

Chapter Objectives

Learners will demonstrate knowledge of the information processing by . . .

- Defining attention, recognition, maintenance rehearsal, and elaborative rehearsal
- Identifying four reasons why we forget
- Identifying four ways to improve memory recall

Learners will demonstrate understanding of information processing by . . .

- Comparing the components and processes of the IPT model with a computer system
- Explaining how information moves from SR to STM to LTM and back to STM
- Describing the role of metacognition in learning
- Defining three types of metacognition
- Developing three different mnemonic devices based on material in the chapter
- Contrasting the three-component, connectionist (PDP), and working memory (WM) models of IPT

Learners will demonstrate appreciation for information processing by sharing a personal experience related to recognition, elaboration, forgetting, or metacognition.

Discussion Questions

1 Define each of the following components and give examples of their operation from your own experience: sensory register, short-term memory, long-term memory, and metacognitive processes.

2 Create a chart comparing short-term and long-term memory on the following characteristics: speed of acquisition, length of retention, stability, and capacity. Use the following terms: volatile, fast, unlimited, long, nonvolatile, limited, short, slow.

3 Define the following types of memory and give two examples of each from your own long-term memory: episodic memory, semantic memory, and procedural memory.

HUMANISTIC LEARNING

Abraham Maslow and Carl Rogers

"For where your treasure is, there your heart will be also."

Matthew 6:21

The secret in education lies in respecting the student.

—Ralph Waldo Emerson[1]

Chapter Rationale

Humanistic learning theory is dead. It was dying in the 1990s when I wrote the first edition (see "Humanism in the 1990s" later in the chapter), but one is hard-pressed to find any contemporary reference to the system in educational psychology textbooks. For years, in one edition of their popular text after another, Biehler and Snowman maintained a separate unit on humanistic learning, but even they have surrendered to the field. Their latest edition (2009) gives eight pages out of 619 to "The Humanistic Approach to Teaching: Student-Centered Instruction." I've found no other contemporary educational psychology textbook that addresses "humanistic learning."

Reasons why this occurred will be given a little later. But make no mistake: the tenets of humanistic learning have not disappeared. Rather they have been absorbed into the ever-growing Constructivist camps, especially Radical Constructivism, as well as broader-based, hybrid learning approaches, such as Cooperative Learning. Textbook designers have moved humanistic theorists like Abraham Maslow and Carl Rogers into chapters on Motivation Theory.

The self-centeredness of humanistic learning has become the water through which our society swims. Entertainment has become our highest virtue. Elections and consumer choices are determined more by personal emotions than reason. Personal choices to gratify sexual desires increasingly replace

God's commands and Christian codes of conduct. These changes are found, not only among the secular society around us, not only among parishioners in the pews, but among Christian leaders, from presidents of evangelical institutions to pastors of prominent churches. Graduate students who cheered "personal freedom," and "choice," and "revolt from the norm" in the 1970s have filled the ranks of professors, curriculum writers, and journalists for years. Today they populate the highest seats of power in education and government. "Self" is the highest reality. "Choice" is the greatest good.

It is for that reason I retained this chapter. The idealistic and Self-centered foundations, laid for "future Man" in the 1960s and 1970s by those who defined society's ills in terms of "repressive forces" of government, traditional education, Church, and God have crumbled. But you will see in this study how we came to where we are today. Humanistic learning theories have been discarded by educational thinkers as ineffective, but Humanism itself lives on in Postmodernism, radical libertarianism, and educational perspectives that continue to reflect the status quo of the 1960s generation and their disciples.

I retained the chapter for one other reason. Much of the learning that goes on in local churches is humanistic in approach. One can attend Sunday school for a lifetime but will never earn a certificate or degree. There are no examinations. No consequences for truancy. No payments for books or class hours. People gather freely and enthusiastically, learning together, ministering to each other, giving freely to support churches and their ministries, volunteering time and energy, growing as citizens of the kingdom (or, as often as not, freely choosing not to).

Humanistic learning theory emphasized the values and attitudes of students rather than their behavior or thinking. Solomon wrote, "Lay hold of my words with all your **heart**; keep my commands and you will live" (Prov 4:4). Jesus said, "Love the Lord your God with all your **heart** and with all your soul and with all your mind" (Matt 22:37). The "heart" is the seat of conviction, values, attitudes, and ideals. It is not enough to simply do the right things (duty, ritual), or think the right thoughts (orthodoxy, intellectualism). Scripture teaches us to **be** right, as people of God—to integrate God's truth into who we are. How do we establish values? How do we help learners change their attitudes toward spiritual truths? How do we help students develop Christian ideals? In this chapter we present the arm of educational psychology that dealt with the affective, the emotional, and the personal aspects of education: humanistic learning theory. We do so because these insights help us in ways humanists never dreamed.

Chapter Overview

➤ Historical Roots

➤ Leading Humanistic Educators

➤ Humanistic Approaches to Education

➤ Three Types of Humanistic Education

➤ Analyzing Humanistic Approaches

➤ Humanistic Learning in the 1990s

➤ Humanistic Learning in the 2000s

➤ Humanistic Learning in the Church

➤ *Chapter Concepts, Chapter Objectives, Discussion Questions*

Historical Roots

Few words evoke resentment and anger among evangelicals like the word "humanism." It has been the rallying cry, the call to arms, of conservative Christians for four decades. The word elicits tangible fear and provokes quick commitment to "defend the faith." Why then should I devote an entire chapter in a Christian textbook to the subject? The answer lies in the definition of the term, whether we speak of "small-h" humanism or "capital-H Humanism."

The American Heritage Dictionary defined "humanism" (small h) ***in 1993*** as a "system of thought that centers on humans and their values, capacities, and worth," or "concern with the interests, needs, and welfare of humans."[2] Evangelical Christians should have little difficulty seeing the importance of such an approach to learning in the Church. We could use the phrase "personalizing the classroom" or "making Bible study relevant" and be confident no one would object. Christ established the Church, died, and rose again *because God loves learners* ("the Son of Man did not come to be served, but to serve, and to give His life—a ransom for many," Matt 20:28). The Church-at-its-best concerns itself with the needs of learners. The teaching ministry of the Church focuses on establishing biblical values in learners. The right side of the Disciplers' Model emphasizes meeting the needs of learners and improving openness and willingness to share in the classroom. These are the small-h humanistic emphases of this chapter.

The updated *American Heritage Dictionary* (2004) adds a single phrase to their previous definition that changes the thrust of the whole: humanism is "a system of thought that ***rejects religious beliefs and*** centers on humans and their values, capacities, and worth," or "concern with the interests, needs, and welfare of humans" [my emphasis].[3] In eleven years, the nuance has changed from "emphasizing the human," as in humane and humanitarian, to an overt secular rejection of religious beliefs.

The *American Heritage Dictionary* further defines (2004) "Humanism" (capital H) as a "cultural and intellectual movement of the Renaissance that emphasized **secular concerns** as a result of the rediscovery and study of the literature, art, and civilization of ancient Greece and Rome" [my emphasis].[4] This definition has not changed since the 1993 edition. Capital-H Humanism has always presented a problem for Christians because of its secular foundation. Though the distinction between the more general humanism and secular humanism is dissolving, we will look at the differences, focusing on secular humanism, classical humanism, and educational humanism. We will conclude with a discussion on the personal dimension of Christian education.

Secular Humanism

Humanism emphasizes man. *Secular* emphasizes "worldly rather than spiritual" matters.[5] Secular humanism emphasizes man but goes farther in excluding God. In 1882 German existential[6] philosopher Friedrich Neitzsche wrote, "Since God does not exist, man must devise his own way of life."[7] In 1946 John Paul Sartre wrote that man must work out his own values by making choices.[8] The Russian Christian, Fyodor Dostoevsky wrote, "If God did not exist, everything would be permitted." This was Sartre's beginning point: God does not exist. Individuals define themselves by making choices and working out their own values.[9] In 1970 John Randall wrote that "Men should place their faith in man himself—in man's infinite possibilities . . . [as well as in] a realistic recognition of man's finite limitations."[10] These existentialists focus on man and exclude God. Such is the nature of secularism, the "religion of humanity."

Secularism has four major tenets. First, secularism emphasizes the *self-sufficiency of man's own natural powers* to direct destiny. Second, secularism *rejects supernatural religion* as little more than superstition. Third, secularism accepts the *scientific method* as a substitute religion. And fourth, the highest values of secularism are *academic freedom* and *civil liberties*.[11] It is no wonder that secular humanism is anathema to Christianity—and vice versa.

The term *humanism* is often used as a shortened form for secular humanism, and such usage, as evidenced in the changing definitions of the *American Heritage Dictionary*, continues to expand. Over the last decade, we have seen the trend: as secular humanism grows, so grow the attacks against religious faith in general, and the Church in particular.

Classical Humanism

Classical humanism has two forms. The first is secular and grew out of southern Europe in the Renaissance, roughly from the fourteenth to seventeenth centuries. Man was placed, philosophically, at the center of all things. This "new horizon" of life was culturally rich, purely human, easily attainable, and without much restraint. It appealed to the emotions and emphasized living for the present. This worldview focused on personal success in terms of fame, pleasure, gratification of human craving, and satisfaction of sensual desires.[12]

The second form of classical humanism is biblical and grew out of northern Europe during the Reformation in the sixteenth century. The authority for teaching was not Man, nor even the Church, but the Bible, which was placed at the center of the curriculum. "Christian humanism"[13] emphasized the sovereignty of God as well as the worth of the individual. Indeed, the individual is deemed worthy precisely because we are created in God's image. Reformation leaders, such as Martin Luther and John Calvin, stressed living a worthy life here on earth, as well as in the hereafter. Schools emphasized high educational standards, including trained teachers, discipline, pleasant methods, and attractive classrooms and materials.[14]

Such a view fits perfectly with Christian education today, where learner needs are met through the study and application of God's Word. Don't we want warm, friendly classes? Don't we want to integrate the needs and interests of our learners into our studies? In church-based education programs, don't we stress contacts, visitation, and ministry to members and prospects because we care about them as people? Aren't we interested in helping learners apply their studies to their own life situations? Of course we are. And each of these desires are "humanistic" in the sense that they focus on the person, the learner, rather than the "lesson." This is the thrust of Christian humanism and opens the door to more general, and acceptable, educational humanism.

Educational Humanism

Humanistic learning theory[15] developed, not in opposition to the Church, but in opposition to the mechanically rigid approach to learning fostered by B. F. Skinner's programmed instruction and Freudian psychoanalysis.[16] Research in the 1940s—pursued by clinical psychologists, social workers, and counselors—focused on the affective (emotional, personal) side of learning.[17] Learners are more than learning machines to be programmed by teachers or computers. Learners are more than minds to be engaged with content. Learners are persons; therefore, life-changing learning engages personal attitudes, emotions, and values. The goal of educational humanism was to *personalize the classroom.*

Educational humanism was concerned with the uniqueness, the individuality, the humanity of each individual learner.[18] It was most concerned with the affective needs of students: emotions, feelings, values, attitudes, predispositions, and morals.[19] Emphases included personal freedom and growth, choice, and self-determination in the educational process.[20] The focus of the humanistic teacher was on the total person—intellectually, emotionally, and socially—and how these factors affected learning and motivation.[21]

The Personal Dimension of Christian Education

How do we teach Scripture so that learners personally integrate it into their lives and life situations? It is one thing to know that it is wrong to cheat. It is quite another to live honestly. It is a good thing to know the Good Samaritan story. It is quite another to be a "good Samaritan." It is wonderful to exegete "By this all people will know that you are My disciples, if you have love for one another" (John 13:35). It is quite another to actually love others. In Christian education, "knowing the right answer" isn't enough. Jesus calls us to a kingdom lifestyle. This requires the integration of affective elements in the teaching process. Humanistic theorists provide suggestions in how to do this.

Leading Humanistic Educators

Abraham Maslow, Carl Rogers, and Arthur Combs were three leading psychologists who influenced humanistic methods of education.

Abraham Maslow (1908–1970)

Abraham Maslow is the father of humanistic psychology,[22] though he is best known for the "Hierarchy of Needs" theory of motivation, which we will discuss in Chapter Fourteen. Maslow believed that children will make wise choices for their own learning when given the opportunity. He encouraged teachers to arrange attractive and meaningful learning situations and then let students select from the several offerings the one they find personally valuable. In this climate, Maslow suggested, teacher-directed classroom management becomes less necessary, due to the motivating power of self-chosen activities. The learning experience itself becomes its own reward.[23] This idealistic view of self-motivated content mastery proved false as standardized test scores plummeted in the late 1970s.

Carl Rogers (1902–1987)

Carl Rogers wrote "In my view education should evoke <u>real</u> learning . . . not the lifeless, sterile, futile, quickly forgotten stuff which is crammed into the mind of the poor helpless individual tied to his seat by ironclad bonds of conformity!"[24] He writes this as if behavioral and cognitive educators embrace lifeless, sterile, futile, quickly forgotten stuff.

Rogers developed person-centered methods for his work as a counselor-therapist. The term "person-centered" refers to the idea that counseling should revolve around the client, as opposed to "directive therapy," which revolves around the counselor. His ideas were not based on objective data, but rather personal answers to questions about individuals. How do they feel? How do they perceive their relationships with others? He focused more on phenomenology, the world as it is perceived by individuals, rather than reality, the world as it may actually be.[25]

As a graduate professor, he transferred his counseling methods to the seminar room. Rogers' fatal flaw, as regards educational theory, was his assumption that he could transfer his interactions with graduate students in a small seminar to classroom instruction. The two situations are worlds apart in terms of interactivity, background, self-motivation, experience, and academic abilities. His principles of teaching emphasized "learner-centered education."[26] In Rogers' view, teachers should trust students to do their work to the best of their ability and provide opportunities for learning.[27] Teachers should be "real persons" before students and not present a facade. They should be sincere and transparent facilitators.[28] Teachers should respect their students as well as their students' feelings and frustrations.[29] Teachers should view learning from the student's point of view.[30] The result of these efforts, according to Rogers, is that students take responsibility for their own learning.[31]

In reality, they didn't. But "personal feelings and frustrations" certainly became more prominent, and continues to dominate American life. A moment's reflection calls up all manner of examples. "How do you feel?" has become the stock question of journalists, whether they cover sports, politics, or personal tragedies. Teachers and administrators show more concern for students' feelings than their performance (so long as students do well enough on government-mandated tests to secure state and federal funds). Advertising is short on facts and long on emotion. Political campaigns focus more on casting an emotional tone than presenting a workable plan, more on style than substance, more on tomorrow's dream than on today's problems.

Arthur Combs (1912–1999)

Arthur Combs wrote "I am not a humanist because I want to go about being nice to people. I am a humanist because I know that when I apply humanist thinking to my teaching, students will learn anything better."[32] Combs stressed the role of *facilitator* for teachers. Much of his emphasis parallels

Jerome Bruner's discovery learning, but Combs placed more emphasis on sharing personal views and less on objective problem-solving. Effective facilitators, according to Combs, are well-informed, sensitive, believe in their students' ability to learn, have a positive self-concept, and use many methods to engage students in the learning process.[33]

For Combs, *meaning was not inherent in the subject matter. The individual instills subject matter with its meaning.* The question, "What does this mean?" asks for an objective explanation. The question, "What does this mean *to you*?" asks for a subjective reflection, or for some expression of relevance. We saw this same view expressed in radical Constructivism. The dilemma in teaching, for Combs, was not how to explain the objective *meaning* of a subject, but how to help students derive personal (subjective) meaning, or *relevance*, from that subject."[34] The emphasis of relevance over meaning has saturated teaching in both the church and the classroom.

Combs' emphasis on "personal meaning" undermined his own assertion that "students will learn anything better" using humanistic methods. Research found, time and again, that academic achievement suffered under humanistic methods[35] as objective meaning was deemphasized. Proponents continued to emphasize such factors as improved attitudes toward school, improved students' self concepts, and improved cooperation among students. But in the end, the star of humanistic teaching, which blazed so brightly in the 1960s and 1970s, burned out in the late 1980s.

I suspect the early successes of humanistic principles came as a result of cognitive skills, previously established by traditional teachers and approaches, which were unleashed by greater freedom to pursue personal interests. By emphasizing personal freedom over understanding and skill, humanistic teachers replaced tangible achievement with intangible appreciation. As the emphasis on understanding and skill development waned, so did the achievement of students. What is amazing is that these giants of educational theory could not predict what would result in educational outcomes from such an emphasis.

Other Key Humanistic Psychologists

Four other psychologists are mentioned for their influence in humanistic learning theory:

C. H. Patterson saw affective education as an antidote to an overemphasis on educational technology. He advocated characteristics in teachers and teaching techniques similar to those of Rogers and Combs. *George Brown*'s Confluent Education stressed the combination of cognitive and affective factors in the learning process but emphasized the affective as more important for long-term learning. *Thomas Gordon* studied with Carl Rogers and applied person-centered therapy to parent-child relationships in his book *Parent Effectiveness Training* (1970). The success of that book led him to write *Teacher Effectiveness Training* (1974) in which he stressed the affective relationship between teachers and students. This relationship is enhanced by openness, honesty, caring and interdependence.

William Purkey's Invitational Learning encouraged teachers to convey messages, both verbal and non-verbal, that students are responsible, able, and valuable. In *Inviting School Success* (1984), Purkey suggested four student factors that are likely to lead to school success: *relating* (students to fellow students), *asserting* (experiencing self-control in the learning process), *investing* (personally participating in learning), and *coping* (meeting school expectations successfully).[36]

Humanistic Approaches to Education

Humanistic teaching methods focused on learner experiences, emotions, values, and choices. While they were promoted as better suited for situations where *appreciation* of subjects was the primary goal,[37] humanistic methods were used across the whole spectrum of instruction. Here are some of the most popular approaches to classroom instruction.

Group Processes

The heart of humanistic methodology in the 1970s was sensitivity training and encounter groups. Groups of learners spent large portions of class time expressing feelings, exploring interpersonal relationships, and sharing personal values. Simulation games and role-playing activities were used to help participants intensify their personal sharing.[38]

Self-Regulated Learning

Humanistic educators emphasized self-directed and self-motivated learning in which students controlled their own learning. Such control included selection of topics and resources, setting goals, and evaluating outcomes with little teacher guidance.[39]

Warm Classroom Climate

Humanistic educators emphasized a relaxed and safe class atmosphere[40] where teachers demonstrate care for learners as individuals. Factors such as open communication, willingness to share, genuine empathy, and warmth were emphasized.[41]

Priority on Affective Outcomes

Humanistic educators believed that providing an environment of freedom, responsibility, caring, and interpersonal sharing was more important than "achieving a few additional points on standardized tests."[42] Achieving personal growth, nurturing enhanced and clarified values, and developing better interpersonal skills took priority over standard curricula, testing, and academic achievement.

"Authentic" Assessment

Humanistic educators avoided grades, standardized testing, and formal evaluations. They preferred to evaluate learners on a pass-fail basis, and emphasized written evaluations for individual students.[43] Value was placed on individual learners as persons rather than their ability to perform.[44]

Individualized Instruction

Humanistic educators molded instruction to student abilities. Students were allowed to progress at their own pace. Students were given responsibility to identify needs, plan activities, and evaluate mastery. Teachers offered a wide variety of activities for achievement of academic goals, and encouraged peer assistance—learners helping each other—and cooperative learning experiences.

Three Types of Humanistic Education

Most humanistic theory focused on attitudes more than specific methods. However, three basic types of educational practice grew, briefly, to prominence from humanistic theory: the Open Classroom, Learning Styles, and Cooperative Learning.

The Open Classroom

My seminary Philosophy of Education class, circa 1974, visited an elementary school that had moved to the Open Classroom concept. The school had few inside walls. Learning areas were separated by book shelves. Bean bag chairs and pillows provided comfortable areas for reading and study. There were no "classrooms" and no "classes." Each student had an individual educational plan that detailed agreed-upon goals, objectives, and activities. Teachers moved from area to area, providing individual help as needed. Time in school was measured by the accomplishment of learning goals rather than scheduled periods for specific subjects.

I remember a fifth grade girl who was involved in a research project. Part of her educational plan included viewing a film. On her own, she moved to the film area, set up the projector, threaded the film, watched the movie—taking notes relevant for her project—and then put the equipment away. At no time did she require teacher help.

The "open classroom" concept focused on the student, not the teacher. Learning stations, projects, and individualized workbooks were used in place of direct instruction. Teachers helped individual students set specific learning goals.[45] There were no set curricula or age-grading. Teacher-student relations were relaxed. Emphasis was placed on learner experiences and the role of emotions. Students were given freedom to move, explore, and discover on their own. There were few formal tests.[46]

For all their popularity in the 1970s, such schools were, by the mid-1990s, rare in North America.[47] The walls have been put back. Children have been organized into classes with teacher-teams who work to achieve specific content objectives. Research has demonstrated that open education methodology did succeed in affective learning, but produced lower achievement in cognitive outcomes.[48] Students learned less and were less motivated to learn than in traditional classrooms.[49]

Learning Styles

"If students have difficulty learning the way we teach, perhaps we should teach the way they learn." This was the central principle of learning styles. Research in the late 1970s and early 1980s demonstrated that learners could be classified by differing abilities to learn. Some learned best through sharing personal experiences. Others learned best through well-organized lectures. Still others learned best through problem-solving and experimentation. Others learned best through projects and hands-on activities. Others learned best through music. In traditional classrooms, students succeed when their preferred learning style matches the predominant style of the classroom. Learning styles emphasized the need to provide learning alternatives so that all students could experience a "best fit" environment.

In a learning styles classroom, students had many options for learning, including individualized activities, group activities, lectures and multimedia presentations. Core subjects were rotated throughout the day to ensure that all students had a turn at their best subject first. Exams were scheduled according to the students' own internal clock. Students were generally more involved in classroom activities because the activities fit student choices better.[50]

While the humanistic "learner-centered" focus is clear, the learning styles approach placed more emphasis on cognitive and academic growth than open classroom structures. Research found that schools employing learning styles' principles produced high academic achievement along with positive attitudes toward school.[51]

While learning styles continues to receive enthusiastic support in some quarters, I have misgivings about how far teachers can go in being all things to all students. While teachers should avoid an overly rigid emphasis in a single learning style—say, all group discussion or all lecture—there are limits to what teachers can do in providing unique learning opportunities for each student in the class. How do we keep track of each person's work? How does writing a poem compare to producing a term paper? How does composing a song compare to leading a group to develop a valid checklist for observing teaching skills? Too much emphasis on personal talents, interests, and choices moves us away from measures of mastery, performance, and excellence in the classroom.

In earlier days I allowed students to choose their own term paper topics. Most students chose topics similar to what they had already studied. In the worst cases, students chose topics about which they had already written a research paper. I now assign research topics in order to stretch students beyond past studies. It does not make them happy at first, but in the long run, most express enthusiasm over the discoveries they made as they tackled new ideas.

A large university in our area experimented with a learning styles approach campus-wide by offering multiple sections of courses geared to four major learning styles. The experiment came to a quick end as soon as it was discovered what an administrative nightmare this caused. Providing options for students geared to different learning styles is certainly possible. But providing as many versions of a course as there are learning styles of students proved unrealistic.

Cooperative Learning

The last manifestation of humanistic theory is Cooperative Learning.[52] Of all the approaches mentioned in the chapter, only Cooperative Learning maintains an important place in the literature. While none of my textbook sources lists Humanistic Learning Theory, and only one[53] addresses Humanistic Approaches to Teaching, *every one of them have entries for Cooperative Learning.*[54] The impact of Vygotsky, Bruner, and Bandura on the social dimensions of learning can take much of the credit for extending the life of this aspect of humanistic learning.

Looking at Cooperative Learning another way, the approach provides flexibility, in that it can be used in a variety of forms. Advocates of Piaget see Cooperative Learning as a way to create disequilibrium as individuals question their own perspectives. Advocates of IPT see Cooperative Learning as a means of promoting rehearsal and elaboration among group members. Advocates of Vygotsky's theory view Cooperative Learning as a means of promoting social interaction, the basis for reasoning and critical thinking.[55] Cooperative Learning finds connections to Cognitive Social Learning (Bandura), Cognitive Learning Theory (Piaget and Vygotsky), Constructivism (Jerome Bruner), Metacognition, and Motivation Theory.

The term *cooperative* in Cooperative Learning stands against *competitive.* Cooperative learning classrooms refrain from grading systems that pit individual students or student teams against each other in a race for limited high grades. High grades can be earned by every student or student team that meets the requirements for excellence. Students are encouraged to help each other learn. Emphasis is given to active participation in *achieving both cognitive and affective outcomes.* Cooperative learning places *more emphasis on academic achievement* than mainstream humanistic approaches did. Cooperative Learning provides *more structure and less freedom* than the open classroom and does not cater to individual student preferences as in learning styles. In a sense, Cooperative Learning is a hybrid cognitive-affective approach to learning. Research has shown that Cooperative Learning *increases achievement* and the *motivation* to learn, develops *higher thinking skills*, and enhances *interpersonal relationships* in students.[56] We investigate several contemporary models of Cooperative Learning in Chapter Fourteen.

Analyzing Humanistic Approaches

How have humanistic pronouncements of the past stood the test of time? The quotes below represent humanistic thinking in the mid-1970s when educational existentialism was in full bloom. We analyze each of these in light of educational realities and more recent research.

"Trust children and let them make their own decisions. Instruction should be learner-centered (Maslow, Rogers)."[57]

Humanistic educators placed too much responsibility for educational decision-making on students. Each student has a life, not to mention other classes, beyond the walls of our classroom. The choices students make to prepare or not prepare for our classes are influenced by these external factors. What other requirements and demands do students have besides those in our classes? If some of our students have a major exam in another class, can we reasonably expect them to spend time reading a chapter of material for our class—particularly if they receive nothing for this preparation beyond the "joy of learning"? Exams determine grades. Reading assignments seldom do. What choice would we make in the same situation?

What prevents students from making wrong choices? Shouldn't teachers provide some direction for student learning? How important is subject mastery? Is it important for students to understand the subject, or is it enough simply to experience something about it?

The move from Bruner's pure Discovery Learning, a more humanistic approach, to Directed Discovery, to Ausebel's reception learning, to Information Processing theory, to Constructivism[58] is evidence that Educational Psychology found "trusting learners too much" led to mediocre performance.

"Effective teachers are trusting, sincere, empathetic, and confident (Rogers, Combs)."

This principle remains important, regardless of teaching approach, because teaching is a highly personal, deeply interactive social process that requires a warm relational bridge. Teachers do well when they look for the best in students, empathize with their problems, and try to see the course work load from their point of view. However, teachers should not allow students to short-circuit course requirements because of personal difficulties or irresponsibility. ["My hard disk crashed at 3 this morning as I was printing my term paper. Will I still be docked for lateness?"] If we excuse one student's irresponsibility and procrastination, we are being unjust to other students who planned properly and submitted their papers on time.

"Affective factors in education are as important as cognitive factors (Brown)."

Educators moved away from this principle in the early 1990s and have shown little interest in returning to its extreme subjectivity. Affective responses rightfully come *after* the subject is mastered. Personal involvement should enhance, but not replace, cognitive learning.

Some of my research students, usually those required to take my course as part of their degree plan, have few "positive affective experiences" during the semester. Their emotions range from fear to anger to frustration to defeat. And yet, at the end of the semester, when it all comes together, and most of the class has earned their A's and B's, there is celebration—a *positive affective response*. If I gave in to student protests and anguish a third of the way through the course, they would fail to achieve the victory, or experience the exhilaration, that they do at the end of the semester. Their deep sense of accomplishment, reinforced by sharpened skills in analysis and clear understanding of research, gives them confidence that comes in no other way than hard, focused work. Affective elements should enhance, not replace, the cognitive.

"Teachers should have positive relationships with students (Gordon)."

Teachers who exhibit harsh and rigid attitudes undermine the learning process. Students learn better when they have confidence that their teachers accept them and believe in their ability to succeed. Still, teachers are more than friendly colleagues since they are assigned the task of equipping students in a given area. Teachers are required to assign a grade to students based on their objective performance in their courses. Assigning grades is not always a friendly act!

The social nature of teaching and learning require positive relationships between teacher and students. Teachers do well to manage classrooms with sensitivity, grace, flexibility, and a listening ear. Teachers do well to befriend every student, but to do so in a professional and educational sense. The focus of friendliness is student learning, not personal relationship.[59]

"Encourage learners to explore their feelings and emotions (Purkey)."

The right pillar of the Disciplers' Model encourages teachers to "remove masks" and "share themselves" with learners, even as we help students to do the same. Openness and transparency build a warm, trusting atmosphere in the classroom. Small group sharing was very popular in the 1970s, but it characterized first-century house churches as well. Humanistic encounter experiences often had little to do with the subject matter. Christian encounter experiences form the very core of New Testament faith, standing on the Written Word and anchored by the Living Word.

If achievement, subject mastery, and understanding are important educational goals, sharing experiences and feelings cannot be an end in itself. Sharing is helpful as a means to integrating subject matter into life. In the context of Bible study, exploring personal feelings and sharing personal testimonies are means to spiritual growth as God's Word speaks, and Bible truths are discovered, personalized, and integrated into the authentic activities of life.

Humanistic Learning in the 1990s

The 1970s Encounter Group phenomenon and Open Classrooms are gone. Clouse explained (1993) the decline of humanistic thinking in the 1980s as having three major causes. The first was its association with the drug counter-culture and its affinity with the occult. The second was a decline in attacks by the Christian Right. During the 1970s a number of Christian leaders and groups vociferously attacked humanism. Such attacks caused humanists to redouble their efforts to explain their position. In the 1980s such attacks declined and the prominence of the movement dwindled. Clouse states the third reason for a decline in humanism was the increased prominence of cognitive psychology,[60] as we saw in the chapters on Cognitive Learning and Information Processing.

Research demonstrated that learning and motivation require more than freedom of choice. Existential individualism leads directly to chaos as each one does what is right in his own eyes. The chaos in American society today can be laid at the feet of existential extremes in education through the 1960s and 1970s. "Choice" became the banner cry of individuals who believed their own wants and comforts are more important than community standards. "Revolt from the norm," the Existential societal goal, became the norm.

Even the secular press dedicated issues and articles to the excess of self-concept and self-esteem. *Newsweek's* cover story of February 17, 1992, was "Hey, I'm Terrific: The Curse of Self-Esteem." *Newsweek* presented an in-depth analysis of the fact that our society went overboard with the idea of self-esteem and positive self-concept. In one telling example, they reported a research study (1992) that showed American high school students were significantly *more confident* in their math and science skills than their Japanese counterparts were. The only problem was that the Japanese high school students proved significantly *more capable* in math and science than American students.[61] For fifty years now, we have worshipped "feel good" at the expense of "think right" and "do well." The result has been more self-esteem problems than ever.

But why should we be surprised at the breakdown of academic achievement at the hand of humanistic educators? How long would a business exist if every worker did as he or she pleased? How effective would a military unit be if it depended solely on the choices of each soldier to do his or her duty? What organization could function as an effective community if every member did as they pleased? When employees submit themselves to work for the good of the business, they help themselves. An effective military unit, submitted to the command and direction of its leader, is more likely to survive and complete the mission than an ineffective one. Organizations are as strong as the commitment of their individual members to that organization. And it follows that teachers should know better what their students need to understand than students do. Teachers can better organize curricula and learning activities than students can. Teachers can explain and illustrate difficult topics better than students can. Let the teachers teach! And help students learn!

On the other hand, business leaders who ignore the needs of workers, military commanders who fail to take care of their soldiers, and organizations that take volunteers' efforts for granted will soon fail. In the same way, teachers who teach *lessons* rather than *learners*, and who demonstrate an uncaring and disinterested attitude toward students, will soon find that meaningful learning has stopped.

In the 1970s, whole chapters of most educational psychology textbooks were devoted to "humanistic learning theory." In the 1990s, few textbooks did.[62] Humanistic principles were moved to chapters on motivation and classroom climate. Humanistic educators drew back from earlier extremes of the past and espoused cooperative learning strategies that emphasize both cognitive and affective outcomes, employed guided discovery methods, and focused on helping students understand, as well as love, a given subject.

Humanistic Learning in the 2000s

One searches in vain among thousands of pages of educational psychology textbooks for any mention of Humanistic Learning theory. From all appearances, the field declares by its silence that Humanistic Learning, as a viable educational system, is no more. Snowman (2009) stands alone in addressing it.[63] In a sidebar on the last of eight pages given to the subject in his 619-page text, he admits that by the "late 1980s, many textbooks had either drastically cut back or eliminated coverage of [humanistic learning theories], fewer papers on humanistic topics were delivered at major conferences, and fewer conceptual and research articles appeared in journals." He cites three reasons for this decline. First, IPT, social cognitive, and constructivist theories "ignited a torrent of research that promised . . . dramatic gains in achievement." Second, he suggests that the theoreticians and researchers who followed Maslow, Rogers, and Combs were not able to sustain interest in humanistic approaches. Third, standardized test scores proved American students were falling behind students of earlier generations, as well as students in other countries. Emotions, values, and individual needs were seen to be "frivolous" in the pursuit of academic achievement.[64]

Snowman points to a come-back of humanistic theories in the form of emphasis on learner needs, social harmony among students, and self-perceptions of students which is "every bit as important to understanding and improving classroom learning as the quality of their thinking." He concludes with great confidence: "So if someone tries to convince you that humanistic theories are dead, tell them that humanistic approaches to education never die; they just hang around waiting to be acknowledged."[65]

Human emotion, personal values, and learner needs remain part of the human experience, to be sure. And they continue to play a large role in any educational process. But one is hard-pressed to find support for Snowman's optimism in contemporary textbooks. The educational pendulum has certainly swung away from the humanistic label. But its extremes continue to reverberate along the corridors of Cooperative Learning and the more subjective forms of Constructivism. The name-brand of Humanistic Learning Theory is dead, but its spirit is alive and well.

The Continuing Legacy of Summerhill

Zoë and Tony Readhead, and the community of Summerhill, no doubt disagree. Summerhill, the quintessential model of humanistic learning, has stood the test of time, continuing a tradition begun in Germany in 1921 by Zoë's father, A. S. Neill, to provide a place where "children can learn in freedom." An introduction to the school is provided in the accompanying text box, and even more details can be found at the school's Web site.

I studied Summerhill as part of my Master's program at Southwestern in 1975. Our group's task for Dr. Terry's *Philosophy of Education* class was an hour-long presentation of "Existentialism in Education." (Since we were supposed to use the philosophical approach in making our presentations, I asked Dr. Terry if we could simply lay out the materials and let our classmates wander around and "freely choose what they wanted to learn," but, being a pragmatist, he would not permit that.)

Summerhill was our "philosophy-in-practice" centerpiece. Beyond the actual practice of existential and humanistic principles, there are two discoveries from that assignment that remain, burned into my memory, after all these years. First, while older children wore swimsuits in and around the pool, younger children had no such restrictions. Mixed "skinny-dipping" was not only allowed, it was encouraged in order to promote a sense of free expression and openness. That was surprising to me, having grown up in West Texas where the Baptist camps had separate pool times for girls and boys, *and we wore swim suits.* More shocking was the additional fact that, following school principles, the *children themselves* decided when they were old enough to don swimsuits. I did not find this particular aspect of Summerhill life mentioned on their 2008 Web site.

Summerhill: Humanistic Learning Theory in Practice

The early days

Summerhill was founded by A. S. Neill in 1921 in Hellerau, a suburb of Dresden. It was a part of an International school called the Neue Schule *[New School-RY]*, but Neill disagreed with the rules imposed by the school administrators. They "disapproved of tobacco, foxtrots, and cinemas—while he wanted the children to live their own lives." He expressed his philosophy this way:

> I am only just realising the absolute freedom of my scheme of Education. I see that all outside compulsion is wrong, that inner compulsion is the only value. And if Mary or David wants to laze about, lazing about is the one thing necessary for their personalities at the moment. Every moment of a healthy child's life is a working moment. A child has no time to sit down and laze. Lazing is abnormal, it is a recovery, and therefore it is necessary when it exists.

He moved his school to a beautiful site, a castle atop a mountain in Sonntagsberg in Austria; but he was not well received by the local Catholic community. So he moved the school to the south of England in 1923, to a town called Lyme Regis, to a house called Summerhill, and began with five students. In 1927, the school moved to Leiston, in the county of Suffolk, where it resides today *[2004]*.

The school was controversial—often referred to in the press as the "Do As You Please" school. Neill, however, did have the respect of many educationalists and well-known personalities such as, among others, Bertrand Russell and Henry Miller.

Enrollment in the school plummeted to 25 in the late 1950s, and the school considered closing its doors. However, an American publisher worked with Neill to publish *Summerhill—A Radical View of Child Rearing.* It quickly became a nationwide best seller, and enrollment increased—many students coming from the U.S.

Neill suffered declining health in 1973 and passed away on September 23 of that year. His wife continued to run the school until her retirement in 1985 when daughter Zoë Readhead, the current head teacher, took over. She and her husband Tony now administer the school and travel around the world, conducting conferences to share their approach to education.

Summerhill today

Summerhill has been successful since 1921 in "providing a happy environment for kids and producing well-balanced men and women." The school maintains Neill's fundamental belief: "The function of the child is to live his own life—not the life that his anxious parents think he should live, nor a life according to the purpose of the educator who thinks he knows best."

"All crimes, all hatreds, all wars can be reduced to unhappiness."

A. S. Neill, founder of Summerhill School

Information drawn from the official Web site of Summerhill, http://www.summerhillschool.co.uk/ , accessed November 18, 2008

The second discovery was a research study of Summerhill graduates who were asked whether they would send their children to Summerhill. The majority said no. When asked why, the most common response was, "Too much freedom." One graduate lamented the fact that he might have been a brain surgeon had his teachers encouraged him in that direction. At the time, he was producing and selling Black Light paintings out of his one-room walk-up in a suburb of London.[66]

A. S. Neill wrote the following in his best seller *Summerhill—A Radical Approach to Child Rearing*.[67]

"We set out to make a school in which we should allow children freedom to be themselves. In order to do this we had to renounce all discipline, all direction, all suggestion, all moral training, all religious instruction. We have been called brave, but it did not require courage. All it required was what we had—a complete belief in the child as a good, not an evil, being. Since 1921 this belief in the goodness of the child has never wavered; it rather has become a final faith."[68]

This quote can be found as the last paragraph on Summerhill's "Policies" Web page. I will leave it to you to visit the Web site and read for yourself the governing principles of the school. You will find in them the embodiment of a secular humanistic system of education.

A. S. Neill has inspired many educational thinkers over the years. You may remember one such contemporary educator from the 2008 presidential campaign.[69] He is William Ayers, Professor of Curriculum and Instruction[70] at the University of Illinois, Chicago. In 2003 William Ayers wrote the book *On the Side of the Child: Summerhill Revisited*[71] in which he "speaks as a parent and educator who has spent years in the classroom experimenting with A.S. Neill's progressive approach."[72]

Perhaps Snowman is right after all. Humanistic theories do not die. They simply hang around waiting to be acknowledged. But one would never know it from reading contemporary textbooks on learning theory.

Humanistic Learning in the Church

Why have I continued to include humanistic learning in this unit on learning theory systems? The answer is that humanistic principles, when stripped of their secular garments and dressed in kingdom garb, are an essential part of Christian education. Much of the learning that goes on in our churches reflects small-h humanism: a "concern with the interests, needs, and welfare of human beings."[73] Effective churches are those that care about people, that minister to the needs of people, and that take seriously the perceptions and problems of the people they serve. Effective Bible study classes are warm, inviting, open, sharing groups of believers who structure their convictions according to God's Word and love each other freely. See Chapter One, "The Right Pillar," for specifics on using affective principles in a Christian context.

In Christian college classrooms and seminary classes, academic standards and instructional goals require attention to honing skills and sharpening understanding. But at the center of the process, and all along the way, stands this never-changing principle: "They will know we are Christians by our love." Not by our doctrines, nor by our institutionalized ministries, important as they are. "By this all people will know that you are My disciples, if you have love for one another" (John 13:35). Secular humanism focuses on self and emotions—"my values, my desires, my choices, without outside interference or restraint." As Neill would say, the goal is for people "to be happy." Christian humanism focuses on others—helping others, caring for others—in Jesus' name.

The Disciplers' Model calls for balance between two extremes. The Thinking Pillar (cognitive meaning) stands on the Foundation Stone of the Bible. The Feeling Pillar (affective relevance) stands on the Foundation Stone of Learner Needs. Both are necessary for growth. Cognition without affect produces impersonal abstraction. Affect without cognition produces superficial meaninglessness. Taken together, Christian teachers help learners understand Scripture *and* discover personal relevance in Scripture. By doing so, teachers produce *personal clarity* of Scripture. The balance—clear

Key Emphases from Humanistic Learning Theory

The following twelve statements summarize essential distinctive of traditional behavioral learning. Use these terms to compare and contrast learning as defined in chapters 6 and 9.

1. The learner is a. . .	**PERSON** Learning involves personal attitudes and values as well as content
2. The focus is on the. . .	**PERSONAL EXPERIENCES** Learners embrace ideas that they've personally experienced
3. Relationship of learning "whole" to its parts	**THE "WHOLE" INCLUDES EMOTIONS** Learners filter content through their own personal values
4. Learning is. . .	**PERSONAL and INTERACTIVE** Learners build value systems out of their social interactions w/ others
5. The target learning domain is. . .	**AFFECTIVE** Building learning through personal responses, values, priorities
6. The goal of learning is. . .	**CHANGE IN ATTITUDES AND VALUES** Learning is growing as a person more than understanding content
7. Learning is strengthened by. . .	**PERSONAL SHARING** Small groups, interaction, creative writing, sharing perspectives
8. Learning is guided by. . .	**PERSONAL SATISFACTION** Learners choose subjects that are personally meaningful
9. Motivation keys on. . .	**PERSONAL FRIENDSHIP AND FREEDOM** Learners are "free to learn" when they feel they "belong" in the group
10. Feedback should be. . .	**PERSONAL, ON EFFORT** Help each learner, at their point of need, to make the best effort
11. Best curriculum is. . .	**ELECTIVE** Learners do best when they are free to choose their own subjects
12. The Theory in Practice is. . .	**SUMMERHILL** *Summerhill: For & Against.* (Paperback, 1970) by Harold H. Hart

understanding ("What does this mean?") on one hand and personal relevance ("What does this mean to me?") on the other—can be applied to any subject of study.

The balance between cognition and affect, reason and emotion, is not a static 50-50. Rather, teachers do well to focus on cognitive approaches as they (pleasantly) engage students' minds in subject matter structure (90-10), then focus on humanistic approaches as they (clearly) engage students' hearts in subject matter relevance (10-90). Success in striking a proper balance over time is difficult, and requires flexibility, careful observation of student actions, and facility with a range of teaching skills. Despite the difficulties, teachers do well to push students toward personal clarity.

As we said at the top of the chapter, it is not enough to simply do the right things (duty, ritual), or think the right thoughts (orthodoxy, intellectualism). Scripture teaches us to **be** right, as people of God—to integrate God's truth into who we are. This chapter gives principles of affective education, emphasizing values and changed attitudes. May God bless your teaching efforts as you love your students and care for them one by one, even as you help them understand.

Chapter Concepts

Affective learning	Learning that emphasizes emotions, values, attitudes, predispositions, and morals
Confluent education	Combining cognitive and affective factors in the learning process (George Brown)
Cooperative learning	Stands against *competitive* learning. A hybrid cognitive-affective approach to learning
Existentialism	Philosophy given to idea that human essence is derived from choices made by self
Humanism—secular	Philosophy focused on humanity; rejects God and supernatural religion (secularism)
Humanism—classical	Philosophy focused on humanity; both secular (Renaissance) and biblical (Reformation)
Humanism—educational	Philosophy focused on personal aspects of learning: experiences, values, priorities
Learning Styles	Educational view that each learner's learning preferences be considered in teaching
Open Classroom	Educational view that walls and classroom teachers be replaced with open learning spaces
Person-centered learning	Educational view that emphasized trust and empathy over performance (Carl Rogers)
Phenomenology	The world as it is perceived by individuals (vs. *reality*, the world as it may actually be)
Relevance	Personal (subjective) meaning from that subject (vs. the objective meaning of a subject)

Secularism	The "religion of humanity": human self-sufficiency, rejection of the supernatural, worship of the scientific method, emphasis on civil and academic freedom
Self-regulated learning	Students controlling their own learning: selection of topics, setting goals, and evaluating outcomes with little teacher guidance
T. E. T.	Teacher Effectiveness Training: stressed the affective (Thomas Gordon)

Chapter Objectives

Learners will demonstrate knowledge of Humanistic Learning Theory by . . .

- Recalling the distinctions among secular humanism, classical humanism, and Christian humanism.
- Identifying a key contribution of the following theorists to the teaching-learning process: Brown, Rogers, Combs, Gordon, Maslow, Patterson, and Purkey.

Learners will demonstrate understanding of Humanistic Learning Theory by . . .

- Explaining the usefulness of educational humanism to the Christian teaching process.
- Contrasting the extreme claims of humanistic educators with recent research findings.

Learners will demonstrate appreciation for Humanistic learning theory by sharing at least three classroom experiences that helped shape their present value system.

Discussion Questions

1 Discuss the similarities and differences among the secular humanism of the Renaissance, the "Christian humanism" of the Reformation, and educational humanism.

2 Describe one or more contributions to humanistic learning by Brown, Rogers, Combs, Gordon, Maslow, Patterson, and Purkey.

3 Explain why principles drawn from educational humanism (affective learning) are useful in Christian teaching.

4 What educational experiences have you had that shaped your present value system?

5 Identify the following questions or activities as cognitive or affective.
  a. Read 1 Corinthians 13. How have you experienced this kind of love in your life?
  b. Compare the responses of Peter and Judas to their betrayal of Jesus.
  c. What does the term "agape" mean?
  d. What experiences of witnessing have you had?
  e. If you had been Nicodemus, what would you have asked Jesus?
  f. Explain "sanctification" in your own words.
  g. Have you experienced the joy Philip must have felt as he led the Ethiopian to faith in Christ? What was it like?

6 Compare and contrast humanism and Humanism. How are they alike? How do they differ?

The Christian Teachers' Triad

A Meta-Theory of Learning

"Love the Lord your God with all your heart, with all your soul, with all your mind, and with all your strength."

Mark 12:30

The best and safest thing is to keep a balance in your life, acknowledge the great powers around us and in us. If you can do that, and live that way, you are really a wise man.

– Euripides

If you are planning for a year, sow rice; if you are planning for a decade, plant trees; if you are planning for a lifetime, educate people.

—Chinese Proverb

Chapter Rationale

The previous five chapters describe three major learning theory systems. Each has its proponents. No doubt, your own views of teaching and learning resonated with one of the systems more than the others. If teachers want to help all students learn in the real world of the classroom, we cannot focus on one system alone. Educational problems do not fall neatly into any one system: some are behavioral, some cognitive, and others affective. Effective teachers move freely from system to system, moment by moment, engaging learners where they are, helping them master the subject, and grow as a result.

The Christian Teachers' Triad helps in two important ways: it balances the various approaches to learning over time and encourages flexibility in response to student needs – head, heart, and hand – in the moment. This chapter defines the Triad, describes the imbalance and harm that can result from giving too much attention to any one system, and relates specific principles of teaching to each component. The flavor of this chapter is small-group Bible study, such as Sunday school classes,[1] but the principles certainly apply to all subjects and Christian contexts.

Chapter Overview

➤ Historical Background
➤ The Triad of Life
➤ The Distortion of Imbalance
➤ Jesus, Master of the Triad
➤ The External Influence of the Teacher
➤ Christ, the Center of the Triad
➤ A Dynamic Synergism of Learning Theory Systems
➤ *Chapter Concepts, Chapter Objectives, Discussion Questions*

Historical Background

The Christian Teachers' Triad first appeared in print in Eldridge's *The Teaching Ministry of the Church* (1995), in my chapter on Christian growth.[2] I had by that time been using the Triad in educational psychology classes for eight years to provide an integration of the three learning theory systems. The Triad reflects not a loose aggregation of psychological perspectives, but the holistic perspective found in the Gospel records of Jesus' approach to teaching.[3] That approach to teaching in general—and to the people He taught specifically—included elements of all three systems. I used the Triad in *Teaching Ministry* as a simple structure around which to discuss the goal of Christian education, which is growth toward Christlikeness.[4]

In 1994 an invitation was extended from B&H Publishers to consider writing another book. The proposed textbook, based on the educational psychology course being taught at the time, became the original edition of *Created to Learn*. Published in 1996, *CTL* used the Triad as a means of formally unifying the three learning theory systems into a single approach to teaching and learning. While the

Triad provided the framework for two later texts,[5] this chapter elaborates on those brief overviews. Since the Triad integrates the three learning systems already discussed, you will find here some degree of redundancy. In earlier chapters we focused on the systems and theories themselves. Here we focus more on the integration—how the various elements support each other in a dynamic synergism of learning and teaching theory.

The Triad of Life

The apostle John summarizes his Gospel record of the life and work of Jesus this way: "Jesus performed many other signs in the presence of His disciples that are not written in this book. But these are written so that you may believe Jesus is the Messiah, the Son of God, and by believing you may have life in His name" (John 20:30–31). John's Gospel, and by extension Scripture as a whole, has been written so that people may believe in—depend on, trust in—Jesus, the Anointed One (Acts 10:38), the express image of Almighty God (Col 1:15) and in His name, have life. This life is not biological life (*bios*) that begins with great potential and energy, grows, declines, and dies. It is God's own life (*zoay*), imparted to us by faith when we are "born again" (John 3:3), grows, and never dies. This life—eternal in quantity and quality—begins *when* we believe—the moment we accept, decide, repent, depend—and grows *as* we believe—deciding, accepting, repenting, depending. John emphasizes both the event ("believe") and the process ("by believing"). Such belief is not self-made, but a response to the wooing, teaching, and leading of God's Spirit. When Peter proclaimed his own belief in Jesus as God's Son, Jesus replied, "Simon son of Jonah, you are blessed because flesh and blood did not reveal this to you, but My Father in heaven" (Matt 16:17–18).

The result of "having believed" and "believing" is life. Not life in general. Not even spiritual life in general. But "life in His name." Life in union with Christ (Col 1:27). Life lived out in the yoke of Christ, in the yoke with Christ, which gives refreshment and renewal (Matt 11:28–30). This spiritual life is not wholly separated from our own experience with life in the world, because we are created in the image of God. God is Triune in His Person—Father, Son, Spirit. He is also Triune in nature, revealing Himself as Rational, Personal, and Active. The life we have as human beings, born into this world, is rational, personal, and active—the very life reflected in the three learning systems. Since we are created in His image, we too are rational, personal, and active. The spiritual "life in His name" we receive by belief and believing is rational, personal, and active. We picture these aspects of life, both natural (three circles) and supernatural (three circles plus overlap), by means of three intersecting circles—the Triad of Life.

The three psychological spheres reflect processes of cognitive (rational), humanistic (personal), and behavioral (active) learning—thinking clearly, feeling and valuing deeply, and doing skillfully. Each sphere is connected to the other two, but develops in its own way. Each sphere can be any size, and can overlap the others in an infinite number of combinations. The two lower diagrams show two examples of distortion naturally found in human beings. We will discuss this later in the chapter.

The larger figure represents an ideal: all three circles are the same size, and all three intersect equally.[6] I say "*an* ideal" because "*the* ideal" is found in Jesus. Were we to draw the Triad depicting Him, we would see all three spheres perfectly overlapped, forming a seamless, single whole. What we lose in that singular perspective is the three-ness of the Triad—essential in discussing human tendencies toward one extreme or another.

In the end, the measure of Christian teaching—teaching that is Christian—is not transmitting lessons or subjects. It is imparting life—rationally, emotionally, actively, and spiritually. Let's look at each sphere, define its connection to learning theory, and its contribution to the life of students.

Thinking

The thinking circle represents the rational or *cognitive* sphere of life: knowing, encoding, conceptualizing, problem-solving, analyzing, synthesizing, and evaluating. This sphere of life reflects the discoveries of Piaget and Bruner, Vygotsky and Köhler, as well as the evolving views of Constructivism, and Information Processing Theory. The multi-layered networks of concepts, principles,

rehearsal, elaboration, schemes, meaningfulness, accommodation, and a hundred others, as well as suggestions for teachers desiring clear understanding in their students, all fall into this Circle of Thinking. All of it speaks to our desire for clear thinking in the Christian context of teaching.

Without a clear focus on "correctly teaching the word of truth" (2 Tim 2:15), we open learners to deception and delusion. The rational confronts, for example, John 3:16 with *conceptual* (objective) questions: What did God do when He *loved* the world? What is the *world* that He loved? What does it mean to *believe* in His Son? What kind of *life* do we obtain through this belief? What does *eternal* add to this life?

Jesus said, "Do not judge, so that you won't be judged." (Matt 7:1). What did Jesus mean by *judge*? Are we not to have an opinion? Are we to go through life without evaluating ideas, priorities, and actions? The apostle John writes, "Test the spirits to see whether they are from God, because many false prophets have gone out into the world" (1 John 4:1). Is this "testing" not a judgment? Did Jesus and John disagree? Is this a contradiction? Just what did Jesus mean by "Do not judge"? These are rational questions (which we will delve into a little later).

The classic hymn "Come Thou Fount of Every Blessing" introduces the second verse with the words "Here I raise my Ebenezer." *What is an Ebenezer?*[7] I sang the hymn for years and never asked this question until I began interpreting for deaf worshippers. The *second phrase* of the second verse helps clarify the meaning: "hither by Thy help I'm come." The sense of the verse is "Here I raise my praise to the Lord, for, right up to now, He has always been my source of help." The hymn was a favorite for years, but until I studied the meaning of the words, I didn't understand what I was singing.

If learners grow rationally in the Lord, it is because they move beyond mere words to clear meanings, beyond pat answers to cogent principles. None of us can grow "in every way into Him who is the head—Christ" (Eph 4:15) without a clear understanding of what God's Word means.

Feeling and Valuing

The feeling and valuing circle represents the emotional or *affective* sphere of life: listening, sharing, loving, valuing, prioritizing, and reflecting spiritual truths in daily life. This sphere represents Maslow and Rogers, Combs and Purkey, as well as the lingering emphases of self-instruction, choice, personal satisfaction, and Summerhill. The multi-layered networks of values, attitudes, priorities, personal experiences, as well as suggestions for teachers desiring openness, transparency, and personal growth in their students, all fall into this Circle of Feeling. All of it speaks to our desire for authentic life change in the Christian context of teaching.

Scripture uses the word "heart" to refer to both "mind"[8] and "emotion." But the Bible often uses the term to refer specifically to the affective elements of life. "A glad heart makes a cheerful countenance, but by sorrow of heart the spirit is broken" (Prov 15:13). Here "heart" refers to feelings of happiness or depression.

The emotional confronts John 3:16 with *personal* (subjective) questions: How has God loved *you*? How have *you* learned to believe in Jesus Christ? What has been the result in *your own life*? How has *your life changed* through your relationship with Jesus? How have *you experienced* "God's kind of life" since you gave your life to Him?

King David writes, "I have treasured Your word in my heart so that I may not sin against You" (Ps 119:11). This was David's way of reflecting his heartfelt commitment to live by God's Word. While he seriously failed to live up to it, he passionately desired to do so. He displayed this passion in his dance before the Lord (2 Sam 6:16–22), and in his deep grief when confronted by his sin (2 Sam 12:13–20). His heart-centered response was to repent and to embrace his Lord. It may be due to these very qualities that Samuel declared this future adulterer and murderer "a man after his [God's] own heart" (1 Sam 13:14 KJV). He suffered dearly for his sin, but he never turned his back on God. He never ran away from God but always toward Him.

If learners grow emotionally in the Lord, it is because they move beyond historical facts to present experiences, from cold doctrine to warm lifestyle. Learners grow as they move from surface feelings to unrestrained devotion to the Lord, from self-centered agendas to God's priorities. None of us can grow "in every way into Him who is the head—Christ" (Eph 4:15) without a humble, loving embrace of the Lord and His ways.

Doing

The doing circle represents the *behavioral*, or skill, sphere of life: imitating, practicing, repeating, honing, exercising, programming, reinforcing, and innovating. This sphere of life reflects the discoveries of Pavlov and Thorndike, Watson and Skinner, as well as the views of Programmed Instruction, and Social Learning Theory (Bandura). The multi-layered networks of stimulus-response bonds,

skills, competencies, feedback, reinforcement schedules, drill and practice, performance-based rewards and a hundred others, as well as suggestions for teachers desiring excellence in student habits and competencies, all fall into this Circle of Doing. All of it speaks to our desire for skillful actions in the Christian context of teaching.

Without a willingness to obey Jesus' declaration—"hears these words of Mine **and acts on them**" (Matt 7:24)—we open ourselves and our learners to great danger. Those who only hear Jesus' words, and fail to act on them, will be swept away by life's storms (7:26–27). Hearing alone is not enough.

The behavioral confronts John 3:16 with competent *ministry outcomes*: How can I love people in my world this next week? How well will I depend on the Lord this week as I face problems, frustrations, disappointments, and temptations? What are ways I can exercise my love skillfully, exercising my dependence on God at work and at home? What evidence of God's tangible actions in our lives do we provide each other week by week as we report on our faithful actions, and God's faithful blessing?

We may clearly "understand biblical love," but—*do we love?* We may "love missions," but *—do we support missions* with personal time, talent, and money? We can "believe in forgiveness" with all our hearts, but—*do we forgive?* What we do with our lives, what we do in our lives, is a window on who we are. Jesus said, "Beware of false prophets. . . . You'll recognize them by their fruit. Are grapes gathered from thornbushes or figs from thistles? In the same way, **every good tree produces good fruit, but a bad tree produces bad fruit**" (Matt 7:15–17) . . . **"for a tree is known by its fruit"** (12:33).

If learners grow behaviorally, skillfully, in the Lord, it is because they move beyond words and feelings to ministry actions, from high-sounding word magic[9] and superficial feelings to disciplined behavior. Further, learners will grow as they eliminate old bad habits and practice new good habits. None of us can grow "in every way into Him who is the head—Christ" (Eph 4:15) without a dedicated, action-oriented obedience to put Jesus' words into practice.

The Distortion of Imbalance

God calls us to prepare *people.* The problem is that people do not come to us prepackaged and pre-equipped to learn and serve. They do not come spin-balanced and ready to roll. Every person tends toward one of the three spheres of the Triad. Some emphasize the rational, others the emotional, and still others the behavioral. But imbalance in life, just as in automobiles, causes vibration and eventual breakdown. Overemphasis of any one sphere creates a danger zone for learning and growth.

Student tendencies toward over-thinking, over-feeling, and over-doing can certainly cause problems in the classroom. But there is greater danger to learning when teachers lead their classes to these extremes. Extremism in any of the three spheres diminishes learning and hampers growth.

Thinkers

Teachers and learners who emphasize the rational over emotional or behavioral elements are "thinkers." Thinkers generally prefer theologically sound hymns over foot-tapping choruses. They prefer factual and conceptual questions over personal and subjective ones. They like well-organized lectures more than group discussions—particularly if the discussion "slogs through" people's feelings and personal experiences more than the Scripture.

Thinkers like studies that are deep, profound, and (mentally) challenging. They actually enjoy grappling with Greek and Hebrew. Context is important, both historically and theologically. They thrive on making comparisons and contrasts among biblical concepts, or conducting word studies. Distilling biblical principles. Considering various (theoretical) applications.

They enjoy developing relationships among the ideas in the passage more than developing relationships with other learners in the class. Classrooms that might seem rather cold and analytical to others are, for thinkers, welcome and safe. Classrooms that are open and spontaneous are, for thinkers, superficial and sometimes dangerous—one never knows when order will be disturbed by a rabbit-chase[10] or an overly personal story. They keep their focus on the topic.

Thinkers define learning itself as primarily conceptual, and the richer, deeper, and more complex the session, the better. The classrooms of thinkers reflect the ambiance of an old library, lined with great books, and furnished with overstuffed chairs, where scholars open their inquiring minds to profound truths.

Such an approach, *taken to extreme*, produces a purely academic process that overemphasizes the rational while dismissing the emotional and behavioral. In this extreme environment, learning is dry, impersonal, and overly abstract. *A cold intellectualism.* Learning tends to wander from one viewpoint to another, seldom touching down in life. While such learning may pique the curiosity of learners momentarily ("deep and mysterious"), it can result in little or no difference in what we value or how we live (which, by the way, may not bother hard-core thinkers).

It is one thing to understand honesty, but quite another to value honesty, or to be competently honest. It is one thing to understand the plan of salvation, quite another to be saved. One thing to understand Matthew 28:19–20, quite another to support and engage in missions. Bible knowledge, doctrinal understanding, Christian principles, and spiritual concepts will lead to spiritual pride unless we integrate them into personal attitudes and actions (1 Cor 8:1–3).

Feelers

Teachers and learners who emphasize the emotional over rational or behavioral elements are "feelers." Feelers focus on feelings, attitudes, values, and personal experiences. Feelers prefer free-wheeling discussions over structured lectures, especially if the discussions engage the lives of learners and touch the heart. Feelers enjoy giving testimonies and hearing the testimonies of others. They want learning to be fun and spontaneous, not heavily structured with explanations of terms or historical background. Feelers want their classroom to be friendly, warm, accepting, and never threatening—and to feelers, the profundities of theology and philosophy are threatening.

Feelers care more about people than principles, more about experiences than teaching points: "More passion and less analysis, please." They consider their relationships with other learners far more important than multi-layered relationships among ideas. If teachers do not "finish the lessons," it is no problem, so long as "we've shared our lives in meaningful ways."

Feelers define learning itself as emotional, celebrative, liberating, and warm. The classrooms of feelers reflect the ambiance of evening campfires, hand-holding and *Kum-ba-ya*, where counselors love the campers unconditionally, hoping they will understand and practice what they've so deeply enjoyed.

Superficial Emotionalism

Such an approach, *taken to extreme*, produces an overly personal Bible study process that focuses on the emotional while dismissing the rational and behavioral. In this environment, learners find themselves immersed in warm, lighthearted, superficial feel-good. Subjective relevance trumps objective meaning. The Bible means *what it means **to me***. Learning tends to wander from one self-centered story to another. While such learning produces a momentary emotional high ("fun and excitement"), it can result in little or no difference in the way we think or live (which, by the way, may not bother hard-core feelers). Worse, such an extremely subjective process, over time, may well leave learners open to emotional manipulation, deception, and delusion.

It is one thing to "get excited" about a mission trip, but quite another to understand its purpose, or develop the skills to actually help others. It is one thing to "share an experience" about faith, quite another to differentiate between "faith" and "presumption." One thing to "freely volunteer" to mow a widow's lawn, quite another to complete the task, and do it well. Joining a group, sharing experiences, having fun, getting excited, "letting go," and opening up will lead to spiritual pride unless we graft these emotions into biblical meanings and Christian actions.

Doers

Teachers and learners who emphasize the behavioral over rational or emotional elements are "doers." Doers focus on practical, tangible outcomes for learning: What are we going to do with this?

How can we use it? How can we live and work more effectively? Doers are passionately utilitarian. They dislike the paralysis of analysis of thinkers, preferring one clear application that learners can actually make during the week over "five possible applications" which never seem to be done. Likewise, they dislike the superficial, inefficient wandering of feelers, preferring a straight-line approach from subject to action. While sessions may begin with a concept or personal experience, doers push toward realistic competence, the mastery of life and ministry skills. They keep their focus on "What doth hinder thee?"

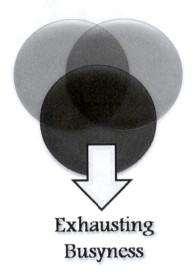

Exhausting Busyness

Doers define learning itself as practical, efficient, and focused. The classrooms of doers reflect the ambiance of busy laboratories and workshops, where engineers convert theory and passion into life practice through on-going action-oriented projects.

Such an approach, *taken to extreme*, produces an action-oriented study process that focuses on the behavioral while dismissing the emotional and rational. In this extreme environment, we find ourselves immersed in mindless, unfeeling busyness—one activity after another, one ministry project after another, which can lead to ritual and eventually to exhaustion. While such learning may spur us to action in some type of practical ministry, at least for a moment, it can result in little or no difference in what we think or value (which, by the way, rarely bothers hard-core doers). Without understanding the why of ministry, without personally owning the ministry, learners simply go through the motions until they burn out and give up.

Pictures of Extremes

I have painted pictures of extremes. And yet these extremes exist in real-world classrooms. In the last fifteen years, I have taught fifty-something classes in educational psychology and principles of teaching. In every one of those classes, I have defined the Triad, and invited students to physically move to one of three areas in the classroom representing the three circles. In nearly every case, with few exceptions, students break themselves out in rough thirds. Every group. Regardless of nationality or ethnicity—American, Russian, Ukrainian, Kyrgyz, Kazakh, Caucasian, Afro-American, Hispanic, Korean, deaf or hearing. Every group breaks themselves down into rough thirds: thinkers, feelers, and doers. When asked to describe, in their groups, what they most like and dislike in classes, they respond with ideas as described above. In fact, these many exercises over the years are the source for the summaries of thinkers, feelers, and doers above.

If the class is large enough,[11] and if there are roughly equal numbers of men and women in the class,[12] then gender breaks out in a systematic way. Despite the myth than "men are thinkers and women are feelers," *both men and women populate all three groups.* Specifically, there are always more men than women in the Thinkers' group. More women and than men in the Feelers' group. Roughly equal numbers of men and women in the Doers' group. "Women thinkers" are closer to "men thinkers" in the way they learn than they are to "women feelers." "Men feelers"[13] are closer to "women feelers" in the way they learn than they are to "men thinkers."

Every group has a mixture of learner types. The natural mixture of learner types helps balance the group as a whole—thinkers pulling the group toward clear meaning, feelers toward authentic values, and doers toward practical action.

Having emphasized the differences among the three groups, it is good to remember, also, that *all learners think, feel and value, and do.* The overlap of the circles is intended to reflect this unity. The extremes develop, not from abilities, but preferences. An extreme in one area does not negate the presence of the other two, but simply dominates them. Thinkers possess both values and skills. But in teaching and learning, thinkers prefer to engage subjects *intellectually.* Feelers possess both concepts and skills. But in teaching and learning, feelers prefer to engage subjects *emotionally* and *relationally.* Doers possess both concepts and values. But in teaching and learning, doers prefer to engage subjects *practically.* Absent an intentional analysis of how we teach and learn, we naturally engage in these distorted approaches without awareness of their impact on learners.

Striking a Balance

The dilemma for teachers is how to strike a balance *over time,* providing learning experiences that touch all three spheres, without overemphasizing any one of them. Effective teaching requires provoking the thinking of learners, but too much focus on thinking leads to a cold, idealistic intellectualism. Effective teaching requires nurturing positive feelings toward the class, the content, and the teacher, but too much focus on feelings leads to mindless, sentimental, impractical fluff. Effective teaching requires leading students to master a range of academic and ministry skills, but too much focus on doing leads to mindless, unfeeling ritual.

One answer to the dilemma is for teachers to stretch into less comfortable spheres. Thinkers tend to be suspicious of emotions and the chaos they can generate in class. It requires courage and an intentional plan to move from the comfort of concepts to affective activities ("sharing") that may bring conflict, confrontation, or confusion. Regardless of preferences, teachers do well to develop biblical concepts and principles, embrace Christian values wholeheartedly, and engage in practical ministries. Proper understanding provides the foundation for biblical values and ministry. Personally embraced biblical values inject life into biblical exegesis and ministry practice. Christ-centered ministry builds the bridge between Bible study (concepts and values) and the world of people in need. In the same way, feelers leave their emotional comfort zones to engage thinkers with deep content and doers with expertise; doers leave their activity comfort zone to engage thinkers with deep content and feelers with care and concern.

A second answer to the dilemma is to intentionally select learning activities in spheres other than our preferred area. Again, teachers tend to choose activities and procedures that reflect their own preferences in teaching, and ignore activities that do not. When feelers intentionally choose to exegete a verse of Scripture, when doers intentionally choose to share a personal experience, when thinkers intentionally make a practical assignment to be done during the week—they stretch themselves as teachers, and their learners as kingdom citizens.

Making this move toward "balance over time"[14] is both frightening and difficult, and requires intentional effort: for thinkers—to embrace personal emotion and practical action; for feelers—to embrace scholarly analysis and practical actions; and for doers—to embrace scholarly analysis and personal emotion. And yet this intentional discomfort is necessary if any of us would succeed at engaging every learner in our classrooms.

Jesus, Master of the Triad

It should be no surprise, then, that the Master Teacher reflected the Triad in His own teaching ministry. God created us in His Image—thinker, feeler, doer—and Jesus reflected that triadic perspective in His life and work as Prophet, Priest, and King.

Jesus as Prophet

Jesus was **a Prophet,**[15] proclaiming the kingdom of God. He used stories and illustrations to explain the kingdom of heaven. He represented God the Father to the people and taught them the meaning of the Word of God. As prophet, Jesus focused on the objective element of faith.

Expounds. Jesus demonstrated a mastery of Old Testament Scripture that cut through the traditions, laws, and interpretations of the religious elite. But Jesus went further and spiritualized the concrete laws of Moses. Jesus made every attempt to lift His disciples and listeners from the concrete *actions* of sin to intangible *thoughts* of sin,[16] connecting sin to its roots in the mind of man. In His "You have heard it said . . . but I tell you" statements, He expounds Kingdom life beyond Old Testament wineskins.

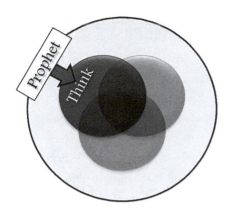

"You have heard that it was said to our ancestors, Do not murder, and whoever murders will be subject to judgment" (Matt 5:21). He was referring to the sixth Commandment (Exod 20:13). "But I tell you, everyone who is angry with his brother will be subject to judgment" (Matt 5:22). Replace irritation and contempt with agape love—an immense desire to be of help.[17]

"You have heard that it was said, Do not commit adultery" (Matt 5:27). He was referring to the seventh commandment (Exod 20:14). "But I tell you, everyone who looks at a woman to lust for her has already committed adultery with her in his heart" (Matt 5:28). Replace sexual fantasy and its titillating siblings with God's love and goodness, which produce respect and purity.[18]

"Again, you have heard that it was said to our ancestors, You must not break your oath, but you must keep your oaths to the Lord" (Matt 5:33). Jesus was referring to the third commandment (Exod 20:7). "But I tell you, don't take an oath at all. . . . But let your word 'yes' be 'yes,' and your 'no' be 'no.' Anything more than this is from the evil one" (Matt 5:34,37). Replace manipulative language—the "song and the dance,"[19] the "sizzle that sells the steak"—with simple, honest information: a yes or a no.

"You have heard that it was said, An eye for an eye and a tooth for a tooth (see Exod 21:24). But I tell you, don't resist an evildoer. On the contrary, if anyone slaps you on your right cheek, turn the other to him also. As for the one who wants to sue you and take away your shirt, let him have your coat as well. And if anyone forces you to go one mile, go with him two. Give to the one who asks you, and don't turn away from the one who wants to borrow from you" (Matt 5:39–42). Dallas Willard writes that these statements cause many to "throw up their hands in despair,"[20] because they mistakenly take Jesus' words as kingdom *laws* (how godly people must act) rather than kingdom *characteristics* (how the godly people normally act).[21] The sensible application of *appropriateness* to these behaviors calls us to evaluate situations and decide, before God, what we should do. Appropriateness includes a larger context of life: responsibilities, prior commitments, family obligations. In each case we must decide if the gift of our "vulnerability, goods, time, and strength is, precisely, appropriate." We make this decision in the moment, before God—for, as "a child of the King, I always live in His presence." As one example, consider the heart surgeon who is on his way to do a heart transplant. He does not have the freedom to "go the second mile." He has another pressing matter that requires his attention. He "must say no and leave at the end of the first mile with best wishes and a hasty farewell."[22]

"You have heard that it was said, Love your neighbor (see Lev 19:18) and hate your enemy.[23] But I tell you, love your enemies and pray for those who persecute you, so that you may be sons of your Father in heaven" (Matt 5:44–45). Those born into God's kingdom live on a higher plane than those who are not. Replace the desire for vengeance with prayer.

Jesus did not waste His time spinning abstract theories about goodness. "He struck powerfully at the heart of human existence: anger, obsessive lust, manipulation, revenge, slapping, suing, cursing, coercing—the stuff of real life."[24]

Transforms. Jesus transformed the thinking of listeners through parables. A parable begins with a familiar, tangible object (concrete operational) and proceeds to use that tangible object to teach about the intangible kingdom of heaven (formal operational). "The kingdom of heaven is like . . ." a "mustard seed" (Matt 13:31), "yeast" (13:33), "treasure, buried in a field" (13:44), "a merchant in search of fine pearls" (13:45), "a large net thrown into the sea" (13:47), "a landowner who brings out of his storeroom what is new and what is old" (13:52). The Kingdom of heaven "may be compared to a man who sowed good seed in his field" (13:24), "a king who wanted to settle accounts with his slaves" (18:23), and "a king who gave a wedding banquet for his son" (22:2). Jesus demonstrated His intellect in creating these comparisons. He then used them to help learners think about the kingdom of God in radically different ways.

Questions. Jesus asked questions. His questions were both objective ("Who do people say that the Son of Man is?" Matt 16:13) and personal ("Who do *you* say that I am?" Matt 16:15). They were informational ("How many loaves do you have?" Matt 15:34) and analytical ("How is it then that David, inspired by the Spirit, calls Him 'Lord'?" Matt 22:43). He asked questions for emphasis ("Whose image and inscription is this?" Mark 12:15) and learning readiness ("What is written in the law? . . . How do you read it?" Luke 10:26). In each case, Jesus engaged the knowledge and experience of His listeners in preparation for teaching.

Jesus also used questions to expose His enemies. "Woe to you, blind guides, who say, 'Whoever takes an oath by the sanctuary, it means nothing. But whoever takes an oath by the gold of the sanctuary is bound by his oath.' Blind fools! For which is greater, the gold or the sanctuary that sanctified the gold? (Matt 23:16–18).

Explains. Jesus clarified His teachings through explanations, especially with His disciples:

"This is the meaning of the parable:" (Luke 8:11).

When two disciples sought power for themselves, Jesus explained the true meaning of kingdom greatness.

"You know that the rulers of the Gentiles dominate them, and the men of high position exercise power over them. It must not be like that among you. On the contrary, whoever wants to become great among you must be your servant, and whoever wants to be first among you must be your slave; just as the Son of Man did not come to be served, but to serve, and to give His life—a ransom for many" (Matt 20:25–28).

Defends Truth. For Jesus, Truth was eternal and objective. The approaches He took to describe and explain the Truth to people varied, but the Truth itself—the Truth Himself—was One: "I am the Truth" (John 14:6). Jesus proclaims, "I tell you the truth" (Luke 9:27; 12:44; 21:3; John 8:40, 45-46, and others). Jesus came into the world to herald the Truth: "I was born for this, and I have come into the world for this: to testify to the truth. Everyone who is of the truth listens to My voice" (John 18:37).

Maintains Objective Standards. Despite His love for people, Jesus maintained objective standards. Despite His desire that all should accept His love and care (Matt 23:37), Jesus did not compromise. When the rich, young ruler came to Him, asking what he should do to be saved, Jesus pointed out the "one thing he lacked"—his love of wealth. When the man refused to do what Jesus said was necessary, he left in grief. *And Jesus let him go* (19:16–23).

In these ways, Jesus showed Himself a Prophet and Thinker. Dallas Willard spends a number of pages in *The Divine Conspiracy* dispelling the myth that "Jesus, while 'nice,' was not very intelligent." Willard declares Jesus the "Master of intellect,"[25] the "Smartest Man in the World,"[26] the Master of Molecules,"[27] and the Master of Moral Understanding."[28] He devotes a section on "The Brilliance of Jesus" as an introduction to the Sermon on the Mount, which itself provides substantial evidence, when properly understood, that Jesus was the world's greatest intellect. We have merely touched these themes here, and I heartily recommend Willard's deeper analysis. Jesus is more, however, than the world's greatest moral philosopher, more than a brilliant intellect. He is also the loving Savior, a Priest-Feeler.

Jesus as Priest

Jesus was a **Priest**.[29] He loved people and gave His life, figuratively and literally, daily and ultimately, for others. He healed their sicknesses and calmed their fears. He ministered to their needs. He was tempted in every way we are, yet remained without sin (Heb 4:15). He moved among the people and lifted them to the Father. As priest, Jesus focused on the subjective element of faith.

Accepts. Jesus welcomed everyone, teaching that "God loved the world in this way: He gave His One and Only Son, so that everyone who believes in Him will not perish but have eternal life" (John 3:16). He accepted women and children, the sick and the lame, the powerful and the outcast.

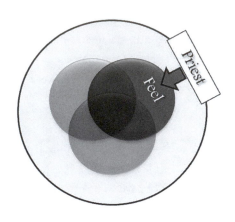

Jesus' heart was open to everyone. Tax collector Zacchaeus approached him in *curiosity*. Tax collector Matthew (Matt 9:9) and a Roman centurion (Matt 8:10) approached Him in *faith*. Pharisee Nicodemus (John 4) approached Him with *skepticism*. Judas (Matt 26:50) approached Him in *betrayal*. He accepted them all.

Cares for. Jesus cared about His **disciples** in tangible ways. "He said to them, 'Come away by yourselves to a remote place and rest a while.' For many people were coming and going, and they did not even have time to eat" (Mark 6:31–32).

He cared about the **crowds** in tangible ways. "I have compassion on the crowd, because they've already stayed with Me three days and have nothing to eat. I don't want to send them away hungry; otherwise they might collapse on the way" (Matt 15:32).

He cared for **women**. To the adulterous woman He said, "Neither do I condemn you . . . Go, and from now on do not sin any more" (John 8:11–12). To the Samaritan woman, He said "If you knew the gift of God, and who is saying to you, 'Give Me a drink,' you would ask Him, and He would give you living water" (4:10). To Mary Magdalene, He said, "Woman . . . why are you crying? Who is it you are looking for?" (20:15). To the Canaanite woman, He said "Woman, your faith is great. Let it be done for you as you want" (Matt 15:28).[30] At a time when culture denigrated sinners, Samaritans, Gentiles, and women, Jesus cared for them, received them, taught them, and helped them.

Jesus cared for **children**. "Let the little children come to Me [to be blessed, v 16]. Don't stop them, for the kingdom of God belongs to such as these" (Mark 10:14–15). "Then He took a child, had him stand among them, and taking him in His arms, He said to them, 'Whoever welcomes one little child such as this in My name welcomes Me. And whoever welcomes Me does not welcome Me, but Him who sent Me'" (9:36–37). Children, like women, were considered unimportant because they had no power, nor could they provide others with power. But Jesus cared for them, demonstrating the loving-kindness of the Father toward all.

Befriends. Jesus and the disciples lived together and ate together, because Jesus specifically "appointed twelve to be with him" (Mark 3:14). They witnessed the miracles of Jesus together. They suffered rejection together. Like coals in a fire, their mutual support and service strengthened them. Pull a coal from the fire, and it soon cools down. Peter's denials. Thomas' doubt. Their scattering at Jesus' arrest. But Jesus fanned the individual sparks of the twelve into a Family of Fire, and within that context, He loved them, taught them, protected them.

The disciples were not merely the *means* of Jesus' ministry. They were the *ends* of it. Jesus did not use—that is, *abuse*—His disciples to reach the crowds. He pulled away from the crowds in order to teach them. They were not tools in the hands of a manipulating leader. They were beloved friends. He poured His heart into them, and after He left, they carried on His work until they died.

"I do not call you slaves anymore, because a slave doesn't know what his master is doing. I have called you friends, because I have made known to you everything I have heard from My Father. You did not choose Me, but I chose you. I appointed you that you should go out and produce fruit and that your fruit should remain, so that whatever you ask the Father in My name, He will give you. This is what I command you: love one another" (John 15:14–17).

Sacrifices. "This is My command: love one another as I have loved you. No one has greater love than this, that someone would lay down his life for his friends" (John 15:12–13).

Jesus is the only Priest who carried His own blood to the mercy seat.[31] By doing so, Jesus completely fulfilled, once and for all, the old Tabernacle system. No longer would worshippers be shut out of God's presence by fences and tents. No longer would the high priest carry the blood of spotless sacrifices to the mercy seat, the meeting place with God. Jesus is High Priest, seated at the right hand of God (Luke 22:69), the One Mediator between God and man (1 Tim 2:5–6), Who interprets our attempts at prayer (Rom 8:27).

Jesus is well-known as Gentle Savior, Kind Friend, but He is more. He is Lord of Lords, King of Kings, our Commander. He is also guiding Leader, a King-Doer.

Jesus as King

Jesus was **King**.[32] He chose twelve apprentices and trained them for action (Matt 10). He sent His followers into the whole world to "make disciples of all nations, baptizing them . . . and teaching

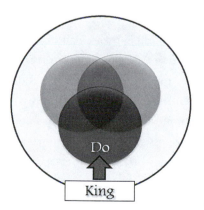

them to obey everything I have commanded you" (28:19–20). He is our Leader, our Lord. He calls us to action (Matt 5–7; John 17:20) and taught that our fruit (actions) exhibits our roots (concepts and values) (Matt 7:16–17). Our spiritual wisdom is shown in how we put His words into action (7:24–27).

Calls. Jesus called men to His service as apprentices, as learners who would become teachers, followers who would become leaders. When He called them, they dropped what they were doing and followed Him. "'Follow Me,' He told them, 'and I will make you fish for people!' Immediately [Peter and Andrew] left their nets and followed Him." And again, "Going on from there, He saw two other brothers, James the son of Zebedee, and his brother John. They were in a boat with Zebedee their father, mending their nets, and He called them. Immediately they left the boat and their father and followed Him" (Matt 4:21–22). As Matthew Henry points out, this was not their first encounter with Jesus. They were disciples of John and became "ordinary disciples" when John pointed to Jesus as "the Lamb of God" (John 1:36). They remained with Jesus for only a day (1:39). But God was working in them to prepare them to respond to the long-term call of Jesus. Now they responded—leaving all their possessions, their very livelihood, to follow this Leader.

Demonstrates. Jesus sealed His *words about ministry* by His *actions as Minister*. He spoke of need-oriented agape love and then practiced His words by meeting others' needs. He spoke about humility in the kingdom (Matt 20:26–28), and then humbly washed their feet (John 13:14–15). He prayed, and the disciples saw its effect and asked Jesus to teach them how to pray (John 11:1). Jesus was the ultimate Player-Coach.

Sends. Jesus gave specific instructions to the Twelve (Matt 10), and then sent them out (10:5) to "announce this: 'The kingdom of heaven has come near.' Heal the sick, raise the dead,[33] cleanse those with skin diseases, drive out demons" (10:7–8). We often think of Jesus' ministry as focused either on the intimate preparation of the Twelve, or a broad teaching ministry to the multitudes. But Dr. Luke tells us also of the seventy who were selected and sent out, two by two, to heal sicknesses and preach the approach of the kingdom of God (Luke 10:1–9). The equipping of disciples by Jesus extended well beyond the Twelve.

Admonishes. The essence of kingdom living is faith. When the Twelve demonstrated lack of faith, Jesus admonished them. "'Lord, save us! We're going to die!' But He said to them, 'Why are you fearful, you of little faith?'" (Matt 8:25–26). On another occasion Peter had enough faith to step out of the boat and walk toward Jesus on the sea. But He took His eyes off Jesus, looked to the swirling winds, and began to sink. Jesus did not congratulate him on his partial success but called him to greater faith. "You of little faith, why did you doubt?" (14:31).

Jesus admonished them for lack of understanding. "'You of little faith! Why are you discussing among yourselves that you do not have bread? Don't you understand yet? Don't you remember the five loaves for the 5,000 and how many baskets you collected? Or the seven loaves for the 4,000 and how many large baskets you collected? Why is it you don't understand that when I told you, "Beware of the yeast of the Pharisees and Sadducees," it wasn't about bread?' Then they understood." (Matt 16:8-12). Jesus gave them power to exorcise demons from the possessed, but there were times they could not. "Then the disciples approached Jesus privately and said, 'Why couldn't we drive it out?' 'Because of your little faith'" (17:19–20).

Jesus admonished the first among the disciples, the one He had so recently blessed (Matt 16:17), when Peter became Satan's tool to tempt Him, yet again, to consider an easier way. "Then Peter took Him aside and began to rebuke Him, 'Oh no, Lord! This will never happen to You!' But He turned and told Peter, 'Get behind Me, Satan! You are an offense to Me because you're not thinking about God's concerns, but man's'" (16:22–23). Correction is not the enemy of true love, but a reflection of it.

Heals. Jesus healed broken **minds** ("They came to Jesus and saw the man who had been demon-possessed by the legion, sitting there, dressed and in his right mind; and they were afraid" Mark 5:15–16).

Jesus healed broken **hearts** (Mary Magdalene was crying, broken hearted, for she did not know where Jesus' body had been taken. Jesus appeared to her, and gave her a message for the disciples, John 20:11–18).

Jesus healed broken **bodies** ("'I tell you: get up, pick up your stretcher, and go home.' Immediately he got up before them, picked up what he had been lying on, and went home glorifying God (Luke 5:24–26).

"And there are also many other things that Jesus did, which, if they were written one by one, I suppose not even the world itself could contain the books that would be written" (John 21:25). Jesus demonstrated in His teaching ministry and life the triadic balance we raise as our standard. He is our Model, our Guide, and our Helper as we seek to emulate this balance in our own life and ministry.

Jesus as Curricula Designer

How, then, did Jesus choose His methodology? How did He decide when to be Prophet-explainer, or Priest-comforter, or King-admonisher? The answer lies, as we declared in Chapter One, in the **needs of those He taught**.

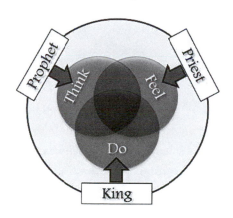

Jesus was not Prophet, *or* Priest, *or* King, moving from one sphere to another. He was Prophet-Priest-King, able to respond from any sphere in the moment.

When He confronted confusion or misunderstanding in His learners, He explained, illustrated, and clarified the message. When He confronted fear, deep hurt, or anger, He comforted, embraced, and empathized. When He confronted lack of skill or inability, He patiently showed how, reinforced skills, and corrected mistakes. He was not constrained or predisposed to any one of the three spheres, but was Master of them all. How then, do we strengthen our triadic approach to learners?

The External Influence of the Teacher

How do we provide a learning environment that permits balanced growth in the rational, emotional, and behavioral spheres of life? How do we help learners think clearly? Or appreciate warmly? Or put into practice skillfully? Here are some practical suggestions.[34]

Helping Learners Think Clearly

A little boy sat in his Sunday school class listening to his teacher intently. She asked, "What is gray, has a furry tail, and stores nuts for the winter?" The little boy thought for a moment and then said, "Well, it sounds like a squirrel—but I'll say Jesus Christ." He was not being irreverent. He was doing his best to answer the teacher's question. And it seemed to him that "Jesus Christ" was the answer to most of her questions. How can we help our learners to think clearly? We will do well if we focus on the meaning of concepts, ask conceptual questions, pose problems, and provide meaningful examples. Let's look more closely at each of these.

Focus on concepts more than words. What does the word "run" mean? The word has several meanings, a variety of concepts. Here are sentences that use nine different concepts of the single word "run":

- Johnny *runs* to second base. (moves swiftly)
- Judy *runs* her business well. (manages)
- Tim *runs* a printing press. (operates)
- The congressman *runs* for office. (campaigns)
- The engine *runs* well. (functions)
- Water always *runs* downhill. (flows)
- Jane has a *run* in her hose. (defect)
- Peter's team scored a *run* in the second inning. (score)
- Fido was kept in a nice dog *run*. (outdoor enclosure)

Earlier in this chapter I asked you several questions about Jesus' statement, "Do not judge, or you too will be judged" (Matt 7:1). Jesus was condemning the nagging, carping, censorious spirit of the Pharisees and religious leaders of His time. He was saying that when we live with a judgmental spirit, we will be criticized by others. Citizens of the kingdom are to avoid the hypercritical, judgmental spirit of holier-than-thou bigotry. It is not enough to say, "Jesus said, 'Don't judge.'" Unless we *explain* what Jesus meant by "judge," we leave learners to define the word in their own way (assimilation). A clear explanation allows learners to accommodate themselves to the term as Jesus used it.

One day a student led the class in a Bible study on the fruit of the Spirit. He described joy this way: "Joy is the kind of joy that only God can give, the kind of joy we'll experience in heaven. Oh! The joy of the Lord is wonderful!" Either this student did not understand the meaning of biblical joy, or he did not know how to explain it. He said nice words about joy, and even expressed deep feeling. But his words were empty. Had he a clear understanding of the term, he might have said something like this:

Joy is similar to the concepts of fun, pleasure, and happiness. In fact, some Christians mistakenly believe that biblical joy means fun or happiness. All these terms are emotional and generally express a sense of gladness or delight. But here's the distinction. The "joy of the Spirit" comes from within and exists despite external circumstances. Fun, pleasure, and happiness all depend on the nature of surrounding circumstances, and in some ways are controlled by them.

Had the student consulted a Bible dictionary, or a Bible commentary or two, he could have easily made such an explanation. Teachers do well to go beyond words to meanings. Learners will be less likely to *eisegete,* reading personal meanings into a passage (assimilation), and more likely to *exegete,* reading God's meaning out of a passage. If personal perceptions differ from God's meaning, learners "renew their minds" (Rom 12:2) by adjusting their conceptions (schemes), or by creating new ones to fit the new meaning (accommodation).

Focus on asking questions more than giving answers. We promote thinking more by the questions we ask than the answers we give. Even a profound answer may strike learners as one more fact, mere information, essentially meaningless. But a well-asked question drives learners into their own memories, class notes, and the text. Questions confront learners with a mental empty space, which they fill with related facts and concepts, processed and networked into an answer. The answers they derive have both objective and subjective meaning. Along the way learners improve the quality and frequency of questions they create on their own, a sure sign that thinking has been engaged.

The *type* of teacher question makes a difference in how much student thinking is enhanced. **Factual** questions do little to enhance thinking, since their answers require little more than recall, e.g., "What theorist defined learning as stamping stimulus-response bonds into the nervous system?" (Thorndike). **Conceptual** questions require learners to paraphrase meanings, or make comparisons and contrasts among similar concepts, e.g., "Thorndike and Skinner both emphasized the bond between stimuli and responses. How did they differ in their views on this relationship?"[35] "When

Jesus commanded us to "*love* our enemies," did He mean we have to *like* them as well?"[36] Such questions move beyond simple recall and test the relevant networks of ideas students possess.

Focus on posing problems more than giving reasons. When teachers give learners "five reasons why we ought to forgive," it may leave them with little more than sound bites. It is better to pose a problem in which "forgiveness" provides the solution. "Based on our study of forgiveness this morning, how would you handle this situation?" A problem emphasizes the application of meaning, while a conceptual question emphasizes the meaning itself.

Listen to their answers. Correct misunderstandings. Suggest alternatives. Lead the class to see the relevance of "biblical forgiveness" in a contemporary situation.

Focus on examples more than facts. Facts are important. Knowledge of facts is also important. But facts simply are. Little thinking is required to master the facts of a subject. But what do the facts mean? Comprehending the way facts interrelate with each other to create concepts requires thought. A German shepherd is a dog (fact). A Collie is a dog (fact). A Dachshund is a dog (fact). All of them are dogs. They all share "dogularity" or "dogness" (concept). By asking for examples, teachers can look into the thinking of learners directly by means of the examples given. Correct examples reveal correct understanding; incorrect examples reveal misunderstanding.

"Love is patient; love is kind. Love does not envy; is not boastful; it is conceited; does not act improperly; is not selfish; is not provoked; does not keep a record of wrongs; finds no joy in unrighteousness; but rejoices in the truth" (1 Cor 13:4–6). These are the facts of love. What do these facts mean? What is an *example* of patient? How do you *describe* kind? *Illustrate* envy and boasting. *Explain* improper actions, selfishness, and how we might be provoked. *How* might I keep a record of wrongs? *Why* would anyone take joy in unrighteousness? *What is the truth* with which I am to rejoice?

The popular *King James Version* of Scripture uses 1611 English that is unfamiliar to most people today. "Charity suffereth long, and is kind; charity envieth not; charity vaunteth not itself, is not puffed up" (1 Cor 13:4 KJV). Learners who are unfamiliar with church talk will choke on the "eth" endings, and words like "suffereth," "vaunteth," and "puffed up." The *New King James* helps, bringing the beauty of the classic text into the twenty-first century. It reads, "Love suffers long and is kind; love does not envy; love does not parade itself, is not puffed up." Even here, unchurched folks may strain at the phrase "love suffers long" and wonder why the Bible is talking about parades. *The Message* paraphrases the verse this way, "Love never gives up. Love cares more for others than for self. Love doesn't want what it doesn't have. Love doesn't strut, Doesn't have a swelled head." While biblical purists wince at the casual feel of *The Message*, there is no argument that it conveys contemporary meaning much better than the Old King James.

Even when we use contemporary versions of Scripture, we can insure accommodation of biblical meanings and prevent assimilation of learners' private meaning only by clear explanations. We must convey the actual meaning of the concept "patient" ["suffers long," "never gives up": *makrothumeo* (mak-roth-oo-meh'-o); to be long-spirited, i.e. (objectively) forbearing or (subjectively) patient; KJV: bear (suffer) long, be longsuffering, have (long) patience, be patient, patiently endure."][37] By focusing on examples, whether the sources are various translations of Scripture, commentaries, or descriptions created by learners in the moment, teachers help learners construct well-structured and accurate networks of meanings.

Helping Learners Feel, Respond, and Value

One day years ago I was having a cup of coffee with a pastor acquaintance. He told me of a boy who had come forward during the invitation. His parents were getting a divorce, he had no friends at school, his grades were bad—he just didn't know what to do. The pastor reported his response this way: "Son, I really don't care to hear about your problems. Do you know that you are a lost sinner? Do you know that if you die tonight without Jesus, you'll spend eternity in hell?" The boy looked at him with wide eyes, brimming with tears. His mouth fell open and, for a moment, time stopped. Then he turned and ran out of the church. I was heartsick. The pastor was proud. "So I guess I put the fear of God in him!"

I never think of that boy without praying that the Lord will send someone to share the love of Jesus with him. The pastor was doctrinally correct, but he lacked compassion for the heartfelt needs of this ten-year-old boy. How much better it would have been had this well-meaning but misguided pastor said something like, "I can tell you are really hurting about these things. I've had some hurt in my own life. And I've found Someone Who has always been ready to listen to me and help me. Someone Who cares deeply about me. His name is Jesus, and He will never leave you, even if your parents get a divorce. He'll be your Friend, even if you have no friends at school. He'll help you study, and learn, and do better in school. Would you like to learn more about this Best Friend of mine?" I can guarantee this ten-year-old would not have run out of the church building in tears. He just might have given his life to The Answer to all his problems.

Hearts are more easily opened in classes where learners find an atmosphere of openness, warmth, and trust. So how do we create such a climate? Teachers make good progress toward emotional warmth in the classroom when they share themselves, share the experiences of class members, accept students as they are (while determining not to leave them that way), use humor appropriately, and build trust. Let's look at each of these more closely.

Focus on personal experiences more than wooden stories. Teachers often tell a story to begin a session. Stories are powerful, because they have the ability to portray concepts, evoke emotions, and suggest actions in a life-like situation. Stories speak to everyone—thinkers, feelers, and doers—simultaneously. Commercial Bible study materials provide suggestions for doing this. "Joan is a single mother, working two jobs" and the like.

Pre-packaged stories offer teachers good suggestion but are not usually the best material: fictitious testimonies, contrived case studies, and artificial anecdotes may do little to warm up learners. No matter how good they are, they are wooden, stilted, often forced, because they do not relate to the life experiences of the teacher or class.

Far better are stories that come from our own experiences or experiences of learners. All of us have experiences of struggle, growth, and victory in the Lord. As these experiences are shared to the glory of God, the class is warmed by His presence and our praise of Him.

When circumstances require the use of pre-packaged stories, teachers do well to follow the story with an invitation for class members to share their own. "Have any of you had an experience like this? (Pause for response). What did you do?" The packaged story is used as a prompt; learner experiences provide more power.

Earning the right versus putting on the spot. Teachers do well to earn the right to ask personal (subjective, revealing) questions. We do not have the right to call on learners to confess sins in front of the group—to put learners on the spot.

A student began his practice teaching session this way: "How many of you haven't had a daily devotional this week?" There was a silent pause. "Just lift your hands." There followed a longer, uncomfortable pause, and some frowns. No one raised a hand. The student teacher was a bit frustrated with the lack of response. "Well now, I know there's *someone* in a class this size who hasn't had a regular time of Bible study and prayer this week. Remember, God is watching and He knows who you are." Tension increased amid a few muffled groans. Then, a young man in the back of the room yielded to the guilt, bowed his head, and slowly lifted his hand.

The student teacher had no right to do this. The effect of his actions went farther than a mistake in practice teaching. He humiliated the learner. He angered the class. It destroyed any sense of openness toward this student teacher and made for a long, tense, ten-minute session. It is not for us to publicly humiliate learners through guilt but to correctly handle God's Word (2 Tim 2:15). The Holy Spirit convicts people of sin (John 16:8), not teachers.

Had the student-teacher "earned the right" to ask his question—sharing his own struggles with having a daily quiet time—this problem would have been avoided. Look at the difference: "This past week I've not spent time in prayer and Bible study as I normally do. Things have gotten so busy and hectic. Are any of you struggling with this problem?" (Several heads would have nodded, including mine). "Let's see what we can discover that will help us give top priority to the Lord."

Such an approach increases openness. It warms the class because the teacher has suggested an area of common struggle. We will work together to find answers from God's Word. When we share ourselves, others are more likely to share as well. Earn the right.

There will be times, as we study a passage and focus on its positive truths, that learners will openly and freely share a time of failure, a testimony of poor choices, a time of sin. Teachers do well to accept those offerings of public confession with sensitivity and understanding, and to use them carefully to illustrate the teaching of the passage. Such confessions require courage and leave confessors vulnerable to self-guilt and criticism. Stories of failure should certainly be received with grace but should never be called for by teachers if our goal is to increase openness and transparency in the classroom.

Focus on acceptance more than judgment. We discussed Jesus' command, "Do not judge, so that you won't be judged" earlier in the chapter. There, we emphasized the **meaning** of Jesus' word "judge" as a carping, censorious spirit, like that of the Pharisees. Here, we focus on the **attitude** that pulls us in the direction of judging others.

The disciples failed in many ways, but Jesus forgave them, loved them, and continued to teach them. Accept learners as they are. Love them, teach them, and encourage them to grow in the Lord. Some grow slower than others. Commitment level of some may never please us. But when our focus is accepting rather than judging, openness and warmth blossom and bear fruit in spiritual growth.

The principle holds true in more academic settings as well. Though students are required to attend class, we cannot force them to study, embrace our subjects, or improve their behavior. In fact, displaying a judgmental attitude insures less study, negative attitudes, and rebellion. It also insures that our students will become more judgmental toward others, even as we tell them not to. Teachers do well to focus on acceptance more than judgment.

Focus on appropriate humor more than feigned solemnity. Appropriate humor relaxes learners and frees the class. Feigned solemnity does just the opposite. Paul was a great Christian philosopher. His letters are deep and often hard to understand.[38] Yet, philosophical reasoning and theological expertise was not, for Paul, the evidence of Christ in our lives. The presence of Christ is displayed in the joy and peace we experience in walking with Him.

- "**Rejoice** in hope; be patient in affliction; be persistent in prayer" (Rom 12:12).
- "For the kingdom of God is not a matter of eating and drinking, but of righteousness, **peace and joy** in the Holy Spirit" (Rom 14:17).
- "May the God of hope **fill you with all joy and peace** in believing, so that you may overflow with hope by the power of the Holy Spirit" (Rom 15:13).

- "May you be strengthened with all power, according to His glorious might, for all endurance and patience, **with joy**" (Col 1:11).

The Bible is a solemn book with a solemn message. We are wise to approach Scripture study with reverence. But positive reverence differs from the stoic, stern, dispassionate logic of the false teachers Paul opposed. *Where the Spirit is free to produce fruit, there is joy* (Gal 5:22).

Teachers do well to insure the humor of the classroom is positive and uplifting. Avoid crude or vulgar jokes, stories with double meanings, and even lighthearted pranks or gags. Humor misfires when it denigrates others, or demeans the sacred task at hand: "Coarse and foolish talking or crude joking are not suitable, but rather giving thanks" (Eph 5:4).

The super-serious have little warmth, the super-silly little depth. While biblical joy is much more than good humor, the proper use of humor can both warm up and settle down a class. Humor can enhance the openness of class members, not just to one another, but to God's Word as well. People who honestly laugh together can also honestly share together, or pray together, or weep together (see Rom 12:15). The natural use of humor enhances openness in the classroom.

Focus on trust more than guilt. There is no doubt that guilt is a strong motivator. Perhaps that is why so many immature leaders use it. It produces quick results but undermines trust, the glue that holds human relationships together. The judgmental student mentioned above used guilt to push students to confess their sins in class and lost them in the process.

Do you remember B. F. Skinner's experiments with electric shock (Chapter Six)? He found that electric shock motivated the rats to learn the maze faster than food. But the shock also taught the rats to fear the maze. Eventually the rats refused to move, regardless of the degree of shock applied, even to the point of death. Guilt is like an electric shock to the personality. It produces quick results but leads to fear in a class or congregation.

Where do we find Jesus, the Lord of lords, teaching this way? "For God did not send His Son into the world that He might condemn the world, but that the world might be saved through Him" (John 3:17). Where do we find Paul, strong personality that he was, teaching this way? Paul's enemies in Corinth claimed he was strong in his letters but weak in person (2 Cor 10:10). Paul responded by pointing out, with tongue in cheek, his weakness: "You put up with it if someone enslaves you, if someone devours you, if someone captures you, if someone dominates you, or if someone hits you in the face. I say this to [our] shame: we have been weak" (11:20–2l).

Rather, Paul loved the church at Corinth and grieved over their problems: "For out of an extremely troubled and anguished heart I wrote to you with many tears—*not that you should be hurt, but that you should know the abundant love I have for you*" (2 Cor 2:4, emphasis mine). By his clear teaching and firm but loving exhortation, Paul led the church at Corinth away from her problems and into a more focused relationship with Christ. Paul was not weak but humble.

Trust grows among people as they live, work, and pray together, as they share needs together, as they forgive one another. Paul underscored this social element of the Christian faith:

> But now you must also put away all the following: anger fury **toward others**, wrath settled hatred **toward others**, malice wishing harm **on others**, slander demeaning the character of **others**, and filthy language abusive talk **toward others** from your mouth.

> Therefore, God's chosen ones, holy and loved, put on heartfelt compassion soft-heartedness **toward others**, kindness helpful actions **toward others**, humility right thinking **toward others**, gentleness tenderness **toward others**, and patience long-suffering **with others**, accepting **one another** and forgiving **one another** if anyone has a complaint **against another**. Just as the Lord has forgiven you, so also you must [forgive].

> Above all, [put on] love—the **perfect bond of unity**. (Col 3:8,12–14).[39]

Paul's words are relational marching orders for pastors and teachers. When we keep in step with them, we find trust levels among members increase.

Guilt is a quick motivator. But it is toxic to learners in every case except in the hands of the Holy Spirit, Who can change guilt into growth when we confess the sins responsible for guilt (1 John 1:9).

Helping Learners Do Skillfully

Years ago my wife and I worked as dormitory counselors at Gallaudet University for the Deaf in Washington, D.C. During our time there, I taught a Sunday school class for deaf college students. One day I ran into Keith, a member of the class and a student at the university, while walking across campus. During our conversation I asked him what he learned in our study the previous Sunday. He shrugged his shoulders and frowned, "That was a long time ago." Yes, I agreed. It had been a few days since class. I asked again what he had learned. "We studied something in the Old Testament, right?" Actually, we studied a passage in Ephesians. "Ephesians! Right! I remember now!" So what did he discover? What did he learn? "I don't remember. That was a long time ago!"

I had spent five or six hours preparing to teach. I had given the presentation my best efforts. Now, on Wednesday, he could not remember the first thing about what we had studied on Sunday. And since he could not remember the study, it was clear he was not living it out.

While behaviors flow directly out of the Doing Circle, they can originate in how we think and what we value. We will look at the influence of all three spheres of life on how we live out what we learn.

A Rational Approach to Doing. Biblical actions can be prompted by biblical concepts as they are understood and integrated into mental networks. We discussed this at length under "Helping Learn-

Actions, Skills Ministries

ers Think Clearly." Those who love the Lord need little more than to understand what He commands to put His words into practice. I write "*can be* prompted" because clear understanding does not guarantee proper action beyond the class. Nevertheless, clear understanding encourages Christian action.

I failed Keith in my teaching because class time was filled with fact-telling and explanations. I focused more on my teaching than Keith's learning, more on my presentation than his thinking. While I spent hours in preparation, it took less than a minute to learn how little I accomplished in Keith's life. This chance meeting on campus changed my view of teaching forever.

An Emotional Approach to Doing. Biblical actions outside the classroom can be prompted through personal sharing with others inside the classroom. We discussed this at length under "Helping Learners Feel, Respond, and Value." The tangible testimonies of Christian actions from *some* make it more likely that *more* will appreciate the relevance of God's Word, and then join them in living it out beyond the classroom.

These two general approaches to learning—understanding concepts and appreciating values—lay a firm foundation for Christian action. But there is a far more direct way to provoke Christian action outside of class.

An Action Approach to Doing: Assignments. The most direct way to encourage learners to "do" their lessons during the week is to make specific assignments. Assignments can vary in their intensity and scope: selected verses to read, specific questions to answer, a simple project, making entries in a journal, words to analyze, and the list goes on. Assignments can be done individually, in pairs, or in groups of various kinds. By giving learners things to do during the week, you give them the opportunity to learn from the Lord on their own. Assignments need not be difficult or complex. But the regular, intentional, and patient assignment of tasks to "put into practice" the session's explanations and discussions pays rich dividends in Christian learning and growth, such as the following.

An out-of-classroom assignment . . .

- Encourages learners to explore biblical topics in more detail (thinking)
- Promotes increased opportunities of elaboration and retrieval (thinking)
- Furnishes mental resources for future learning through increased sharing (thinking)
- Increases interest in personal Bible study (feeling)
- Increases enthusiasm for teaching sessions themselves (feeling)
- Increases the variety of learning experiences (feeling)
- Builds rapport between teacher and members through sharing (feeling)
- Helps shy members to become more involved with others (feeling)
- Develops ministry skills as Scripture is put into practice in "the real world" (doing)
- Recognizes and develops the gifts of learners (doing)
- Develops teaching skills in learners (doing)
- Expands the teaching session beyond the classroom (doing)
- Reduces dependence on the teacher as it increases independent study (doing)
- Reduces teacher study time as learners share in teaching (doing)

Learners in many Bible study classes come to quietly receive, and sadly, many teachers seem to like it that way. Moving a group of teenagers or adults to action takes time. To move the group away from "Sit and Listen" to "Go and Teach" is a major achievement for teachers who see this as a central part of their teaching ministry.

Christ, the Center of the Triad

Teachers who model a thoughtful-passionate-skillful approach to life create the best environment for learning. This environment of thoughtful, passionate, skillful action is a veritable greenhouse for human growth. We have taken a Christian view of thinking-feeling-doing in this chapter, but the triadic balance need not be Christian.

In the early days of the Russian revolution, Vladimir Ilyich Ulyanov, better known as Lenin, set up a state security agency known as the *Cheka*. The motto of the *Cheka* was triadic: "the Chekist is a man with a 'warm heart, a cool head, and clean hands.'"[40] The *Cheka* later morphed into the more familiar K.G.B., which carried on the triadic formula, as well as the twin symbols of *shield*—to defend the Revolution—and the *sword*—to defeat its enemies.

The first time I read the Chekist motto, a cold chill swept over me. I had been using the Christian Teachers' Triad in conferences for nearly ten years, and now I read that its essential *head, heart, and*

hand reflected the essence of the Soviet Secret Service? I could not form words to pray, so I simply groaned to God: What had I done? Then I saw it differently: the Triad did not reflect the Chekist motto; the Chekist motto reflected God's fundamental design of Man: *head, heart, hand.*

The three circles of the Triad overlap at the center, shown at left as a darkened circle. This is the seat of the will, the ego, the "I" of the personality. Those without Christ determine the course of life for themselves: what *I* think, what *I* value, what *I* choose to do. We quoted Dostoyevsky in the last chapter, "If God did not exist, everything would be permitted," and pointed out this was precisely the beginning point of existential philosophers like Sartre: "God does not exist, so everything is permitted. Make your choices."

By contrast, Paul wrote, "But the natural man does not welcome what comes from God's Spirit, because it is foolishness to him; he is not able to know it since it is evaluated spiritually" (1 Cor 2:14).

After we accept Christ as Lord and Savior, He lives in us (Col 1:27). If *'I'* continues to reign—determining what *'I'* think, what *'I'* value, and what *'I'* do—there may be little perceptible differ-

ence between our lives and the lives of the unredeemed "good people" who live around us. (In the diagram at left, such a condition would have "I" above the line, in charge, and "Christ" below the line, where He is available as needed, but conveniently out of the way.)

Earlier, we looked at *psychological* elements of thinking-valuing-doing, an integration of the learning theory systems of Chapters Six to Ten. Now we turn to the *spiritual* elements of the Triad that are energized by Christ, Who lives within us by faith. He does not force his way into our life spheres, nor does He dominate them. He gives us freedom to invite Him in or lock Him out, to our blessing or hurt. His promise is sure: "I stand at the door and knock. *If anyone hears my voice and opens the door*, I will come in and eat with him, and he with me" (Rev 3:20). As we invite Him to lead us, to teach us, to mold us into what He desires, He helps us to think, to value, and to do—according to His will. How do we do this?

Jesus said, "If anyone wants to come with Me, he must deny himself, take up his cross daily, and follow Me" (Luke 9:23). Deny self. Follow Christ. This makes all the difference, for it engages Christ as Internal Teacher. Spiritual growth is learning how to let Jesus be Teacher and Lord, both learning from Him and obeying Him. Paul knew this: "I have been crucified with Christ; and I no longer live, but Christ lives in me. The life I now live in the flesh, I live by faith in the Son of God, who loved me and gave Himself for me" (Gal 2:19b–20). We provoke our learners to grow in the Lord as we teach them to depend on Him. "Christ in you" and "Christ in charge" makes all the difference. Let's see how.

CHRISTian Thinking

"We haven't stopped praying for you. We are asking that you may be filled with the **knowledge** of His will in all **wisdom** and spiritual **understanding**, so that you may walk worthy of the Lord, fully pleasing to Him, bearing fruit in every good work and growing in the knowledge of God" (Col 1:9b–10).

The knowledge Paul prays for the Colossians to have is not head knowledge *(gnosis),* which inflates with pride (1 Cor 8:1), but an intimate, relational knowledge *(epignosis)* which comes through devotion to Christ. The message of Scripture is more than words printed on a page, because we can read into the text our own definitions. As we depend on the Lord, His Spirit illumines the Word and enlightens us, so that we grow in the *epignosis* of God's message.

But the mental result is more than not knowledge alone. The Lord leads us into spiritual understanding—that is, what Scripture *means.* As we walk with the Lord, He explains the meanings of the words, just as He did with the two disciples on the road to Emmaus. "Weren't our hearts ablaze within us while He was talking with us on the road and explaining the Scriptures to us?" (Luke 24:32).

But not understanding only. The Lord leads us beyond understanding into "wisdom." Paul, a philosopher by training, rejected human philosophy, emphasizing rather the ability "to judge correctly and to follow the best course of action, based on knowledge and understanding."[41] This harmonizes well with Jesus' own words: "Therefore whoever hears these sayings of Mine, and ***does them***, I will liken him to a wise man . . ." (Matt 7:24 NKJV, emphasis mine).

Doing in the Lord begets broader knowledge of His Word, which begets deeper understanding, which begets more effective doing. The cycle of rational development proceeds *under the direction of the Lord* Who lives within and teaches us. The means: knowing what the Bible says, understanding what the Bible means, and putting it into practice—as Jesus leads. The result: learners being "transformed by the renewing of their mind" (Rom 12:2).

CHRISTian Valuing

The apostle Paul is more widely known for his warrior spirit, militant missiology, and theological depth than for his soft and open heart. And yet he wrote, "Rejoice in hope; be patient in affliction; be persistent in prayer. Share with the saints in their needs; pursue hospitality. Bless those who persecute you; bless and do not curse. **Rejoice with those who rejoice; weep with those who weep.** Be in agreement with one another. Do not be proud; instead, associate with the humble. Do not be wise in your own estimation" (Rom 12:12–16). The rebellion of the Corinthian Christians broke his heart, and he shed many tears because of his love for them. "For out of an extremely troubled and anguished heart I wrote to you with many tears—not that you should be hurt, but that you should know the abundant love I have for you" (2 Cor 2:4).

Emotional attributes such as anger, instability, harshness, insecurity, bitterness, selfishness, hatred, and the like plague Christians just as they plague others. We suffer from emotional problems when we live in our own power and according to our own will. Jesus declared kingdom beatitudes and behaviors in the Sermon on the Mount (Matt 5) that are humanly impossible, in our strength and wisdom, to develop. The Lord within helps develop these kingdom elements of action.

Scripture underscores the progression Christians make in removing the negative and growing in the positive, a progression called sanctification.[42] Paul emphasized several positive values in the above passage: joy, hope, patience, persistence, benevolence, hospitality, blessing, empathy, agreement, relationships. Each of these affective qualities is developed out of the tangible fabric of everyday social situations: conflicts, misunderstandings, disappointments, and loss. The positive outcomes spring from humble hearts and denial of self. Perhaps Paul remembered his former arrogance as a religious bounty hunter, and the chilling question put to him when he first met the risen Lord: "Saul, Saul, why are you persecuting Me? It is hard for you to kick against the goads" (Acts 26:14).

All believers experience affective challenges as they move from pagan to believer to teacher and leader to missionary: To love, and not hate. To forgive, and not harbor anger. To be steadfast, and not unstable. To be gentle, and not harsh. To be courageous, and not insecure. To be sweet, and not bitter. To be generous, and not selfish. The affective component of spiritual growth revolves around openness, values, priorities, and commitments in classroom and congregation.

Christian affective growth is humanistic, in that human beings were created to love God and one another. But Christian affective growth is not secular, and diametrically opposed to it. We see it in the present culture war between traditionalists and progressives. Christians and their churches are no longer simply ignored. They are increasingly attacked by secularists who are both angry and afraid, opposed to any who declare their "self-chosen values" to be violations of the Lord's commands.

As we walk with the Lord, He teaches us by means of each day's struggle how to put off the negative and put on the positive. Seeking His values produces dramatic positive results, not only in our own lives, but also in the lives of those around us.

CHRISTian Doing

"All of you, **take up My yoke** and learn from Me, because I am gentle and humble in heart, and you will find rest for yourselves. For My yoke is easy and My burden is light" (Matt 11:29–30).

As our understanding of God's Word (head) and commitment to the Lord (heart) deepens, our actions change (hand). Old habits die, new habits grow. How do we refine those habits? How do we learn the skills of spiritual living as Jesus lives within us and teaches us?

Jesus shows us the way. He says "take up My yoke." *Take up* denotes a voluntary action. I can take the yoke or I can leave the yoke. *Yoke* refers to a wooden beam that ties two oxen together. Two can pull a load more easily than one, and the yoke ties them together. *My* refers to Whose yoke it is. Jesus invites us to accept is His yoke—not our parents', nor our pastors', nor our friends' yokes. The yoke of the Lord is ministry—that which the Lord wants each of us to do. All believers are gifted (Eph 4:7) in order to edify—strengthen—the church (4:12). 'Where should we serve? What should we do? "Take up my yoke," Jesus says.

Why should we give up what we want to do in order to do what the Lord wants? The answer strikes at the very heart of natural self-centeredness: The yoke of Jesus is the only place where we find "rest"—"relief and ease and refreshment and recreation and blessed quiet" *(Amplified Bible)*.

The invitation of Jesus is not to learn more *about* Him, but to "learn *from* Him"—to observe Him and imitate Him. As a young man, my grandfather trained young horses to pull a plow by hitching them alongside a steady plow horse. The colt always fought the traces, being unaccustomed to the restraints. After a time of fighting, the colt settled down and learned to cooperate with the mature horse in pulling together. He found it meant getting back to the barn and oats sooner, and it took less effort. In the same way, the Lord invites us to hitch ourselves to Him in order to learn from Him how to minister. This practical training in know-how does not diminish the importance of knowledge gained from books, conferences, or seminary classes, since the most effective writers, leaders, and professors share what they have experienced in the Lord's yoke. But it is essential when the Lord calls us to a ministry for which no books have been written, no conferences offered, no classes developed. In those situations, we can depend on the Lord to teach us as we pull with Him in the yoke He has chosen for us.

His yoke is "easy"—*comfortable*—and his burden is "light"—*easy to be carried*. Rough wooden beams would irritate, chafe, and even cut the shoulders of oxen. Jesus the Carpenter had shaped many beams for a custom fit—an "easy" fit—to the shoulders of the animals. The yoke distributed the load across the oxen, and so made the burden lighter. Jesus custom-fits our ministry to who we are, making even our sacrificial service comfortable, making our burdens light. In His will, pulling with Him, going His direction, there is restoration and renewal, even in the work. Ministry burnout, on the other hand, comes from work done in our own will, when we pull alone, in our own strength, going our own direction.

As Christ grows in our lives, the center of the triad expands. Notice how the larger circles overlap more, reflecting a more balanced approach to learning. This integration of learning—thinking, valuing, and doing—is not limited to spiritual things. Secular theories have moved a long way toward integration of the three learning systems in the past ten years. Increasingly, secular theories present a synergistic approach to learning.

A Dynamic Synergism of Learning Theory Systems

The Triad represents a dynamic synergism of the three learning systems. The Triad is *dynamic* in that the three components individually push us toward the imbalances of cold intellectualism, warm fluff, and burnout. It represents the struggle to balance thinking, valuing and doing.

The Triad is a *synergism* in that all three **together** do far more than any one system alone. Bandura's social learning theory is a behavioral theory that integrates cognitive elements. Information Processing Theory is a cognitive theory that blends behavioral elements. The growing emphasis on self-regulation in behavioral theory (self-reinforcement) and cognitive theory (personal goal-setting) integrates humanistic elements in both systems. Secular theorists increasingly speak of balance among conceptual, affective, and behavioral elements, reflecting the triadic perspective first laid out in 1995–1996,[43] though they certainly use different words to describe it.

In Summary

The goal of Christian teaching is Christ-likeness in our learners. The teacher helps by provoking clear thinking, nurturing passionate valuing, and shaping skillful doing. We, of course, cannot produce Christ-likeness in our learners. "I planted, Apollos watered, but God gave the growth" (1 Cor 3:6–7). But we are living instruments in the Master's hand, and can cooperate with Him in the process.

In the end, when we honor Jesus as Teacher and Lord, when we teach others as He teaches us, when we love others as He loves us, we will influence them toward Christ-likeness. May God richly bless our teaching efforts as we depend on Him to bring oneness out of the three spheres of life. "In any case, we should live up to whatever we have attained" (Phil 3:16).

The Triad unifies the three systems of learning psychologically. How do we translate learning theory into classroom practice? Educators use overarching goal statements and measurable indicators to provide the framework around which learning sequences are planned. We turn to this technical side of learning in the next chapter.

Chapter Concepts

Burn-out	Result of over-emphasis on doing without understanding or commitment
Doing	The behavioral emphasis of the Triad: behaviors, habits, and skills
Dynamic synergism	Mutual influence and interaction of the three spheres of the Triad
Earn the right	Teachers share an experience before asking students to share

Eisegesis	Reading *into* Scripture from one's own thinking. Assimilation. Sin.
Emotionalism	The state of being controlled by emotion. Emotionally driven.
Epignosis	Intimate, relational knowledge that comes through devotion
Exegesis	Reading *out of* Scripture God's message. Accommodation. Life.
Feeling	The emotional emphasis of the Triad: affect, values, priorities
Gnosis	Intellectual knowing (head knowledge) that causes pride (1 Cor 8:1)
Intellectualism	The state of being controlled by rationality. Rationally driven
King (leader)	One of the three biblical references to Jesus, related to Triadic *Doing*
Priest	One of the three biblical references to Jesus, related to Triadic *Feeling*
Prophet	One of the three biblical references to Jesus, related to Triadic *Thinking*
Thinking	The rational emphasis of the Triad: facts, concepts, principles

Chapter Objectives

Learners will demonstrate knowledge of the Christian teachers' triad by drawing and labelling the complete diagram from memory.

Learners will demonstrate understanding of selected principles of teaching by identifying them as behavioral, cognitive, or humanistic.

Learners will demonstrate understanding of the Christian teachers' triad by describing the relationships between the three spheres and Jesus' work as Prophet, Priest, and King.

Learners will demonstrate understanding of the Christian teachers' triad by developing examples in which imbalance impairs the learning process.

Learners will demonstrate appreciation for the triad by sharing personal experiences they've had in classrooms where either an imbalance (negative) or balance (positive) existed.

Discussion Questions

1 Read the following statements and determine whether they reflect **B**ehavioral, **C**ognitive, or **H**umanistic principles of teaching.

_____ **1. Teach learning strategies.** Instruct your students on how to study, how to take notes, how to organize, and how to remember what they need to know. Don't assume they know how to study, nor leave them to their own devices.

_____ **2. Encourage openness.** Develop a relaxed, open class atmosphere. Avoid negative tones and moralizing, as this hinders learner participation. Focus on the positive.

_____ **3. Provide factual foundation.** Provide an adequate foundation of terminology, concepts, and examples to support the main focus of learning: the discovery of meaning of the subject.

_____ **4. Clarify learning task.** Use objectives, tests, outlines, or other advance organizers to provide _clear direction_ for the student. Know where you're going, and share it with your learners.

_____ **5. Correct responses.** Avoid erroneous teaching ("sharing of ignorance"). Explain, then question. Teach, then test. Lead students to competence step by step.

_____ **6. Call on volunteers.** Let those who wish to share positive experiences do so. Do not call on learners to confess failures publicly.

_____ **7. Gain and retain attention.** Work to gain and retain the attention of your students. Vary the level of intensity in the class through the use of visual aids, meaningfulness, and personal enthusiasm. Create surprise by using a variety of learning activities.

_____ **8. Discussion of concepts.** Provide time in class for large-group or small-group discussion of key ideas and principles.

_____ **9. Permit deviation from the routine.** Avoid following a repetitious pattern in every class. Add spontaneity to the class process. Encourage learners to ask questions, make comments, share experiences, and even "chase rabbits" within reason.

_____ **10. Elaborative rehearsal.** Help learners relate new material to what they've already learned. Conversely, don't make each class hour separate and distinct from the next. Help learners bridge from the known to the unknown. Elaboration strategies include paraphrasing, creating analogies, answering questions, and describing how new material relates to existing knowledge.

_____ **11. Simplicity.** Take small steps. Move from simple to complex. Move from concrete (experienced truths) to abstract. Teach in a logical sequence.

_____ **12. Model the role.** How we live speaks louder than what we say. Be an "example to the flock" (1 Pet 5:3).

_____ **13. Chunking.** Divide material to be learned into meaningful chunks. Either present material "prechunked" or encourage (older) learners to "chunk" for themselves.

_____ 14. **Have learners practice.** Use active, rather than passive, recall. Distribute drills throughout the session to reduce boredom.

_____ 15. **Contrast.** Help learners define concepts and principles by comparing and contrasting terms ("Must I *like* the people Jesus commanded me to *love*?")

_____ 16. **Structure.** Help learners discover the structure of the course material, the major and minor points. Focus on the meaning of the material more than discrete bits of information.

_____ 17. **Use small groups.** Sub-groups within the class provide for greater participation and volunteering, because they are less intimidating.

_____ 18. **Delayed Feedback.** Help learners evaluate their own understanding. Ask questions. Pose problems. Make specific comments on written work.

_____ 19. **Organize material.** Clearly present what you expect your students to learn. Use advance organizers, outlines, pre-tests, or key words *to structure the material* to be learned.

_____ 20. **Build relationships.** React positively to positive responses. React in a neutral manner to negative responses. Avoid criticizing or embarrassing learners. Use natural humor to relieve tension.

_____ 21. **Reward.** Provide tangible rewards for good performance and good effort. Personal rewards (smiles, hugs, pats on the back) are more enduring than stars or candy.

_____ 22. **Guessing and mistakes.** Allow learners to make guesses and risk answering with incomplete information. Then allow the class to evaluate their responses. Provide explanations and allow the class to critique your views.

_____ 23. **Provoke thinking.** Your task is to help students think creatively: to comprehend, illustrate, devise, examine, sift, condense, summarize, synthesize, evaluate, compare and contrast, integrate. Your task is to help change your learners' mental representations to better reflect life as it really is.

_____ 24. **Worthy learners**. Treat each learner as a person of worth, as a worthwhile individual. Love (for students) covers a multitude of sins (in teaching). Encourage learners to probe their own personal experiences with the topic under consideration.

_____ 25. **Empathize.** Your task is to empathize with your students. Be open and sincere with them, particularly when they ask questions or express confusion and frustration. Handle learner comments with care and respect. Strive to see the learning situation from the *learners'* point of view.

_____ **26. Sequence material.** Properly sequence course material for optimum learning. Set goals, order learning experiences, provide feedback, test, motivate, and reward successful accomplishments.

2 Draw the Christian Teachers' Triad from memory. Include the following elements: Christ, priest, thinking, superficial emotion (warm fluff), prophet, doing, feeling, intellectualism, burnout, king (leader)—Colossians 1:27,9-10; Romans 12:15; and Matthew 11:29–30.

3 Which of the three circles of the triad best reflects your preferred teaching/learning style? Which of the three circles least reflects your preferred teaching/learning style? List three things you will do to strengthen your weakest area. Before the next class session, share these answers with at least two other classmates.

INSTRUCTIONAL TAXONOMIES

Setting Up Targets for Teaching

"Friends, don't get me wrong: By no means do I count myself an expert in all of this, but I've got my eye on the goal, where God is beckoning us onward— to Jesus. I'm off and running, and I'm not turning back. So let's keep focused on that goal, those of us who want everything God has for us. If any of you have something else in mind, something less than total commitment, God will clear your blurred vision— you'll see it yet! Now that we're on the right track, let's stay on it."

Philippians 3:13–16, *The Message*

Who begins too much accomplishes little.

—German proverb[1]

Man is a goal-seeking animal. His life only has meaning if he is reaching out and striving for his goals.
—Aristotle[2]

Chapter Rationale

Unit 2 presented the range of social and intellectual skills of learners. Unit 3 presented the scope of learning perspectives. We now turn to converting educational theory into classroom practice. The first step is to determine what our learners need to learn and how they demonstrate they have learned it.

Learners achieve better because they know where they are going and what teachers expect of them on the way. How are approaches selected from the variety that exists? What are the expected results of the course? What implications do these questions have for long-range and short-range planning?

This chapter addresses the role of instructional taxonomies and objectives in planning, teaching, and testing. The classic learning taxonomies of Bloom, Krathwohl, and Simpson provide the foundation for writing objectives and planning sessions, units, and courses. We consider two new taxonomies that have been developed to overcome the flaws of the classic perspectives: Anderson and Krathwohl's *Revised Taxonomy* (2001), an expansion of Bloom's Cognitive Taxonomy, and Marzano and Kendall's *New Taxonomy* (2006–2008).

Chapter Overview

➤ What Is An Instructional Objective?

➤ Why Have Instructional Objectives?

➤ How Objectives Strengthen the Teaching-Learning Process

➤ Kinds of Objectives

➤ Historical Roots

➤ The Taxonomies of Educational Objectives—Bloom, Krathwohl, and Simpson

➤ Writing Instructional Objectives

➤ Writing Course and Unit Objectives—The Behavior-Content Matrix

➤ Building a Course of Study

➤ Instructional Objectives in the 2000s

➤ *Chapter Concepts, Chapter Objectives, Discussion Questions*

What Is An Instructional Objective?

An instructional objective is a "statement about the type of performance that can be expected of students once they have completed a lesson, a unit, or a course."[3] These *statements of intent* focus more on students than on content,[4] more on what students will do more than what teachers will do. Objectives are not descriptions of teaching, but terminal indicators[5] that students have learned what we intended for them to learn. The term "indicator" refers to student behaviors that demonstrate learning. For this reason, instructional objectives are often referred to as "behavioral objectives."[6] Some object to this terminology because it appears to focus only on behavior and ignore equally important cognitive and affective outcomes.[7] This concern misses the point of instructional objectives. If there is no overt demonstration of learning, teachers cannot know if learning has occurred. But we will see in this chapter that there are specific ways students can demonstrate learning in all three spheres—cognitive, affective, and behavioral. "Behavioral" objectives do not limit teachers to behavioral methods of teaching.

Why Have Instructional Objectives?

When I was ten years old, my family lived in El Paso, Texas. On Christmas I received a bow and arrow set. Since it was a balmy 65 degrees outside, I eagerly attached my bull's eye target to a cardboard box and proceeded to play Robin Hood. I drew back my first shot and let it fly. The arrow missed the target, missed the box, hit the stone fence behind, and split right down the middle.

I had two arrows left, so I decided to invent a game that let me shoot arrows without breaking them. I moved out to the center of the yard. Pulling the bowstring back as far as I could, I shot the arrow straight up. I watched as it travelled higher and higher, then turned and made its way back down. I stayed under the falling arrow—watching it play in the wind. At the last moment, I stepped my foot out toward where I thought the arrow would land (and not get hit, of course). It was great fun. I began to adapt the game. I walked to one side of the yard, put some angle into my shot, then I would run across the yard, search and find the arching arrow, and see how close I could get my foot to the impact point. This went well until my Mom saw what I was doing from the kitchen window and threatened to take my bow away. I tried to play my game at night but found that so much harder that I soon gave up.

The point of my telling this story is that *I never learned to be an archer*. Archers have the ability to put arrows in the center of targets intentionally. How do they learn to do that? They begin the same way I began, by shooting at a target and missing. The difference is that skilled archers keep shooting and missing, each time adjusting their aim. Shoot, miss, adjust. They repeat the cycle thousands of times. In the process of shooting, missing, and adjusting, they develop the skills—tension, aim, windage, and distance—needed to put an arrow in a target. I never developed those skills because I refused to use targets, fail, and break my arrows.

Years later I began teaching a Sunday school class. I found myself following the same pattern. I would talk about the Bible (shooting an arrow into the air) and watch what the Holy Spirit did in the class (watch the wind buffet the arrow). Then, I considered the session successful no matter where we were at the end (I moved my foot to where the arrow landed). The Lord still blessed the teaching of His Word, but *I didn't grow as a teacher*. I had no targets to hit, no intentional expectations to meet. My teaching was all process with no predetermined destination.

This kind of teaching is certainly not limited to Sunday school. A college professor can entertain his history classes with stories and anecdotes about the Civil War. But if he asks them to "describe and explain the five major causes of the Civil War" on an exam, he has not been consistent in his teaching and testing.[8] The disconnect between teaching and testing can be remedied by instructional objectives, which guide both. The remedy is essential for those who teach in accredited institutions.

Accrediting agencies take seriously their requirements for "statements of measurable goals and objectives" as part of every course in a degree plan. "Statements of measurable goals and objectives" is the focus of this chapter.

How Objectives Strengthen the Teaching-Learning Process

The subtitle of the chapter—"Setting Up Targets for Teaching"—underscores the rationale for writing objectives. There are at least six ways instructional objectives strengthen the teaching-learning process.

Focuses Student Attention

Classroom teaching involves many verbal activities. These activities—like lectures, films, guest speakers, projects, and readings—are often loosely organized and make it difficult for students to organize course content. Objectives focus student attention on key ideas and attitudes.[9]

Clarifies Teacher Expectations

Objectives help clarify teacher's expectations for students' learning.[10] Rather than providing students with word magic—"to become good citizens," or "to engender the highest ideals of science," or, "to be exposed to the early Church Fathers"—objectives help specify the knowledge, understanding, values and skills teachers expect their students to achieve in units and courses.

Guides Students in Preparing for Tests

When objectives are used to guide teaching and testing, students are able to study more effectively, and achieve better scores on tests.[11] Their grades are based on mastery of course material rather than answers to arbitrary test items or subjective impressions. Objectives target essential facts and concepts in the course. Students focus their study far better than when they are simply told to "know everything."

Student Attitudes Improve

When courses are structured by objectives, and tests are constructed to measure those objectives, frustration is decreased, and attitudes toward the course, learning experiences, and the professor improve.

Improves Session Planning

Teachers facilitate learning by providing activities and experiences tied to the material to be learned. What activities should be provided? In what order should these activities be done?[12] If teaching is directed by specific objectives, then activities can be selected that move students toward those outcomes. Selecting activities by objectives provides continuity in the class sessions,[13] establishes cohesiveness in learning experiences, and gives students a sense of *going somewhere*.

Some object to the use of objectives because they "oversimplify" course structure, in effect reducing the academic level of courses. This objection is either a misrepresentation of how objectives can be used, or a misconception of objectives in general. Instructional objectives can be written to any level of academic sophistication.

Improves Unit and Course Planning

Just as objectives provide a sense of *going somewhere* in a single session, so they can provide a road map for a unit or entire course of study. Objectives are written for units and courses based on what teachers specifically want students to be able to do at the end of the unit or course. Lesson plans are then slaved to lead to these outcomes. This "backward planning" process—course to units to sessions—ends with specific learning activities that moves students to unit and course indicators.

Improves Teacher Performance

Archers become proficient as they shoot, miss, and adjust. Teachers become proficient as they target their teaching, evaluate the outcome, and revise. Instructional objectives provide the tangible means by which teachers measure how well they accomplish their plans.[14] Are objectives too demanding? Are they too shallow? Do objectives fit student abilities? Do teaching procedures fit stated objectives? Do evaluation means—tests, portfolios, research papers, essays, presentations—match course objectives? What changes need to be made so that objectives can be achieved more effectively?

No one likes to be evaluated. No one wants clear evidence that their teaching is lacking. No one, that is, except those who desire to become skillful teachers. Archers who refuse to be evaluated by firing arrows into targets will never improve. Teachers do well to distribute written instructional targets appropriate for "this subject" and "these learners," select classroom activities and out-of-class assignments to support achievement of course objectives, and evaluate the results. Teachers who open themselves to evaluation, and make adjustments where needed, continue to grow.

Kinds of Objectives

The literature presents a variety of objective types. Some objectives are so broad that they are worthless as instructional guides. Examples include "developing intellect" or becoming "good citizens,"[15] or, "Students should understand evolutionary theory."[16] How do we know that students have developed their intellect? What constitutes a good citizen? How will students show they understand evolution? These questions point to the need for measurable indicators to be included in objective statements.

Some objectives are so specific and trivial that they limit both the quantity and quality of learning. Examples of these include "recall selected definitions" or "reconstruct the flowchart,"[17] or "Students should write from memory two Darwinian laws of evolution."[18] These statements all target the lowest level of cognitive learning and do not lift students into conceptual thinking, critical analysis, or higher-order synthesis and evaluation.

Woolfolk suggests a middle ground for objectives that provides direction for students but allows for a broad range of learning. Here's one example she cites:

> In class, without access to notes, given three presidential elections between 1900 and 1944, write a 200-word essay describing how domestic policy might have changed if the defeated candidate had been elected. (The test specified the election years 1900, 1912, and 1940.)[19]

Students know from this objective what the teacher expects them to do. They know the range of material required to satisfy this objective. They understand the focus of study to be domestic policy of both the elected and defeated presidential candidates. Such flexible structure avoids confusion on the one hand and trivialization on the other.

Before discussing levels of learning and writing objectives, it is helpful to place present thinking in its historical context by looking at four major contributors to the science of instructional design.

Historical Roots

Four theorists have greatly influenced the development and use of instructional objectives. These are Robert Mager (1962, 1975[20]), Norman Gronlund (1972, 1975, 1991, 2009[21]), E. W. Eisner (1967[22]) and Leroy Ford (1978 [2002], 1991 [2003][23]).

Robert F. Mager

In *Preparing Instructional Objectives*, Mager proposed writing three-part objective statements. The first part answers the question, "What will the student do?" The second part answers the question "How will this behavior be tested?" The third part answers the question "What is the criteria for acceptable performance?"[24] Here are several examples of Mager's performance objectives:

- When given a series of instances of government activities, the student can identify the instance as the proper interest of the legislative, judicial, or executive branch of government (8 of 10 correct).[25]
- Given pictures of ten trees, correctly identifies at least eight as either deciduous or evergreen.[26]
- Students correctly define in their own words six of the nine Fruit of the Spirit (Gal 5:22–23).

Critics refer to Mager's system as being best suited for outcomes of simple recall or skill.[27] In fact, the tight specifications of Mager's work has been criticized for leading to an overly rigid system[28] of "hopelessly trivial"[29] statements of performance. This was not Mager's intent, nor is this bent toward course trivia found in his writings. He includes suggestions for all levels of learning, but his broader perspective is demonstrated in his book *Developing Attitude Toward Learning*, in which he applies his system to affective outcomes.

Educators who use Mager's approach may tend to write trivial objectives. Course trivia are easier to test than are higher cognitive skills. It may be the improper *use* of Mager's system, not Mager's system *per sec*, that draws the criticism. Still, Mager's insistence on performance criteria opens the door to criticisms of rigidly structured courses.

E. W. Eisner

Eisner believed Mager's approach to writing objectives was too narrow. The "performance" objectives approach restricts the curriculum, discourages a range of learning outcomes, and (despite Mager's book on developing attitudes) "does not recognize student attitudes as important."[30] While Mager would not agree with these criticisms, Eisner suggested more emphasis on what he called "expressive" objectives.

Expressive objectives include intangible outcomes as well as the tangible. For example, a teacher should teach reading, a measurable outcome, but should also "instill positive attitudes toward reading."[31] But *how will teachers know* if positive attitudes have been instilled in their students?

Some will argue that teachers do not need to know what students are learning. This is like arguing that a doctor does not need to know the effects of prescribed medicines, or that aeronautical engineers do not need to know the effects of their design changes on the flight characteristics of aircraft. If Mager leads us toward the hopelessly trivial, then Eisner leads us toward the "impossibly cosmic."[32]

Norman Gronlund

Mager begins with the specific and Eisner begins with the intangible. Norman Gronlund[33] begins with general objective statements, followed by a *list of sample behaviors* that clarify how teachers know the objective has been reached. The general objective statement uses terms like *know*, *understand*, *solve*, and *appreciate*. Then the sample behaviors clarify how students will demonstrate achievement of the objective. Rather than a large number of specifically targeted behaviors, Gronlund suggests a few central objectives. Research has generally favored this approach.[34] Here's an example of Gronlund's approach for an introductory course in educational psychology.

General objective:

- Students will understand how to use instructional objectives in preparing teaching procedures.

Sample behaviors:

- Defines the levels of learning in the cognitive, affective, and psychomotor domains.
- Analyzes instructional objectives and determines which level of learning they target.
- Given a Bible passage and a level of learning, writes an appropriate instructional objective.
- Evaluates selected objectives written by classmates according to unit criteria. (Yount)

Gronlund's approach targets teacher expectations for students while allowing flexibility in specific methods and evaluation procedures.

Leroy Ford

Leroy Ford served the Sunday School Board[35] of the Southern Baptist Convention for seven years (1959–1966), majoring on curriculum design issues, before beginning his teaching ministry at Southwestern Seminary in Fort Worth, Texas. He chaired the Religious Education[36] School's Curriculum Committee for years and served as editor of the *Course Descriptions for Master's Degree Programs, School of Religious Education*. Every course offered by the School was listed in this Course Description Guide, complete with a course rationale, course and unit objectives, major teaching procedures, and bibliography. Every student entering the School of Religious Education received a copy of the *Course*

Descriptions so that they could choose the courses that best fit their ministry needs. Though Ford retired in 1984, the manual continued to be updated and revised every two years by the Curriculum Committee. Increasing printing costs and rapid curriculum changes led to the demise of the *Course Descriptions* guide in the 1990s. However, the *Course Descriptions* has been recently updated (2008), and serves as the foundation for documenting the "new" course design requirements of SACS and ATS[37] as we approach our next accreditation visits.

Ford's approach to instructional objectives follows Gronlund. Ford calls the general objective a "goal," which he defines as "a broad statement of learning intent which identifies the domain of learning and states the subject in a chewable bite."[38] He calls the sample behaviors "indicators" or "objectives," which he defines as a phrase that "states what the learner will do to prove or *indicate* achievement of a goal." The term indicator reflects more accurately the *function* of an objective.[39] Simple instructional objectives can be stated in a single statement. The **goal** part of the statements below is shown in normal type. The **indicator** is shown in *italics*.

Learners will demonstrate knowledge of the Great Commission (Matt 28:19–20) *by writing it from memory.*

Learners will demonstrate understanding of the Great Commission (Matt 28:19–20) *by defining the terms "go," "baptize," and "teach" in their own words.*

Learners will demonstrate appreciation for the Great Commission (Matt 28:19–20) by sharing a personal experience in which they intentionally shared the Gospel with another.

Ford's system also permits indicators that are more complex, along the lines of Gronlund's "sample behaviors." The first instructional objective at the end of this chapter reflects this complex form:

Learners will demonstrate knowledge of the levels of learning by doing such things as

- listing the 18 levels of learning in the three domains
- matching level of learning with its definition.

As you can see, students have a clear picture of the nature and process of the course from these statements. Yet the statements are general enough to allow teachers flexibility in choosing specific content and procedures.

Ford's latest book on curriculum design[40]—*A Curriculum Design Manual for Theological Education: A Learning Outcomes Focus*—applies the principles of learning outcomes to theological studies. *Design Manual* is must reading for any administrator or professor involved in designing courses or leading institutional self-study efforts for re-accreditation. Appendices in the book include sample course descriptions for theological education, suggestions for creating interactive instruction in correspondence school materials, and guidelines for teaching for knowledge, understanding, skills, attitudes, and values. While viewpoints on instructional objectives and course design continue to evolve, the fundamentals of constructing learning systems remain the same. Ford's book presents these fundamentals in the same professional way that he taught—systematically and practically.

We have used general terms such as *knowledge* and *understanding*—as well as specific terms such as *define*, *analyze*, and *design*—in the examples above. These terms come from various taxonomies of learning domains and levels, which have been used by educators since the 1950s. A taxonomy is a collection, or "framework," of elements that "lie along a continuum,"[41] forming a hierarchy. Three such taxonomies have been used by educators and administrators for decades. We turn our attention to these now.

The Taxonomies of Educational Objectives—Bloom, Krathwohl, and Simpson

The spheres of learning (*Triad*, Chapter Eleven) reflect well established domains of learning: the *cognitive* (knowing and understanding), the *affective* (feeling and valuing), and the *psychomotor* (competency and skill).[42] Each of these is related, in turn, to one of the learning theory systems—cognitive, humanistic, behavioral—as we saw in Chapters Six through Ten. The elements do not form mutually exclusive relationships with each other, since behaviorists, cognitivists, and humanists do not limit their theories to psychomotor, cognitive, and affective learning *per sec*. But the case can be made that cognitive theories (facts and concepts) fit best in the cognitive domain, humanistic theories (personal feelings and values) fit best in the affective domain, and behavioral theories (skills) fit best in the psychomotor domain. Since learners are unified persons, learning in one domain often affects the others—producing the dynamic synergism we discussed in Chapter Eleven. Still, from a design point of view, teachers do well to select methods and activities that intentionally target desired kinds of learning. The taxonomies of Bloom, Krathwohl, and Simpson provide the framework for doing so.

Benjamin Bloom of the University of Chicago led a team of educators to formulate the first educational taxonomy in 1956 and defined six levels of learning in the **cognitive domain**.[43] The book presenting this work is called *Taxonomy of Educational Objectives, The Classification of Educational Goals, Handbook I: Cognitive Domain*. The book has been translated into more than twenty languages (as of 1994) and has provided a basis for test design and curriculum development in the U. S. and around the world.[44] In 1964 **David Krathwohl** of Syracuse University led a team of educators, including Benjamin Bloom, to formulate a second taxonomy for the **affective domain**.[45] Their work was published in 1964[46] in the book *Taxonomy of Educational Objectives: The Classification of Educational Goals, Handbook II: Affective Domain*. In 1972, **Elizabeth Simpson** of the University of Illinois developed a taxonomy for the **psychomotor domain**,[47] published as *The Classification of Educational Objectives in the Psychomotor Domain.*[48]

There are newer taxonomies emerging to replace these classic frameworks. We will discuss two[49] of these in due course: the "Revised Taxonomy" of educational objectives (2001)[50] and *The New Taxonomy of Educational Objectives* (2001, 2007).[51] The classic taxonomies of Bloom, Krathwohl, and Simpson, defined below, are so widely accepted, however, that it could be years before the newer systems permeate the educational community. No lesser educator-theorist than Norman Gronlund used the taxonomies of Bloom, Krathwohl, and Simpson as the framework for his most recent (2009) text on writing instructional objectives,[52] though he does include Anderson and Krathwohl's "Revised Taxonomy" in appendix C. He defends the use of the older taxonomies by the fact that "many teachers still use the original" because "that's the framework they learned to use, and because it's very useful."[53]

Each of the three domains of learning contains **levels** of learning. There are six levels of learning in the cognitive domain, five levels in the affective, and seven levels in the psychomotor. These domains and levels of learning provide the basis for writing instructional objectives.

The Cognitive Domain

The six levels of learning in the cognitive domain are knowledge, comprehension, application, analysis, synthesis, and evaluation. The Left Pillar of the Disciplers' Model and the Thinking Circle of the Teachers' Triad correspond to this domain of learning.

Knowledge. The lowest level of learning in the cognitive domain is knowledge, defined as the ability to recall previously memorized facts,[54] or, to remember or to recognize[55] information. This information can range from individual facts to complete theories. Verbs associated with this level of learning include *identify, recall, recognize, describe, name, state, select, reproduce, list, quote, define* (verbatim), and *match.* "All that is required is the bringing to mind of the appropriate information."[56]

An example of a knowledge indicator would be "*to recall the historical context and exegetical outline of Jesus' command to 'Love your enemies'.*" An essay question that asks students to "list and describe the twelve causes of the fall of Rome" is difficult, but

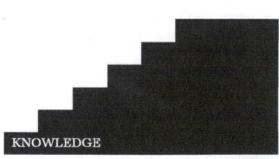

KNOWLEDGE

Cognitive Domain

is a knowledge level question requiring recall of previously learned facts: *"to recall and describe the twelve causes of the fall of Rome."*

While many dismiss rote memory as unimportant, the truth is that much of the Bible teaching done in churches fails to achieve this lowest level. How much of last Sunday's study do our learners remember this Sunday? How much of last Sunday's sermon do we remember today? Much of the "teaching" in our churches is little more than words spoken in the air. We speak volumes of religious words, but how many of these words do learners *remember*? If they can't remember, how can they live out the Word?

I was disappointed one day in 1972 when I met a member of our deaf college Sunday school class while walking across campus.[57] I asked him about any discoveries he might have made during the study. He could not remember the study. "Long, long time ago," he signed. He guessed we had studied something from the Old Testament—"Right?" We had studied an Ephesians passage, one that I had spent six or seven hours preparing to teach. Seeing my disappointment, he remarked, "But you don't understand. You teach so much that it goes in one eye and out the other!" Information, not knowledge. Learners remember facts, definitions, and truths presented by their teachers when they learn at the knowledge level. I was over-doing information and under-doing knowledge.

Aristotle said, "Unless we remember we cannot understand." Martin Tupper, British author and poet (1810–1889) wrote, "Memory is not wisdom; idiots can by rote repeat volumes. Yet what is wisdom without memory?"[58] Higher level thinking requires a foundation of knowledge—terms, words, phrases, jargon, definitions, diagrams, symbols—an idea we've encountered before from Jerome Bruner and Information Processing theorists. In our humanistic-laden world, teachers seldom lead students in exercises that promote ready access, easy retrieval, and correct recollection of essential facts.

These exercises follow specific principles for teaching for knowledge, which stand separate from learning strategies aimed at understanding. In my Principles of Teaching classes, I use the principles in the text box to help the class memorize ten principles for teaching for knowledge.

Knowledge—defined in Bloom's Taxonomy as the ability to recall previously learned facts, theories, and principles—is often displaced by personal experiences, personal opinions, and spontaneous perceptions. Without focused knowledge of a subject, it is impossible to think clearly about that subject.

While "Knowledge" is the lowest level of learning in Bloom's Taxonomy, it is not, in reality, the lowest level of learning. Some teachers focus on "giving information" to students. They lecture, show videos, walk through PowerPoints, and assign hundreds of pages of reading. Students are expected to "know everything," but little is done during class time to help them commit key ideas to memory, let

---

Principles for Teaching for Knowledge

Subsumption:	Relate new facts to established facts
Overview:	Display the list of facts to be memorized at the beginning of the session
Avoid Errors:	Avoid discussion, group work. Practice a small group of phrases, and then test
Active Recall:	Have learners repeat the phrases aloud
Drills short and frequent:	Practice a group of 3-4 phrases, and then explain their meaning
Novel ways of recall:	Have learners recall the phrases in different ways
Relationships:	Help learners understand the common theme in the list
Use Facts:	Help learners use the facts in some activity or project
Space Practice:	Distribute practice throughout the entire session
Knowledge of Results:	Test learners' recall and let them see how well they remembered

---

alone prioritize, systematize, synthesize, or otherwise process the information into meaningful forms. Establishing the core knowledge of a discipline is an essential beginning. But it is only the beginning if we expect students to be able to use what they learn in any meaningful way.

Comprehension. Bloom's cognitive domain is divided into two major sub-domains: knowledge and understanding. Understanding encompasses the upper five levels of the cognitive domain.

Comprehension is the second level of the cognitive domain, and the first level in the understanding sub-domain. There is a qualitative change in learning as we move from knowledge to comprehension. Texts define comprehension as "obtaining meaning from communication,"[59] "processing information,"[60] "translating information from one form to another (words to numbers), interpreting material (explaining or summarizing)."[61]

I find a lot of confusion among writers who give specific examples of levels of learning. Gronlund, for example, proposes the phrase "justifies methods and procedures" as a comprehension level example. But to "justify" suggests a type of evaluation, which is the highest level of cognitive learning. Gronlund also includes the term "distinguishes,"[62] which reflects the comparison and contrast of analysis, a higher level. In fact, Gronlund uses the same term for that level as well, underscoring the ambiguity of interpretation permeating the whole system. Ambiguity among those who create

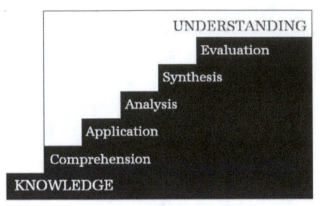

Cognitive Domain

these examples leads to confusion in using the taxonomy. After nearly forty years of using and teaching these taxonomies, I have developed less ambiguous meanings for these levels. They are perhaps overly simplistic, but are certainly more focused and usable than the contradictions we often find in the literature.

Comprehension's clearest meaning is found in the definition and explanation of singular, simple concepts such as love, joy, hope, salvation (Bible); knowledge, affect, skill, feedback (educational psychology); correlation, regression, significance, power (statistics). Learners functioning at this level of learning can give examples, paraphrase a passage, translate from a verbal form to graphical or mathematical form, explain a term or phrase (correctly!)[63] in their own words, or illustrate the term verbally or graphically. Terms which focus on this level include such as these: draw, explain, illustrate, rephrase, translate, convert, infer, interpret, or estimate. An example of a comprehension indicator would be *to define in their own words the terms 'love' and 'enemies' as used by Jesus in the command 'Love your enemies'.* What did Jesus mean by "love"? Are we required to like our enemies? Are we to feel warm and tingly toward them? Who are our enemies? Terrorists who kill Americans? What do these terms mean?

Jesus used the words *agapao*—"wish well to, regard the welfare of,"[64] or to act in another's best interest—and *echthros*—an adversary, an enemy, a foe[65]—in His command. When others act against us, we are to act in their best interest. Or, as He says in clarification[66], "do good to those who hate you" (Luke 6:27). "To love" in this context means "to do good," regardless of feelings. "Enemy" in this context means "those who hate you personally, those close to you." Explaining what singular, simple concepts mean—love, joy, salvation, heaven, Trinity, homoscedasticity, statistical power— occurs at the comprehension level. It requires more than simply recalling memorized definitions but does not allow learners to use the meaning to answer questions or solve problems. That occurs at the next level.

Application. The term application is often used in Christian educational materials in its broadest sense, as in "to apply the Bible to life." This broad sense includes learners' personal experiences and commitments. Such is not the focus of Bloom's third level. Built on comprehension, application refers to "using a concept to solve a particular problem"[67] or "using information in a novel situation"[68] or simply answering a conceptual question correctly. Gronlund includes the application of rules, methods, principles, laws, and theories in "new and concrete situations."[69] Again, some of this application actually happens at higher levels, since some methods, laws, and theories are themselves products of higher level thinking.

I would emphasize application as *the ability to use single, simple concepts to answer conceptual questions, or solve concrete situational problems.* Terms which focus on this level include such as these: *apply, employ, transfer, use, solve, construct, prepare, demonstrate,* and *calculate.*

An example of an application indicator in a Bible study would be "*to explain how agape love could be used to solve case studies involving family conflict."* The focus here is the meaning of *agape* love. An example from educational psychology would be, "*to give two (original) examples of the 'comprehension' level of learning."* The focus here is the meaning of *comprehension.*

The levels of comprehension and application focus on **singular, simple concepts**. What do these words and phrases mean? How can we use these meanings to answer questions or solve problems? As we move to the next level, we pass from consideration of single, simple concepts to **multiple, complex concepts.** An example of a multiple, complex concept is the Christian Teachers' Triad, or the Disciplers' Model,

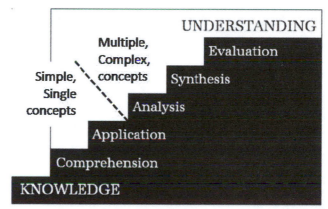

Cognitive Domain

because they are concepts made up of several interrelated (singular) concepts.

Analysis. As we move to analysis, we move into what educators call, collectively, "higher levels of learning." The three higher levels—analysis, synthesis, and evaluation—focus on multiple or complex concepts.

At the level of analysis, learners "break something down into its parts"[70] or "separate something into its components"[71] so that "its organizational structure may be understood."[72] This level includes classifying or categorizing concepts according to specifications, comparing and contrasting concepts within a body of knowledge, or discovering the relationships among concepts. Terms which focus on this level include such as these: *analyze, categorize, compare, contrast, exegete, discriminate, outline,* and *diagram*. Gronlund adds two terms to the mix—*distinguishes* (which he also uses for comprehension) and *identifies* (which he also uses for knowledge)—which adds ambiguity. But notice the reflection of multiple or complex concepts in these terms.

When we analyze (i.e., exegete) 1 Corinthians 13, we create an outline such as the following:

I. Introduction
    A. Love vs. angelic languages
    B. Love vs. prophecy and faith
    C. Love vs. personal sacrifice

II. What Love Is
    A. Patient
    B. Kind
    C. Rejoicing in truth
    D. Protects
    E. Trusts
    F. Hopes
    G. Preserves

III. What Love is Not
    A. Envious
    B. Boastful
    C. Proud
    D. Rude
    E. Self-seeking
    F. Not easily angered
    G. Keeps no record of wrongs
    H. Does not delight in evil

IV. Conclusion
    A. Love stands—prophecies, tongues, knowledge will cease
    B. Childish emotions put away by mature emotions
    C. Faith, hope, love: Love is the greatest

Notice the many singular concepts involved in this passage. Through analysis, we have identified these concepts and listed them under their broader conceptual headings, "what love is."

An example of an analysis indicator in Bible study would be "to exegete five selected passages to determine their teaching on agape love as expressed by Jesus' command to 'Love your enemies.'" Learners will use commentaries and Bible dictionaries to break apart the meanings of five passages of Scripture in order to discover how they reinforce the meaning of agape love.

An example from educational psychology is *to compare and contrast 'social interaction' as used by Piaget and Vygotsky.*" The concept *generally refers* to the give and take of individuals in a group context (comparison), but the two theorists describe the purpose of the process differently (contrast). Do learners understand the similarities and differences of social interaction in the two theories?[73] Any assignment that requires learners to break down research articles and books—to compare and contrast writers, or to determine key ideas and related concepts—moves them to the analysis level. Any assignment that requires learners to compare and contrast perspectives, philosophies, theologies, theories, schools of thought, or opinions engages learners at the level of analysis.[74] The level of analysis assumes that learners *comprehend* each of the concepts produced by the analysis; otherwise, learners produce outlines of meaningless words.

Synthesis. At the level of synthesis, learners "create something new by combining different ideas."[75] The emphasis of synthesis is learner creativity,[76] and includes such things as writing an original speech or lesson plan, constructing a integrated research plan, or creating a new way to depict complex relationships among ideas. Using the interrelated multiple concepts derived through analysis, learners put ideas together in a new, *yet correct*, way.[77] The smooth narrative of a term paper, built upon many articles and books, organized according to key concepts, written in the required academic style is the result of synthesis.

Terms focusing on this level include such as these: *combine, formulate, organize, produce, integrate, design, or create.* Gronlund adds "rewrites" and "summarizes" (which he also uses for *comprehension*) and "compiles," [78] which refers more to a collection of objects (the result of analysis) than the condensing quality of synthesis.

An example of a synthesis indicator in a Bible study would be *"to write an essay on God's kind of love (agape) based on a study of Jesus' command to 'Love your enemies,' (1 Cor 13, and 1 John 4:7–10)."* In this statement, we find learners combining key ideas drawn from an analysis of two passages in order to define "God's kind of love." An example in educational psychology would be *"to define a Christian approach to improving emotional maturity in high school students based on the ideas of Abraham Maslow, Lev Vygotsky, Albert Bandura, and the apostle Paul in Romans 12."*

Dr. Leroy Ford's curriculum design classes at Southwestern led students through a semester-long assignment that required the creation of an "original model" illustrating the interrelationships of several dozens of elements of curriculum design.

Synthesis is a volatile level of learning because it causes learners to confront issues in a complex way. We "know" divorce is wrong, and yet God commanded divorce when He told the Israelites to separate themselves from their foreign wives (Ezra 10:10–11).[79] At about the same time, Esther is praised for marrying a foreigner—the pagan King Xerxes (Esth 2:16–17) and saving the Jewish people from destruction (Esth 9). We "know" that we should not be "unequally yoked with unbelievers" (KJV), yet God commanded Hosea the prophet to marry a prostitute (Hos 1:2; 2:5). Care must be taken to understand the whole counsel of God in Scripture, and not take each truth, each instance, as a stand-alone truth. This tendency leads us to contradictions (some hold to "whosoever shall call upon the Lord" (Rom 10:13) and *over*emphasize free will; others hold to "God's elect" (Titus 1:1) and *over*emphasize sovereignty of God. The truth is neither one nor the other, but an integration of both, a synthesis. God is sovereign, and He has made us free moral agents. We are free, but even a free man cannot make a spiritual choice when he is spiritually dead. We must be quickened by God.[80] Does He quicken everyone (and some refuse to believe—*free will*) or does He only quicken the elect (resigning the rest to hell—*Sovereign God*)? And the debate goes on, each side choosing its proof-texts respectively.[81]

God is love and God is wrath. How can He be both? The answer is found in synthesis. The fire that warms cold hands is the same fire that burns them. The difference is in the relationship between hands and fire. Those rightly related to God are warmed by His love. Those who refuse His love, who reject His offer of grace, are left to be burned by His wrath. He is not love or wrath. He is love-wrath, which exists like two sides of a single coin.[82]

Integration is essential for correct understanding. Rather than holding unrelated bits of truth as True in isolation, leading us to misunderstanding, or even heresy, we do well to fit individual Bible truths into the context of the Scripture-as-a-Whole. Some religious leaders take Hebrews 13:17—"Obey your leaders and submit to their authority"—as a license to be lords over their churches. This is misinterpretation (and sin) because Hebrews 13:17 is written to church *members*, not church *leaders*. Jesus taught, and Peter wrote (under the inspiration of the Holy Spirit) that leaders are not to be lords, but servants, shepherds, and examples (Matt 20:25–26; Mark 9:35; 10:44; 1 Pet 5:2–3).

The truth is found in proper synthesis. Pastors and professors are servants, not lords, placed in leadership for the good of their flocks, not their own personal agendas. As leaders give away their own lives for the good of the flock, the flock is wise to follow and obey. Where there is a humble, servant-oriented pastor and humble, serving-oriented church members, there is peace. Where there is a tyrannical pastor (violating Jesus and Peter), there will be rebellion (violating the writer of Hebrews). Where there is rebellion and unrest among the people, there will be a requirement for increased leader power and more rules. If either pastor or people act for "self" rather than "others," there will be contention. Where both pastor and people do what is best for the other, and for the community and world beyond (*agape* love), there is peace. Proof-texting is a dangerous business and can lead to all sorts of error. Spiritual synthesis helps us rightly handle the truth.

Evaluation. At the level of evaluation, learners objectively[83] "judge the value of material according to specific criteria."[84] "These may be internal criteria (organization) or external criteria (relevance to the purpose), and the student may determine the criteria or be given them."[85] Bloom's highest level of learning is a thoroughly cognitive process, rationally appraising a concept or procedure according to definite standards. Terms focusing on this level include such as these: *appraise, argue, assess, judge, evaluate, validate, critique, weigh,* and *examine.*[86] For me, evaluation focuses on making objective critiques of views, ideas, systems, and perspectives on the basis of stated criteria.

An example of an evaluation indicator in Bible study is *"to evaluate how well learners love others, using criteria established from Jesus' command to 'Love your enemies,' (1 Cor 13, and 1 John 4:7–10)."* The criteria may be developed by learners (synthesis), or given to learners. The criteria are applied at the evaluation level. An example from educational psychology would be *"to evaluate the quality of selected test items according to the criteria given in Chapter Fifteen."*

In my Principles of Teaching class, students write five instructional objectives (synthesis) as a homework assignment. In the following session, they write one of their objectives on the class chalkboards. The result is five lists containing four objectives each, or a display of twenty objectives. Students evaluate each statement based on their understanding of the material. We debrief their evaluations as a class. Some evaluations are correct and suggestions are made for improving the objective. Some evaluations are wrong, and proper principles are reinforced by re-thinking them. Understanding grows as students work at every level of the cognitive domain to evaluate the statements.

With greater understanding comes greater confidence. While this increased understanding and confidence does not help their grades on this minor assignment,[87] it provides a powerful foundation for writing clear objectives for the teaching plans they have yet to write. In another evaluation exercise, students evaluate the MicroTeach[88] sessions of their classmates using a standard checklist.[89]

In summary. The cognitive domain focuses on knowing (recalling and identifying) facts and understanding (explaining, using, and integrating) concepts and principles. It consists of six levels: knowledge, comprehension, application, analysis, synthesis, and evaluation.

The Affective Domain

In 1964 David Krathwohl and a team of educators formulated a taxonomy for the affective domain.[90] Five levels comprise this domain: receiving, responding, valuing, organizing, and characterizing. The Right Pillar of the Disciplers' Model and the Feeling Circle of the Teachers' Triad correspond to this domain of learning. Just as educational publishers have moved away from humanistic theories of learning, so they have largely abandoned the affective domain of learning. Woolfolk (2004) devotes a half-page to the original list, noting that the affective domain has yet to be revised.[91] Snowman, the only contemporary writer to tip his hat toward humanistic approaches to instruction, lists the levels of affective learning as well, stating rather optimistically that, "virtually all teachers are interested in encouraging the development of attitudes and values."[92] The problem for secular educators, particularly in Postmodern times, is what values to instill. No such problem exists for Christian educators, and so we gladly focus on levels of learning in the affective domain.

Affective Domain

Receiving. The first level of the affective domain involves the "willingness to listen"[93] or "attending to something"[94] such as "classroom presentations [and] textbooks."[95] Teachers can prepare wonderful learning procedures, but, as emphasized in IPT, if students are not tuned in and focused, they will not learn. Teachers do well to provide learning experiences that capture the interest and attention of their students. Woolfolk provides an interesting series of examples that I will use throughout this section. She begins with *receiving*: "I'll listen to the concert but I won't promise to like it."[96]

Terms focusing on this level include such as these: *listen, concentrate, observe, follow, watch, view* (a film), *attentive to, focused on.* An example of a receiving indicator in a Bible study would be "*to listen attentively to an explanation of Jesus' command 'Love your enemies'.*" An example of a *receiving* indicator in educational psychology would be "*to give attention to the PowerPoint explanation of the various levels of learning in cognitive and affective domains.*"

While we might consider this level trivial—how can students learn if they are not engaged?—it is vital, since learning ceases if this level is not achieved. You may recall the example I gave in a previous chapter, in which I place a word, or phrase, or partially-completed diagram on the classroom marker board. To the extent that class members look at the prompts and begin to consider the study, they demonstrate *receiving*.

In lesson construction, we talk about learning readiness activities, which engage the learners' mind or heart in preparation for the study of the day. The aim of learning readiness is to secure learners at the affective level of receiving.

Responding. Learners at the second affective level of learning engage in "active participation indicating positive response or acceptance of an idea"[97] by "reacting to it in some way."[98] Learners express their opinions. They willingly answer questions. They share personal experiences related to the subject. They ask questions of their own and participate in group discussions. Following Woolfolk's example (responding): The person attending the concert "might applaud" or "hum some of the music the next day."[99]

Terms focusing on this level include such as these: *share, answer, ask, volunteer, comply, assist,* and *testify.* An example of a responding indicator in a Bible study would be *"to share personal experiences in which they loved another or was loved by another as Jesus commanded."* An example from educational psychology would be *"to share how the lack of instructional objectives (or any type of course guidelines) affected the motivation to learn in the course."*

Moving learners from receiving to responding requires an environment of openness and safety. Without these, voluntary sharing suffers and dies. If teachers are domineering or harsh, learners will not risk speaking out. Teachers affect the climate of the classroom (Chapter Fourteen) by the manner in which they interact with students.

Perhaps the greatest hindrance to openness in a classroom is the perceived lack of time. If teachers prepare too much information for a given session, there is always pressure to reduce learner comments and stories in order to provide more time for teacher explanations. It is better to build in time for student responses, "cover" less information, and process the essentials more deeply, more personally. Unless sufficient time is given for responding, learners will not be ready or able to progress to the next stage, a stage that is critical for the development of values and priorities.

Valuing. The third level of affective learning targets "personal involvement or commitment"[100] and "expressing a belief or attitude about the value or worth of something."[101] It is the worth or value that *students* attach to the material. While values are internal, and thus unseen, a valuing outcome emphasizes consistent and stable behaviors that reflect desired values.

Learners see the importance of the subject for their own work and ministry. They are willing to take a position on the subject and defend it. They share class experiences with friends and family outside of class. They go beyond required assignments to learn more. Following Woolfolk's example (valuing): "a person might choose to go to a concert rather than a film."[102]

Terms focusing on this level include such as these: *justify, commit, defend, initiate, appreciate, select, value,* and *work.*[103] An example of a valuing indicator in a Bible study would be *"to encourage others to be loving in their behavior toward one another and speak against unloving actions within their churches."* An example from educational psychology would be *"to defend the use of instructional objectives in teaching and testing against those who consider the time and energy required to write them could be better spent in research and lecture preparation."*

"Values are more caught than taught."[104] We cannot force our values on others, but we can teach in a way that encourages learners to catch our values. We can live in a way that causes others to imitate our actions. Dr. Bill Reynolds taught for years in Southwestern's School of Church Music. Periodically he led the congregational singing during Chapel. He motivated whole-hearted singing like no other. I never heard him berate a congregation for weak singing. He never told us to sing louder, or placed a hand to his hear, feigning an inability to hear us. He simply led us in singing the hymns *as if they were important.* Beating out the tempo with a dramatic fist, and large arm swings, we caught his love for signing, and we sang our hearts out.

Teaching is much the same. Teachers do well to believe in what they teach, to believe in the value of the subject, and in the importance of mastering it. In fact, if we ever get to the place where we have lost our way, lost our love for the subject, lost that sense of "life change" embodied in what we teach, we would do well to work, study, and pray until it returns. We do our students no favors with yellowed notes and jaundiced lectures. Once renewed, students will catch our enthusiasm for understanding the material and will give themselves even more to learn it for themselves. Our conviction will be "caught" and translated into personal study. Study creates deeper meaning. Deeper meaning yields an increased sense of inherent value, which drives students from within to learn even more. When done right, the greening of the class, the blooming of learning, is a beauty like no other, a beauty intoxicating any who hold learning in high regard. But I am getting ahead of myself. *Valuing* focuses on the creation of single values. *Organizing* focuses on the priorities of values in one's value system.

Organizing. The fourth level of affective learning emphasizes "integrating new values into one's general set of values,"[105] "resolving conflicts between" values,[106] and "organizing values into an internalized system."[107] In short, learners prioritize personal values by importance to themselves. Following Woolfolk's example (organizing): "making long-range commitments to concert attendance,"[108] which reflect a sense of prioritizing.

Terms focusing on this level include such as these: *prioritize, integrate, reorder, compare,* and *combine.*[109] An example of an organizing indicator in a Bible study would be *"to make 'loving enemies' a priority in their lives."* The on-going goal for teachers is to help students move good values to a higher priority and poor values to a lower priority. In terms of Bible studies, the goal is to move biblical values higher and worldly values lower in priority. Such reordering of values—the transformation of personal value systems in light of God's Word—requires consistent influence over a long period of time.

Years ago I was discussing levels of learning in a Doctor of Ministry seminar on educational psychology. A pastor asked, "How can I get my congregation to attend Church Training[110] instead of staying home and watching the Dallas Cowboys play football?" I asked, "If you were away from home, sitting in a motel room on Sunday afternoon, would you attend a Church Training class at a nearby church, or would you stay in your room and watch the Cowboys play?" A low murmur spread across the class. The pastor just smiled and said, "I'd probably watch the game."

"So, it's not the value of Church Training that's in question," I continued. "You're just jealous because, as pastor, you have to be at church, and your members have the freedom to stay home and watch football if they choose." "Murmur, murmur," said the class, stronger this time, like a painful moan. Another pastor spoke up and said, "What we do is get all our people in Church Training, and then my education minister and I walk down to my office and watch the game in my office!" The class burst into one boisterous, good-natured "Boooo!" at the hypocrisy![111]

The issue, truthfully, is one of priority. If minister-leaders want people to participate in church programs, then it is only fitting that we provide programs that church members deem valuable. Over time, programs that prove themselves worthy of members' time will be supported by members' participation. Over time, members will give higher priority to them because they have greater worth than a football game.

More recently I was talking with a regional Baptist leader in Ukraine on our way to a Sunday evening service in a small town a hundred miles from where I was teaching. Along the way, he said, "It is our duty as pastors to prepare and preach sermons. It is the members' duty to come and listen to us." Such an attitude may have worked under autocratic rule, but it holds little long-term value where personal freedom has set in. People can choose. If we wish them to choose training over a dozen other activities, it is incumbent upon us to provide training they value. Programs that help participants grow, develop ministry skills, and become more effective in their life and work will be supported. Supporting unhelpful church programs out of a sense of religious duty is no longer valuable in and of itself, whether in the former USSR or the US. Programs that help participants grow, develop ministry skills, and become more effective in their life and work will be supported.

In terms of Christian academic classrooms, teachers do well to understand the reality that their assignments compete for the attention of our students against other classes and outside interests. Do learners see the inherent value in the assignments we make? If they do, they will spend time and energy on them. If not, we can expect learners to take academic short-cuts to reduce their work load.

Characterizing. The fifth level of affective learning involves "acting consistently with a new value"[112] or the process in which one's "value system becomes a way of life."[113] At this level, learners behave in ways that are "pervasive, consistent, and predictable."[114] Learners live out personalized values that have been drawn from their studies. They consider history as a historian does. They plan research studies in the same way professional researchers do. They actually become what they have learned. Others know them by their personalized values. Following Woolfolk's example (characterizing): "a person would be firmly committed to a love of music and demonstrate it openly and consistently."[115]

Terms focusing on this level include such as these: *reflect, display, practice (as in practice what you preach), act, demonstrate.*[116] An example of a characterizing indicator in a Bible study would be "*to be known by others as lovers of enemies.*" It is one thing to know the Good Samaritan story, or to understand the key principles found in the story. But it is quite another to *be* a Good Samaritan, to live day by day as a Good Samaritan as a natural outflow of one's life.

Suppose a high school student develops an aversion to math because of bad experiences in his classes. He enters college dreading his first math class. But to his surprise, the teacher is clear in her explanations, helpful when he runs into problems, and generally facilitates his success in the course. At the end of the semester, he earns an "A." Beyond the grade, the student considers majoring in math—perhaps becoming a math teacher so he can help others overcome their bad attitudes toward the subject. Not only did his teacher lead him to develop understanding of the material, but she led him to the affective level of characterizing as well.

Early in my seminary career, I had a student who was studying to become a minister of youth. One day during an after-class conversation, I asked him about his journey. He told me he was headed the wrong way in life. When he was 16, a friend invited him to a Sunday school class. The teacher was a young lady who seemed happy to meet him, and happier to teach him and others from the Bible. He began attending, finding in the teacher someone who cared about him. He was deeply drawn to this teacher. Then he began to see that what made her so attractive was her enthusiasm, her love for the Bible. And he was drawn to study the Bible more. Then he discovered that her love for the Bible was generated by her personal relationship with Jesus Christ. He asked questions and learned what it meant to become a Christian. He gave his life to Christ, and now he was in seminary, preparing to help other teenagers find the Lord. His teacher had impact because she had reached the level of characterization and was living out what she had learned from Scripture, from Jesus Himself. Now her student was doing the same.

In summary. The affective domain focuses on attitudes and values and consists of five levels of learning: receiving, responding, valuing, organizing, and characterizing.

The Psychomotor Domain

The psychomotor domain focuses on skill development and emphasizes physical actions.[117] Characteristics of psychomotor development include such things as speed, accuracy, integration, and coordination. Adjectives that describe psychomotor learning include such terms as *correctly*, *appropriately*, and *efficiently*.[118] The psychomotor domain receives much less attention in educational psychology texts than the cognitive and affective domains. This may be due to the perception that psychomotor learning is limited to sports, wood shop, band, or penmanship. Or it may be that cognitive and affective learning dominate classroom activities. However, psychomotor learning principles can be applied to other types of skills, such as writing teaching plans, preparing sermons, witnessing—any activity requiring a high degree of proficiency.[119]

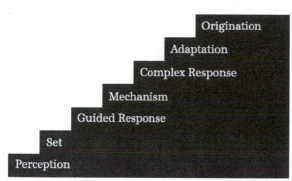

Psychomotor Domain

Elizabeth Simpson developed a taxonomy for the psychomotor domain in 1972.[120] The seven levels of the domain are perception, set, guided response, mechanism, complex or overt response, adaptation and origination.

Perception. The first level of psychomotor learning is perception, where learners "use their senses to obtain cues to guide motor activity."[121] Learners listen to sounds made by an instrument before tuning it, observe the proper grip on a golf club, or watch how to set up a drill press. Terms focusing on this level include: *listen*, *observe*, *choose*, and *detect*.

In learning how to share the gospel, learners would accompany a skilled witness and observe how to move from general conversation to discussing spiritual matters. In learning how to apply a mathematical formula, learners would follow a demonstration of the procedure given in class, or presented by PowerPoint or video.

Set. The second level of psychomotor learning is set, which emphasizes "being ready to perform a particular action." Set involves mental readiness (*knowing* the proper steps), emotional readiness (being *willing* to perform the action), and physical readiness (being properly *positioned*).[122] Terms focusing on this level include: *begin*, *start*, *proceed*, *show*.

In learning to share the gospel, learners would prepare mentally by learning key points of the presentation, and emotionally by practicing presentations with fellow learners. Learners would prepare to use the formula (cognitively) by memorizing it and (affectively) by working through completed examples of work sets.[123]

Guided Response. The third level of psychomotor learning is guided response, which emphasizes "performing under the guidance of a model."[124] Learning at this level focuses on imitation and trial and error as the model (teacher) provides skilled direction to the learner. Terms focusing on this level include: *assemble, fix, manipulate, perform, imitate.*

In learning to share the gospel, learners would share part of the gospel presentation—for example, a personal testimony—during an actual evangelistic visit. A skilled observer (one that is experienced in witnessing) would be present to assist if needed and to provide evaluation after the visit. In learning to use the formula, learners would be given data and required to execute part of the procedure under supervision.

Mechanism and Complex Response. The fourth and fifth levels of psychomotor learning merely extend Guided Response into higher levels of proficiency. Mechanism involves the "*ability to perform a task habitually* with **some confidence and proficiency**."[125] Complex Response involves "*performing a task* with a **high degree of proficiency and skill**."[126] Terms focusing on these levels are the same as for Guided Response[127]—with expectations of greater skill.

In learning to share the gospel, learners continue to practice their skills in simulations and actual witnessing experiences in order to become more proficient in the process. The same is true for learning to use the formula.

Adaptation. The sixth level of psychomotor learning is adaptation, which introduces the element of creativity. Learners at this level use "previously learned skills to perform new but related tasks."[128] Terms focusing on this level include: *adapt, modify, change, improve, extend, elaborate,* and *enhance.*

In learning to share the gospel, learners adapt their presentation dialogue to include persons of different religious backgrounds or cultures or languages.

Origination. The seventh and final level of psychomotor learning is origination, which involves "creating new performances after having developed skills."[129] Terms focusing on this level include: *create, develop, invent, design, compose,* and *devise.*

In learning to share the gospel, learners at this level develop new ways to witness, or new ways to train others to witness, in order to clearly present the Old Story to an ever-changing society.

Had I known about the psychomotor domain when I was ten years old, I could have used its sequence of levels to master arrow-shooting.

Perception: What important cues need attention?

- Distance to target, wind, tension on the bow, distance of draw, elevation of aim.

Set: Am I ready to shoot the arrow?

Guided Response: Is there a mentor to correct my faulty efforts?

Mechanism and Complex Response: practice, practice, practice!

Adaptation and Origination: what new ways can I use these skills to do new things?

While Simpson articulated seven levels in her psychomotor taxonomy, we can simplify the process of developing skills—whether they be physical (serving a tennis ball), mental (writing an instructional objective), or emotional (willingness to forgive our enemies)—to a cycle of demonstration and practice with feedback. Repeat the cycle until every learner has mastered the skill.

Summary of Domains and Levels of Learning

As you can see, learning is far more complex than "acquiring information." We have defined eighteen levels of learning in three domains. Each of these eighteen levels can serve as an instructional target. We have described eighteen possible outcomes. Now let's focus on actually writing the statements.

Three Domains and a Star Trek Analogy

It is hard for me to believe that the original Star Trek television series with William Shatner (Kirk, the ship's captain), Leonard Nimoy (Spock, the science officer), DeForest Kelley (Bones, the doctor), and James Doohan (Scottie, the chief engineer) aired between 1966 and 1969. But then, it was even more startling to realize that I've **used** these characters to illustrate the three domains of learning in seminary classes for nearly thirty years. So I present this historical look as a sidebar.

While I've never been able to confirm this, I believe that Gene Roddenberry, creator of the original Star Trek concept, must have been a student of educational psychology and formed the four major characters named above as reflections of the three domains.

Lt. Commander Spock: Cognitive Domain

Spock, half Vulcan and half human, repressed his emotional human self and focused on his rational Vulcan self. He is portrayed in the series as a walking Cognitive Domain: rational,

---

cerebral, objective, factual. If he were to engage in Bible study, he would be able to operate "logically" in the six levels of the cognitive domain without any problems.

Doctor Leonard "Bones" McCoy: Affective Domain

McCoy was a medical doctor and could deal rationally with medical problems. But his relationships with people were always characterized by rampant emotions: anger, frustration, joy, love, impatience. He was portrayed as a walking Affective Domain.

McCoy and Spock were often pitted against each other. Spock detested McCoy's irrational emotions, and McCoy detested Spock's "infernal logic." From time to time, the Captain would be spirited away to some other planet and either Spock or McCoy would be left in charge. Disaster always followed. Spock was logical but could not humanize his logic in order to deal with others. McCoy never made a decision because he was confused by mixed emotions.

Chief Engineer Montgomery Scott: Psychomotor Domain

"Scottie" was a technical genius. He knew how to coax "jest a wee bit murrr" speed out of the warp engines. He lived in schematics and technical manuals. He kept all the systems of the *Enterprise* in excellent condition and knew how to combine systems to do things their designers never considered. He was able to do this in the midst of one crisis after another.

Captain James T. Kirk: The Balance

Captain Kirk demonstrated an overdramatic balance of all three domains. He could think rationally like Spock, feel deeply like McCoy, and readjust a faulty transporter as skillfully as Scottie. James T. Kirk was a balance of all three domains. It was he who, in every episode, burst upon the scene just in time to save the day and win the girl.

Balance Is What We Need

The Teachers' Triad (Chapter Eleven) reflects a balanced, integrated approach to these three domains and eighteen levels. Now we focus on how to actually use these domains and levels of learning to set up meaningful teaching targets.

Writing Instructional Objectives

Good instructional objectives, based on the approach of Gronlund and Ford, have four characteristics. First, instructional objectives should be written from the *learners' point of view*. **What will learners do to demonstrate their learning?**

Second, objectives should state a general goal for learning. **What is the desired outcome of learning:** to establish knowledge, develop understanding, change an attitude, or master a skill?

Third, objectives should state how students will demonstrate the achievement of that goal. **What is the measurable *indicator*** that demonstrates performance at a given level of learning?

And fourth, objectives should express these elements in a clearly understood format, such as this: ***Learners will demonstrate (domain) of (content)* by (action)**. The underlined portion is the "goal statement," and the action component is the "indicator." Here are several examples of instructional objectives for John 3:16 and Ephesians 6.

Knowledge

Learners will demonstrate knowledge[domain] of John 3:16[content] by writing the verse from memory.[knowledge action (indicator)]

Learners will demonstrate knowledge[domain] of the armor of God (Eph 6)[content] by recalling the pieces of Roman armor and their spiritual counterparts. [action (indicator)]

Comprehension

Learners will demonstrate understanding[130] of John 3:16 by explaining the terms "love," "world," "believe," and "eternal life" in their own words.

Learners will demonstrate understanding of the armor of God (Eph 6) by explaining how faith is like a shield, how truth is like a belt, and how righteousness is like a breastplate.

Application

Learners will demonstrate understanding of John 3:16 by explaining how God's kind of love might solve problems presented in case studies.

Learners will demonstrate understanding of the armor of God (Eph 6) by explaining how faith, truth, and righteousness protect Christians from spiritual attacks.

Analysis

Learners will demonstrate understanding of God's kind of love (John 3:16) by comparing and contrasting it to *phileo* (brotherly love) and *eros* (sexual love).

Learners will demonstrate understanding of the armor of God (Eph 6) by contrasting faith and presumption, truth and perception, and righteousness and ritual.

Synthesis

Learners will demonstrate understanding of John 3:16 by writing a research paper defining God's kind of love.

Learners will demonstrate understanding of the armor of God (Eph 6) by developing an original teaching plan (understanding) focusing on faith, truth, and righteousness.

Evaluation

Learners will demonstrate understanding of John 3:16 by appraising various ministries of the church in terms of how they demonstrate "God's kind of love for the world."

Learners will demonstrate understanding of the armor of God (Eph 6) by judging their own preparation to face spiritual attack.

Receiving

Learners will demonstrate appreciation of John 3:16 by listening to an explanation of the verse.

Learners will demonstrate appreciation of the armor of God (Eph 6) by viewing a PowerPoint presentation of church members who have successfully withstood Satan's attacks.

Responding

Learners will demonstrate appreciation for John 3:16 by sharing their personal testimonies of salvation with the class.

Learners will demonstrate appreciation for the armor of God (Eph 6) by sharing a personal experience in which faith shielded them from the fiery darts of Satan.

Valuing

Learners will demonstrate a change in attitude concerning John 3:16 by committing themselves to witness to at least one person this week.

Learners will demonstrate a change in attitude concerning the armor of God (Eph 6) by making a commitment to strengthen the armor in their lives.

Organizing

Learners will demonstrate a change of attitude concerning John 3:16 by placing greater priority in loving the world as God did in sending His Son.

Learners will demonstrate a change of attitude concerning the armor of God (Eph 6) by placing higher priority on "putting on God's armor" before beginning each day.

Characterizing

Learners will demonstrate a change of attitude concerning John 3:16 by consistently sharing the love of God (the Gospel) with others.

Learners will demonstrate a change of attitude concerning the armor of God (Eph 6) by consistently praying on the armor of God before beginning their daily activities.

Psychomotor Domain

Psychomotor objectives focus on performing a task correctly and proficiently. The term "correct" is defined by the teacher's standards or demonstration. The phrases "as demonstrated in class" or "as illustrated in the film" are often used to guide students in seeing what is expected of them.[131] Here are two examples:

Learners will demonstrate skill in using commentaries to explain scripture by exegeting selected verses as demonstrated in class.

Learners will demonstrate proficiency in writing teaching plans by composing a plan on a specified Bible passage as demonstrated in class.[132]

Writing Course and Unit Objectives—The Behavior-Content Matrix

We have focused on writing single session objectives to this point. The danger of emphasizing the session alone is that, given the limited time in a single session, objectives tend to huddle near the bottom of the taxonomies. Session by session, instructional objectives may never climb above comprehension or responding.

Teachers do well to avoid this by using larger frameworks for planning, such as a "behavior-content matrix,"[133] (see below) to identify unit or course content and levels of learning. The BCM provides a visual way to structure units and courses in such a way to insure a range of learnings in their students.

Behavior-Content Matrix							
Content	Behaviors (Levels)						Total
	K	C	Ap	An	Syn	Ev	
Area 1	1	1	1				3
Area 2			1	1			2
Area 3					1		1
Area 4					1	1	2
Area 5	2	2					4
Total	3	3	2	1	2	1	12

Based on Gage and Berliner, 46, Woolfolk (1993), 447

Building a Course of Study

Sunday school materials provide pre-planned structures for sessions, units, and quarters of study. Teachers in church schools and Christian colleges often have to develop courses from little more than a textbook. Courses consist of units, which in turn consist of single sessions. Desired course outcomes (What do we intend for learners to gain?) are broken down into unit outcomes (How does each unit build toward course outcomes?), which are in turn broken down into single session emphases (How does each session support unit outcomes?). By targeting the appropriate concepts, attitudes, and skills of the course, we provide the framework for preparing specific sessions, units, and assessments that lead students to intentional achievement.

The School of Educational Ministries at Southwestern Seminary has a long history of developing course descriptions that go far beyond the paragraph-long course entries one normally finds in academic catalogs. LeRoy Ford initiated this work in the mid-1960s and led the faculty to design course descriptions for every course offered by the School. He led this effort for more than twenty years, retiring in 1984. The *Course Description Handbook* provided every incoming religious education student a detailed structure of every course in our curriculum. The *Handbook* continued to be revised and updated periodically until the cost of printing became prohibitive. *Handbooks* were made available in faculty offices and the Curriculum Lab. This last year, as part of our accreditation process, we updated course descriptions, made them available on-line, and provided them in CD formats.

The most recent revision was completed in May 2008. The sample course description below is for the course *FOUND 3303 Educational Psychology*, a course that uses this text as its base.[134] Though it has been 24 years since Ford directed the efforts of faculty to produce these descriptions, and many new courses have been developed in that time, you will see his system clearly reflected in the statements below. You will notice that each unit of the course has a single goal with multiple indicator statements, which parallels in substance, if not form, Gronlund's use of "general objectives" followed by "specific outcomes."

FOUND 3303 EDUCATIONAL PSYCHOLOGY

RATIONALE FOR THE COURSE

This course focuses on the following student competencies as expressed in the objectives of the School of Educational Ministries:

Functions creatively with other professional staff and other church members

Leads in developing, evaluating, and administering curriculum plans; functions as a resource person in curriculum areas

Models the role of an effective teacher and provides opportunities for persons to exercise self-initiative in learning

---

COURSE DESCRIPTION

A biblical analysis of essential educational theory systems in the context of Christian discipling and equipping. Topics include developmental theories (personality, cognitive, moral), instructional objectives, theories of learning, motivation for learning, classroom management, and effective testing practices. The educational psychology of Jesus concludes the course. Three hours.

COURSE GOAL AND OBJECTIVE

Students will demonstrate understanding of the nature and conditions of learning in a Christian context by formulating practical applications from the field of educational psychology.

UNIT GOALS AND OBJECTIVES

Unit 1: "Christian Education and Educational Psychology"

Students will demonstrate understanding of the relationship between the practice of Christian teaching and the field of educational psychology by achieving objectives such as these:

Explains the meaning of the seven elements of the Discipler's Model, and the Model as a whole, as it relates to the process of spiritual discipleship.

Compares and contrasts the Disciplers' Model with the educational psychology emphases of the course

Differentiates between faith-knowing and scientific-knowing

Differentiates between Greek and Hebrew mind-sets, explaining the dilemma of the American Christian in learning and growing in the Lord

Unit 2: "Stage Theories of Development"

Students will demonstrate understanding of the Christian implications of the stage theories of Erik Erikson, Jean Piaget, and Lawrence Kohlberg by achieving objectives such as these:

Explains the implications of selected developmental stages for the teaching-learning process

Correctly identifies the appropriate theorist and appropriate stage of development when given learner characteristics

Evaluates the developmental theories in relation to the Christian teaching process

Unit 3: "Instructional Objectives"

Students will demonstrate understanding of the creation and use of instructional objectives in evaluating learner performance by achieving objectives such as these:

Differentiates among the three domains of learning

Classifies instructional objectives as to their domain and level of learning

Writes an instructional objective for a given domain and level of learning.

Unit 4: "The Nature of Learning and Motivation"

Students will demonstrate understanding of the theories of learning and motivation by doing such things as these:

Defines selected terms from learning theory and motivation

Classifies learning characteristics as to their appropriate learning theory, demonstrating flexibility in meeting learner needs with the appropriate approach to teaching.

Classifies principles of teaching in a Christian context as to appropriate learning theory

Evaluates strengths and weaknesses of each learning theory system for Christian teaching and motivation

Formulates a holistic approach, The Christian Teacher's Triad, to Christian teaching from the three learning theory systems

Unit 5: "Becoming An Effective Teacher"

Students will demonstrate an understanding of attitudes and skills required for effectiveness in Christian teaching by achieving objectives such as these:

Differentiates among four views of motivation: behavioristic, cognitive, humanistic, and attribution theory

Defines the role of personal attitudes toward one's subject, students, and self in improving teaching effectiveness

Distinguishes between class atmospheres under competition and cooperation classroom structures

Defines structuring, soliciting and reacting teacher's behaviors in terms of learner achievement

Identifies good and bad examples of lecturing and questioning strategies

Analyzes present approaches in Church Education programs in light of the teaching approach of Jesus, the Master Teacher

Methods of Instruction

Methodology for the course grows out of the statements of unit goals and objectives. Methods include conversational lectures, class dialogue, directed reading, question and answer, small group discussion, and problem-solving activities.

Tests and Evaluations

Periodic examinations are given over the course content. These examinations are conceptual in nature and administered under a mastery learning approach. Evaluations will also be made of written work submitted in preparation for class discussions.

Bibliography

Biehler, Robert F. and Jack Snowman. *Psychology Applied to Teaching,* 11th ed. New York: Houghton-Mifflin, 2004

Eggen, Paul and Kauchak, Don. *Educational Psychology: Classroom Connections,* 5th ed. New York: Prentice Hall College Division, 2000

Issler, Klaus. *How We Learn: A Christian Teacher's Guide to Educational Psychology.* Wipf and Stock Publishers, 2002.

Slavin, Robert E. *Educational Psychology: Theory and Practice,* 8th ed. Boston: Allyn and Bacon, 2005

Woolfolk, Anita, *Educational Psychology,* 10th ed., Boston: Allyn and Bacon, Inc., 2006

Yount, William R. *Created to Learn: A Christian Teachers' Introduction to Educational Psychology.* Nashville: Broadman & Holman, 1996

Instructional Objectives in the 2000s

Two new systems have emerged as possible replacements for Bloom's Taxonomy. The first, the *Revised Taxonomy*, is an "update" to Bloom's original, and shares both strengths and weaknesses with it. The second, the *New Taxonomy*, is presented as a "replacement" for Bloom's, its authors offering it as a solution to "the inherent flaws in the original."

New perspectives provide different ways to look at the educational process, so we will cover them here. This is not an exhaustive exposition for several reasons. First, the classic principles shared earlier in the chapter remain the most popular and widely used by educators. Recent textbooks that address instructional objectives spend their pages on Bloom, Krathwohl, and Simpson. Only two textbooks mention the Revised Taxonomy (2001). None mention the New Taxonomy (2006, 2007), but this may be due to lag time in textbook revisions.

Textbook Coverage of Instructional Objective Systems

	Mager	Gronlund	Bloom cognitive	Krathwohl affective	Simpson psychomotor	Revised cognitive
Snowman (2009)	d	d	d	d	d	--
Eggen & Kauchak (2007)	d	d	m	--	--	m
Ormrod (2006)	--	--	d	--	--	--
Woolfolk (2004)	d	d	d	d	m	m
Sternberg (2002)	d	d	d	d	m	--

d = discussion   m = mention

Second, the two major books I'm using as resources for the two new taxonomies contain nearly 500 pages of explanation between them. We simply can't do justice to this level of complexity in the limited space of this text.

Third, only time will tell whether the newer taxonomies will replace the classics, and in what form. The classics will serve you better now. The newer approaches may fall by the educational wayside in a few years. Hopefully the following will prepare you to make the choice between the established and reformed views.

The Revised Taxonomy (Anderson and Krathwohl, 2001)

In the original taxonomy, Bloom's committee positioned "knowledge" as the lowest level of cognitive learning. It always struck me as odd, since teaching for a gain in knowledge had far more in common with behavioral principles than cognitive. More troubling was the confusion of content and process. While "knowledge" was defined as remembering, or recall, of facts, the examples of content residing at the knowledge level seemed far more sophisticated than factual recall. After listing "recall of specific facts," other examples include the "ways and means of dealing with specifics (conventions, *trends* and *sequences, classifications* and *categories, criteria, methodology*); *universals* and *abstractions* in a field (*principles* and *generalizations*, theories and structures)"[135] *(italics mine)*.

The Revised Taxonomy Table

The Knowledge Dimension	The Cognitive Process Dimension					
	1. Remember	2. Understand	3. Apply	4. Analyze	5. Evaluate	6. Create
A. Factual Knowledge						
B. Conceptual Knowledge						
C. Procedural Knowledge						
D. Metacognitive Knowledge						

Anderson and Krathwohl (2001), 28

The Revised Taxonomy solves this problem by proposing a two-dimensional model: **knowledge type** is one dimension, and **cognitive process** is the second. The **four knowledge types** form the four rows of the Table: *Factual, Conceptual, Procedural,* and *Metacognitive.* The **six cognitive processes** form the six columns of the Revised Taxonomy Table: *Remember, Understand, Apply, Analyze, Evaluate, Create.*[136] Let's define each of these briefly.

Factual knowledge refers to the "basic elements students must know to be acquainted" with a subject.[137] *Factual knowledge* has two sub-divisions. *Knowledge of terminology* refers to elements like technical vocabulary and symbols. *Knowledge of specific details* refers to elements like major natural resources or reliable sources of information.

Conceptual knowledge refers to the "interrelationships among basic elements within a larger structure." *Conceptual knowledge* has three sub-divisions. *Knowledge of classifications* refers to elements like periods of geological time or types of business ownership. *Knowledge of principles and generalizations* refers to elements like the Pythagorean Theorem or the law of supply and demand. *Knowledge of theories, models, and structures* refers to elements like the theory of evolution or the structure of Congress.

Procedural knowledge refers to how to do things and includes methods, skills, algorithms, and techniques. *Procedural knowledge* has three sub-divisions. *Knowledge of subject-specific skills* (skills used in painting with water colors, whole number division), *Knowledge of subject-specific techniques* (interviewing techniques, scientific method), and *Knowledge of criteria for determining when to use procedures* (criteria for using a particular method or technique).

Metacognitive knowledge refers to the awareness and knowledge of one's own cognition. *Metacognitive knowledge* has three sub-divisions. *Strategic knowledge* (knowledge of tools, such as outlining to capture the structure of a text chapter), *knowledge about cognitive tasks* (types of tests teachers use, cognitive demands of given tasks), and *self-knowledge* (awareness of one's own knowledge, as well as personal strengths and weaknesses).

The first three types of knowledge—factual, conceptual, and procedural—existed as sub-divisions under "Knowledge" in the original taxonomy. However, conceptual and procedural types were often overlooked, reducing Bloom's classic knowledge level to recall of facts.[138] The impact of Information Processing Theory is clearly seen in the addition of the metacognitive type.

Let's turn now to the **six cognitive processes**. Notice that the major elements ("Remember") are stated as simple verbs, while the sub-divisions ("recognizing") are stated as gerunds ("-ing").

Remember refers to the retrieval of relevant knowledge from long-term memory and is divided into two sub-divisions: *recognizing and recalling*.[139]

Understand refers to the construction of meaning from "instructional messages, including oral, written and graphic communication." *Understand* has seven sub-divisions. *Interpreting* (paraphrasing), *exemplifying* (giving examples), *classifying* (grouping similar objects), *summarizing* (writing a short summary of events on a videotape), *inferring* (inferring rules from examples), *comparing* (comparing historical events to contemporary situations), and *explaining* (explaining the causes of).

Apply refers to using a procedure in a given situation. *Apply* has two sub-divisions. *Executing* (carrying out a calculation, such as dividing one whole number by another), and *implementing* (determining in which situations a physical law is appropriate).

Analyze refers to breaking material into its constituent parts and determining how those parts relate to each other. *Analyze* has three sub-divisions. *Differentiating* (distinguishing between similar concepts), *organizing* (structuring information in a historical situation into evidence for and against a particular historical explanation), and *attributing* (determining the point of view of an author of an essay).

Evaluate refers to making judgments based on standards. *Evaluate* has two sub-divisions. *Checking* (determining whether a scientist's conclusions follow from observed data) and *critiquing* (judging which of two methods is best for solving a given problem).

Create refers to putting elements together to form a coherent or functional whole, or reorganizing elements into a new pattern. Create has three sub-divisions. *Generating* (generating hypotheses to account for observations), *planning* (developing a research plan on a given topic), and *producing* (writing an original research paper).

The major change in the sequence of six cognitive processes is exchanging the two top levels, placing *Create* (synthesis) above *Evaluate* (evaluation).

The "X" in the table below marks the placement of a specific instructional objective, such as **"The student will learn to apply the reduce-reuse-recycle approach to conservation."** The major verb in the objective is "**apply**." The major noun in the objective is "reduce-reuse-recycle approach," which is **procedural knowledge** ("how to").[140] The table looks very much like a Behavior-Content Matrix, with specific subject areas being replaced by the more general types of knowledge. Such a visual may help teachers see the variety of knowledge types and cognitive processes that are being employed in class sessions.

The suggested format of the objectives departs from the more standard goal-indicator format: "The student will learn . . .," "The student will be able to . . .," or "The student should be able to . . .". Dr. Ford's incessant question rings in my head, "*How will you know* the student is able?" When given an answer, he would say, "So, the student *demonstrates* (some ability) by (doing something specific)." The objective statements suggested by Anderson and Krathwohl lack indicators, the means by which the goal is measured.

The Revised Taxonomy Table

The Knowledge Dimension	The Cognitive Process Dimension					
	1. Remember	2. Understand	3. Apply	4. Analyze	5. Evaluate	6. Create
A. Factual Knowledge						
B. Conceptual Knowledge						
C. Procedural Knowledge		X				
D. Metacognitive Knowledge						

Anderson and Krathwohl (2001), 28

The authors provide a "silly example"[141] regarding *doodling*. While they admit that an objective about doodling is unlikely in an academic setting, they used it to illustrate how even this could be classified in the Revised Taxonomy Table. Here is the objective: **"The student will learn that doodling helps him or her to relieve stress temporarily when working on difficult problems."** The authors declare this "might" be a strategy within *metacognitive knowledge*. Further, the phrase "will learn that" suggests simple recall. The objective, then, would take the more general form of "remember metacognitive knowledge"[142] and can easily be located on the Table. As we learned in Chapter Nine (IPT), learning to relieve stress by doodling is certainly a metacognitive outcome. There is concern, however, that the Revised Taxonomy makes the targeting of kinds of knowledge and levels of cognitive processing so specific—24 distinct cubby holes—that the system will simply overwhelm many teachers.[143]

Anderson and Krathwohl provide extensive explanations of all of these elements and give many pages of examples of how to use the Revised Taxonomy Table for objectives, activities, and assessments. The Table ties in nicely with discoveries from Information Processing Theory, and its two-dimensional structure emphasizes the complexity of knowledge (in the philosophical sense) beyond simple recall or identification of facts. Any benefit, however, from an improved understanding of how information is processed into various kinds of knowledge may not be enough to overcome the additional complexity of the two-dimensional model.

Marzano and Kendall (2007) criticize the Revised Taxonomy at the very point of its close connection with Bloom's original. Specifically, it "suffers from the same inherent weakness of that work—the tacit assumption that its levels are ordered hierarchically in terms of difficulty."[144] Difficulty here refers not to effort—*memorizing* Psalm 23 is obviously more difficult than *paraphrasing* Psalm 23, a higher level—but to cognitive complexity. *Understand* is more cognitively complex than *Remember*. *Create* is more cognitively complex than *Evaluate*. (My suspicion about why Bloom placed evaluation above synthesis in the original taxonomy, which I've never been able to verify, is that learners must create standards [synthesis] before those standards can be used to judge something [evaluation]. It is obvious, again, that creating something new, such as a sermon or lesson plan, is far more difficult than critiquing it, and the Revised Taxonomy is correct in this.)

Additionally, Marzano and Kendall criticize the fact that the Revised Taxonomy, as an update to Bloom's alone, addresses cognitive processes with little attention to affective or psychomotor outcomes.[145] They propose a replacement system that attempts to solve these problems.

The New Taxonomy (Marzano and Kendall, 2006–2008)

The New Taxonomy is so new that it has not made its way into contemporary (2007–2009) educational psychology textbooks. Marzano et al present their ideas in two books. The first, now in its second edition, is *The New Taxonomy of Educational Objectives*, 2nd ed., (Thousand Oaks, CA: Corwin Press, 2007). The companion volume is *Designing & Assessing Educational Objectives: Applying the New Taxonomy*, (Thousand Oaks, CA: Corwin Press, 2008).

The New Taxonomy differs from the Revised Taxonomy in three ways. First, the New Taxonomy "**explicitly addresses cognitive, affective, and psychomotor** aspects of learning," and not cognitive processes alone. Secondly, the New Taxonomy **places metacognition above cognitive** processes, representing a type of processing. The Revised Taxonomy locates metacognition (metacognitive knowledge) in the same dimension as subject matter content. Yet Anderson, et al, admits that metacognitive knowledge "does not have the same status as the other three status types."[146] The third difference is the **treatment of self-thinking**. The Revised Taxonomy places self-thinking within metacognitive knowledge. The New Taxonomy places self-thinking at the top of the hierarchy because it controls both the decision to engage a learning task, as well as the energy given to tasks that are engaged.[147]

The New Taxonomy is similar to the Revised Taxonomy in that it uses a two-dimensional structure. The two dimensions are "**Levels of Processing**" and "**Domains of Knowledge**." The table below, while in a different format from Marzano, et al, displays the two dimensions of the New Taxonomy. Many pages are given to defining each level of the two domains. The next section will provide enough overview to give you a sense of this new system.

The New Taxonomy defines three levels of knowledge: information, mental procedures, and psychomotor procedures. **Informational knowledge** (declarative knowledge in Information Processing Theory) refers to the "what" of human knowledge: vocabulary terms, facts, time sequences, generalizations, and principles, which themselves form a hierarchy from simple to complex. (Just to make the point as clear as possible: elements of declarative knowledge can be processed across all six levels of processing. At retrieval [lowest level], students remember a generalization that has been committed to memory. At self-system [highest level], students examine the effect the generalization has on them—importance, emotional impact, and usefulness. We will define levels of processing in a moment.)

Mental Procedures (procedural knowledge in Information Processing Theory) refers to the "how-to" of human knowledge: processes and skills (which can further be divided into tactics, algorithms, and single rules). Tactics are procedures for accomplishing tasks, such as reading a bar graph. Algorithms are basic sets of steps that are applied in the same way to given problems and become, with practice, automatic, such as addition and subtraction. A single rule is a simple "*if* situation X occurs, *then* perform action Y." These single rules can be used in sets to solve problems that are more complex.[148]

Psychomotor procedures refer to the same elements as Simpson's psychomotor domain, which were never addressed by Bloom's panel. The New Taxonomy considers psychomotor procedures as a type of knowledge for two reasons. First, they are "stored in memory in a fashion identical with mental procedures." Second, psychomotor skills are developed in ways very similar to the acquisition of mental procedures—first learned as information, shaped through practice, and finally learned to a level of automaticity.[149] Psychomotor procedures are sub-divided into skills and processes. *Skills* refer to foundational procedures (finger dexterity, control precision) and simple combinational procedures (shooting a free-throw in basketball) involving the interaction of many foundational procedures. *Processes* refer to complex combinational procedures (the actions involved in playing defense in basketball).

The New Taxonomy

Domains of Knowledge	Levels of Processing					
	1. Retrieval (cognitive)	2. Comprehension (cognitive)	3. Analysis (cognitive)	4. Knowledge Utilization (cognitive)	5. Metacognitive System	6. Self-system
Information						
Mental Procedures						
Psychomotor Procedures						

Based on Marzano and Kendall, the New Taxonomy, 13

The New Taxonomy defines six levels of mental processing. The first four levels form the cognitive system, the fifth level forms the metacognitive system, and the sixth level forms the self-system.[150] **Retrieval** (cognitive system) refers to the "activation and transfer of knowledge from permanent memory to working memory,[151] where it can be consciously processed."[152] Retrieval is seen in both *recognition*—the unconscious and automatic decoding of information in order to compare with sensory experience—and *recall*—the intentional recollection of information previously learned. Retrieval is closely related to Bloom's Knowledge level, though "Bloom confounded the object of retrieval (i.e., knowledge) with the processes of retrieval (i.e., recall and recognition). The New Taxonomy does not."[153]

Comprehension (cognitive system) refers to the process of encoding sensory information in permanent memory in a complete and structured format. Comprehension involves two related processes. *Integrating* refers to the distillation of information "down to key characteristics, organized in a parsimonious, generalized form." *Symbolizing* refers to the translation of information into two modes: linguistic and imagery. The linguistic mode is semantic in nature (word-based), while imagery is episodic in nature (picture-based). There is strong correspondence between the comprehension levels in both Marzano, et al, and Bloom.[154]

Analysis (cognitive system) refers to the elaboration of knowledge as comprehended,[155] going beyond the information given to "generate new information not already possessed by the individual." Analysis consists of five processes. *Matching* (similarities and differences between knowledge components), *Classifying* (organizing information into meaningful categories), *Analyzing errors* (addresses the logic or accuracy of knowledge), *Generalizing* (constructing new generalizations from information already known), and *Specifying* (generating new applications of a known generalization or principle). Analysis in the New Taxonomy corresponds to elements of analysis, synthesis and evaluation in Bloom's.[156]

Knowledge Utilization (cognitive system) refers to knowledge employed to accomplish specific tasks. Knowledge utilization consists of four general categories. *Decision-making* is employed when an individual must choose among alternatives. *Problem-solving* is employed when "an individual attempts to accomplish a goal for which an obstacle exists." *Experimenting* is the process of generating and testing hypotheses in order to understand "some physical and psychological phenomenon" on the basis of statistical hypothesis testing. *Investigating* is the process of generating and testing hypotheses about "the past, present, or future" on the basis of "rules of evidence" and "a well-constructed argument." Knowledge utilization corresponds closely to the synthesis level in Bloom's taxonomy.[157]

Metacognition is responsible for "monitoring, evaluating, and regulating the functioning of all other types of thought," and corresponds to metacognition in IPT. The metacognition system has four functions. *Specifying goals* refers to the determination of learning outcomes as well as the planning for milestones, deadlines, and resources needed to insure success. *Process monitoring* is a quality control function that monitors how well mental procedures are being carried out. *Monitoring Clarity* and *Monitoring Accuracy* are quality control functions that monitor how well information processing is proceeding in constructing clear and accurate knowledge. There is no corresponding component of metacognition in Bloom's Taxonomy.[158]

Self-System Thinking refers to attitudes, beliefs, and emotions, and their interaction to determine motivation and attention. It is the processing of the self-system that determines the quality of learning in learners for it is here that the decision is made to engage a task or not, and to what energy level the task will be engaged. Once the decision is made to engage a task, all the other systems are brought into play. For most of us, the concept of "human will" fits nicely here.

There are four types of self-system thinking. *Examining importance* refers to the inherent value of the information to the learner and corresponds to Krathwohl's *Valuing* level in the affective domain. *Examining efficacy* refers to the learner's belief that they possess the resources, ability, and power to "gain competence relative to a specific knowledge component." *Examining emotional response* refers to the awareness learners have concerning emotional reactions to learning. *Examining overall motivation* refers to an awareness of the synergistic effect of the previous three components—value, efficacy, and emotional response—which determines how learners engage new tasks, or increase competence in established tasks.[159]

Critique of The New Taxonomy

It is obvious that the New Taxonomy has taken advances in IPT very seriously in attempting to create a taxonomic system for the twenty-first century. As a teacher, I question whether the level of detail being identified and labeled in this system will actually translate into better classroom performance. My concern is deepened as I turn to the examples of instructional objectives given in the text, which mirror the same format as Anderson and Krathwohl: "Students will be able to . . ." I find myself asking Dr. Ford's question, "How will you know?"

More disturbing is the analytical way Marzano, et al, handles the affective dimension of learning. After criticizing the Revised Taxonomy for its lack of emphasis on affective and psychomotor elements, the New Taxonomy shows the same deficiency, focusing more on the *evaluation* of emotional responses than the generation of them. Under *Examining importance*, for example, Marzano, et al, illustrates the level with the statement, "The student *will be able to identify how important* the information, mental procedure, or psychomotor procedure is to him or her and the reasoning underlying this perception" (emphasis mine). Similar statements are given for *Examining efficacy* ("be able to identify his or her beliefs"), *Examining emotional response* ("be able to identify his or her emotional responses") and *Examining motivation* ("be able to identify his or her overall level of motivation").

This sounds like cold, intellectual analysis. Where is the affect, the joy, the openness, the freedom of expression, the passion to defend? It is the difference between two teenagers sitting in an ice cream shop, sharing one milk shake with two straws, eyes glued to each other (*enjoying* the emotional response of infatuation) and a social scientist observing their behavior (*identifying* the emotional response of infatuation). It is the difference between a neurologist who studies pain (*identifying* pain in its various types) and a neurologist who breaks one of his teeth (experiencing personal pain).

While the brain may process emotional and rational experiences in similar ways, the effects of emotions and reason are very different in learning experiences. While I may focus on understanding goal-objective statements for official documents, I am always looking for ways to open up the class, to increase personal responses and questions, and make the process of learning more humane. Perhaps the lack of affective sensitivity in the New Taxonomy results from its foundation in IPT, which likewise gives little attention to emotional responses.

Even so, it is helpful to have a single system, albeit complex, that attempts to subsume all three spheres of learning into a cohesive whole. The New Taxonomy leads educators to embrace a triadic view of learning—head, heart, and hand—and this is an improvement over the three distinct taxonomies of the past.

In Summary

Why write objectives?

We write objectives to target teaching efforts and to improve planning, testing, and the objective evaluation of students' learning. Instructional objectives help *us*.

We write objectives to focus student learning, to structure their study, and to guide them in preparation for testing. Instructional objectives give students the sense that teachers are "going somewhere," which is crucial in establishing confidence in the course and the professor. Instructional objectives help *them*.

The cost is high, there's no doubt about it. Writing good objectives is difficult, but then, producing anything of quality is difficult. Writing good objectives is time-consuming. Yet aimless teaching wastes the time of students as well as the teacher—to what end?

Research shows that objectives improve *intentional* learning, but hinders *incidental* learning.[160] While incidental learning increases in loosely structured discussions and projects, focused learning and subject mastery will suffer in those same situations. The kind of instructional objectives emphasized in this chapter, based on Gronlund and Ford, expand opportunities for incidental learning beyond the Mager model, even while providing intentional guidelines for students. This is no small matter, since intentional guidelines have been shown to produce the most effective learning situations[161] over time—*and for good reason*, for "if the trumpet makes an unclear sound, who will prepare for battle?" (1 Cor 14:8–9).

Chapter Concepts

Adaptation	Psychomotor domain: sixth level (creativity in modification)
Affective domain	Sphere of emotions, values, and priorities
Analysis	Cognitive domain: fourth level (outlining, exegesis)
Application	Cognitive domain: third level (solving problems)
Behavior-Content Matrix	Planning tool to insure distribution of content over learning levels
Performance objectives	Mager: objectives consisting of behavior, test, and criteria
Characterization	Affective domain: fifth level (learning reflected in life)
Cognitive domain	Sphere of facts, concepts, and principles
Complex response:	Psychomotor domain: fifth level (increased skill over mechanism)
Comprehension	Cognitive domain: second level (explaining, illustrating simple concepts)
Expressive objectives	Eisner: objectives contain tangible (cog) and intangible (aff) components
Evaluation	Cognitive domain: sixth level (judging by a standard)
General objectives	Gronlund: broad learning intent
Goal statement	Ford: general statement of learning outcome (domain, content)
Guided response	Psychomotor domain: third level (attempting skill with guidance)
Indicator	Ford: specific measurable behavior that indicates achievement of goal
Mechanism	Psychomotor domain: fourth level (increased skill over guided response)
New Taxonomy	New two-dimensional Taxonomy: Marzano and Kendall (2006–2008)
Origination	Psychomotor domain: seventh level (creativity in design)
Revised Taxonomy	Revised (Bloom) Taxonomy: Anderson and Krathwohl (2001)
Sample Behaviors	Gronlund: suggested ways teachers measure achievement of general objective

| Set | Psychomotor domain: second level (preparing to execute skill) |
| Perception | Psychomotor domain: first level (listening,, observing) |

Chapter Objectives

Learners will demonstrate knowledge of the levels of learning (Bloom, Krathwohl, Simpson) by doing such things as

- listing the 18 levels of learning in the three domains
- matching level of learning with its definition.

Learners will demonstrate understanding of levels of learning (Bloom, Krathwohl, Simpson) by identifying the domain and level of learning of stated instructional objectives.

Learners will demonstrate understanding of instructional objectives by writing appropriate objectives for given Scripture passages and learning levels.

Learners will demonstrate appreciation for instructional objectives by sharing personal experiences of two classes—one that did not use objectives and one that did.

Discussion Questions

1 Jesus was the greatest Teacher Who ever lived. Yet we can safely assume He never wrote an instructional objective to guide His teaching. Why do you suppose He didn't? Why do you suppose we should?

2 Read Ephesians 4:11–12 and determine what concepts, values, and skills reside there for ministers to master.

3 Write complete instructional objectives, using the suggested format given in the chapter, for the following:
   a. 1 Corinthians 13 and comprehension
   b. Revelation 2–3 and synthesis
   c. Matthew 28:19–20 and responding
   d. Colossians 3:8–12 and analysis

UNIT 4

Educational Psychology and Motivation

Unit 3 presented key principles from three theory systems—cognitive, humanistic, and behavioral—that govern the learning of facts, concepts, attitudes, and skills. Learning theories help us understand *how* students learn.

But what can we do to arouse interest or make the attainment of educational goals attractive? What effect do grading structures have on learning? What effect do teacher personality factors have on classroom climate? How do teacher behaviors influence the atmosphere in the classroom? How do evaluation practices help or hinder learning? These kinds of questions focus on *why* students learn. In Unit 4, we present an introduction to motivation and answer each of these key questions in four chapters.

Chapter 13: Provoking the Desire to Learn

A common misunderstanding of the idea of motivation is this: motivation is the means by which we make others do as we wish. At the heart of this understanding stands the desire to overcome the will of the follower-learner by the will of the leader-teacher. We can insist that learners be quiet, sit up straight, and look at us, but we cannot insist that they listen, or learn, or think about what we say. We can set objectives according to any system of learning, but students do not achieve our objectives simply because we set them.

Without the self-willed, internal desire of learners to listen, respond, and participate, our demands do little more than create a toxic environment for learners and learning. While it is possible to force students to do as we wish for a short time, such an approach always breeds, in the end, rebellion. Along the way, and often early on, learners simply stop learning. All true motivation comes from within the individual. The question is how to stimulate this inner motivation, so that learners choose to learn.

Out of this distinction flow several questions. Why do some students desire to learn while others do not? Why do some students persist in their efforts while others give up? Why do some students attribute their success to effort while others attribute it to luck? If our desire is to help students achieve certain learning goals, how do we energize them so that they can succeed? This chapter answers these questions by addressing motivation in six ways, employing rewards, models, curiosity, meaningfulness, friendship, and successful experiences to stimulate the efforts and achievement of learners.

Chapter 14: The Teacher and Classroom Climate

James writes, "Not many of you should presume to be teachers, my brothers, because you know that we who teach will be judged more strictly" (Jas 3:1). God holds teachers to a higher standard because we deal in human personality. Any mismanagement or misdirection of the "little ones" entrusted to our care carries heavy condemnation by the Lord (Matt 18:6; Mark 9:42; Luke 17:2). Students sitting in classrooms, under our control and management, certainly qualify as "little ones."

Classrooms where students experience a triad of clarity, warmth, and productivity find a stable climate that maximizes motivation and minimizes misbehavior. Effective teachers create such a climate; ineffective teachers do not. In this chapter, we analyze teacher variables such as personality traits, teaching behaviors and reward structures that facilitate a positive learning environment. Finally, we will view classroom climate from the perspective of the Christian teachers' triad.

Chapter 15: Measurement as Motivation: Evaluation of Learning

As far as we can gather from Scripture, Jesus never administered a formal examination. But He did evaluate His disciples. He assessed them *by their actions* when they were caught in a storm on the sea of Galilee (Matt 8:26; Mark 4:40). He assessed their *understanding* of His mission: "Who do you say that I am?" (Matt 16:15; Mark 8:29). He assessed the kingdom *values and personal devotion* of Peter when He asked him, "Do you love me?" (John 21:15ff). Although Jesus "knew what was in man" (John 2:24–25), He asked questions and posed problems to reveal what His listeners understood and believed.

There are many creative ways to evaluate learning. No doubt you have experienced portfolios, group projects, creative presentations, and the ubiquitous research paper. This chapter focuses on the area of evaluation that produces the greatest amount of sin in Christian academics: objective examinations. The material in this chapter helps us consider ways to sharpen skills in writing items, grading items, and analyzing the examinations themselves. Teaching is a process of leading learners to a specific destination. Objective evaluation, properly done, determines whether they arrived—in a fair and unbiased way.

PROVOKING THE DESIRE TO LEARN

"Christ is all and in all."
Colossians 3:11—Christ at the center of Christian motivation

"Forgive as the Lord forgave you.
Colossians 3:13 NIV—Imitative Doing

"And let the peace of the Messiah . . . control your hearts. Be thankful"
Colossians 3:15—Devoted Feeling

"Let the message . . . dwell richly among you, teaching and admonishing one another in all wisdom."
Colossians 3:16—Wise Thinking

"Why wasn't this fragrant oil sold for 300 denarii and given to the poor?" [Judas] didn't say this because he cared about the poor but because he was a thief. He was in charge of the money-bag and would steal part of what was put in it.
John 12:5–6

A man may well bring a horse to the water, but he cannot make it drink.
—John Heywood "The Proverbs of John Heywood" (1546)[1]

Chapter Rationale

All true motivation comes from within the individual. Teachers can insist that learners be quiet, sit up, and pay attention, but we cannot force them to actually listen, or learn, or think about what we say. While it may be possible to force learners to do as we wish for a short time, such an approach always breeds, in the end, rebellion. Along the way, and often early on, learners simply cease to learn.

Without the internal desire of learners to learn, teacher demands do little or nothing but create a toxic environment. The question is how to stimulate this inner motivation so that students choose to be learners.

Out of this distinction between outer force and inner desire flow several questions. Why do some students desire to learn while others do not? Why are some students persistent in their efforts while others quickly give up? Why do some students attribute their success to effort while others attribute it to luck? If our desire is to help learners achieve our goals, how do we energize them so that they can succeed? This chapter answers these questions by addressing motivation in six ways: employing rewards, models, curiosity, meaningfulness, friendship, and successful experiences to stimulate the efforts and achievement of learners.

Chapter Overview

- ➤ What Is Motivation?
- ➤ The Nature of Motivation
- ➤ The Locus of Motivation
- ➤ Motivation as Direct Reinforcement
- ➤ Motivation as Providing Appropriate Models
- ➤ Motivation as Creating Curiosity
- ➤ Motivation as Increasing Meaningfulness
- ➤ Motivation as Meeting Personal Needs
- ➤ Motivation as Providing Successful Experiences, Parts 1 and 2
- ➤ *Chapter Concepts, Chapter Objectives, Discussion Questions*

What Is Motivation?

Motivation is a "hypothetical construct used to explain the initiation, direction, intensity, and persistence of goal-directed behavior."[2] It is a force that energizes and directs behavior toward a goal."[3] It is a "directive, sustaining quality that energizes and maintains learning activities."[4] Motivation is related to Learning Theory, and shares much common ground. But they are distinct emphases. *Learning Theory* focuses on the establishment and strengthening of new behaviors, attitudes, and concepts. *Motivation* focuses on the energy, vitality, and intensity of learning, on the learner's own *intention* to learn.[5] Learning Theory emphases the learning *what*, motivation the learning *why*. Where there is proper motivation for learning, there is better achievement, better student attitudes and fewer classroom problems.[6]

The Nature of Motivation

Motivation can be general or specific. **General motivation** toward learning is an enduring and broad disposition to master a variety of learning situations. It is the kind of motivation found, for example in the "industry" pole of Erikson's "Industry-Inferiority" stage of personality development. General motivation is stable over time and situation, and resides in the learner rather than the teacher or class.

Specific motivation energizes a student toward a particular learning situation. It is unstable, changing from class to class and even from topic to topic within a given class. Specific motivation resides primarily in the teacher and the particular content to be learned.[7]

The Locus of Motivation

Motivation can be extrinsic or intrinsic. **Extrinsic motivation** is impersonal and is based on rewards that originate from outside the learner.[8] Students achieve in order to win parents' approval, or to gain the praise of their teacher, or to earn high grades.[9] Under an extrinsic system of motivation, learners are passive players. They engage in appropriate behavior only when offered attractive incentives or to avoid aversive consequences.[10] Excessive use of extrinsic motivation can make learners dependent on the rewards. When the rewards stop, so does the behavior.[11]

Intrinsic motivation is based on the personal satisfaction derived from achieving learning goals. Students achieve because of their own personal desire to learn. They enjoy the subject, or they are personally interested in mastering it.[12] Intrinsic motivation depends on the learner being an active player in learning process. Such students engage in appropriate behavior because they want to grow, and learn, and master their subjects.[13]

Both are important. Extrinsic motivation may be required to get students started in a new subject and to initially direct them down the right path.[14] Students who do not enjoy learning for learning's sake, who are not interested in a given subject, or are disadvantaged in some tangible way may need the motivational boost of external rewards to initiate their learning. If successfully tied to the quality of students' performances, these rewards can actually raise the level of their intrinsic motivation.[15]

Learning is complex—and *motivating* students to learn is complex as well, requiring a variety of motivational approaches. We will present motivation as a matter of reinforcing desired behavior (traditional behaviorism), providing appropriate models for behavior (social learning theory), creating a sense of curiosity (cognitive learning theory), making material meaningful (information processing theory), meeting personal needs (humanism), and encouraging achievement through successful experiences (aspiration and achievement theories).

Motivation as Direct Reinforcement (Traditional Behaviorism)

Traditional behaviorism emphasizes the regulation of future actions by the control of the consequences of present behavior.[16] Behaviorists look for the cues that elicit desired behaviors and the reinforcers that sustain them.[17] Behavioral motivation is extrinsic and majors on rewards that learners earn through proper behavior. Rewards include things such as specific teacher praise, "happy faces" drawn on assignments, high test scores, and so forth.[18] The cumulative consequences of past learning behaviors, called the learner's "reinforcement history,"[19] produce the learner's present level of motivation.[20]

Behavior Modification

The motivational theory which developed out of behaviorism is called **behavior modification**. Teachers select appropriate reinforcers for each student and then tie those reinforcers to desired behaviors. An appropriate reinforcer is an activity that a particular student enjoys doing: reading a book, working on a computer, talking quietly with a friend. When students successfully complete required assignments, they are rewarded by being allowed to spend time in their preferred activities.[21] Selectively using reinforcement strategies to move students toward particular goals is called **shaping**. One particular system that used reinforcers to shape behavior is called a **token economy**. Tokens or tickets were given to students for specific behaviors. These tokens were saved and exchanged for desired activities or items.[22]

The Decline of Direct Reinforcement

Direct reinforcement strategies were most popular in the 1960's. Educational theory and practice has moved away from excessive use of behavior modification strategies for several reasons. First, direct reinforcement decreased intrinsic motivation in students.[23] If a student is interested in a particular subject, providing rewards in that subject actually decreases interest. Students who were given rewards for correct solutions to problems chose less difficult problems than students who received no rewards

Motivational Dilemmas: What Would You Do?

What would you do to create a positive learning climate in each of the following dilemmas?

Situation One

Students are required to take an introductory course in mathematics as part of their degree plan. Most of the students dislike math and some admit an outright fear of the course. Your challenge is to help students overcome negative attitudes and master the course.

Situation Two

You teach a class entitled the Teaching Ministry of the Church. The aim of the class is to prepare educational ministers and pastors for the practical problems they will face when their first church calls them to serve. Since most of the students have little or no local church staff experience, they have difficulty understanding the problems they will face. Your challenge is to make the suggestions you give credible and "real world."

Situation Three

Your Baptist History course requires a hundred pages of reading a week. Your lectures "augment," rather than explain, what students read. By mid semester, many in the class have fallen behind, and frustration is growing. The midterm examination is fast approaching. Your challenge is to relieve the distress and re-energize their learning.

Situation Four

A median adult class gathers to study the story of the Good Samaritan. As you enter the classroom you overhear one of the members sarcastically remark to another, "Again? The Good Samaritan story? (sarcastically) I can't wait!" Several folks laugh in agreement. Your challenge is to engage them in a meaningful study of the passage.

Situation Five

You are teaching a class in introductory Hebrew. Most of your students have no background in the language. The curious alphabet, the unfamiliar grammar, even reading from right to left have students nervous.

at all. Worse yet, giving rewards simply for completing an assignment, rather than meeting some standard of performance, resulted in decreased motivation.[24]

Second, educators found that direct reinforcement narrowed student focus in the learning process. Interesting class discussions were short-circuited by the simple question, "Will this be on the test?" Rewards gained through "passing a test" became more important than learning.[25] Other types of motivation were sought to broaden the learning spectrum.

Third, the logistical problems associated with selecting, using and tracking reinforcers for each student became an administrative burden. Token economies were developed to help ease the burden, but eventually the system was discarded as too tedious and time consuming.[26]

Fourth, and most important, is the fact that direct reinforcement ignored important aspects of learning. These overlooked aspects were the perceptions and beliefs of students.[27] The rise of Bruner's discovery learning and information processing theory moved educators away from behavior modification systems of motivation.

Suggestions for Using Behavioral Principles

Direct reinforcement is effective in motivating behavior in disadvantaged learners as well as in students who are not intrinsically interested in the subject at hand. By clearly explaining course requirements and expectations you set up specific targets for students to hit. Using frequent, consistent, specific and immediate reinforcement will direct students toward achieving course skills.[28] Praising student achievements appropriately increases their level of effort.[29] Encouraging student efforts for completing course tasks increases their expectation of success.[30] By engaging student attention on specific course tasks and providing successful class experiences through the semester, not only will many of your students master the required skills, but they will also develop positive feelings about you, the subject and themselves.

Teacher Praise

Research demonstrated that the most effective reinforcer is teacher praise. Praise is more than objective feedback on performance. It also provides information on the student's personal worth. This last element is a powerful motivator.[31]

But praising students effectively is a complex skill. Praise should be contingent on specific tasks[32] because random or indiscriminate praise is ineffective.[33] Praise should be given in moderation because too little is ineffective and too much is meaningless.[34] Praise should be perceived as credible, believable and sincere. Praise should provide informative feedback and not simply be warm and fuzzy positive reactions.[35] Praise should focus on student performances and not teacher perceptions.[36] Praise should be given for student performance and not mere participation.[37] Praise should be individual—that is, not given to everyone all the time.[38] Use prior performances as a benchmark for a student's improvement rather than the performance of peers.[39]

Situation One Revisited

Students are required to take an introductory course in mathematics as part of their degree plan. Most of the students dislike math and some admit an outright fear of the course.

The course is required. Students enroll because someone in power determined the course is "good for them." Strike one. Most students—especially ministerial students—dislike math as a subject. Most disliked courses they took in high school, and some entered the ministry because they were sure to escape "the dreaded maths." Strike two. Some are afraid of this particular course because their friends have told them how hard the material is, and now unfair the teacher is. The first is an exaggeration and the second is untrue. But the gathering students do not know this. Strike three. How would direct reinforcement be effective in motivating students to master the course content?

Direct reinforcement of specific behaviors helps students focus on completing specific tasks for a specific reward, usually a grade. Complex reinforcement schedules, popular in the 1960's, have given way to other approaches to motivation. Teacher praise, however, remains a powerful reinforcer.

Provide students a proper foundation for the course. Overview the various units of study and why they are important to the subject, and more, why they will be helpful in future studies and ministry. Provide small, frequent assignments, which can be graded and returned quickly. Begin simply so that all students can complete them correctly and receive maximum positive reward. Beyond good grades, use specific praise to reinforce individual performance. This works best *outside of class*, either as personal e-mails or when meeting students on campus. When students ask good questions, compliment the questions—"that's a good question!"—before answering it, reinforcing questioning behaviors. When students ask bad questions, avoid criticism of student and question. Simply ask for a clarification—"I don't quite understand your question. Would you ask it again, please?" Never treat student questions as interruptions. Never display frustration over requests for more explanation, or for repeating an explanation. Welcome these as signs of interest in learning. If time is a factor, welcome students to stay after class and ask their questions.

Assignment by assignment, question by question, explanation by explanation, help students understand and use correctly the math skills you teach. As the semester progresses, assignments can become longer and less frequent, helping to strengthen self-motivated behaviors such as distributing work over time and meeting deadlines.

Discipline in the Class: Step by Step

Principle one: The teacher is the leader of the class, and sets the boundaries for behavior.

Principle two: Clearly establish class rules on the first day of class.

Principle three: Begin disciplinary interventions softly and escalate only if the misbehavior continues.

You notice that two students are talking to each other in whispers while you are making explanations of the day's material. What will you do? Consider the following incremental steps.

1. Non-verbal intervention. We can often correct minor misbehaviors by gentle, unspoken actions.

   a. Ignore the whispering. Students may be talking about the material. One may be explaining something to the other. The whispering may stop in a moment or two without any intervention. (But whispering continues.)

   b. While continuing your explanations, look at the students. One of the students will soon see you are looking at them, and stop whispering. (The whispering may soon begin again).

   c. While continuing your explanations, catch the eye of the whispering students and gently shake your finger or head "no." (Students stop but may start again).

   d. While continuing your explanations, physically move toward the whisperers. (Whispering stops. By this point, most students will have gotten the message to stop their whispering, without any words being spoken. If the whispering continues . . . .)

   e. While continuing your explanations, stand next to the whisperers. (Continues?)

   f. If whispering continues, (and the students are children or youth), gently touch or pat the shoulder of one of the students. (Continues?)

2. Verbal interventions. When non-verbal approaches fail to control the misbehavior of learners, teachers intervene verbally.

   a. Ask one of the whispering students a question about the topic. Many times the student will not be able to answer, because he/she has not been paying attention. This causes mild humiliation, brought about by his/her own misbehavior. Most students will stop whispering and pay closer attention. (Students continue to whisper sporadically?)

b. Directly confront the students with a question: "John, Jimmy – do you know you two are whispering to each other? (Of course they know, but now the teacher has focused the class' attention on their whispering. Students stop for a while, but soon continue.)

c. Direct the students to proper behavior. "John and Jimmy, please, listen.» (They stop for a moment but then continue.)

d. Directly correct the misbehavior. "John and Jimmy, stop whispering." (They continue to whisper sporadically.) There is little more we can do verbally than directly require silence from the students. Ninety-nine percent of misbehavior will have stopped by this time. If the behavior continues, it reflects overt rebellion. If allowed to continue, the rebellion will spread, and misbehavior will increase. Interventions must now move from verbal to physical.

3. Logical Consequences. Bad behavior must result in negative consequences for the misbehavers. These negative consequences have been signals and verbal directions to this point. Now teachers take physical steps to end the misbehavior. The general principle is this: "Students have a choice: obey or you will suffer the consequences."

a. "John, if you continue to talk to Jimmy, I will move you to the back of the room." Continue your remarks to the class without a direct confrontation. (John continues to whisper to Jimmy.)

b. "John, since you have chosen to continue whispering, move yourself and your things to the back of the room." (John has lost the option to simply stop whispering. He must now move. He does not move.)

c. "John, either move to the back of the room now, or you and I will stay after class to discuss your behavior. Move there now, please." (Wait for John to move. He doesn't.)

d. "John, you have one more opportunity to do the right thing. Move to the back, or we will have a meeting with (your parents, the principal, the pastor, the director of camp – whoever is the most appropriate authority in your situation). You decide."

Even if John refuses to move, his whispering behavior will have long since stopped. We have moved John in the right direction, but he has revealed that his bad behavior is part of a larger problem. We have connected his bad actions with negative consequences. John has chosen the negative consequences. Ultimately, John can lose the privilege of being in the class through his insistence on misbehaving.

For all but the most obstinate students, these behavioral measures will prompt engagement with the subject. Engagement begets understanding, and understanding begets confidence. "Love for math" may be an unrealistic expectation in this situation, but the majority of learners will achieve success, and that is a major victory.

Motivation as Providing Appropriate Models (Albert Bandura's Social Learning Theory)

Some behaviorists found direct reinforcement too limited an explanation for learning.[40] While behavioral purists have held on to traditional behaviorism, most have integrated cognitive processes[41] that cannot be directly observed—expectations, thoughts, and beliefs.[42]

As we saw in Chapter Seven, Bandura used the term reinforcement for his fourth stage of learning, but his definition was broader than Skinner's. He went beyond Skinner's **direct reinforcement**—an observer watches a model's behavior, imitates the behavior, and is directly reinforced or punished for the action[43]—to include a second type, called **vicarious reinforcement**.[44]

Vicarious reinforcement emphasizes the *consequences to the model* rather than the observer. An observer watches a model's behavior, and further observes how the model is rewarded or punished for that behavior.[45] If the model is rewarded, the observer tends to imitate the behavior. If the model is punished, the observer tends to avoid that behavior. Vicarious reinforcement—the heart of Social Learning Theory—allows observers to learn from the consequences of others' behavior.[46] A great deal of classroom reinforcement is vicarious.[47] Praising one student for asking a good question encourages others to ask good questions.[48]

The contagious spreading of behaviors in a group, whether the behaviors are good or bad, by means of imitation is called the **ripple effect**.[49] The fact is that many of our most persistent habits and attitudes[50] result from simply watching and thinking about the actions of others.[51] We can learn complex behavior with a single observation without cuing or reinforcement.[52]

In general, then, students are prompted to master desired skills when they observe others modeling the mastery of those skills.[53] Teachers are effective models of new behaviors as they demonstrate, clearly and systematically, the skills under study. We do this by focusing attention on critical elements of the skill. We think aloud as we consider student questions.[54] We use step-by-step demonstrations, explaining each step along the way. We contrast good and bad examples of the skills.[55]

Students who break rules, misbehave, submit work late, or engage in other inappropriate behavior will encourage others to do the same, unless their behavior is corrected. A warm but firm reprimand of those who misbehave will decrease misbehavior by others. We do well to begin softly, moving to stricter measures only if students continue their misbehavior. See the "Discipline" text box in the last section for details. There the focus was on direct consequences on the misbehavers. Here, the focus is on the impact of consequences on the rest of the class, who merely observe the corrections of misbehavers (see p. 431).

Students refrain from asking questions in our classes when they observe other students reprimanded (in other classes) for "asking dumb questions." We overcome this inhibition by encouraging students intentionally to ask questions. I assure my students—especially in my hardest classes—that "there is no such thing as a dumb question," so long as it is an *honest* question. I receive every question with patience, and reward it with as much explanation as necessary. We also soften this inhibition by giving appropriate praise for questions asked. "Good question," I often say.

I encourage students to ask questions because their questions help me see where they need further explanation. The Ripple Effect insures that praise of one question encourages others. Monologue turns to dialog, and learning improves.

Teachers are, by our natural position in the classroom, influential and accessible as role models for students. We have high status in the classroom at the beginning, simply because we are in charge of the classroom.[56] We strengthen our influence as models by demonstrated competence—making clear presentations, highlighting key ideas, answering questions, creating a sense of relevance for our subjects. We maintain student attention by the use novelty and surprise.[57] We help change student behaviors by focusing attention on critical aspects of desired behaviors.[58]

Teachers do more than model proper behaviors. Through our interactions with students, we model personal traits (honesty, fairness), personal values and beliefs (life, justice, love), and personal mastery of academic skills, such as problem-solving and creative thinking.[59]

Situation Two Revisited

You teach a class entitled the Teaching Ministry of the Church. The aim of the class is to prepare educational ministers and pastors for the practical problems they will face when their first church calls them as a minister. Since most of the students have little or no local church staff experience, they have difficulty understanding the problems they will face. Your challenge is to make the answers you give credible and "real world." How might you apply principles of Social Learning Theory to enhance the real world emphasis of this course?

Provide the students with "real world" role models. The most effective role models are the teachers themselves, if in fact they have been successful educational ministers. Weaving personal experiences of success and failure into the recitation of program principles and ministry guidelines makes the course material resound with reality. These stories are most effective during the early years of a professor's tenure when personal experiences are relevant and timely. Unless the professor lives a dual life of teacher/local church minister, personal experiences become quickly dated.

Provide students with "real world" models from regional churches. Invite educational ministers and pastors into the classroom to discuss course topics in light of their own ministerial experiences. Insure relevancy to course themes by meeting with these ministerial models ahead of time to discuss major topics and specific areas to address. Well-meaning visitors can damage our credibility by promoting approaches to ministry inconsistent with material in the course.[60]

Secure a list of model churches in the area and engage pastors and staff ministers as mentors for student groups to visit, interview, and question. Provide model questions to students and mentors, so that students connect course material and "real world" church work in the interviews and observations. Provide time for students to report their findings in class, thereby sharing the small group experiences with the class as a whole. Secure models and model behaviors from printed publications,[61] and assign these resources for students to read and analyze.

Theoretical solutions are, by definition, general. The principles we teach in our classes, based on our personal experiences, are both abstract and obsolete. They are abstract in that they illustrate general themes. They are obsolete in that they point to past realities—the longer we teach, the more obsolete our experiences.[62] Contemporary role models, in person or in print, provide relevant, tangible illustrations for timeless truths.

Motivation as Creating Curiosity (Cognitive Learning Theories)

We saw in Chapters Eight and Nine that Cognitive Learning Theory is concerned with how we know, think and remember.[63] Basic to cognitive theories is the idea that *thought processes* control behavior.[64] In Chapter Four, we introduced you to Jean Piaget and his concept of equilibration. Equilibration is the *natural tendency to maintain a balance* between what one already knows, the cognitive network, and what one experiences in the world.[65] When this balance is disturbed—that is, when we experience something that does not fit what we know—we experience anxiety, discomfort, or confusion. Piaget called this confusion **disequilibrium**.[66] The discomfort caused by disequilibrium compels us to reduce the disequilibrium by restoring the balance, or *equilibrium*, between our understanding of the world and experiences in the world. Piaget called the process of restoring equilibrium **equilibration**.[67]

Cognitive theorists see motivation in terms of creating disequilibrium—more commonly known as curiosity—in the minds of learners. Specific suggestions were made in Chapter Four for cognitive teaching which are, themselves, motivational. The tension created by optimal discrepancy prompts the mind to probe new territory without anger or fear. Direct experience raises rational questions as learners try out new ways of seeing the world. Social interaction prompts questions as learners struggle with differing viewpoints in the group. Thought-provoking questions challenge unexamined positions by pitting one concept against another ("Must we *like* the enemies Jesus commands us to *love*?" If students say "yes," then their definition of love is wrong). Problem-solving activities confront learners with dilemmas that call for creative thought and practical application of theory. The use of open-ended questions can create a sense of surprise, or provoke discussion, or provide contradictory points of view, or prompt student discovery.[68]

Situation Three Revisited

A Baptist History course requires a hundred pages of difficult reading a week and the lectures "augment," rather than explain, what students read. They are falling farther behind and becoming frustrated. How might we apply cognitive learning principles to enhance this classroom environment?

Along with the long reading assignments, assign thought-provoking questions that have contemporary significance, but which the readings answer. The questions provide a rational framework for processing the reading. Such structure provides a direction for thinking, and motivates focused attention on the text.

Have students write out one personal experience they have had in their lives which reflects the Baptist history themes they are reading. Have students share these personal experiences in class as illustrations of the reading.

Break students into groups of 4–5 to discuss the major themes of the readings. More knowledgeable students will teach the less knowledgeable, which will help both. The social interaction of students around the reading will highlight major themes. Holding students individually accountable for the reading, through exams for example, will minimize the tendency of some to ignore the reading assignments and depend on the group to do their work for them.

Thoughtfully consider whether 100 pages of reading per week is a reasonable requirement, given the other courses students are required to take. Such assignments can be so general, so arbitrary, that they are meaningless. Consider whether fewer pages of targeted reading might produce better results. Structure lectures to augment what students read. Use question and answer techniques to draw out students' views from the reading, and then extend that understanding with new material. Focus more on reinforcing clear concepts from Baptist History, and less on the number of pages read by students. As history is conceptualized, and applications are made to contemporary problems, students will grow in their desire to read more.

Motivation as Increasing Meaningfulness (Information Processing Theory)

Organization, according to Piaget, is the *natural tendency* to make sense of experiences by integrating them into cognitive structures that are logically related.[69] This natural tendency to make sense of the world is the cognitive definition of motivation.[70] We saw in Chapter Nine that information processing theory focuses on how humans process information from the environment through sensory registers and short-term memory, in order to store it in long-term memory. We suggested several ways to approach motivation from this perspective. Attract and hold attention with attractive displays, voice changes, or simple diagrams. Encourage students' thinking about their own learning. Teach students how to learn in order to place more control in the hands of students. Organize presentations with outlines, flow charts, advance organizers and the like to provide information in a pre-processed form. Avoid confusion and information overload since they undermine motivation. Use elaboration to increase meaningfulness. Do this by building on previous learning, relating new material to old, and asking questions that require comparisons, relationships and patterns. Use analogies and illustrations to make explanations more clear. Teach students how to use mnemonic devices to make learning tedious material more enjoyable. Provide clear expectations for conceptual retrieval so that learners know what they must remember. Teach students the skills of self-questioning and productive note-taking, which increases their probability for success.

Situation Four Revisited

A median adult class gathers to study the story of the Good Samaritan. As you enter the classroom you overhear one of the members sarcastically remark, "Oh boy, the Good Samaritan story again. I can't wait!" Several folks laugh in agreement. How might you apply information processing principles to enhance this classroom environment?

Obviously some of the class members are so familiar with the story that it has lost its meaningfulness. It is essential to gain the attention of the class in a creative way. Rather than reading the overly familiar story, ask class members to define the term "Good Samaritan" by way of someone who has been a Good Samaritan to them. What did they do? What was their attitude while doing it? How helpful were they? What was your reaction? How do you suspect their actions affected them?

Elaborate the shared experiences by connecting them with characteristics in the text. Tie personal experiences in the class with the biblical story. Ask open-ended questions regarding the text, drawing on previous studies the students have had. Be ready with clear explanations of themes in the story, but focus on drawing out the viewpoints of class members. Ask members, "To whom have you been a

Good Samaritan?" Elaborate on their stories by asking questions. What did they do? Why did they help? What was the reaction of the one helped? What was the impact of helping on you? Summarize key ideas toward the end of the lesson, and close with an open prayer time focused on helping "each of us seek out situations in which we can be Good Samaritans to others." Spend a few minutes the following week asking members to share their "Good Samaritan" attempts.

Motivation as Meeting Personal Needs (Humanistic Perspectives)

Humanistic learning theories, as we discussed in Chapter Ten, have disappeared from contemporary texts. Not so with humanistic approaches to motivation. The emphasis on the autonomy, dignity, worth of the self,[71] and personal growth[72] of the student lives on under other names. The basis for humanistic motivation is the learner's self-concept and how the school contributes to that self-concept.[73] Humanist pioneer Arthur Combs wrote (1962) "People are always motivated; in fact, they are never unmotivated. They may not be motivated to do what we would prefer they do, but it can never be truly said they are unmotivated."[74] While this is certainly true, it is unhelpful for those who wish to secure motivation in particular learners at particular times for particular learning tasks. Would such a "narrow" focus be considered too repressive for a truly humane environment?

The key to motivation for the humanistic founders was to allow learners freedom to choose what they desired to learn. Abraham Maslow believed that all human beings have an innate drive for self-actualization, defined as the unfolding and fulfillment of one's personal potential. The unfolding process draws its energy from the satisfaction of physical, social, emotional, and intellectual needs.[75] Maslow proposed a "Hierarchy of Needs" as his description of how persons move toward fulfillment.[76]

The Hierarchy of Needs consists of seven levels. Maslow called the first four levels **deficiency needs**. Until these personal needs are satisfied, learners have little or no motivation to learn. The four levels are *survival, safety, belonging and love,* and *self-esteem.* He called the higher levels **growth needs**. These include *knowing and understanding, aesthetic appreciation, self-actualization,*[77] *and transcendence.*[78] These higher needs, unlike the lower deficiency needs, are never satisfied, but rather expand as people grow.[79]

Deficiency Needs

Survival, or physiological, needs refer to one's immediate existence. Without shelter, physical warmth, sufficient food and water, or sleep, persons seek little else. Motivation to learn is swallowed by the desire to live. When basic life needs are adequately satisfied, then one is free to consider the next level.

Safety needs refer to one's present environment. Without a sense of security, order, and some degree of predictability in the immediate surroundings, persons seek little else. Motivation to learn is swallowed by the desire to secure psychological safety. When personal safety is to some degree secured, then one is free to consider the third level.

Belonging and love needs refer to one's social environment. Without love and acceptance from family, friends, teachers, and classmates, absent a sense of being wanted by others, lacking relationships with others, persons seek little else. Motivation to learn is swallowed by the desire to be accepted. When community has been to some degree secured, then one is free to consider the fourth level.

The need of **Self-esteem** refers to one's acceptance of self. Without some sense of self-respect or personal competence, absent a sense of social status, lacking recognition and approval, persons seek little else. Motivation to learn is swallowed by the desire for being. Some writers prefer to think of self-esteem as a growth rather than a deficiency need.[80]

Hunger, sexual and physical abuse, rejection, and a sense of inferiority defeat the best efforts of teachers to engage learners in work, thought, or group interaction. Survival, safety, belonging, self-worth—until these person-focused needs are sufficiently met, there is little desire for learning or growth. When they are adequately satisfied, learners are ready to grow, and are free to move to the fifth level.

Growth Needs

The need for **intellectual achievement** refers to the desire to know how to do things, and to understand the meanings of things, events, and symbols. This need is never satisfied: the capacity to learn objectively, to know and understand the surrounding reality of the world, expands as learners grow rationally. Knowing begets a greater desire to know, and understanding a greater desire for understanding, so long as the deficiency needs remain satisfied. In the process of intellectual growth, one is free to consider the sixth level.

The need of **aesthetic appreciation** refers to the desire to experience beauty, order, truth, justice, and goodness in the world and in one's personal experience. This need is never satisfied: the capacity to learn subjectively, to appreciate and value the surrounding beauty of the world, expands as learners grow affectively. Experiencing justice and goodness begets a greater desire to experience justice and goodness, and appreciating the arts—music, literature, painting—a greater desire for the arts, so long as the deficiency needs remain satisfied. In the process of affective growth, one is free to consider the seventh level.

The need for **self-actualization** refers to the desire to develop one's talents, capacities, and potential. It is, according to Maslow, "the desire to become everything that one is capable of becoming." Characteristics of the self-actualized person include such things as acceptance of self and others, spontaneity, openness, democratic relations with others, creativity, positive humor, and independence. Self-actualized individuals appreciate natural events—the beauty of a sunrise or a splash of daffodils—more intensely than others do. These occasional intense experiences, which Maslow called "peak experiences," produce profound changes that "involve a momentary loss of self and feelings of transcendence . . . the feeling of limitless horizons opening up and of being simultaneously very powerful, yet weak."[81]

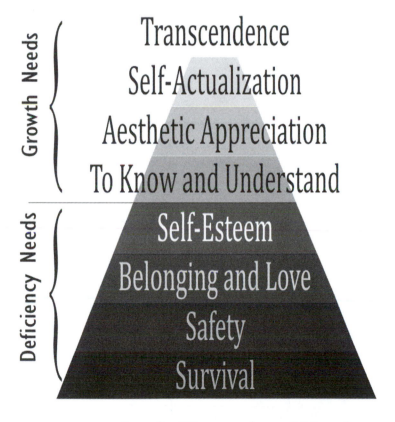

Maslow's Hierarchy of Needs

Maslow refined his views on peak experiences and, in 1968, added an eighth level to the Hierarchy of Needs. **Transcendence** refers rather vaguely to the "spiritual need for broader cosmic identification."[83] Hamachek suggests this eighth stage is "an important addition," because it is "consistent with what the religions of the world have always talked about."[84] This may be so, but secular theorists rarely confuse human psychology with religion, and never with biblical faith.

Self-actualizing **Non-Transcenders** Stage 7	Self-actualizing **Transcenders** Stage 8
Practical Doers	**Cosmic Dreamers**[82]
Actualize capabilities within Self	**Actualize beyond Self** **Family** **Community** **World**
Intense personal experiences are important	**Peak experiences are highest priority** **Intense interest in beauty** **Hunger for becoming more** **Striving toward Being** *Perfection, Goodness, Truth, Unity*
Loveable	**Loveable** **but more likely to be** **Awe-inspiring** **Revered** **Considered "great"**

The chart above depicts Maslow's attempt to distinguish between characteristics of transcending and non-transcending self-actualized adults.[85] In time, Maslow himself became confused by the overlapping, abstract distinctions made between Levels Seven and Eight. He eventually gave up the attempt to squeeze spiritual reality out of naturalistic humanity, lamenting before he died, "It is unfortunate that I can no longer be theoretically neat at this level."[86]

The Mockery of Secular Transcendence

Secularists emphasize self-awareness, the expansion of personal human qualities, and the embrace of subjective realities in the natural world. Human beings discover and develop Inner Being by moving beyond Self to others and abstracts. The goal is to become whomever we choose to be.

The matter of transcendence in old age is quite puzzling. Why would secular thinkers encourage "formation of spirit" just prior to death and the end of existence? Why theorize ways to help senior adults develop beyond self-actualization—"having become all they were meant to be"—to a vague eighth level of Being, when they soon will not be? How can such theoretical propositions be helpful to senior adults? These propositions merely impose another standard against which they can fail, just before they cease to exist. There comes a time in the natural span of life that reality mocks the theoretically positive stages of such developmental theories. To add an abstract "cosmic" level to this secular reality merely twists the mockery into something quite ugly. Might this explain why recent texts[87] exclude both Maslow's "transcendence" and Erikson's "gerotranscendence" (Chapter Three). **These concepts have simply not been accepted by mainstream educational psychologists.**

One could claim this is due to the school-age focus of the textbooks. But since the books include the entire range of the original stages—which obviously extend beyond school age—this claim falls to the ground. It is more likely that secular writers consider conceptions of transcendence, even as defined by a fellow secularist, irrelevant to secular educational theory.

Fortunately, the depressing juxtaposition of transcendence and death does not plague evangelical Christians. More than *self*-awareness, Christians emphasize *God*-awareness and find meaning for self in the One Who made us. Rather than emphasizing *personal, self-centered* human abilities, Christians emphasize the expansion of *Spirit-given and Spirit-quickened capabilities* (head, heart, and hand) through union with God through Christ. Rather than embracing *subjective realities* in an idealized world of goodness, Christians embrace the *Objective Reality* of the Holy Spirit, Who is working in us and the world as it is. The goal is to make us more like Christ. These distinctions are critical for Christian teachers.

An Evangelical Christian View of Transcendence

Alfred Edershiem, a profound nineteenth-century Jewish-Christian scholar, writing in 1886, gives us a very different view of spiritual formation from that of secular humanists. ". . .there must be work to do for Christ, for which the **preparation is in this life** by faithful application for Him of what He has entrusted to us—be it much or little. This gives quite a new and blessed meaning to **the life that now is**—as most truly and in all its aspects part of **that into which it is to unfold.**"[88]

Dallas Willard, writing in 1997, mirrors the theme as he describes the life-after-death we spend our lives preparing for:

> We will not sit around looking at one another or at God for eternity but will join the eternal Logos, "reign with Him," in the endlessly ongoing creative work of God. It is for this that we were each individually intended, as both kings and priests (see Exod 19:6; Rev 5:10).

> Thus, our faithfulness over a "few things" in the **present phase of our life** develops the kind of character that can be entrusted *[in the future, after death—RY]* with "many things" . . . **His plan is for us to take our place in the ongoing creativity of the universe.**[89]

Evangelicals see growth here and now as having eternal consequences for life there and then. This places far greater importance on spiritual development in senior adults since physical death is not the end—there is an eternal existence for which to develop. The continued *becoming* and *on-going re-definition of reality* postulated by Lars Tornstam **only has meaning if we move from physical existence to spiritual existence at death.** Jesus Himself made this clear in His parable of the Talents:

"His master said to him, 'Well done, good and faithful slave! You were faithful over a few things; I will put you in charge of many things. Share your master's joy!'" (Matt 25:21).

And again in the parable of the Returning King:

"'Well done, good slave!' he told him. 'Because you have been faithful in a very small matter, have authority over 10 towns'" (Luke 19:17).

In both parables, Jesus referred to His own future return, and the future reign with Him of His followers. There is within the human heart an innate desire for life after death. We see it in Egyptian burial rituals: mummification, and the provision of foods and tools for the afterlife. We see it in Norse rituals, as they place provisions in funeral boats along with the dead—which are then set afire and pushed out to sea. We see it in the burial mounds of England. The question comes to us naturally, "What will become of us?" As Willard points out, all of this "touches on a general human need, built into our nature as intelligent, active beings. . . . Human life and consciousness require, by its very nature, a projected future."[90]

It is *in that projected future* we find the fulfillment of "in charge of many things" and "have authority over 10 towns" of Jesus' parables. *In that projected future*, we live out the transcendent personality we have developed in union with Christ, walking with Him here.

Spiritual formation for senior adults is not a matter of meetings, or services, or studies. While these activities may be helpful, growth of Spirit does not come by repeated attempts, in our own strength, to carry out what Christ said long ago. C. S. Lewis, a Christian apologist-philosopher of

Erikson's era, writes, "The real Son of God is at your side. He is beginning to turn you into the same kind of thing as Himself. He is beginning, so to speak, to 'inject' His kind of life and thought, His *Zoe* (spiritual life), into you; beginning to turn the tin soldier into a live man. The part of you that does not like it is the part that is still tin."[91]

Spirituality for the evangelical Christian is not a matter of becoming more religious (that is, doing more religious things), but rather is a matter of developing as a citizen in the kingdom of God. "That senior adults are coming to the end of their life, 'life in the flesh,' is of little significance. What is significant is the kind of person they have become."[92]

Space does not permit an extensive discussion of the process, but it is perhaps instructive to list briefly Willard's five dimensions of the "eternal kind of life" we have been defining. Willard does not use the term *Christian transcender* in his descriptions, but we use the term to contrast evangelical Christian transcendence and the secular constructs of Maslow.

1. Confidence and Reliance on Jesus. Christian transcenders have complete confidence in and reliance upon Jesus as the One appointed to save them. This confidence is not mere intellectual assent to religious dogma, but rather a true manifestation of "life from above." It is not a normal human capacity.

2. Apprentices of Jesus. Christian transcenders have a desire to be apprentices of Jesus ("All of you, take up My yoke and learn from Me," [Matt 11:29] living in the kingdom of God, putting His teachings into practice, and integrating their entire existence into the "glorious world of eternal living."[93]

3. Obedience and Love. Christian transcenders experience abundant inner life through apprenticeship to Jesus, which leads to obedience. The teaching we have received and our experience of living it brings us to love the Lord with our whole being: heart, soul, mind, and strength. The love of Jesus sustains us through continued discipline and makes obedience possible.

4. Inner Transformation. Christian transcenders, having been obedient and in turn loved, experience the pervasive inner transformation of the heart and soul. Genuine characteristics of self-giving love, joy unhampered by external circumstances, inner peace undisturbed by surrounding conflicts, patience in the face of trying circumstances, (as well as kindness, goodness, faith, meekness, and self-control) become real in their deepest core. These qualities are called "fruit of the Spirit" because they are not direct effects of our own efforts to produce them, but grow indirectly as we admire and emulate Jesus and do whatever is necessary to learn how to obey Him.

5. Experience Power. Christian transcenders, being transformed in heart and soul, experience power to do the works of God's kingdom. Such power is dangerous, since it can lead to a sense of spiritual superiority. Great power requires great character if it is to be a blessing rather than a curse, and that character is something Christian transcenders can only grow toward.[94]

Of course, such an expansion of heart, mind, and soul makes little sense if life ends at death, that is, if the transcender's existence is extinguished. But to those who have within them the confident hope of life eternal, the construction of a framework for continued spiritual formation for adults, even senior adults, in preparation for even greater work in a continuing kingdom existence—"training for reigning"—is a blessing indeed. This is not mere idle speculation or wishful thinking. Two recent studies (2005) found evidence that senior adults make just this kind of progress toward biblical transcendence in tangible, practical ways.[95]

Motivation by Satisfying Needs of Becoming and Being

The hierarchy of needs model is helpful in the educational process, whether teachers are secular or Christian. Teachers do well to help students satisfy their deficiency needs. Fatigue, hunger, and abuse diminish the desire of students to learn. If there are threats of embarrassment or humiliation in the class, achievement will suffer.[96] Avoid head-to-head competition among students[97] as a means to motivate greater excellence. Excessive competition rewards a few advantaged students but punishes many more "weaker students" who experience ongoing failure. (Consider the connection with "Industry—Inferiority," Chapter Three).

Be conscious of self-esteem factors in the classroom.[98] Take advantage of student interests.[99] Promote feelings of success by making appropriate assignments, providing positive feedback on effort, and giving credible rewards.[100] Display a caring attitude toward students.[101] Personalize the content so that students can integrate it into their own experiences.[102] Help students set their own goals.[103] Provide alternative learning activities from which students can choose.[104] Provide a safe, supportive classroom climate. Set high, but attainable, standards.[105]

Situation Five Revisited

You are teaching a class in introductory Hebrew. Most of your students have no background in the language. The curious alphabet, the unfamiliar grammar, even reading from right to left have students nervous.

Any time we stand before a group of students with an unfamiliar and potentially frightening subject to teach, we do well to create a climate of safety for them. A course syllabus helps reduce anxiety of the unknown by explaining teacher expectations and providing assignment due dates and guidelines. Examination objectives provide learners a tangible way to direct efforts and focus study time for success.

Teacher availability to answer questions by office visit, or Internet—and certainly within the class sessions themselves—provides a sense of belonging. Create a course grading structure that allows students to earn grades by the work they, individually, do. Do not force students to compete for a limited number of high grades. Avoid comments and critiques that humiliate or embarrass learners, whether in public or private. Discuss individual poor performance on assignments and tests in private. Suggest ways students can improve their study and achievement. Provide a selection of passages that teach similar forms of Hebrew grammar and allow students to choose which passages to study.

Choose Hebrew Bible passages for translation that teach biblical truths that are personally relevant to contemporary students. Connect Hebrew texts to parallel New Testament passages. Structure the course so that students experience personal success as they apply themselves to the study of Hebrew. Show students you care about them, and want to help them even when they fail in learning tasks. Support their efforts generally by course structure, and individually by specific attention to their progress in the course.

Teachers do well to befriend their students appropriately,[106] especially when teaching difficult subjects. The sense that teacher and student are in the process together warms student hearts and motivates higher levels of effort.

Motivation as Providing Successful Experiences Part 1 (Achievement Theories)

H. A. Murray (1938) defined achievement motivation as the "need to accomplish something difficult, to excel oneself, to rival oneself and others."[107] People who have a high achievement need strive for excellence for the *sake of achieving* and not for a reward.[108] John Atkinson (1964) proposed a theory of achievement motivation. His research classified students as **success-oriented** or **anxiety-ridden**. Success-oriented students are motivated to achieve without the need of external rewards. They are success-seekers. Anxiety-ridden students are motivated to avoid failure and therefore are hesitant to take risks. They are failure-avoiders. Families and cultures support the development of achievement motivation by encouraging autonomy, initiative, and industry (Erikson, Stages 2, 3, and 4) where parents and teachers do not criticize failures, but help children to solve problems on their own.[109] These differences are summarized below.[110]

A **second type** of achievement motivation emphasizes the reasons learners give for their experiences of success and failure.[111] *To what* do learners *attribute* their success or failure? This aspect of achievement motivation is called **Attribution Theory**.

	Success Seekers	Failure Avoiders
History of . . .	Success	Failure
Self-confidence	High	Low
Success	High	Low
Locus of control	Self-reinforcement	Praise and approval of others
Goals Set	Moderate difficulty*	Difficulty too high or too low**
Source of failure	Lack of effort	Lack of ability
Result of Failure	Increases future efforts	Decreases future efforts
Outcomes of success and failure	*Intermediate goals challenge success-seekers, but offer a high probability of success. The challenge makes success satisfying. Success reinforces future efforts.	**High goals excuse failure, because task was too difficult. Achieving low goals is unrewarding, because the task was too easy. Blame for failure is avoided on the one hand, but pride in achievement is lost on the other.

Motivation as Providing Successful Experiences Part 2 (Weiner's Attribution Theory)

Attribution theory is an attempt to describe systematically student explanations for their successes and failures in the classroom.[112] Student attributions affect the level of motivation for future tasks. Bernard Weiner has done extensive study in attribution theory.[113] His model emphasizes two dimensions of attribution: *stability* and *locus of* control.[114] Under these dimensions, he suggests four attributions: ability, effort, task difficulty, and luck.[115] The two dimensions and four attributions are shown at left.

Stability refers to the *durability* of attributions. **Stable** attributions of success or failure remain consistent over time. Ability and difficulty are stable over time. The *ability* of learners changes slowly, developing gradually over time. The level of task *difficulty* is relatively similar for a given course of study.

Unstable attributions change from task to task. Personal *effort* changes from task to task, depending on personal circumstances and choices. The *luck* of studying the appropriate material

	Stability	
	Stable	Unstable
Internal	Ability	Effort
External	Difficulty	Luck

Locus of Control

for a given examination changes from exam to exam. A sense of luck is more likely when teachers neglect giving students study guidelines, leaving their preparation to guesswork.

Locus of control refers to the source of success or failure in a given situation. An **internal** locus perceives the control of success or failure as being the students themselves. Students determine their own *ability* over time. Students determine personal study *effort* for each and every task.

An **external** locus perceives the control of success or failure as belonging to the circumstances of task. The *difficulty* of the task is determined by teachers, and *luck* determines whether student guesswork matches the actual test questions. Both are beyond the students' control to determine whether their efforts are sufficient for success.[116]

Stability

Locus of Control	Stable	Unstable
Internal	I'm bad at statistics! *Ability*	I didn't study enough! *Effort*
External	That was a tough test! *Difficulty*	I guessed wrong on what to study! *Luck*

Failure Attributions

Stability

Locus of Control	Stable	Unstable
Internal	I'm good at statistics! *Ability*	I studied hard for this exam! *Effort*
External	That was an easy test! *Difficulty*	I guessed right on what to study! *Luck*

Success Attributions

Students who perform poorly on a test tend to explain their failure in one of four ways.

"I'm bad at statistics!" (ability)

"That was a tough test!" (difficulty)

"I didn't study enough." (effort)

"I guessed wrong about what to study." (luck)

Students who perform well on an examination tend to explain their success in one of four ways.

"I'm good at statistics!" (ability)

"The test was easy!" (difficulty)

"I studied hard for this exam!" (effort)

"I guessed right about what to study." (luck)

Stable attributions (ability and task difficulty) build expectations for future successes or failures.[117] That is, perceptions of low ability or high difficulty tend to increase expectations of future failure. Perceptions of high ability or low difficulty tend to increase expectations of future success.

Internal attributions (ability and effort) produce feelings of pride or shame in students.[118] That is, perceptions of low ability or lack of effort produce feelings of shame. Perceptions of high ability or diligent effort produce feelings of pride.

Over time, repeated success or failure can lead to **rigid attributions** in students, and changes the perspectives of high-achievers and low-achievers toward success and failure. **High achievers** view success as the result of ability and hard work, and failure the result of laziness[119] Failure does not discourage high-achievers,

Achiever Status

Outcome		High	Low
	Success	*Ability and Hard Work*	*Luck*
	Failure	*Laziness*	*Lack of Ability*

Persistent Attributions

nor does it diminish the expectancy of success. On the contrary, failure proves they underestimated the amount of work necessary for success and drives them to work harder. **Low achievers** view success as a result of luck and failure as confirmation of their lack of ability.[120] How can we change low-achievers into high-achievers?

Difficulty and *Luck* are beyond the control of learners, and so offer little help in the transformation. *Ability* changes gradually over long periods of time, and requires sustained, consistent success. So, **personal *Effort*** offers the greatest potential for improving student achievement. The amount of effort students give to *each and every learning task* is the greatest motivational difference between high achievers and low achievers. Teachers do well to help low-achievers focus on *the personal effort* they make in learning.[121] Low-achievers will grow toward a high-achiever perspective only when they *believe* their success is not a matter of luck or faith, but strictly a matter of their own personal effort in study. One must persist in behaving like a high-achiever before becoming a high-achiever! Unfortunately, ***the most difficult task in teaching*** is changing low-achievers' entrenched toxic self-concepts, into a proactive, positive one that allows students apply themselves in high-achiever behavior.[122]

We attack the problem, however, in several tangible ways. We lift low-achievers toward success when we help them develop basic **learning skills and strategies**.[123] Emphasize **progress** by reviewing previous material to show how "easy" it was, or by encouraging students to **redo projects** when they have learned more.[124] Support low achievers with assignments that offer a **high probability of success**, particularly at the early stages of learning.[125] **Model a "mastery orientation"** for learners: those who have a mastery orientation value achievement for its own sake, believe they have the ability to improve, do not fear failure, are willing to take risks, are self-confident and energetic, and welcome feedback.[126] These suggestions will help low achievers build a ***history of successes*** *tied to* ***their own effort***, which is the best antidote for low achievement.

Teachers do well to challenge high achievers as well. High-achievers are motivated with assignments that offer a mix of potential success and failure. The possibility of failure motivates high achievers to work harder.[127]

In Summary

Learning theories describe the "What?" of learning and growth. Motivation describes the "Why?" At the beginning of the chapter, we raised several questions. Why do some students desire to learn while others do not? We have provided some answers. Some desire to learn in order to gain a reward. Others in order to imitate a respected model. Or, to answer a question. To make sense of a subject. To satisfy a personal need. To achieve success.

Why do some students persist in their efforts, while others give up? When effort secures desired gains, effort persists. When it does not, effort decreases, resulting in lower achievement. The longer the trend, positive or negative, the stronger the response, until success or failure is achieved.

Why do some students attribute their success to effort while others attribute it to luck? When effort repeatedly succeeds in producing sharper skills, broader knowledge, deeper understanding, or greater appreciation, it is reinforced, embraced, and increased. When effort repeatedly fails, it is rejected, and only luck remains to explain random successes.

If our desire is to help learners achieve course goals, how do we energize learner efforts that success requires? We can offer a tangible reward. Provide appropriate models. Provoke curiosity. Insure meaningful content. Satisfy a need toward becoming and belonging. Engineer successful outcomes.

All true motivation comes from within. We cannot guarantee success for any learner. We can, however, provide an environment in which every learner has an opportunity to succeed. We have now discussed many specific elements in terms of learning and motivation, but we turn now to the larger scope of classroom environment.

Motivation Summary	
Motivation Theory	**Associated Learning Theory**
Employing rewards	Traditional Behaviorism
Modeling Skills	Social Learning Theory
Provoking Curiosity	Constructivism
Insuring Meaningfulness	Information Processing Theory
Engaging Learner Needs	Humanistic Learning Theory
Stressing Realistic Attributions	—

Chapter Concepts

Ability	Stable/Internal: competence in learning tasks due to previous experience and training
Aesthetic appreciation	Maslow: the (growth) need to experience beauty, order, truth, justice, and goodness
Behavior modification	Desired behaviors are established and strengthened by appropriate reinforcers
Belonging and love	Maslow: the (deficiency) need to be accepted and respected by one's group
Deficiency needs	Maslow's Hierarchy: physical and psychological needs that hinder learning and growth
Direct reinforcement	Bandura: observers are rewarded for specific behaviors (Skinnerian reinforcement)
Effort	Unstable/internal: the amount of exertion and time given to a learning task
Extrinsic motivation	Motivation from outside the learner: tokens, stars, praise
General motivation	An enduring and broad disposition to master a variety of learning situations (stable)
Growth needs	Maslow's Hierarchy: the desire to grow intellectually, artistically, and personally
Intellectual achievement	Maslow: the (growth) need to understand the meanings of things, events, and symbols.
Intrinsic motivation	Motivation from within the learner: aspirations, desires, personal goals, standards
Locus of control	Internal/external: the source of success or failure in a given situation
Luck	Unstable/external: the probability that study is applied to material that is tested
Ripple effect	The contagious spreading of behaviors in a group by means of imitation
Safety	Maslow: the (deficiency) need for physical and psychological security in the classroom
Self-actualization	Maslow: the (growth) need to unfold one's person and fulfill one's potential.

Self-esteem	Maslow: the (deficiency) need to develop a sense of acceptance of self and competence
Self-reinforcement	Rewarding one's own behaviors
Shaping	Selectively using reinforcement strategies to move students toward particular goals
Specific motivation	A specific disposition to work in a particular learning situation (unstable)
Stability	Stable/Unstable: the durability of attributions
Survival	Maslow: the (deficiency) need to exist: food, water, shelter
Task difficulty	Stable/external: the degree of difficulty in a given learning task
Token economy	Tokens (reinforcers) given for specific behaviors. Exchanged for desired activities or items
Transcendence	Maslow: the (growth) need to experience a spiritual reality beyond self
Vicarious reinforcement	Bandura: observers are motivated when respected models are rewarded for their behavior

Chapter Objectives

Learners will demonstrate understanding of motivation by . . .

- Explaining five views of motivation in the classroom based on the three systems of learning theory.
- Explaining motivation according to achievement and attribution theories.
- Properly categorizing teacher actions by motivation type

Learners will demonstrate understanding of Maslow's Hierarchy of Needs by giving examples of each of the eight stages.

Learners will demonstrate understanding of transcendence by . . .

- Comparing and contrasting secular and biblical views of transcendence.
- Evaluating their own stage of Christian transcendence by Willard's five stages

Learners will demonstrate appreciation for proper motivation principles by sharing personal classroom experiences related to behavioral motivation, cognitive motivation, humanistic motivation, achievement motivation, and attribution theory.

Discussion Questions

1 Choose any two of the five situations presented at the beginning of the chapter and apply principles of motivation from a different system than given in the text. For example, the text applied behavioral principles to situation one. Discuss this situation with any other system.

2 Consider recent experiences of success or failure in your studies. What attributions did you make to explain them? Did you focus on ability, effort, task difficulty, or luck?

3 Discuss examples of motivation (or lack of motivation) in classes you have taken. What type of motivation was applied? Was it effective in motivating you to achieve? Why or why not?

THE TEACHER AND CLASSROOM CLIMATE

*"I . . . urge you to walk worthy of the calling you have received, with all humility and gentleness,
with patience, accepting one another in love, diligently keeping the unity of the Spirit
with the peace that binds [us].*

Ephesians 4:1–3

*I exhort the elders among you: shepherd God's flock among you, not overseeing out of
compulsion but freely, according to God's [will]; not for the money but eagerly; not lording it over
those entrusted to you, but being examples to the flock. And when the chief Shepherd appears,
you will receive the unfading crown of glory.*

1 Peter 5:1b–4

"Power lasts ten years; influence not more than a hundred."

—Korean Proverb[1]

Chapter Rationale

James writes, "Not many should become teachers, my brothers, knowing that we will receive a stricter judgment" (Jas 3:1). God holds teachers to a higher standard because we deal in human personality. Any mismanagement or misdirection of persons entrusted to our care carries the heaviest condemnation. "But whoever causes the downfall of one of these little ones who believe in Me—it would be better for him if a heavy millstone were hung around his neck and he were drowned in the depths of the sea!" (Matt 18:6; Mark 9:42; Luke 17:2). Christian students, sitting in our classrooms under our control and management, certainly qualify as "little ones."

Classrooms where students experience a triad of clarity, warmth, and productivity find a stable climate that maximizes motivation and learning, while minimizing misbehavior. Effective teachers create such a climate while ineffective teachers cannot. What makes the difference? In this chapter, we analyze teacher variables such as personality traits, teaching behaviors, and reward structures that facilitate a positive learning environment. Some of this material may seem redundant. In earlier chapters, we made practical suggestions in microcosm, based on specific theories. Here we make suggestions in macrocosm, looking at the classroom as a whole. While overlap is unavoidable, perhaps the repetition from different perspectives will prove helpful.

Chapter Overview

➤ Teacher Effectiveness: A Complex Issue
➤ Teacher Personality and Classroom Climate
➤ Global Teacher Behaviors and Classroom Climate
➤ Instructional Teacher Behaviors and Classroom Climate
➤ Competition, Cooperation, and Classroom Climate
➤ A Triadic View of Motivation
➤ *Chapter Concepts, Chapter Objectives, Discussion Questions*

Teacher Effectiveness: A Complex Issue

What is an effective teacher? Some say "one that explains things so I can understand"; others say "one that cared about me"; and still others say "one that showed me how to meet his expectations."[2] Some define teacher effectiveness in terms of student ratings (more often than not a measure of popularity[3]). Others define teacher effectiveness in terms of student outcomes.

In general, we might define teacher effectiveness as *creating a stable classroom climate* where students experience a triad of clarity, warmth, and productivity.[4] Such a climate stimulates maximum motivation to succeed. In the previous chapter, we looked at specific ways to motivate learners. Here we discuss two macro-factors of classroom climate, the foundation of teacher effectiveness. These are teacher *personality* and teacher *behaviors* (both global and instructional). We take each of these in turn.

Teacher Personality and Classroom Climate

Personality is a global concept that describes the "distinctive qualities of a person, especially those distinguishing personal characteristics that make one socially appealing."[5] Teaching is a social enterprise. It follows that persons who are socially appealing—who can relate to others in a positive way—can create a better climate for learning than persons who are socially inept.

For the last 15 years, I have begun educational classes and conferences by asking participants to consider teachers they have had. I ask them to focus on their best teacher, and write down words or simple phrases that describe this "best teacher." Americans, Russians, Ukrainians, Kyrgyz, and Kazakhs answer the same way. Some point to competency in the classroom: punctuality, order, teaching skills. Some point to clarity of understanding: understandable lectures, good questions, focused explanations. Most, however, point to relationships: cared about students, willing to listen, flexible, helpful.

Then I ask them to describe their worst teachers. Again, the answers are the same from Fort Worth to Kiev, from Moscow to Bishkek. Some point to the lack of order and discipline, others to confusion and superficiality. Most, however, point to a lack of relationship: anger, humiliation, threats, arbitrary punishments, and favoritism. The "link of life" between teacher and student is more important to learning than any particular educational system.[6] "If possible, on your part, live at peace with everyone" (Rom 12:18). We look now at four critical personality factors that create and strengthen these links of life: warmth, enthusiasm, flexibility, and emotional maturity.

Warmth

Teachers who are warm, caring, and friendly set a positive emotional tone in the classroom. Contrast this with teachers who are cold, uncaring, and aloof. The former treats students as persons, the latter as objects. The former emphasizes interaction, the latter on telling. The former concentrates on engagement, the latter on domineering. The former desires student learning, the latter student subservience. The former welcomes student questions, the latter confronts their ignorance. It is clear which kind of classroom produces more openness, curiosity, and freedom to ask questions.

Consider the words of Jesus the week before He died, as He entered Jerusalem: "Jerusalem, Jerusalem! The city who kills the prophets and stones those who are sent to her. How often I wanted to gather your children together, as a hen gathers her chicks under her wings, yet you were not willing!" (Matt 23:37).

In the face of Jerusalem's violent history and His own impending death, Jesus spoke words of warm embrace, of togetherness and love. Later, when Judas the betrayer approached Jesus in the garden, Jesus accepted his kiss of greeting and called him "friend" (Matt 26:49–50). Earlier He chose twelve men to "be with him" (Mark 3:14). The Lord of the Universe did not consider His learners as servants, but "friends" (John 15:15). The Teacher loved His students and encouraged them to love each other (John 13:34). Warm is always better than cold.

Enthusiasm

Enthusiasm refers to "great excitement for or interest in a subject or cause,"[7] and manifests itself as intensity, vigor, movement, joy, surprise, frustration, and delight.[8] Such elements reflect an intense interest in the subject as well as zeal for communicating that subject to others. Teacher enthusiasm brings life and energy into the classroom.

Contrast this with teachers who move through their material methodically and monotonously, with little change of pace. Their focus is their notes, often yellow with age. They seem unmoved by the excitement of students whose thinking is stirred by the truths for the first time.

Students are rarely excited by teachers who seem bored by their own subjects. Such was the contrast between the teaching of the scribes and Pharisees, who quoted prominent rabbis, and the teaching of Jesus, Who spoke with authority. "You have heard that it was said to our ancestors . . . But I tell you . . ." (Matt 5:21–22). Jesus' teaching had such intensity, such authority, that "the crowds were astonished at His teaching" (7:28–29). Enthused is always better than bored.

Flexibility

"Teaching flexibility" means the appropriate use of teaching methods, whether direct or indirect, according to the learning needs of students. Direct methods include lecturing, explaining, and correcting. Indirect methods include questioning, listening, and accepting students' opinions and feelings.[9] Flexibility is the most repeated adjective used to describe good teachers.[10]

Rigid teachers tend to use the same procedures in the same way, regardless of student outcomes.[11] They tend to have low expectations of student ability and performance. They are more authoritarian and prone to bias and prejudice. They depend more on first impressions and past records than flexible teachers do.[12]

Flexible teachers employ whatever means are necessary to secure student learning. They are more positive and more democratic than rigid teachers, and students in all subjects learn more under their guidance.[13] Matthew 23 reflects the difference between the flexibility of Jesus' understanding of the Law and the rigidity of the Pharisee's religion. Jesus understood kingdom principles and used them appropriately to teach and minister. The Pharisees held rigid traditions and religious formulas and burdened their followers with them: "The scribes and the Pharisees" (Matt 23:2) "tie up heavy loads that are hard to carry and put them on people's shoulders, but they themselves aren't willing to lift a finger to move them (23:4). Flexible is always better than rigid.

Emotionally Mature

Emotionally mature teachers display a sense of humor, have a pleasant manner, and are fair and disciplined.[14] Such teachers work well with others, manage their impulses, express good feelings without embarrassment, refrain from worry, and can accept constructive criticism.[15]

Contrast this with immature teachers who tend to be unpleasant, impulsive, irritable, rash, anxious and short of temper.[16] College and seminary students may be able to avoid such teachers by choosing others. But for elementary and secondary students, required by law to attend school with little or no choice in their teachers or subjects, immature teachers can make school an unbearable experience.

The experience of Jesus and Lazarus reflects the difference in emotional maturity between Jesus and the Pharisees. Jesus was late. Lazarus was dead (John 11:17). Martha was distraught (John 11:21). Jesus' response, in word and action, was measured and calm. He raised Lazarus from the dead. And the response of the Pharisees upon hearing of the miracle? "If we let Him go on like this [performing miracles, v. 47], everyone will believe in Him, and then the Romans will come and take away both our place and our nation" (John 11:48). Immature teachers always consider their *position* more important than their *mission*, which is helping students learn. Mature is always better than immature.

Warmth, enthusiasm, flexibility, and emotional maturity are powerful influences in creating a positive classroom climate. If teachers want to increase their effectiveness in the classroom, they would do well to focus on these four personal attributes. Teacher behaviors also have a direct impact on the climate of the classroom.

Global teacher behaviors refer to general behaviors that support a good classroom climate through ***preparation for*** *teaching*. Instructional teacher behaviors refer to specific behaviors that influence classroom climate in the ***practice of*** *teaching*.

Global Teacher Behaviors and Classroom Climate

Global behaviors refer to overarching activities that provide structure for classroom climate. These include content-communication balance, performance skills, organizational clarity, scholarship, responsibility, and self-evaluation.

Content-Communication Balance

A common fallacy among teachers and students alike is that teaching is ***delivering content***—telling students what one knows. Wherever I go in the world, students define teaching as "giving information," and learning as "getting information."[17] Since *telling students* emphasizes teacher knowledge, it is assumed that the best teacher is one with command of the subject matter.[18] While teacher knowledge is a necessary basis for effective teaching, it is not sufficient. If students process this "rich content" poorly, it remains foreign, artificial, and unhelpful.

Another common fallacy among teachers is that teaching is ***humanizing content***—addressing less content, but making it relevant to student experiences through interactive methods. Since *communication skills* are primary in interaction, it is assumed that the best teacher is one with command of good interpersonal communication skills—listening, sharing, questioning, discussing. While communication skills are necessary for effective teaching, they are not sufficient. If students over-process less content, it may seem superficial and less challenging.

Effective teachers know their subjects well, yet plan activities that are relevant to students' lives, needs, and ministries. They use lecture, discussion, projects, questions, and problems to help students integrate new material into their thinking. Serious scholarship provides depth. Genuine relationship provides warmth, interaction, and relevancy. Proper planning provides the flexible balance between content and communication.[19] This balance offers a winning combination for effective learning.

Performance skills

Skilled performance in any endeavor requires years of consistent hard work. Most of this work is done alone, off the platform. Olympic athletes give years of their lives in private practice in order to perform publicly at the Games. Years of effort for a moment of excellence. Comedians appear to be "naturally funny," and yet they often spend months developing a new joke.[20] Months of word craft for a momentary laugh. Teaching is a complex social skill. Effective teachers work behind the scenes to make their teaching skills appear "natural."

Platform skills. One performance skill set consists of ***platform*** **skills**, the on-stage characteristics of presence, poise, and calmness. Teachers with good platform skills appear unhurried, confident, and in control of themselves, as well as the class—*they seem to be going somewhere important*. Effective teachers focus performance skills more on students than themselves, more on students than the equipment used to teach them. When the elements are just right, students can hear "drums and bugles in the distance" as they march to conquer a new field of study.

Teachers who lack platform skills appear to be distracted, anxious, and confused—working hard but going nowhere. They fidget with things; are easily frustrated; appear unsure of what to do, as if they repeatedly lose their place in the notes, forgetting where they have been or where they are going. Inanimate objects stymie them. They break out in a cold sweat when machines refuse to cooperate. They tend to worry about themselves and manifest a sense of dread toward students. Without platform skills, the best academic preparation is rendered unappetizing, like a freshly grilled steak served on a dirty plate. But there are other skill sets.

Speaking skills. Speaking skills relate to control of the voice to provide emphasis, pacing, and structure to conversational lectures. *Pitch* refers to the tone of the voice, from high to low. *Pitch range* refers to the difference between the highest and lowest pitches. Speaking with a small pitch range (monotone speech) over time is boring. Use higher pitches to emphasize. Lower pitches to draw attention. Middle pitches to convey information. *Volume* refers to loudness of speech. Speaking at a steady volume over time is boring. Use louder speech to emphasize. Softer speech to draw attention. Middle loudness to convey information. *Pace* refers to the speed of speech. Speaking at the same pace over time is boring. Use a faster pace to emphasize. A slower pace to draw attention. A middle pace to convey information.

Effective communicators combine these speech characteristics for greater effect. A faster, louder, higher voice dramatically confronts listeners. A slower, softer, lower voice calmly, yet powerfully, draws in listeners.

Too much emphasis in either direction hampers communication. Speech that is *too high-loud-fast* is overly dramatic and reduces credibility. Speech that is too *low-soft-slow* is boring and reduces attention. We are not, after all, performers on a stage, but teachers. Breathy stage-whispers and boisterous rabble-rousing belong to charlatans and demagogues. Variety is the key. Teachers do well to use middle ranges in the main, raising pitch, volume, and pace as needed for emphasis, lowering pitch, volume, and pace for dramatic effect. Teachers do well to study effective speakers (pastors, teachers, politicians) to see how they use pitch-volume-pace to emphasize key words, convey information, and draw in listeners. The use of personal video tapes, recorded in class while we teach, allows us to analyze our own speech patters.

Verbal pauses distract attention from the message being conveyed. A verbal pause is an audible sound made to connect one word to another, one phrase to another, or one sentence to another. For example, a teacher might say, "The next major event in the last week of Jesus' life was **uhhhh** the Passover celebration with His disciples." The teacher had to think just a moment to find the proper "next event." As she mentally searched for the next event, she unconsciously filled the silence with "uhhhh." "Ahhh," "eeee," and "ehhh" are also common sounds. We find these same verbal pauses in all spoken languages. Even deaf people "verbally pause" by drawing out movements of their hands.

A few verbal pauses in an hour's lesson or a 40-minute sermon causes little problem. But when we use verbal pauses repeatedly and often, listeners notice them—and may even begin to count them. When that happens, we have lost them to our message. Teachers do well to avoid verbal fillers altogether.

"Listen" to two speakers deliver a paragraph. Perhaps you will be able to "hear" the difference between the two, even as it is presented in written form.

Ahhh The work of the Lord, *ehhh* which is done *uhhh* by means of the Lord, always *uh* succeeds. *Ehh* When we have *uh* spiritual success on *ehh* one level, the Lord*ahh* lifts us to another, in order to*ahhhhh* teach more and to*uhhhh* help others *uh* more.

Did you get the message? How hard did you have to work to ignore the verbal clutter and concentrate on the thoughts being conveyed? I *wrote* the sentences above and have difficulty following the theme. Now try the same words, using the principles of speech control. Sentences are broken into phrases, which indicate slight pauses. Bold indicates emphasis. Bold with underline indicates heavier emphasis. Ellipses indicate slower pace and lower volume.

The **work** of the **<u>Lord</u>**,
when done **by <u>means</u> of the** Lord,
always succeeds.
When we have spiritual success on **<u>one</u> level**,
the Lord lifts us to **another**,
. . . in order to **teach more** . . .
. . . and to **<u>help others</u>** more.

These skills grow with practice, most easily done by telling stories to illustrate content. Colorful speech is not limited, however, to stories. Verbal emphasis can be used to highlight key points, ask pointed questions, relax the pace of a lecture, or draw attention to easily confused concepts. So much of what we do in the classroom is verbal, and colorful speech helps students separate wheat from chaff, essential from support, principles from footnotes.

Explaining skills. Explaining skills refer to the ability to convey difficult concepts in simple ways, so that essential meaning (structure) is lifted from non-essential verbiage. Once students understand the essence of a difficult concept, they can more easily build networks on this core ("Elaboration," IPT, Chapter Nine). Explaining skills include the use of *parables, illustrations, examples, non-examples,*[21] *analogies, synonyms, antonyms,* and relevant *stories.*

Questioning skills. Questioning skills refer to the ability to ask clear and understandable questions. Questions can be used to review previous material ("Yesterday, we discussed behavioral learning. What is the primary focus of this approach?"), probe for deeper meaning ("Good answer, but what do you mean by 'understanding the verse?' How will you know if students understand?"), contrasting two concepts ("How would you differentiate assimilation and accommodation?"), call for personal response ("Fine, but how would *you* describe the term?"), call for public testimonies ("When have you experienced the care of a Good Samaritan?"), or summarize a discussion ("Given our discussion of the Teachers' Triad today, how would you define 'teaching' and 'learning'?").

Teachers do well to plan questions ahead of time, to space them throughout the sessions, and to balance type and focus. The highest form of questioning skill is found in the ability to generate meaningful, probing, engaging questions "in the moment." Intentional practice in planning future questions produces better abilities in generating questions spontaneously.

Listening skills. Listening skills refer to the ability to focus attention on student questions, explanations, and personal stories. Listening involves eyes and facial expressions, as well as the ears. Eyes engage the student's, not glancing at notes or watches. Facial expressions indicate a connection with student comments—concern for concern, smile for smile. Nodding the head slightly "yes" conveys agreement with what the student is saying. Turning the body in the direction of the student indicates greater interest than merely looking over at the student. While these suggestions may seem contrived, I do not mean them to be. These are actions teachers take when they absorb themselves in listening to students.

Discipline skills. Discipline skills refer to the ability to manage a class of students, and especially to intervene when student behavior distracts from learning. We discussed the step-by-step approach to discipling students in Chapter Thirteen. Chaotic classrooms create a toxic climate. Postmodern or not, teachers are responsible for maintaining order in the classroom.

Long-range planning skills. Long-range planning skills refer to the ability to create individual lessons, units of lessons, and courses in which students are moved, step-by-step, through material and exercises to secure stated goals and objectives in learning. Issues include writing instructional objectives and learning readiness activities, selecting and sequencing appropriate teaching methods, measuring outcomes, and creating interconnections among lessons, units, and courses. See Chapter Six in *Called to Teach* (Yount, 1999), or download a free copy of *The Disciplers' Handbook* and see Chapter Two, "The Disciplers' Method" for specific guidelines on lesson planning in Bible study situations.

Aristotle wrote, "Excellence is an art won by training and habituation. We do not act rightly because we have virtue or excellence, but we rather have those because we have acted rightly. We are what we repeatedly do. Excellence, then, is not an act but a habit."[22] What we understand, we do.

What we do, we become. Being skilled in these behaviors instills confidence that teachers not only understand their subjects, but that they can lead students to that understanding as well.

Organizational Clarity

Teachers who create organizational clarity in their classrooms arrange the elements of learning—units, session plans, learning readiness activities, major and minor tasks, visual aids, transitions, assignments, due dates, examination dates—in a way that minimizes confusion. Learning in a disorganized and confusing classroom is like hunting for a favorite shirt in a dark closet. All the shirts seem to look alike—dark shapes in the shadows. Turn on the closet light, and suddenly one can see distinctive colors and patterns, and can easily find the favorite. Organizational clarity enables learners to see the *flow* of learning—its starts and stops, its essentials and their supports—as well as the *structure* of learning—assignments, time lines, and tests. It follows from our discussion of IPT (Chapter Nine) that meaningful learning springs from organizational clarity. Such a climate results in higher student morale, more positive student attitudes, and higher achievement.[23]

Scholarship

Effective teachers are scholars, pursuing the evolving issues in their fields of study. Times change. Students change. Needs change. Effective teachers blend new studies, new theories, and new discoveries into their class structure in order to keep current. Since class time is fixed, adding new material requires culling older material from courses. As hard as it is, we do well to cull cherished stories, favorite examples, and choice approaches—irrelevant to contemporary students—from long-used notes, moving them from active files to memoirs. The longer we teach, the harder such culling becomes. Regardless, on-going scholarship and the willingness to give up "tried-and-true" for approaches more relevant for *today's students*, increases effectiveness, and more: it provides an excellent model of life-long learning.

Effective teachers go beyond scholarship in their majors, but study supplementary areas such as science, literature, and music. These supplementary areas provide "fertile sources of analogies and relationships."[24]

Responsibility

Effective teachers *accept personal responsibility* for how well their students learn. While we cannot force any student to learn, we can certainly hinder learning by our own poor performance. We do well to build bridges to struggling students, seeking ways to engage them and help them learn. Most students respond well to this support. If students refuse our help, and refuse to do better, there is little we can do but be fair in our evaluations of their failure.

Ineffective teachers deny personal responsibility for student difficulties, and often blame hard-working (yet poor-performing) students for failure. They tend to use threats and make demands to motivate better performance.[25] Such behavior reveals the taproot of their ineffectiveness, a smallness of the person behind the teacher's mask.

Self-evaluation

The apostle Paul evaluated himself and found he was lacking in Christian maturity (Phil 3:12). "I do not consider myself to have taken hold of it." He saw himself as a continual learner in God's kingdom. He lived in an upward spiral, "forgetting what is behind and reaching forward to what is ahead." Paul pushed himself to fulfill all that God called him to be in Christ. "I pursue as my goal the prize promised by God's heavenly call in Christ Jesus" (3:14). His goal was not to be better than others, but to be everything God called him to be.

Our goal is not to be better teachers than others, but to be better at teaching today than we were yesterday, and better yet tomorrow, for the sake of the Lord. Teachers do well to reflect on strengths and weaknesses as revealed in student evaluations and comments, and make appropriate changes.[26] Regular self-evaluations help to reduce weaknesses and polish strengths. Effective teachers are thoughtful about their work ("How can I explain this better?") and monitor their instruction ("How are my students responding to this approach?"). They reflect on the connection between planning and actual instruction in class[27] and improve plans for future sessions by addressing these discrepancies.

These **global behaviors** construct, over time, a strong foundation for classroom ministry, where we decide, act, and react in the moment. We turn now to consider these instructional behaviors.

Instructional Teacher Behaviors and Classroom Climate

Instructional behaviors refer to specific discipling actions that influence classroom climate "in the moment." We consider *structuring*, *questioning*, and *reacting* behaviors[28] now.

Structuring Behaviors

We define "structuring" as *setting the global context* for learning in general, and classroom behavior in particular. Teachers structure courses with advance organizers[29] such as course objectives and outlines. Too much structure represses spontaneity and student freedom and produces a rigid atmosphere. Too little structure invites spontaneity and student freedom and produces a chaotic atmosphere. Both extremes decrease achievement.[30]

Challenge and Encourage. Effective teachers balance challenge and encouragement.[31] On the one hand, teachers provoke ever-higher levels of achievement in students, *expecting* them to succeed. On the other, teachers nurture and support student efforts, encouraging them when they fail. Ineffective teachers respond to student failures with frustration and impatience. "Don't you know *that*?!"[32]

Personal Feedback. Effective teachers provide specific, informative feedback to individual students. Ineffective teachers tend to provide global feedback to the class as a whole.[33] Review the section on "Teacher Praise" in Chapter Six.

Relate and Expect. Rapport is a relationship—a bond between teacher and student—that creates the interpersonal medium in which learning flourishes. Effective teachers establish positive rapport with their students and among their students.

Along with rapport, effective teachers establish high, yet achievable, expectations for students.[34] The combination of rapport and high expectations produces a warm, productive classroom climate.

Manage Time for Learning. *Allocated time* refers to the amount of time set aside for learning.[35] In a Sunday morning Bible study program, the allocated time might be 9:30 to 10:30. *Engaged time* refers to the time spent actively learning.[36] In Sunday school, *engaged time* excludes time given to greetings, announcements, prayer requests, and refreshments. The effectiveness of learning is directly related to the amount of time students are engaged in learning.[37]

Follow a Specific Outline. Effective teachers follow an explicit teaching format. This format includes such components as *review* of the previous day's work, an *overview* of goals, *guided practice*, *feedback* on performance, and *time to practice*.[38] These components provide structure and direction to the allocated class time.[39]

Structure and direction limit the number of tangential "rabbits"[40] that pop up in classes. When students raise a question that veers away from the session direction, we must decide whether to chase the rabbit or let it go. If the question is important, and captures the interest of students, teachers do well to follow the rabbit for a while—just to see where it leads. Spontaneous learning is often more effective than planned activities. If the question seems trivial, and fails to capture the interest of students, we do well to bring the focus back on topic. Structure and direction help us make that critical choice.

Giving Signals. As we have seen, it is good for a teacher to have an explicit organizational plan for each session. It is better when students recognize that class time is intentionally organized. "Signal giving" refers to the skill of providing definite starts and stops throughout the session. These starts and stops emphasize transitions in the organization of the material. "We have discussed the concept of justification ("stop"). Now let's move to sanctification ("start")."

Signal giving includes the use of "mands"—words that draw attention to important points.[41] "Listen!" "Look!" "Write this down!" "Take note of this!" "Never forget!" "If there's one thing to remember, it's that . . ." Signal giving attracts attention and helps students separate more important from less important material. Teachers do well to use mands sparingly since frequent use renders them ineffective. When overused, mands become verbal static, like highlighting every third sentence in a text. In the use of mands, less is better.

Orchestration of Activities. An orchestra is composed of various instruments, playing many notes. Under the direction of the conductor, musicians play their various instruments in *coordination and harmony*. The result is a complex and transforming sound that touches the hearts and minds of listeners. Without coordination and harmony, musicians produce irritating noise. In the same way, effective teachers orchestrate the various activities in the class—readiness, direction, explanation, questioning, discussion, group work, summary—to create coordination and harmony in learning.

Tempo is likewise critical in orchestral music. Fast sections followed by slow movements. The pace of classroom activities, like the pace of speech discussed earlier, affects the learning climate. When the pace of activities is too slow, boredom sets in. Teachers do well to read student boredom—rolling eyes, heavy sighs, fidgeting, tapping pencils, glances at watches—and quicken the pace with a question, an illustration, or a relevant story. When the pace is too fast, confusion sets in. Teachers do well to read student confusion—the furrowed brow, the cocked head, the look of lostness—and slow the pace with a reflective question, a review of recently explained material, or a slower delivery with longer pauses.

Questioning Behaviors

The way *teachers ask questions* affects classroom climate. We do well to present material before asking a question about that material. While this may seem obvious in theory, in practice, teachers often ask questions first "in order to discover what students already know."[42] When students give awkward, incomplete, or incorrect answers, teachers respond by explaining the material and answering the questions. If this is a habitual practice, students will grow to feel incompetent and will stop answering questions altogether. Teach, then test. Explain, then question. Students are better able to understand the material, the context, and the question. They can respond more clearly and confidently, demonstrating their understanding in a positive way.

The way *students answer questions aloud* demonstrates the quality of their understanding. This is not only a problem for teachers; it is a problem for learners themselves! There exists an irrational, *internal* sense of learning—*everything seems to make sense in our own heads*. When teachers ask a vague "Do you have any questions?" and receive silence as the response, there is a problem. Teachers do not know if learners understand. Learners may not realize they do not understand.

The internal sense of things must be tested with the external world. It is not until learners reduce their "sense" to language (spoken or written) that they demonstrate (to themselves or others) the correctness of understanding. The student who says, "I know the answer, but I just don't know how to explain it" does not, in fact, know the answer or understand the material.

When teachers ask focused, conceptual questions, they provide specific opportunities *for learners to display* understandings they have already created from their studies, and *for teachers to gauge* the correctness of the understandings expressed. If the understandings are correct, teachers move to the next area. If they are wrong, further processing is necessary. Other more specific issues in questioning include question *frequency, cognitive level, pauses, directing, redirecting*, and *probing*.

Frequency of Questions. In general, the more questions teachers ask, the more students learn.[43] Questions call for analysis of the question itself ("What is she asking?"), selective recall of relevant information ("What do I need to answer this question?"), synthesis of an answer ("How do I put all this together in order to answer?"), and conversion from thought to speech ("How do I phrase the answer?"). Repetition of these precesses—analyzing, searching, synthesizing, communicating —transforms sterile facts into coordinated concepts, which learners use to solve problems—in the class and in life.

Teachers do well to gauge the number of questions they ask. Too many questions create a sense of oppression in the classroom, a taste of an educational inquisition. We might call this "Testing without teaching."

Too few questions allow students' minds to drift away on the distant hum of teacher talk. "Teaching without testing." Interlacing clear explanations with conceptual questions provides new material for processing, and the means to process it. Teachers do well to structure their lectures as packets of facts-concepts-questions. "Teach, then test," mentioned above, reflects this middle ground.

Cognitive Level of Questions. Cognitive level refers to Bloom's taxonomy of the cognitive domain (see Chapter Twelve): knowledge (*recall*), understanding (*comprehension, application, analysis, synthesis, evaluation*). In general, the higher the cognitive level of question, the more students learn from answering it.[44]

Comprehension questions are better than *knowledge questions* (simple recall of facts). Comprehension questions call for students to interpret, compare, and explain simple, single concepts (love, joy, salvation, constructivism). Words such as describe, illustrate, and rephrase characterize this level. *Application questions*, which call for students to use simple, singular concepts to solve problems, produce higher achievement than comprehension questions. Words such as apply, solve, classify, choose, and employ reflect this level.

The three higher levels of learning focus on complex, multi-faceted concepts. *Analysis questions* call for students to identify causes and motives, as well as the internal structure of a subject. The theological word for analysis is *exegesis*, the process of breaking complex concepts (e.g., *agape* love in 1 Cor 13) into its constituent parts. Each of these separate parts (e.g., "is not provoked," v. 5) are concepts, which must be comprehended in order to understand the passage. Words such as analyze, conclude, infer, distinguish, and outline reflect this level.

Synthesis questions require students to create a new complex concept, principle, or definition. The creation of essays, research papers, lesson plans, and sermons require synthesis. Words such as predict, construct, originate, design, and plan reflect this level.

Evaluation questions call for students to judge or appraise the work of others—most often the result of synthesis. Words such as judge, argue, decide, and critique reflect this level.

Simplistic, leading, and rhetorical questions are common in sermons, where preachers do not expect listeners to respond. But these kinds of questions are deadly in a teaching environment. They undermine classroom climate and student achievement.

A *simplistic* question asks students to express agreement with the teacher. "So you see that asking questions is important in a classroom, right?" (Of course, *sigh*).

A *leading* question points directly to the answer, which is often a simple fact. "So we see in Col 1:27 that 'Christ in us' gives us the hope of . . . what?" (glory, *sigh*).

A *rhetorical* question is one that teachers answer themselves. "And so, what is hope? Hope is the confident expectation that . . . ." (La la la la, *sigh*). My personal rule concerning rhetorical questions in teaching situations is to **never ask them. Ever.** Regular use of rhetorical questions teaches students NOT to answer questions. They learn to wait for teachers to answer our own questions. Some teachers make the situation worse by chastising students for doing what they have been taught—*not answering questions*.[45] Teachers do well to ask questions only when they want student answers, and then pause for students to answer. Rather than asking simplistic, leading, or rhetorical questions, it is much better to make *direct statements*.

Pausing after asking a question. Effective teachers pause after asking questions to give learners time to answer them. Gage and Berliner call this intentional pause after asking the question "Wait Time I" and state that it gives students time to consider the question, process relevant information, and formulate an answer.[46]

Thirty years ago Craig Pearson conducted a classic study on the amount of time elementary school teachers paused after asking a question. After analyzing the pausing behavior of several hundred teachers, he found the average pause between the end of a question, and the teacher answering the question herself, was nine-tenths of a second (0.9 seconds). Pearson instructed the teachers to ask a question and then count silently "1001, 1002, 1003" before saying anything else. This simple three-second pause changed student behavior significantly.

Pearson reported that

- Student answers were longer (students had more to say).
- More students volunteered answers (questions engaged more students).
- Inflected answers[47] decreased (students were more confident of their answers).
- Students worked together more (cooperation increased).
- More students *asked* questions (curiosity grew).
- Students that teachers considered "slow" showed considerable improvement (they had more time to consider the answer).[48]

The higher the cognitive level targeted by a question, the longer Wait Time I needs to be.[49]

Directing Questions. Every child in an elementary or secondary classroom should have an equal opportunity to succeed or fail. Teachers insure this distribution of opportunity by directing questions to all learners over time. Managing this equal opportunity requires some system[50] for directing questions equitably, which reduces anxiety and increases achievement. Without such a system, teachers tend to ask questions of "better" students and deprive less able students their equal chance to respond.[51]

When teaching *adults*, my preference is to allow *volunteers* to answer questions. Some adults learn better from listening. Others fear being embarrassed. Teachers generate better rapport in the adult classroom when they remove the anxiety produced by random questions. I engage quiet students before or after class, or during small group work. As trust and confidence grows, they will more likely volunteer to answer questions in future sessions.

Redirecting Questions. There are times when teachers ask a question and receive a wrong answer. This is particularly true when teachers ask questions at higher cognitive levels. Effective teachers redirect the question—asking the question again to another student or to the class as a whole—to keep it before the class.[52] Teachers can also redirect questions that are *asked by students* rather than answering the questions themselves. Redirecting questions engages students but also gives teachers time to consider the question and how best to answer it.

Probing Questions. A student's initial response to a question may be shallow—"off the top of the head."[53] Less effective teachers tend to accept shallow responses and move on or may choose to provide more explanation themselves. Effective teachers ask follow-up questions—more specific, more detailed—to "probe student understanding" more deeply. Probing questions compel students to make more effort to answer.

Teachers do well to use probing questions carefully, with sensitivity. Students take personal risks to answer our questions. When we respond with a second, direct, more detailed question, they may not be able to answer and can be embarrassed. The degree of embarrassment depends on the teacher's behavior toward wrong answers. Berating responses curtail student willingness to respond at all. Probing works much better with success-seekers than with failure-avoiders.

Reacting Behaviors

Having generally structured class time and specifically solicited responses from students, teachers now react to student responses. *How teachers react* influences the climate of the classroom.

Pausing After Student Response. As mentioned above, Q&A sessions can take on an oppressive feeling if the pace of questions is too fast. By pausing briefly *after students respond*, teachers slow down the session pace. Such pauses encourage others to consider the question and respond. Gage and Berliner call this *after-response pause* "Wait Time II." Achievement increases as teachers slow down.[54]

Use Positive Reactions. Effective teachers acknowledge *correct answers* with a word or two of praise (behavioral). They engage *incorrect answers* with simpler questions that help students pull together the necessary elements to find the correct response. We might call this a reverse questioning sequence (cognitive). Teachers encourage students by working with them, supporting them, warmly accepting them[55] as worthy persons (humanistic) despite their momentary inability to answer a specific question correctly.

Avoid Negative Reactions. Effective teachers do not criticize, humiliate, or embarrass students for their incorrect responses.

A certain professor was well-known for warning students on the first day of class, *every* class, to refrain from "wasting class time" by asking "stupid questions" since they "lacked the depth of understanding necessary to ask meaningful ones." Every semester a student would forget the warning and violate the rule. And lightning would fall: "That's the dumbest question I've ever heard. Let's get back to the lecture." He was certainly committed to "brotherly love" at church (1 Thess 4:9–10) and at home—he simply disassociated brotherly love and his academic work. He separated Christian faith and Christian teaching, creating a climate that offended many adult "little ones" who loved the Lord. It was a habit, his common practice, because he repeated this behavior semester after semester for years. While his lectures were excellent, "stupid student questions" was the core of his reputation among students. He taught them well—students learned very quickly not to ask questions in his

"You are still my brother"

I was in the first few minutes of introducing a week-long course in Bishkek, Kyrgyzstan (2005). I had just revealed a PowerPoint slide showing the Discipler's Model when a young pastor-student raised his hand. I acknowledged him and he asked, rather bluntly, "Where did this model come from?!" I explained that we would be discussing the Model in detail over the next few hours, but to answer his question, I had created it myself. As I continued my comments, he jabbed his hand into the air. "Where did YOU get it?!" Now I was frustrated, because the rudeness of this student was hijacking my agenda of smoothly moving into a discussion of the Model itself. "We'll get into that in a few minutes, but as I said, I created it years ago." As I continued my comments, he flailed the air with his arm and not waiting for me to call on him, shouted out "But where did you GET these ideas?!" I called him by name and said, calmly, "As I said, I will explain this at the proper time. For the present, do not ask any more questions." My neutral response did not strike him as positive. He looked at me with more anger than I deserved, but he asked no more questions. He slid down in his seat and pouted for the remaining 40 minutes of the session. We had a 10-minute tea break, and as the students filed out past me, I saw Rusland coming toward me. I needed to move from neutral to positive. I needed to attempt to re-establish some basis for a positive relationship. This brief battle in class could set our relationship crossways for the next two weeks. I prayed for wisdom in what to say, and I prayed for the Russian I needed to say it. He began to pass by me, eyes averted, and I quietly said to him, «**Руслан, вы ещё мой брат, и мой друг.**» ("Rusland, you are still my brother, and my friend.")

He was startled that I spoke to him, and more so that I spoke to him in Russian. As he became aware of my words, his eyes registered surprise, but said nothing in reply. The students returned after the break to begin the next session. During that session Rusland raised his hand. "May I ask a question now?" he asked. Yes. He proceeded to ask a relevant, serious question—though I cannot remember what it was. I gave him a relevant, serious answer, and our relationship had a whole new beginning. Over the next four days, he sat close to me at meals and asked questions. He invited me to his church (75 miles from the school) on Sunday evening to speak to his congregation on "Why We Need to Teach Adults in the Church." He was one of the best students in the class, and though I did not see him on my 2009 trip, I heard that he is doing great work in a region of eastern Kyrgyzstan.

classes! One can only imagine how his students, once graduated and called as pastors, staff leaders, and missionaries, greeted questions from church members.

Teachers do well to avoid any behavior that demeans their students. As teacher criticism increases, student achievement decreases.[56]

Use Neutral Reactions. There will be times in the course of teaching that students will respond negatively. Effective teachers react to negative responses—complaining, criticizing, or arguing—in a neutral manner.[57] Since teachers are human, it is easy for us become entangled in emotional battles with belligerent or uncooperative students. Angry responses invariably hinder future teaching opportunities.

Effective teachers are able to balance responsibility to the teaching task with concern for students. We said it in the Preface, but it bears saying again. The best teachers weave together content and communication, grace and justice, nurture and control in order to help learners grow. Teaching is art in that this weaving of elements happens spontaneously, in the very process of teaching: framing the right question on the spot, responding appropriately to learners "in the moment," using humor appropriately to dispel tension or drive home a sensitive point. This is art and flows out of the personality of the teacher. The teacher's personality both envelopes and fills the classroom, creating a climate in which learning is helped or hampered.

Competition, Cooperation, and Classroom Climate

Competition means to "strive with another or others to attain a goal, such as attaining an advantage or winning a victory."[58] Footballs' *Super Bowl*, basketball's *Final Four*, baseball's *World Series*, and the *Olympic Games* all testify to the high excitement generated by striving to be the best.

The question is whether learning should be considered a sport. Research suggests it should not. Hamachek reports it is "almost impossible to find research studies that praise competition as a motivator" in the classroom. While competitive methods produce a few winners, it produces many more losers—and this causes problems in school.[59] Other studies have found that competitive methods produce higher anxiety, lower self-esteem, and less responsibility for and value toward fellow students.[60]

While students readily and aggressively compete on the playground, the classroom is different. They *choose to compete* at recess. Competitive grading structures in the classroom give students no choice. On the playground, students are *free to quit* a game anytime. They cannot quit the classroom. School feels like forced labor under these conditions, especially to low-achievers. Under these conditions, competition is more destructive than constructive.

Destructive Competition

When teachers emphasize rank order and relative performance among students, the quality of learning declines for most students. No matter how much work is done, or how successful the outcomes, someone in the class must finish last. Under these conditions, students refocus their efforts from attacking learning tasks and seeking success to playing it safe and avoiding failure. As we saw in the previous chapter, failure-avoiders seldom achieve the way success-seekers do. Teachers do well to reject methodologies that force students into destructive structures.

The destructive nature of competition is made much worse when relative performance is made public. My wife has a pleasant alto voice but she never sings in public. She was made to stand before her third grade class and sing as part of a class competition. When she finished, the teacher laughed and told her she would never ask her to sing again. I wonder if this teacher *intended* to scar her nine-year-old student for life?

Constructive Competition

Competition is not always destructive. There are ways to use competitive methods in a constructive way. Competition motivates students when they are prepared to *compete on an equal basis*.[61] Competition is helpful when students focus on *personal improvement* rather than relative standing in the class. Competition is helpful when *grades are kept confidential*. Competition is softened when students are allowed to demonstrate their learning in a *variety* of ways.[62]

Cooperative Learning

Cooperation means to "work or act together toward a common end or purpose.[63] In Chapter Ten, we discussed Cooperative Learning, reporting that it improves achievement, motivation, thinking skills, and interpersonal relationships in students.[64] It also improves student self-esteem and even the acceptance of handicapped students.[65] How might we engage students in cooperative learning activities? We turn to those now.

Reciprocal Questioning. One of the simplest approaches to Cooperative Learning is *reciprocal questioning*, which requires no special materials or testing procedures. After a lecture or presentation, students "are assigned to work in pairs or triads to ask and answer questions about the material." The teacher provides a list of question stems to students who are then taught how to create questions from the stems. Examples of question stems are "What is a new example of . . . ?", "Explain why . . . ?", "Explain how . . . ?", and "What would happen if . . . ?" The students create questions and then take turns asking and answering. This approach encourages deeper thinking than traditional discussion groups, as well as connections to previous lessons.[66]

Student Teams-Achievement Divisions (STAD). Assign students to four- or five-member heterogeneous groups to study materials in preparation for competition against other teams. Study groups discuss the material and answer questions. Students then individually take twice-weekly quizzes. Based on test performance, each team member earns one to three points for their group based on their Individual Learning Expectation (ILE)[67] score and their quiz score. Due to the nature of the ILE, every member of the group, regardless of ability level, is able to contribute a maximum number of points to the group. *The ILE encourages every member to work hard.* Every week the group scoring the highest number of points is declared the winner.[68] Every two to three weeks, groups are re-assigned so that students have opportunity to work with others in the class.[69]

Jigsaw I and II. Jigsaw is a "cooperative structure in which each member of a group is responsible for teaching other members one section of the material."[70] Assign students to heterogeneous groups. Give each student in the group individual study materials and assignments that form part of a learning whole. When these are completed, have group members meet together to share what each member has learned. Test students individually on the whole material.[71] Jigsaw II (1995) added the element of "expert meetings" to the original (1978) approach. Students from all groups who are assigned the same topic meet together to "compare notes, go over material, and plan how to teach their group members."[72] Jigsaw activities encourage the interdependence of group members.[73]

Group Investigation (GI). Like Jigsaw, Group Investigation is a technique in which students work together in heterogeneous groups of two to six members. Each group is given a sub-topic to research, discuss, and prepare for presentation. Groups then present their findings to the whole class.[74] The major difference between Jigsaw and GI is that teachers form groups in Jigsaw while students form their own groups in GI.[75]

Reciprocal Teaching (RT) is a text-based instructional approach in which groups of students work together to make sense of specific subject matter. Group members use the comprehension strategies of summarizing (capturing the main idea), questioning (probe understanding), clarifying (clear up misconceptions), and predicting (make reasoned guesses about what the author will share next) to build an understanding of the text. Each group has a student-facilitator, under the guidance of the teacher.[76]

Scripted Cooperation (SC). Like Reciprocal Teaching, *Scripted Cooperation* operates as student-led groups. Like RT, the goal of SC is for group members to build a shared understanding of the text, problem, or writing assigned to them. However, in SC, students work in pairs rather than small groups. One member of the pair serves as the "recaller" (summarizes an assigned reading) and the other as "listener" (corrects or expands the summary of the recaller), decided by a coin toss. SC pairs follow a general script provided by the teacher, which provides steps the pair should follow in conducting their study.[77] SC works well for analyzing readings, solving math problems, and editing writing drafts. Partners work together to elaborate the information—creating "images, mnemonics, ties to previous work, examples, analogies, and so on." The partners switch roles of recaller (summarizer) and listener (elaborator) for each new section or problem.[78] RT and SC are sometimes called **collaborative** techniques.[79]

As in any teaching strategy, careful planning is required to make cooperative activities effective. This is due to the fact that poorly organized activities can result in "less learning than whole-group lessons."[80]

Suggestions for organizing cooperative learning exercises include the following:

- Seat group members together to save time moving from whole-class to group activities.
- Have materials ready for easy distribution.
- Introduce students to cooperative learning with short, simple tasks.
- Make objectives and directions clear.
- Specify the amount of time students have to accomplish the task.
- Keep work times relatively short.
- Monitor groups as they work.
- Require students to produce a product (written answers to questions).[81]
- Test students individually to prevent uneven effort within the groups.[82]

Advocates see cooperative learning as a supplement to, not a replacement for, direct instruction. Cooperative learning accomplishes this by its support of interactive learning, the reduction of anxiety created by competitive structures, the natural development of interpersonal skills, and the fact that it produces many more "winners" in the class.[83]

A Triadic View of Motivation

The Christian Teachers' Triad provides a means for synthesizing suggestions of the chapter and unit into three key principles for provoking student performance and securing a positive classroom climate.

Motivation in the Rational Sphere: Light Rather Than Dark

Light refers to the rational clarity of structured presentations, organized lectures on relevant topics, focused questions, well-framed problems, and meaningful exercises. *Dark* refers to chaotic presentations, meandering and self-centered lectures, vague questions, superficial problems, and busy work. When teachers make sense, the rational climate is improved, and learners understand both content and process better. Such a cognitive climate challenges, confronts, stretches, and probes student thinking.

Motivation in the Emotional Sphere: Warm Rather Than Cold

Warm refers to the emotional warmth of the classroom produced by teacher openness and availability, classroom safety, and mutual rapport. *Cold* refers to the emotional coldness of the classroom produced by teacher detachment and indifference, classroom uncertainty and fear, and personal isolation. When teachers treat learners as persons of worth, the emotional climate is improved, and classroom activities are more inviting and reassuring. Such a humane climate supports, encourages, nurtures, and cares for students as they learn.

Motivation in the Behavioral Sphere: Active Rather Than Passive

Active refers to the productive engagement of students as co-laborers in learning through participation, interaction, and mutual contribution in the educational process. *Passive* refers to the stagnant non-engagement of learners, treating them as dormant receptacles of whatever teachers deem important. When teachers engage learners in meaningful activity—whether mental, relational, or skill-building—the productive climate is improved, and classroom activities are more useful, challenging, and relevant to real-world applications. Such an active climate trains, reinforces, and "models the role" for students.

"Good teachers," writes Hamachek, ". . . rather like life; are firm but fair; expect a lot from themselves and their students; have a sense of humor; and enjoy, at least most of the time, their work.[84] We can certainly see the Triad at work in his observations.

Motivation from the Spiritual Center

Emanating from the center of the Triad is the spiritual focus of Christian teaching. Spiritual growth is stimulated as teachers integrate the spiritual qualities of faith, hope, and love into the methods we employ every day. Infusing the human interactions we experience in classrooms with the fruit of the Spirit—love, joy, peace, patience, kindness, goodness, faithfulness, goodness and self-control—balances the toxic extremes we often see in academic settings: to stretch yet support, confront yet care, persuade yet permit, lecture yet listen, and challenge yet charm those whom God has sent us to teach.

"Lord, I am Your instrument of learning in this time and place. I am a Christian who teaches. Enable me to become Christian in my teaching. Confronting ignorance while loving students. Setting high standards and helping students achieve. Explaining objectively and listening attentively. Judging fairly, and correcting warmly.

Make me aware of my faults, and give me the strength to change, so that every one of my students can grow to become the servants *You* want them to be. For Your kingdom's sake, Lord, I ask this in Your strong name. Amen."

Chapter Concepts

Allocated time	The amount of time set aside for a group or class to meet. (vs. engaged time)
Competition	Students or groups work against each other to secure limited high grades
Collaboration	Cooperative learning approaches that emphasize the achievement of consensus
Content-communication balance	The tension between scholarship ("tell") and relationship ("discuss") in a class
Cooperative learning	Students work together toward a common educational end or purpose
Directing questions	Distributing questions to every learner in the classroom in a systematic way
Engaged time	The amount of time students are engaged in learning. (vs. allocated time)
Enthusiasm	Intense interest in a subject; zeal for communicating that subject to others.
Flexibility	Use of teaching methods according to the learning needs of students

Group investigation	Group members research sub-topics, then synthesize and present as a whole
Jigsaw	Group members study sub-topics and teach the group what they find
Mand	Words that draw attention to important points. "Listen!" "Look!"
Negative reactions	Criticizing, humiliating, or embarrassing students for incorrect responses.
Organization	Arranging course elements (content and structure) in an understandable way
Positive reactions	Working with, supporting, warmly accepting students as worthy persons
Probing questions	Follow-up questions that call for deeper reflection or greater discrimination
Reciprocal questioning	Students in pairs or triads create questions from "stems" and test each other
Reciprocal teaching	Students in groups summarize, question, clarify, and predict—teaching each other
Redirecting questions	Reflecting student questions back to the class for consideration and response
Responsibility	Teachers' accountability for what happens in the classroom
Scholarship	Teachers' commitment to on-going research into subjects they teach
Self-evaluation	Willingness to reflect on student evaluations and make appropriate changes
Signal giving	Organizing lecture material with verbal starts and stops
Structuring	Setting the context for learning in general, and classroom behavior in particular
STAD	"Student Teams-Achievement Divisions"—a Cooperative Learning structure
Wait time I	Amount of time teachers pause after asking a question
Wait time II	Amount of time teachers pause after a student answers a question

Chapter Objectives

Learners will demonstrate understanding of teachers' influence on classroom climate by . . .

- Comparing and contrasting destructive competition, constructive competition, and cooperation in assigning grades
- Giving one definitive example, either good or bad, of teacher personality factors, global behaviors, and instructional behaviors (3 examples) from their own previous classes
- Defining the terms structuring, signal giving, mands, organization, wait time I, wait time II, directing questions, redirecting questions, probing, and positive reactions, and negative reactions as ways to improve classroom climate.

Learners will demonstrate appreciation for the importance of classroom climate by sharing specific personal experiences related to the best and worst teachers they have had.

Discussion Questions

1 Choose two of the four teacher personality factors discussed in the chapter. Define the factor in your own words. Describe teachers you have had that possessed these factors. Describe teachers you have had that did not possess these factors. How did these four teachers affect classroom climate?

2 Choose any five of the following terms: structuring, signal giving, mands, organization, wait time I, wait time II, directing questions, redirecting questions, probing, and positive and negative reactions. Define each term and give an example of its use in class.

3 Choose two types of cooperative learning procedures and describe them.

4 Consider the teachers you have had in school or church. Who was the best teacher you ever had? Who was the worst teacher you've every had? Write their names at the top of a sheet of paper, separated by a vertical line down the page. Review the chapter and identify the characteristics that differentiate these two teachers. At the bottom of the page, summarize in four or five sentences what you learned about teachers and classroom climate from this exercise.

MEASUREMENT AS MOTIVATION

Evaluation of Learning

*You are to have honest balances, honest weights, an honest dry measure, and an honest liquid measure; I am the L*ORD *your God, who brought you out of the land of Egypt.*

Leviticus 19:36

*You must have a full and honest weight, a full and honest dry measure, so that you may live long in the land the L*ORD *your God is giving you. For everyone who does such things and acts unfairly is detestable to the L*ORD *your God.*

Deuteronomy 25:15–16

*Honest balances and scales are the L*ORD*'s; all the weights in the bag are His concern.*

Proverbs 16:11

*Differing weights and varying measures—both are detestable to the L*ORD*.*

Proverbs 20:10

Can I excuse wicked scales or bags of deceptive weights?

Micah 6:11

It would be better for him if a millstone were hung around his neck and he were thrown into the sea than for him to cause one of these little ones to stumble.

Luke 17:2

There is no luck except where there is discipline.

—Irish proverb[1]

Chapter Rationale

As far as we can gather from Scripture, Jesus never administered a formal examination. But He did evaluate His disciples. He assessed them *by their actions* when they were caught in a storm on the sea of Galilee (Matt 8:26, Mark 4:40). He assessed their *understanding* of His mission: "Who do you say that I am?" (Matt 16:15, Mark 8:29). He assessed the kingdom *values and personal devotion* of Peter when He asked him, "Do you love me?" (John 21:15ff). Jesus "knew what was in man" (John 2:24–5). Yet He asked questions and posed problems to reveal what His listeners understood and believed.

There are many creative ways to evaluate learning. No doubt, you have experienced portfolios, group projects, creative presentations, and the ubiquitous term paper. This chapter focuses on the area of evaluation that produces the greatest amount of sin[2] in Christian academics: examinations. The material in this chapter helps us consider ways to sharpen skills in writing items, grading items, and analyzing the examinations themselves. Teaching is a process of leading learners to a specific destination. Objective evaluation, properly done, determines whether they arrived—in a fair and unbiased way.

Chapter Overview

- ➤ Why Evaluate?
- ➤ Measuring Cognitive Learning
- ➤ Item Analysis: The Discrimination Index
- ➤ Testing as a Motivational Tool
- ➤ *Chapter Concepts, Chapter Objectives, and Discussion Questions*

Why Evaluate?

We defined "education" in the Preface as the process of developing the innate capacities of learners, especially by schooling or instruction. How do we know whether our students have developed their innate capacities? How do we know whether our educational efforts produce meaningful learning? We periodically check student learning[3] for several reasons.

Evaluations provide information on **student progress** toward instructional goals[4] and—in elementary situations—form a communication bridge between the school and home.[5] They reveal which students need **additional help**.[6] Evaluations provide a **basis for honors**, promotion, graduation, and probation.[7] They provide feedback on the **quality of instruction**.[8] Evaluations in the form of tests and quizzes produce **incentive for greater efforts**[9] because research has shown students learn more in courses that use tests than in those that do not.[10] Measuring student performance and assigning grades for student achievements cause anxiety and stress. But evaluation is necessary because too much depends on the information it provides.[11]

The movement toward student- and group-centered methods has also produced more student- and group-friendly approaches to evaluation. Portfolios allow students to display their best work. Assignments are often allowed to be re-worked for a higher grade. Semester-long research projects allow students freedom to work at their own pace, in their own time, to read and develop a topic of their own choosing. Group presentations permit a team-approach to learning, where members of the group produce individual elements, and then synthesize these into a coordinated, multi-faceted whole. Each of these humanistic approaches has its advantages and disadvantages for student learning. But none of them distinguishes the various degrees by which **individuals** in a given course **master** common terms, principles, practices, or skills. If those terms, principles, and practices are important, they need to be evaluated accurately and fairly for every learner in the class.

Formal evaluations, such as those made by objective quizzes, examinations, and performance observations, help teachers make decisions regarding learning activities and time allotment.[12] Systematic evaluations prevent faulty assessments based on student activity level (active or passive) or appearance (attractive or unattractive).[13]

Nothing affects student attitudes in an academic setting more than the **quality of the tests** teachers use. Poorly written test items, subjectively graded essays, and unclear requirements make "objective" evaluation unsettling. Grades—and future opportunities—depend on fair evaluations of student performance. When teachers subject students to unfair examinations, students suffer the consequences of lower grades, and teachers suffer the consequences of lower student evaluations.[14]

Formal testing is rarely if ever done in the non-academic settings of Sunday school or discipleship classes in local churches. Yet, the principles that govern the writing of test items help teachers in any setting learn how to frame clear and direct questions more effectively. The purpose of this chapter is to focus on the writing of fair, accurate, and objective examinations that can test student learning across the spectrum of cognitive learning.

Measuring Cognitive Learning

Despite recent attempts to update Bloom's 1956 taxonomy of cognitive learning, this classic framework of learning levels remains the most popular foundation for test-item development. In

Chapter Twelve, we outlined the use of broad domain-related goal statements ("Learners will demonstrate understanding of John 3:16") and specific level-related indicator statements ("by explaining the terms 'love,' 'world,' 'believe,' and 'eternal life' in their own words") to set up targets for teaching (see suggestions under "Ford"). We described the behavior-content matrix, sometimes called a table of specifications,[15] as a means to track subject content areas and levels of learning addressed in class. The behavior-content matrix provides a clear direction for writing test items and constructing examinations. If examinations are to provide fair, accurate, and objective measures (Prov 16:11; 20:10), they must possess three qualities of measurement.

The Measurement Trio: Validity, Reliability, Objectivity

Tests that provide correct, systematic, and unbiased information on student achievement possess three characteristics. These are validity, reliability, and objectivity.[16]

Validity refers to the appropriateness of a test. A test is *valid* if it actually measures what it purports to measure. A "valid" intelligence test measures *degree of intelligence* rather than some other construct (socioeconomic status, quality of education, family support).[17] This may seem obvious, but all tests are grounded in assumptions. If the assumptions are wrong, tests build on them are not valid. Deaf sixth grade school children regularly score at the "imbecile" level of functioning on the *verbal skills portion* of a state-required intelligence test because they lack experience with spoken language and English vocabulary. These same grade school children score at the "college" level of functioning on *three-dimensional reasoning*, since their manual language is a three-dimensional reality. So do these deaf sixth graders function as imbeciles or college students? Obviously, this state-mandated intelligence test is not valid for deaf grade school students. Intelligence tests that use a specific vocabulary set, experience with classical music, exposure to foreign language study, and middle class social values will produce different results depending on who takes the test. A teenager raised in the inner city may be very intelligent but will likely score poorly on such a test.

There are several types of test validity. *Concurrent validity* refers to how well a smaller, more convenient form matches the score of a longer, more complex test. If the two tests have high concurrent validity, the smaller test produces the same results as the longer one. *Construct validity* refers to how well a test measures a given construct, or psychological concept, such as intelligence or spiritual maturity. *Predictive validity* refers to how well a test predicts future behavior, as in aptitude tests.[18] *Content validity* refers to how well the content of a test matches the universe of learnings the test covers. That is, a test designed for a given unit of study should contain items from that unit. Items should reflect major issues (vocabulary, trends, principles). Including items from other units, or from supplementary material (footnotes, optional readings), lowers the content validity of the test.

A behavior-content matrix assures content validity, because the test items match the outcomes targeted by the unit or course.[19]

Reliability refers to the *precision* of the test—how accurately the test measures student achievement. Poorly written questions inject random noise into student scores and lowers test reliability. The principles provided here improve the quality of test items, which in turn improves the reliability of tests.[20]

Objectivity refers to absence of personal bias in stating questions and scoring answers. "Objective" tests are so called because answers are specifically right or wrong.[21]

How do we write such objective tests? How do we construct the questions? What are the various types of questions that lend themselves to objective evaluation? We turn now to these issues.

Constructing Objective Tests

An objective test consists of questions that students answer with a word, a short phrase, or by circling a given answer. Answers to objective questions are either correct or incorrect. Graders do not need to interpret student responses.[22] Different graders will be able to award the same score for the same answer for each student.[23]

Objective tests have several advantages over essay tests. Asking 100 objective questions over a given content field provides a much better sampling of student knowledge and understanding than asking three or four essay questions. The diagram

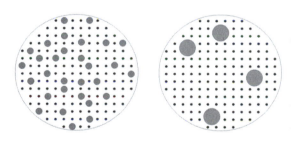

at left illustrates this principle in a simple form. The dots represent facts and concepts in the unit of study. The gray circles represent test items. It is obvious that asking more questions allows the exam to cover more material in the unit. Many more objective questions can be asked in a given amount of time than essay questions. The grading of objective items is easier to do and the test scores provide a more reliable measure of what the student knows.[24]

Writing good objective questions is more difficult and time-consuming, however, than writing essay questions.[25] Perhaps this explains why teachers favor the essay type question. Benefits to student learning and attitude, however, outweigh the cost of time and effort for those committed to fairness in evaluation.

Critics lament that use of objective questions forces students to take a "simplistic" view of great academic themes, reducing complex principles to factual recall. The lament mistakes "simple recall" for "objective." As we shall see, such is not the case. The most common types of objective questions[26] are the supply question,[27] the true-false question,[28] the multiple-choice question,[29] and the matching question.[30]

The SUPPLY question, sometimes called "completion"[31] or "fill in the blank"[32] question, presents a statement with one or more missing words. Blanks replace these words in the statement. The student answers the question by filling in the blank with the most appropriate term in order to correctly complete the statement. This question type is best used when the correct response is a single word or brief phrase.[33] Here is an example:

> When different graders obtain the same scores for a given test, the test is said to have the measurement characteristic known as _____. (objectivity)

Advantages. Supply items are relatively easy to construct.[34] They are efficient in that students can answer more statements of this type than others in a given length of time.[35] Since *recalling* a term is more difficult than *recognizing* it, supply items discriminate better than other types of objective questions.[36] Perhaps its greatest advantage is that a supply item offers little opportunity for guessing.[37]

Disadvantages. Supply items are notorious for being ambiguous. It is difficult to write a supply item that is clear and plainly stated. Grading can be arbitrary and unfair, depending on how synonyms—different words with the same meaning[38]—are handled.[39] More than one word may adequately fill the blank, requiring equal credit for alternative (correct) answers.[40] Finally, overuse of completion items can lead to overemphasis on memorization.[41] Supply items should be supplemented by other types of objective questions.

Writing supply items. The following guidelines will help you avoid major pitfalls in writing supply items.

1. **Limit the number of blanks**. Use only one or two blanks in a supply item. The greater the number of blanks, the greater the item ambiguity.[42] Dembo uses the term "mutilated" to describe supply items with too many blanks.[43]

   > Poor: Piaget wrote that _____ consists of _____ and _____.
   > Better: Piaget wrote that **adaptation** consists of _____ and _____.
   >   (assimilation, accommodation)

2. **Only one correct answer**. Write the item in such a way that only one explicit term or definite word[44] will correctly complete the statement.[45] If there are equally acceptable terms for a given concept, then credit should be given for either answer.[46]

3. **Omit important terms.**[47] Leave only important terms blank. Blanking out minor words makes the item trivial.[48]

> Poor: "Appropriateness" is a _____ for test "validity." (synonym)
>
> Better: "Appropriateness" is a synonym for test "_____." (validity)

4. **Place blank at or close to the end of the statement.** In most cases, it is preferable to place the blank at the end of the statement, allowing the entire sentence to provide the basis for supplying the term. Blanks placed at the beginning reverses this natural process and can confuse prepared as well as unprepared students.[49]

> Poor: _____ is the father of Social Learning theory.
>
> Better: The father of Social Learning theory is _____. (Bandura)

5. **Avoid irrelevant clues.**[50] Do not provide irrelevant clues to the correct answer. An example of an irrelevant clue is to make the length of the blank equal to the number of characters in the word. Make all blanks the same length.[51] Another irrelevant clue is the use of "a" or "an" before the blank (word begins with a vowel or consonant). Use "a(n)" before the blank.

6. **Avoid text quotes.**[52] Do not use directly quoted sentences out of required reading as supply items. Sentences taken out of context are usually ambiguous. Write the supply item based on a clear concept, not a specific quote.

The TRUE-FALSE question, sometimes called the constant alternative question,[53] presents the student with a factual statement, which students judge to be either true or false.[54]

> T   F   According to our course material on learning, students are more
> concerned with the quality of lectures and classroom activities than they
> are with the quality of examinations. (false)

Advantages. True-false test items are efficient and potent. They are *efficient* in that a large number of items can be answered in a short time.[55] They are *potent* because they can directly reveal common misconceptions and fallacies in student thinking.[56] Scoring true-false items is fast and easy.[57]

Disadvantages. A good true-false item is hard to write.[58] An item that makes good sense to the writer may confuse even well-informed students. Statements require careful wording, evaluation, and revision. True-false items encourage guessing.[59] A student can earn fifty percent on a test by simply guessing at the right answer.[60]

Writing True-False items. The following guidelines help avoid major pitfalls in writing true-false test items.

1. **Focus each question on one central idea.**[61] Each statement should focus on one central idea in order to minimize irrelevant confusion.

> Poor: T   F   B. F. Skinner developed operant conditioning principles **and** Jerome Bruner developed the hierarchy of needs.
> (The first part is true and the last part is false)
>
> Better: T   F   B. F. Skinner developed the hierarchy of needs. (false)[62]

2. **Avoid specific determiners.**[63] Specific determiners are words like "only," "all," "always," "none," "no," or "never." True-false items containing these words are usually false. On the other hand, items containing terms like "might," "can," "may," or "generally" are usually true. Write items without using these terms.

> Poor: T   F   Consistent use of instructional objectives will **always** improve student achievement. (Depends on student cooperation in studying)
>
> Better: T   F   Consistent use of instructional objectives helps to improve student achievement. (true)

3. **Call for an absolute answer.**[64] Base true-false items on absolutely true (or absolutely false) statements.[65] Avoid statements that are true under some conditions but not others, unless the conditions are specifically stated. Well-prepared students will have greater difficulty analyzing obscure or confusing statements correctly because they have more information to process in trying to understand what the item is asking.

> Poor: T   F   The bell curve **is helpful** in distributing grades among students in a class.
>
> Better: T   F   The bell curve unfairly forces an arbitrary distribution of grades in a class. (true)

The first statement confuses test-takers with the word "helpful." The bell curve may be helpful to teachers in distributing grades, but it is always harmful in the way it forces fewer As and more Fs in the class.[66]

4. **Minimize the use of negative statements.**[67] State items in a positive, rather than a negative, way to reduce confusion.[68] Avoid double negatives altogether.[69]

Poor:	T F	It is **not infrequently** observed that three-year-olds play cooperatively in groups.
Better:	T F	Three-year-olds play cooperatively in groups. (false: parallel play)

The latter item tests knowledge of three-year-olds and social development. The former requires this knowledge plus skill with mental gymnastics and sentence structure manipulation. This kind of linguistic complexity is especially difficult for international students.

5. **Use precise language.**[70] Avoid using terms like "few," "many," "long," "short," "large," "small," or "important" in test items. These terms are ambiguous. How much is enough for a true-false answer? How big is "big"? How many is "many"?

Poor:	T F	Writing clear test items **is important** in motivating students to study for exams.
Better:	T F	Students are encouraged to study for exams when teachers write clear test items. (true)

The word "important" is ambiguous.

6. **Avoid direct quotes.**[71] Do not use direct quotes from class notes or required readings as the basis for true-false items. First, use of direct quotes overemphasizes rote memory.[72] But statements quoted out of context are too ambiguous to use as a test item. It is better to focus on meanings rather than exact words.[73]

Poor:	T F	Maslow wrote, "It is quite impossible for the student to discover for himself any substantial part of the wisdom of his culture."
Better:	T F	Maslow opposed Bruner's discovery approach to education on the grounds of self-initiated learning. (false)

Maslow welcomed self-initiated learning. It was Skinner the behaviorist who opposed Bruner for his emphasis on cognitive processing. The "better" item focuses on the conceptual difference, not the quote.

7. **Attribute opinion to a source.** Give the source of an opinion statement. Doing this informs the student that the statement is asking whether or not the source, and not the student, holds that opinion.[74]

> Poor: T   F   It is not possible for students to discover for themselves any substantial part of their culture's wisdom.
>
> Better: T   F   **Skinner believed that** it is not possible for students to discover for themselves any substantial part of their culture's wisdom. (true)

The first statement is unclear—is it asking for the student's own view or the view of another? Link the statement with the source to remove this ambiguity.

8. **Insure that item length is not a clue to the answer**. True statements often require qualifications to insure they are absolutely true.[75] Qualifications tend to make true statements longer than false statements, which provides an irrelevant clue to correct answers: "shorter statements tend to be false; longer statements tend to be true." Since some statements must be longer than others, avoid the problem by writing both true and false statements of varying lengths. Students will not be able to use item length as a clue to the answer.[76]

9. **Avoid complex sentences**. Complex grammatical constructions and obscure language confuse students unnecessarily. Write items that are simple statements of truth or misconception.[77]

> Poor: T   F   It is, in the opinion of many scholars, an epistemological dilemma for knowledge to be obtained in a manner inconsistent with objective reason, that is, through rational correspondence to the truth as we experience it in the natural world.
>
> Better: T   F   Valid human knowledge is obtained through an objective study of the natural world. (false)

10. **Include more false items than true items**.[78] A true-false examination should consist of roughly sixty percent false statements.[79] False items discriminate—separate prepared from unprepared learners—better than true items, and produce a more reliable measure.

The MULTIPLE CHOICE question, sometimes called the changing alternative question,[80] is the most popular type of objective question.[81] It consists of a sentence or **question stem** and **several responses**.[82] One response is correct. The others, called distractors,[83] are incorrect but plausible. The most common form of this type is the multiple choice question with four or five responses.[84]

The measurement characteristic related to the precision (accuracy) of a test is

    a. validity   (appropriateness of test—wrong)
    b. subjectivity   (unrelated to question—wrong)
    c. reliability   (correct)
    d. objectivity   (lack of bias—wrong)

Advantages. Multiple-choice questions can be written with less ambiguity and greater structure than true-false or short answer questions.[85] Guessing is reduced[86] since the probability for selecting the correct answer by chance is one in four (25%) or one in five (20%) instead of one in two (50%) for true-false items. Multiple-choice items demand more conceptual discrimination than other forms of objective questions. Multiple-choice items can test at higher levels of learning than other question types.[87] Because students can process multiple-choice questions faster than short-answer essay questions, more questions can be asked, providing a better sampling of student mastery.[88]

Disadvantages. Writing good multiple choice questions is both time-consuming[89] and difficult.[90] Effective distracters—wrong but plausible—are hard to create,[91] particularly if you are providing a fifth or sixth response.[92] Multiple choice tests are less efficient than other objective types because students can process fewer multiple choice items in a given time.[93] Snowman (2009) cites two more disadvantages of multiple-choice items. First, they measure what students know, but reveal nothing about what students can do with that knowledge." And second, multiple-choice tests lead "students to believe that learning is merely the accumulation of universally agreed-upon facts."[94] These two statements are true only if teachers insist on using multiple-choice questions for lower levels of learning. One can construct multiple-choice questions that test higher levels of learning just as effectively as short-answer and essay tests.[95]

Writing Multiple Choice Items. The following guidelines will help you avoid major pitfalls in writing changing alternative items.

1. **Pose a singular problem**. The question stem should pose a clear, definite, singular problem.[96] A common mistake in multiple-choice questions is the use of an incomplete stem.[97] Make the stem a complete sentence or a direct question[98], rather than a sentence fragment.[99]

        Poor: Behavior modification is

                   a. punishment

                   b. classical conditioning

                   c. self-actualization

                   d. reinforcement contingencies

        Better: Which of the following alternatives best characterizes the modern clinical use of behavior modification?

a. punishment

b. classical conditioning

c. self-actualization

d. reinforcement contingencies (correct)[100]

2. **One and only one correct answer**.[101] Be sure that one and only one response is correct. Avoid using synonyms or overlapping responses.[102]

Poor: Which of the following types of research describes a current situation?

a. experimental

b. descriptive   (overlaps c)

c. correlational   (overlaps b)

d. ex post facto

(Correlational research is descriptive research. Both **b** or **c** are correct.)

Better: Which of the following types of research describes a current situation?

a. experimental   (no: future treatment, future situation)

b. base-line design (no: history of measurements)

c. correlational   (correct: contemporary data)

d. ex post facto   (no: based on past events)

3. **Minimize negative stems**.[103] Avoid negative stems if possible. Negative items can confuse students who might otherwise understand the material. If you must use a negative in the stem, emphasize it with boldface or italics.[104]

Poor: Which of the following is not an example of an objective item?

Better: Which of the following is an example of an objective item? (avoids <u>not</u>)

Better: Which of the following is **<u>not</u>** an example of an objective item?

(emphasizes <u>not</u>)

4. **Make response choices similar**. The correct response should not differ from the incorrect alternatives in grammar, length, or construction. Make all responses similar so that the form of the response is not a clue to the correct answer.[105]

Poor: The boiling point of water is

a. 424° F

b. 282° F

c. 212° F at sea level, in an open container

d. 98° F

Requiring Students to Make False Items "True"

One way to make true-false items more reliable is to require students to change specified words or phrases in false statements to make them true. Adding this element combines the potency of a true-false item with the deeper recall of the supply item. Identify the term or phrase students must correct by underlining it.[106] Look at the following, which tests whether students understand the broad categories of research and null hypotheses, and their relation to types of hypotheses:

Original statement: T F Jesus as Prophet reflects the Doing sphere of the Triad. (false)

Inventive answer: T F Jesus as Prophet ^{does not} reflects the Doing sphere of the Triad.
(artificially true!)

Improved: T F Jesus as <u>Prophet</u> reflects the Doing sphere of the Triad. (false)

Correct answer: T F Jesus as ~~Prophet~~ ^{KING} reflects the Doing sphere of the Triad.
(The student made the false item true appropriately)

Better: The boiling point of water at sea level, in an open container, is
- a. 424° F
- b. 282° F
- c. 212° F   (correct)
- d. 98° F [107]

5. **Make responses equally plausible.**[108] Alternative responses should be equally plausible and attractive to the less-prepared student.[109] Each response should be credible and logical.[110]

Poor: Which of the following is **not** an objective-type question?
- a. constant alternative   (objective)
- b. essay   (correct: subjective)
- c. completion   (objective)
- d. large-group discussion   (not credible)

Better: Which of the following is **not** an objective-type question?
- a. constant alternative   (true-false = objective)
- b. essay   (correct)
- c. completion   (supply = objective)
- d. changing alternative   (multiple-choice = objective)

6. **Randomly order responses.**[111] Teachers unwittingly place the correct answer in the middle of the set more often than in the first (a.) or last (d.) positions. Randomly order responses for each question.[112]

7. **Avoid sources of irrelevant difficulty.**[113] Avoid irrelevant sources of difficulty in the stem (question) and the alternative responses. The key word here is "irrelevant." Questions ought to test student understanding of course material by using course vocabulary. Students who do not understand the meaning of required course vocabulary will not be able to read the questions correctly. However, teachers should not confuse students by using unnecessarily complex vocabulary or convoluted sentence constructions. Use foreign language phrases (Latin, Greek) only if students know this is an expectation.

8. **Eliminate extraneous material.**[114] Do not include extraneous material in a question. That is, do not attempt to mislead students by including information not necessary for answering the question. Misleading material makes the determination of each question's emphasis (unfairly) more difficult.

9. **Avoid responses such as "none of the above."**[115] Alternative responses such as "none of the above," "all of the above," and "both b and d" should be eliminated if possible. These responses reduce the number of possible correct choices.[116]

10. **Test at higher cognitive levels.**[117] Multiple-choice items can set a complex case (theological, historical, political, educational, or social) and present alternative explanations for the case. Charts, maps, or graphs can be used in conjunction with a series of multiple-choice questions that call for analysis, synthesis, and evaluation. Avoid testing at the knowledge level—recall of facts—predominantly.

The MATCHING question presents students with two columns[118] of words or phrases that relate to each other. A common version of a matching question has a **numbered item list** on the left and a **lettered response list** on the right.[119] Here is an example:
Match the educational psychology terms on the left with the theorists on the right by writing the appropriate letters in the numbered blanks.

(f) _____ 1. Programmed Instruction	a. Erikson
(c) _____ 2. Life Space	b. Kohlberg
(e) _____ 3. Equilibration	c. Lewin
(a) _____ 4. Trust-Mistrust	d. Maslow
(d) _____ 5. Hierarchy of Needs	e. Piaget
	f. Skinner
	g. Thorndike

Advantages. The matching item can test a large amount of factual material simply and efficiently.[120] Test writers can draw response pairs from various texts, class notes, and additional readings to form a summary of facts. Grading is easy.[121]

Disadvantages. A good matching item is difficult to construct. As the number of response pairs grows, so does the difficulty in processing the combinations required to answer it. Several suggested test-writing principles listed below address this issue directly. Matching items are restricted to measuring factual information[122] and simple concepts.

Writing matching items. The following guidelines will help you avoid major pitfalls in writing supply items.

1. **Limit number of items in the matching question**. Do not create a single matching question with more than eight[123] to ten[124] items. Matching questions that contain more than ten pairs test student intelligence—the ability to manipulate multiple combinations quickly—more than course mastery. IQ testing is not the purpose of course exams. In addition to limiting questions to no more than ten pairs, design the question so that it is contained entirely on one page.[125]

2. **Make the response list longer than the item list**. If a response is correctly used once, and only once, in a given question, then include more responses than numbered items (see the example above). This prevents students from answering the last item simply by elimination.[126] Opinions vary on how much longer to make the response list. Suggestions range from two to three items[127] to fifty percent[128] longer. However, if students can correctly use responses more than once, then both lists can be the same length.[129]

3. **Insure only one correct match**.[130] Insure that each numbered item (left column) matches one and only one word or phrase in the response list (right column). Response options, however, may be used multiple times, creating a type of multi-level multiple-choice question,[131] as shown below.

   (c) _____ 1. Edward Thorndike   a. Thinking
   (b) _____ 2. Abraham Maslow   b. Feeling/Valuing
   (a) _____ 3. Constructivism   c. Doing
   (c) _____ 4. Reinforcement
   (a) _____ 5. Jerome Bruner

4. **Maintain a single central theme for each matching question**.[132] A matching question should contain matched pairs that relate to one central theme. Avoid mixing names, dates, events, and definitions in a single matching item. If various themes must be tested in this way, construct separate matching items, each with a central theme: dates-events, terms-definitions, authors-writings, and so forth.[133]

5. **Keep responses simple**.[134] Place longer statements in the item list (left column) and the shorter answers in the response list (right column). This helps students rapidly scan the response list for the correct match.

6. **Make the response list systematic**.[135] Arrange the answers in the response options column in some systematic way. This might be alphabetical order (names) or chronological order (dates).[136] Ordering responses makes the task of searching through the responses less taxing and allows students to concentrate on answering correctly. Notice in the example question that the response list is ordered alphabetically by theorist's name.

7. **Specific instructions**.[137] Provide clear instructions on how the matching is to be done. Specifically indicate whether students can correctly use answers more than once.[138] Show an example, if necessary.

Essay Tests

Essay tests are constructed from unstructured or "open-ended" questions that require students to collect related thoughts, formulate an answer, and write out their response. For example:

> Discuss educational motivation from the perspective
> of the three major learning theory systems.

Advantages. Essay test items are easy to construct.[139] They allow much greater flexibility and freedom in answering. Since grammar, structure, and content of the answer are left to students, teachers gain insight into students' abilities to organize, integrate, and synthesize concepts in the course.[140] Essay items permit testing at higher levels of learning than most types of objective questions,[141] though many teachers use essay type questions for factual recall as well.[142] Essay questions permit a greater range of answers than objective items, and eliminate guessing.[143]

Disadvantages. Essay questions are difficult to score consistently.[144] Student answers are more ambiguous, more subjective than the constrained responses of objective questions.[145] The result is that test reliability is lower for essay questions than objective items over the same content.[146] Essay tests pose content validity problems,[147] because, as we have already noted, essay items target less course material than objective types.[148] Essay answers are tedious and time-consuming to grade.[149]

Writing essay items. The following guidelines will help you avoid major pitfalls in writing essay items.

1. **Use short-answer essays**.[150] It is much better to use several short answer essay items than one or two long ones. One author defines "short-answer" as a half page.[151] If the testing period is one hour, it would be better to ask six ten-minute essays than two 30-minute essays.

Six shorter questions improve the sampling of course material over the two longer questions. Six questions focus the essays sufficiently to increase reliability of grading, and produces a better measure of what students know.[152]

2. **Write clear questions**.[153] Give sufficient information to guide students toward your intended response.[154] Insure questions are limited in scope so they can be credibly answered within the examination time frame. Dr. Leroy Ford underscored this point, jokingly suggesting the following question: "Define God and give two examples."[155] The following comparison illustrates the principle:

> Poor: Discuss learning theory and its role in Christian education.
>
> Better: Describe the three major learning theory systems. Choose one system and explain how it can be used in a Christian teaching context.

3. **Require all students to answer all questions.**[156] A common contemporary practice, growing out of the influence of humanistic and postmodern personal choice, is to allow students to choose a subset of questions to answer. For example, a teacher might list ten essay questions and allow students to choose any four to answer. While this may increase one's student evaluations, it reduces the reliability of the test scores. Students are not being evaluated on the same questions. It is better to set course objectives, teach according to those objectives, and systematically test whether students achieve those objectives.

4. **Develop a grading key**. Develop a specific grading key[157] or model answer[158] for each essay item. Award points for each element in the key. Major elements of the key should receive more points than minor elements. Award a point or two for grammar, punctuation, organization, and the like.[159] *A grading key provides a systematic guide for **objectively grading** a subjective essay answer.* Without such a key, the score is as much a result of the perception of the grader as it is a measure of the knowledge of the student. Grade each test without knowing its author[160] to avoid any sort of personal bias. Grade one question at a time for all papers.[161] These practices increase the reliability and objectivity of the scoring.

5. **Consider assigning essays as homework.**[162] Rather than confronting students with essay-type questions on an examination, assign essays as homework. The lack of time pressure and availability of resources will permit students to write better papers. Use objective tests to evaluate—individually, reliably, and systematically—the level of understanding achieved by each student in the class.

Item Analysis: The Discrimination Index

Item analysis is a procedure for determining which items in an objective test discriminate between prepared and unprepared students. A test's purpose is to measure students along a scale of achievement. A *discriminating* test separates students from one another based on their objective achievement on the test. It is vitally important that this discrimination be done *fairly, without bias.*

To this end, test writers design examinations such that *every item in a test* contributes to this objective process. When a test item does not contribute positively to the overall score of the test, it should be revised or eliminated altogether. A popular method of item analysis is a procedure called the *Discrimination Index.*

I began using this procedure as a young professor. Inevitably, while going over an examination in class, a student would shout out, "Why did I get number 15 wrong?" Even after I explained the question, and why the correct answer was correct, students would argue for their interpretation of the question: "If we assume such and such and if conditions were this and that, the answer could be so and so." My response of "That's not what the question asked" was seldom good enough to settle the complaints.

With the DI, I could say, "Item 15? This is an excellent discriminating question. Nine of the top 10 students answered it correctly, and only one of the bottom 10 students answered it correctly. Overall, 70 percent of the class answered it correctly." Arguments over personal interpretations of questions ceased. The DI also proved to the class that there were no "bad questions" on the exam, and that when questions separated students into "right" and "wrong" groups, they did so fairly.[163]

There was another, unexpected, benefit. Since I demonstrated the fairness of the tests, and certified that better prepared students scored reliably better than less prepared students, most students expended more effort in preparation. Learning improved. Grades improved overall. Attitudes improved as well,[164] in spite of the difficulty and quantity of the material. See tables on the following pages for a detailed example. Apply the Discrimination Index procedure as follows[165]

- create a spreadsheet with test item numbers across columns and students across rows
- enter 1 (correct) or 0 (incorrect) for each item for each student
- compute total score by adding item scores across columns
- rank order students (with all scores) by sorting on total score
- select the top and bottom 25 percent[166] of scores
- add the item scores for "top" and "bottom" groups separately
- subtract the bottom total from the top total

Enter answers

	1	2	3	4	5	6	7	8	9	10	11	12	13	14	15	16	17	18	19	20	21	22	23	24	25	
	d	b	d	c	c	a	c	b	a	c	c	a	d	b	c	a	d	a	a	c	a	a	c	c	c	item # key
1	a	b	d	c	c	a	c	c	c	a	c	c	a	d	b	c	a	d	c	a	a	c	a	a	d	c	answers
2	d	d	d	b	d	a	c	d	b	c	c	b	c	b	a	a	d	c	b	b	c	b	d	a	c	
3	d	b	d	c	c	a	c	b	a	a	c	a	d	b	c	a	d	a	a	a	c	a	a	c	c	Each row
4	c	b	d	c	d	a	c	c	a	a	c	b	d	b	b	c	a	d	c	a	c	c	b	a	b	a	represents
5	d	b	d	c	c	a	c	d	a	c	c	a	d	b	c	a	d	c	a	a	c	a	a	c	c	one student.
6	a	b	d	c	c	b	c	b	a	c	d	c	a	d	b	c	a	d	c	a	a	c	b	a	d	c	
7	a	b	d	c	c	a	c	b	a	a	c	a	d	b	c	a	a	c	a	a	a	c	a	a	b	c	
8	d	d	d	d	c	a	c	b	a	c	c	a	d	b	c	a	d	c	a	a	c	a	a	d	c	
9	d	b	d	c	c	a	c	b	a	a	c	c	d	b	c	a	d	a	b	a	c	a	a	d	c	
10	d	b	d	d	c	a	c	c	a	c	c	b	d	c	c	a	d	a	a	a	c	a	a	c	c	
11	d	b	d	c	c	b	c	b	a	c	c	a	d	b	c	d	d	b	a	a	c	b	d	e	a	
12	d	b	d	c	c	a	c	b	a	c	c	a	d	b	c	a	d	a	a	a	c	a	a	c	c	
13	d	b	d	a	c	a	c	b	a	c	c	a	d	b	c	a	d	a	a	a	c	a	a	c	c	
14	a	b	d	c	c	b	c	b	a	c	c	a	d	b	c	a	d	a	a	a	c	d	a	d	c	
15	d	b	d	c	c	a	c	b	a	c	c	a	d	b	c	a	d	a	a	a	c	a	a	c	c	
16	d	b	d	a	c	a	c	d	a	a	c	a	d	b	c	a	d	c	a	a	c	a	a	d	c	
17	d	b	d	d	c	a	c	d	a	a	c	a	d	b	c	a	a	a	a	a	c	a	a	d	c	
18	c	b	d	c	c	a	c	b	a	c	c	a	d	b	c	a	d	c	a	a	c	a	a	c	c	
19	a	c	d	c	c	b	c	c	a	c	c	b	c	b	c	a	d	a	a	b	c	a	a	d	c	
20	d	b	a	d	c	a	c	b	a	a	c	a	d	b	c	a	a	c	a	a	c	b	b	d	c	
21	d	d	d	a	c	b	c	c	a	d	c	b	d	b	c	a	d	c	a	a	c	b	a	d	a	
22	d	d	d	c	c	a	c	c	a	c	c	a	d	b	c	a	d	c	a	a	c	a	d	a	c	
23	a	b	d	c	c	b	c	b	a	a	d	b	d	b	c	a	d	c	a	a	c	a	b	a	c	
24	c	b	d	c	c	b	c	a	a	a	c	c	a	d	c	c	a	a	c	d	a	c	b	a	d	c	
25	d	b	d	c	c	b	c	b	a	c	c	a	d	b	c	a	d	c	a	a	c	a	a	c	c	
26	d	b	d	d	c	b	c	b	a	c	c	a	d	b	c	a	d	a	a	a	c	a	d	a	c	
27	c	b	d	c	c	a	c	b	a	c	c	a	d	b	c	a	d	c	a	a	c	a	a	c	c	
28	d	b	d	d	c	b	c	b	a	c	a	c	b	d	b	c	a	d	a	a	a	c	b	a	c	c	28 students

^ student id

IF(N7=N6$,1,0)

If the value of the item at location N7 (answer) equals the value at N6 (key), enter '1' otherwise enter '0'

Convert answers to 1's (correct) and 0's (incorrect)

	1	2	3	4	5	6	7	8	9	10	11	12	13	14	15	16	17	18	19	20	21	22	23	24	25	total	score
1	0	1	1	1	1	1	1	0	1	1	1	1	1	1	1	1	1	0	1	1	1	1	1	0	1	21	84
2	1	0	1	0	0	1	1	0	0	1	1	0	0	1	0	1	1	0	0	0	1	0	0	0	1	11	44
3	1	1	1	1	1	1	1	1	1	0	1	1	1	1	1	1	1	1	1	1	1	1	1	1	1	24	96
4	0	1	1	1	0	1	1	0	1	0	1	0	1	1	0	1	1	0	1	0	1	0	1	0	0	15	60
5	1	1	1	1	1	1	1	0	1	1	1	1	1	1	1	1	1	0	1	1	1	1	1	1	1	23	92
6	0	1	1	1	1	0	1	1	1	1	0	0	1	1	1	1	1	0	1	1	1	1	0	0	1	18	72
7	0	1	1	1	1	1	1	1	1	0	1	1	1	1	1	1	0	0	1	1	0	1	1	0	1	19	76
8	1	0	1	0	1	1	1	1	1	1	1	1	1	1	1	1	1	0	1	1	1	1	1	0	1	21	84
9																								0	1	21	84
10																								1	1	21	84
11																								0	0	18	72
12																								1	1	25	100
13																								1	1	23	92
14																								0	1	20	80
15																								1	1	25	100
16																								0	1	20	80
17																								0	1	20	80
18	0	1	1	1	1	1	1	1	1	1	1	1	1	1	1	1	0	1	1	1	1	1	1	0	1	23	92
19	0	0	1	1	1	0	1	0	1	1	1	0	0	1	1	1	1	0	1	0	1	1	1	0	1	17	68
20	1	1	0	0	1	1	1	1	1	0	1	1	1	1	1	0	0	1	1	1	0	0	0	1	1	17	68
21	1	0	1	0	1	0	1	0	1	0	1	0	1	1	1	1	1	0	1	1	1	0	1	0	1	15	60
22	1	0	1	1	1	1	1	0	1	0	1	1	1	1	1	1	1	0	1	1	1	0	0	1	1	19	76
23	0	1	1	1	1	0	1	1	1	0	0	0	1	1	1	1	1	0	1	1	1	1	0	0	1	17	68
24	0	1	1	1	1	0	1	0	1	0	1	1	0	1	1	0	1	0	0	1	1	0	1	0	1	15	60
25	1	1	1	1	1	0	1	1	1	1	1	1	1	1	1	1	1	1	1	1	1	1	1	1	1	24	96
26	1	1	1	0	1	0	1	1	1	1	1	1	1	1	1	1	1	1	1	1	1	1	0	1	1	21	84
27	0	1	1	1	1	1	1	1	1	1	1	1	1	1	1	1	1	0	1	1	1	1	1	1	1	23	92
28	1	1	1	0	1	0	1	1	1	1	1	0	1	1	1	1	1	0	1	1	1	0	1	1	1	20	80

total * 4 = score

Overlay detail (inset):

	1	2	3	4	5	6	7	8	9	10	11	12
	d	b	d	c	c	a	c	b	a	c	c	a
1	a	b	d	c	c	a	c	c	c	a	c	c	a
2	d	d	d	b	d	a	c	d	b	c	c	b

(row labels 4, 5, 6, 7, 8 shown at left)

- divide the difference between top and bottom totals by the number of scores in one group
- the result is the Discrimination Index

Enter Student Answers

In a spreadsheet program—I am using Excel 2007 here—enter labels for the question numbers (see row 5 above). Enter the correct answers (key) for each question in the next row. Letters can be used as I have here for this multiple-choice exam, or 't' and 'f' for true-false questions, or numbers. It is possible to use the DI procedure for essay questions, but the results are questionable.[167] Enter student names or ID across rows (see column B). Enter student answers in rows for each item.

Set up the next section to convert answers into 1's and 0's to indicate right (1) and wrong (0). Excel uses the 'IF' command to do this. The next table uses a specific example for question 12 (column N) for students 1 and 2. The formula in cell N41 (student 1, item 12) is '**=IF(N7=N$6,1,0)**.' **N7** refers to the answer of student 1 for item 12. **N$6** refers to the correct answer (key) in row 6. The dollar sign ($) keeps the '6' from changing as the formula is copied to other cells. When this formula is copied to other columns, the 'N' in N7 will change, as will the '7' in N7 and the 'N' in N$6. The '6' will not change. This means we need type in the formula only once, and then copy it across 24 columns, and 27 rows, and all the formulas will refer to the proper student answer and key answer.

The formula in cell N42 is '**IF(N8=N$6,1,0)**.' (N41 and N42 are marked on the previous page.).

The insert on the previous page shows the correct answer for item 12 is 'a,' that student 1 answered 'a' and student 2 answered 'b.' After conversion, the table above shows a '1' for student 1 and '0' for student 2 on item 12.

Add the 1's and 0's across columns. The sum is placed in column AB. The formula in the cell AB41 is '**=SUM(C41..AA41')**.'' The row numbers change automatically as the formula is copied from cell AB41 to AB68. If you want scores based on 100 points, multiply the total by 4. The formula in cell AC41 is '**=AB41*4**.' Copy this formula down column AC to each row.

Rank Order Students by Overall Test Grade

Copy the entire section shown above and "paste special" to an area below it. Check "values and number formats," and click OK. This changes all the ***formulas*** (which converted answers "a, b, c, or d" to numbers 1 or 0) to the ***values*** (1,0). Rank order students high to low by their overall grade on the exam. Their rank, high to low, reflects their overall preparation for the examination (see next table). In the spreadsheet, highlight **student names and all 1's and 0's** so they are kept together as

Rank order items by difficulty, low to high (sort columns on sum, row 104)

#	24	18	10	8	1	4	6	12	22	23	2	17	19	20	25	5	11	13	14	3	9	15	16	21	7			
12	1	1	1	1	1	1	1	1	1	1	1	1	1	1	1	1	1	1	1	1	1	1	1	1	1	25	100	high
15	1	1	1	1	1	1	1	1	1	1	1	1	1	1	1	1	1	1	1	1	1	1	1	1	1	25	100	
3	1	1	0	1	1	1	1	1	1	1	1	1	1	1	1	1	1	1	1	1	1	1	1	1	1	24	96	top
25	1	1	1	1	1	1	0	1	1	1	1	1	1	1	1	1	1	1	1	1	1	1	1	1	1	24	96	25%
5	1	0	1	0	1	1	1	1	1	1	1	1	1	1	1	1	1	1	1	1	1	1	1	1	1	23	92	
13	1	1	0	1	1	0	1	1	1	1	1	1	1	1	1	1	1	1	1	1	1	1	1	1	1	23	92	
18	1	0	1	1	0	1	1	1	1	1	1	1	1	1	1	1	1	1	1	1	1	1	1	1	1	23	92	
27	1	0	1	1	0	1	1	1	1	1	1	1	1	1	1	1	1	1	1	1	1	1	1	1	1	23	92	
1	0	0	1	0	0	1	1	1	1	1	1	1	1	1	1	1	1	1	1	1	1	1	1	1	1	21	84	
8	0	0	1	1	1	0	1	1	1	1	0	1	1	1	1	1	1	1	1	1	1	1	1	1	1	21	84	
9	0	1	0	1	1	1	1	0	1	1	0	1	1	1	1	1	1	1	1	1	1	1	1	1	1	21	84	
10	1	1	1	0	1	0	1	0	1	1	1	1	1	1	1	1	1	1	0	1	1	1	1	1	1	21	84	
26	0	1	1	1	1	0	0	1	1	0	1	1	1	1	1	1	1	1	1	1	1	1	1	1	1	21	84	
14	0	1	1	0	1	0	1	1	1	0	1	1	1	1	1	1	1	1	1	1	1	1	1	1	1	20	80	
16	0	0	0	0	1	0	1	1	1	1	1	1	1	1	1	1	1	1	1	1	1	1	1	1	1	20	80	
17	0	1	0	0	1	0	1	1	1	1	0	1	1	1	1	1	1	1	1	1	1	1	1	1	1	20	80	
28	1	0	1	1	0	0	0	0	1	1	1	1	1	1	1	1	1	1	1	1	1	1	1	1	1	20	80	
7	0	0	0	1	0	1	1	1	1	1	1	0	1	1	1	1	1	1	1	1	1	1	0	1		19	76	
22	0	0	0	0	1	1	1	1	0	0	1	1	1	1	1	1	1	1	1	1	1	1	1	1		19	76	
6	0	0	1	1	1	1	0	0	0	1	1	1	1	1	0	1	1	1	1	1	1	1	1	1		18	72	
11	0	0	1	1	1	1	0	1	0	0	1	1	1	1	0	1	1	1	1	1	0	1	1			18	72	
19	0	1	1	0	0	1	0	0	1	0	1	0	1	0	1	1	0	1	1	1	1	1	1			17	68	
20	0	0	0	1	0	1	1	0	1	0	1	0	1	1	1	1	1	0	1	1	1	1	1			17	68	
23	0	0	0	1	0	1	0	0	1	0	1	1	1	1	1	0	1	1	1	1	1	1	1			17	68	bottom
4	0	0	0	0	0	1	1	0	1	1	1	0	0	0	1	1	1	1	1	1	1	1	1			15	60	25%
21	0	0	0	0	1	0	0	0	0	1	0	1	1	1	1	1	1	1	1	1	1	1	1			15	60	
24	0	0	0	0	1	0	0	0	1	0	1	1	1	1	1	0	1	1	1	1	1	1	1			15	60	
2	0	0	1	0	1	0	1	0	0	0	1	0	0	1	0	1	0	0	1	1	1	1				11	44	low
sum	10	12	14	17	18	18	18	19	19	22	23	24	25	25	25	26	26	26	26	27	27	27	27	27	28			

^ most difficult (least # right)   easiest item (most # right) ^

rows are sorted. *Do not highlight the item numbers across the top.* SORT high to low on "total score" (column AC) so that the highest grade is at the top and the lowest grade on the bottom.

Sum the number correct for each item by using the formula '**=SUM(C76..C103)**.' Copy the formula across columns, so that 'number right' is computed for each item (see row 104 below).

Rank Order Items by Number Correct

Rank items by number correct across columns. Highlight item numbers and all 1s and 0s so that columns are kept together when they are sorted. *Do not include student names (IDs) or student totals and scores.* SORT left to right on row 104 *sums*. Sort low to high, so that the smallest number (most difficult item) is on the left, and the largest number (least difficult item) is on the right.

Divide Students into Top and Bottom Groups

Identify top and bottom proportions of students to compare. You can choose a percentage ranging from 10 to 40 percent. Twenty-five percent is common and gives you the top and bottom quarters of the class. Ten percent results in a sharper discrimination but should only be used in larger classes (40 or more students). Forty percent results in a looser discrimination.

	A	B	C	D	E	F	G	H	I	J	K	L	M	N	O	P	Q	R	S	T	U	V	W	X	Y	Z	AA	AB	AC	AD

107 Eliminate all rows except top ten and bottom 7 (25%). *Add 1's and 0's for each item and for each group separately.*

109 *Top seven (25%)*

110	24	18	10	8	1	6	4	12	22	23	2	17	19	20	25	5	11	13	14	3	9	15	16	21	7		
111 12	1	1	1	1	1	1	1	1	1	1	1	1	1	1	1	1	1	1	1	1	1	1	1	1	1	25	100
112 15	1	1	1	1	1	1	1	1	1	1	1	1	1	1	1	1	1	1	1	1	1	1	1	1	1	25	100
113 3	1	1	0	1	1	1	1	1	1	1	1	1	1	1	1	1	1	1	1	1	1	1	1	1	1	24	96
114 25	1	1	1	1	1	1	0	1	1	1	1	1	1	1	1	1	1	1	1	1	1	1	1	1	1	24	96
115 5	1	0	1	0	1	1	1	1	1	1	1	1	1	1	1	1	1	1	1	1	1	1	1	1	1	23	92
116 13	1	1	0	1	1	0	1	1	1	1	1	1	1	1	1	1	1	1	1	1	1	1	1	1	1	23	92
117 18	1	1	1	1	0	1	1	1	1	1	1	1	1	1	1	1	1	1	1	1	1	1	1	1	1	23	92
118	7	5	5	6	6	6	6	7	7	7	7	7	7	7	7	7	7	7	7	7	7	7	7	7	7		

119 ^ sum of correct scores in *top* 7 for hardest item

121 *Bottom seven (25%)*

122 19	0	1	1	0	0	1	0	0	1	1	0	1	1	0	1	1	1	0	1	1	1	1	1	1	1	17	68
123 20	0	0	0	1	1	0	1	1	0	0	1	0	1	1	1	1	1	1	0	1	1	1	1	1	1	17	68
124 23	0	0	0	1	0	1	0	0	1	0	1	1	1	1	0	1	1	1	1	1	1	1	1	1	1	17	68
125 4	0	0	0	0	0	1	1	0	0	1	1	1	0	0	0	1	1	1	1	1	1	1	1	1	1	15	60
126 21	0	0	0	0	1	0	0	0	0	1	0	1	1	1	0	1	1	1	1	1	1	1	1	1	1	15	60
127 24	0	0	0	0	0	1	0	1	0	1	1	0	0	1	1	1	0	1	1	1	1	1	1	1	1	15	60
128 2	0	0	1	0	1	0	1	0	0	0	0	1	0	0	1	0	1	0	0	1	1	1	1	1	1	11	44
129	0	1	2	2	3	4	3	2	2	4	4	5	5	4	5	5	6	5	6	6	6	6	7	7	7		

130 ^ sum of correct scores in *bottom* 7 for hardest item

132	7	4	3	4	3	2	3	5	5	3	3	2	2	3	2	2	1	2	1	1	1	1	0	0	0

133 ^ difference between top and bottom sums. Divide by 7 (25% of 28 students) to produce the discrimination index for this item

135 item	24*	18	10	8	1	6	4	12	22	23	2	17	19	20	25	5	11	13	14	3	9	15	16	21	7
136	1.000		0.429		0.429		0.429		0.714		0.429		0.286		0.286		0.143		0.143		0.143		0.000		0.000
137		0.571		0.571		0.286		0.714		0.429		0.286		0.429		0.286		0.286		0.143		0.143		0.000	

138 ^ discrimination index

140 excellent	0.700 - 1.000
141 good	0.300 - 0.699
142 weak	0.001 - 0.299
143 barrier	0.000
144 bad	less than 0.000

Summary:
Out of 25 questions, there are 3 excellent discriminators, 8 good discriminators, 11 weak discriminators, and 3 barrier questions. There are no bad questions (=negative index)

The section above uses 25 percent of 28 students, producing the top seven and bottom seven students. These sections are shaded and boldfaced above. In the next table, the middle rows have been deleted, leaving only the top seven and bottom seven students and their scores.

Count Correct Answers

For each question in the exam, count how many students in the top group answered correctly (1's) (HIGH count) and how many in the bottom group answered correctly (LOW count). If the question fairly separates students by their level of preparation, more of the top group will have answered it correctly than in the bottom group. HIGH will be greater than LOW.

In the table above, the 1's and 0's are added across the rows of the top ten students (see row 118). Do the same for the bottom block (see row 129). This produces HIGH and LOW counts for every question.

Compute the Discrimination Index

Compute the Discrimination Index by subtracting LOW from HIGH to computer a DIFFERENCE (see row 132). The formula in cell C132 is '**=C118-C129.**'

The DI is computed by dividing the DIFFERENCE between high and low counts by the NUMBER of scores in one group. In the table above, NUMBER is 7. The DI for the hardest question on the exam—#24—is equal to (7-0)/7 = 1.000. The formula in cell C136 is '=**C132/7**' (which is the equivalent to DIFFERENCE/NUMBER).

While only 10 of 28 students answered #24 correctly, it is a perfect discriminator.[168]

Interpreting the Index

A discrimination index ranges from -1.00 to +1.00. **Negative indices** indicate faulty questions because more "bottom" students answered these correctly than "top" students. Questions with negative indices are faulty in some way, causing *more informed* students (based on total score) to answer them correctly less often than *less informed* students.

Positive indices indicate that questions *fairly* separate more informed from less informed students—the larger the index, the more discriminating the question. Questions that produce indices very close or equal to zero *do not discriminate* between upper and lower groups. This does not make them bad questions because there are some items we expect every student to answer correctly. These questions are called "barrier" questions.

In summary, DI scores between +0.00 and +0.30 identify weak discriminating questions ("discriminators"). Values between +0.30 and +0.70 identify good discriminators. Values above +0.70 identify excellent discriminators.[169]

Using Indices to Revise Tests

Analyze all items scoring less than 0.00 on the Discrimination Index. Consider whether items were determined faulty because of their own structure, or because of lack of emphasis in classroom learning. When "top students" answered a question wrong, *how did* they respond? Which multiple choice alternative *did* they select? How *did* they attempt to correct false items? What words *did* they supply in blanks? What matches *did* they make? An analysis of the responses of top students helps clarify their points of confusion. Make notes of these areas to insure that you make essential distinctions in class. If the items appear to be faulty because of vague structure, rewrite or eliminate them.

Consider the mix of discrimination and barrier questions in your exam. A good starting place is 60 percent barrier items and 40 percent discriminating items. Tests can be made *legitimately* more difficult by increasing the percentage of discriminating questions (say, from 40% to 60%) and by selecting questions with higher discrimination indices (increase the number of questions with a DI greater than 0.70).

Base Discrimination index values on as many students as possible. In classes of less than 40 students, indices become less reliable, so use them with caution. DI scores are not permanent, nor do they determine which students are the class are the best. They simply reflect the degree of preparation of students on a particular test.

Using the Discrimination Index, however, solves one of the most frustrating problems students face in school: vague and arbitrary testing. Properly used, the discrimination index insures that examinations yield valid and reliable measurements of student learning by evaluating answers on every question against total score. Such fairness in "weights and measures" used to judge the achievement of our "little ones" is sure to please the Lord, Who made abundantly clear His views on measurements.

Testing as a Motivational Tool

The overarching theme of the present unit is motivation, and we turn now to consider the impact that testing has on student motivation. No matter how well students understand their assigned subjects, poorly written tests prevent them from demonstrating what they have learned. When course grades are determined by arbitrary or faulty measurements, they are not valid indicators of student learning. This is unfair in secular settings, but it is nothing short of sin in a Christian context. Millstones (Matt 18:6). The motivation to study deteriorates quickly among students caught in such a situation.

Slavin describes seven characteristics that *enable tests to be motivational tools*. Tests should focus on **"important"** subject matter.[170] That is, write test items in a way that emphasizes major ideas, terms, and principles. Avoid trivial questions.

Tests should be **"soundly based."**[171] That is, tests should measure, fairly and accurately, the actual knowledge and understanding of students. The focus should be on mastery of the prescribed subject, and not on extraneous issues that "students should know by now."

Tests should set **"consistent standards."**[172] Requirements should be the same for all students. Avoid giving students the choice of questions to answer.

Tests should have **"clear criteria"**[173] for grading. Students should know the requirements for earning high marks.

Tests should receive **"reliable interpretations."**[174] The grading of objective tests is far more reliable, and much less open to question, than essay tests. Essay exams require objective checklists so that graders can evaluate questions objectively. In either case, students' answers need objective evaluation.

Students should receive **"frequent evaluations."**[175] Administering shorter quizzes, more frequently, maintains higher student achievement than larger, less frequent examinations. Teachers can also supplement larger examinations by homework assignments, problem-solving exercises, group work tasks, and other evaluation activities.

Finally, students benefit from **"challenging evaluations."**[176] Motivation suffers when tests are either too easy or too difficult. Motivation is highest when tests are challenging for all, and impossible for none.

Teachers consistently promote high levels of motivation for their students when they provide an inviting classroom, clear explanations of the subject, and consistently fair and challenging examinations.

In Summary

As Christian educators, we are held to higher standards than our secular counterparts (Jas 3:1). We deal with the "little ones" of the Lord—children, youth, or young adults—students who look to us as representatives of Christ to teach them. Shoddy examinations frustrate their best efforts to demonstrate success and undermine future opportunities for study and service.

Old Testament Law is clear: "You must not act unfairly in measurements of length, weight, or volume. You are to have honest balances, honest weights, an honest dry measure, and an honest liquid measure; I am the LORD your God, who brought you out of the land of Egypt" (Lev 19:35–36).

Isaiah writes, "Woe to those enacting crooked statutes and writing oppressive laws to keep the poor from getting a fair trial and to deprive the afflicted among my people of justice" (Isa 10:1–2a).

Jesus reflected these sentiments in His chastisement over power: "You know that the rulers of the Gentiles dominate them, and the men of high position exercise power over them. It must not be like that among you. On the contrary, whoever wants to become great among you must be your servant, and whoever wants to be first among you must be your slave; just as the Son of Man did not come to be served, but to serve, and to give His life—a ransom for many" (Matt 20:25–28).

It is a matter of simple ethics that the evaluations of students—believers who look to us for learning in a Christian context—should be as accurate and fair as possible. We do well to challenge our students toward excellence, but we undermine that very possibility with arbitrary scales and vague measures.

Christian teaching is far more than scholarly discourses. It includes the work of the shepherd as well as the instructor in terms of nurture, guidance, and support. Our Master has warned us: He will evaluate us the way we evaluate others: "By the measure you use, it will be measured and added to you" (Mark 4:24). Are there learned scholars among us who think this kingdom principle excludes Christian classrooms? Obviously, to our shame, there are.

But it need not be so. We need not abuse our students in the way we ourselves were abused. Neither do we need to give up objective evaluation altogether for the soft, vague, relativistic methods of Postmodernism. We have ways to test with grace and justice. We can learn from Another, a Teacher Who washed students' feet. "For I have given you an example that you also should do just as I have done for you. . . . If you know these things, you are blessed if you do them (John 13:15,17).

Chapter Concepts

Barrier question	Test item with low positive discrimination index that all students are expected to know
Changing alternative	Alternative name for the multiple-choice question
Constant alternative	Alternative name for the true-false question
Content validity	Type of validity that reflects correspondence between test and course material
Discriminating question	Question that separates more-prepared from less-prepared students
Discrimination index	Numerical value that reflects strength of discrimination of a given question
Distracters	Alternative choices in multiple-choice questions that are incorrect but credible
Grading key	List of correct answers
Informal evaluation	Judgment of student progress by personal observation of participation in class
Irrelevant cues	Hints that permit students to answer questions correctly without understanding
Item analysis	Process to evaluate the quality of individual questions in a test
Negative index	Discrimination Index value less that 0.00. Indicates a faulty question
Objective test	Test consisting of items whose answers are either correct or incorrect (right/wrong)
Objectivity	A quality of measurement that indicates absence of personal bias in questions

Positive index	Discrimination Index value greater than 0.00. Indicates a good question
Reliability	A quality of measurement that indicates level of precision in a test.
Specific determiners	Clue-words in items like "only" (usually false) and "might" (usually true)
Supply question	Question type that requires student to complete a statement by "filling in a blank"
Validity	A quality of measurement that reflects the appropriateness of a test for given content.

Chapter Objectives

Learners will demonstrate knowledge of test writing principles by matching given principles with their definitions.

Learners will demonstrate understanding of proper principles of writing test items by . . .

- determining whether selected test items are correctly written.
- writing two questions of each type on the material contained in the chapter
- properly evaluating the questions of at least three classmates.

Learners will demonstrate appreciation for writing clear test items by sharing experiences of good and bad testing experiences.

Discussion Questions

1 Explain why objective tests produce more reliable scores than essay tests.

2 Evaluate the questions below based on material in the chapter. Write a "G" for "good" questions, "P" for "poor" questions, and "?" if you are not sure. *Explain why* you evaluated the question as you did.

_____ 1. _____ and _____ are major influences on identity formation (Erikson).

_____ 2. T F Carl Rogers, one of the founding fathers of humanistic psychology, grew up in a conservative, Bible-believing home.

_____ 3. Jean Piaget

     a. founded the Behaviorism School in America

     b. understood human thinking to be stable from childhood to adulthood

     c. laid the foundation for humanistic psychology

     d. developed principles of affective, as well as cognitive, development.

_____ 4. Kohlberg's fourth stage, related to society's need for organization and harmony, is called _____.

_____ 5. T F   Piaget is to humanism what Skinner is to cognitive theory.

3 Create two questions of each of the five objective types using guidelines in the chapter.

4 Describe your best and worst test experience in writing. Evaluate the experiences and explain what made these experiences as good/bad as they were.

UNIT 5

Educational Psychology and the Brain

President George H. W. Bush declared 1990–2000 the "Decade of the Brain" on July 17, 1990. He anchored the importance of brain research to overcoming a variety of diseases, such as Alzheimer's, and disabilities, such as stroke, schizophrenia, autism, impairments of speech, language, and hearing, as well as drug addiction and AIDS. The proclamation generated millions of dollars for research.[1]

Research has proceeded at a rapid pace, and discoveries in the last two decades have overturned one hundred years of established scientific views of brain structure and function. "In fact, 95% of what we know about the brain has been learned in the last fifteen years" (2008).[2]

Chapter 16: Mind Over Matter: Teaching Brains by Teaching People

In Chapter Sixteen, we analyze the revolution in brain science, evaluate the questionable leap from brain science to classroom practice, focus on the role of mental attention, suggest implications for the teaching ministries of the Church, and recommend several cautions when reading materials intent on "teaching brains."

Recent research findings, and the tremors they are sending through the materialistic dogmas of the past century, reinforce much of what we already do, by experience, in Christian teaching and discipleship. They reinforce our best approaches in startling ways, and help us in ways brain scientists never dreamed.

MIND OVER MATTER

Teaching Brains by Teaching People

For it was You who created my inward parts; You knit me together in my mother's womb.
I will praise You, because **I have been remarkably and wonderfully made.**
Psalm 139:13–14, emphasis mine

So if you have been raised with the Messiah, **seek what is above,** *where the Messiah is, seated at the right*
hand of God. **Set your minds on what is above,** *not on what is on the earth.*
Colossians 3:1–2, emphasis mine

Pay careful attention, *then, to how you* walk—*not as unwise people but as wise*—*making the most of*
the time, because the days are evil.
Ephesians 5:15–17, emphasis mine

Give your attention *to public reading, exhortation, and teaching. . . .* **Practice** *these things;* **be**
committed *to them, so that your progress may be evident to all.*
1 Timothy 4:13,15, emphasis mine

Man's power of choice enables him to think like an angel or a devil, a king or a slave.
Whatever he chooses, mind will create and manifest.
—Frederick Bailes[1]

Chapter Rationale

Advanced medical technology in the form of "positron emission tomography (PET), single pro-
ton emission computed tomography (SPECT), magnetic resonance imaging (MRI), and functional
magnetic imaging (fMRI)," has provided the means in recent years to measure brain functioning in

real time,[2] even color-coding areas of the brain that "light up" in response to stimuli. Research has proceeded at a rapid pace, and discoveries in the last two decades have overturned one hundred years of established views of brain structure and function. "In fact, 95% of what we know about the brain has been learned in the last fifteen years" (2008).[3]

Educators have been quick to claim these discoveries for the "improvement" of the classroom, creating a new educational industry called "Brain-based learning." Some would say this has developed too quickly. They caution against many of the confident pronouncements of those who advocate this new wave of education, which some refer to as "teaching the brain."

Much of this material is suspect, making leaps of logic from synapses, lobes, and neurotransmitters to specific teaching procedures. Brain structure and function are so complex that specific connections to teaching strategies remain, at best, questionable, and at worst, dangerous. New brain discoveries render previous ones obsolete, and at times, completely wrong—and this happens repeatedly. It is difficult to stay current, or to say anything with certainty, since tomorrow may bring, *will* bring, another discovery that undoes today's accepted truth.

A more basic question begs an answer: Is it necessary for teachers to understand how brains function to "produce thought"? Do we really need to understand, for example, how potassium ions leap across synapses[4] in order to effectively disciple learners? We certainly do not need to understand Ohm's Law[5] in order to turn on the lights, or comparative theories of light—*Does light consist of continuous frequency waves or packet-like photons?*—to use a digital projector. Is brain-based learning (2000s) yet another educational fad, soon to fade into the grand warehouse of educational tools like Instructional Television (1950s), Computerized Instruction (1960s), Open Classrooms (1970s), "Authentic Assessment" (1980s), and Learning Styles (1990s)? Or, are there discoveries in recent brain research that can help us develop as teachers and disciplers long-term?

In fact, there is. Discoveries in neuroscience have revolutionized thinking concerning the relationship between the mind (philosophy, consciousness, free will) and the brain (physiology, neuro-networks, genetic determinism). These findings reinforce much of what we already do, by experience, in Christian teaching and discipleship. They reinforce our approaches in startling ways. We analyze the revolution itself, evaluate the leap from brain science to classroom practice, focus on what is, for me, the most exciting brain-based discovery of all, and then suggest implications for the teaching ministries of the Church and cautions concerning the onslaught of materials intent of "teaching brains."

Chapter Overview

- ➤ A Wealth of Information—The Riches of Confusion
- ➤ Confusion Personified—Left-Brain Right-Brain Dichotomies
- ➤ The Sciences and Christian Education
- ➤ The Decade of the Brain: Stimulus for Research
- ➤ The Complexity of Brain Development
- ➤ The Leap from Brain Research to Educational Practice
- ➤ The Key to Physiological Brain Change: Mental Attention
- ➤ A Scriptural Call to Attention
- ➤ The Influence of God's Mind on Our Brains
- ➤ Implications for "Teaching the Brain"
- ➤ Negotiating the Evolving Field of Brain-Based Learning
- ➤ One Major Question Remains
- ➤ *Chapter Concepts, Chapter Objectives, Discussion Questions*

A Wealth of Information—The Riches of Confusion

In the past ten years, a tsunami of books and articles about "teaching the brain" has hit educational circles. I take a considerable risk in focusing a single chapter on the subject. On one hand, there is no way this chapter can wrap itself around the mountain of material available for study. Whatever I choose as my sample of sources will fail to provide a balanced evaluation of the range of viewpoints, which seem to extend from exuberant devotion to indifferent rejection. Views are fluid because researchers continue to make astounding discoveries. And that's "the other hand": whatever we write here may well be replaced in a very few years by new discoveries—discoveries that are being made every day.

In 2000, Daniel Drubach wrote an illustrated book with the audacious title *The Brain Explained*. There on the front cover is a standard depiction of the human brain, color-coded by brain structure. The implication is that regions of the brain are fixed, as are the functions those regions perform. Experimental evidence throughout the 1990s demonstrates, however, that brain structures are not fixed, that in fact the brain is quite capable of remapping itself. In 1995 researchers "studied six men whose devastating left-hemisphere stroke had largely destroyed" the area critical to understanding speech.[6] All six had "severe impairments in their ability to use and comprehend spoken words." After intensive therapy, all six regained their ability to speak and communicate. When PET[7] scans were done, it was discovered that regions in the *right* hemisphere had become active and had taken over the functions of the left brain's damaged language zones.[8]

Such changes also happen "naturally" as a result of genetic disabilities. Brain regions that are responsible for processing sound in individuals with normal hearing actually remap themselves to process visual stimuli in congenitally deaf individuals.[9] The regions and functions of the brain are not permanently fixed.

In 2002, Joseph LeDoux equated human personality to the tiny space between the axon of one neuron and the dendrite of another.[10] Daniel Schacter, chairman of Psychology at Harvard University, writes on the back cover, "Synapses, the spaces between neurons, are the channels through which we think, act, imagine, feel, and remember. In short, they enable each of us to function as a single, integrated individual—from moment to moment, from year to year."[11]

LeDoux himself writes in his "Acknowledgments," "The bottom-line point of this book is 'You are your synapses.'"[12] In other words, these profound thinkers of the twenty-first century define the very essence of "you" as the empty spaces between neurons in your brain. This strikes me as comparable to reducing a family's Disney World car trip to the tiny gaps across which their motor's spark plugs fire.

Writers have applied brain research to the field of ethics. In 2007, Walter Gannon edited a book of essays entitled *Defining Right and Wrong in Brain Science: Essential Readings in Neuroethics*. An overarching goal of the text is to answer this question: "What can brain scans tell us about our capacity for moral reasoning and *whether individuals are able or unable to control their impulses* when they act?" *(emphasis mine).*[13] Apparently, these moralists wonder if we can choose right over wrong. Obviously, God knew the answer to the question—that is, "man *is able*"—when He directly commanded us to do just that in the Ten Commandments.[14]

Confusion Personified—Left-Brain Right-Brain Dichotomies

Roger Sperry proposed in 1973 the idea that left and right hemispheres of the brain function differently. "There appear to be two modes of thinking, verbal and nonverbal, represented *rather separately* in left and right hemispheres respectively . . . . Our education system, as well as science in general, tends to neglect the nonverbal form of intellect. What it comes down to is that modern society discriminates against the right hemisphere" (emphasis mine).[15] From Sperry's work developed the idea that we tend to be "left-brained" or "right-brained" in terms of thinking preferences. This dichotomy of thinking inspired many self-help books that exhorted people to "liberate their right brains and avoid too much sterile left-brain thinking."[16]

Carole Philips, associate professor of education at the Harvard Graduate School of Education, continues (in 2009) to offer an on-line quiz to "help you learn whether you are a left-, right-, or middle-brained teacher." She maintains the dichotomous view, explaining that *Right-brain dominant* means thinking and decisions are guided by "your intuitive, emotional right hemisphere," and *Left-brain dominant* means thinking and decisions are guided by the sequential, time-oriented left hemisphere." She adds a new category, *Middle-brain dominant*, in which people

LEFT BRAIN FUNCTIONS	RIGHT BRAIN FUNCTIONS
uses logic	uses feeling
detail oriented	"big picture" oriented
facts rule	imagination rules
words and language	symbols and images
present and past	present and future
math and science	philosophy & religion
can comprehend	meaning
knowing	believes
acknowledges	appreciates
order/pattern perception	spatial perception
knows object name	knows object function
reality based	fantasy based
forms strategies	presents possibilities
practical	impetuous
safe	risk taking

http://www.viewzone.com/bicam.html

struggle to overcome confusion as the two halves battle for dominance. Such thinking is "flexible" and often "vacillate[s] between the two hemispheres," sometimes becoming "confused when decisions need to be made."[17]

The problem is that the "left-right brain" dichotomy is false. John McCrone, writing in 2000, declared that this "myth" of brain dichotomy—coldly logical and verbal *Left* versus imaginative and emotional *Right*—is viewed by "most neuroscientists . . . as simplistic at best and nonsense at worst." McCrone used brain scans to describe how *both sides* of the brain play an active, *cooperative role* in mental functioning. While differences in hemispheric functioning exist, these differences are more in processing styles than content.

McCrone used language and spatial perception as examples. Language was long thought to be a left-brain (i.e., verbal) function. Research in the 1990s showed that language is represented on *both sides* of the brain. The left side handles core aspects of speech, such as grammar and word production, while the right side manages intonation and emphasis. Both sides of the brain function in a cooperative, simultaneous way to produce "language." As we saw in the 1995 study of six stroke victims, the brain can create new structures to control language when "standard" structures are damaged or destroyed.

Spatial perception, long thought to be a right-brain function, actually involves *both hemispheres* in complex ways. The right side is more active in "a general sense of space," while the left side is more active "when someone thinks about objects at particular locations."

McCrone's conclusion, stated briefly above, was straightforward: the simple dichotomies "that inspired so many self-help books exhorting people to liberate their right brains and avoid too much sterile left-brain thinking" are out. "It is how the two sides of the brain complement and combine that counts."[18]

Jerry Larsen wrote *Religious Education and the Brain: A Practical Resource for Understanding How We Learn about God* in 2000.[19] Larsen emphasized the newer thinking style over the older structural preference view of left- and right-brain functioning. Yet it is difficult to escape the sense of dichotomy even as we read his seven ("left/right") processing pairs: logical-intuitive, intellectual-sensual, rational-mythical, abstract-concrete, sequential-holistic, verbal-visual/spatial, and scientific-poetic.[20] "Evaluating human cognitive abilities just in terms of left-right thinking skills is a bit too simple."[21] Indeed, and yet such descriptions continue.

The brain.web-us.com Web site emphasizes contrasts between left and right *styles* of thinking. Yet, as we read over the tabled contrasts below, is there not a sense in which these specific "style" characteristics categorize people just as the older Left/Right dichotomy did? One could use the characteristics listed below to create a test to determine whether learners are "Left Style" or "Right Style."

Carole Phillips is far from alone in continuing the idea of left- and right-brain dichotomies. Andrew Curran (2008) devotes a chapter (24 small pages, 12 of these filled with large crayon drawings) to the left/right brain perspective. Granted, he struggles to include the newer findings of complementary functioning in his analysis. Ameliorating phrases include such as these, "Obviously there is a *great deal of shared function* between the two parts [of the brain]." "Lateralization however should be thought of in terms of '*complementary hemispherical specialization*.' "Both your hemispheres carry equal functionality."[22] "This [dichotomy] is an *extremely simplistic way* of looking at brain functioning as *both hemispheres in fact contain both these functions* . . . " (emphasis mine).[23]

In the end, however, he lays out the classic verbal/nonverbal [dichotomous] view. "For this discussion, *I want you to imagine* that one hemisphere dominates the other in terms of these functions" [emphasis mine]. And so the Left/Right brain perspective continues in a 2008 publication, subtitled "The True Story of Your Amazing Brain," and on a 2009 Web site created by an education professor at Harvard University. Phillips and Curran are far from alone.

Left Hemisphere Style	Right Hemisphere Style
Rational	**Intuitive**
• Responds to **verbal** instructions	• Responds to **demonstrated** instructions
• Problem solves by **logically and sequentially** looking at the parts of things	• Problem solves with **hunches**, looking for **patterns and configurations**
• Looks at **differences**	• Looks at **similarities**
• Is **planned** and **structured**	• Is **fluid** and **spontaneous**
• Prefers established, **certain information**	• Prefers elusive, **uncertain information**
• Prefers **talking and writing**	• Prefers **drawing** and manipulating objects
• Prefers **multiple choice** tests	• Prefers **open ended** questions
• **Controls feelings**	• **Free with feelings**
• Prefers **ranked authority structures**	• Prefers **collegial authority structures**
Sequential	**Simultaneous**
• Is a **splitter**: distinction important	• Is a **lumper**: connectedness important
• Is **logical**, sees cause and effect	• Is **analogic**, sees correspondences, resemblances
Draws on previously **accumulated, organized information**	Draws on unbounded **qualitative patterns** that are not organized into sequences, but that cluster around images

http://brain.web-us.com/brain/right_left_brain_characteristics.htm, *bold emphases mine*

I recently googled "Left Brain," and was given 7,100,000 references.[24] I looked through the first ten pages of references, and every one of them reflected the "accepted truth" of the Left-Right brain functioning. Whether the authors intend to convey the older dichotomous myth or the newer cooperative/shared view is often hard to discern, as in the examples above. Regardless, teachers are urged, repeatedly and passionately, to move away from "cold, rational" Left Brain teaching approaches, in order to embrace the "warm, spontaneous" Right Brain approaches.[25]

Popular theories die hard even when they are thoroughly debunked by valid, albeit more complex, scientific evidence. Older publications set error in an obsolete frame of reference. Newer publications quote them, re-energizing the misconceptions. Our brains function, we now know, through complementary processes of both hemispheres, and, as we have already noted, when a function in the left hemisphere is disabled, the brain is quite capable of reconstructing that same function in the right hemisphere.[26] The structure of the brain is not fixed, nor does it determine the choices we make, nor how we make them.

The confusion will continue because the human mind is "the most complex creative thing known to us."[27] The point of this chapter, then, is to provide a meaningful framework to use as you begin your study of this rapidly evolving field. Like the rest of the text, I orient the framework from the teacher's point of view. From that viewpoint, I promise educational gold before we are through. We begin our prospecting journey by seeing how neuroscience fits into the overall picture of Christian education.

The Sciences and Christian Education

We discussed the relationship between science (educational psychology) and faith (Christian education) in Chapter Two. The relationship between neuroscience[28] and Christian education is more complex. Aristotle's Form-Matter Hypothesis provides a helpful perspective. Aristotle observed that the world consists of two elements: *matter* and *form*. *Matter* is the material out of which everything in the (physical) world is made. *Form* is the structure each material object takes. From this observation, he developed the Form-Matter Hypothesis, often illustrated as a triangle. At the base of the triangle, he placed matter without form—the very earth beneath our feet. Ascending the triangle, matter takes greater form—from soil to rocks, to plants, to simple organisms, to animals, to human beings, to angels, and finally to God, Who is Pure Form, a Being without matter.[29] Using this hierarchy (see left diagram, next page) as a frame of reference, we can picture the physical, mental, and spiritual aspects of man as follows (center diagram). We see the brain (physical body) toward the bottom. Next is the natural mind, and then the spirit, or spiritual mind.[30] The gap between Brain and Mind represents the unknown ("?") between the physical functioning of the brain, which operates according to fixed laws of physics, and the mental functioning of the mind, "which seems not to." Neither neuroscientists nor philosophers have bridged this gap "for one inescapable reason: a neural state is not a mental state."[31] Philosopher Colin McGinn describes the situation well: "The problem with materialism is that it tries to construct the mind out of properties that refuse to add up to mentality."[32] And yet, even here, we see the clash of worldviews, indeed the differing foundations of human thought, as materialistic, mental, and spiritual. Each of these reflects in its own sphere of study, which stands over against others (below, right).

Physiology (*physis logos*—the study of living things) emphasizes the general study of the physical functions of living organisms. Neuroscience studies the physiology of the nervous system, which includes the brain. What are the physical characteristics of the brain? How does the brain function? How does the brain learn?

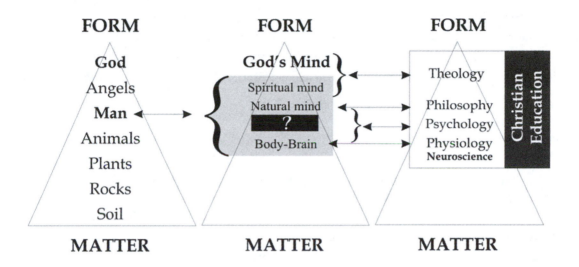

Philosophy (*phileo sophos*—the love of wisdom) focuses on consciousness, rational thought, and reason. Philosophy is the study of metaphysics (What is real?), epistemology (What is true? and How do we know it?) and axiology (What is valuable?), further divided into ethics (What is right?) and aesthetics (What is beautiful?).

To the three fundamental questions of metaphysics, epistemology, and axiology, the educational philosopher adds five: What is the Teacher? What is the Learner? What is the Method? What is the Outcome? What is the Social Impact? Classical educational philosophies provide coherent answers to all these questions: Idealism, Realism, Neo-scholasticism, Pragmatism, and Existentialism.

Psychology (*psyche logos*—the study of the soul) developed from the marriage of physiology and philosophy and focuses on thought processes, motivational states, and behaviors of individuals. Educational psychology emphasizes these processes in the context of teaching and learning—and is the focus of this text. We have seen that the earliest psychological theories of learning were behavioral (physiological) and defined learning as physical stimulus-response bonds stamped into the nervous system by experience and tangible satisfaction. Later psychological theories of learning, both cognitive (rational) and humanistic (emotional), focused on the mind. Each of these systems of learning theories finds their connection to the various sub-systems of the brain.

Theology (*theos logos*—the study of God) emphasizes the Characteristics, Works, and Word of God. The spiritual aspect of human life is a supernatural connection with God through faith and prayer. New Testament theology expresses this supernatural connection in terms of a personal relationship with Jesus Christ (John 3:16, Col 1:27).

Christian education draws on all of these areas, in order to draw the lost to Christ, to stimulate growth in the Lord, to disciple believers into a kingdom lifestyle, and to equip them to carry the kingdom to the whole world through ministry, evangelism, and missions. Given the complexity of brain functioning, and the confusion surrounding application of neuroscience to educational processes, what role does brain science play in Christian education? It is to that question we now turn our attention.

The Decade of the Brain: Stimulus for Research

President George H. W. Bush declared 1990–2000 the "Decade of the Brain" on July 17, 1990. He anchored the importance of brain research to overcoming a variety of diseases, such as Alzheimer's, and disabilities, such as stroke, schizophrenia, autism, impairments of speech, language, and hearing, as well as drug addiction and AIDS.[33] The proclamation generated a great deal of research.

Early Research: A Focus on the Role of Genes

One branch of neuroscience focused on the role of DNA and human genetic code, asking whether all human behavior could be reduced to specific genes. Scientists hypothesized that human behavior is determined at conception by the genetic code one inherited. If true, this would remove the need for moral codes or conceptions of right and wrong. Comedian Flip Wilson's famous "The devil made me do it!" would be replaced by a far more serious, scientific, proposition that "Our genes make us do it"—whatever *it* might be. Is obesity the result of an improper diet and lack of exercise, or a "fat" gene? Is anti-social behavior the fault of bad choices made by delinquents, or could it be connected to a "delinquency" gene?

What makes some people "inherently religious" while others are not? The October 25, 2004, front cover of *TIME* Magazine featured a story suggesting that some human beings bear a gene that gives them a "predisposition to episodes interpreted by some as religious revelation." Please read that phrase again, carefully. A "predisposition to episodes interpreted by some as religious revelation." Such a definition for religious experience lies a long way from Mount Sinai, and farther still from an empty tomb.

The article pointed to Dr. Dean Hamer, a geneticist at the National Cancer Institute at the National Institutes of Health,[34] who wrote *The God Gene: How Faith Is Hardwired into our Genes*. According to Hamer's hypothesis, the God gene "is not an encoding for the belief in God itself but a physiological arrangement that produces the sensations associated, by some, with the presence of God or other mystic experiences, or more specifically spirituality as a state of mind." If this strikes you as verbiage created by someone who has no idea at all what "belief in God" actually is, the article only gets worse.

"The loose interpretation is that monoamines correlate with a personality trait called self-transcendence. Composed of three sub-sets, self-transcendence is composed of 'self-forgetfulness' (as in the tendency to become totally absorbed in some activity, such as reading); 'transpersonal iden-tification' (a feeling of connectedness to a larger universe); and 'mysticism' (an openness to believe things not literally provable, such as ESP). Put them all together, and *you come as close as science can to measuring what it feels like to be spiritual* (emphasis mine). This allows us to have the kind of experi-ence described as religious ecstasy."

The article continues, "What evolutionary advantage this may convey, or what advantageous effect it is a side effect of, are questions that are yet to be fully explored. However, Dr. Hamer has theorized that self-transcendence makes people more optimistic, which makes them healthier and likely to have more children."[35]

Materialist Hamer reduces "belief in God" to certain genetically based sensations of emotional attachments (personal activities, a larger world than Self, and a willingness to consider the improb-able), which gives us a "kind of experience" which "some might describe" as religious ecstasy. Hamer tells us, quite seriously, that this is as close as science can get to a definition of "spiritual."

As it turns out, *TIME* simply reported bad science. Carl Zimmer suggested a more accurate title for Hamer's article in an article for ***Scientific American*** in the same month. "A Gene That Accounts for Less Than One Percent of the Variance Found in Scores on Psychological Questionnaires Designed to Measure a Factor Called Self-Transcendence, Which Can Signify Everything from Belonging to the Green Party to Believing in ESP, According to One Unpublished, Unreplicated Study."[36]

Homosexual Rights' activists were quick to use the backdrop of DNA research to suggest, with-out evidence, that homosexuality was determined by a specific "homosexual gene," present in inher-ited DNA. Such a discovery would end the controversy over whether homosexuality is an in-born trait, like blue eyes, or a preference, like a chosen profession. A homosexual gene would remove per-sonal responsibility for homosexual behavior since no choice is involved. While such a view clashes with Scripture—especially the apostle Paul's view in Romans[37]—it certainly would strengthen the culturally chic notion that "victims need tolerance and understanding"—especially those victimized by their own gene pool.

The hypothesis for a homosexual gene was set forth by the same Dean Hamer mentioned above.[38] Despite great fanfare in the secular press, South Bank University in London, England, published a report in 2002 declaring, *"Although researchers are hopeful,* a single gene [predicting homosexuality] has not yet been identified"[39] (emphasis mine).

What is not mentioned in most articles is the fact that Dean Hamer is himself homosexual, as he shares in a personal info-interview on You-Tube.[40] His deeply personal vested interest—explaining away God (along with Scripture, the Church, and long-standing religious objections to homosexual behavior) and supporting a genetic (amoral) basis for homosexuality—undermine his credibility as an objective researcher. The simple fact is that the brain is so complex that its development, not to mention the higher level development of human personality, cannot be controlled by genetic code alone.

Brain Complexity and Genes

There are only 35,000 genes present in human DNA. Only half of those are active in the brain. There are 100 billion (to 1 trillion)[41] neurons in the human brain. Each neuron connects to a few thousand to 100,000 other neurons. A conservative estimate is that the adult brain boasts 100 trillion connections, or synapses. Some put the number at 1,000 trillion connections.[42] How big a number is this?

The human heart beats on average about 60 times per minute. This produces 3600 beats an hour, 86,400 beats in a day, 32 million a year, 32 billion in 1000 years, 32 trillion in a million years, 320 trillion in 10 million years, and 1000 trillion in a little more than 30 million years.

The human brain is "more complex by far than anything else known in the universe."[43] The trillions of connections make possible "virtually endless mental activity."[44] Ralston Holmes III provides a helpful analogy: "Compare how many sentences can be composed by rearranging the 26 letters of the English alphabet." Then extrapolate that to 100 billion neurons and 1000 trillion connections.[45]

It is mathematically impossible for 18,000 genes to control the growth of all of these connections[46]—*and it is in these connections that we find all human behavior, thought, and emotion.* Human DNA is simply too limited to spell out the wiring diagram for the human brain,[47] whether it be "gay" or "God." What *does* control the wiring and structure of our brains is the most exciting scientific discovery I have experienced in my lifetime. And for that, we turn to brain development.

The Complexity of Brain Development

Not only is the human brain the most complex organism known to man, it is incredible in its complexity of development. While the limited number of human genes is insufficient to account for the weaving of billions of brain cells and trillions of connections, DNA does a great deal, especially during early brain development. While neuroscientists do not know how genes accomplish what they do, it is "reasonable to assume, given that fetal brains follow the same sequence of development, and that they reach the same milestones at about the same time, that the overall pattern is under some sort of genetic control."[48]

The human brain is born soon after a sperm fertilizes an egg. After fourteen days of cell-divides, the human being is a ball of hundreds of cells.[49] On or about this fourteenth day, this ball folds in on itself, until the cells on the outer surface reach the center. In the process, the ball transforms itself into a tube. One end of this tube will become the spinal cord. The other will become the brain. At about three weeks after conception, the embryo begins to produce "protoneurons" (immature neurons that will become fully developed at the proper time in the sequence) at a rate of about 500,000 every minute, and maintains this rate until about the eighteenth week. From there until the end of nine months, and birth, the embryo produces 250,000 neurons per minute. The newborn enters the world with about 100 billion neurons. More than 90 percent of these were produced in the first four and a half months of development.[50]

Beginning in the second trimester of pregnancy, protoneurons begin to migrate outward in a journey so incredible, it is hard to imagine. Dr. Jeffrey Schwartz likens the journey to a baby crawling from New York to Seattle and winding up in the "precise neighborhood, on the right street, at the correct house that he was destined for from the moment he left Manhattan." These baby neurons travel a network, not unlike the interstate highway system, laid down by cells called *radial glia*. The network is complete with rest stops that allow the glial cells to nourish the protoneurons along the way. Six separate waves of protoneurons move, one after another, each wave moving beyond the previous one, until all six cortical layers are populated. When all the immature neurons are in place, the glial network disappears. How neurons "know" they are in place remains a mystery, but only when they are in place do they become full-fledged neurons and anchor down. Then, they begin to produce dendrites, from which they will receive electrical impulses from other neurons, and axons, by which they pass electrical impulses on to other neurons.[51]

While genetics control the individual production, migration, and inter-connection of brain cells, it also controls the timing of brain organization as a whole. Sub-structures of the brain appear at what seems to be genetically programmed times. By the third trimester, most neurons have found their place, and the brain's major structures have formed.[52]

Systems continue to develop after birth. The spinal cord and brain stem are almost fully functional at birth (these systems regulate body heat, heartbeat, and the reflexes of grasping and sucking). Over the next two years, various sub-systems come on-line as nerve cells become encased in a fatty coating of myelin that enables them to carry electrical signals.

The somatosensory cortex, which processes the sense of touch, is a good example of sub-system development. At birth, the neurons from different parts of the body converge in cortical regions that overlap so much that newborns cannot tell where they are being touched. Through *experiences* of touch, the somatosensory cortex develops a precise map, proceeding from head to toe, and beginning with the mouth, until every speck of skin is represented. Touch a pin to a point on your cheek, and you will feel the precise place the pin touches.

Development continues over time with motor regions (physical movements), and then parietal, temporal, and frontal cortices (associated with judgment, reason, attention, planning, language). Some higher-order sub-systems continue to form into the late teen years.[53]

These discoveries forced neuroscientists to change what the field had long held as true. For nearly a hundred years, neuroscience held that the fundamental structure—the wiring together of billions of neurons—was no longer pliable, no longer plastic, after the age of six. As late as the 1970s, it was "established fact" that the structure and wiring of the human brain is fixed—hardwired like an electronic calculator—by age six.

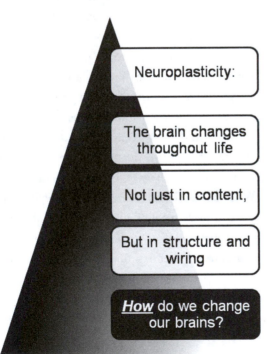

Neuroplasticity:

The brain changes throughout life

Not just in content,

But in structure and wiring

How do we change our brains?

By the 1980s technological advances demonstrated that brain structures remain plastic into late adolescence. And later, research pushed plasticity into young adulthood. Mike Merzenich, an early proponent of neuroplasticity,[54] estimated that in the early 1990s, only "10 to 15 percent" of neuroscientists accepted the existence of adult neuroplasticity. Just *ten years later*, however, "there remained no question that the brain remodels itself throughout life."[55] Since the early 2000s, studies have shown beyond any doubt that the neuroplasticity of the brain "extends throughout life"[56]—the brain never stops changing in structure or wiring.[57] This is a profound discovery for adult educators.

But the complexity does not stop at mere quantity of neurons (100–1000 billion) and their interconnections (300–1000 trillion), nor in the perfectly orchestrated structural developments of the brain. "Moving a few billion neurons to a particular site doesn't give you a working brain any more than throwing a few million integrated circuits into a plastic box gives you an iMac." Billions of neurons have to make the *right* connections with each other.[58] Schwartz describes this incredible complexity for just one sub-system: vision.

A functional pathway must be formed from the rods and cones of the retina (eye) to the visual cortex (brain), where visual data are interpreted. Neural signals move from rods and cones to interneural cells, which hand them off to retinal ganglion cells (comprising the optic nerve), and then to a relay station called the *lateral geniculate nucleus* (LGN), where axons from the left eye alternate with axons from the right eye to form eye-specific layers. From there, the signals travel to cells in the primary visual cortex all the way in the back of the brain, where clusters of neurons receiving signals from the left eye form separate, alternating layers with clusters of neurons receiving input from the right eye. In order for this to happen, axons from the eye must grow to the correct spot in the LGN. Axons growing from the LGN "must resist the urge" to terminate in synapses in the auditory or sensory cortex (where they arrive first), and continue to grow until they reach the appropriate target all the way back in the primary visual cortex. The ultimate goal is for each cluster of several hundred neighboring neurons in the visual cortex to form synapses only with the neurons responding to the same little region of the baby's visual field. How does this happen?[59]

The answer, as with touch, is "experience."[60] The fetal brain produces twice as many neurons, some 200 billion, as it will have at birth. Neurons that fail to form functional synapses (connections) simply vanish. Synapses begin forming in the spinal cord five weeks after conception. One estimate is that 1.8 million synapses form every **second** from the second month of gestation to the child's second birthday! Which synapses remain, and which whither away, *depends on which ones are used*. One estimate is that 20 billion synapses are pruned every day between childhood and early adolescence. Experience determines which neurons and synapses remain, and which die. "The ultimate shape of the brain . . . is the outcome of an on-going active process that occurs where lived experience meets both the inner and the outer environment."[61]

As prefrontal circuitry (responsible for decision-making) develops, *volitional choice* becomes a primary force in modifying brain structures that were formed by genetics and shaped by the environment.[62] *That is, what we choose to experience, where we choose to place our attention, shapes the structure and function of our own brains.* This shaping continues, following the choices we make, as long as we live. We will soon delve into the mechanics of choice, attention, and brain change. But we need to take a step back and chronicle the journey brain science has taken in educational practice.

The Leap from Brain Research to Educational Practice

Educators are quick to harness new scientific discoveries for the classroom. In the introduction to the chapter, I listed educational fads of the past five decades—Instructional Television (1950s), Computerized Instruction (1960s), Open Classrooms (1970s), "Authentic Assessment" (1980s), and Learning Styles (1990s). "Brain-based learning" is the flavor of the 2000s.

Educational Fads and Educational Practice

It is easy to be cynical about educational fads, but the truth is that much of our educational experience today is built on the fads of the past. The Instructional Television of the 1950s offered little more than "talking heads." The cost of creating films and tapes, as well as maintaining school-wide television systems, quickly dampened the initial excitement. And yet, who can argue the benefits produced by popular educational television programs like *Sesame Street* and *Mister Rogers*, brought into our living rooms, free of charge. Televisions have the potential to enrich learning, but they have not replaced teachers in classrooms.

The costs of programming and equipment also dampened the initial enthusiasm for computerized instruction. As a systems engineering major in the mid-1960s, my professors were convinced that, long before the turn of the century, the "archaic and inefficient approaches" of human teachers engaging classrooms of human learners would be gone. In their place would be computerized learning labs, where each student would study just what they needed, without frustration or wasted time, programmed by Skinnerian-based computer modules. Learning labs exist today, but more often than not we find them used by disadvantaged students who need persistent and regular feedback—step by step—on the work they do. Computers have the potential to enrich learning, but they have not replaced teachers in classrooms.

Open Classrooms suggested that children could teach themselves and would be more likely to do so in a relaxed, open environment. School administrators removed walls and managed the educational process by means of individualized learning contracts. Children moved from learning area to learning area, fulfilling their contracts, under the roving supervision of teacher-monitors. It did not last the decade. Educators discovered that Maslow's "Trust the Children" had limits and that too much trust and not enough direction led to lower performance in general. Administrators rebuilt the walls and assigned students to particular grade levels, teachers, and classrooms. Self-motivated learning is a positive goal (and we have seen its emphasis in earlier chapters), but it requires nurture by responsible teachers who care for learners.

Learning Styles developed from the discovery that learners have personal preferences in how they learn, and indeed actually learn better when those preferences are addressed by particular methodologies. Growing from a humanistic view of educational psychology, proponents pressed for every child to be engaged in his or her own "preferred style," at least for part of the day. One university went so far as to create four different courses—one for each learning style proposed by David Kolb[63]—for every subject. Administrators dropped the project quickly as they realized how difficult it was to create four approaches to a given subject, and, more realistically, how expensive such duplication was. A learning styles approach to teaching tends to overextend teachers as they attempt to meet the preferences of a classroom of children. However, there is value in children learning to adapt to others. Placing emphasis on the learner as the most important element in the classroom is justified, since only learners can learn. Satisfying every personal preference is not.

I fully expect the same to happen in the current wave of "brain-based learning." I predict that most teachers will discover that "Teaching the Brain" is a lot like teaching people. As we will see in the next section, the brain is an organic machine that creates the neuro-networks to support the "tone and tenor of our day-to-day, and even our second-to-second, experience."[64] When students learn, under the proper conditions, their brains naturally follow. And yet the debate among educators continues.

Brain Research and Educational Practice: Taking Sides

Leonard Abbeduto edited the fourth edition of *Taking Sides: Clashing Views in Educational Psychology* (2006). Issue 12 asked the question, "Do recent discoveries about the brain and its development have implications for classroom practice?" Mariale Hardiman[65] answered, "Yes." John Bruer, "No."

Hardiman bases her argument for the connection between brain research and the classroom on her own school's improvement in state performance tests.[66] The school implemented R. J. Marzano's Dimensions of Learning model (1992) in 1994, and "has steadily improved the achievement of its 1,350 students during the past six years." (We discuss Marzano's 2007 version of *Dimensions of Learning* in Chapter Twelve).

With all due respect to her efforts, and successes, in leading her school to become a "Blue Ribbon School of Excellence," her arguments supporting brain-based learning suffer from unsubstantiated leaps of logic. Her approach is common among proponents. Here are several specific examples.

Dimension One (Marzano, 1992) is Positive Attitudes. Hardiman writes, "Students' attitudes and perceptions serve as filters that enhance or inhibit natural learning. *Although educators may have long suspected that attitudes affect learning*, brain research clearly supports the link between emotion and cognition" (emphasis mine). Such a link seems obvious. Would we believe a study finding no link between rationality and emotion, given our common experience of interaction between thoughts and feelings?

Given this obvious and long-established finding ("may have long suspected"), Hardiman chronicles practical things her teachers do to apply this "finding of brain science." They assign a "peer buddy" as a homework helper, arrange for tutoring in study skills, demonstrate [an] acceptance of diversity, and "to cement long-term memory, connect emotions to learning." She elaborates on how to connect emotions to learning: "Tell a funny instructional story at the beginning of class to foster a relaxed yet supportive atmosphere."[67]

I have no quarrel with any of these interventions. To suggest, however, that these practical steps are based on the discovery of neural pathways between the limbic system (emotions) and the frontal lobes (decision-making system) is, to be kind, a loose interpretation of the findings.

Marzano's Dimension Two is Acquiring and Integrating Knowledge. Hardiman underscores new discoveries in brain science that support the *use of repetition* in learning facts. "Learning occurs through the growth of neural connections, stimulated by the passage of electrical current along nerve cells and enhanced by chemicals discharged into the synapse [sic] between neighboring cells. The more often the 'trail is blazed,' the more automatic a task or memory becomes." Based on this new discovery in brain science, Hardiman recommends we "allow students to repeat learning tasks to cement them in memory . . . especially important for activities that require an automatic response, such as . . . mastering math facts."[68]

She has the matter backwards. The findings she cites are not discoveries of new ways of learning. Repetition is an ancient way of learning. Thorndike established the Law of Exercise[69] to promote repetition of important facts nearly a hundred years ago. We quoted earlier the ancient Russian proverb, "Repetition is the mother of learning." No doubt, thousands of ancient Israelites used repetition to commit the Books of Moses to memory. No, what brain science shows us is *how* the brain functions to support memory work, not the importance of memory work. We find this faulty logic used repeatedly: connecting what is already known with a neurological discovery, and then calling the discovery a "new approach to learning."

Hardiman recommends integrating "art, music, and movement into learning activities to activate multiple parts of the brain and enhance learning." She fails to connect this "best practice" with any of the brain-based learning research cited in the preceding paragraph and does not explain how such integration enhances learning. Then she recommends, "Students can learn how the earth's tilt and rotation create seasons through body movements—tilting the body toward the center of the circle to simulate spring; turning and tilting away from the center to simulate fall."[70] This reminds me of another educational enthusiast who recommended "using brain-based discoveries" to teach geography. She gave each student an orange. They peeled the oranges (smelling the aroma), ate the oranges (tasting both flavor and texture), and then used the peels to make a miniature map of the world. This multiple use of the senses "was proven to enhance learning." Perhaps such an approach would be appropriate for preschoolers, but she was teaching seniors in high school. I still wonder what her students actually learned about geography from this exercise.[71]

The problem is not with Hardiman's suggestions, which, used within proper age-appropriate guidelines, are no doubt effective. I take issue, however, with the way she describes these general, educational recommendations as new approaches derived from brain research. Neuroscientists are discovering the underlying processes of the brain, the biochemical mechanics, which support these (long-known) educational principles. Reporting these discoveries may provide reinforcement for what we already know, but it is disingenuous to market these recommendations as "new."

John Bruer makes a different case in his opposition to the relevancy of brain science for classroom practice. He bases his opposition on the misapplication of scientific findings in educational recommendations. "What we need to be critical of is not the ideas [from brain research itself], but how they are interpreted for educators and parents." Bruer tackles three "big ideas" arising from brain science: 1) rapid synaptic development early in life, 2) critical periods of brain development do exist, and 3) enriched environments have a profound effect on brain development in the early years. While these are true statements, and have been known "for 20 or 30 years," we need to be careful in the implications we draw from them.[72]

There is a current (1999) fixation, says Bruer, on early development and critical periods. But there is little to suggest that teachers can meaningfully harness early synaptic development or critical periods of development in the classroom. Bruer further warns against the confusion between "complex" (a neurological term) and "enriched" (an educational term) when describing learning environments. For scientists, "complex" means "a wild or natural environment." For many educators, "enriched" means "Mozart, piano lessons, [and] playing chess."[73] It is easy to slide from "describing complexity" to "prescribing enrichment." And that is a mistake from the viewpoint of neuroscience.

Another problem, says Bruer, is that neuroscientists have little idea how brain-based realities translate into the complex world of teaching and learning. He warns against using "neuroscience to provide biological pseudo-argument in favor of our culture and our political values and prejudices." Since his article appeared three years before Hardiman's, he was not responding directly to her article, but he no doubt had others like her in mind. Given Hardiman's leaps of logic from neuroscience to educational practice, we can see the wisdom of Bruer's warning. Bruer concludes, "Our appeals to this research are often naive and superficial . . . . Educators seeking to base practice on the best science might want to assess recommendations stemming from these ideas even more carefully and critically."[74]

A Sampling of Educational Recommendations from Brain Science

A 2005 article by Madrazo and Motz[75] describe numerous positive considerations for education from brain research. I have listed nine here. As you read these recommendations, consider whether these approaches are actually new—derived from cutting-edge brain technology—or merely restatements of teaching principles educators have promoted for years. I have appended my own reactions.

1. Students retain learning best when they teach others, practice by doing, and discuss content in groups. [Educators have long known that student activity is better than student passivity in learning.—RY]

2. Shorter, diverse lessons with different means of instruction may be more effective than an ongoing lecture environment. [Educators have long known that variety of method is better than any one method, especially an "on-going lecture" environment.—RY]

3. Classroom setting and the emotions of students play significant roles in the ability to learn.[76] [Christian educators in the Reformation promoted classrooms that provided pleasant surroundings and attractive materials for students. See "classical humanism" in Chapter Ten.—RY]

4. Teachers need to apply multiple strategies and opportunities for oral communication (talking, listening, reading) as well as written ways of communication (reading and writing). [A rather vague repetition of "variety" and "activity."—RY]

5. Open-ended questioning is valued because it allows for reflective thought, creative response, and unique commentary. [A rather vague recommendation that has little connection with brain science.—RY]

6. Allow students to process and challenge the information they hear or seek through personal discovery.[77] [Would any educator *forbid* students to process and challenge what they discover personally? Is it possible to do so?—RY]

7. Cater to the learning styles and diversity of learners [In what ways? How far do teachers go in catering to learner differences? Is it not possible for older student brains to adjust to styles different from their own?—RY]

8. Allow students to learn by reviewing and reflecting on their work, not simply completing a task or listening to a lecture. [Perhaps *generating directive ways for students to review and reflect* on their work would be more effective than "allowing students" to do so. Does any serious educator advocate

"listening to a lecture" as an effective means of learning? Lectures are the beginning, not the end, of learning.—RY]

9. Encourage processing time instead of automatically asking students to repeat back information they have just covered or heard in lectures.[78] [Piaget declared decades ago that "learning by heart is not learning." He promoted processing by group-oriented problem-solving. See Chapter Four.—RY]

Madrazo and Motz conclude by stating, "A growing understanding of the way the brain functions offers new insights into the minds of students at all stages of development. . . . Teachers must promote active learning through incorporation of research on brain-based education and the corresponding needs of the student."[79]

If these suggestions are examples of "incorporation of research on brain-based education," most teachers would do well without it. The article provides a general overview of vague educational principles more than specific applications of brain research. In all likelihood, the appearance of "Brain Research" and "Implications" in the title, along with some references to brain studies, provided the impetus for its publication.

Returning to John Bruer, we find in him a scientific purist in the sense that he wants us to take brain science for what it is, and as it is. He is no doubt uncomfortable with any kind of generalization of scientific findings into more useful "life" applications, since such interpretations often say more about interpreters than the facts. It is helpful to keep in mind that, while he is being quoted in a 2006 publication, he actually wrote his criticisms more than a decade ago, in 1998. His bibliography spans the years of 1977, ancient history in terms of brain research, to 1998, just as The Revolution was breaking out of the laboratories. Leading the charge was Jeffrey Schwartz, who has a very different view of the implications, and practical applications, of brain research and neuroplasticity.

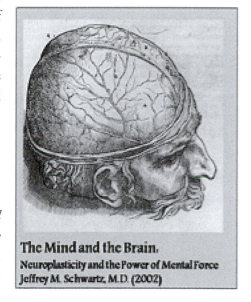

The Mind and the Brain,
Neuroplasticity and the Power of Mental Force
Jeffrey M. Schwartz, M.D. (2002)

The Key to Physiological Brain Change: Mental Attention

Dr. Jeffrey Schwartz's 2002 book *The Mind and the Brain: Neuroplasticity and the Power of Mental Force* is one of the most fascinating books I've read in years. Schwartz's passion for real-world application of brain-based studies overshadows the confusion and word magic often found in educational writing. His conclusions have been both affirming and challenging. His focus has been my most significant discovery in eighteen months of study and is profound in its support for what we do in the classroom every day.

Experiments with Obsessive-Compulsive Disorders

In the 1980s, Schwartz, a medical doctor and neuro-psychiatrist, was working with Obsessive-Compulsive disorders (e.g., compulsive hand washing). Until the mid-1960s, the psychiatric and psychological associations considered OCD *"treatment-intractable*: nothing could be done to release patients from its grip."[80] He found the psychoanalytical treatments of the late 1970s not only dehumanizing,[81] but also ineffective.[82] Schwartz wanted to find a better way to help patients overcome their obsessive thoughts.

Schwartz is also a student of Buddhism,[83] a naturalistic religion of the mind. The mounting scientific evidence of adult neuroplasticity and the emphasis of mental force in Buddhism led him to consider a focused mental approach to OCD. Is there a way, he wondered, to replace faulty brain circuits—the cause of OCD—with healthy ones by the use of focused mental attention? Put another way, is it possible to change the physical structure of neuron networks in our own brains by changing the focus of our minds?[84]

In OCD, the faulty brain circuit representing "wash your hands" begins firing repeatedly. This firing represents over-activity in the OCD circuit, which connects several major sub-systems of the brain.[85] The faulty circuit continues to fire, increasing its intensity, until the associated behavior is engaged—patients wash their hands. But unlike an itch that scratching relieves, obsessive thoughts are reinforced by the compulsive behaviors they demand. "It's like chronic poison ivy of the mind: the more you scratch it, the worse it gets."[86]

In the early 1990s, Schwartz and his colleagues began using PET scans to determine if changes in OCD behavior were associated with changes in the brain. In their first study, eighteen drug-free OCD patients signed on for a ten-week Four Steps[87] treatment program. These patients exhibited moderate to severe symptoms. Twelve (66%) made significant improvement in the ten weeks. In these twelve patients, PET scans showed "significantly diminished metabolic activity in both the left and right caudate (sub-systems associated with OCD)."[88] There was also a significant decrease in the abnormally high (and pathological) correlations of brain activity among the sub-systems associated with OCD.[89] As a result of these findings, Schwartz added PET scans to the therapy process: he showed patients exactly where their obsessive thoughts were being created.[90]

Schwartz's approach to OCD therapy was to introduce *an alternative idea* to washing one's hands. One such alternative idea was to "go to the garden." By focusing on this new idea, patients activated new planning circuits in their brains' prefrontal cortex. They quite literally created new brain circuits ("neurogenesis") by mentally focusing on the new behavior "going to the garden."

Schwartz spends an entire chapter describing quantum physics[91] in order to explain how mental force changes the probabilities determining which of two co-existing brain circuits will fire. I will simply summarize by stating the situation this way. Two biochemical paths exist in our example. One is the faulty OCD circuit (wash hands) and the other is the new circuit (go to the garden). When the faulty circuit begins to fire, the patient, through mental effort, can choose to focus on going to the garden. Simply by doing so, patients strengthen the "Garden" circuits, and weaken the "Wash Hands" circuits. Still, the stronger OCD circuit is more likely to fire, and patients are more likely to wash their hands than not.

By continuing to expend mental effort, patients, "by the laws of quantum physics,"[92] were able to change the odds of circuit firings in favor of "go to the garden." Patients could act on this thought and choose to go to the garden rather than to the sink. The action of going to the garden, *even if patients did this only in their minds*, continued to strengthen the "garden" circuits, as shown by PET scans.

The importance of this last sentence, thought versus action, is worth a small diversion. Experiments in 1995 proved that *thinking* about a behavior produces the same changes in the motor cortex as *engaging* in that behavior. One group of volunteers practiced a five-finger piano exercise, and a comparable group merely thought about practicing it, essentially focusing on each finger movement, playing the piece in their head. Both groups produced the same changes in the motor cortex. "Merely *thinking about* moving produced brain changes comparable to those triggered by actually moving."[93]

Jesus' words immediately spring to mind: "You have heard that it was said to our ancestors, Do not murder, and whoever murders will be subject to judgment. But I tell you, everyone who is angry with his brother will be subject to judgment" (Matt 5:21–22). And again, "You have heard that it was said, 'Do not commit adultery. But I tell you, everyone who looks at a woman to lust for her has already committed adultery with her in his heart'" (Matt 5:27–28). As far as the brain is concerned, *thought of an action* and *the action itself* have the same effect. But I am getting ahead of myself.

As patients regularly responded with a "Garden" response, the "Garden" circuits took over, and the faulty "Wash Hands" circuitry dissipated. With these changes in the brain, less mental effort was required to avoid the obsessive behavior and engage the positive behavior.[94] Because the new circuit was not faulty, patients did not replace one obsession ("washing") with another ("garden"), but replaced a faulty circuit with a healthy one. Going to the garden was not an obsession, but a relief. The sub-structures, locked in a faulty loop creating obsessive thoughts and compulsive behaviors, were set free from them. "Therapy had altered the metabolism of the OCD circuit. Our patients' brain lock had been broken."[95]

Brain Mapping, Violinists, and Driving Taxis

Other studies followed that reinforced the reality of adult neuroplasticity. A 1995 study found that, "with the decision to play the violin well and resolute practice, string musicians alter the structural configuration of their brains to facilitate the differential use of left and right arms—fingering the strings with one and drawing the bow with the other."[96]

Another study showed that "musicians enhance their hearing sensitivity to tones, enlarging the relevant auditory cortex by 25 percent compared with non-musicians."[97]

A study published in 2000 analyzed the differences in brain structure between a group of sixteen London taxi drivers aged 32 to 62 and fifty "ordinary right-handed men of the same age." The brain structures looked the same with the exception of the hippocampus.[98] The back part of the hippocampus was significantly larger in the taxi drivers than in the controls, and the front part was significantly smaller. Perhaps, thought the researchers, the taxi drivers were born with a "big rear hippocampus" that predisposed them to be good at navigation. Eleanor McGuire correlated the "size of the hippocampus" with "years of driving experience" in the taxi drivers group. *Length of time spent driving* correlated positively with the *volume of the right posterior hippocampus*. Acquiring navigational skills by driving in London caused a "redistribution of gray matter in the hippocampus" as the drivers' mental maps grew larger and more detailed with experience.[99]

The pattern of findings has been consistent now for a decade. What we give focused attention to, where we place our mental effort, causes changes in the actual structure and wiring of our brains. Let this thought roll over your mind for a moment. Consider its implications. *What we give our focused attention to—to this action and not that one, to this attitude and not that one, to this thought and not that one—changes the actual structure and wiring of our brains. For as long as we live.*

Neuroscientists have come to accept the overwhelming evidence that these kinds of physical changes, produced by experience and focused attention, are "an exaggerated version of a continuous mapping process that goes on in everyone's brain as their life experiences vary."[100] This may be true for motor skills, some may say—driving a taxi, playing the a violin or piano, learning a second language—but it does not apply to higher cognitive functions, like achieving a graduate degree. While it is true that motor skills are highly localized in the brain, and that "scientists have no way to measure the global synaptic changes" required in higher education, "[there is] every reason to believe they are there."[101]

Schwartz concludes his book, "The life we lead . . . leaves its mark in the form of enduring changes in the complex circuitry of the brain—footprints of the experiences we have had, the actions we have taken."[102]

Schwartz's discoveries intrigue me for the simple fact that, through 420 pages of text, he has reminded me in profound ways, through the issues of mind and attention, of the truth and power of the Scriptures. Not that Schwartz gives any hint of supernatural interest or inclination. It is fascinating to me that one can understand the intricacies of brain development and function, and yet ignore every hint of, every signpost pointing to, the Designer-God. But then Schwartz lays out the explanation of this in clear and unmistakable language. By focusing on naturalistic explanations and rejecting the supernatural constructs of creation and Spirit, naturalists develop brains that are increasingly hostile to the idea of God. The brain eventually prunes such thoughts, if they ever existed, from consciousness.

We learned from Jean Piaget that "what we know" affects how we react to "what we experience" in the world (see Chapter Four). The cognitive structure performs a screening function for incoming stimulation. We learned from Information Processing theory that this screening function is provided by memories stored in Long Term Memory, which provide a pattern by which we evaluate incoming sense perceptions (see Chapter Nine). Brain science physically places this "screening function" in the frontal lobes, and posits there a warning system that determines if incoming information is acceptable or not. Nerves extend from the frontal lobes to regions in the stomach. These nerves produce an unsettled or queasy feeling about suspicious signals long before the rational mind detects them. Past choices determine the nature of mental warnings. "The life we lead . . . leaves its mark in the form of enduring changes in the complex circuitry of the brain." This circuitry determines largely what we will accept, consider, tolerate, or reject. The brain circuitry is amoral, and merely processes what the mind pursues. What we give attention to—God or self, pure or polluted, love or lust, dry or drunk, lively or lazy—is the quintessential existential act, setting in motion the forces that make us who we are. Where the mind leads, the brain follows by supporting our willful thoughts through neurogenesis, warning us of any thought that differs from our established viewpoint.

A Scriptural Call to Attention

The Scriptures are filled with warnings and pleadings concerning where to place our attention. Many observers, especially those outside church circles, describe such warnings in terms of religious duty, church requirements, or simply a dark and troubling foreboding. The scores of millions around the world who know the God of the Book understand these pleadings in the context of a mother's love or a father's good direction, and they find comfort in them. Those who do not know God simply cannot understand them at all. Indeed, they cannot tolerate them long enough to consider, even for a moment, the possibility of their value. For they have wired themselves closed to God, and He is little more to them than an unsettled feeling that eventually goes away.

One of the profound purposes of Scripture is to focus our attention in the One Direction that gives us life. "Jesus performed many other signs in the presence of His disciples that are not written in this book. But these are written so that you may believe Jesus is the Messiah [the Christ], the Son of God, and by believing you may have life in His name" (John 20:31). Many familiar passages call us to focus attention on God through His Word, which is "a lamp for [our] feet and a light on [our] path" (Ps 119:105).

God said through Moses, "**Do not have other gods besides Me**. Do not make an idol for yourself, whether in the shape of anything in the heavens above or on the earth below or in the waters under the earth" (Exod 20:3–4, *emphasis mine*). When we make gods for ourselves—whether it be ambition, wealth, popularity, or notoriety; career, family, or hobby—we make them in our own image. We worship our gods in our own ways in the hopes of getting what we want. As such, "our gods" reflect our own evil desires. But the God Who made us, Who knows the number of hairs on our heads (Matt 10:30), calls us to **focus only on Him**. As we focus our attention on God's character, on God's ways, on God's commands and instructions—literally on God Himself—we develop ways of thinking, valuing, and behaving that reflect Him. And this is always, in the long view of such things, a deep and abiding blessing.

The oxymoron of "blessed enslavement" to God is reflected in Jesus' words, "Take up My yoke and learn from Me, because I am gentle and humble in heart, and you will find rest for yourselves. For My yoke is easy and My burden is light" (Matt 11:29). Jesus promises rest in terms of refreshment and renewal—from a yoke? But this is His yoke, carved to my specifications ("easy"), a yoke in which we pull together ("light"). He teaches me as I focus on Him ("learn from me"). And because of Who He is, this yoke leads me to rest. "Come to Me, all of you who are weary and burdened, and I will give you rest" (Matt 11:28). Jesus freely offers His invitation to focus on Him, join Him in His yoke, and find life. The choice is ours to make. The choice has been made by millions who can attest to the validity of the restful yoke of Christ.

King David certainly focused his attention on the Lord. "How can a young man keep his way pure? By **keeping Your word**. I have **sought You** with **all my heart**; don't let me wander from Your commands. I have **treasured Your word** in my heart so that I may not sin against You" (Ps 119:9–11). It was sentiments such as these—a deep desire to live according to God's ways—that made David a "man after His [God's] own heart" (1 Sam 13:14, *Amplified Bible*). If he had but maintained his attention on God's ways and God's Word, how much trouble he could have saved himself, his family, his nation, and his legacy. His power as king and lust for Bathsheba opened the way for a different kind of thinking. He re-focused his attention away from God and His Laws and became an adulterer and murderer. His subsequent repentance renewed his relationship with God, but the consequences of his actions remain to this day.

King Solomon wrote, "**Listen closely**, **pay attention** to the words of the wise, and **apply your mind** to my knowledge. For it is pleasing if **you keep them within you** and if they are **constantly on your lips.** I have instructed you today—even you—so that your confidence may be in the LORD" (Prov 22:17–19, *emphasis mine*). Solomon says that when we focus "constantly" on "words of the wise," which come from the Lord, the result is increased confidence in the Lord.

Jesus said, "Blessed are those who **hunger and thirst for righteousness**, because they will be **filled**" (Matt 5:6, *emphasis mine*). Those who focus their minds on the righteousness of God's kingdom will be filled with God's righteousness. Give focused attention to "right actions" that reflect a kingdom lifestyle—like the thirsty give attention to water and the hungry to bread—and those actions will be wired into our lives. The result is God's blessing, a direct consequence of right action.

On the other hand, those who hunger and thirst for **un**righteousness are never filled. They only desire more, pushing the envelope of un-right actions until their lives become a curse for themselves and others. The unrighteous run from God's blessings because they run from God. They wire themselves against God and against His ways. The freely chosen end is death, the wage sin pays (Rom 6:23).

The apostle Paul connects the process to mental effort and attention. "Though they knew God, they did not glorify Him as God or show gratitude. Instead, **their thinking became nonsense, and their senseless minds were darkened**. Claiming to be wise, they became fools and exchanged the glory of the immortal God for images resembling mortal man, birds, four-footed animals, and reptiles. Therefore, **God delivered them over in the *cravings of their hearts*** to sexual impurity, so that their bodies were degraded among themselves" (Rom 1:18–24, *emphasis mine*). Brains wire into neurological reality what hearts (the emotional and volitional centers of the brain: desire and will) crave. Once wired, any behavior seems reasonable to the brain that is so wired.

To the Ephesians, Paul warned, *"Pay careful attention,* then, to **how you walk** [that is, how we live our lives]—not as unwise people but as wise—making the most of the time, because the days are evil (Eph 5:15–17, *emphasis mine*). We live in a world governed by time. Where we focus our attention makes a difference in real time. Paul urges us to focus wisely on the choices we make day by day, "because the days are evil."

To the Colossians, Paul writes, "So if you have been raised with the Messiah, *seek* what is above, where the Messiah is, seated at the right hand of God. *Set your minds on what is above*, not on what is on the earth" (Col 3:1–2, *emphasis mine*). There is heavenly, and there is earthly. Those who focus their attention on heavenly things have an inner security, grounded in God's nature and kingdom, which protects them against—and sometimes *through*—the ever-changing circumstances of the world.

As if expounding on his words above, Paul writes to the Philippians, "*Don't worry* about anything, but **in everything, through prayer and petition with thanksgiving, let your requests be made known to God**. And the **peace of God**, which surpasses every thought, will **guard your hearts and your minds** in Christ Jesus. Finally brothers, whatever is **true**, whatever is **honorable**, whatever is **just**, whatever is **pure**, whatever is **lovely**, whatever is **commendable**—if there is any **moral excellence** and if there is any **praise**—*dwell on these things* (Phil 4:8, *emphasis mine*). Peace in the face of distress comes through focusing on the right things.

God
Written Word

Focused attention

Brain ← **Mind**

Focused attention, mental force, changes our brains to think God's recorded thoughts

To young pastor Timothy, Paul gives fatherly advice for his spiritual growth and the growth of his church: "**Give your *attention* to public reading, exhortation, and teaching. . . . Practice these things**; *be committed to* **them**, so that your *progress may be* **evident** to all (1 Tim 4:13,15, *emphasis mine*). What we do in reading, preaching, and teaching makes a difference in the lives of our listeners and learners as they focus on God's Word. The very acts of teaching, preaching, singing, praying change our own brains to support spiritual thinking. Commitment to these things inwardly, as well as the regular practice of these things outwardly, results in resilient changes that are external, visible, "evident to all."

In his second letter to Timothy, the last letter written before his martyrdom, Paul expressed his concern that Timothy remain focused on the right things. In the final chapter of the final letter, Paul writes, "Proclaim the message; *persist* in it **whether convenient or not**; **rebuke, correct, and encourage** with great **patience** and **teaching**. For the time will come when **they *will not tolerate* sound doctrine, but *according to their own desires*, will accumulate teachers for themselves** because they have an itch to hear something new. **They will *turn away from hearing the truth* and will**

turn aside to myths. But as for you, **keep a *clear head* about everything, *endure* hardship,** do the work of an evangelist, ***fulfill* your ministry**" (2 Tim 4:1–5, *emphasis mine*).

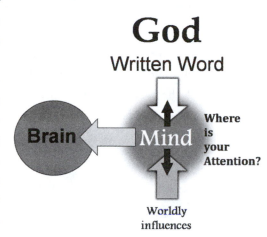

Desires direct mental attention. Mental attention directs physical changes in the brain. These neural changes support perspective and worldview in the natural world in which we live. Where is our attention? On truth or deception? On the honorable or dishonorable? On justice or injustice? On the pure or the tainted? On the lovely or the freakish? On the commendable or the shocking? Neuroscientists have shown that the answers to these questions make a difference in how the brain remaps itself here. God tells us the answers to these questions make a difference in who we become, both in this natural world, and in the world to come.

Of course, Jeff Schwartz and most proponents of neuroplasticity would read these words and most likely laugh at my naiveté, my lack of scientific "reality." But they cannot have it both ways. Either the brain wires itself as a result of focused attention, or it does not. Since the late 1990s we've known that "there [is] no question that the brain remodels itself throughout life."[103] The force behind the reshaping of "neural circuitry and cortical maps" is the "power of attention . . . the exercise of the will."[104]

In matters of faith and spirit, the atheist wires himself against God-thoughts by focusing on a godless frame of reference and naturalistic explanations of life. Christians wire themselves open to God-thoughts by focusing on a godly frame of reference, which includes both natural and supernatural viewpoints. The whole of Scripture warns against the former as deadly foolishness and urges the latter as life-giving wisdom. Whether the *object* of mental attention is true or not is a matter of faith, not science. After all, Schwartz declares that literally "going to a garden" or merely "thinking about going to a garden" makes no difference in terms of brain wiring. The brain obediently goes where the mind leads, mechanically wiring what the mind attends.

Three thousand years of biblical history and two thousand years of Church history declare that where we focus our attention makes a difference in the way we live. Ten years ago neuroscience agreed.[105]

The Influence of God's Mind on Our Brains

Focusing our attention "in Christ Jesus"[106] on the actions, values, and principles of Scripture creates, for lack of a better term, a more biblical brain, which "naturally" supports a biblical lifestyle.[107] With the application of mental force, the brain takes over repetitive thoughts, requiring less mental effort to think them.[108] We might well consider such a process the neurological aspect of sanctification. But God does not only speak to us through Scripture. He speaks to us directly through the medium of dreams and conscious thoughts. As His mind speaks to ours, and we attend to what He says, our brains weave the circuits to think His thoughts.

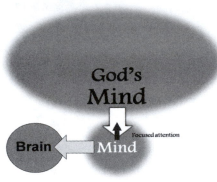

God speaks, through dreams and conscious thoughts, and changes the way we think

Speaking Through Dreams

In countries where the Bible is banned, and speaking Jesus' name is forbidden, missionaries report startling experiences of God revealing Himself directly through dreams. At a missions meeting in England just a few years ago, I heard a first-hand account of one such incident. "A Man Who called Himself Isa told a Bedouin Arab to go to a nearby city, to a certain street, to a certain building which had a certain carving on the door, and 'ask them to tell you about Me'." The Arab immediately got up, dressed, and set out for the city. It was 3:00 am. He went to the street and found the building with the recognizable "carving on the door." The carving was the logo of the Southern Baptist International Mission Board. The door belonged to their mission station.

He knocked on the door. It was 6:00 am. Two very surprised and sleepy mission attendants appeared. He said, "Tell me about Isa." Fearful that he might be someone making trouble, they shut the door in his face. He knocked again. A missionary opened the door. "I had a dream. Isa said you would tell me about Him." The missionary brought him inside, gave him some tea, and, after a discussion of his dream and the Scriptures pertaining to repentance and salvation, this Arab gave his life to Christ.

His life changed immediately. He worshipped enthusiastically. He helped around the mission by straightening chairs and distributing songbooks for the services. He read his Arabic Bible voraciously and shared his faith in public more openly than he "should have." He secured a job and began buying Bibles to hand out to interested persons he met around the city. His Christian friends warned him that such actions were very dangerous. But he insisted it was what Isa wanted him to do.

Eventually the authorities arrested him and, over several days, "roughly" questioned him. The authorities ordered him not to distribute Bibles or tell others about Isa. But upon his release, he continued his ministry, both inside and outside the mission station. The last report I heard, and this was several years ago, was that the authorities had arrested this Arab "brother in Christ" again. He was awaiting execution for refusing to return to Islam.

I was teaching at Kiev Theological Seminary (Ukraine) in March 2009 when I received an unexpected confirmation of the above account. My roommate was another visiting professor, Dr. Frank Martin, a man who works in Turkey among Muslims.[109] I asked him if he had any personal experiences with God's use of dreams as depicted in this first-hand account. He did not hesitate. "Evangelical churches in Turkey are only about ten years old. Nearly every believer converting from Islam to Christ reports receiving a similar message from the Lord. Where the Bible is scarce, and where religious oppression hinders the preaching of the Gospel openly, God is using dreams to speak directly to the minds of those looking for Him. And He is doing so by the thousands."

Speaking Through Conscious Thoughts

There are also experiences in which God speaks directly to His children, Mind to mind, while we are awake. The most startling for me happened nearly forty years ago. My wife and I were expecting, but something had gone terribly wrong. She was experiencing abdominal pain at home—*increasingly severe pain*—and I called 911. She passed out just as help arrived and was still unconscious as the paramedics placed her into the ambulance. I took my place beside her, and we were off to the hospital, sirens blazing. Suddenly she sat straight up on the gurney and screamed. She fell back, unconscious. Had she died? A few moments later she sat up and screamed again, falling back unconscious. And then once more as we pulled into the emergency entrance. She was rushed into the emergency room, and I was sent down the hall to the waiting room.

Over the next three hours, I waited. Others smoked away the time, but I did not smoke. Some nervously cleaned their glasses, repeatedly, but I did not wear glasses. Some paced back and forth, but I could only sit in a fog of conflicted emotion. And pray. It did not seem to help me feel any better, and with no word from doctors or medical staff, I had no evidence my prayers were getting past the ceiling. But what else was there for me to do? And so I prayed. "Please let her live, please let her live."

Sometime during the second hour, a phrase stirred in my mind. It appeared, out of the confused darkness, like a tiny match struck in a very large and very dark room. There was no voice. No thunder or lightning. No vision. But the impression was as clear as if whispered by someone sitting very close. The phrase could not be ignored: "Everything will be all right."

Instantly, and with excitement, I silently spoke an inward response to the phrase. "So, Barb's going to live!" And just as quickly another phrase replied. *"I did not say that."*

I was stunned. Without thinking, I silently shouted at God: "What is the value of faith if my wife still dies?" In the long pause that followed, I stepped away from myself to consider what I had just demanded to know. I didn't like what I found. Did I still consider God little more than a doting grandfather, One Who existed to provide me what I wanted? A sanctified Santa Claus? After all the years of sermons, Bible studies, and personal surrenders, I was surprised at the questions that continued to bubble up in my mind, and which kept coming despite my surprise. "If You are not going to give me what I want, what I *need*, then what good are You to me?" I couldn't believe I was asking these things. It was such a self-centered perspective, and yet, this was real! My wife's life was at stake! So did my faith only work when it wasn't needed? Was faith supposed to work in any real sense at all? In what ways does it work? To get me what I wanted?

"Everything will be all right."

I sat there in my own little world, alone, surrounded by a mass of chain-smoking, eyeglass cleaning strangers. As time passed, the fog of self-centered religion slowly morphed into the clarity of God's presence. I began to ask myself more objective questions. "Isn't God with Barb right now?" Of course He is. "Does He not love her and care for her?" Of course He does. "If she were to die, would He not continue to care for her, to take her home, where there would be no more pain?" Of course He would. And then the questions became more personal.

But what about me? I cried. I would be left alone! "Am I not with you right now?" Yes. Will I still be with you if Barb dies?" Of course You will. "Will I not take care of you?" Yes, Lord, just as You always have.

"All things work together for good to them who are called according to his purpose." *Even the death of a loving spouse, because God is greater than death.* "Everything will be all right, because I am with you both." Somewhere during this internal discussion, I began my third hour of waiting, and as I waited, I prepared myself for the news that Barb was gone.

It began slowly, oh, so slowly, yet welling up within me, starting from somewhere way down deep, came a sensation of . . . peace. It was literally like a river rising out of its banks, flooding and rising again, swallowing fear and self-pity. Higher and higher it rose, overwhelming my conflicted emotions. And then, just behind it, another sensation, another river, another wave, another flood began to rise as well. It was a river of joy. How many times in my twenty years on this earth had I sung the old spiritual? But for the first time I understood the life-connection of its words: "I've got peace like a river . . . I've got joy like a river . . . *in my soul.*"

I certainly was not *happy*. I was worried. I was grieving. The sitting and waiting were not pleasant but burdensome. I felt no sense of pleasure. Happiness and pleasure are natural emotions that are heightened or diminished by external circumstances. The rivers of peace and joy presently flooding my soul were not natural feelings—they were *super*natural gifts. I did not fully understand it at the time, but I was being given a graduate course in distinguishing Creator and creation, Ruler and rules, Faith and sight, Trust and treats, God and get.

"Everything will be all right."

"Yes, Lord, I know. Whatever comes, I am Yours. Help Barb know You are near her as well." I looked up to see a doctor approaching. I studied his face for a clue, but his somber expression did not change as he came closer. He remained businesslike, detached in his demeanor. Straight as an arrow, he came right up to where I was seated. It was not a good sign. I stood and shook his hand, waiting for his words. "Your wife has had a hard time of it. Her blood pressure was nearly zero when she arrived. She had been bleeding internally a long time. We thought at one point we were going to lose her, but, *about an hour ago*, she took a surprising turn for the better. She is very weak and needs to rest, but she's in her room now, and you can go see her. I'll be up later to check on her."

Whether she lived or died, everything would be all right, because God's kingdom is "at hand" (Matt 4:17 KJV), all around us, and He cares for everyone who calls on Him. I learned that day that *He* is the Prize, not the things He gives us. With *Him*, we get everything we need to live, even after we die. Those profound thoughts did not come directly from any given Bible study or sermon and certainly were not derived by my own rational synthesis of religious beliefs. I've pondered it over the years and can come to only one conclusion. God spoke His words of comfort and instruction in those hours, congruent with His Written Word, but startling in their clarity and pointed application to a life and death situation. And by focusing on those thoughts, my brain began immediately constructing the neurological support to think in this new way. The supremacy of God's presence in the life of a believer has never left me, and I've never had to ask any of my self-serving questions again. I received the answer, Mind to mind. That answer has been the foundation of my life ever since, reflecting the golden declaration of the apostle Paul: "God wanted to make known to those among the Gentiles the glorious wealth of this mystery, which is Christ in you, the hope of glory" (Col 1:27).

I told this story to our Sunday school class one Sunday morning and asked the twenty-something members who were present how many of them had ever had a similar experience. Every member raised a hand in affirmation. We spent the rest of the hour sharing various experiences of God speaking Mind to mind, and how He changed our lives.

God created us to learn about Him and from Him. He created us in His image, able to think as He thinks. He created us in a physical body, in a physical world, with a physical brain capable of recording in flesh what our minds process. Medical technology has opened a new window on just how complex this learning flesh is. What are the implications of these recent discoveries, these on-going discoveries, for teaching?

Implications for "Teaching the Brain"

As we saw in the section on Education Practice, educators hold a variety of opinions concerning the value of recent discoveries in brain science for classroom practice. We can safely reject the extreme views at either end of a continuum. At one end, we have those who suggest there is nothing to learn from brain science at all. Interesting, perhaps, they say, but not especially helpful to the classroom teacher. These writers remind me of the Studebaker Corporation at the turn of the twentieth century, who viewed the automobile as "an interesting novelty," while continuing to expand their development of horse-drawn wagons. The best horse-drawn wagons ever built were designed and constructed by Studebaker just before the internal combustion engine replaced horsepower altogether.[110] This chapter demonstrates that there is much for teachers to gain from these discoveries, if nothing else than the confident encouragement that good teaching makes sound and enduring changes in the minds (and brains) of our students.

At the other end of the continuum, we have those who consider the dawn of brain-based learning a new age in educational practice, set apart from all that has gone before. As we have seen, many of the purported "new applications" developed to "teach the brain" simply reflect well-established techniques re-written in neurological language. Reading these specialists is like listening to the latest *Tide* commercials, promoting "new and improved" cleaning action. Whether *Tide* has little green crystals, or blue color-safe bleach bits, or lemon-fresh deodorizers, it is laundry soap. Still, its promoters have claimed "newness" for as long as I can remember hearing or seeing *Tide* commercials—and that's nearly 60 years. The call for caution in making a leap from brain discovery to educational application is a valid one.

Cautions When Considering Brain-Based Discoveries for Educational Practice

Folk wisdom urges caution before making changes. Look before you leap. Measure twice, cut once. Making broad-based changes in educational institutions—whether they are national, state, private, or local—is serious business. Basing those changes on the direct application of narrowly defined, ever-changing scientific discoveries, or the vested interests of educational businesses, requires the same kind of caution.

The Nature of Scientific "t"ruth. Scientists make discoveries every day that challenge what other scientists thought to be true. The pace of these discoveries in neuroscience is mind-numbing. So volatile is the knowledge base in brain science that one is hard-pressed to use the term "status quo" in speaking of it. Scientific truth is, by definition, contemporaneous and changing—*truth* written with a small "t." Neurological discoveries push ever deeper into biochemical processes and sub-system communication processes. So complex is the operation of the human brain that one regularly runs into the phrase "we simply do not know how that happens." Holmes flatly states (2005) "What we do not know [in neuroscience] vastly exceeds what we know."[111]

Two scientists stand at a large blackboard. Formulas and mathematical symbols cover every square inch of the massive surface, and arrows connect one calculation to another. On the right side of the board, there is a small open space with the notation "(Then a miracle happens)." Just to the right of that is the observed result they were seeking to explain. Science is self-limited, since its work demands explanations without miracles, designs without a Designer, and the detailed analysis of creation without a Creator. It is wise to keep that limitation in mind as you read their work.

Schwartz himself continues to delve into the mysteries of quantum physics to provide stronger support for the "other worldliness"[112] of mind-brain functions. For him, the light that will illuminate the Dark Unknown lying between the *deterministic functioning of brain cells* and the *free will of the mind* is focused attention, operating by quantum principles, which change the probabilities of which brain circuits fire at any given moment. His latest article, written in 2005, deals with this very topic.[113] There is so much about the brain that remains unknown, and that which *is* known is fragmented and contradictory. It is dangerous to leap from scientific fragments into general recommendations for broad-based classroom teaching.

The Nature of Experimental Research. A second caution comes from the nature of scientific experimentation, which is, by definition and intention, narrow. In 1997 researchers placed adult mice in an enriched (wild) environment[114] and found that the **formation of neurons** (neurogenesis) increased 15 percent in a region of the hippocampus over the course of the experiment. In 1998 researchers demonstrated the existence of **neurogenesis** in the adult *human* hippocampus. In 1999 a study connected the **creation of new neurons** to learning tasks involving the hippocampus. Another study in 1999 showed that exercising on a wheel **produced neurogenesis** in the hippocampus of adult mice. In 2001 researchers demonstrated that the process of acquiring new memories is associated with **generating new neurons**. These were stunning discoveries since adult neurogenesis "had long been dismissed by the field."[115] The dramatic demonstrations of neurogenesis continued to propel changes in brain science begun by neuroplasticity, re-energizing the revolution in neuroscience. How, then, do we translate these findings into our classrooms?

We certainly want to "provide an enriched environment for students," but what results from that? Even when we believe teaching helps students "create new neurons," how do we practically direct these changes? What startling new things can teachers do to harness these changes to the teaching of prescribed curricula? Those who are publishing answers to these kinds of questions give us little more than reiterations of established practices, or whacky suggestions like orange-peel geography. While recent educational psychology texts cite research from brain science, they couch the findings—wisely, it seems to me—within the larger context of established educational psychology.

While the brain's complex functioning supports all personality, cognition, emotion, memory, motor skills, and motivation, we have yet to breach the barrier that exists between neural states and mental states. The educational applications in this chapter on "brain" tie us back to the previous six on "learning theory." Educational processes sit more comfortably within higher-level cognitive contexts than lower-level synaptic ones. Perhaps that will change in the next decade. For now, we will do well to remember how dangerous it is to leap directly (and precipitously) from the narrow findings of scientific experiments to general classroom practices.

The Power of Money. We find a third caution in the power of money. Those in the business of selling books, journals, educational programs, or school curricula find in brain-based learning a way of offering, like *Tide*, "something new" for profit. Yet, as we just said, the literature tying recent discoveries in brain science to educational practice too often repeat what we already know from experience. Such repetition does not hinder established approaches to classroom teaching and learning, but neither does it provide us the "new, improved" variety of learning that many claim. The temptation is understandable. Who would buy a textbook that claims to be a rehash of what readers already know?

Mike Merzenich, mentioned earlier, provides what may well be the best example of this business perspective. By the mid-1990s, Merzenich and his research team had twenty years of animal research behind them.[116] In 1994 his team began to focus on dyslexia, asking whether "carefully manipulated sounds could drive changes in the human auditory cortex."[117] The problem facing them was that the brains of dyslexic children cannot process certain consonant sounds fast enough to recognize them. The *B* in *Bah* lasts just 40 milliseconds before sliding into the *ah* sound, while the *M* in *Mall* lasts 300 milliseconds. Dyslexics, able to process consonants longer than 200 milliseconds, recognize the *M* in *Mall*, but not the *B* in *Bah*. *Bah* sounds like *Dah,* because dyslexics only hear the vowel.[118]

Using a process called Modified Speech, the Merzenich team created computer games to stimulate the growth of new neurons in the auditory processing circuits. In the summer of 1995, 22 SLI[119] children, aged five to nine, spent 20 days playing the games. One game would display a rake and a lake on the screen, and verbally ask the child to point to a rake. In another game, children clicked the mouse when a spoken *K* broke a series of spoken *G*'s.

The computer began consonant lengths at 300 milliseconds. In the *rake* example above, the computer exaggerated the *R*, as in *RRRRRRake*. When the children recognized a difference in prompts at 300 milliseconds, the computer shortened the transition to 280 milliseconds. The goal was to push the auditory cortex to faster processing speeds. "After a few months of receiving twenty to forty hours of training, all the children tested at normal or above in their ability to distinguish phonemes. Their language ability rose by two years." *Fast ForWord* was born.[120]

Merzenich had witnessed the frustration experienced earlier by Edward Taub, another pioneer in neuroscience. As early as 1987, Taub demonstrated conclusively that constraint-induced movement therapy[121] was effective in rehabilitating limbs affected by stroke.[122] In 1992 and 1993, the National Institute of Health rejected applications for research funding because his proposed stroke therapy was "so beyond the pale."[123] Despite repeated and varied successes in treating stroke victims,[124] the rehabilitation community remained resistant to his findings and slow to change their methodologies.[125]

Merzenich decided the fastest way to get the science "out of the lab and into the brains of children" was to sell the program as a business product. In October 1996, Merzenich secured capital and launched *Scientific Learning, Inc.* The next month they demonstrated *Fast ForWord* at the annual meeting of the American Speech-Language-Hearing Association. A year later, "19 schools in 9 districts across the country" had participated in the *Fast ForWord* program, having enrolled 450 SLI students. By 2000, the number reached 25,000.[126] By 2005, the number was nearly 125,000.[127]

Early critics of *Fast ForWord* cited its high cost—school districts pay $30,000 per school per year plus $100 for teacher training materials (2005 figures). Were the achievements cost-effective?[128] Others criticized the program's "rush to market" without subjecting it to independent testing. The greatest criticism, however, focused on the claim that *Fast ForWord* "reshapes the brain." Schwartz defended that claim through fMRI scans of dyslexic and normal adults undergoing the *Fast ForWord* treatment. Results of one study showed that three of the four dyslexics undergoing treatment experienced "significantly greater activation" of the targeted area of the brain along with "the greatest improvement . . . in their processing of rapid auditory signals and language comprehension." The fourth showed neither. The research conclusion of these independent studies was that there was a "clear connection between intensive training and differential sensitivity to sounds."[129] From everything I have read, there appears to be consistent evidence that *Fast ForWord* improves the ability of the brain to process sounds.

In the fullness of time, however, *Scientific Learning* began marketing their programs for use in **improving reading achievement**. Such a claim would naturally draw the attention, and the accompanying lucrative sales, from educational specialists and administrators. The 2009 *Fast ForWord* Web site invites educators to "find out how you can invest today's stimulus dollars to help struggling students **achieve lasting reading gains**"[130] (emphasis mine). But does *Fast ForWord* do for **reading achievement** what it does for **auditory training**? Research suggests it does not.

The Coalition for Evidence-Based Policy reports the findings of two independent studies of the *Fast ForWord* program on reading achievement. In a 2004 study, researchers conducted a "randomized controlled trial of 512 third through sixth grade students reading substantially below grade level in four elementary schools in an economically disadvantaged, urban school district. Students were randomly assigned within each school and grade into either a group that used *Fast ForWord* as an add-on to their regular reading instruction, or a control group that did not. . . . **No significant effect on students' reading achievement** [was found], as measured by their scores on the state's standardized reading assessment, as well as other researcher-administered standardized tests"[131] (emphasis mine).

In a 2005 study, researchers conducted a "randomized controlled trial of 415 second and seventh grade students[132]. . . reading well below the national average, from eight Baltimore schools. Students were randomly assigned within each school and grade into either a group that used *Fast ForWord* as an add-on to their regular reading instruction, or a control group that did not. "At the end of the intervention (i.e., two months after random assignment)," the program showed **"no significant effects on students' reading comprehension or language skills**, as measured by standardized tests"[133] (emphasis mine).

We find the context for resolving the apparent contradiction between Schwartz and the Coalition at the bottom of the Coalition Web site. "One well-designed randomized controlled trial did show promising evidence of an effect on students' **awareness of the sounds within words and letter-sound correspondences** [which was Schwartz's emphasis], but did not measure *Fast ForWord*'s effect on **ultimate reading ability** . . ."[134] [which was the Coalition's concern].

Scientific Learning has pushed the use of *Fast ForWord* beyond their initial scientific foundation (neuroplasticity, rehabilitating auditory processing) to a more general application in reading education. Their leap from brain science to reading education was a lucrative business move, but it has brought them a barrage of criticism as well. In searching the Web for *Fast ForWord* evaluations, I found a reasonably balanced view in a Web post. "Sandy" responded to a mother's request about *Fast ForWord* this way: "It has worked for many and seems to be **best suited for those who have auditory processing difficulties**. . . . Fast for Word [sic] has been compared (by a child) to 'glasses for the ears.' **It helps students hear consonants they cannot otherwise distinguish.** Then reading instruction can be more effective, just as getting glasses will not, by itself, create a better reader. . . . Where combined with good reading instruction, it has worked well"[135] (emphases mine). *Fast ForWord* improves auditory processing. Reading instruction improves reading achievement.

Beware the jump from scientific discovery to classroom practice, especially when there is a profit motive—computer programs, books, articles, conferences—standing behind the leap. You can see the generalized claims of Scientific Learning at http://www.scilearn.com/index.php.

Validation of Experienced-based Educational Practice

I have been suspicious of those touting "teach the brain" methodologies since I first began to explore the field. As we have discovered, the brain obediently goes where the mind leads, mechanically wiring what the mind attends. What I do find, however, is that many of the discoveries of educational psychologists over the last one hundred thirty years are being validated by new discoveries of the mechanics of brain support for learning. Many of the articles on "Brain-based learning" are reiterations of earlier practices re-cast in neurological terms. But especially heartening for me personally are the connections I find to principles laid down in the Disciplers' Model thirty years ago.

In 1971 I began teaching a Bible study class for deaf college students. There were no books on the subject, and so I simply asked the Lord to help me teach. Over the next six years, through personal teaching discoveries with deaf young adults at Gallaudet College in Washington D.C. (1971–1973), deaf median adults at First Baptist Church, Irving, Texas, and seminary studies in Fort Worth (1973–1978), I developed an approach to teaching that included rational explanations, emotional connections, and mutual relationships. This journey ultimately led to the creation in 1977 of the Disciplers' Model (see Chapter One), which provided a synergistic approach to "how to teach so that learners grow in the Lord." Based upon educational research studies from the 1960s and 1970s, and personal teaching discoveries I made with deaf learners, I:

- Advocated focusing content (the Bible in Bible studies) on the needs of learners (Needs).
- Suggested that the emotional tone of the classroom, as well as emotional needs of students, are essential elements of the learning process (Feeling/Valuing).
- Emphasized the role of social interaction and the development of relationships within the class (Relating).
- Underscored the importance of structure, clarity, and meaningfulness in explaining concepts (Thinking).

Given these elements, I found that learners grow rationally, emotionally, and socially. I found Scriptural support for these elements in the teaching ministry of Jesus, and in the philosophical and theological expositions of the apostle Paul.

Each of these elements connect to theories of learning already presented. They also connect to recent discoveries in brain science regarding cognitive processing, emotional processing, and social processing. Daniel Goleman has made a significant mark for himself in his books on *Emotional Intelligence* (1995, 2006) and *Social Intelligence* (2006, 2007).

The last element of the Disciplers' Model, the Holy Spirit as Teacher, quickens the natural human process with supernatural learning, as the Lord Himself helps learners understand God's principles, value God's priorities, and build godly relationships with each other. This Element, of course, has no counterpart in educational psychology texts or brain research. It does have, however, consistent and dramatic support from the experiences of biblical characters in Scripture.

Prayer, Study, and Attention in Evangelism, Discipleship, and Missions

Prayer and study are both aspects of focused attention. Prayer focuses the mind on God—whether the prayers are for forgiveness, petition, praise, or intercession for others. By giving regular and focused attention to God as Provider, the locus of the universe is moved away from Self.

Bible study focuses the mind on the Word of God. By giving regular and focused attention to the history, commands, examples, principles, and admonitions of Scripture, the locus of our minds is moved out of our own particular frame of reference.

Such moves are not natural, since natural man "does not welcome what comes from God's Spirit, because it is foolishness to him; he is not able to know it since it is evaluated spiritually" (1 Cor 2:14). Neither is it *un*natural, since we are designed after the image of God in order to know Him. Rather these moves are *super*natural: "Flesh and blood did not reveal this to you, but My Father in heaven" (Matt 16:17).

Despite the supernatural essence of these changes of focus from self to God, they are reflected in our flesh, in our brains. Just as Schwartz's OCD patients required less mental effort, over time, to think "Garden" than "Wash Hands,"[136] so we require less mental effort, over time, to think biblically. The brain takes over more of the details of the Object of our Attention, allowing us to think more deeply and more clearly, with less effort.

These general transformations reshape our brains, reducing the influence of national, cultural, and familial patterns, increasing the influence of God's Pattern—allowing us to think His way, to receive His thoughts, and to live according to His directions. "Do not be conformed to this age, but be transformed by the renewing of your mind, so that you may discern what is the good, pleasing, and perfect will of God" (Rom 12:2). The process of mental renewal and its subsequent shaping of the brain have specific implications for the teaching ministries of the Church.

Evangelism. The frontal lobes are the informational gate keepers of the brain. Believing parents expose their children to spiritual behaviors, attitudes, and thoughts from their earliest days. A friend of mine has three children, ages three, five, and eight. He and his wife are missionaries, living in

Ukraine. They pray at every meal. Worship twice on Sundays. Read the Bible as a family. All three children pray at mealtimes and bedtimes. The three-year-old amazes his father with the kinds of things he thanks God for—a slice of cake, a walk with his mom, a favorite cartoon. The eight-year-old has already made her profession of faith and is active in sharing her faith with Ukrainian friends at school. The five-year-old is asking questions about salvation and faith. These children have been surrounded by faith-language and faith-action all their lives. Their brains have woven it all into their thinking. These faith-shaped brains are quite content to allow the children access to more of the same. The realities that set off their warning bells for them are lying, cheating, stealing, fighting, and disobedience. "Teach a youth about the way he should go; even when he is old he will not depart from it" (Prov 22:6).

The longer persons live in the natural world, focusing on natural thoughts, engaging in natural behaviors, and prioritizing natural values, the less likely they are to consider spiritual things. Living without God becomes the norm, and for them, the realities that set off alarm bells are spiritual ones. Unlike the three-year-old (or a 60-year-old like me) who can easily and enthusiastically thank God for a piece of cake, naturalists find such religious ideas uncomfortable at best, and outrageous at worst. They find rational comfort in their godless existence, and their brains naturally follow their desires to wire themselves against outside interventions by anything God-like. They easily and confidently reject any thought of God. This is the safer course, because if they discover God really does exist, He might hold them accountable for the choices they make. Such thoughts of accountability are uncomfortable, and with the proper mental force against anything godlike, their brain obediently reinforces the materialist wiring and makes it easier to think in these ways.

I just returned from a Central Asian country working to impose a new "religious freedom" law. A more honest name would be "freedom *from* religion." Modeled after similar laws in the former Soviet Union, one section forbids teaching religion to children, even by their own parents, until they reach eighteen years of age. While children may accompany parents to church, parents will be in violation of the law if they keep their children in church with them. Bible studies, children's choirs, and summer camps will be banned. Given what we know about the brain, it is easy to recognize that eighteen years of brain wiring, without a thought toward God, will set up a materialistic brain pattern that is very resistant to change. This, of course, is the goal.

Baptist leaders who have given testimony (2008, 2009) before the government committee drawing up the new law show a different kind of brain wiring, also resistant to change. Said one leading pastor, "You can command us not to breathe, but we will breathe as long as we live. You can command us not to tell others about Jesus, but we will continue to do so as long as we live. It is who we are. All you will succeed in doing is drive us underground."

Those who harden themselves against God come to the end of their lives highly resistant to change. There is little hope of winning them to faith in Christ. Their minds have chosen, and their brains have followed. The probability of changing their thinking is small. A neighbor of ours was dying of cancer and was in the last days of his life. His Christian wife had prayed for him for years. But he was a hard case, and God does not crash our parties (Rev 3:20). She asked my wife if I might go by the hospital and visit him, one last time, to share the gospel. On my way I prayed for wisdom, and I prayed for the Lord to go before me and prepare him for what the Lord would have me say. I had no idea what that was going to be as I made the 20-minute drive to the hospital.

When I walked into his room, I saw his wife and forty-something son sitting on either side of his bed. He was awake and sitting up, breathing tubes attached. He looked at me and chuckled. "Well, now, what are *you* doing here?!" I told him I had come by to see him. Was there anything I could do for him?

"No, I don't suppose there is. I'm checking out of here in a day or two." I asked if he wanted to talk about spiritual things, future things, his relationship with God. His response was firm and confident.

"I have lived my 65 years without God, and I'll be damned if I'm going to play the hypocrite now." Damned was exactly what he was, but he seemed numb to the reality of it. "If there's a hell, I deserve it. And heaven isn't much of a place if they let me in now. No, I'll play the cards I've held all my life. There is no sense trying to change the deck now." I began to reply. I wanted to explain that God's reality is not ours. That it wasn't too late to make a change. But his son stood, unsmiling, and moved toward me. He asked me to leave, and he was serious. I looked over at his wife, who sat quietly weeping. I thanked them all for their time, and I left. He died the next day.

The brain wires itself according to the choices we make, the lives we lead. Neuroplasticity says, however, that the brain is not deterministic. The structure of our brain today need not be its structure forever. By focusing attention differently, we open neurological doors to new ways of thinking. My neighbor *could* have re-thought his situation, his life, and God's offer. Cancer and approaching death often do that. His brain would have immediately begun remapping circuits to think in new ways. But he chose not to.

At another time and place, another unbelieving husband went on a hunting trip. He was a likable fellow, but adamantly opposed to the Church and all things religious. He and his hunting partners separated when he went back to his jeep to get water. He decided to move the jeep, and as he did, it became tangled in some branches. When he moved around to the front of the jeep to clear the obstructions, the transmission somehow slipped into *drive*. The jeep lurched forward and knocked him down. His heavy coat caught on the bumper so that he was dragged along under the front of the jeep. As the jeep lumbered over fallen trees and old logs, his body was pummeled and broken. He passed out knowing he was going to die. Apparently there was a prayer on his lips as he lost consciousness. The jeep hit a tree and stopped. His friends found him an hour later and rushed him to the hospital. Internal organs were badly bruised, some were crushed. Nearly every bone in his body was broken. He lay in a coma for two weeks.

When he came out of the coma, his wife's testimony is that the first words out of his mouth were words of thanks to God for saving his life. He began to read the Bible his wife had bought him years ago. He talked to our pastor. He gave his life to Christ. And six months later, after he had healed enough to walk, he made a public profession of faith and was baptized. His mental outlook on life had changed completely, and his brain followed.

Such stories need not be so dramatic. Neuroplasticity says that anything we focus our attention on sets in motion the natural forces of the brain to either rewire circuits that exist, or create new ones. An Arab man reads about Jesus in the Koran and learns that He sits at the right hand of God (Mohammed does not). Jesus performed miracles (Mohammed did not). Jesus was sinless (Mohammed was not). It shocks him and raises many questions. He determines to learn more about Jesus and locates an Arabic Bible. He finds answers to every question in the New Testament, but when he reads Jesus' words "Love your enemies, do good to them who persecute you," he gives his life to Christ. Now he witnesses to Arabs all over his native country of Kyrgyzstan, first using the Koran, and then the Bible.

A deaf man learns from his doctor that he will die in two years unless he stops drinking. "Can Jesus help me?" he asks. The answers lead him to repentance and faith.

A woman is washing clothes by a stream, crying out to God for help because her marriage is dead and her religion is empty. A book comes floating by. She picks it up and finds that the book is a Bible (a leader in the village upstream had thrown it in the river). She dries it out and begins to read it. When a missionary team visits her village the following week, she offers her home as a meeting place and soon becomes a Christian. Her home becomes the meeting place for a newly established church, which grows, despite opposition from the village.

My father rejected Christ for years because "everyone knows the Bible is full of contradictions." This faulty tenet of unbelief had kept him safe from 15 years of my mother's attempts to witness to him. Then two men from the church where my mother and I attended came to visit him. One of the men, hearing Dad's perspective, challenged him to take the week and find a single contradiction. Dad was intrigued since he knew he could find many. He worked at it, struggling every night that week to prove his point, finding what he thought were contradictions, and then having to scratch them off his list.[137] His time was running out, and he was not making progress. Finally, in great frustration, and an explosion of temper, he threw his note pad and pencils across the room, grabbed his Bible and, shaking it at the ceiling, yelled at God: "If You are Who You say You are, then You will just have to show me!" I have never heard a pastor suggest this as an appropriate way to approach God. But Dad's testimony was that his heart was strangely warmed, and when he opened his Bible, he found that it was a different Book. He made his profession of faith the next Sunday and later became a Bible class teacher, and eventually a deacon. A challenge unsettled his mind and raised questions. Questions pursued answers. Answers changed perspective. And through all these things, his brain re-wired itself to support the processing of these new thoughts.

Life's problems create questions. Events shake apathy. Tragedies, celebrations, and life's unexpected difficulties can all shake one's perspective, and open up new opportunities for sharing the gospel. If we are sensitive to these changes in perspective, we can help those who are beginning to question anew the purpose of life and find new openings for sharing the gospel.

Discipleship. The *super*natural course of growth in a Christian's life follows a life cycle much like that of a tree, which moves through repeated phases of rapid growth and recovery. We see the tangible evidence of these cycles in the concentric growth rings in logs. These same cycles exist in the upward growth of the Christian. Rapid changes followed by consolidation. Each series of rapid changes result from some stimulus—a moral dilemma, a theological puzzle, contradictory thoughts in a sermon, a personal conflict—and the spiritual resolution of that conflict. Each cycle leaves us changed by the experience, and those changes are recorded in the woof and weave of neurological networks. These cycles are not comfortable experiences, and some choose to avoid them by isolating themselves from conflicts, changes, and even other people. This results in what Erikson called "stagnation." Personal growth stops.

Bibles studies, ministry opportunities, worship services, fellowships, witnessing, visiting the sick—these activities provide many kinds of stimuli—rational, emotional, behavioral—to energize cycles of growth. Every time we sing a hymn, read a Scripture, help another person, accept help from others, listen to a sermon, write a note, have a conversation—we reinforce ideas, attitudes, and actions that have been laid down before. The more consistently we engage these activities, and the more deeply we engage other people, the deeper and more lasting are the changes made in our brains.

As a teacher, I am not as concerned about controlling neurogenesis in my students as I am in the fact that, whatever I do, however I do it, I am creating changes—for better or worse. As we saw in the Triad chapter, some students will focus more on thoughts, others on values and feelings, still others on behaviors. But in every case, brains are being re-wired as learners focus on God and His Word:

"Speaking the truth in love, let us grow in every way into Him who is the Head—Christ" (Eph 4:15). Our goal is to teach in such a way that learners grow in positive ways.

Missions. Evangelism and discipleship take on complex challenges when we move into a culture different from our own. Meanings are created from cultural frameworks, and people of the same culture share those meanings. Something as simple as a greeting can cause misunderstandings. An American greets another by saying, "Hi. How are you?" The other responds, "Fine, thanks. And you?" But neither goes into details about "how they are." The question is just part of the greeting. A Russian student once asked me, "Dr. Rick, when Americans ask you how you are, they really don't want to know, do they?" An American had asked him "How are you?" as part of the greeting, and then cut him off when the student began telling him. Worldviews, perspectives, word choices, standards of morality, and a whole host of "meanings" divide cultures.

Attitudes appropriate in one culture are inappropriate in another. Americans laugh easily (and loudly). Ukrainians are initially reserved, even somber in their demeanor. Americans very quickly "become friends" with new acquaintances, but the friendships tend to be superficial. Ukrainians are slow to open their hearts to new acquaintances, but when they do, they hold them dear for a long time.

I once had a difficult conference with an African-American student in Fort Worth. As I was discussing the problem with her, she kept looking at the floor, refusing to look at me. It made me very uncomfortable. As a child, I had been punished for "such rude behavior" (looking at the floor when my father spoke to me). When I asked her to look at me when I was talking to her, she became very uncomfortable and finally explained that, when she was a little girl, she had been punished for "such rude behavior" (looking at her father when he spoke to her). Once that cultural barrier was removed, our discussion went much better.

Behaviors appropriate "here" are inappropriate "there." When one couple invites another for dinner in America, we rarely take flowers or candy. We simply return the favor. In Ukraine, guests always take candy. And the Ukrainian hosts serve the candy at the end of the meal. American hosts who are unaware of this custom usually serve their own dessert and save the candy brought by Ukrainian guests for their own use later. The Americans consider serving the gift candy rude. The Ukrainians consider *not* serving it—keeping the candy for themselves—rude.

Cultural and linguistic wiring sets up additional barriers to sharing the gospel, or even teaching believers in other cultures. Cultural and social warning signals differ. Changes are possible (neuroplasticity) but are often difficult to secure (cognitive structures resist change). Mike Barnett and I deal with these issues extensively in *Called to Reach: Equipping Cross-Cultural Disciplers*, (without the connection to brain science).[138]

In the end, we do not "teach brains," we teach people. Whenever we intensely engage the minds of learners in interesting, warm, and useful activities, we can be reasonably sure their brains will follow.

Negotiating the Evolving Field of Brain-Based Learning

Given the confusion, the complexity, and the sensationalism swirling around brain-based studies, how do we negotiate the rapidly evolving field of brain science? I suggest five elements to keep us focused.

Nothing New Under the Sun

"What has been is what will be, and what has been done is what will be done; there is nothing new under the sun. Can one say about anything, "Look, this is new"? It has already existed in the ages before us" (Eccl 1:9).

Psychologist William James (1842–1910) foreshadowed many of the recent "discoveries" regarding mental effort and material changes discussed in this chapter. But he could not mesh his ideas of free will and the power of mental effort with classical physics[139] and the materialist perspective of the late nineteenth century. John Watson's Behaviorism did mesh with Newtonian laws of physics and materialism and became a powerful force in replacing free will with determinism. As behavioral theories grew stronger, so did the denial of the reality of thoughts and emotions—"indeed, of any sort of inner life." James' ideas of the power of the mind had to wait, not only for breakthroughs in neurological technology, but, more importantly, for a revolution in physics.[140] The newest discoveries anchor deeply in the past, even to the point of reflecting Scriptural truths regarding the connections among attention, meditation, behavior, and spirituality.

Choice and change. Modern neuroscience is now demonstrating what James suspected more than a century ago: that "attention is a mental state (with physically describable brain state correlates)" that allows us, moment by moment, to "choose and sculpt how our ever-changing minds will work, [to] choose who we will be the next moment in a very real sense. . . . Those choices are left embossed in a physical form on our material selves."[141] What we choose, we become, not simply in a psychological sense, but in flesh and spirit too.

Clay and flame. James wrote, "Nature in her unfathomable designs has mixed us of clay and flame, of brain and mind, that the two things hang indubitably together and determine each other's being, but how or why, no mortal may ever know (*Principles of Psychology*, Chapter VI)."[142] The clay cannot produce the flame. "A neural state is not a mental state."[143]

Chris Frith disagrees. Writing in 2007 *(Making Up the Mind: How the Brain Creates Our Mental World)*, he said, "I have emphasized how much my brain knows and does without me being aware of it. My brain makes me afraid of things I am not aware of seeing and can control complex limb movements without my knowing what I am doing. There seems very little left for consciousness to do. So, rather than asking how subjective experience can arise from activity in neurons, I ask the question, "What is consciousness for?"[144]

It is an interesting question, given the fact that Frith used nine personal pronouns in four sentences, unconsciously separating self from brain. One hundred twenty years before Frith asked the question, James made the "justifiable" case for human consciousness. "On the basis of evolutionary biology, that consciousness must have had a selective advantage for it to 'exist, and persist, in nature. . . . What possible selective advantage could consciousness offer if it is only a functionless phantasm? Could consciousness ever have evolved in the first place if, in and of itself, it does nothing? . . . "The conclusion that [consciousness] is useful is . . . quite justifiable. But if it is useful, it must be so through its causal efficaciousness.'"[145] Human consciousness does something important; it is not the imaginary step-child of the brain.

Possibilities and actualities. On the subject of mental possibilities becoming physical actualities, James foreshadows quantum mechanics: "At various points . . . ambiguous possibilities shall be left open, either of which, at a given instant, may become actual. One branch of these bifurcations become[s] real."[146]

Attention as free will. On the subject of attention, James suggested the capacity to "emphasize, reinforce or protract certain thoughts at the expense of others percolating into consciousness"—an ability he identified with attention—reflects what philosophers refer to as human will. Human (free) will "derives not from the freedom to initiate thoughts, but to focus on and select some while stifling, blocking—or vetoing—others."[147] As you can imagine, James' writings are being reconsidered in light of the recent advances in both medical technology and quantum physics. The former provides the means to measure the physical changes in brain function, and the latter provides a framework to understand how brain-based minds work.

We would be wise, therefore, to reject the naive notion promoted by many brain-based proponents that "new is better and never existed before." Anchoring our thoughts, attitudes, and actions in the long history of ideas will help us keep balanced as we face the ever-changing flow of information, materials, and programs surrounding the study of the brain.

Limitations of Science

We discussed the issue of faith and science in Chapter Two and the limitations of scientific experimentation and truth earlier in this chapter. The scientific method is a powerful tool for gathering unbiased data in order to solve questions inherent in the natural order. I have taught the scientific method and principles of research design and statistical analysis to ministerial students for thirty years. The development of critical thinking skills—analysis, synthesis, and evaluation of hypothetical solutions to real-world problems—is an exceptionally helpful component in ministerial training.

Science limits itself, however, to nature. It confines itself, by definition and with pride, to a closed-system of reality. God is not part of that system.[148] Indeed, scientists—as *scientists*—reject out of hand any suggestion of supernatural design or Designer. This self-imposed limitation makes for interesting reading in the field of brain-mind studies.

Ralston Holmes III quotes from a recent study on whether animals have language[149] and declares **humans unique in their use of language**. "It seems relatively clear, after nearly a century of intensive research on animal communication, that **no species other than humans** has a comparable capacity to recombine meaningful units into an unlimited variety of larger structures, each differing systemically in meaning." The operative word here is "comparable capacity." Experiments on chimpanzees, especially one named Washoe in the 1970s, demonstrated what researchers claimed was a surprising capacity for human-like thinking through the use of American sign language. But even the most optimistic would not argue Washoe had a capacity for language comparable to (adult) humans.[150]

Humans are unique in their transmission of culture.[151] "Discovery of the nature and origins of human language, making possible this emergence of culture, is quite possibly 'the hardest problem in science.'"[152] Obviously human culture exists, and obviously, human beings transmit their culture from generation to generation. This unique capacity begs for explanation, but explanations must be made without reference to any type of Design or Designer outside the box of natural processes. What results, of course, is the attribution of *intentional creative powers to natural processes*.

Holmes continues. ". . . whatever the proximate explanations about how an infant develops a brain and a mind, a *more comprehensive framework is the evolutionary process* (which is the dogmatic *given* in scientific discussions—RY); ***brains must have been good for something***. Fish have fins, birds have wings, humans have brains—**all for adaptive success**. Fish must swim, birds must fly, and **humans must be cultured**. That seems obviously what the distinctive human brain is for."[153]

Why must humans be cultured? Are all human beings cultured? What drove human beings to become cultured? Recognizing the blatant circular reasoning at play here, we move on to Holmes' sophisticated explanation of how this unique human brain came about—given present culture and the requirements of language for it.

Holmes describes the inability of genes, which change over "centuries and millennia," to account for the rapid changes in culture. "The **best strategy for slow-paced genes** that need to succeed in fast-paced culture is **not to build a relatively inflexible mind** whose pace and preferences are genetically biased toward one culture or another, since these biases could misdirect persons in the rapidly shifting vicissitudes of culture. Rather, **genes will need to build a flexible mind**, which can make preferences independently of any genetic/cultural biases. . . . **the genes will need to develop** so as to **favor** teachability above all. . . . the **genes will have to abandon tight control** of behavior and **cast their luck** with launching a human organism whose behavior results from an education **beyond their control**. . . . If the **genes supply intelligence** in sufficient amounts, they need not themselves be closely tuned to **directing behavior** that can track environmental changes; **they turn this over** to the general intelligence **they have created**" [emphases mine].

I predict Holmes' next book will be entitled, *Sovereignty of Genes—Free Will of Man*. Such is the best naturalists can do from inside their self-imposed box. Human DNA is the creator, the designer, of all that is human. To ask where DNA comes from, or how genes develop the *proper mind-set* to direct this development, invites one of two serious responses. Naturalists will step back in time to discuss evolutionary processes that might account for such genes, no doubt themselves produced through natural selection in their environment. Or, having stepped back as far as they can, glibly reply that such questions are "beyond the scope of science" and therefore not important.

Take scientific discoveries for what they are: hypothetical explanations of how the world works. Take scientific discoveries in context with what you already know by experience. Take scientific discoveries in the context of their self-imposed limitations. Remember that what scientific theories dogmatically assert from one series of experiments can be, and often is, refuted by the next. Scientists see this as a positive process, gathering, sifting, and synthesizing empirical data into temporary scientific truths, which, as we've already seen, they always spell with a lower case *t*.

Sensationalism of Pop Culture and the Media

We provided a few examples of pop culture's sensationalism of brain research earlier in the chapter (Hamer's gene-based explanations of faith and homosexuality). Patricia Wolfe, an educational consultant writing in 2001, relates two instances where media reports distorted the actual findings of research. One recommended music as a means to increase IQ, and the other sugar as a means to enhance memory.

In the first study, media reports declared the amazing finding that "17 of 19 school children who received music lessons for eight months increased their IQs by an average of 46 percent." In reality, the study measured increases in "spatial temporal reasoning," *not IQ*.

Circular Reasoning Inside the Naturalistic Box

James' explanation of the human consciousness and its selective advantage prompts several irritating questions. If consciousness must have had a selective advantage for it to exist and persist in nature, why do "most species (plants, insects, crustaceans) survive quite well with little intelligence and develop no more over the millennia"?[154] Why is the human brain the only known brain in the universe to process language and transmit culture?[155] If the success of natural selection is based on probabilities for survival, why is the human brain the only one to develop these traits? How did we come to have intelligence, consciousness, self-awareness, and the ability to analyze our own thinking, when no other product of evolutionary biology comes close?[156]

Theodosius Dobzhansky supplies the naturalistic answer, declaring again the creative powers of human genes. "Human genes have accomplished what no other genes succeeded in doing . . ." in that they "formed the biological basis for a superorganic culture, which proved to be the most powerful method of adaptation to the environment ever developed by any species . . ." which shows "regularities not found in biological nature" (emphasis mine).[157] Human genes create the human mind that operates beyond biological principles, and that mind develops by means of experience beyond what genes are capable of controlling. In short, as Holmes concluded, "The genes outdo themselves."[158]

Schwartz admits, however, that neuroscientists have yet to discover how human genes do what they do.[159] Even an avowed evolutionist admits being "impressed by the incredible improbability of intelligent life ever to have evolved."[160] When the wise of the world wire themselves closed to God, they can only scratch their heads at the obvious inconsistencies. "And God created man in His own image, male and female . . . lower than the angels for a short time; [He] crowned him with glory and honor, and subjected everything under his feet." See Genesis 1:27; Hebrews 2:7–8. RY.

In the second study, researchers divided elderly people into two groups. They gave one group lemonade with glucose, and the other lemonade with a sugar substitute. Researchers found the elderly subjects receiving the glucose improved their memories. Wolfe writes, "what was not reported, however, was that these findings did not prove true for college students, and that no research was conducted with K-12 students . . . [and yet,] some teachers are giving their students peppermint candy because 'research proves that candy improves memory.'"[161]

Time and space do not permit a detailed analysis of the vapid nature of stories created to sell magazines and newspapers. But perhaps it is enough to call your attention to the magazine rack at your local bookstore or supermarket any given week, or Web headlines seeking additional clicks to linked sites, increasing ad revenues. There we find articles touting "new brain discoveries" that offer ways to transform our lives through brain-based weight loss, success, romance, and wealth. Educators, as we have seen, are not immune to this pop culture perspective.

Helping Learners Learn

We teach learners, not brains. The students sitting before us are far more than collections of nerves and synapses. As we focus their attention on our subjects, engaging them rationally (head), emotionally (heart), and physically (hand), their brains follow, naturally supporting student learning by the physical creation of neuronal networks that help them think clearly, value deeply, and perform skillfully.

As you read brain-based articles and books, soften their rhetoric and word magic with common sense questions. The answers are already familiar to us.

How do we provide skill-developing sequences that lead to success?

[See Chapter Six: Traditional Behavioral Theory].

How do we develop effective role models for student behavior?

[See Chapter Seven: Observational Learning].

How do we engage learners with each other, using the inherently different perspectives of students to produce disequilibrium, problem-solving opportunities, and social growth?

[See Chapter Eight: Constructivism].

How do we engage minds with curiosity and meaningfulness, or structure learning sequences that help students encode studies into long-term memory stores?

[See Chapter Nine: Information Processing].

How do we insure relevance of subjects for learners?

[See Chapter Ten: Humanistic Theory].

How do we synthesize all of these disparate processes into a coherent whole?

[See Chapter Eleven: Christian Teachers' Triad].

The study of lobes and synapses, electrical impulses, and potassium ions is interesting for many. I sincerely doubt that it has direct relevance to what happens in a classroom, or any intentional educational process. I began the chapter with two questions: "Is brain-based learning (2000s) yet another educational fad, soon to fade into the grand warehouse of educational tools like others of the last five decades? Or, are there discoveries in recent brain research that can help us develop as teachers and disciplers long-term?" The answer to both questions is "Yes."

Like the educational fads that preceded it, interest will wane, and brain-based learning will lose much of the hyperbole that has driven it the last ten years. We see signs of that already. The Web-based screening site for McGraw Hill's popular *Annual Editions: Educational Psychology* lists **forty-three** suggested articles for evaluation and recommendation for inclusion in the upcoming 2009–2010 edition. **None** of the forty-three addresses brain-based learning.

Real-time teacher-practitioners in classrooms across the country will sift brain-based discoveries, derived theories, and proposed methodologies as they engage students day by day. The promotional chaff will be blown away, and the transformational wheat will remain. That which survives the sifting will become part of our common experience in teaching.

The Greatest Discovery: Mind's Control over Brain's Structure

What has been earth-shaking for me, as a teacher, is the open recognition by many brain scientists that immaterial mind[162] has creative control over material brain. That recognition, and the evidence behind it, has profound implications for what we do, for better or worse, every time we step before a class of students. It compels me to keep fighting the pervasive idea that teaching is "simply telling what you know."

Teaching, discipling, and equipping find their power in the consistent and persistent focusing of learners' minds on biblical concepts and conceptual relationships, spiritual attitudes and priorities, and ministry skills—through the wide variety of principles laid down in earlier chapters—with the intent of changing each learner for the better. Teaching is creating a learning environment that evokes, energizes, and maintains student attention on the truths, values, and skills of God's kingdom—indeed, on God Himself—that will transform them. Brain science now agrees with Scripture that the choices we freely make matter. We eventually become—head, heart, and hand—what we attend to. The revolution in neuroscience is helping us in ways it never imagined.

One Major Question Remains

All developmental theories end at death. For naturalists, it is the end of everything. The highest levels of human development, transcendence, and cosmic perspective have a hollow ring in the face of natural death. For Schwartz, it is enough that our brains profile in their myriad connections every experience, choice, and action of our lives. It is a different matter for Christians, who understand death, not as the end of life, but a doorway to another kind of life altogether. Here in this world, biological brains support mental operations that surpass biology. When the brain dies, *the mind as we know it here* ceases to exist. And yet it remains.

The apostle Paul writes, "Brothers, I tell you this: flesh and blood cannot inherit the kingdom of God, and corruption cannot inherit incorruption. Listen! I am telling you a mystery: We will not all fall asleep, but **we will all be changed**, in a moment, in the twinkling of an eye, at the last trumpet. For the trumpet will sound, and the dead will be raised incorruptible, and we will be changed. Because this corruptible must be clothed with incorruptibility, and this mortal must be clothed with immortality. Now when this [happens. . .], then the saying that is written will take place: **'Death has been swallowed up in victory. O Death, where is your victory?** O Death, where is your sting?' Now the sting of death is sin, and the power of sin is the law. But thanks be to God, who gives us the victory through our Lord Jesus Christ! Therefore, my dear brothers, be steadfast, immovable, always excelling in the Lord's work, **knowing that your labor in the Lord is not in vain** (1 Cor 15:50–58).

Since "we" continue to exist, how are the moment-by-moment experiences of our lives recorded in the 1000 trillion physical connections of our brains, transformed into a purely mental state? Do we possess immaterial minds throughout life, connected to physical brains in this world, holding immaterial copies of the information processed by axons and synapses in real time, and then released at death? Or is there an instantaneous transfer of brain-mind personality and memories into a purely mental form? Given the way the Lord speaks to us in the moment, Mind to mind, it seems we live in two parallel universes. There is the natural world, perceived by biochemical brains, functioning "miraculously above" the laws of biology. And there is the spiritual world, the kingdom of God, "at hand," perceived by immaterial mind.

We can be thankful, however these questions are answered, that all we do with the Lord, for the Lord, and as a result of the Lord's presence in our lives, is kept safe. Our labor in the Lord is not in vain, for even Death cannot overcome who we are in Christ. Until that day, we can rest in the sure knowledge, promised by God, demonstrated in the lives of the faithful since creation, and now verified by twenty-first century neuro-technology, that our choices, experiences, and focus determine our destinies. We can say with Joshua, "Choose for yourselves today the one you will worship. . . . As for me and my family, we will worship the Lord" (Josh 24:15).

> "Listen closely, pay attention to the words of the wise, and apply your mind to my knowledge.
> For it is pleasing if you keep them within you, and if they are constantly on your lips.
> I have instructed you today—even you—so that your confidence may be in the LORD"
> (Prov 22:17–19)

Chapter Concepts

Attention	Selecting one thought or action so that it prevails over all others
Axon	The sending nerves of a brain cell. Ends in a synapse with neuron/dendrite/axon.
Brain-based learning	Teaching methods based on discoveries in neurological research
Complementary functioning	Both Left and Right hemispheres function in interactive, cooperative ways
Complex environment	Wild or natural environment (as opposed to lab cages)
Decade of the Brain	Declared by President George H. W. Bush: the 1990s: Emphasis on research
Dendrite	The receiving nerves of a brain cell. Receive impulse from axons.
DNA	**D**eoxyribo**N**ucleic **A**cid. Holds genetic codes for living things
Enriched environment	Culturally enhanced: classical music, chess, language study
Frontal Lobes	Sub-section of brain: executive functions: self-control, judgment; warning system
Gene	Part of DNA. Holds information for building and maintaining cells; biological traits
Hippocampus	Sub-section of the brain that helps regulate emotion and memory
Left Brain functioning	Thinking characterized by logic, objectivity, analysis, rationality, parts (outdated)
Mental force	Exertion of conscious mental effort that results in tangible changes in the brain
Modified speech	Process of slowing consonant sounds so that SLI children can process them
Neurogenesis	The ability of the brain to create new neurons throughout life
Neuron	Brain cell. Between 100 billion and 1 trillion neurons exist in an adult human brain

Neuroplasticity	The ability of the brain to change in structure and wiring
Neuroscience	The study of the nervous system, including the brain. Brain science.
Newtonian physics	Objects exist independently of observation. Mind and world distinct.
OCD	Obsessive-Compulsive Disorders (e.g., repeatedly washing one's hands)
Philosophy	Emphasizes the general study of consciousness, rational thought, and reason.
Physiology	Emphasizes the general study of the physical functions of living organisms.
Psychology	Emphasizes the general study of individuals: rational, emotional, behavioral.
Quantum physics	Objects do not exist independently of observation. No separation of mind/world.
Right Brain functioning	Thinking characterized by randomness, subjectivity, synthesis, intuitiveness, wholes
SLI	Specific Language Impairment. Best-known form of SLI is dyslexia
Synapse	Small space between sending axon and receiving dendrite/neuron
Theology	Emphasizes the study of God: His Characteristics, Works, and Word

Chapter Objectives

Learners will demonstrate knowledge of brain-based learning by . . .

- Recalling the findings of the studies of taxi drivers, violinists, and the five-finger piano exercise
- Recalling the distinctions of treatment and outcome between the approaches of Schwartz and psychoanalysts for OCD.

Learners will demonstrate understanding of brain-based learning by . . .

- Describing the treatment used by Schwartz with OCD patients.

- Describing the nature of the neurological revolution of the 1990s
- Explaining the three "cautions" concerning brain-based learning
- Contrasting the views of James, Frith, and Holmes concerning human consciousness.

Learners will demonstrate appreciation for brain-based learning by sharing an experience of changed perception through God's speaking to them directly or through Scripture.

Discussion Questions

1 Choose any of the Learning theory chapters (6–10) and find concepts that correspond to the discussion of brain science in this chapter.

2 Explain Schwartz' treatment for OCD. How does his treatment process compare or contrast with regular worship (Bible study, prayer, ministry)?

3 How has regular worship (Bible study, prayer, ministry) changed your thinking? How do experiences in these activities confirm or refute the suggestions made in this chapter on neuroplasticity?

4 Search the Internet for "brain-based teaching suggestions" posted in the past five years. Choose at least four suggested approaches and evaluate them. Do you find them to be new approaches, or established approaches recast in neurological terms?

5 I shared an experience in which God spoke dramatically to me Mind to mind. Have you ever had such an experience? What did you learn?

EPILOGUE

"Set your minds on what is above, not on what is on the earth."

Colossians 3:2

I was finishing up six weeks of teaching and preaching in Central Asia. The director of the seminary visited class the day I presented slides and material on "The Brain and Spiritual Growth." At the end of the day, he invited me to speak to his church-based "small-group" of 40 Baptist men, who met every week for Bible study, prayer, and fellowship, on Tuesday evenings. He specifically asked me to share the material on brain development, mental force, and the Bible's call for attention to godly things.

During the discussion of several Scripture passages, a man volunteered this testimony:

"I was a prisoner in the Soviet Prison System for 17 years. I was not imprisoned for my political or religious views. I was a criminal. Within the Soviet prison system, there is a brotherhood, a network of gangs of the worst-behaved prisoners. I was a member of that inner circle of criminals.

The Soviets tried everything to change our mentality and behavior. They used cattle prods (electric shock), deprivation of sleep and food, isolation, chemical injections, and heavy labor. But nothing they did broke our spirits or changed our views. We had a prison library with a thousand books in it, but none of the books helped us at all.

When Perestroika[1] came, a box arrived at the prison addressed to the library. The box contained Bibles.

We were curious about what the Bible said since we knew that possession of a Bible was illegal under Soviet law. So members of our criminal underground began meeting in the library to read the Bible. And the Bible completely changed our thinking, because the Bible led us to God, and God changed us. No other book in that library, no punishment, no reward could change us. But the Bible changed all of us in our Bible reading group."

This man is now a deacon in one of the largest Baptist churches in his city—over 500 gathered for worship the Sunday I preached there. I learned that five other criminals from that prison Bible study are now members of that church. All of them are active in witnessing and sharing Scripture in their city. "God loved us. God forgave us. God gave us new minds and new lives. And only the Bible showed us the way."

Such is the power of Scripture: to lead us to the One Who gives life.

Since Scripture is so powerful, why have we spent sixteen chapters dealing with science and psychology as it applies to teaching and learning? We write these chapters for the same reason that others write books on prayer, evangelism, pastoral ministry, and theology in general. These sixteen chapters have been written about scientific discoveries and psychological applications to teaching and learning because, in a simple phrase, *they help us*—usually, as we have said, in ways they never intended.

We certainly are *not* saying that psychological theories have equivalence with God's Word. "These are written so that you may believe Jesus is the Messiah, the Son of God, and by believing you may have life in His name" (John 20:31). "Written," "believe," "have life." The Holy Bible has no equivalents, no peers, for that outcome.

Further, there is nothing in the science of education, *in itself*, that imparts spiritual life. But then again, there is nothing in the science of theology, *in itself*, that imparts spiritual life. All sciences are man-made. To pit psychology against Scripture is a false argument. Anyone who has been changed by the One to Whom Scripture points, including criminals in a Soviet prison, knows there is no equivalence between man's views and God's message. "No other book."

The national leaders of seminaries and Bible Institutes in Ukraine and Central Asia—strongly conservative and strongly evangelistic—invite me to return repeatedly to teach the material you find in this text. Even now as I write these words in mid-2009, invitations are in place for two schools in Ukraine (2010) and two schools in Central Asia (2011). Lord willing, I will be there to teach much of what you have read here.

I say this in order to assure you, without the slightest fear of contradiction, that these conservative leaders would never invite me to shape and train their future leaders with these ideas if they had the slightest concern about them. These leaders assume personal and unwavering responsibility to protect their churches and schools from any hint of theological liberalism. Yet they see great value in these psychological theories when they are anchored—as they are here in this text—in the Eternal message of Scripture.

As one teacher to another, I hope and pray *your experience* in reading this text mirrors brothers and sisters half a world away: that your confidence in Scripture has been confirmed, and your views of teaching, learning, and spiritual growth have been expanded. I pray that your study of this text has helped you, is helping you, and will continue to help you as you set the minds and hearts of your learners on God, His Word, and His work in a very real world.

Jesus assures us that nothing done in His name—even to the giving of a cup of water—will be forgotten: "He will never lose his reward" (Mark 9:40–41). May God richly bless you as you learn from Him, depend on Him, and follow Him to transform *your assigned portion of the nations* through Christian teaching—here at home and to the ends of the earth.

Your fellow teacher,

RY

NOTES

Preface Notes

1. The very first book I wrote was *Ephphatha! Introduction to Ministry with the Deaf*—self-published and sold directly to students in a Southwestern Seminary Continuing Education class, as well as to ministers of the deaf, in 1975. This book was formally published in 1976 by Broadman Press as *Be Opened! An Introduction to Ministry with the Deaf*.

2. Richard Wurmbrand was director of a ministry to the Underground Church in the Soviet Union. This early newsletter later became *Voice of the Martyrs*, which is still published. Richard Wurmbrand died in 2001.

3. Wikipedia has an interesting overview of fMRI at http://en.wikipedia.org/wiki/Functional_magnetic_resonance_imaging.

4. These recent texts are *Called to Teach* (B&H, 1999); *Called to Reach* (B&H, 2007); and *Teaching Ministry of the Church* (2nd ed., B&H, 2008). Chapter Fifteen, "Jesus, the Master Teacher"—in the original *Created to Learn*—has been eliminated from this edition since it now appears as Chapter Four in *Teaching Ministry of the Church*, 2nd ed. (2008). The material of the original chapter, dealing with the triadic elements of Jesus' teaching ministry, has been moved to Chapter Eleven, "The Christian Teachers' Triad," in this edition.

5. Most obvious will be the stages of faith development by Bruce Fowler.

Unit 1 Notes

1. Refers to cognitive (head), humanistic (heart) and behavioral (hand) spheres of learning, and continuing theme through the text.

2. *The American Heritage Dictionary of the English Language,* 4th ed., http://dictionary.reference.com/ browse/educare. Accessed August 28, 2008. Actually, the debate among educators is far more complex and befuddling. Does "education" come from "educare" (to bring up, to mold) or "educere" (to lead out)? Do we preserve the (classic) past or prepare for the (unknown) future? See V. Randall Bass and J. W. Good, "Educare and Educere: Is a Balance Possible in the Educational System? (*The Educational Forum,* Winter 2004.) http://findarticles.com/p/articles/ mi_qa4013/ is_200401/ ai_n9389288, or check my discussion of this in *Teaching Ministry of the Church,* 2nd ed., (Nashville: B&H Publishers, 2008), p. 5. *American Heritage Dictionary* does not have information regarding "educere."

3. Ibid., http://dictionary.reference.com/browse/educate

4. Ibid., http://dictionary.reference.com/search?q=psych-

5. Ibid., http://dictionary.reference.com/search?q=-logy

6. God provides guidance through laws and commands (v. 5)—"Head." God is near to His people and communicates with them (v. 7)—"Heart." God teaches by His actions (v. 3). People learn by observing what God does, as in the Baal of Peor—"Hand." See Exod 4:15; Pss 25:12; 32:8; 71:17; Isa 2:3; 48:17; Jer 32:33; and Ps 81:10–14.

7. Lucien Coleman, *Why the Church Must Teach,* (Nashville: Broadman Press, 1984), 15–27.

8. Ibid., 29–48.

9. George R. Knight, *Philosophy & Education: An Introduction in Christian Perspective,* 4th ed., (Berrien Springs, MI: Andrews University Press, 2006), 9.

Chapter 1 Notes

1. http://www.great-quotes.com/cgi-bin/viewquotes.cgi?action=search&orderby=&keyword=ideal&startlist=45. Carlyle was a Scottish poet who lived 1795–1881.

2. *Called to Reach: Equipping Cross-Cultural Disciplers* (B&H, 2007), *The Teaching Ministry of the Church* (B&H, 2008), or the self-published *Disciplers' Handbook2* (1981–2006). You may obtain a free download of *The Disciplers' Handbook* as a series of PDF files from www.napce.org. Two additional chapters, "The Disciplers' Method" and "The Disciplers' Manner," expand the discipling focus of teaching and equipping ministries.

3. How he came to be in the front row is another (though tangential) teaching story. This pastor began the class sitting as far away from me as he could get, in a back corner desk, alone. During the first day, several hours into the course, I asked a question. He answered, and I took the occasion of his answer to expand. He took my response to be a criticism of his answer. He raised his hand and said, "I wish to apologize to the professor for the inadequacy of my answer. I will try to do better in the future." I was surprised—I had never had an *American* student say any such thing. But it also made me wonder about teachers in his past who had impressed on him the importance of adequate answers.

I responded this way: "Your answer was correct, and it was certainly adequate. But it also caused me to think of something else I wanted to discuss. I call that *teaching*. But you certainly owe me no apology for your answer."

After the next tea break, this pastor moved to the very front of the room, as close to me as he could get. He was no longer just physically in the room, but psychologically in the class. It is interesting that my openness to him, which brought him up front, was also an open door for his later vocal and public criticism of the Model. While he was rude in the way he made his point, it was a good one. It was a point he might never have made without the bridge of relationship we established on the first day.

4. From *gnosis* is derived "Gnosticism," a cult of pre-Christian and early Christian centuries distinguished by the conviction that matter is evil and that emancipation comes through *gnosis*, knowledge. Zodhiates, Spiros: *The Complete Word Study Dictionary: New Testament*. electronic ed. Chattanooga, TN: AMG Publishers, 2000, c1992, c1993, S. G1108, *PC Study Bible*, v. 5E, 2007, "knowledge."

5. Bratcher, Robert G.; Nida, Eugene Albert: *A Handbook on Paul's Letters to the Colossians and to Philemon*. New York: United Bible Societies, 1993, *PC Study Bible*, v. 5E, 2007, "knowledge."

6. Friberg, Timothy; Friberg, Barbara; Miller, Neva F.: *Analytical Lexicon of the Greek New Testament*. Grand Rapids, MI: Baker Books, 2000 (Baker's Greek New Testament Library 4), S. 163, *PC Study Bible*, v. 5E, 2007, "knowledge."

7. Professor of New Testament at Southwestern Seminary, 1950–1995. For Dr. Vaughn's obituary, see http://www.bpnews.net/bpnews.asp?ID=20424.

8. Personal conversation with Dr. Curtis Vaughn in the spring of 1995.

9. Wiersbe, Warren W.: *The Bible Exposition Commentary*. Wheaton, IL: Victor Books, 1996, c1989, S. Col 1:9, *PC Study Bible*, v. 5E, 2007, "knowledge."

10. *PC Study Bible*, 1995, *Strong's Greek/Hebrtew Dictionary*, Col 1:9, "understanding."

11. Walvoord, John F.; Zuck, Roy B.; Dallas Theological Seminary: *The Bible Knowledge Commentary: An Exposition of the Scriptures*. Wheaton, IL: Victor Books, 1983–c1985, S. 2:670–71, *PC Study Bible*, v. 5E, 2007, "Col 1:9."

12. Melick, Richard R.: *Philippians, Colossians, Philemon*. electronic ed. Nashville: Broadman & Holman Publishers, 2001, c1991 (Logos Library System; The New American Commentary 32), S. 201, *PC Study Bible*, v. 5E, 2007, "knowledge." (*Knowledge* was the search term that collected a variety of resources reflected here.)

13. Walvoord, John F.; Zuck, Roy B.; Dallas Theological Seminary: *The Bible Knowledge Commentary: An Exposition of the Scriptures*. Wheaton, IL: Victor Books, 1983–c1985, S. 2:670–71, *PC Study Bible*, v. 5E, 2007, "Col 1:9."

14. Matthew Henry, *Matthew Henry's Commentary on the Whole Bible: Complete and Unabridged in One Volume*. Peabody: Hendrickson, 1996, c1991, S. Col 1:9, *PC Study Bible*, v. 5E, 2007, "Col 1:9."

15. Pollyanna was the heroine of a novel of the same name written by Eleanor Porter (1868–1920). A *Pollyanna* is a "person regarded as being foolishly or blindly optimistic," http://www.thefreedictionary.com/Pollyanna, accessed June 18, 2009.

16. In the heady humanistic times of the 1970s, "spiritual" Christians were known by the frequent use of this phrase. Whatever misfortune or frustration came, the "spiritual" reaction was "Praise the Lord, anyway!" Some even shortened this to "PTLA!" The worst instance of this emotional distortion occurred to me while I was a seminary student in the mid-1970s. I greeted one of my classmates on the way into our classroom one afternoon and asked how he was doing. He looked at me with a big smile on his face and said "PTLA! My grandmother died yesterday!" I thought he was kidding at first. Sadly, he was not. I have often wondered what he did with his grief when he finally allowed himself to consider

his actual loss. He somehow missed Paul's words on empathy, "Weep with those who weep" (Rom 12:15), and would not allow himself to weep or others with him.

17. Subjective questions move learners *into themselves* to consider their own experiences: "If you had been Nicodemus, what would *you* have asked Jesus?" Objective questions move learners *into the text*. "How did Nicodemus view Jesus?" (John 3).

18. North American Professors of Christian Education (NAPCE) is an excellent professional organization for those who teach in the various fields of Christian Education. Marlene LeFever of David C. Cook Communications has been a driving force in NAPCE for years. Years ago Marlene introduced a new adult Bible study curriculum line on behalf of Cook and likened it to steel-belted radials. Steel wheels wear well, she said, but produce a hard ride. Rubber tires, on the other hand, ride well, but wear out too soon. Steel-belted radials provide both durability and comfort. It was a great analogy for the Bible-based, people-oriented curriculum. She ended her presentation by giving away a set of four steel-belted radial tires. I can never think of steel-belted radial tires without thinking of that NAPCE event.

19. Minister of Education, Columbia Baptist Church, Falls Church, VA, December 1976 to August 1981.

20. Both Paul and Peter use the terms "Holy Spirit" and "Spirit of Christ" interchangeably. Paul uses "Holy Spirit" 15 times and "Spirit of Christ" twice; Peter uses "Holy Spirit" twice, and "Spirit of Christ" twice.

21. "But this has been our room for ten years!" (even though we have 15 members using a room that holds 50, and another class needs more room because it is reaching many new members).

22. "We do not want to use Curriculum A (which is being used by the rest of the adult division)—we prefer Curriculum B" (rendering teachers' meetings educationally untenable, since different curricula focus on different passages).

23. "We like the organization we have, and do not want to change it" (even though the group is not reaching out to unchurched members of the community, even when they visit the church).

24. "You cannot have Mrs. Jones teach in the third grade department. She is one of the most faithful members of my class!" (as if we need to enlist unfaithful Sunday school members to teach in other areas; as if Mrs. Jones would not be helped to grow more by teaching third graders than sitting in her adult class).

25. There is an excellent example of this inability of science to define "spiritual" as most of us have experienced it in Chapter Sixteen. Look for the discussion on "the God gene."

Chapter 2 Notes

1. http://creativeproverbs.com/cgi-bin/sql_search3cp.cgi?keyword=science&boolean= and&field=quote&frank=all&database=all. Search for "science," accessed June 22, 2009

2. Ontology is a branch of metaphysics that focuses on the nature of "existence."

3. Axiology is further divided into aesthetics, "What is beautiful?," and ethics, "What is good?"

4. George R. Knight, *Philosophy & Education: An Introduction in Christian Perspective*, 4th ed., (Berrien Springs, MI: Andrews University Press, 2006), 9.

5. Janet M. Ruane, *Essentials of Research Methods: A Guide to Social Science Research*, (Malden, MA: Blackwell Publishing, 2004), 8.

6. Ibid., 7.

7. Jeffrey M. Schwartz, M.D., and Sharon Begley, *The Mind and the Brain: Neuroplasticity and the Power of Mental Force*, (New York: HarperCollins Publishers, 2003), 366.

8. Ruane, 4.

9. Knight, 24.

10. Ruane emphasizes a more subjective view than Knight and defines intuitive knowledge as "gut feelings" and "hunches" (8, 9). "Intuition/Revelation" is often placed under neo-thomist (neoscholastic) philosophy which forms the foundation for Catholic catechetical education. One often finds the promotion of the study of difficult and impractical subjects—Latin and geometry, for example—in order to "train the brain" to think naturally.

11. David R. Krathwohl, *Methods of Educational and Social Science Research: An Integrated Approach*, (New York: Longman, 1993), 48.

12. I am thinking here of personal revelation, of the way God reveals Himself to each of us through personal experiences and circumstances that are, themselves, unique to us. I am not referring here to the settled revelation of God through the Scriptures, which of course is objective Truth. Wise believers measure personal, subjective truths by the Gold Standard of God's Objective Truth. Placing personal experience—central to postmodern thought—above God's self-revelation in Scripture is tantamount to creating our own gods, in our own image, and this is idolatry. Still, God reveals Himself to us individually in the weave and woof of our life experiences, which personalizes Objective Truth.

13. Matt 28:19–20, the Great Commission of Jesus to the Church: going, baptizing, teaching, evangelism, discipleship and ministry, missions.

14. Textbooks in educational psychology in the 1970s and 1980s presented humanistic theories of learning on equal par with cognitive and behavioral theories. Over those same years, school leaders employed humanistic approaches predominantly, reducing emphasis on mastery and skill by emphasizing student attitudes. Today (2009), one is hard pressed to find a textbook that presents humanistic ideas as learning theory. The reason for this has been the dismal record of humanistic approaches in facilitating standardized mastery of subjects. You will find humanistic ideas treated here as part of a learning synergism, the Christian Teachers' Triad, because of the importance of subjective, personal, attitudinal aspects of Christian education as part of a holistic approach to learning.

15. The process is called the Delphi technique, which can be used in a manipulative way. Some researchers suggest sending the general ranking back to individuals with both the average response and the individual's response depicted. Individuals are then allowed to change their opinion to fall more in line with the group. This last step does have a manipulative effect, pressuring individuals to change their responses to "agree more" with the group. I recommend letting the rankings, as synthesized from individual responses, stand on their own by omitting this last "pressure toward consensus" step.

16. Some point to scientific laws, such as gravity or the boiling point of water, as approaching absolute Truth, but even these examples are not "the same everywhere and at every time."

17. I qualify these definitions by the term *honest* because scientists, being human, are subject to the same problems of political correctness and bias as any other observer.

18. An operational definition defines a term by how it is measured. "Intelligence is defined by subject score on the <named> intelligence inventory." A verbal definition defines a term by other words. "Intelligence is the capacity for learning, reasoning, understanding, and similar forms of mental activity". "intelligence," Dictionary.com. Dictionary.com Unabridged (v 1.1). Random House, Inc. http://dictionary.reference.com/browse/intelligence (accessed: September 29, 2008).

19. Gail G. Linam, "A Study of the Reading Comprehension of Older Children Using Selected Bible Translations," (Ed.D. dissertation, Southwestern Baptist Theological Seminary, 1993), 225 pages.

20. Denise E. Thatcher, "The Interaction Between Love Language and Marital Alignment on Marital Satisfaction for Selected Married Individuals," (Ph.D. dissertation, Southwestern Baptist Theological Seminary, 2004), 144 pages.

21. Knight, 68–69

22. "empiricism," Dictionary.com. Merriam-Webster's Medical Dictionary. Merriam-Webster, Inc. http://dictionary.reference.com/browse/empiricism (accessed: September 06, 2008).

23. Deut 25:13,15; Prov 16:11; 20:10,23; Ezek 45:10; Mic 6:11.

24. "closure," Dictionary.com. Dictionary.com Unabridged (v 1.1). Random House, Inc. http://dictionary.reference.com/browse/closure (accessed: September 06, 2008).

25. Schwartz, 7

26. Kerlinger, 6

27. "Stephen Hales," The Columbia Dictionary of Quotations is licensed by Microsoft Bookshelf from Columbia University Press. Copyright 1993 by Columbia University Press. All rights reserved.

28. Ibid., "Maria Mitchell."

29. Phillip Johnson, *Reason in the Balance* (Downers Grove, IL: InterVarsity Press, 1995), 8.

30. Ibid., 9.

31. The Columbia Dictionary of Quotations, "Science."

32. Johnson, 8.

33. Ibid., 7.

Chapter 3 Notes

1 Virgil (70 BC–19 BC). http://www.quotationspage.com/search.php3?Search=twig&startsearch=
Search&Author=&C=mgm&C=motivate&C=classic&C=coles&C=poorc&C=lindsly. Accessed June 26, 2009.

2. Norman A. Sprinthall, Richard C. Sprinthall, and Sharon Nodie Oja, *Educational Psychology: A Developmental Approach,* 7th ed. (New York: McGraw-Hill, Inc., 1998), 151.

3. "Tell me the first thing that comes to mind."

4. Sprinthall, 152.

5. Ibid., 152-53.

6. Ibid., 154-56.

7. Jack Snowman, Rick McCown, and Robert F. Biehler, *Psychology Applied to Teaching* 12th ed., (Boston: Houghton Mifflin Company, 2009), 26

8. Material on Erik Erikson's life drawn from Biehler and Snowman, 41–42, Woolfolk (1993), 66, and John J. Gleason, *Growing Up to God*, (Nashville: Abingdon Press, 1975), 13–15.

9. Don Hamachek, *Psychology in Teaching, Learning, and Growth*, 4th ed., (Boston: Allyn and Bacon, 1990), 44.

10. "epigenetic," Dictionary.com. Dictionary.com Unabridged (v 1.1). Random House, Inc. http://dictionary. reference.com/browse/epigenetic (accessed: September 12, 2008).

11. Snowman, 26.

12. Erik Erikson, Joan M., and Kivnick, Helen Q., *Vital Involvement in Old Age: The Experience of Old Age in Our Time* (New York: W. W. Norton and Company, 1986), 32–33.

13. My major reference books make no reference to Erikson's ideas of prenatal development: Sprinthall, Snowman, Ormrod, Woolfolk, Mayer, Elliot, Sternberg, and Alexander. In fact, none of these texts reference Erikson's *Vital Involvement* (1986) at all.

14. I did not have the courage to transfer my classroom approach to writing in the first edition, fearing it would be confusing. I have regretted that ever since.

15. Jeanne Ellis Ormrod, *Educational Psychology: Developing Learners,* 5th ed., (Columbus: Pearson Education, Inc., 2006), 69.

16. Myron H. Dembo, *Applying Educational Psychology,* 5th ed., (New York: Longman, 1994), 443.

17. Robert E. Slavin, *Educational Psychology: Theory and Practice,* 4th ed., (Boston: Allyn and Bacon, 1994), 56.

18. Ormrod, 69.

19. Ibid.

20. Eggen and Kauchak, 70.

21. Snowman, 28.

22. Dembo, 439.

23. Ibid.

24. Ormrod, 69.

25. Erikson (1980), 103.

26. Slavin, 56.

27. Dembo, 444.

28. Eggen and Kauchak, 70.

29. Snowman, 27.

30. Eggen and Kauchak, 76.

31. Dembo, 443.

32. Erikson, *Vital*, 103.

33. Gage and Berliner, 170.

34. Dembo, 439.

35. Ormrod, 69.

36. Snowman, 27.

37. Paul Eggen and Don Kauchak, *Educational Psychology: Classroom Connections,* 2nd ed., (New York: Macmillan College Publishing Company, 1994), 73.

38. Thomas L. Good and Jere E. Brophey, *Educational Psychology: A Realistic Approach,* 4th ed., (New York: Longman, 1990), 103.

39. Dembo, 443.

40. Robert J. Sternberg and Wendy M. Williams, *Educational Psychology,* (Boston: Allyn and Bacon, 2002), 84.

41. Paul Eggen and Don Kauchak, *Educational Psychology: Windows on Classrooms,* 7th ed. (Columbus: Pearson Education, Inc, 2007), 71.

42. Snowman, 27.

43. Ormrod, 69. Note: Biehler and Snowman's texts, 7th and 12th editions, of *Psychology Applied to Teaching* change the singular "a close and committed intimate *relationship with another person*" (1993) to the plural "close and committed intimate *relationships with other people*" (2009).

44. Snowman, 27.

45. Sternberg, 84.

46. Eggen and Kauchak (1994), 75.

47. Dembo, 439.

48. "12–18" years was Erikson's original age range for Stage 5. In the 1950s when Erikson wrote his first book, most American teenagers graduated from high school, married, and went to work. Few went to college. By the 1990s many more teenagers were entering college and postponing marriage. Sprinthall (1994) extended Stage 5 through the college years. In fact, some research in the early 2000s reported adolescence extending to "the early thirties," pushing personality development much later than Erikson's original theory. I expected to find "early thirties" reinforced in the most recent batch of university texts. Yet what I found was a return to Erikson's original "12–18" years. A few used "the adolescent years" as a general label, but only one, Sprinthall, extended Stage 5 beyond 18 to "through the college years," and one, Parsons, suggests "mid-twenties." The implication is a serious one in terms of "intimacy" and "generativity." If the end of adolescence does not come until the mid-twenties, this helps explain the obvious increases in isolation (despite sexual freedom) and self-absorption (due to the lack of identity and the inability to establish long-term relationships). My sense is that the move from adolescent to adult is being increasingly delayed by single adults until "school is finished."

49. Sprinthall (1998), 167.

50. Richard D. Parsons, Stephanie Lewis Hinson, and Deborah Sardo-Brown, *Educational Psychology: A Practitioner-Researcher Mode of Teaching,* (Belmont, CA: Wadsworth/Thomson Learning, 2001), 93.

51. Sprinthall (1998), 167.

52. Parsons, 92.

53. Good and Brophey, 100.

54. Snowman, 27.

55. Sprinthall (1998), 167.

56. Ormrod, 69.

57. Richard D. Parsons, Stephanie Lewis Hinson, and Deborah Sardo-Brown, *Educational Psychology: A Practitioner-Researcher Mode of Teaching,* (Belmont, CA: Wadsworth/Thomson Learning, 2001), 91.

58. Eggen and Kauchak (1994), 75.

59. Patricia A. Alexander, *Psychology in Learning and Instruction,* (Upper Saddle River, New Jersey: Pearson Education, 2006), 50.

60. Major sources are James E. Marcia, "Development and Validation of Ego Identity Status," (*Journal of Personality and Social Psychology,* 1966, 3, 441–558); "Identity Six Years After," (*Journal of Youth and Adolescence,* 1976, 5, 145–160); "Identity and Self-Development" in R. Lerner, A. Peterson, & J. Brooks-Gunn, Eds., *Adolescent Identity Formation,* (Newbury Park, CA: Sage, 1991, 173–192).

61. Sprinthall (1998), 171.

62. Sternberg, 85.

63. Parsons, 94.

64. Table information drawn from Sternberg, 85 as well as descriptions by Ormrod, 71, and Snowman, 31.

65. Ormrod, 71.

66. Sternberg, 85.

67. Ibid.

68. Ormrod, 71.

69. Ibid.

70. Sternberg, 85.

71. Good and Brophey, 100.

72. Ormrod, 72.

73. Choi found that Korean American Christians who lacked interest in their (Korean) ethnic identity or had no understanding of their ethnic identity issues also demonstrated a weak sense of relationship with God (religious well-being) and with others (existential well-being). Those who had been exposed to ethnic identity issues, understood the effects of ethnicity in their lives, and achieved a positive ethnic identity also had a stronger sense (affect) of relationship with God and with others than those who had an unexamined ethnic identity. This is not to say "being more Korean in an American culture" *causes* greater spiritual maturity. The findings were correlational. Perhaps the best way to describe the findings is to say, "The more one understands himself ('achieves personal identity,' including cultural acceptance), the more one can give himself to God." Jung Ki Choi, Ph.D., in "Foundations of Education" (2009) Southwestern Baptist Theological Seminary.

Choi's research was based on the theoretical perspective of J. S. Phinney, "Ethnic Identity in Adolescents and Adults: Review of Research," *Psychological Bulletin* 108, no. 3 (1990): 499–514; and J. S. Phinney, "A Three-Stage Model of Ethnic Identity Development in Adolescence," in *Ethnic Identity: Formation and Transmission among Hispanics and Other Minorities,* ed. M. E. Bernal and G. P. Knight. (Albany: State University of New York Press, 1993), 61–79.

74. Dembo, 439.

75. Snowman, 31.

76. Hamachek, 49.

77. Snowman, 31.

78. Parsons, 90.

79. Snowman, 27.

80. Ormrod, 69.

81. Good and Brophey, 99.

82. Sprinthall (1994), 155.

83. Parsons, 90.

84. Snowman, 27.

85. Parsons, 90.

86. Hamachek, 49.

87. Dembo, 439.

88. Parsons, 90.

89. Erikson used generic terms for age ranges: "play age," "school age," and the like. Snowman (2009) maintains the traditional breakdown of Erikson's first three stages: 0–1, 2–3, and 4–5 years of age respectively. Other authors modify these age ranges slightly. Eggen and Kauchak (1998, 70) list "Birth to 1 year," "1–3" years, and "3–6" years; Parsons (88) lists "Birth to 1 year," "1–3" years, and "3–5" years; Slavin (53–55) lists "Birth to 18 months," "18 months–3 years," and "3–6" years. I follow Snowman here, who reflects the traditional age ranges.

90. Parsons, 89.

91. Eggen and Kauchak (1994), 72.

92. Slavin, 55.

93. Interview with Dr. Marcia McQuitty, Associate Professor of Childhood Education, Southwestern Baptist Theological Seminary, Fort Worth, TX, February 22, 2005.

94. Good and Brophey, 99.

95. Eggen and Kauchak (1994), 72.

96. Good and Brophey, 99.

97. Hamachek, 49.

98. Dembo, 439.

99. Parsons, 89.

100. Ormrod, 69.

101. Eggen and Kauchak (1998), 70.

102. Ormrod, 69.

103. Snowman, 27.

104. Eggen and Kauchak (1994), 73.

105. Good and Brophey, 98.

106. Eggen, 72.

107. Sprinthall (1994), 157.

108. Good and Brophey, 98.

109. Ibid.

110. Sprinthall, 157.

111. Good and Brophey, 98.

112. Eggen, 72.

113. Good and Brophey, 99.

114. Hamachek, 49.

115. Dembo, 439.

116. Ormrod, 69.

117. Toddlers need a balance of freedom and restraint. Too much freedom leads to danger, such as inserting a knife into an electrical socket, or running into the street. Too much restraint leads to a lack of confidence in one's abilities.

118. Snowman, 27.

119. Ormrod, 69.

120. Ibid.

121. Good and Brophey, 97.

122. Eggen and Kauchak (1998), 82.

123. Slavin, 53.

124. Snowman, 27.

125. Good and Brophey, 97.

126. As noted elsewhere, "one year" is extended by some to 18 months and even two years. This does not change the focus of the first stage.

127. Snowman, 27.

128. Ormrod, 69.

129. Good and Brophey, 97.

130. Dembo, 439.

131. See http://www.businessballs.com/erik_erikson_psychosocial_theory.htm#erikson's_maladaptations_malignancies.

132. Erikson, Vital, 33.

133. Ibid., 41.

134. Erikson's last book, *Vital Involvement in Old Age* (1986), has been largely ignored by contemporary authors. Perhaps this is due to his position on prenatal personality development. But also ignored are his modifications to the original eight stages. Of all my resource texts, only two mention Erikson's later work.

Sprinthall (1998) folds brief mentions of adaptive strengths into his discussions of the original eight, and Elliot (2000) includes the eight adaptive strengths in a table. None of the texts discuss the extreme poles Erikson proposed.

Perhaps this is due to space limitations, or a desire to focus on Erikson's original theory. Perhaps it is a way of ignoring his 1986 work altogether. Much of the information in the following sections is taken from a Web site on Erikson's theory (see note 131).

135. Erikson, *Vital*, 42.

136. Snowman, 27.

137. Erikson, *Vital*, 42.

138. Ibid., 41.

139. Ibid., 34.

140. Snowman, 27.

141. Erikson, *Vital*, 48.

142. Snowman, 27.

143. Erikson, *Vital*, 34.

144. Sprinthall (1994), 150.

145. Erikson, *Vital*, 35.

146. Ibid., 43.

147. Ibid.

148. Ibid., 35.

149. Ibid., 49.

150. "fanaticism," Dictionary.com. *The American Heritage® Dictionary of the English Language, Fourth Edition.* Houghton Mifflin Company, 2004. http://dictionary.reference.com/browse/fanaticism (accessed: September 17, 2008).

151. Snowman, 27.

152. Erikson, *Vital*, 43.

153. Ibid., 35.

154. Snowman, 27.

155. Ibid., 43.

156. Ibid., 37.

157. Ibid., 50.

158. Ibid., 27.

159. Ibid.

160. Ibid., 44.

161. Ibid., 72.

162. Ibid., 27.

163. Ibid., 288.

164. Ibid., 289.

165. Ibid., 51.

166. Ibid., 27.

167. Ibid., 37–38.

168. Sprinthall (1998), 163.

169. Lars Tornstam, "Gerotranscendence: A Reformulation of the Disengagement Theory." *Aging: Clinical and Experimental Research,* (Vol. 1, 1, 55–63, 1989), 60.

170. Ibid.

171. Lars Tornstam, "Gerotranscendence—A Theoretical and Empirical Exploration." In Thomas, L.E., and Eisenhandler, S.A. (Eds.). *Aging and the Religious Dimension.* Greenwood Publishing Group, Westport. 1994.

172. Erik Erikson and Joan M. Erikson, *The Life Cycle Completed, Extended Version,* (New York: W. W. Norton & Company, 1997), np.

173. Tornstam, 1989.

174. Erikson, 1997, 124.

175. Verbraak, Annekatrien. "Gerotranscendence: An Examination of a Proposed Extension to Erik Erikson.s Theory

of Identity Development." A thesis submitted in partial fulfillment of the requirements for the degree of Master of Science in Psychology. University of Canterbury. New Zealand. 2000. http://www.soc.uu.se/research/gerontology/pdf/verbraak. pdf.

176. Lars Tornstam, "Gerotranscendence and the Functions of Reminiscence." *Journal of Aging and Identity,* (4 (3), 155–166, 1999), 11.

177. Edward Prager, "Meaning in Life: An Organizing Theme for Gerontological Curriculum Design." *Educational Gerontology* 23, No. 1. January/February 1997), 2.

178. Snowman, 32.

179. Ibid.

180. Good and Brophey, 103.

181. Sprinthall (1998), 179.

182. Sprinthall (1994), 153.

183. Snowman, 33.

184. LifeWay Christian Resources offers a series of books on age-related teaching approaches. Go to www.lifeway.com and search for the latest resources related to "teaching preschoolers (children, youth, adults)."

185. Hamachek, 45

186. Stephen N. Elliot, Thomas R. Kratochwill, Joan Littlefield Cook, and John F. Travers, *Educational Psychology: Effective Teaching, Effective Learning,* (Boston: McGraw-Hill, 2000), 73.

187. Elliot, 75.

188. Sternberg, 84.

189. Hamachek, 46.

190. McQuitty, 294.

191. Pamela R. Rothstein, *Educational Psychology,* (New York: McGraw-Hill, 1990), 64.

192. Elliot, 75.

193. Anita Woolfolk, *Educational Psychology,* 9th ed., (Boston: Pearson Education, Inc., 2004), 68.

194. Ibid.

195. Elliot, 75.

196. Woolfolk, 72.

197. Ibid., 70.

198. Ibid.

199. Ibid.

200. Verbraak, 14.

Chapter 4 Notes

1. http://creativeproverbs.com/cgi-bin/sql_search3cp.cgi?keyword=candle+understanding&boolean=and&field=all&frank=all&database=all. Accessed September 9, 2008.

2. Robert E. Slavin, *Educational Psychology: Theory and Practice,* 4th ed., (Boston: Allyn and Bacon, 1994), 31.

3. Norman A. Sprinthall, Richard C. Sprinthall, and Sharon N. Oja, *Educational Psychology: A Developmental Approach,* 6th ed., (New York: McGraw-Hill, Inc., 1994), 97.

4. Sprinthall (1994), 98

5. See Sprinthall (1994), 100 and Slavin, 31.

6. Barry J. Wadsworth, *Piaget's Theory of Cognitive and Affective Development,* 3rd ed., (New York: Longman, 1984), 9.

7. Don Hamachek, *Psychology in Teaching, Learning, and Growth,* 4th ed., (Boston: Allyn and Bacon, 1990), 148.

8. Ibid.

9. Material for the Life of Piaget drawn from Biehler and Snowman, 57; Sprinthall (1994), 100–101; Barry Wadsworth, *Piaget's Theory of Cognitive and Affective Development,* 3rd ed. (New York: Longman, 1984), 2; Slavin, 31; Eggen and Kauchak (1994), 225; Hamachek, 147; Bonnidell Clouse, *Teaching for Moral Growth: A Guide for the Christian*

Community: Teachers, Parents, and Pastors, (Wheaton: Victor Books, 1993), 225; and Thomas L. Good and Jere E. Brophey, *Educational Psychology: A Realistic Approach*, 4th ed., (New York: Longman, 1990), 55 and Sprinthall (1994), 53.

10. Wadsworth, 10.

11. Anita Woolfolk, *Educational Psychology*, 5th ed., (Boston: Allyn and Bacon, Inc., 1993), 28.

12. Robert F. Biehler and Jack Snowman, *Psychology Applied to Teaching*, 7th ed., (Boston: Houghton Mifflin Company, 1993), 59.

13. Woolfolk (1993), 28.

14. Jack Snowman, Rick McCown, and Robert F. Biehler, *Psychology Applied to Teaching*, 12th ed., (Boston: Houghton Mifflin Company, 2009), 35.

15. Glover notes that Piaget differentiated between a scheme (pl. schemes) and a schemata (pl. schema). The first refers to learned behaviors, such as tying a shoelace. The second refers to factual knowledge, such as "Birds have wings." Most texts, however, use the term *scheme* to generally refer to the basic building block of the cognitive structure. John A. Glover and Roger H. Bruning, *Educational Psychology: Principles and Applications*, 3rd. ed., (Glenview, IL: Scott, Foresman/Little, Brown Higher Education, 1990), 115.

16. Biehler and Snowman, 59.

17. Woolfolk (1993), 28.

18. Wadsworth, 11.

19. Ibid., 13.

20. Woolfolk (1993), 29.

21. Biehler and Snowman, 60.

22. Ibid., 59.

23. Paul Eggen and Don Kauchak, *Educational Psychology: Classroom Connections*, 2nd ed., (New York: Macmillan College Publishing Company, 1994), 35.

24. Biehler and Snowman, 59.

25. Glover, 115.

26. Biehler and Snowman, 59.

27. N. L. Gage and David C. Berliner, *Educational Psychology*, 3rd ed., (Boston: Houghton Mifflin Company, 1984), 143.

28. Guy R. LeFrancois, *Psychology for Teaching*, 8th ed., (Belmont, CA: Wadsworth Publishing Company, 1994), 58.

29. Hamachek, 149

30. Myron H. Dembo, *Applying Educational Psychology*, 5th ed., (New York: Longman, 1994), 355.

31. Glover, 115.

32. Eggen and Kauchak (1994), 35.

33. Good and Brophey, 118.

34. Woolfolk (1993), 29.

35. Wadsworth, 14.

36. Glover, 116.

37. Biehler and Snowman, 59.

38. Gage and Berliner, 143.

39. Dembo, 355.

40. Good and Brophey, 55.

41. LeFrancois, 58.

42. Woolfolk (1993), 29.

43. LeFrancois, 58.

44. Good and Brophey, 55.

45. Wadsworth, 16.

46. Textbooks written over the last decade (2000s) continue to redefine Piaget's position on objective reality. Radical

---

constructivism is the strongest example of the shift toward subjective reality, but cognitive and social constructivism are pushing in that direction as well. This is discussed in Chapter Eight.

47. Ibid., 17.
48. Good and Brophey, 55.
49. Anita Woolfolk, *Educational Psychology*, 9th ed., (Boston: Pearson Education, Inc., 2004), 68.
50. Glover, 120.
51. Biehler and Snowman, 63.
52. Patricia A. Alexander, *Psychology in Learning and Instruction* (Upper Saddle River, NJ: Pearson Education, 2006), 50.
53. Watch a video demonstrating differing responses of a 4-year-old and 7-year-old on conservation of volume. www.youtube.com/watch?v=MpREJIrpgv8 . Accessed June 27, 2009.
54. Paul Eggen and Don Kauchak, *Educational Psychology: Windows on Classrooms*, 7th ed. (Columbus: Pearson Education, Inc, 2007), 38.
55. Woolfolk (1993), 33.
56. Eggen and Kauchak (1994), 46.
57. Biehler and Snowman, 65.
58. Glover, 120 and Eggen and Kauchak (1994), 46.
59. Eggen and Kauchak (2007), 38.
60. Biehler and Snowman, 65.
61. Eggen and Kauchak (2007), 39.
62. Very often conflicts in church or the classroom are caused by the inability to see the same reality from different points of view. This might be expressed like this: "If you do not see this the way I do, you are wrong."
63. We will see this 80-year-old idea again in Information Processing Theory ("long-term memory controls what we give attention to," Chapter Nine) and in the most recent discoveries in brain science ("neural networks provide the basis for the frontal lobes to determine what to process and what to ignore," Chapter Sixteen).
64. Glover, 114.
65. Sprinthall (1994), 98.
66. Woolfolk (1993), 30.
67. Ibid.
68. While abilities do not disappear, the use of those abilities may fade. The fantasy of preschoolers (imaginary playmates, Santa Clause, and the Tooth Fairy) gives way to the tangible logic of the elementary years. Imagination can be overwhelmed by logic to such a degree that adults lose the ability to think beyond what they know.
69. Wadsworth, 9.
70. Glover, 114.
71. Sprinthall (1994), 105.
72. Eggen and Kauchak (1994), 44. This explains why "peek-a-boo" games surprise infants—over and over again.
73. Sprinthall (1994), 105–6.
74. Eggen and Kauchak (1994), 44.
75. Sprinthall (1994), 106.
76. Ibid.
77. Parents know that babies cry differently when they are hungry, wet, tired, or sleepy. Learning to interpret these cries is the beginning of communication between parent and child.
78. Sprinthall (1994), 110.
79. Glover, 122.
80. Eggen and Kauchak (1994), 45.
81. Glover, 122.
82. Ibid.
83. Sprinthall (1994), 107.

84. Eggen and Kauchak (1994), 45.

85. Sprinthall (1994), 110.

86. Eggen and Kauchak (1994), 44.

87. Sprinthall (1994), 109.

88. Ibid.

89. Ibid.

90. Glover, 122.

91. Sprinthall (1994), 107.

92. Ibid., 108.

93. Dembo, 359.

94. Ibid., 360.

95. Ibid.

96. Ibid., 361.

97. Eggen and Kauchak (1994), 45.

98. Sprinthall (1994), 109.

99. Glover, 124.

100. Marcia McQuitty, "Teaching Preschoolers" in William R. Yount, ed., *Teaching Ministry of the Church*, 2nd ed., (Nashville: Broadman & Holman, 2008), 295–96.

101. Eggen and Kauchak (1994), 48.

102. Sprinthall (1994), 109.

103. Ibid., 110.

104. Dembo, 361.

105. Eggen and Kauchak (1994), 45.

106. Ibid., 49.

107. Glover, 124.

108. Ibid., 125.

109. Ibid., 362.

110. Dembo, 361.

111. Glover, 125.

112. Eggen and Kauchak (1994), 50.

113. LeFrancois, 68.

114. Eggen and Kauchak (1994), 50.

115. LeFrancois, 68.

116. Dembo, 362.

117. Norma Hedin, "Teaching Children," in Daryl Eldridge, *Teaching Ministry of the Church*, 1st ed., (Nashville: Broadman & Holman, 1995), 233. quoted by Karen Kennemer, "Teaching Children," in W. R. Yount, *Teaching Ministry of the Church*, 2nd. ed., (Nashville: Broadman & Holman, 2008), 313–14.

118. Karen Kennemer, "Teaching Children," in W. R. Yount, *Teaching Ministry of the Church*, 2nd. ed., (Nashville: Broadman & Holman, 2008), 315–19.

119. Eggen and Kauchak (2007), 40.

120. Eggen and Kauchak (1994), 50.

121. Glover, 128.

122. Eggen and Kauchak (1994), 50.

123. Glover, 128.

124. Eggen and Kauchak (1994), 50.

125. Ibid., 51.

126. Woolfolk (1993), 40.

127. Sprinthall (1994), 113.

128. LeFrancois, 69.

129. Neal Jones, long-time pastor of Columbia Baptist Church, Falls Church, VA, made the comment regarding the disconnect between what we say at church and how we live the rest of the time. From a sermon in the early 1970s.

130. Malcolm Knowles, *The Modern Practice of Adult Education: From Pedagogy to Andragogy*, rev. & updated (Chicago, IL: Follett, 1980), 56.

131. Jack Snowman, Rick McCown, and Robert F. Biehler, *Psychology Applied to Teaching*, 12th ed. (Boston: Houghton Mifflin Company, 2009), 43; Gage and Berliner, 144; and Dembo, 364.

132. Snowman, 43 and LeFrancois, 71.

133. Snowman, 43; Dembo, 364; and LeFrancois, 71.

134. T. H. Epstein, "Brain Growth and Cognitive Functioning" in *The Emerging Adolescent: Characteristics and Educational Implications* (Columbus, OH: National Middle School Association, 1980) as cited in Biehler and Snowman, 70.

135. Constance Kamii, "Autonomy: The Aim of Education Envisoned by Piaget," *Phi Delta Kappan*, 65(6), 410–15 as cited in Biehler and Snowman, 70.

136. N. A. Sprinthall and R. C. Sprinthall, *Educational Psychology: A Developmental Approach*, 4th ed. (New York: Random House, 1987) as cited in Snowman, 43.

137. Snowman, 43.

138. Ibid., 43–44.

139. Dembo, 364.

140. Woolfolk (2004), 42–43.

141. Gage and Berliner, 144.

142. Sprinthall (1994) (1998), 114.

143. Ibid.

144. Alexander (2006), Eggen and Kauchak (2007), Ormrod (2006), Snowman (2009), Sternberg (2002), Woolfolk (2004).

145. LeFrancois, 72.

146. Dembo, 366.

147. Ibid., 367.

148. Ibid., 366.

149. "People to People," William J. Reynolds (Nashville: Broadman Press, 1971) in Baptist Hymnal (Nashville: Convention Press, 1975), 308.

150. Glover, 132.

151. Slavin, 46.

152. LeFrancois, 73 .

153. Dembo, 365.

154. LeFrancois, 74.

155. Dembo, 366.

156. This "understanding how we understand" is called a metacognitive process and figures prominently in Information Processing Theory (Chapter Nine).

157. A four-year-old's attempt at the Pledge of Allegiance: "and to the Republic, for which it stands."

158. Slavin, 45.

159. Woolfolk (1993), 33.

160. A doctoral student used the word *heuristic* during his presentation. I thought it important that students understand what the word means and so asked the presenter to explain it. "It was in a quote," he said. "Yes, and what does the word mean in that quote?" "I don't know." We then laid down a principle for class presentations: do not use words in presentations that you cannot explain.

161. Glover, 131.

162. Dembo, 367.

163. For examples of Paul's uses of the terms, see Rom 8:9 and Phil 1:19; then Rom 9:1, 1 Cor 6:19; 2 Cor 6:6. For Peter's, see 1 Pet 1:11 and 4:14.

164. From "Piaget Rediscovered," 5, as quoted in Herbert Ginsburg and Sylvia Opper, *Piaget's Theory of Intellectual Development: An Introduction* (Englewood Cliffs, NJ: Prentice-Hall, Inc., 1969), 231–32.

165. Eggen and Kauchak (2007), 45.

166. Ibid., 46.

167. Woolfolk (2004), 45.

168. Alexander, 47.

169. Eggen and Kauchak (2007), 50.

170. Snowman, 47.

171. Ibid., 46.

172. Eggen and Kauchak (2007), 45.

173. Woolfolk (2004), 45.

174. Snowman, 46.

175. Eggen and Kauchak (2007), 45.

176. Ibid., 47.

177. Woolfolk (2004), 45.

178. Eggen and Kauchak (2007), 47.

179. Ibid., 47.

180. Ibid. Note: Self-talk, or private speech, can be external (audible) or internalized (silent). In either case, it represents conversations with ourselves, not with others.

181. Woolfolk (2004), 49.

182. Snowman, 47.

183. Ibid.

184. Ibid.

185. I was greatly helped in understanding certain aspects of deaf culture by my 1975 study of Value Orientation Theory (1961) developed by F. R. Kluckhohn and others. VOM delineates various views of cultural issues such as human nature, man-nature relationship, time sense, activity, and social relations. "Most studies of the dominant Euro-American culture in the United States find that it is future oriented, focused on doing, emphasizes individualism, aspires to be dominant over nature, and believes that human nature is mixed, some people are good and some are bad (e.g., Carter, 1990). By contrast, most studies show that Native cultures are past oriented, focused on being, emphasize collateral (group) relations, aspire to be in harmony with nature, and believe that people are fundamentally good (e.g., Russo, 2000a). A helpful overview is located at http://www.joe.org/joe/2001december/tt1.php. Accessed on June 29, 2009.

186. Alexander, 47.

187. Ibid. A four-year-old child of evangelical missionaries prays at the dinner table—not by repeating memorized prayers, but by praying for heartfelt needs in the moment. These are simple needs ("Thank you for Daddy and Mommie. Thank you for hot dogs on the table."), but complex thoughts. The nine-year-old son of a chess champion plays competitive chess at levels far above the norn for his age group. These "social context" examples reinforce Vygotsky's ideas.

188. Woolfolk (2004), 43.

189. Snowman, 48.

190. Ibid., 49.

191. Vygotsky, 345.

192. Ibid., 339.

193. What is confusing in the literature is how different writers frame this difference, especially regarding the lower end of the zone. Sternberg says ZPD is the range between a child's "level of independent performance and the level of performance a child can reach with expert guidance" (56–57). Ormrod writes that the ZPD is the "range of tasks children cannot yet perform independently but can perform with the help and guidance of others" (36). So, which is it? Ability

or inability? Most focus on "ability" and are referring to area "A" in the illustration. Those who focus on "inability" are referring to the area just inside the line between "A" and "B" since a new task that falls in ZPD is one that learners cannot do without help.

194. Mayer, 462.

195. Eggen and Kauchak (2007), 49.

196. Snowman, 50.

197. Mayer, 462.

198. Snowman, 50.

199. Woolfolk (2004), 52.

200. Ibid.

201. Snowman, 50.

202. Woolfolk (2004), 52.

203. James Atherton at http://www.learningandteaching.info/learning/constructivism.htm (last up-dated 23 May 2009). Accessed June 28, 2009.

204. The types of scaffolding are drawn from Eggen and Kauchak (2007), 50.

205. Snowman, 51.

206. Lev S. Vygotsky, *Educational Psychology* translated by Robert Silverman, (Boca Raton, FL: St. Lucie Press, 1997 (1926)), 344.

207. Ibid. Russian quote from the Russian edition of the text. ... ., ..., (......: ....-....., 1999), 311. (Lev S. Vygotsky, *Pedagogical Psychology* [Moscow: Pedigogic-Press, 1999])

208. Ibid., 345.

209. Vygotsky may have been criticizing Piaget here, since Piaget based his theory in a "universal biological process" of development. Soviet education would produce a higher sociobiological type of humanity as it reorganized the cultures of the world to provide a proper socialistic environment for learning.

210. Ibid., 351.

211. Eggen and Kauchak (2007), 45.

212. Snowman, 49.

213. Eggen and Kauchak (2007), 51.

214. Vygotsky, 345.

215. Eggen and Kauchak (2007), 51.

216. Woolfolk, 53.

217. Eggen and Kauchak (2007), 51.

218. Woolfolk, 53.

219. Ormrod, 38.

220. Woolfolk (2004), 53.

221. Ormrod, 38.

222. I just recently returned from six weeks in a Central Asian nation (predominantly Muslim, former Soviet Republic) where I met with Baptist teachers, pastors, and church members in three different regions. As we talked of the things of the Lord, I realized I had more in common, culturally, with these Asian Baptists, eleven time zones from home, than I had with unbelieving Americans who live in my city. God, church, Bible, salvation, baptism, abortion, homosexuality, alcoholism, drugs, smoking, juvenile delinquency, leadership—the list goes on and on. Walking into a Baptist church on the other side of the world, I felt completely "at home."

223. Eggen and Kauchak (1994), 35.

224. Sprinthall (1994), 117.

225. Biehler and Snowman, 59.

226. Glover, 117.

227. Ibid., 123.

228. Ibid., 120.

Chapter 5 Notes

1. http://creativeproverbs.com/cgi-bin/sql_search3cp.cgi?keyword=honest+steal&boolean=and&field=all&frank=all&database=all. Accessed June 28, 2009.

2. Paul Eggen and Don Kauchak, *Educational Psychology: Classroom Connections*, 2nd ed., (New York: Macmillan College Publishing Company, 1994), 63.

3. Jack Snowman, Rick McCown, and Robert F. Biehler, *Psychology Applied to Teaching*, 12th ed., (Boston: Houghton Mifflin Company, 2009), 54.

4. Ibid., 55.

5. Robert E. Slavin, *Educational Psychology: Theory and Practice*, 4th ed., (Boston: Allyn and Bacon, 1994), 58. Snowman says "four to seven," 55.

6. Robert F. Biehler and Jack Snowman, *Psychology Applied to Teaching*, 7th ed., (Boston: Houghton Mifflin Company, 1993), 73.

7. Slavin, 58.

8. Snowman et al. says ages 7–10, 73.

9. Ibid.

10. Slavin, 59.

11. Snowman, 55.

12. Ibid.

13. Slavin, 59.

14. Eggen and Kauchak (1994), 63.

15. Quoted from Jean Piaget, *The Moral Judgement of the Child*, (Glencoe, IL: Free Press, 1948), 118 by Biehler and Snowman, 74.

16. Don Hamachek, *Psychology in Teaching, Learning, and Growth*, 4th ed., (Boston: Allyn and Bacon, 1990), 170.

17. Ibid.

18. Slavin, 59.

19. Biehler and Snowman, 73.

20. Anita Woolfolk (1993), *Educational Psychology*, 5th ed., (Boston: Allyn and Bacon, Inc., 1993), 79.

21. Biehler and Snowman, 74.

22. Woolfolk (1993), 79.

23. Guy R. LeFrancois, *Psychology for Teaching*, 8th ed., (Belmont, CA: Wadsworth Publishing Company, 1994), 42.

24. Slavin, 59.

25. Biehler and Snowman, 73, Hamachek, 171.

26. Woolfolk (1993), 78.

27. Ibid., 79.

28. Biehler and Snowman, 78.

29. Woolfolk (1993), 79.

30. LeFrancois, 42.

31. Slavin, 61.

32. Eggen and Kauchak (1994), 63, Slavin, 60, Biehler and Snowman, 74.

33. Bonnidell Clouse, *Teaching for Moral Growth: A Guide for the Christian Community: Teachers, Parents, and Pastors*, (Wheaton, IL: Victor Books, 1993), 243.

34. Norman A. Sprinthall, Richard C. Sprinthall, and Sharon N. Oja, *Educational Psychology: A Developmental Approach*, 6th ed., (New York: McGraw-Hill, Inc., 1994), 182.

35. Lawrence Kohlberg, "My Personal Search for Universal Morality," *Moral Education Forum* 11:1 (1986), quoted in Clouse, 234.

36. Clouse, 235.

37. Ibid.

38. Sprinthall (1994), 182.

39. Clouse, 235.

40. Sprinthall (1994), 182.

41. Dembo, 218.

42. Eggen and Kauchak (1994), 63.

43. Hamachek, 172.

44. Clouse, 235.

45. Sprinthall (1994), 182.

46. Clouse, 235.

47. Ibid.

48. Stephen N. Elliot, Thomas R. Kratochwill, Joan Littlefield Cook, and John F. Travers, *Educational Psychology: Effective Teaching, Effective Learning,* (Boston: McGraw-Hill, 2000), 86; Robert J. Sternberg and Wendy M. Williams, *Educational Psychology,* (Boston: Allyn and Bacon, 2002), 103; Jeanne Ellis Ormrod, *Educational Psychology: Developing Learners,* 5th ed., (Columbus: Pearson Education, Inc., 2006), 69.

49. Ormrod, 90.

50. LeFrancois, 43.

51. Slavin, 61.

52. Snowman, 57.

53. Slavin, 62.

54. Thomas L. Good and Jere E. Brophey, *Educational Psychology: A Realistic Approach,* 4th ed., (New York: Longman, 1990), 55, and Sprinthall (1994), 108.

55. LeFrancois, 43.

56. John A. Glover and Roger H. Bruning, *Educational Psychology: Principles and Applications,* 3rd. ed., (Glenview, Illinois: Scott, Foresman/Little, Brown Higher Education, 1990), 230.

57. Ormrod, 90.

58. They place emphasis either on the simple inability of children to think differently or on the value of obedience.

59. Sternberg, 103.

60. Elliot, 87.

61. Clouse, 208.

62. Ormrod, 90.

63. Slavin, 62.

64. LeFrancois, 43.

65. Slavin, 62.

66. Eggen and Kauchak (1994), 65.

67. Glover and Bruning, 230.

68. Clouse, 228.

69. Anita Woolfolk, *Educational Psychology,* 9th ed., (Boston: Pearson Education, Inc., 2004), 68.

70. LeFrancois, 43.

71. Eggen and Kauchak (1994), 65.

72. Norman A. Sprinthall, Richard C. Sprinthall, and Sharon Nodie Oja, *Educational Psychology: A Developmental Approach,* 7th ed., (New York: McGraw-Hill, Inc., 1998), 194.

73. Eggen and Kauchak (1994), 65.

74. Ormrod, 90.

75. Snowman, 57.

76. Biehler and Snowman, 77.

77. Glover and Bruning, 230.

78. Eggen and Kauchak (1994), 65.

79. Norman A. Sprinthall, Richard C. Sprinthall, and Sharon N. Oja, *Educational Psychology: A Developmental Approach,* 6th ed., (New York: McGraw-Hill, Inc., 1994), 179.

80. Sternberg, 103.

81. Sprinthall (1998), 197.

82. Clouse, 234.

83. Elliot, 87.

84. Eggen and Kauchak (1994), 65.

85. Good and Brophey, 108.

86. Woolfolk (2004), 81.

87. Slavin, 62.

88. LeFrancois, 43.

89. Snowman, 57.

90. Ormrod, 90.

91. Slavin, 62.

92. Sprinthall (1998), 194.

93. Eggen and Kauchak (1994), 65.

94. Glover and Bruning, 230.

95. Biehler and Snowman, 77.

96. Clouse, 229.

97. Ibid._

98. Ibid., 247.

99. Sprinthall (1998), 195.

100. Dembo, 217.

101. LeFrancois, 43.

102. Sprinthall (1998), 195.

103. Clouse, 229.

104. Glover and Bruning, 231.

105. LeFrancois, 43.

106. Slavin, 62.

107. Eggen and Kauchak (1994), 66.

108. Snowman, 57.

109. Eggen and Kauchak (1994), 66.

110. Slavin, 62.

111. Eggen and Kauchak (1994), 65.

112. Clouse, 247.

113. Elliot, 88.

114. Sternberg, 103.

115. Woolfolk (2004), 81.

116. Elliot, 87.

117. Sprinthall (1998), 195.

118. Slavin, 62.

119. Sprinthall (1994), 183.

120. LeFrancois, 43.

121. Slavin, 62.

122. Eggen and Kauchak (1994), 66.

123. Clouse, 234.

124. Clouse, 232.

125. Sprinthall (1998), 197.

126. Glover and Bruning, 231.

127. Sprinthall (1994), 181.

128. LeFrancois, 43.

129. Snowman, 57.

130. Eggen and Kauchak (1994), 66.

131. Clouse, 232.

132. These differences are described by Clouse (232)—except she identifies the lower-level lawbreaker as Stage II when her descriptions fit Stage I much better.

133. Sternberg, 103.

134. Dembo, 217.

135. Clouse, 238.

136. Elliot, 89.

137. Parsons, 79.

138. Biehler and Snowman, 78.

139. Sprinthall (1998), 197.

140. Excerpts from Wallace's life taken from James MacKay, *William Wallace: Braveheart,* (Edinburgh: Mainstream Publishing, 1995).

141. Sternberg, 105.

142. http://www.brainyquote.com/quotes/authors/m/mother_teresa.html.

143. For additional insights into the way Mother Theresa left home to serve God in India and then left the security of the Calcutta convent to serve the dying poor in the streets, depending on God alone for sustenance, see her Nobel Prize biography at http://nobelprize.org/nobel_prizes/peace/laureates/1979/teresa-bio.html

144. Sprinthall (1994), 183.

145. Biehler and Snowman, 78.

146. Ormrod, 90.

147. LeFrancois, 43.

148. Slavin, 62.

149. Sprinthall (1998), 198.

150. Woolfolk (2004) and Sprinthall (1998) use asterisks to report Kohlberg's suspension of Stage VI. A few others report the stage is rarely encountered in life (Eggen and Kauchak, 2007, 82; Parsons, 77; Elliot, 89; Ormrod, 90; Sternberg, 105; Snowman, 57).

151. Quoted from Dr. M. L. King, Jr., *Why We Can't Wait* (New York: Harper & Row, Publishers, 1963), 84–85 by Sprinthall (1994), 184.

152. Sprinthall (1994), 184.

153. This means only that I should treat a criminal as I would wish to be treated if I were a criminal. It does not excuse criminal behavior but protects against unbridled abuse.

154. Clouse, 233.

155. Elliot, 87.

156. Sternberg, 103.

157. Elliot, 89.

158. Sprinthall (1998), 197.

159. Ronald Duska and Mariellen Whelan, *Moral Development: A Guide to Piaget and Kohlberg* (New York: Paulist Press, 1975), 86–99.

160. Ibid., 86.

161. Ibid.

162. Ibid., 87.

163. Ibid., 88.

164. Ibid., 91.

165. All God's children—in the sense that He created us all.

166. "For God so loved the world."

167. Duska and Whelan, 99.

168. Woolfolk (2004), 82; Eggen and Kauchak (1994), 67.

169. LeFrancois, 45.

170. Sprinthall (1998), 201.

171. This is logical since the theory is anchored in Piaget's cognitive development theory, which is itself sequential and fixed.

172. Glover and Bruning, 236.

173. Eggen and Kauchak (1994), 67.

174. Woolfolk (2004), 82.

175. Eggen and Kauchak (1994), 68.

176. Woolfolk (1993), 81.

177. Ibid., 82.

178. Ibid.

179. Elliot, 87.

180. Sternberg, 105.

181. Woolfolk (2004), 81.

182. Clouse, 232.

183. Sternberg, 106.

184. Woolfolk (1993), 82.

185. Good and Brophey, 111.

186. Clouse, 248.

187. Gilligan's views had an immediate impact on psychology and the wider community—as she was named Woman of the Year by a leading feminist magazine. Sprinthall (1998), 206.

188. Carol Gilligan, *In a Different Voice: Psychological Theory and Women's Development* (Cambridge, MA: Harvard University Press, 1982).

189. Clouse, 249.

190. Ibid., 250.

191. Woolfolk (2004), 83.

192. Jaffee, Hyde, and Shibley (2000) cited in Snowman, 60–61.

193. Elliot, 92.

194. Ormrod, 92.

195. Snowman, 60.

196. Eggen and Kauchak (1994), 67.

197. Ibid.

198. Eggen and Kauchak (2007), 85.

199. Elliot, 93.

200. Biehler and Snowman, 85.

201. Elliot, 91.

202. Ormrod, 93.

203. LeFrancois, 47.

204. Ibid.

205. Eggen and Kauchak (2007), 87.

206. Biehler and Snowman, 85.

207. Sternberg, 106.

208. Biehler and Snowman, 85.

209. LeFrancois, 46.

210. *Ibid.*, 45.

211. Biehler and Snowman, 85, Elliot, 90.

212. Eggen and Kauchak (1994), 69.

213. Eggen and Kauchak (2007), 87.

214. See item 1 under Criticisms of Kohlberg's Theory.

215. Good and Brophey, 112.

216. "One of them, Caiaphas, who was high priest that year, said to them, "You know nothing at all! You're not considering that **it is to your advantage that one man should die for the people rather than the whole nation perish.**" He did not say this on his own, but being high priest that year he prophesied that Jesus was going to die for the nation, and not for the nation only, but also to unite the scattered children of God. So from that day on they plotted to kill Him" (John 11:49–54).

217. Clouse, 233.

218. Galatians 3:24, pedagogue. "The slave employed in Greek and Roman families of the better class in charge of the boy from about six to sixteen. The paedagogue watched his behaviour at home and attended him when he went away from home as to school. Christ is our Schoolmaster and the law as paedagogue kept watch over us until we came to Christ. (Robertson's *Word Pictures in the New Testament*, Electronic Database. Copyright © 1997, 2003, 2005, 2006 by Biblesoft, Inc. Robertson's *Word Pictures in the New Testament*. Copyright © 1985 by Broadman Press, *PC Study Bible*, version 5.0E, Biblesoft, 1988–2007).

219. Charles M. Sell, *Transitions through Adult Life* (Grand Rapids, MI: Zondervan Publishing Company, 1991), 107.

Unit 3 Notes

1. Parsons, 206.

Chapter 6 Notes

1. http://creativeproverbs.com/cgi-bin/sql_search3cp.cgi?keyword=praise+blossom&boolean=and&field=all&frank=all&database=all. Accessed June 29, 2009.

2. The three systems are the behavioral (skills, hand), the cognitive (concepts and principles, head), and the humanistic (attitudes and values, heart).

3. Ralph Garry and Howard Kingsley, *The Nature and Conditions of Learning*, 3rd ed., (Englewood Cliffs, NJ: Prentice-Hall, Inc., 1970), 76. Dr. George Boeree lists a fourth: *frequency*. The more often two elements are linked together, the stronger the link between them. "Psychology: The Beginnings," (2000) http://webspace.ship.edu/cgboer/psychbeginnings.html. An article on the "New Advent" Web site lists three laws of association, relegating "frequency" to secondary status. I also recall from earlier studies the law of "sequence" (we associate elements in a sequential list: "this after that"), but I have not found any reference for that.

4. Aristotle broke with his teacher Plato who posited "reality" in the spiritual world of a Universal Knower. The objects in our world, and the world itself, were an imperfect reflection of the real, which consisted of ideas (Idealism). Aristotle asked of the world, "What do I see?" "Of what does it consist?" "What form does it take?" From these questions, he developed his form-matter hypothesis and focused on the physical world as real (Realism).

5. George Boeree, "Aristotle." http://webspace.ship.edu/cgboer/athenians.html , accessed September 12, 2008.

6. Garry and Kingsley, 76.

7. George R. Knight, *Philosophy & Education: An Introduction in Christian Perspective*, 4th ed., (Berrien Springs, MS: Andrews University Press, 2006), 50.

8. D. C. Phillips and Jonas Soltis, *Perspectives on Learning* (New York: Teachers College Press, 1985), 13.

9. Bonnidell Clouse, *Teaching for Moral Growth: A Guide for the Christian Community: Teachers, Parents, and Pastors*, (Wheaton, IL, Victor Books, 1993), 167.

10. Phillips and Soltis, 13.

11. Norman A. Sprinthall, Richard C. Sprinthall, and Sharon N. Oja, *Educational Psychology: A Developmental Approach*, 6th ed., (New York: McGraw-Hill, Inc., 1994), 241.

12. Boeree, "Aristotle." http://webspace.ship.edu/cgboer/athenians.html , accessed September 12, 2008.

---

13. Phillips and Soltis, 13.

14. Traditional behaviorists believe the mind is irrelevant to understanding why people behave as they do. Sprinthall (1994), 232. Behaviorists emphasis "nervous system" and "brain" rather than "mind."

15. http://www.indiana.edu/~intell/wundt.shtml.

16. Sprinthall (1994), 212.

17. Go to http://www.elementsdatabase.com/ to see a table of the 103 elements, the atomic building blocks of the universe. Wundt wanted to find the "building blocks" of human personality and learning.

18. Garry and Kingsley, 77.

19. Myron H. Dembo, *Applying Educational Psychology*, 5th ed., (New York: Longman, 1994), 41.

20. Robert E. Slavin, *Educational Psychology: Theory and Practice*, 4th ed., (Boston: Allyn and Bacon, 1994), 154.

21. Paul Eggen and Don Kauchak, *Educational Psychology: Classroom Connections*, 2nd ed., (New York: Macmillan College Publishing Company, 1994), 257

22. Anita Woolfolk, *Educational Psychology*, 5th ed., (Boston: Allyn and Bacon, Inc., 1993), 199.

23. Thomas L. Good and Jere E. Brophey, *Educational Psychology: A Realistic Approach*, 4th ed., (New York: Longman, 1990), 55. and Sprinthall (1994), 155.

24. John A. Glover and Roger H. Bruning, *Educational Psychology: Principles and Applications*, 3rd. ed., (Glenview, IL: Scott, Foresman/Little, Brown Higher Education, 1990), 270.

25. Slavin, 155.

26. Good and Brophey, 153.

27. Guy R. LeFrancois, *Psychology for Teaching*, 8th ed., (Belmont, CA: Wadsworth Publishing Company, 1994), 87.

28. Good and Brophey, 154; Eggen and Kauchak (1994), 261; Woolfolk (1993), 200.

29. Good and Brophey, 154.

30. Eggen and Kauchak (1994), 260.

31. Given the basic S-R bond, behaviorists prefer to talk about "organisms" rather than human learners. As we shall see, behaviorists prefer to study pigeons, rats, and cats because they are simple. The laws governing learning in these simple organisms apply directly to human learning on which Cognitivists disagree.

32. Woolfolk (1993), 200.

33. Eggen and Kauchak (1994), 258.

34. Chapter One introduced you to The Disciplers' Model. In the original text, *The Disciplers' Handbook,* you will find Chapter Three: "The Disciplers' Manner," which describes teaching in terms of how we lead based on the leadership principles of Jesus with the Twelve. You may obtain a copy of this chapter as a free PDF download at www.NAPCE.org/resources.

35. Dembo, 42.

36. Good and Brophey, 155.

37. LeFrancois, 88.

38. Dembo, 42.

39. Good and Brophey, 156.

40. Ibid., 155.

41. Ibid., 156.

42. Dembo, 42.

43. Ibid.

44. Good and Brophey, 156.

45. LeFrancois, 91.

46. Dembo, 42.

47. Good and Brophey, 156.

48. Slavin, 156.

49. LeFrancois, 91.

50. Good and Brophey, 156.

51. Sprinthall (1994), 215.

52. Dembo, 44.

53. Наука есть вернейший путь к овладению жизнью (Pov-ta-RYEN-ee-yeh mat' abu-CHYEN-ee-ya.) Repetition—mother of learning.

54. Good and Brophey, 157.

55. Sprinthall (1994), 215.

56. LeFrancois, 91.

57. Eggen and Kauchak (1994), 262.

58. Dembo, 44.

59. Woolfolk (1993), 198. The term "S-R bond" was actually coined by E. L. Thorndike. LeFrancois, 90.

60. LeFrancois, 90.

61. Sprinthall (1994), 215.

62. Ibid.

63. Woolfolk (1993), 202.

64. Eggen and Kauchak (1994), 262.

65. Sprinthall (1994), 232.

66. Eggen and Kauchak (1994), 262.

67. Material for this biography was drawn from Clouse, 156 and Sprinthall (1994), 230–1.

68. Woolfolk (1993), 202.

69. Eggen and Kauchak (1994), 262.

70. Woolfolk (1993), 201.

71. LeFrancois, 92.

72. Woolfolk (1993), 201.

73. Hamachek, 231.

74. Woolfolk (1993), 202.

75. LeFrancois, 94.

76. Eggen and Kauchak (1994), 262.

77. Glover and Bruning, 275.

78. Woolfolk (1993), 203.

79. Eggen and Kauchak (1994), 262.

80. Slavin, 158; Woolfolk (1993), 203.

81. LeFrancois, 94.

82. Slavin, 158.

83. Woolfolk (1993), 203.

84. Dembo, 51; Slavin, 158.

85. Descriptions of positive and negative reinforcement, punishment I and II, and schedules of reinforcement are described by recent writers as they were in the first edition. Jack Snowman, Rick McCown, and Robert F. Biehler, *Psychology Applied to Teaching,* 12th ed., (Boston: Houghton Mifflin Company, 2009), 222–3; Richard D. Parsons, Stephanie Lewis Hinson, and Deborah Sardo-Brown, *Educational Psychology: A Practitioner-Researcher Mode of Teaching,* (Belmont, CA: Wadsworth/Thomson Learning, 2001), 221; Robert J. Sternberg and Wendy M. Williams, *Educational Psychology,* (Boston: Allyn and Bacon, 2002), 245; Anita Woolfolk, *Educational Psychology,* 9th ed., (Boston: Pearson Education, Inc., 2004), 204–5.

86. LeFrancois, 97.

87. Skinner believed the word *reward* carried subjective undertones which he rejected. Dembo, 44.

88. Woolfolk (1993), 204.

89. Slavin, 159.

90. Hamachek, 234; LeFrancois, 97.

91. Sternberg, 247.

92. Woolfolk (1993), 205.

93. Dembo, 51.

94. LeFrancois, 97.

95. Dembo, 51.

96. It is more effective to inform learners of consequences ahead of time: "If you do not clean your room when you come home from school, you may not watch television this evening."

97. Woolfolk (1993), 205.

98. Dembo, 51.

99. Eggen and Kauchak (1994), 269.

100. LeFrancois, 97.

101. Richard D. Parsons, Stephanie Lewis Hinson, and Deborah Sardo-Brown, *Educational Psychology: A Practitioner-Researcher Mode of Teaching*, (Belmont, CA: Wadsworth/Thomson Learning, 2001), 221.

102. Elizabeth Gershoff (2002) "analyzed eighty-eight studies conducted over the past sixty years and concluded that corporal punishment was strongly associated with negative behaviors and experiences [such] as low internalization of moral rules, aggression, delinquent and antisocial behavior, low-quality parent-child relationships, and being the recipient of physical abuse." Gershoff's findings were challenged on the basis of her definition of corporal punishment, which was more severe than most parents administer. When the studies were re-analyzed with the narrower definition, a much weaker relationship between spanking and aggressive behavior was found. The conclusion was that "a blanket condemnation of spanking cannot be made on the basis of existing research." Snowman, 235.

103. Sternberg, 252.

104. Ibid., 225.

105. Woolfolk (1993), 205.

106. Eggen and Kauchak (1994), 274.

107. "Right." "Very good." "Exactly right." "Excellent."

108. Woolfolk (1993), 205.

109. Eggen and Kauchak (1994), 274.

110. Woolfolk (1993), 205.

111. Ibid.

112. Eggen and Kauchak (1994), 276.

113. Ibid.

114. Woolfolk (1993), 206.

115. Eggen and Kauchak (1994), 276.

116. Slavin, 167.

117. Eggen and Kauchak (1994), 276.

118. Woolfolk (1993), 205.

119. Ibid., 206.

120. Slavin, 167.

121. Woolfolk (1993), 206.

122. Slavin, 167.

123. Woolfolk (1993), 207.

124. Ibid.

125. "Superstition and Psychology," http://encyclopedia.thefreedictionary.com/Superstitious+reinforcement, accessed October 10, 2008.

126. Glover and Bruning, 283.

127. Eggen and Kauchak (1994), 278.

128. Sprinthall (1994), 234.

129. Dembo, 54.

130. Parsons, 228.

131. Snowman, 223; Woolfolk (2004), 207.

132. Snowman, 225.

133. Sprinthall (1994), 235.

134. Eggen and Kauchak (1994), 271.

135. Slavin, 172.

136. Eggen and Kauchak (1994), 271.

137. Sprinthall (1994), 235.

138. Eggen and Kauchak (1994), 271.

139. Woolfolk (1993), 201.

140. Dembo, 46.

141. Slavin, 171.

142. Parsons, 224.

143. Ibid.

144. Ibid.

145. Dembo, 56.

146. Woolfolk (1993), 209.

147. Jeanne Ellis Ormrod, *Educational Psychology: Developing Learners*, 5th ed., (Columbus: Pearson Education, Inc., 2006), 310; Woolfolk (2004), 211.

148. Ormrod, 310–1.

149. Woolfolk (1993), 211.

150. Eggen and Kauchak (1994), 272; Woolfolk (2004), 210.

151. Eggen and Kauchak (1994), 272.

152. Woolfolk (1993), 212.

153. They do both activities together, which is far more effective than saying, "When you pick up your toys (alone), then you can watch a video (alone)."

154. Parsons, 225.

155. Snowman, 231; Sprinthall (1998), 288; Sternberg, 244.

156. Hamachek, 236.

157. Snowman, 232.

158. Ibid.

159. Woolfolk (2004), 219.

160. Snowman, 232.

161. Ibid.

162. Sternberg's term is not to be confused with humanistic self-reinforcement in which learners choose to act in certain ways based on personal values. The focus in humanism is "self-chosen." Sternberg seems to be connecting supervised skill development with the outcome of self-sufficiency, which he sees as reinforcing.

163. Sternberg, 256.

164. Snowman, 231.

165. Hamilton and Ghatala, 61.

166. Biehler and Snowman (1993), 337.

167. Ibid., 336.

168. Hamachek, 240.

169. Hamilton and Ghatala, 62.

170. Hamachek, 240.

171. A program may have twenty frames and prompts for a given subseries within the program. If a student answers five of the first five questions correctly, demonstrating understanding of the material, the program can skip to the next series, eliminating fifteen frames of material and prompts—necessary for the less experienced learner but boring to one who already understands it. A linear program would force every student to process every frame.

172. Sprinthall (1998), 289.

173. Snowman, 227.

174. Ibid.

175. LeFrancois, 333.

176. Slavin, 337.

177. LeFrancois, 334.

178. Snowman, 243.

179. Ibid.

180. Ibid., 241.

181. Sprinthall (1998), 290.

182. Biehler and Snowman (1993), 338.

183. Slavin, 339.

184. LeFrancois, 332.

185. Snowman, 229.

186. A meta-analysis is a study of studies that aims to synthesize the findings of many into a single, integrated whole.

187. Snowman, 228.

188. Ibid., 241.

189. Ibid.

190. Ibid.

191. Woolfolk (1993), 216.

192. Ibid., 217.

193. Eggen and Kauchak (2007), 179.

194. Woolfolk (1993), 216.

195. Ibid.

196. Eggen and Kauchak (1994), 281.

197. Woolfolk (1993), 216.

198. Eggen and Kauchak (1994), 281.

199. Sprinthall (1994), 235.

200. Eggen and Kauchak (2007), 179.

201. Ibid.

202. Ibid.

203. Woolfolk (1993), 217.

204. Ibid.

205. Eggen and Kauchak (2007), 179.

206. Snowman, 237.

207. Ibid.

208. Ibid., 240.

209. Klaus Issler and Ronald Habermas, *How We Learn: A Christian Teacher's Guide to Educational Psychology*, (Grand Rapids, MI: Baker Books, 1994), 209.

210. Sprinthall (1994), 239, quoting B. R. Hergenbahn, *An Introduction to Learning Theories*. 2nd ed., (Englewood Cliffs, NJ: Prentice-Hall, 1988), 84.

211. Phillips and Soltis, 29.

212. Ibid.

213. At least, no one had seen a quark at the time they wrote. Quarks are theoretical particles, which are studied by analyzing their effects. By 1995, all six "flavors" of quarks had been observed. http://en.wikipedia.org/wiki/Quark.

214. Phillips and Soltis, 30.

215. Ibid., 31.

216. Sprinthall (1994), 242.

217. http://nobelprize.org/nobel_prizes/medicine/laureates/1904/pavlov-bio.html.

218. Gage and Berliner, 295.

219. One technique presents a series of pictures of food. Some of the pictures show healthy foods arranged beautifully on a plate; others show favorite foods covered with all manner of vermin. Good choices are accompanied by pleasing music, while bad choices are accompanied by a mild electric shock. Over time, they think more positively about healthy choices and tend to avoid bad choices. In another technique, the client is asked to bring their favorite forbidden food with them. When the session begins, they are invited to eat some of their favorite food. As they begin to chew, a new rule is added. They cannot swallow. After they chew for a while, they are encouraged to eat more. Eventually, the clients are chewing large masses of unswallowed mush. Clients often become ill during the process, and they rarely eat their favorite bad food again.

220. Gage and Berliner, 296.

221. Ibid., 297.

222. By recent, I mean textbooks published between 2003 and 2009.

223. Ormrod, 321.

224. The Center for Effective Collaboration and Practice, "Functional Behavioral Assessment," http://cecp.air.org/fba/, accessed October 20, 2008.

225. Ormrod, 322.

226. Ibid., 324.

227. Ibid., 177.

228. Ibid., 178.

229. Eggen and Kauchak (2007), 179.

Chapter 7 Notes

1. http://creativeproverbs.com/cgi-bin/sql_search3cp.cgi?keyword=models+critics&boolean=and&field=all&frank=all&database=all.

2. Anita Woolfolk, *Educational Psychology*, 5th ed., (Boston: Allyn and Bacon, Inc., 1993), 220.

3. Thomas L. Good and Jere E. Brophey, *Educational Psychology: A Realistic Approach*, 4th ed., (New York: Longman, 1990), 55 and Sprinthall (1994), 166.

4. Woolfolk (1993), 220.

5. Anita Woolfolk, *Educational Psychology*, 9th ed., (Boston: Pearson Education, Inc., 2004), 315.

6. Bruner published three earlier works: A. Bandura, and Richard H. Walters, *Adolescent Aggression: A Study of the Influence of Child-Training Practices and Family Interrelationships*, (New York: Ronald Press, 1959); A. Bandura and R. H. Walters, *Social Learning and Personality Development*, (New York: Holt, Rinehart, & Winston, 1963); A. Bandura, *Aggression: A Social Learning Analysis*, (Englewood Cliffs, NJ: Prentice-Hall, 1973).

7. Richard D. Parsons, Stephanie Lewis Hinson, and Deborah Sardo-Brown, *Educational Psychology: A Practitioner-Researcher Mode of Teaching*, (Belmont, CA: Wadsworth/Thomson Learning, 2001), 209.

8. Norman A. Sprinthall, Richard C. Sprinthall, and Sharon N. Oja, *Educational Psychology: A Developmental Approach*, 6th ed., (New York: McGraw-Hill, Inc., 1994), 230.

9. Englewood Cliffs, NJ: Prentice-Hall. 1986.

10. Woolfolk (1993), 220.

11. Sprinthall (1994), 259.

12. Paul Eggen and Don Kauchak, *Educational Psychology: Classroom Connections*, 2nd ed., (New York: Macmillan College Publishing Company, 1994), 282.

13. Robert F. Biehler and Jack Snowman, *Psychology Applied to Teaching*, 7th ed., (Boston: Houghton Mifflin Company, 1993), 346.

14. Bruner published three earlier works: A. Bandura and Richard H. Walters, *Adolescent Aggression; A Study of the Influence of Child-Training Practices and Family Interrelationships*, (New York: Ronald Press, 1959); A. Bandura and R. H. Walters, *Social Learning and Personality Development*, (New York: Holt, Rinehart, & Winston, 1963); A. Bandura, *Aggression: A Social Learning Analysis*, (Englewood Cliffs, NJ: Prentice-Hall, 1973).

15. Woolfolk (2004), 317.

16. Biehler and Snowman (1993), 346.

17. Woolfolk (1993), 221.

18. Eggen and Kauchak (1994), 284.

19. Eggen and Kauchak (1994), 284; Myron H. Dembo, *Applying Educational Psychology*, 5th ed., (New York: Longman, 1994), 57.

20. Dembo, 57.

21. Eggen and Kauchak (1994), 282; Dembo, 57.

22. Woolfolk (1993), 220.

23. A Bobo doll is a plastic, inflatable punching bag that sits on the floor. The bag is decorated with an image of a clown, which stands about four feet tall. The bag is weighted on the bottom so that, when the clown's face is punched, the doll springs back up into a standing position. Bobo dolls were popular toys in the 1950s.

24. Dr. C. George Boeree, http://webspace.ship.edu/cgboer/bandura.html, accessed October 22, 2008.

25. Biehler and Snowman (1993), 349.

26. Robert J. Sternberg and Wendy M. Williams, *Educational Psychology*, (Boston: Allyn and Bacon, 2002), 253.

27. Dr. C. George Boeree, http://webspace.ship.edu/cgboer/bandura.html, accessed October 22, 2008.

28. Woolfolk (2004), 317.

29. Sternberg, 254–55.

30. Biehler and Snowman (1993), 348.

31. Sports heroes and Hollywood stars cannot truthfully claim they have no responsibility when fans imitate their immoral behavior. Their high status insures their behavior will be imitated—whether they intend to be imitated or not. Teachers and pastors can establish bad behaviors merely by behaving badly—even when they do not intend to. "I exhort the elders among you: shepherd God's flock among you . . . not lording it over those entrusted to you, but *being examples to the flock*" (1 Pet 5:1–4).

32. Eggen and Kauchak (1994), 286.

33. Robert E. Slavin, *Educational Psychology: Theory and Practice*, 4th ed., (Boston: Allyn and Bacon, 1994), 174.

34. Biehler and Snowman (1993), 348.

35. Eggen and Kauchak (1994), 285.

36. Biehler and Snowman (1993), 348.

37. Ibid.

38. Sprinthall (1994), 259.

39. Eggen and Kauchak (1994), 286.

40. Slavin, 174.

41. I once had a student whose youth minister "gained their attention" by throwing a firecracker into the middle of their group. From a general learning view, this was a poor choice. Students were shocked, and they were not ready to learn what the youth minister planned to teach. Yet, from a behavioral view, the youth minister modeled "good teaching by firecracker." It would be interesting to know how many of those young people later threw firecrackers to gain attention in their groups! This underscores a macro-principle of behavioral learning: Bad behaviors are learned by the same mechanisms as good behaviors.

42. Eggen and Kauchak (1994), 286.

43. Good and Brophey, 168.

44. N. L. Gage and David C. Berliner, *Educational Psychology*, 3rd ed., (Boston: Houghton Mifflin Company, 1984), 335.

45. Biehler and Snowman (1993), 348.

46. Woolfolk (1993), 221.

47. Biehler and Snowman (1993), 348.

48. Sprinthall (1994), 259.

49. Woolfolk (1993), 222.

50. The term "lights up" refers to the firing of neurons during brain functions. These electrical impulses can be seen and photographed, in color, by advanced imaging equipment. PET and fMRI technology developed over the last decade has revolutionized neuroscience and overturned 100 years of "established truth" concerning the human brain and brain functioning. See Chapter Eleven, Brain-based Learning.

51. A 1995 experiment by Alvaro Pascual-Leone demonstrated the *same changes in the physical structure* of the motor cortex of the brain between two experimental groups. One group practiced a five-finger piano exercise, while the other group merely thought about practicing it. The second group focused on each finger movement in turn, essentially playing the piece in their heads. "Merely thinking about moving produced brain changes comparable to those triggered by actually moving." Jeffrey M. Schwartz, M.D., and Sharon Begley, *The Mind & the Brain: Neuroplasticity and the Power of Mental Force* (New York: HarperCollins, 2002), 217. We'll investigate this far more in Chapter Eleven, Brain-based Learning.

52. Bandura used the term "reproduction" (Eggen and Kauchak, 288) to refer to this stage, but most recent texts use the term "production."

53. Woolfolk (1993), 222.

54. Eggen and Kauchak (1994), 288.

55. Woolfolk (2004), 318.

56. I'm following recent texts that call this fourth stage "motivation" rather than Bandura's own "reinforcement." Dembo, 59; Eggen and Kauchak, 289; Elliot, 222; Parsons, 236; Slavin, 175; Woolfolk (2004), 318.

57. Woolfolk (1993), 222.

58. Biehler and Snowman (1993), 349.

59. Woolfolk (1993), 222.

60. Good and Brophey, 166.

61. Eggen and Kauchak (1994), 289.

62. Dembo, 61.

63. Ibid., 60.

64. Woolfolk (1993), 222.

65. Slavin, 174.

66. Eggen and Kauchak (1994), 289.

67. Skinner was adamant in his defense of traditional behaviorism to the end of his life. Speaking to the American Psychological Association just days before his death, he said, "Cognitive science . . . is an effort to reinstate that inner initiating-originating-creative self, or mind, which, in scientific analysis, simply does not exist. . . . I think it is time for psychology, as a profession and as a science, to realize that the science which will be most helpful is not cognitive science searching for the inner mind or self but selection by consequences represented by behavioral analysis." Quoted by Sprinthall, 231.

68. I have not seen a Pontiac commercial in years; but in the early 1990s, GM advertised the car by using the phrase, "We build excitement—Pontiac!" In one commercial, a beautiful woman skips out of an office building—followed by a handsome fellow carrying a suitcase. He drops the suitcase in the back seat of a brand new Pontiac and the two head out, through a radiant autumn forest scene, to a cute, isolated cabin. "We build excitement—Pontiac!" There were other, more sexually blatant commercials following the same theme; but I will not describe them here. The message was clear. Buy a Pontiac, and romance will be yours.

69. Good and Brophey, 166.

70. Richard D. Parsons, Stephanie Lewis Hinson, and Deborah Sardo-Brown, *Educational Psychology: A Practitioner-Researcher Mode of Teaching* (Belmont, CA: Wadsworth/Thomson Learning, 2001), 237.

71. Albert Bandura Lecture—Bing Distinguished Lecture Series, "The Power of Social Modeling: The Effects of Television Violence" by Christine Van De Velde, 1997–2002, accessed October 22, 2008, http://www.stanford.edu/dept/bingschool/rsrchart/bandura.htm.

72. Statement is from the citation that accompanied the awarding of the Rogers Award to Albert Bandura in 2007 by the Academy for Television Arts & Sciences. http://www.learcenter.org/pdf/Rogers07Winner.pdf., accessed October 22, 2008.

73. Parsons, 237.

74. Eggen and Kauchak (2007), 184.

75. Ibid.

76. Biehler and Snowman (1993), 347.

77. Ibid. LeFrancois combines inhibition and disinhibition into the "inhibitory-disinhibitory effect." Guy R. LeFrancois, *Psychology for Teaching*, 8th ed., (Belmont, CA: Wadsworth Publishing Company, 1994), 109.

78. Eggen and Kauchak (2007), 184.

79. Ibid.

80. Ibid., 182.

81. Ibid.

82. Woolfolk (2004), 319.

83. Woolfolk (1993), 223.

84. John A. Glover and Roger H. Bruning, *Educational Psychology: Principles and Applications*, 3rd ed., (Glenview, IL: Scott, Foresman/Little, Brown Higher Education, 1990), 313.

85. Woolfolk (2004), 319.

86. Ibid.

87. Woolfolk (1993), 223.

88. I put "gracious" in quotes because letting deadlines "slide" is cheap grace and destructive to classroom learning. If the student is ill or has a death in the family, grace (giving the student additional time) is appropriate.

89. Albert Bandura, *Social Foundations of Thought and Action: A Social Cognitive Theory* (Englewood Cliffs, NJ: Prentice-Hall, 1986).

90. A word of caution. Some textbooks merely replace the "Social Learning" Theory label with a "Cognitive Social" Theory label, making no distinction between them (for example, Eggen and Kauchak, 2007, 180). Others make a distinction between them, pointing to a higher order cognitive functioning in Cognitive Social Theory (for example, Woolfolk, 2004, 317). In a sense, Bandura's theory is still evolving since he continues, presently in his eighties, to work and expand his ideas.

91. Ormrod, 331.

92. I recommend Snowman (2009), 274–321 for a healthy overview.

93. Ormrod, 331.

94. Ibid.

95. http://www.learcenter.org/pdf/Rogers07Winner.pdf., accessed October 22, 2008.

96. Ibid.

97. Then there is the dark side of social learning in the church in which immature leaders model bad behaviors, attitudes, and perspectives for those they lead.

98. Quotes taken from Wuest's *Word Studies from the Greek New Testament*, copyright 1940–55 by William B. Eerdmans Publishing Company, copyrights © renewed 1968–73 by Jeannette I. Wuest. All rights reserved. (*PC Study Bible* V5, Biblesoft, 2007)

99. Quotes taken from Wuest's *Word Studies*

Chapter 8 Notes

1. http://creativeproverbs.com/cgi-bin/sql_search3cp.cgi?keyword=mind+listen&boolean=and&field= quote&frank= all&database=all. Search on "mind and listen," accessed June 22, 2009.

2. By "attitude," I refer to the affective or emotional part of life. When we normally refer to one's attitude, we mean to convey something about their feelings or values. However, there are some who would define, quite correctly, "attitudes" as triadic (see Chapter Twelve), containing rational, emotional, and behavioral components.

3. Paul Eggen and Don Kauchak, *Educational Psychology: Classroom Connections*, 2nd ed., (New York: Macmillan College Publishing Company, 1994), 305.

4. Robert F. Biehler and Jack Snowman, *Psychology Applied to Teaching*, 7th ed., (Boston: Houghton Mifflin Company, 1993), 378.

5. Bonnidell Clouse, *Teaching for Moral Growth: A Guide for the Christian Community: Teachers, Parents, Pastors* (Wheaton, IL: BridgePoint Books, 1993), 223.

6. Norman A. Sprinthall, Richard C. Sprinthall, and Sharon N. Oja, *Educational Psychology: A Developmental Approach*, 6th ed., (New York: McGraw-Hill, Inc., 1994), 213.

7. Robert E. Slavin, *Educational Psychology: Theory and Practice*, 4th ed., (Boston: Allyn and Bacon, 1994), 188.

8. Sprinthall (1994), 220.

9. Slavin, 188.

10. Sprinthall (1994), 245.

11. Slavin, 225.

12. http://www.indiana.edu/~intell/wundt.shtml, accessed October 29, 2008.

13. Sprinthall (1994), 213.

14. http://www.science.uva.nl/~seop/entries/ernst-mach/, accessed October 29, 2008.

15. Morris L. Bigge, *Learning Theories for Teachers*, 3rd ed., (New York: Harper & Row, 1976), 61.

16. *The Analysis of Sensations*, originally published in 1886. Read the 1897 edition of this book at http://books.google.com/books?id=hPEMAAAAIAAJ&printsec=titlepage&source=gbs_summary_r&cad=0.

17. Sprinthall (1994), 220.

18. Joseph Plateau of Belgium is generally credited with the invention of the stroboscope in 1832 when he used a disc with radial slits that he turned while viewing images on a separate rotating wheel. Plateau called his device the "Phenakistoscope." There was a simultaneous, independent invention of the device by the Austrian Simon von Stampfer, which he named the "Stroboscope"; and it is his term that is used today. The etymology is from the Greek words *strobo(s)*, meaning "whirling," and *scope* meaning "to look at." http://en.wikipedia.org/wiki/Stroboscope, accessed October 27, 2007.

19. "Max Wertheimer," in Watson, Sr., R.I., *The Great Psychologists*, 4th ed., (New York: J. B. Lippincott Co., 1978), np., http://educ.southern.edu/tour/who/pioneers/wertheimer.html, accessed October 27, 2007.

20. The psychological phenomenon of perceiving movement where no movement exists. "Two lines were exposed in two different places on the face of the tachistoscope. Each exposure lasted a very short time and was separated from the next exposure by varying lengths of time. If there was too long a time between the exposures, the subject would see the lines successively. If the time was too short, he would see the lines simultaneously. However, *if the time interval between the exposures was at an optimal length, the subject saw, not two lines successively or simultaneously, but **one line move from one place to another**.* The experience is that of a single line which visibly moved—despite the fact that actually there are two successively exposed stationary lines separated by an interval of time. Variations, such as exposing a vertical line followed by a horizontal line for which the *observer saw a line swinging around through ninety degrees, gave the same result—an impression of motion of lines.* This apparent movement Wertheimer called phi phenomenon." "Max Wertheimer," in Watson.

21. "Max Wertheimer," in Watson, Sr., R.I., *The Great Psychologists*, 4th ed., (New York: J. B. Lippincott Co., 1978), np., http://educ.southern.edu/tour/who/pioneers/wertheimer.html, accessed October 27, 2007.

22. Ibid.

23. http://en.wikipedia.org/wiki/Stroboscope, accessed October 27, 2007.

24. Sprinthall (1994), 218.

25. Slavin, 188.

26. Wertheimer formally stated his position in 1912 in a paper entitled "Experimental Studies of the Perception of Movement."

27. Charles E. Skinner, Ira Morris Gast, and Hartley Clay Skinner, *Readings in Educational Psychology* (New York: Appleton & Cook, 1958), 407.

28. Sprinthall (1994), 219.

29. Ibid., 221.

30. Ernest R. Hilgard and Richard C. Atkinson, *Introduction to Psychology*, 4th ed., (New York: Harcourt, Brace and World, 1967), 227.

31. Ralph Garry and Howard L. Kingsley, *The Nature and Conditions of Learning*, 3rd ed., (Englewood Cliffs, NJ: Prentice-Hall, 1970), 109.

32. Hilgard and Atkinson, 225.

33. Ibid.

34. Ibid.

35. Ibid.

36. "Max Wertheimer," in Watson, http://educ.southern.edu/tour/who/pioneers/wertheimer.html, accessed October 27, 2007.

37. http://faculty.frostburg.edu/mbradley/psyography/wolfgangkohler.html.

38. Ibid.

39. Köhler may have had more on his mind than learning as he conducted his experiments. There is evidence that he was actually using his lab as a cover for spying activities for Germany during World War I. Sprinthall (1994), 220.

40. Dr. Norma Hedin, Professor and Fellow, B. H. Carroll Theological Institute, e-mail comment, June 15, 2009.

41. Hilgard and Atkinson, 178.

42. Sprinthall (1994), 220.

43. Hilgard and Atkinson, 178.

44. Sprinthall (1994), 220.

45. Stephen S. Sargent, *The Basic Teachings: The Greatest Psychologists* (New York: Barnes & Noble, 1957), 150.

46. "Max Wertheimer," in Watson.

47. Hilgard and Atkinson, 178.

48. Morris L. Bigge, *Psychological Foundations of Education*, 2nd ed., (New York: Harper & Row, 1968), 342.

49. His name is pronounced variously as "La-VEEN" and "LOO-in." Both are correct—the first being German and the second American.

50. "Max Wertheimer," in Watson.

51. Bigge, *Psychological*, 342.

52. Garry and Kingsley, 112.

53. Hilgard and Atkinson, 273.

54. http://findarticles.com/p/articles/mi_g2699/is_0000/ai_2699000048. *Encyclopedia of Psychology*, "Jerome Bruner," accessed October 29, 2008.

55. Sprinthall (1994), 245.

56. Ibid., 243.

57. Guy R. LeFrancois, *Psychology for Teaching*, 8th ed., (Belmont, CA: Wadsworth Publishing Company, 1994), 158.

58. Sprinthall (1994), 243.

59. Information drawn from Biehler and Snowman (1993), 425; Leon Marsh, *Educational Psychology for Christian Education,* (Fort Worth, TX: Southwestern Baptist Theological Seminary, 1982), 186; Daniel Smith, *Educational Psychology and Its Classroom Applications,* (Boston: Allyn and Bacon, 1975), 43; Glen Snelbecker, *Learning Theory: Institutional Theory and Psychological Design* (New York: McGraw-Hill, 1974), 411; Sprinthall (1994), 244–45.

60. Biehler and Snowman, 427.

61. Sprinthall (1994), 247.

62. Biehler and Snowman, 427.

63. Ibid.

64. Slavin, 249.

65. Ibid., 245.

66. Biehler and Snowman, 426.

67. Woolfolk, 319.

68. Daryl Eldridge served in the Foundations of Education division, School of Educational Ministries, SWBTS from 19xx until he became dean in 19xx. He retired from Southwestern, moved to Springfield, Missouri, and founded Rockbridge University in 2002.

69. For years, Piaget was criticized for making cognitive development a matter of biological age. Recent brain research indicates he may well have been right after all. The brain goes through cycles of rapid development, and these waves of neuron production match quite nicely with Piaget's stages of cognitive development. See Chapter Sixteen.

70. Sprinthall (1994), 247.

71. Ibid., 243.

72. Ibid., 247.

73. Ibid., 248.

74. Ibid., 243.

75. Ibid., 244.

76. A disinterested learner is one who lacks "natural curiosity" for a given subject. Disinterest can be a chronic condition, stemming from bad experiences in early development (Erikson stages 1–4) or an acute condition related to a specific subject.

77. From *Piaget Rediscovered*, as quoted in Herbert Ginsburg and Sylvia Opper, *Piaget's Theory of Intellectual Development: An Introduction*, (Englewood Cliffs, NJ: Prentice-Hall, Inc., 1969), 231–32

78. B. F. Skinner, *The Technology of Teaching*, (New York: Appleton-Century-Crofts, 1968), 110.

79. Robert F. Biehler, *Psychology Applied to Teaching*, 3rd ed., (Boston: Houghton Mifflin Co., 1978), 355ff.

80. LeFrancois, 160.

81. Slavin, 230.

82. LeFrancois, 160. To *subsume new ideas* means to relate them to existing concepts, to established understanding.

83. Some writers use the term "guided discovery." Dembo, 270.

84. Jerome Bruner, *Toward a Theory of Instruction* (New York: Norton, 1966), 72.

85. I suggested then that Christians could certainly embrace the more objective approach to constructivism—accommodating one's thinking with Scripture—but would find the more existential aspects of reality creation in subjective constructivism uncomfortable. Yount, *Created to Learn* (1996), 202. That was before the postmodern wave hit evangelical thought, bringing into question the whole matter of "What is Truth?" What is interesting to me is that the debate continues. Woolfolk summarizes her view of the situation this way: "Constructivists debate whether knowledge is constructed by mapping external reality, by adapting and changing internal understandings, or by an interaction of [both]. . . . Most psychologists posit for both internal and external factors, but differ in how much they emphasize one or the other." Anita Woolfolk, *Educational Psychology*, 9th ed., (Boston: Pearson Education, Inc., 2004), 343. This *difference in emphasis* keeps the whole field in a state of confusion.

86. Ibid., 323.

87. Woolfolk (2004), 326.

88. Ibid., 323.

89. Ibid., 325.

90. Sternberg does not mention "social constructivism" but includes some of its tenets under constructivism. Robert J. Sternberg and Wendy M. Williams, *Educational Psychology* (Boston: Allyn and Bacon, 2002), 296. Eggen and Kauchak define both cognitive and social constructivism but use the more general term when listing characteristics. Paul Eggen and Don Kauchak, *Educational Psychology: Windows on Classrooms*, 7th ed., (Columbus: Merrill Prentice Hall, 2007), 235–36, 238.

91. Woolfolk (2004), 323.

92. Bruner argues that the cognitive revolution, with its current (1990) fixation on mind as "information processor," has led psychology away from the deeper objective of understanding mind as a creator of meanings. Only by breaking out of the limitations imposed by a computational model of mind can we grasp the special interaction through which mind both constitutes and is constituted by culture. (Review of Harvard University Press) http://en.wikipedia.org/wiki/Jerome_Bruner, accessed October 29, 2008.

93. Bruner, *Toward a Theory of Instruction*, 249.

94. Woolfolk (2004), 323.

95. Eggen and Kauchak (2007), 235.

96. Snowman, 326.

97. Eggen and Kauchak (2007), 235.

98. Ibid., 236.

99. Ibid., 237.

100. Patricia A. Alexander, *Psychology in Learning and Instruction* (Upper Saddle River, NJ: Pearson Education, Inc., 2006), 69.

101. Alexander, 69.

102. Chart data drawn from Woolfolk (2004), 322–25; Alexander, 67–70.

103. Ibid., 238.

104. Ibid.

105. Jack Snowman, Rick McCown, and Robert F. Biehler, *Psychology Applied to Teaching,* 12th ed., (Boston: Houghton Mifflin Company, 2009), 325.

106. Ibid., 327.

107. Eggen and Kauchak (2007), 241.

108. Ibid., 236.

109. Ibid., 248.

110. Ibid., 250.

111. Woolfolk (2004), 328.

112. Actually, the groups shout out "touchy-feely!" more often than anything else; but it seemed too slangish for a textbook!

113. Snowman, 327.

114. Dr. Barnett is *Elmer V. Thompson Chair of Missionary Church Planting* at Columbia International Seminary, Columbia, S.C. At the time of the first course, he was a faculty colleague in the missions division at Southwestern. He and I wrote *Called to Reach: Equipping Cross-cultural Disciplers* (Broadman & Holman, 2007) as the foundation for this course, which is cross-listed in both Missions and Educational Ministries degree plans.

115. Ibid., 329.

116. Ibid., 334.

117. Woolfolk (2004), 323.

118. "Empty Nesters" are married adults whose children have left home.

119. Ibid., 325.

120. Snowman, 35.

121. Ibid., 323.

122. Ibid., 328.

123. Woolfolk (2004), 323.

124. Alexander, 68.

125. Stephen N. Elliot, Thomas R. Kratochwill, Joan Littlefield Cook, and John F. Travers, *Educational Psychology: Effective Teaching, Effective Learning*, (Boston: McGraw-Hill, 2000), 256.

126. Elliot, 257.

127. Snowman, 326.

128. Elliot, 257.

129. Ibid.

130. Snowman, 326.

131. Lewis Carroll (Charles Lutwidge Dodgson), *Alice's Adventures in Wonderland*, 1864. Kindle Books edition, Location 1719.

132. http://www.worldnetdaily.com/index.php?fa=PAGE.view&pageId=77734, accessed November 1, 2008.

133. The idea of God's love-wrath and its association with a warming, burning fire came from Dr. William Hendricks in his spring 1975 class on "The Theology of Paul and John," Southwestern Seminary.

Chapter 9 Notes

1. http://www.great-quotes.com/cgi-bin/viewquotes.cgi?action=search&orderby=rate&Category=Education&startlist=120 "Edward M. Forster," accessed June 29, 2009.

2. Ibid.

3. Many cognitive writers use the term "knowledge" to refer to the entire cognitive domain. This is more a philosophical use of knowledge. When we discuss levels of learning in Chapter Thirteen, "knowledge" (recall) will be defined as the lowest of the cognitive levels of learning. It is helpful to keep these two definitions of knowledge distinct.

4. Jack Snowman, Rick McCown, and Robert F. Biehler, *Psychology Applied to Teaching*, 12th ed., (Boston: Houghton Mifflin Company, 2009), 247.

5. Examples are neurons (brain cells), synapses (the empty space between the end of one neuron and the cell body of another) as well as specific regions of the physical brain: the frontal lobes, amygdala, and others.

6. Snowman, 247.

7. Norman A. Sprinthall, Richard C. Sprinthall, and Sharon N. Oja, *Educational Psychology: A Developmental Approach*, 6th ed., (New York: McGraw-Hill, Inc., 1994), 285.

8. http://fac.hsu.edu/ahmada/3%20Courses/2%20Learning/Learning%20Notes/Tolman.pdf, accessed November 4, 2008.

9. Sprinthall (1994), 285.

10. Robert F. Biehler and Jack Snowman, *Psychology Applied to Teaching*, 7th ed., (Boston: Houghton Mifflin Company, 1993), 378.

11. Ibid., 379.

12. Biehler and Snowman, 379.

13. Patricia A. Alexander, *Psychology in Learning and Instruction* (Upper Saddle River, NJ: Pearson Education, Inc., 2006), 67.

14. Ibid. "Automatic processing"—the unconscious recording of every event in our lives—should not be confused with "automaticity," which is the overlearning of information such that it is readily available without conscious effort. Multiplication tables (12x12=144) and John 3:16 ("For God so loved . . .") are two examples that leap to mind.

15. Sprinthall (1994), 288.

16. Biehler and Snowman, 379.

17. Dual-core processors provide two parallel paths for data processing. Quad-core processors provide four parallel paths. A rough analogy of parallel processing is the amount of traffic that can be handled by single-lane, dual-lane, and four-lane highways. Parallel processing nearly doubles (dual core) or quadruples (quad core) the amount of information computers process.

18. Paul Eggen and Don Kauchak, *Educational Psychology: Classroom Connections*, 2nd ed., (New York: Macmillan College Publishing Company, 1994), 306.

19. Eggen and Kauchak (1994), 307.

20. Snowman, 245.

21. Sight, sound, smell, taste, and touch are sometimes referred to as visual, auditory, olfactory, gustatory, and tactile stimuli, respectively. Snowman, 248.

22. Ibid., 248.

23. Sprinthall (1994), 288.

24. Hamachek, 195.

25. Snowman, 250.

26. Sprinthall (1994), 288.

27. Hamachek, 195.

28. Eggen and Kauchak (1994), 310.

29. Ibid., 311.

30. Sprinthall (1994), 288. Snowman reports "seven unrelated bits of information" for "20 seconds"—whether this is a newer finding or simply a different perspective is unclear (Snowman, 250). In his 1998 edition, Sprinthall uses the

term "7 ± 2" rather than "five to nine" and centered on Snowman's "7." Given the fact that learners have varying STM capacities, the range appears to be more appropriate.

31. Eggen and Kauchak (1994), 311.

32. Norman A. Sprinthall, Richard C. Sprinthall, and Sharon N. Oja, *Educational Psychology: A Developmental Approach*, 7th ed., (New York: McGraw-Hill, Inc., 1998), 307.

33. Sprinthall (1994), 288.

34. Eggen and Kauchak (1994), 312.

35. Robert E. Slavin, *Educational Psychology: Theory and Practice*, 4th ed., (Boston: Allyn and Bacon, 1994), 188.

36. While the Three-Component model depicts STM as a single entity, more recent models emphasize various sub-components. We will describe the Parallel Distributed Processing (PDP) and Working Memory (WM) models under "IPT in the 2000s" later in the chapter. The Three-Component model remains the most common depiction of IPT.

37. Hamachek, 197.

38. Eggen and Kauchak (1994), 312.

39. Ibid.

40. Biehler and Snowman, 387.

41. Sprinthall (1994), 289.

42. Ibid.

43. Slavin, 193.

44. These irretrievable memories are known to researchers because direct electric stimulation of various parts of the brain causes specific memories to be recalled. One report I read detailed the ability of an adult to remember details of his third birthday party—cooking smells in the house, the dress his mother wore, the presents he received, the names of his friends. Each of these memories was verified as accurate by his mother and others present at the party. Scientists were not able, however, to know where specific memories were stored; so the recalled events were randomly remembered.

45. But not *automatic*. Learning how to compute a formula is intentional. When the formula is learned well enough, it can be used without thinking about it—it is implicit, but not automatic, knowledge.

46. Alexander uses the term "tacit memory" to refer to "that portion of our knowledge base that lies outside our direct awareness." Patricia A. Alexander, *Psychology in Learning and Instruction*, (Upper Saddle River, NJ: Pearson Education, Inc., 2006), 79.

47. The term "memory" (singular) usually refers to cognitive storage, while the term "memories" (plural) usually refers to the information stored. We might say, "Explicit memory (cognitive structure) stores explicit memories (life events, meanings)." The distinction between "container" and "contained" is blurring as discoveries in neuroscience—over the past fifteen years—demonstrate that all human learning, experience, and memory are composed of networks of brain cells.

48. Anita Woolfolk, *Educational Psychology*, 9th ed., (Boston: Pearson Education, Inc., 2004), 247.

49. Slavin, 193.

50. Myron H. Dembo, *Applying Educational Psychology*, 5th ed., (New York: Longman, 1994), 95.

51. Woolfolk (2004), 252.

52. Ibid., 251.

53. Woolfolk (2004), 247.

54. Eggen and Kauchak (1994), 313.

55. Woolfolk (2004), 249.

56. Sign language is not English. A judge once demanded that an interpreter "translate literally" what was said in the courtroom. Then he instructed the deaf defendant, "Please state your name." The interpreter signed, "Please, s-t-a-t-e, your, name." The deaf man responded, quite correctly, "Texas" because, in sign language, the sentence asked the name of his state (please, s-t-a-t-e your, name). The judge was confused. The interpreter explained the difficulty of "literal translation," and the judge relented. The judge said again, "Please state your name." The interpreter signed, "Your name—what?" The deaf man immediately responded with his name.

57. There is an apparent contradiction here between the definitions of (explicit, conscious) semantic memories

and the unconscious use of semantic memories (as in asking "What is your name?" without thinking about how). The contradiction is solved by overlearning and automaticity, which we discuss a little later in the chapter.

58. Woolfolk (2004), 249.

59. Ibid., 250.

60. Biehler and Snowman, 388.

61. In a moment, we will contrast this with *procedural* memory ("I know how to").

62. Eggen and Kauchak (1994), 314.

63. Woolfolk (2004), 249.

64. Robert J. Sternberg and Wendy M. Williams, *Educational Psychology* (Boston: Allyn and Bacon, 2002), 275.

65. Hamachek, 199.

66. Woolfolk (2004), 252.

67. Ibid., 249.

68. Ibid., 252.

69. Eggen and Kauchak (1994), 317.

70. Slavin, 216.

71. Ibid., 191.

72. Biehler and Snowman, 382.

73. Eggen and Kauchak (1994), 308.

74. Woolfolk (2004), 240.

75. Biehler and Snowman, 382.

76. Ibid., 383.

77. Ibid.

78. Slavin, 188.

79. Eggen and Kauchak (1994), 323.

80. Biehler and Snowman, 382.

81. Eggen and Kauchak (1994), 322.

82. Biehler and Snowman, 384.

83. Eggen and Kauchak, 322.

84. Eggen and Kauchak (1994), 312.

85. Not to be confused with "automatic processing" in which every experience in life is encoded into LTM.

86. Ibid.

87. Sprinthall (1994), 288.

88. Ibid., 290.

89. Biehler and Snowman, 384.

90. Ibid.

91. Eggen and Kauchak (1994), 326.

92. Ibid.

93. Slavin, 191.

94. Remember that these descriptions apply to intentional learning. Automatic processing occurs whether we engage in these processes or not.

95. Eggen and Kauchak (1994), 327.

96. Sprinthall (1994), 290.

97. Paul Eggen and Don Kauchak, *Educational Psychology: Windows on Classrooms*, 7th ed., (Columbus: Merrill Prentice Hall, 2007), 209.

98. Eggen and Kauchak (1994), 329.

99. Ibid.

100. Ibid., 16–17.

101. Eggen and Kauchak (2007), 214.

102. If you take the three "Key Issues" charts (behavioral, cognitive, humanistic) and combine them in a 12x3 table, the twelve issues running down the left, the three learning theory systems across the top, and the specific characteristics filling the boxes where the two sets of headings intersect, you will have created a conceptual matrix.

103. Eggen and Kauchak (1994), 333.

104. Sprinthall (1994), 290.

105. Woolfolk (2004), 252.

106. Eggen and Kauchak (2007), 216.

107. Woolfolk (2004), 253.

108. Eggen and Kauchak (1994), 336.

109. Biehler and Snowman, 394.

110. Dembo, 108.

111. Biehler and Snowman, 396.

112. Woolfolk (2004), 261.

113. N. L. Gage and David C. Berliner, *Educational Psychology*, 3rd ed., (Boston: Houghton Mifflin Company, 1984), 223.

114. Biehler and Snowman, 395; Slavin, 209.

115. Dembo, 108.

116. Biehler and Snowman, 395.

117. Eggen and Kauchak (1994), 338.

118. Dembo, 108.

119. Biehler and Snowman, 395.

120. Gage and Berliner, 223.

121. Biehler and Snowman, 397.

122. Dembo, 109.

123. Biehler and Snowman, 397.

124. Ibid.

125. See the "Key Terms in Learning Theories" at the end of this chapter for an example of a matrix.

126. Woolfolk (2004), 263.

127. The principle of subsumption states that new material should be connected to previous studies and established knowledge. Connecting the current learning task with prior studies provides a framework that helps memorization.

128. Teachers use *passive recall* when they remember for their students what has been learned. "Class, you remember that we studied cognitive levels of learning last week and that the lowest level is called knowledge—correct?" Teachers use *active recall* when they force students to remember on their own. "Class, what is the lowest level of learning in the cognitive domain?"

129. Long sessions of massed practice produce fatigue and low motivation. It is better to drill students on a portion of a list or passage and then explain the meaning of the words or phrases being memorized. Drill a portion. Explain. Drill again. Explain more. Drill again. Explain more. Move to the next portion. Repeat through the list or passage.

130. Distribute the short drills throughout the class session. Fill the space between drills with explanations, so the memorized words and phrases are meaningful to the students.

131. We usually end a Gain in Knowledge session with a test. "Take out a sheet of paper, and write the list from memory." After a minute or two, say the list aloud together so that students can grade their own papers. Their score is a silent indication of how well they memorized the list.

132. Jeanne Ellis Ormrod, *Educational Psychology: Developing Learners*, 5th ed., (Columbus: Pearson Education, Inc., 2006), 212.

133. Stephen N. Elliot, Thomas R. Kratochwill, Joan Littlefield Cook, and John F. Travers, *Educational Psychology: Effective Teaching, Effective Learning*, (Boston: McGraw-Hill, 2000), 283.

134. Dr. Smith is Senior Fellow and Professor of Religious Education at B. H. Carroll Theological Institute,

Arlington, Texas (since 2003). Before that, he served as Professor of Foundations of Education at Southwestern Seminary, Fort Worth (1979–2003).

135. Ormrod, 214.

136. Elliot, 284.

137. Eggen and Kauchak (1994), 339.

138. Slavin, 200.

139. Elliot, 284.

140. Ormrod, 212.

141. Sprinthall (1994), 299.

142. Dembo, 95.

143. Eggen and Kauchak (1994), 339.

144. Biehler and Snowman, 390.

145. Ibid., 307; Snowman, 259.

146. Ibid.

147. Eggen and Kauchak (1994), 347.

148. Ibid., 349.

149. Ibid., 350.

150. Biehler and Snowman, 390.

151. Elliot, 281. Elliot declares this "present shift in IPT thinking" (writing in 2000) from memory stores to levels of processing by quoting studies done in 1972 and 1990. Such is the reality found in educational psychology texts. The common approach to IPT is the Three-Component model I have presented.

152. Sternberg, 281.

153. Ibid., 282. Writing in 2000, Sternberg quotes research from 1972 to 1998.

154. Ibid., 283.

155. Ibid., 283–84.

156. Woolfolk (2004), 243.

157. Ormrod, 193. Ormrod quotes five studies from 2000 to 2004.

158. LOP was first proposed in 1972, but Sternberg (2000) and Woolfolk (2004) continue to cover it. Neuroscience describes brain functioning in terms of networks of billions of neurons (brain cells) formed by trillions of connections (axons, dendrites, and synapses). The alternative models reflect the convergence of IPT and brain functioning.

159. Sternberg, 285.

160. Ibid.

161. Ibid., 281–83.

162. Ibid., 284.

163. Sternberg suggests "expert teachers" will correct misconceptions in learners by asking learners what they know about "people in another country," showing a film or reading a story about people in that country, and then having students compare what they first thought about people in the country with what the film or story suggests. (284) Teachers have long used this approach to provoke learners to contrast established viewpoints and new information.

164. Alexander (2006), 67; Eggen and Kauchak (2007), 203; Ormrod (2006), 191; Snowman (2009), 248; Sternberg (2000), 270; Woolfolk (2004), 239.

165. Eggen and Kauchak (2007), 203.

166. Biehler and Snowman, 406.

167. These examples were actually used by youth ministers to "secure attention." Such attention is toxic to learning.

168. Biehler and Snowman, 406.

169. Eggen and Kauchak (1994), 342.

170. Dembo, 99.

171. Eggen and Kauchak (1994), 342.

172. Biehler and Snowman, 410.

173. Dembo, 123. An advance organizer is a general statement given before instruction that structures new information (for example, objectives, list of important terms).

174. Glover, 135.

175. Eggen and Kauchak (1994), 342.

176. Biehler and Snowman, 407.

177. Dembo, 122.

178. Ibid., 123.

179. Eggen and Kauchak (1994), 343.

180. Ibid.

181. Ibid., 112.

182. Ibid., 123.

183. John A. Glover and Roger H. Bruning, *Educational Psychology: Principles and Applications*, 3rd ed., (Glenview, IL: Scott, Foresman/Little, Brown Higher Education, 1990), 135.

184. Dembo, 122.

185. Eggen and Kauchak (1994), 343.

186. Biehler and Snowman, 412.

187. Eggen and Kauchak (1994), 343.

188. Biehler and Snowman, 411.

189. Slavin, 239.

190. This is not to say, of course, we should avoid biblical analogies. We are simply saying that biblical analogies had far more impact on learners then than on learners now because of familiarity. We do well then to use contemporary analogies in addition to biblical ones.

191. Jerome Bruner's emphasis on structure, economy, and power suggests that one cannot learn everything about anything. Yet many teachers—especially in college and seminary classrooms—expect novices to master subjects they themselves have studied for years. I once asked one of my professors what we needed to know in preparation for the first exam. I was looking for some sort of study guidelines or instructional objectives. His reply was short—both in length and tone: "You are expected to know it all." It was unhelpful—to say the least. It is also unrealistic.

192. Eggen and Kauchak (1994), 343.

193. Biehler and Snowman, 383.

194. Dembo, 122.

195. Ibid., 408.

196. Biehler and Snowman, 394.

197. Ibid., 414.

198. Dembo, 123.

199. Ibid., 398.

200. Ibid., 399.

201. Ibid., 414.

202. Ibid., 399.

203. Ibid., 414.

204. Dembo, 110.

Chapter 10 Notes

1. http://www.great-quotes.com/cgi-bin/viewquotes.cgi?action=search&orderby=rate&Category= Education& startlist=180, accessed December 1, 2008.

2. humanism. *The American Heritage [Computerized] Dictionary*, 3rd ed., (Wordstar International, 1993).

3. humanism. Dictionary.com. *The American Heritage® Dictionary of the English Language*, 4th ed., (Houghton Mifflin Company, 2004) http://dictionary.reference.com/browse/humanism (accessed: November 16, 2008).

4. Ibid., "Humanism."

5. Ibid., "secular." It is interesting that the words "temporal" and "profane" have been dropped from the 1993 definition.

6. "Essence" refers to the intrinsic or indispensable properties that characterize or identify something. "Existence" refers to the fact or state of being. In traditional philosophies, essence precedes existence. The nature or design of mankind precedes the actual existence of individuals. Existentialism reverses this order and states that individuals are born first and then define themselves by the choices they make. First, existence, then essence. A fundamental principle of existentialism is "freedom of the individual from societal restraints." Daniel Smith, *Educational Psychology and Its Classroom Applications,* (Boston: Allyn and Bacon, 1975), 187.

7. *The Joyful Wisdom* (1882) quoted in Colin Brown, *Philosophy and the Christian Faith* (Downers Grove, IL: InterVarsity Press, 1968), 139.

8. From *Existentialism and Humanism* (1946), quoted in Colin Brown, *Philosophy and the Christian Faith* (Downers Grove, IL: InterVarsity Press, 1968), 183.

9. Brown, 183.

10. John Herman Randall, "What Is the Temper of Humanism?", *The Humanist* (Nov/Dec 1970), 34. Quoted in Van Cleve Morris and Young Pai, *Philosophy and the American School,* (Boston: Houghton Mifflin Company, 1976), 391.

11. John S. Brubacher, *Modern Philosophies of Education,* (New York: McGraw-Hill Book Company, Inc., 1950), 279ff.

12. Paul A. Keniel, *Philosophy of Christian School Education,* (Whittier, CA: Association of Christian Schools International, 1971), 156.

13. Some may object to the term "Christian humanism" as an oxymoron, but Keniel makes the point that the Reformation did place emphasis on the worth of the individual. This was not a result of man's innate goodness—as in the Southern European Renaissance—but from Scripture and the creation of man. Keniel himself does not use the term "Christian humanism," but many of the reforms in education—pleasant methods, trained teachers, and attractive classrooms—focus on the learner.

14. Keniel, 158.

15. Purely humanistic theorists—like Maslow, Rogers, and Combs—certainly have this view. It is interesting that Skinner believed himself to be a humanist. He was a signatory to the [secular] Humanistic Manifesto I and II, the blueprint for [secular] humanistic doctrine. Skinner saw programmed instruction as "humanistic" because it provided a pleasant learning environment that minimized failure and maximized reinforcement. In fact, many of the theorists we have discussed signed the Humanistic Manifesto documents, including Jerome Bruner and Abraham Maslow. This is why I made the distinction early in the text between understanding and using appropriate principles from these theorists without "believing" in them or their philosophical underpinnings.

16. Anita Woolfolk, *Educational Psychology*, 5th ed., (Boston: Allyn and Bacon, Inc., 1993), 338.

17. Myron H. Dembo, *Applying Educational Psychology*, 5th ed., (New York: Longman, 1994), 202.

18. Guy R. LeFrancois, *Psychology for Teaching*, 8th ed., (Belmont, CA: Wadsworth Publishing Company, 1994), 240,

19. Dembo, 201.

20. Woolfolk (1993), 339.

21. Paul Eggen and Don Kauchak, *Educational Psychology: Classroom Connections*, 2nd ed., (New York: Macmillan College Publishing Company, 1994), 432.

22. Eggen and Kauchak, 439; Glover and Bruning, 246.

23. Glover and Bruning, 252.

24. Carl Rogers, "Freedom to Learn" [Extracts] in Noel Entwistle, ed., *New Directions in Educational Psychology: 1. Learning and Teaching* (London: Falmer Press, 1985), 121.

25. LeFrancois, 241.

26. Robert F. Biehler and Jack Snowman, *Psychology Applied to Teaching*, 7th ed., (Boston: Houghton Mifflin Company, 1993), 475.

27. Dembo, 209–10.

28. LeFrancois, 246.

29. Ibid., 247.

30. Ibid., 244.

31. Dembo, 207–8.

32. Carl Rogers, *A Personal Approach to Teaching: Beliefs That Make a Difference* (Boston: Allyn & Bacon, 1982), 135.

33. Biehler and Snowman, 476.

34. Dembo, 203.

35. Thomas L. Good and Jere E. Brophey, *Educational Psychology: A Realistic Approach*, 4th ed., (New York: Longman, 1990), 471 and Dembo, 227.

36. Biehler and Snowman, 476–79.

37. Robert E. Slavin, *Educational Psychology: Theory and Practice*, 4th ed., (Boston: Allyn and Bacon, 1994), 296.

38. LeFrancois, 250.

39. Slavin, 298.

40. Eggen and Kauchak, 433.

41. LeFrancois, 250.

42. Slavin, 297.

43. Ibid.

44. Eggen and Kauchak, 433.

45. Slavin, 298.

46. Dembo, 225; Smith, 201; and LeFrancois, 251.

47. LeFrancois, 251.

48. Dembo, 227 and Good and Brophy, 471.

49. Slavin, 298.

50. LeFrancois, 252.

51. Ibid., 252.

52. Cooperative Learning emphasizes the grouping of students together for shared learning experiences. This is not to be confused with Cooperative Teaching in which *two or more teachers* work together to plan and deliver instruction.

53. Snowman carries on the tradition set over the years since the 1960s.

54. Specifically, these texts include Alexander, Eggen, and Kauchak (2007); Elliot, Mayer, Ormrod, Parsons, Snowman, Sprinthall (1998); Sternberg; and Woolfolk (2004).

55. Anita Woolfolk, *Educational Psychology*, 9th ed., (Boston: Pearson Education, Inc., 2004), 493.

56. LeFrancois, 253–54.

57. Quotes based on material in Biehler and Snowman, 485.

58. The pendulum appears to be swinging back toward more subjective forms of Constructivism and away from the more mechanical IPT. In education, the pendulum never stops swinging, and educators continue to rediscover the same, old "new approaches" in an attempt to improve student learning.

59. Even in secular situations, personal relationships, in the sense of "friendship," are unethical. The power differential between teachers and students can lead to disastrous outcomes if not held in check by the teacher. If a single teacher and a single student find themselves attracted to one another during a course, it behooves both to wait until the semester is over to pursue the relationship.

60. Bonnidell Clouse, *Teaching for Moral Growth: A Guide for the Christian Community: Teachers, Parents, Pastors,* (Wheaton, IL: BridgePoint Books, 1993), 325–27.

61. Jerry Adler et al., "Hey, I'm Terrific: The Curse of Self-Esteem," *Newsweek,* (February 17, 1992), 46–51.

62. Of the nearly thirty recent (1990–95) educational psychology texts I have in my library, only seven devote chapters to humanistic learning. Only two of these seven discuss humanistic approaches under "learning theory." The remainder discuss these principles under motivation.

63. Alone, that is, among the fifteen texts I have used as my base.

64. Jack Snowman, Rick McCown, and Robert F. Biehler, *Psychology Applied to Teaching,* 12th ed., (Boston: Houghton Mifflin Company, 2009), 392.

65. Ibid.

66. While this study was burned into my memory in graduate school, I have searched in vain for it. I did find a quote from Max Rafferty along the same lines: "I would as soon enroll a child of mine in a brothel as in Summerhill" from *Summerhill: For and Against,* (Hart Publishing, 1970), accessed at http://en.wikipedia.org/wiki/ Summerhill School on July 13, 2009.

67. According to amazon.com, the two books referenced on the site should be *Summerhill School: A New View of Childhood* and *Summerhill: A Radical Approach to Child Rearing*—often referred to simply as *Summerhill* . Both books were originally released in 1960, according to dates given on the Amazon Web pages. http://www.amazon.com/s /ref=nb_ ss_b?url=search-alias%3Dstripbooks&field-keywords=Summerhill&x=8&y=16.

68. http://www.summerhillschool.co.uk/pages/school_policies.html (final paragraph), accessed November 19, 2008.

69. Bill Ayers is known by some as a "social activist and educator." He is known by others as an "unrepentant domestic terrorist" for his leadership in the Weathermen, a.k.a. Weather Underground, organization—responsible for several bombings and deaths as a part of the anti-Vietnam War movement. He cites A. S. Neill as one of his educational heroes.

70. Information accessed on the University of Illinois, Chicago Web site (updated 2008), November 19, 2008.

71. Published by Teachers College Press, 160 pages.

72. From the product description, http://www.amazon.com/Side-Child-Summerhill-Revisited-Between/dp/ 0807743992/ref=sr_1_3?ie=UTF8&s=books&qid=1227078486&sr=1-3 , accessed November 19, 2008.

73. "humanism," Dictionary.com. *The American Heritage® Dictionary of the English Language*, 4th ed., (Houghton Mifflin Company, 2004), http://dictionary.reference.com/browse/humanism, accessed: November 16, 2008.

Chapter 11 Notes

1. This has been intentional and a response to some professors expressing concern that CTL focuses too much on the Christian academy and overlooks local church educational contexts. The principles are the same. Only the content differs—academic subjects in the former and the Bible in the latter.

2. Daryl Eldridge, ed., *Teaching Ministry of the Church*, (Nashville: Broadman & Holman, 1995). Six Foundation of Education professors (Daryl Eldridge, Norma Hedin, Terrell Peace, William "Budd" Smith, Jack Terry, and myself) wrote the text to serve a new course in the teaching ministry of the Church.

3. My two major professors in seminary were Dr. Leon Marsh and Dr. Leroy Ford. Dr. Marsh was a devotee of Jerome Bruner and reflected a strong cognitive focus in his classes. He also took a special interest in students personally and reflected some of the humanistic flavor of Bruner's writing. As a result, he focused on our thinking while using methods that were student-centered. Dr. Ford, a consultant at the Baptist Sunday School Board, was known for his behavioral perspective and was invited to join the faculty by Dr. Marsh as a balancing factor. Dr. Ford became Professor of Programmed Instruction and used behavioral principles predominantly in his classes.

4. That theme was maintained in the second edition of the text. William R. Yount, *Teaching Ministry of the Church*, 2nd ed., (Nashville: Broadman & Holman, 2008). Thirteen professors of the School of Educational Ministries (SWBTS) built on the foundation laid in *TMC* to rewrite the text.

5. The Triad was used as the organizing framework for *Called to Teach*—published in 1999. It was further used, along with the Disciplers' Model, to structure the application of discipling and equipping principles to the field of missions in *Called to Reach: Equipping Cross-Cultural Disciplers* (2007). If you are familiar with the books mentioned above, especially our newest *Teaching Ministry of the Church*, this chapter will be an expansion of those introductions.

6. You may have seen such a figure before. It is one of a set of diagrams, referred to as *Venn diagrams*.

7. Afterwards, Samuel took a stone and set it upright between Mizpah and Shen. He named it *Ebenezer* [Rock of Help], explaining, "The LORD has helped us to this point" (1 Samuel 7:12).

8. "With the **heart** one believes, resulting in righteousness" (Romans 10:10). Strong's number 2588 *kardia* (kar-dee'-ah); "the heart, i.e. (figuratively), the *thoughts* or *feelings* (*mind*)."

9. *Word magic* refers to statements that sound important but are actually empty: "If we truly believe, then we will walk forever in His steps!" "We must see people with God's eyes!" Statements like these draw hearty "Amens!," but what do they mean?

10. *Chasing rabbits* refers to leaving the main point of the study to venture off in tangential pursuits. The term *rabbit trails* is also used. For thinkers, rabbits are usually a waste of time because they seldom support the points being made in the study.

11. Greater than 15 students.

12. Many of the classes in Russian Baptist seminaries have no women students. Interestingly, the men in these classes break out roughly in thirds!

13. Men who place themselves in the Feeler group are not less "manly" than thinkers or doers. They are, however, more interested in relationships, freedom, spontaneity, and personal values than men in the other two groups.

14. Just to be sure I'm saying this clearly enough, we are not suggesting 33-33-33 every session. There will be times when a difficult passage or course topic needs to be explained clearly and in detail. There will be other times when a testimony is shared that captures the hearts of the class, and we need to let go of our notes and go with the Lord in sharing. The "balance over time" means that over the course of a series of sessions, all three spheres are addressed.

15. Matthew 13:57; 21:11; Luke 24:19; John 6:14.

16. In Piaget's language, Jesus made every attempt to lift His disciples and listeners from Concrete Operational thinking (Stage Three) to Formal Operational thinking (Stage Four).

17. Dallas Willard, *The Divine Conspiracy: Rediscovering Our Hidden Life with God*, (New York: HarperCollins, 1997), 146.

18. Ibid., 168.

19. Ibid., 175.

20. Ibid., 177.

21. Ibid., 178.

22. Ibid., 179.

23. "Hate your enemy" is not a direct teaching of Old Testament Scripture, but an inference made by Old Testament commentators. Perhaps the inference was based on passages such as this: "Never seek peace or friendship with them ("Ammonite or Moabite," v. 3) as long as you live" (Deut 23:6), (from *Holman Christian Standard Bible*® Copyright © 1999, 2000, 2002, 2003 by Holman Bible Publishers).

24. Ibid., 129.

25. Ibid., 91.

26. Ibid., 93.

27. Ibid., 94ff.

28. Ibid., 129ff.

29. Hebrews 3:1; 4:14.

30. The statements of Jesus just preceding this seem outright rude, however. "I was sent only to the lost sheep of the house of Israel" (v. 24). And again, "It isn't right to take the children's bread and throw it to their dogs" (v. 26). There is no worse insult one can render another in the Middle East than to call them a dog. Edershiem explains that the woman's approach to Jesus was "not as the Messiah of Israel but an Israelitish Messiah . . . this was exactly the error of the Jews that Jesus had encountered and combated, like when He resisted the attempt to make Him King, in His reply to the Jerusalem Scribes, and in His Discourses at Capernaum. To have granted her the help she so entreated would have been, as it were, to reverse the whole of His Teaching and to make His works of healing merely works of power. . . . And so He first taught her, in such manner as she could understand, that which she needed to know—before she could approach Him in such a manner—the relation of the heathen to the Jewish world and of both to the Messiah, and then He gave her what she asked. Jesus healed her demon-possessed daughter on the basis of a proper relationship. What appears to be rudeness is actually heartfelt care that this Gentile woman properly understand who He was before He granted her request.

31. Jesus was the sacrifice. Jesus was the priest. Jesus was the mercy seat, the "propitiation for our sins" (Rom 3:25). The mercy seat, or propitiatory, was the lid of the ark of the covenant upon which the sacrificial blood was sprinkled and from which God spoke to Israel. The picture is clear. God is brought near His people through Jesus. (See Albert Barnes, *Notes on the New Testament*, [London: Blackie & Son, 1884–85] on Romans 3:25).

32. Mark 15:2; Luke 23:3; John 18:37; Acts 17:7.

33. Matthew Henry suggests this means the "dead in sin" to spiritual life since there is no evidence that the disciples raised anyone from the dead (commentary on Matt 10:7–8).

34. Much of this material is also found in Chapter Eleven, "The Goal of Christian Education: Christlikeness" in *The Teaching Ministry of the Church,* 2nd ed., (2008). There have been revisions and additions made to this chapter, however.

35. Without more context, there are several correct answers to this question. I would focus on the difference between "S-R" bonds (Thorndike) and "R-S" bonds (Skinner). Thorndike's third Law of Learning (S-R+) states that a pleasant response strengthens the bond and an unpleasant response weakens the bond. Skinner converted the response satisfaction ("R+") into a "reinforcing stimulus (R)" so that his R-S bond reflected essentially the same truth as Thorndike's S-R+ bond.

36. In the way we use the words *like* and *love*, we intend a progression. I meet someone; I grow to like them. If I like them very much over a long time, I may eventually love them. These concepts do not relate to Jesus' command. He used the word *agape* (love) and not *phileo* (like brotherly love). Jesus' command had nothing to do with liking people who persecute or abuse us but "meeting their needs." If my enemy has a need, I am to "do good" to them, to help them with their need. While it does not say I must like them in the process, it is true that if I *agape* someone long enough, I may well grow to like them as well.

37. Biblesoft's *New Exhaustive Strong's Numbers and Concordance with Expanded Greek-Hebrew Dictionary.* Copyright © 1994, 2003, 2006 Biblesoft, Inc. and International Bible Translators, Inc. *PC Study Bible*, Version 5.0, accessed November 28, 2008.

38. Even Peter had trouble understanding him sometimes! (2 Pet 3:16).

39. All superscripted words inserted by the author—as well as bold-face emphases.

40. Andrew Christofer and Vasili Mitrokhin, *The Sword and the Shield: The Mitrokhin Archive and the Secret History of the K.G.B.,* (New York: Basic Books, 1999), 23.

41. "wisdom," *Nelson's Illustrated Bible Dictionary*, copyright © 1986, Thomas Nelson Publishers. *PC Study Bible* v5.0E, Biblesoft (1988–2007).

42. There are three tenses of salvation: justification (I have been saved by faith), sanctification (I am being saved day by day), and glorification (I will one day be completely saved, "made whole").

43. *Teaching Ministry of the Church* (1995) and *Created to Learn* (1996).

Chapter 12 Notes

1. http://creativeproverbs.com/cgi-bin/sql_search3cp.cgi?keyword=Who+begins+too+much+ accomplishes+ little+&boolean=and&field=all&frank=all&database=all. Accessed June 29, 2009.

2. http://www.great-quotes.com/cgi-bin/viewquotes.cgi?keyword=Aristotle&action=search, accessed December 6, 2008.

3. Guy R. LeFrancois, *Psychology for Teaching*, 8th ed., (Belmont, CA: Wadsworth Publishing Company, 1994), 354.

4. Thomas L. Good and Jere E. Brophey, *Educational Psychology: A Realistic Approach*, 4th ed., (New York: Longman, 1990), 55 and Norman A. Sprinthall, Richard C. Sprinthall, and Sharon N. Oja, *Educational Psychology: A Developmental Approach*, 6th ed., (New York: McGraw-Hill, Inc., 1994), 142.

5. *Terminal* means the indication of learning comes at the end of the session. "Indicator" refers to student actions, which demonstrate learning at a given level.

6. LeFrancois, 355.

7. Good and Brophey, 143.

8. A disgruntled professor wrote to me not long ago, scoffing at the very idea of instructional objectives. "I decide what I'm going to lecture over as I walk down the hall to my class." Then he wondered why his students were frustrated with his exams, which never seemed to follow his spontaneous lesson planning.

9. Anita Woolfolk, *Educational Psychology*, 5th ed., (Boston: Allyn and Bacon, Inc., 1993), 437.

10. Ibid.

11. Daryl Eldridge wrote his Ed. D. dissertation on the subject of behavioral objectives and student achievement. He showed that students did significantly better when given instructional objectives than when they were not. Eldridge, Daryl

Roger. "The Effect of Student Knowledge of Behavioral Objectives on Achievement and Attitude toward the Course," Ed. D. diss., Southwestern Baptist Theological Seminary, 1985.

12. Woolfolk (1993), 437.

13. Robert F. Biehler and Jack Snowman, *Psychology Applied to Teaching*, 7th ed., (Boston: Houghton Mifflin Company, 1993), 298.

14. LeFrancois, 356.

15. Woolfolk (1993), 438.

16. LeFrancois, 356.

17. Woolfolk (1993), 438.

18. LeFrancois, 356.

19. Woolfolk (1993), 440.

20. These dates refer to his first book, *Preparing Instructional Objectives.* Other books include *Measuring Instructional Intent, Goal Analysis, Analyzing Performance Problems, Developing Vocational Instruction,* and *Developing Attitude toward Learning.*

21. Gronlund wrote *Stating Behavioral Objectives for Classroom Instruction* (1972), *Determining Accountability for Classroom Instruction* (1975), *Measurement and Evaluation in Teaching* (5th ed., 1985), *How to Write and Use Instructional Objectives* (4th ed., 1991), and *Gronlund's Writing Instructional Objectives* (8th ed., 2009).

22. LeFrancois, 357.

23. Leroy Ford, Professor of Foundations of Education at Southwestern Seminary in Fort Worth, Texas 1966–84. He has had as great an influence on Christian educators' views of instructional objectives as any contemporary writer. Ford's classic text on instructional objectives is *Design for Teaching and Training: A Self-Study Guide to Lesson Planning,* (Nashville: Broadman Press, 1978). This text was republished by Resource Publications in 2002. Ford's most recent book is *A Curriculum Design Manual for Theological Education: A Learning Outcomes Focus* (Nashville: Broadman Press, 1991). This text gives detailed procedures to developing a theological curriculum, using instructional objectives. It was republished by Wipf and Stock in 2003. Both books can be easily found at amazon.com.

24. Woolfolk (1993), 439.

25. N. L. Gage and David C. Berliner, *Educational Psychology*, 3rd ed., (Dallas: Houghton Mifflin Company, 1984), 44.

26. Biehler and Snowman, 290.

27. Ibid., 291.

28. Good and Brophey, 143.

29. Sprinthall and Sprinthall, 356.

30. LeFrancois, 357.

31. Ibid.

32. Sprinthall and Sprinthall, 356.

33. Norman Gronlund is Professor Emeritus, University of Illinois at Urbana-Champaign. Norman E. Gronlund and Susan M. Brookhart, *Gronlund's Writing Instructional Objectives*, 8th ed., (Upper Saddle River, NJ: Pearson Education, Inc., 2009), title page.

34. Woolfolk (1993), 439.

35. Now LifeWay Christian Resources.

36. Now School of Educational Ministries.

37. Southern Association of Colleges and Schools and Association of Theological Schools are the two accrediting agencies of Southwestern Seminary in Fort Worth, Texas.

38. Leroy Ford, *A Curriculum Design Manual for Theological Education: A Learning Outcomes Focus* (Nashville: Broadman Press, 1991), 295.

39. Ibid., 296.

40. *A Curriculum Design Manual for Theological Education: A Learning Outcomes Focus* (Wipf & Stock Publishers, 2003), 352 pages.

41. Lorin W. Anderson and David R. Krathwohl, eds., *A Taxonomy for Learning, Teaching, and Assessing* (New York: Longman, 2001), 4.

42. The *psychomotor* refers to physical competence—eye-hand coordination, manual dexterity, completing a specific task.

43. Benjamin S. Bloom, ed., *Taxonomy of Educational Objectives,* (New York: David McKay Company, Inc., 1956).

44. Anderson and Krathwohl, xxi.

45. David Krathwohl, ed., *Taxonomy of Educational Objectives: Handbook II: Affective Domain,* (New York: David McKay Company, 1964), iv.

46. Ibid.

47. Elizabeth Simpson, *The Classification of Educational Objectives: Psychomotor Domain,* (Urbana: University of Illinois Press, 1972).

48. Washington, D.C.: Gryphon House, 1972. Simpson's work was adapted from Krathwohl and Bloom's work in *Handbook II: Affective Domain.*

49. "Over 20" new taxonomies have been developed since Bloom's was published in 1956. Marzano and Kendall, 9.

50. The "Revised Taxonomy" is found in Anderson and Krathwohl, eds., *A Taxonomy for Learning, Teaching, and Assessing* (New York: Longman, 2001). This book presents an update of Bloom's original.

51. The "New Taxonomy" is found in Robert J. Marzano and John S. Kendall, *The New Taxonomy of Educational Objectives*, 2nd ed., (Thousand Oaks, CA: Corwin Press, 2007). This book presents a replacement for Bloom's original.

52. Norman E. Gronlund and Susan M. Brookhart, *Gronlund's Writing Instructional Objectives*, 8th ed., (Upper Saddle River, NJ: Pearson Education, Inc., 2009), 155 pages.

53. Ibid., 52.

54. Myron H. Dembo, *Applying Educational Psychology*, 5th ed., (New York: Longman, 1994), 380.

55. Woolfolk (1993), 443.

56. Gronlund and Brookhart, 128.

57. Gallaudet University, where my wife and I served as dormitory counselors from 1970–3, before heading to Southwestern Seminary. During those years, we established a deaf ministry at Columbia Baptist Church in Falls Church, Virginia. They were three of the happiest years of our lives.

58. http://www.great-quotes.com/cgi-bin/viewquotes.cgi?keyword=Tupper&action=search.

59. LeFrancois, 359.

60. Sprinthall and Sprinthall, 357.

61. Gronlund and Brookhart, 128.

62. Gronlund and Brookhart, 129.

63. An old Charlie Brown cartoon leaps to mind when his teacher asks Charlie Brown to explain the meaning of *longitude* and *latitude* in his own words. Charlie Brown says, "Glik gimbal thut," then looks at the reader and says, "I just love loopholes." The assumption of "in one's own words" is that the answer will be correct but not rote.

64. "agapaoo," *Thayer's Greek Lexicon*, Electronic Database. *PC Study Bible*, v. 5E, Copyright © 2000, 2003, 2006 by Biblesoft, Inc., accessed December 9, 2008.

65. "Enemy," *Vine's Expository Dictionary of Biblical Words*, Copyright © 1985, Thomas Nelson Publishers. *PC Study Bible*, v. 5E, accessed December 9, 2008.

66. Saying the same thing in different words is common in Hebrew teaching and poetry. It is called parallelism. http://dictionary.reference.com/browse/parallelism, accessed December 8, 2008.

67. Woolfolk (1993), 443.

68. Dembo, 380.

69. Gronlund and Brookhart, 128.

70. Woolfolk (1993), 443.

71. Sprinthall and Sprinthall, 357.

72. Gronlund and Brookhart, 128.

73. Notice that *learners* are required to demonstrate learning at these various levels. If a teacher does the analysis and simply talks through it, learners receive little more than information. Pastors do the analysis of Bible passages for their sermons and then talk through their analysis, leaving worshippers as little more than "hearers only." It is hard to disciple

from a pulpit. Pastors do well to engage their parishioners in smaller groups—in homes, prayer groups, and classes as well as overseeing the training of teachers who can gather learners in learning groups to move beyond listening.

74. On a humorous note, I discovered a Web site the other day, offering a twenty-page term paper "breaking down the theories of William R. Yount in *Created to Learn*. Students required to write such a paper can save themselves hours of study and writing simply by buying the ready-made paper, sight unseen, *for $239!* On a serious note, those who would waste their money on a paper that might require ten hours of analysis (earning themselves $23.90 per hour) are also hypnotizing themselves to think they are learning by submitting a paper they did not write. Teachers do well to assign paper topics that relate given themes to current problems in ways not readily found in dishonest paper mills.

75. Woolfolk (1993), 443.

76. Gronlund and Brookhart, 128.

77. If you have slipped into postmodern thinking, you may well react negatively to this statement, "Who's to define 'correct'?" In a word, the teacher (in the context of the classroom). Synthesis is not the product of personal imagination but of rational creativity. "Anything I dream up" is not the basis for a correct synthesis of materials. Synthesis is not about "what I feel about the subject" but about "what the subject means."

78. Ibid., 129.

79. *The Bible Knowledge Commentary* (Ezra 10:10–12) remarks that God was not condoning divorce but emphasizing national purity. The emphasis was not on the nationality of the wife as much as her focus of worship. A "foreign wife" was one who worshipped idols, and each marriage was examined to determine whether this was true. Presumably, those who worshipped Jehovah God were no longer considered "foreign" (consider Ruth, the Moabitess, King David's grandmother.) The problem was widespread, and it took several months to complete the examinations. Presumably, the wives and children were returned to their home countries; but this is not explicitly stated. *PC Study Bible*, Version 5.0E, accessed December 16, 2008.

80. I cannot, of course, resolve the free will sovereignty debate here. Scholars have argued these viewpoints for centuries. But the debate illustrates the challenge of synthesis.

81. For what it is worth, my best attempt at synthesis is that God "foreknows" who will be saved because He does not reside in time as we do. He sees all from beginning to end, and He knows each one of us. Further, there seems always to be an interaction between God's quickening and man's response. Moses sees a bush burning in the desert—not an uncommon sight, given lightning strikes and other natural causes. But there is something in *this* Burning Bush that causes him to "turn aside." When he changes his direction, God speaks to him. He quickens, and we respond (or not). He speaks, and we listen (or not). He teaches, and we learn (or not). God's method, His plan of salvation was foreordained (Hershel Hobbs, SBC pastor and writer). The sign over Heaven's gate reads, "Whosoever will, may come." As we pass through the gate and look on the backside of the sign, we read, "You have not chosen Me, but I have chosen you." Scripture teaches both truths, and we live in the tension of the two by faith.

82. Key points in a lecture by Dr. William Hendricks in his course "The Theology of Paul and John," Spring 1974, Southwestern Seminary.

83. I emphasize the word *objectively* because much of the evaluation done in our humanistic society is subjective: Value is judged by how something makes us *feel*. "How would you evaluate the sermon?" "I really liked it!" This is "valuation." "Evaluation" is anchored in principles and concepts: "The sermon was well constructed. The opening story engaged listeners well and led directly into the passage. Two major points would have been made more effectively if he had used illustrations to clarify contemporary application." (Evaluation is not concerned with *liking or not liking*; it is concerned with *correct or incorrect—based on a standard*.)

84. Dembo, 380.

85. Gronlund and Brookhart, 128.

86. Gronlund lists "describes" at the level of evaluation, which he also uses for the lowest level of learning (knowledge). Obviously, "describing" a fact at the level of knowledge and "describing" a system at the evaluation level of learning are two very different processes; but Gronlund does not differentiate the two different uses (same word, different meanings). Gronlund and Brookhart, 129.

87. I once allowed students to rewrite their objective statements, allowing everyone to make a very good grade. It

also took away any struggle to make the original statements "correct." Students learned they could turn in mediocre work and be allowed to redo it correctly, simply by copying down comments made in class. "A clearly written instructional objective" is worth a letter grade on the teaching plans. They are better prepared to write teaching plans through this process.

88. Each student teaches a Scripture verse, concept, or attitude. They lead the class toward a specific objective for ten minutes, and they are videotaped for self-evaluation. Their teaching plans are graded by the professor.

89. In reality, students rarely (objectively) evaluate their classmates over weaknesses; but they are far more likely to give pats on the back for the positives. Still, the process calls students to compare the "ideals" of the course with the "real" of the MicroTeach sessions.

90. David Krathwohl, ed., *Taxonomy of Educational Objectives: Handbook II: Affective Domain,* (New York: David McKay Company, 1964), iv.

91. Woolfolk (2004), 436.

92. Snowman, 365.

93. Biehler and Snowman, 281.

94. Woolfolk (1993), 444.

95. Gronlund and Brookhart, 128.

96. Woolfolk (2004), 436.

97. Biehler and Snowman, 281.

98. Gronlund and Brookhart, 128.

99. Woolfolk (2004), 436.

100. Woolfolk (1993), 444.

101. Biehler and Snowman, 281.

102. Woolfolk (2004), 436. My concern here is the comparison with another activity, which seems to reflect priority of concert over film—more associated with organization than valuing. Liking concerts, defending concerts, expressing pleasure over attending concerts reflect valuing better than the comparison.

103. Gronlund uses terms like *describes, differentiates,* and *explains* that refer more closely to comprehension in the cognitive domain. Better terms include *initiates, invites, justifies, proposes,* and *studies.* Gronlund and Brookhart, 129.

104. This bromide emphasizes the misconception of teaching as telling. When students "catch their values" from teachers, they are being taught by way of personal example rather than verbiage. Bandura's learning by imitation certainly emphasizes this concept. Teaching is more than telling.

105. Woolfolk (1993), 444.

106. Gronlund and Brookhart, 128.

107. Biehler and Snowman, 282.

108. Woolfolk (2004), 436.

109. Gronlund suggests other terms for Organizing: explains (comprehension), identifies (knowledge), compares (analysis), and synthesizes (synthesis). More useful suggestions include *alters, arranges, integrates, modifies, orders,* and *organizes*—so long as these are used with values rather than concepts.

110. "Church Training," now called "Discipleship Training," is a regular Southern Baptist program, which focuses on Christian Life issues: history, doctrine, polity, Christian living.

111. Doctor of Ministry seminar, "Educational Psychology: Pastor as Teacher," Summer 1984.

112. Woolfolk (1993), 444.

113. Biehler and Snowman, 283.

114. Gronlund and Brookhart, 128.

115. Woolfolk (2004), 436.

116. Gronlund includes in characterizing such terms as *discriminates* (analysis), *listens* (receiving), and *modifies* (organization). More useful terms include *acts, performs, serves,* and *uses.* Gronlund and Brookhart, 129.

117. John A. Glover and Roger H. Bruning, *Educational Psychology: Principles and Applications,* 3rd ed., (Glenview, IL: Scott, Foresman/Little, Brown Higher Education, 1990), 366.

118. Ibid., 367.

119. Based on the work of James Cangelosi (1990). Woolfolk (2004), 437.

120. Elizabeth Simpson, *The Classification of Educational Objectives: Psychomotor Domain* (Urbana: University of Illinois Press, 1972).

121. Biehler and Snowman, 283.

122. Ibid.

123. The purpose of this is not so much to develop the skill but to accustom students to the new procedure in order to reduce fear and anxiety.

124. Ibid.

125. Ibid., 284.

126. Ibid.

127. Gronlund and Brookhart, 133.

128. Ibid.

129. Ibid.

130. "Understanding" is the goal for cognitive levels of learning from comprehension through evaluation.

131. Glover and Bruning, 367.

132. Is this "psychomotor" (skill) or actually "synthesis (understanding)"? Certainly, "synthesis" is required to put together the components of a teaching plan in a correct way. But the focus of this objective is on "**proficiency** in synthesis," which reflects *skill* and fits the broader context of psychomotor objectives (Cangelosi, 1990). Students synthesize teaching plans; but as they cycle through writing, feedback, revising, rewriting, and feedback, they develop **greater skill in synthesis**.

133. Woolfolk (1993), 447.

134. One of the faculty debates we have had several times over the twenty-seven years I have been at Southwestern is whether affective goals should be formally stated as a part of the course descriptions. While we all seek affective changes in our students, we have opted every time to focus on cognitive goals (with specific knowledge and skill goals as appropriate in particular courses). To set out affective goals with measurable indicators is to invite hypocrisy. If students know they can earn 10 points on their semester grade by "reflecting a positive attitude toward the subject," students will be sure to reflect that positive attitude—whether it is real or not—because they want the 10 points. It is only when students freely reflect a positive attitude, without a payoff, that the affective response is real.

135. http://krummefamily.org/guides/bloom.html, accessed December 10, 2008.

136. Anderson and Krathwohl, 5.

137. The definitions of knowledge types are displayed in Table 3.2 in Anderson and Krathwohl, 29.

138. Anderson and Krathwohl, 265.

139. The definitions of cognitive process levels are displayed in Table 3.3 in Anderson and Krathwohl, 31.

140. Anderson and Krathwohl, 28.

141. Ibid., 106.

142. Ibid.

143. My emotional reaction is similar to the one I had with educational programming and its increasingly complex targeting of specific reinforcers for each student and task in a class.

144. Marzano and Kendall, *The New Taxonomy*, 17.

145. Ibid., 17–18.

146. Anderson and Krathwohl, 44. Quoted in Marzano and Kendall, 18.

147. Marzano and Kendall, 18.

148. Ibid., 30.

149. Ibid., 31. Automaticity, you may recall, means learning procedures to the point that they can be used without intentional thought or focus. When a child is learning to tie their shoe laces, it takes all of their attention. A teenager, however, can tie his shoes "without thinking" while carrying on a conversation with a friend.

150. Marzano et al. base their taxonomy on recent research in Information Processing (Chapter Nine) and memory.

151. Marzano et al. use the term "permanent memory" in the place of long-term memory and "working memory" in place of short-term memory, following the single-memory model discussed in Chapter Nine.

152. Marzano and Kendall, *The New Taxonomy*, 37.

153. Ibid., 40.

154. Ibid., 43-44.

155. Keep in mind that the New Taxonomy defines "knowledge" as broad as the old cognitive domain. To those of us used to the classic views, the phrase "knowledge as comprehended" is nonsense since knowledge is recall and comprehension is understanding. It is helpful to think of "cognitive structure" (Piaget) when you read "knowledge" under this system. We found the same situation with Information Processing, where the cognitive structure in long-term memory is also considered "knowledge."

156. Marzano and Kendall, *The New Taxonomy*, 44–51.

157. Ibid., 52–53.

158. Ibid., 53–55.

159. Ibid., 55–58.

160. Biehler and Snowman, 300.

161. Good and Brophey, 145.

Chapter 13 Notes

1. http://www.phrases.org.uk/meanings/you-can-lead-a-horse-to-water.html, accessed July 14, 2009.

2. Thomas L. Good and Jere E. Brophey, *Educational Psychology: A Realistic Approach*, 4th ed., (New York: Longman, 1990), 360.

3. Paul Eggen and Don Kauchak, *Educational Psychology: Classroom Connections*, 2nd ed., (New York: Macmillan College Publishing Company, 1994), 427.

4. Richard Hamilton and Elizabeth Ghatala, *Learning and Instruction* (New York: McGraw-Hill, Inc., 1994), 328.

5. Myron H. Dembo, *Applying Educational Psychology*, 5th ed., (New York: Longman, 1994), 147.

6. Eggen and Kauchak (1990), 427.

7. Eggen and Kauchak (1994), 427.

8. Hamilton and Ghatala, 329.

9. Don Hamachek, *Psychology in Teaching, Learning, and Growth*, 4th ed., (Boston: Allyn and Bacon, 1990), 265.

10. Hamilton and Ghatala, 329.

11. Hamachek, 265.

12. Ibid., 264.

13. Hamilton and Ghatala, 329.

14. Hamachek, 267.

15. Ibid.

16. Guy R. LeFrancois, *Psychology for Teaching*, 8th ed., (Belmont, CA: Wadsworth Publishing Company, 1994), 274.

17. Good, 360.

18. Eggen and Kauchak (1994), 428.

19. Hamilton and Ghatala, 331.

20. Ibid., 328.

21. Eggen and Kauchak (1994), 341.

22. Ibid., 431.

23. Ibid., 340.

24. Ibid., 341.

25. Ibid.

26. Ibid.

27. Ibid.

28. Hamilton and Ghatala, 331.

29. Eggen and Kauchak (1994), 436.

30. Hamachek, 272.

31. LeFrancois, 275.

32. Ibid.

33. Hamachek, 271, 274; Anita Woolfolk, *Educational Psychology*, 5th ed., (Boston: Allyn and Bacon, Inc., 1993), 377.

34. LeFrancois, 275.

35. Hamachek, 275; Woolfolk (1993), 377.

36. LeFrancois, 275.

37. Ibid.

38. Hamachek, 271.

39. Hamachek, 275; Woolfolk (1993), 377.

40. Woolfolk, 220.

41. Good, 166.

42. Woolfolk (1993), 220.

43. Ibid., 222.

44. Biehler and Snowman, 349.

45. Woolfolk (1993), 222.

46. Good, 166.

47. Dembo, 61.

48. Eggen and Kauchak (1994), 289.

49. Woolfolk (1993), 223.

50. Norman A. Sprinthall, Richard C. Sprinthall, and Sharon N. Oja, *Educational Psychology: A Developmental Approach*, 6th ed., (New York: McGraw-Hill, Inc., 1994), 259.

51. Eggen and Kauchak (1994), 282.

52. Good, 166.

53. Eggen and Kauchak (1994), 436.

54. Woolfolk (1993), 223.

55. Glover, 313.

56. Eggen and Kauchak (1994), 286.

57. Slavin, 174.

58. Eggen and Kauchak (1994), 286.

59. Good, 168.

60. Years ago Southern Baptists introduced a concept of building the numerical base of churches called "The Growth Spiral." The Growth Spiral was an effective planning tool because it provided a means to realistically look at the organizational structure required to support a given growth rate or membership goal. "If our average class size is 14 and we have 200 adults in Bible study classes, how many rooms and teachers will we need to support an average attendance of 300 if we maintain present class size?" An increase of 100 in average attendance, with an average class size of 14, requires 7 new classes—7 new teachers and 7 new classrooms. Such information helps educators and administrators plan for this growth, enlisting and training new teachers and securing places for them to meet.

However, a former student surprised me one day as he was showing me around his church facilities. We entered the sanctuary, and there on a side wall was a huge banner of the Growth Spiral planning tool—perhaps 10' wide x 6' tall—complete with quarterly goals and teacher names. One of the class numbers—along with the teacher name—was displayed in red. "Mrs. Smith's" class failed to meet their Growth Spiral goal for the quarter, and every member of the church could see that as they met to worship. I was shocked, for such humiliating behavior is the last thing I would want any of our students to carry away from seminary.

61. LifeWay Christian Resources has a wide variety of leadership periodicals to support ongoing professional development and ministry evaluation. If you teach courses in Christian education at the college or seminary level, be

sure to join the North American Professors of Christian Education organization and attend the annual meetings held in October. Go to www.napce.org for more information. Check out the publishing sponsors who support NAPCE for more helps with leadership models.

62. Unless, of course, we continually update our experiences, shedding old formulas and methods for creative approaches that convey timeless truths in contemporary ways. "The way we built our programs in 1970" will hardly connect with issues in 2010.

63. LeFrancois, 274.

64. Good, 360.

65. Wadsworth, 11.

66. Biehler and Snowman, 60.

67. Ibid.

68. Woolfolk (1993), 370.

69. Wadsworth, 10.

70. Hamilton and Ghatala, 337.

71. LeFrancois, 274.

72. Good, 360.

73. Eggen and Kauchak (1994), 433.

74. "Motivation and the Growth of Self" in Perceiving, Behaving, and Becoming, the Association for Supervision and Curriculum Development Yearbook (Washington, DC: National Education Association, 1962), 83–98.

75. Paul Eggen and Don Kauchak. *Educational Psychology: Windows on Classrooms*, 6th ed., (Upper Saddle River, NJ: Pearson Education, Inc., 2004), 354.

76. Anita Woolfolk, *Educational Psychology*, 9th ed., (Boston: Pearson Education, Inc., 2004), 353.

77. Eggen and Kauchak (2004), 354.

78. Abraham Maslow, "The Various Meanings of Transcendence," *Journal of Transpersonal Psychology*, Vol. 1, 1969, 31.

79. Woolfolk (2004), 353.

80. Robert J. Sternberg and Wendy M. Williams, *Educational Psychology*, (Boston: Allyn and Bacon, 2002), 366.

81. "motivation," <http://www.britannica.com/eb/article?tocId= 12712>, accessed March 5, 2009.

82. This is my term—based on the other traits.

83. Hamachek, 58.

84. Ibid., 57.

85. Maslow, "Transcendence," 31.

86. Ibid.

87. Eggen and Kauchak (2004); Jeanne Ellis Ormrod, *Educational Psychology: Developing Learners*, 5th ed., (Columbus: Pearson Education, Inc., 2006); Sternberg and Williams (2002); and Woolfolk (2004).

88. Alfred Edersheim, *The Life and Times of Jesus the Messiah*, Vol. II, (Grand Rapids: Wm. B. Eerdmans, 1969 [first published in 1886]), 462.

89. Dallas Willard, *The Divine Conspiracy: Rediscovering Our Hidden Life in God*, (San Francisco: Harper, 1997), 378.

90. Willard, 376.

91. C. S. Lewis, *Mere Christianity*, (New York: Macmillan, 1956), 148.

92. Willard, 376.

93. Willard, 367.

94. Ibid., 368.

95. See William R. Yount, "An Evangelical View of Transcendence and Senior Adult Attitudes," *Journal of Religion, Spirituality, and Aging*, Volume 21, Issue 1, (2009), 88-103.

96. Eggen and Kauchak (1994), 440.

97. Glover and Bruning, 262.

98. Eggen and Kauchak (1994), 440.

99. Glover and Bruning, 262.

100. Ibid., 261, 250.

101. Eggen and Kauchak (1994), 436.

102. Ibid.

103. Hamilton and Ghatala, 355.

104. Eggen and Kauchak (1994), 436.

105. Ibid., 433.

106. A "personal relationship" between teacher and student is dangerous. Teachers have power over students, and emotional attachments between led and leader can quickly spin out of control. This is obvious when teacher and student are different genders, but same-sex unions are becoming more common in our "progressive" society. We do well to create "educational" relationships with learners—much as pastors create "pastoral" relationships with members of their congregations." Deeply personal friendships are best established outside classrooms and congregations.

107. Hamilton and Ghatala, 338.

108. Woolfolk (1993), 350.

109. Woolfolk (1993), 351. The balance is important. Help children (through guidance) solve problems on their own (autonomy).

110. Ibid., 257; Glover and Bruning, 254, 257.

111. Dembo, 154.

112. Eggen and Kauchak (1994), 444.

113. Some of Weiner's writings include "An Attributional Analysis of Achievement Motivation," *Journal of Personality and Social Psychology*, 15, (1970), 1–20; *An Attributional Theory of Motivation and Emotion*, (New York: Springer-Verlag, 1985); "Understanding the Motivational Role of Affect: Lifespan Research from an Attributional Perspective," *Cognition and Emotion*, 4, (1989), 401–19; *Human Motivation: Metaphors, Theories and Research* (London: Sage Publications, 1992).

114. Weiner includes a third variable, called responsibility, which refers to the student's ability to control the cause of success or failure. The categories are "controllable" and "uncontrollable" (Woolfolk, (1993), 353). I have omitted this variable to simplify the discussion of attribution effects of stability and locus of control.

115. Dembo, 154.

116. Ibid., 155.

117. Biehler and Snowman, 522.

118. Ibid.

119. It is one thing when high achievers drive *themselves* to succeed. It is quite another when they project this drive to succeed on others. Professors tend to be high achievers and can view low achievement in their students as the result of low ability or lack of initiative. If professors demand more than students can reasonably give—"How can I learn in one semester what my professor has taught for 20 years?"—and blame student failures on their *lack of effort*, they create a toxic environment that destroys motivation.

Professors pass on such attitudes to ministerial students. If students graduate from such a system, they will reflect these same perspectives in the churches they serve. Trained in theology, Bible, Christian education, and church organization, high-achiever ministers tend to attribute success to ability and hard work. When faced with little church progress (often measured by numerical growth in membership and program participation), they often attribute it to the lack of ability or laziness of church members.

The frustration of high achievers—in colleges, seminaries, or churches—does little to help low achievers excel.

120. Ibid., Glover and Bruning, 259.

121. LeFrancois, 284.

122. Ibid.

123. Ibid., 285. See Chapters Six through Eleven for suggestions.

124. Woolfolk (1993), 360.

125. Ibid., 280.

126. Woolfolk (1993), 359.

127. Hamachek, 279.

Chapter 14 Notes

1. http://www.great-quotes.com/cgi-bin/viewquotes.cgi?action=search&orderby=&keyword=memory&startlist=120, accessed September 19, 2008.

2. Common student comments from around the world—addressed in more detail in Chapter Eleven ("Triad").

3. Research suggests that student ratings have little to do with how much they actually learn in a class. M. Daniel Smith, *Educational Psychology and Its Classroom Applications* (Boston: Allyn and Bacon, 1975), 155. Regardless, positive student attitudes are important to the classroom climate.

4. Two general factors of teacher effectiveness are teacher *personality* and teacher *behavior*.

5. "personality," *American Heritage Dictionary*.

6. This exercise is critical for quickly bridging the gap between "American teacher" and students of Ukraine, Russia, Kyrgyzstan, or Kazakhstan. By demonstrating how the personal experiences of the students themselves fit the theoretical perspective of the Triad, students immediately want to learn more about this perspective. The Triad provides a biblical gateway into the science of learning and neutralizes the normal defensiveness of East against West.

7. AHD, "enthusiasm."

8. Hamachek, 399.

9. Ibid., 414.

10. Ibid., 417.

11. Ibid.

12. Ibid., 401.

13. Ibid., 417.

14. Ibid., 402.

15. *The Discipler's Handbook*, 28.

16. Ibid.

17. There is a great difference between "getting information" and "processing information" (IPT, Chapter Nine). The former implies teacher talk and the latter student analysis.

18. Ibid., 403.

19. "Flexible balance" in that content and communication is not a 50-50 proposition. Today is delivery; tomorrow, discussion. Over time, there is a flexible balance between deepening the content mastery of students and leading them to process that content interactively so that it becomes personally relevant.

20. Years ago, I heard comedienne Phyllis Diller describe the steps she takes to create a single, new one-liner. She jots a thought down on paper. Massages the words. Tweaks the timing. She tries the new joke on friends. Revises the line. Maximizes the punch. Rehearses facial expressions. She frequented the Improv, a comedy club where new talent can try out their wares. If the joke worked there, she refined it. If it didn't, she discarded it and started over.

21. A nonexample is an example of what a concept is *not*. Agape love is *not* a greater degree of "like." Jesus did not command us to "like" our enemies but to "agape" them (to do what is best for them). Jesus commanded us to "do good" to them who persecute us. I can give a cup of cold water to someone I dislike because he is thirsty. I have "loved" him. I still do not like him. Jesus did not command us to like them. What is interesting to me is that if we "agape" our enemies long enough, we may actually grow to like them.

22. http://www.great-quotes.com/cgi-bin/viewquotes.cgi?action=search&orderby=&keyword=Aristotle&startlist=180, accessed December 15, 2008.

23. Hamachek, 404; Smith, 154.

24. Hamachek, 405.

25. Ibid., 406.

26. Not all student criticisms are valid. Evaluate each criticism against the realities of the course (time, outcomes, class size, resources).

27. Hamachek, 407

28. N. L. Gage and David C. Berliner, *Educational Psychology*, 3rd ed., (Boston: Houghton Mifflin Company, 1984), 628ff.

29. The term "advance organizer" refers to an overview of expectations. A course advance organizer presents students with course requirements, expectations, grading parameters, and deadlines. An examination advance organizer presents study questions or exam objectives to guide students' study. A single session advance organizer presents a list of key words, principles, or events. It is an overview of what is coming in the hour, unit, or course.

30. Gage and Berliner, 628.

31. Hamachek, 408.

32. Ibid.

33. Hamachek, 410; Robert E. Slavin, *Educational Psychology: Theory and Practice*, 4th ed., (Boston: Allyn and Bacon, 1994), 373.

34. Slavin, 499.

35. Anita Woolfolk, *Educational Psychology*, 9th ed., (Boston: Allyn and Bacon, Inc., 2004), 397.

36. Ibid.

37. Hamachek, 411; Anita Woolfolk, *Educational Psychology*, 5th ed., (Boston: Allyn and Bacon, Inc., 1993), 403.

38. Hamachek, 413.

39. Gage and Berliner, 630. There were few things more frustrating for us in college and seminary classes than professors who began their classes by asking, "So what would you like to talk about today?" We found it insulting, quite frankly, that professors cared so little for their subject that they would open the floor to whatever random thoughts came to any student's mind in the moment. Fifty minutes of meandering discussion resulted in no significant learning, no new discoveries, no explanations.

40. "Chasing rabbits" refers to following unrelated ideas away from the main topic under discussion. Getting "off-track."

41. Gage and Berliner, 629.

42. This "question-first" practice is appropriate in learning readiness. It is not appropriate throughout the session for reasons given in the text.

43. Gage and Berliner, 632. This principle is more important with children and youths than with adults. Adult students have a large reservoir of previous study, learning, and experience and can ask themselves questions during presentations and explanations. Even so, all learners benefit from responding to questions.

44. Ibid., 633.

45. When students ask, after a long pause, "Is this a question?" it means they cannot distinguish between rhetorical questions (that they should not answer) and real questions (that they should).

46. Gage and Berliner, 636

47. Inflected answers end with the upward tone of a question.

48. Craig Pearson, "Can You Keep Quiet For Three Seconds?," *LEARNING: The Magazine for Creative Teachers*, Vol. 1, No. 6 (Palo Alto, CA: Education Today, February 1980).

49. Gage and Berliner, 636.

50. My wife Barb teaches three levels of American Sign Language at the main campus of Crowley High School just south of Fort Worth. She has a Q&A coffee can for each of her classes. Each can holds Popsicle sticks—each stick has the name of one of her students. She asks a question and then lets a student choose a stick at random. The student whose name is drawn has an opportunity to answer the question. She puts the sticks aside until all of the sticks have been drawn; then the sticks are replaced and the cycle restarted. Students like the system. They know she is not picking favorites or picking on failures since she does not pick students at all. They also know that everyone gets a chance, and the teacher singles out no one unfairly.

51. Gage and Berliner, 637–38.

52. Ibid., 638.

53. I have heard teachers call for such answers: "Answer this question with the first thought that comes to mind." These answers will seldom be satisfactory but will provide an opportunity for the teacher to demonstrate his or her knowledge. Much better is to say, "Don't answer immediately. Think for a moment about this question." The following answers will be much better.

54. Ibid., 641.

55. Ibid.

56. Ibid.

57. Ibid.

58. "compete," *AHD*.

59. Hamachek, 287.

60. Norman A. Sprinthall, Richard C. Sprinthall, and Sharon N. Oja, *Educational Psychology: A Developmental Approach*, 6th ed., (New York: McGraw-Hill, Inc., 1994), 542.

61. Robert F. Biehler and Jack Snowman, *Psychology Applied to Teaching*, 7th ed., (Boston: Houghton Mifflin Company, 1993), 527.

62. Hamachek, 288.

63. "cooperate," *AHD*.

64. Ibid., 253–54.

65. Woolfolk (1993), 376; Dembo, 581.

66. Eggen and Kauchak (2007), 433; Woolfolk (2004), 497–98.

67. The ILE is computed from each student's previous test scores. If students score 10 or more points above their ILE on a given quiz, their group earns three points. Five to nine points above ILE contributes two points to the group. Four points below to four points above ILE contributes one point to the group. Five or more points below ILE contributes zero points. Every two weeks, ILE scores need to be recalculated for each student. Woolfolk (2004), 498.

68. Woolfolk (2004), 499–500.

69. Hamachek, 293; Dembo, 171; Robert J. Sternberg and Wendy M. Williams, *Educational Psychology*, (Boston: Allyn and Bacon, 2002), 453.

70. Woolfolk (2004), 496.

71. Dembo, 171-2; Sprinthall (1994), 543.

72. Sternberg, 454.

73. Ibid., 453; Eggen and Kauchak (2007), 433.

74. Dembo,172; Hamachek, 293.

75. Patricia A. Alexander, *Psychology in Learning and Instruction*, (Upper Saddle River, NJ: Pearson Education, Inc., 2006), 250.

76. Ibid., 251.

77. Alexander, 251–52; Eggen and Kauchak (2007), 433; Woolfolk (2004), 499.

78. Woolfolk (2004), 499.

79. Alexander, 251.

80. Eggen and Kauchak (2007), 432.

81. Ibid.

82. Dembo, 171-2; Sprinthall (1994), 543.

83. Hamachek, 293.

84. Hamachek, 419.

Chapter 15 Notes

1. http://www.great-quotes.com/cgi-bin/viewquotes.cgi?action=search&orderby=&keyword=memory&startlist=120, accessed July 15, 2009.

2. Here are some actual examples of this sin—committed in the name of Christian higher education. Sadly, they are all true.

A student averages a 96 percent on four course exams but earns a D in the course because many students in the course scored better than he did. The grading scale for that semester, given at the end of the semester, was 99 percent (A), 98 percent (B), 97 percent (C), 96 percent (D), and less than 96 percent (F). Simple fairness dictated that every student should have received an A.

A teacher copies sentences out of the course textbook and converts them into true-false questions. (This practice always produces faulty items because the sentences are taken out of context.)

A teacher examines students over footnotes and captions under graphics. (If the information were of major importance to the author, he would not put it in footnotes or relegate it to captions.)

A teacher makes an exam so difficult that only 50 percent of the students pass. He brags to colleagues that the exam scores dropped his students (who had, in his opinion, done "too well in his course that semester") into an "appropriate" spread of grades. He admitted that one of his students cried when his course grade dropped a letter grade as a direct result of his "killer of a final."

A teacher requires students to read 20 books for the course in addition to taking detailed notes of his lectures. One question on the final exam takes a random paragraph from one of the texts and scrambles the words. The students must "reorganize the words of the paragraph into its original form." When confronted over this travesty by a friend of his who was taking his class, he explained, "Students who have thoroughly read the texts should be familiar enough with the authors to enable them to reproduce the appropriate paragraph from the scrambled words." His friend gave him another view of the testing approach. (There are no grounds in testing theory, or the Scripture, to justify this practice.)

A teacher asks arbitrary, trivial questions to find out if "students listened closely" in class. "When missionary X sailed for China, what was her cabin number?" "In the story of missionaries Y and Z in Kenya, what animal figured prominently in their first witnessing encounter?" Students learned quickly to write down every word written on the board and every factoid of every story told in class because any bit of information—no matter how trivial—might well find its way into their next examination. Studying for examinations meant memorizing this mass of trivia rather than understanding underlying concepts, major principles, or creative applications for their life and work in the Lord.

3. Robert E. Slavin, *Educational Psychology: Theory and Practice*, 4th ed., (Boston: Allyn and Bacon, 1994), 499.

4. N. L. Gage and David C. Berliner, *Educational Psychology*, 3rd ed., (Boston: Houghton Mifflin Company, 1984), 730.

5. Slavin, 499.

6. Ibid.

7. Gage and Berliner, 731.

8. Guy R. LeFrancois, *Psychology for Teaching*, 8th ed., (Belmont, CA: Wadsworth Publishing Company, 1994), 377.

9. Gage and Berliner, 731.

10. LeFrancois,377; Slavin, 499.

11. Gage and Berliner, 731.

12. Ibid., 646.

13. Ibid.,647.

14. In today's postmodern climate, even the best teaching practices do not guarantee good student evaluations. The best teaching I do happens in the hardest course I teach: research and statistics. I always receive my lowest student evaluations in that class. It is the perfect storm: required course, difficult material, limited time, objective evaluation of understanding. All my efforts to make two interrelated and difficult subjects understandable cannot overcome the students' assumption that "learning should be fun."

15. Myron H. Dembo, *Applying Educational Psychology*, 5th ed., (New York: Longman, 1994), 575.

16. Eggen and Kauchack (1994), 647.

17. "Other constructs" include variables like socioeconomics status, education level, or exposure to classical music.

18. The SAT measures the supposed aptitude for high school students to do well in college. The GRE purports to report the aptitude for college students to do graduate-level studies. Years ago I did research for our School of Theology on GRE scores and doctoral GPAs over a five-year period. I found a very low correlation between recorded GRE scores from MDiv students and their PhD GPA. This means that scores on the GRE test had little relationship to degree of success in their doctoral program. The test was not valid as an indicator for PhD work for our theology students.

19. William Yount, "Collecting Dependable Data," *Research Design and Statistical Analysis for Advanced Studies*, (Fort Worth: self-published, 2006), 1–3.

20. Ibid., 4–5.

21. Care should be taken to grade essay questions, which are notorious for subjectivity, as objectively as possible. Honest student grades stand on objective evaluations of their learning. This can be done by the use of objective checklists that insure consistency across essays.

22. Slavin, 509.

23. Don Hamachek, *Psychology in Teaching, Learning, and Growth*, 4th ed., (Boston: Allyn and Bacon, 1990), 374.

24. Gage and Berliner, 709.

25. LeFrancois, 369.

26. Slavin, 509.

27. David A. Payne, *The Assessment of Learning: Cognitive and Affective*, (Lexington, Massachusetts: D. C. Heath and Company, 1974), 101. This is a classic text in the area of tests and measurements.

28. Jum C. Nunnally, *Educational Measurement and Evaluation*, (New York: McGraw-Hill Book Company, 1972), 160. This is a classic text in the area of tests and measurements.

29. Ibid., 169.

30. Ibid., 166.

31. Hamachek, 378.

32. Nunnally, 163.

33. Biehler and Snowman (1993), 581; Hamachek, 378.

34. Ibid.

35. Nunnally, 164.

36. Biehler and Snowman (1993), 581; Slavin, 513.

37. Hamachek, 378.

38. Biehler and Snowman (1993), 581.

39. Payne, 112.

40. In research design, the terms "universe" and "population" have the same meaning. If this concept were to be used in a supply item, both words would be accepted as correct. Otherwise, the grading is arbitrary and unfair.

41. Hamachek, 378.

42. Nunnally, 164.

43. Dembo, 581.

44. Payne, 102.

45. Dembo, 581.

46. Nunnally, 164. See note 39 for an example.

47. Dembo, 581.

48. Nunnally, 165.

49. Ibid.

50. Payne, 104.

51. Dembo, 581.

52. Biehler and Snowman (1993), 581; Nunnally, 166.

53. Payne, 104.

54. Nunnally, 160.

55. Dembo, 581; Robert F. Biehler and Jack Snowman, *Psychology Applied to Teaching*, 7th ed., (Boston: Houghton Mifflin Company, 1993), 582.

56. Payne, 105.

57. Dembo, 581.

58. Payne, 105.

59. Anita Woolfolk, *Educational Psychology*, 5th ed., (Boston: Allyn and Bacon, Inc., 1993), 160; Dembo, 581.

60. Slavin, 512; Payne, 108.

61. Dembo, 581; Hamachek, 376.

62. You may wonder why this question is not a trivial one. "Who will care in twenty years if I know who established the Hierarchy of Needs?" Skinner and Maslow are classic giants in the field of education. We strengthen our credibility among professional teachers in our churches when we demonstrate we understand the basics of the field.

63. Dembo, 581; Nunnally; 162, Payne, 106.

64. Dembo, 581; Payne, 107.

65. Tom Kubiszyn and Gary Borish, *Educational Testing and Measurement: Classroom Application and Practice,* (Glenview, IL: Scott, Foresman and Company, 1987), 73.

66. Since teaching is an intervention, success is reflected when students master the material and fairly earn higher grades. Students should not be punished arbitrarily by an enforced bell-curve distribution.

67. Dembo, 581.

68. Hamachek, 376.

69. Dembo, 581.

70. Payne, 107.

71. Hamachek, 374; Payne, 108.

72. Payne, 108.

73. Hamachek, 374.

74. Dembo, 581.

75. Biehler and Snowman (1993), 582; Payne, 108; Kubiszyn and Borish, 73.

76. Some readers may wonder why we *shouldn't* "help students get the right answer" through such irrelevant clues. The goal is not to help students get the right answer but to measure the level of knowledge of understanding possessed by students. If they are well prepared, they will do well; if they are not, they will not. This is a just approach to evaluation of student achievement.

77. Biehler and Snowman (1993), 582; Payne, 108; Kubiszyn and Borish, 73.

78. Payne, 106

79. Not all authors agree with the 60-40 split. Biehler and Snowman (582) and Hamachek (377) both suggest an equal number of true-and-false items.

80. Inventive students can make a statement true without knowing the answer unless the phrase to be changed is specified.

81. Payne, 109.

82. Kubiszyn and Borish, 77.

83. Slavin, 509.

84. Biehler and Snowman (1993), 583.

85. Slavin, 510.

86. Biehler and Snowman (1993), 584.

87. Dembo, 579.

88. Nunnally, 172; Kubiszyn and Borish, 86–87.

89. Dembo, 583.

90. Biehler and Snowman (1993), 584.

91. Dembo, 581.

92. Woolfolk (1993), 547.

93. Biehler and Snowman (1993), 584.

94. Payne, 110.

95. Jack Snowman, Rick McCown, and Robert F. Biehler, *Psychology Applied to Teaching,* 12th ed., (Boston: Houghton Mifflin Company, 2009), 480–81.

96. Snowman, 480.

97. Dembo, 578; Payne, 110; Kubiszyn and Borish, 87.

98. Nunnally, 172.

99. Hamachek, 374; Payne, 110.

100. Slavin, 510.

101. Ibid.

102. Kubiszyn and Borish, 87.

103. Nunnally, 180; Payne, 112.

104. Biehler and Snowman (1993), 584; Nunnally, 178, 112.

105. Dembo, 579.

106. Biehler and Snowman (1993), 584; Dembo, 578; Hamachek, 375; Nunnally, 174; Payne, 112.

107. Nunnally, 174.

108. Kubiszyn and Borish, 87.

109. Nunnally, 173; Payne, 113; Slavin, 512.

110. Hamachek, 374.

111. Dembo, 579; Nunnally, 174.

112. Biehler and Snowman suggest listing the responses alphabetically (584). That is, list the four answers alphabetically by the first letter of the answer.

113. Nunnally, 176.

114. Ibid., 174.

115. Nunnally, 174; Payne, 113; Kubiszyn and Borish, 87.

116. Slavin, 511.

117. Payne, 116–26; Kubiszyn and Borish, 84–87.

118. Matching items can be made more complex by adding an additional column of related material such as "authors," "books," and "major themes." But two-column matching questions are the most common.

119. Nunnally, 167.

120. Biehler and Snowman (1993), 582; Payne, 128.

121. Biehler and Snowman (1993), 582.

122. Ibid.

123. Nunnally, 167.

124. Biehler and Snowman (1993), 583.

125. Dembo, 580; Kubiszyn and Borish, 77. One of my student's college professors routinely created matching questions with fifty pairs or more—stretched over three pages of the exam.

126. Dembo, 580.

127. Payne, 129.

128. Nunnally, 167.

129. Kubiszyn and Borish, 77.

130. Nunnally, 167.

131. The left column might list 8–10 "stems" while the right column lists 4–5 responses that can be used more than once. Such a format reduces 8 to 10 multiple-choice questions to a single matching question. An example of this is presenting the student with 8 to 10 teaching procedures (items), which they match with one of the three spheres of the Triad (repeated responses).

132. Nunnally, 167.

133. Biehler and Snowman (1993), 583; Kubiszyn and Borish, 74.

134. Payne, 129.

135. Payne, 129; Kubiszyn and Borish, 74.

136. Dembo, 580.

137. Kubiszyn and Borish, 75.

138. Ibid., 77.

139. Ibid., 103.

140. Ibid., 98.

141. Ibid., 103.

142. "List and describe the twelve reasons for the fall of the Roman Empire." This essay-type question tests ability to recall the list and meanings given in class (knowledge, lowest level of learning).

143. Kubiszyn and Borish, 104.

144. Eggen and Kauchack (1994), 661.

145. Dembo, 582.

146. Kubiszyn and Borish, 105.

147. Dembo, 582.

148. This is due to the longer time required to analyze the question, formulate an answer, and write answers in complete sentences.

149. Biehler and Snowman (1993), 586.

150. Kubiszyn and Borish, 106.

151. Nunnally, 182.

152. Payne, 143.

153. Biehler and Snowman (1993), 587; Kubiszyn and Borish, 106.

154. Nunnally, 182.

155. Unfortunately, actual test questions come close to Dr. Ford's exaggeration. Not long ago a student shared this question from one of his exams: "Explain the doctrine of God (10 points)." Scholars have devoted lifetimes to answering this question. It is much too broad and vague and worth only 10 percent of the test grade.

156. Ibid., 184.

157. Kubiszyn and Borish, 106–12.

158. Dembo, 584.

159. Slavin, 515.

160. Dembo, 584.

161. Ibid., 585.

162. Biehler and Snowman (1993), 587.

163. The DI also revealed bad questions on my exams. For any question on the exam scoring a negative DI, I simply added the question's value (usually 2 points) to every student's grade. This did not penalize students who actually answered the ambiguous question correctly but also did not punish students who answered it incorrectly.

164. There are a few curmudgeons who remain disgruntled because their poor performance cannot be blamed on the professor or the examination. Their poor efforts result in poor scores, and these few express frustration at this "unfairness."

165. Biehler and Snowman (1993), 592–94; Glover 421–23; Nunnally, 186–96; Payne, 274–76; Kubiszyn and Borish, 122–30.

166. 25 percent is standard. A lower percent (10 percent) sharpens the discrimination; a higher percent (40 percent) lessens the discrimination.

167. For example, if an essay question is worth 10 points, one might award a "1" for any score 6 and above and a "2" for any score 5 or less. This is imprecise but do-able.

168. This is a tedious process to do by hand and not easy even by spreadsheet, but it is well worth the effort when you review test results with students. Demonstrating that your test items are fair reduces the number and intensity of student complaints. But better than quelling student complaints is the fact that every item in your test *is shown to be good!* "Bad items"—defined as items with negative DIs—must be revised or eliminated altogether.

169. These values vary from text to text, but those listed here provide a good basic standard.

170. Slavin, 501.

171. Ibid.

172. Ibid.

173. Ibid.

174. Ibid.

175. Snowman, 479.

176. Slavin, 502.

Unit 5 Notes

1. http://www.loc.gov/loc/brain/proclaim.html, (accessed January 14, 2008).

2. Andrew Curran, *The Little Book of Big Stuff about the Brain*, (Carmarthen, Wales: Crown House Publishing, 2008), iv.

Chapter 16 Notes

1. http://www.worldofquotes.com/author/Frederick-Bailes/1/index.html, accessed November 8, 2008. Frederick Bailes (1889–1970) is known for his Science of Mind philosophy. He taught principles for healing physical diseases by right thinking. See http://frederickbailes.wwwhubs.com/. I include his quote here—not because I agree with his philosophy—but because his statement reflects, at least partially, the idea that mind, through choice, has power over the physical structure of the brain.

2. Leonard Abbeduto, *Taking Sides: Clashing Views in Educational Psychology*, 4th ed., (Dubuque, IA: McGraw-Hill Contemporary Learning Series, 2006), 251. *Wikipedia* has an interesting overview of fMRI at http://en.wikipedia.org/wiki/Functional_magnetic_resonance_imaging.

3. Andrew Curran, *The Little Book of Big Stuff about the Brain*, (Carmarthen, Wales: Crown House Publishing, 2008), iv.

4. A synapse is the tiny gap between the "tail" of a sending nerve cell and the body of another. Electric pulses travel from nerve cell to nerve cell—so long as the impulse is strong enough to "jump the gap."

5. Basic law of electric current. $I = E/R$ where I refers to electric current (amps), E to voltage (volts), and R to resistance (ohms).

6. The region is called Wernicke's area.

7. "PET" stands for "positron emission tomography" and measures important body functions—such as blood flow, oxygen use, and sugar (glucose) metabolism—to help doctors evaluate how well organs and tissues are functioning. PET scans are useful in evaluating "brain abnormalities—such as tumors, memory disorders and seizures and other central nervous system disorders" as well as to "map normal human brain and heart function." http://www.radiologyinfo.org/en/info.cfm?PG=pet, accessed March 8, 2009.

8. Jeffrey M. Schwartz and Sharon Begley, *The Mind & The Brain: Neuroplasticity and the Power of Mental Force* (New York: ReganBooks, 2002), 197.

9. Abbeduto, 252.

10. Picture a nerve cell with appendages extending from it—like arms of an octopus. Some of these arms are receivers, accepting electrical impulses from other cells; these are dendrites. Other arms are senders, sending electrical impulses to other cells; these are axons. When an axon interfaces with another neuron, there is a tiny gap. Only impulses strong enough to jump the gap continue along their pathways. This gap is called the synapse.

11. Joseph LeDoux, *The Synaptic Self: How Our Brains Become Who We Are* (New York: Penguin Books, 2002), back cover.

12. Ibid., ix.

13. Walter Gannon, *Defining Right and Wrong in Brain Science: Essential Readings in Neuroethics* (New York: Dana Press, 2007), xv.

14. Exodus 20.

15. http://www.viewzone.com/bicam.html, accessed December 17, 2008.

16. John McCrone, "'Right Brain' or 'Left Brain'—Myth or Reality?" in *The New Scientist* (July 21, 2000).

17. http://www2.scholastic.com/browse/article.jsp?id=3629, accessed December 17, 2008.

18. John McCrone, "'Right Brain' or 'Left Brain'—Myth or Reality?" in *The New Scientist* (July 21, 2000).

19. Jerry Larson, *Religious Education and the Brain: A Practical Resource for Understanding How We Learn about God* (New York: Paulist Press, 2000).

20. Larsen references S. Springer and G. Deutsch, *Left Brain, Right Brain*, (San Francisco: W. H. Freeman & Co., 1989), 284, in *Religious Education and the Brain: A Practical Resource for Understanding How We Learn about God*, (New York: Paulist Press, 2000), 18.

21. Larsen, 18.

22. Curran, 101.

23. Ibid., 102.

24. December 18, 2008.

25. This false dichotomy reflects the cognitive/humanistic debates of the 1970s. The "cold, logical" (cognitive) Left Brain is pitted against the "warm, spontaneous, creative" (humanistic) Right Brain. The humanistic idealism of the 1970s failed but has reappeared—dressed up in popular brain pseudo-science. It is little wonder our high school graduates embrace world peace, global warming, and diversity but cannot diagram an English sentence, solve a simple math problem, or deliver a coherent five-minute critique of a current political issue.

26. Patients lost their ability to process speech due to stroke damage to the left-side control region but regained the ability to speak. PET scans showed that "regions in the *right* hemisphere had become active, and had taken over the functions of the left brain's damaged language zones." Schwartz, 197.

27. Holmes Rolston III, "Gods, Brains, Minds: The Human Complex," in Kelly Bulkeley, ed., *Soul, Psyche, Brain: New Directions in the Study of Religion and Brain-Mind Science*, (New York: Palgrave Macmillan, 2005), Kindle edition.

28. Neuroscience is a broad field, which encompasses the study of the nervous system, including the brain. A good overview of the field can be seen in *Wikipedia* at http://en.wikipedia.org/wiki/Neuroscience.

29. For Aristotle, "God is a being with everlasting life, and perfect blessedness, engaged in never-ending contemplation." Anonymous essay found at http://www.iep.utm.edu/a/aristotl.htm, *The Internet Encyclopedia of Philosophy.* IEP is seeking an author to write a replacement for this lengthy article. Accessed March 7, 2009.

30. I am not interested in debating a dyad or triad model of human personality. I will leave that to others. I simply use the practical distinctions among the physical body (for example, brain, nervous system), the nonphysical natural mind (for example, Buddhism and mental force, philosophy), and the nonphysical supernatural spirit/mind ("flesh and blood did not reveal this to you, but My Father in heaven" (Matt 16:17).

31. Schwartz, 29. Of course, other writers disagree. Blakesee and Blakesee analogize the mind as a neurological jazz band, where multiple players—without music scores or conductor—play the music of life in perfect harmony. There is no self, no independent mind—just the grand "irreducible illusion of being the conductor of your life's music in all its complexity, emotional nuance, crescendo and diminuendo—the ballad that is the you-ness of you." Sandra Blakesee and Matthew Blakesee, *The Body Has a Mind of Its Own: How Body Maps in Your Brain Help You Do (Almost) Everything Better*, (New York: Random House, 2007), 20

Perhaps the most depressing end to a book on the subject belongs to Chris Frith in his *Making Up the Mind: How the Brain Creates Our Mental World*, (Malden, MA: Blackwell Publishing, 2007). Taking a strong position on "Brain creates (the illusion of) mind," he writes, ". . . this book is not about consciousness. . . . I have emphasized how much my brain knows and does without me being aware of it. My brain makes me afraid of things I am not aware of seeing and can control complex limb movements without my knowing what I am doing. There seems very little left for consciousness to do. So, rather than asking how subjective experience can arise from activity in neurons, I ask the question, 'What is consciousness for?' Or more particularly, 'Why does my brain make me experience myself as a free agent?' My assumption is that we get some advantage from experiencing ourselves as free agents. So the question is, 'What is the advantage?' My answer is, for the moment, pure speculation." 190. Dr. Frith uses the words "me," "my," and "I" as if he thought of himself as a conscious being—even as he proclaims the very idea a neurological illusion.

32. Schwartz, 30.

33. http://www.loc.gov/loc/brain/proclaim.html, accessed January 14, 2008.

34. See Al Mohler, "The God Gene: Bad Science Meets Bad Theology," http://www.beliefnet.com/News/Science-Religion/2004/10/The-God-Gene-Bad-Science-Meets-Bad-Theology.aspx?p=1, accessed June 2, 2009. One need only Google "Dean Hamer" to find numerous articles on his materialistic views of faith and morals.

35. http://en.wikipedia.org/wiki/God_gene, accessed January 14, 2008.

36. Carl Zimmer (October 2004), "Faith-Boosting Genes: A Search for the Genetic Basis of Spirituality," *Scientific American,* http://www.sciam.com/article.cfm?articleID=000AD4E7-6290-1150-902F83414B7F4945, accessed March 28, 2009.

37. "For though they knew God, **they did not glorify Him as God** [*choice*] or show gratitude. Instead, their thinking

became nonsense, and their senseless minds were darkened. Claiming to be wise, they became fools and exchanged the glory of the immortal God for images resembling mortal man, birds, four-footed animals, and reptiles. **Therefore, God delivered them over in the cravings of their hearts to sexual impurity**, so that their bodies were degraded among themselves. They exchanged the truth of God for a lie, and worshiped and served something created *[choice]* instead of the Creator, who is blessed forever. Amen.

"This is why God delivered them over to degrading passions. For even their females exchanged natural sexual intercourse for what is unnatural. The males in the same way also left natural sexual intercourse with females and **were inflamed in their lust for one another**. Males committed shameless acts with males and received in their own persons the appropriate penalty for their perversion. And because they did not think it worthwhile to have God in their knowledge *[choice]*, God delivered them over to a worthless mind to do what is morally wrong" (Rom 1:21–28).

38. Reference found on Dean Hamer's home page http://rex.nci.nih.gov/RESEARCH/basic/biochem/hamer.htm. S LeVay and DH Hamer, "Evidence for a Biological Influence in Male Homosexuality," *Scientific American,* 1994; **270**: 20–25.

39. http://serendip.brynmawr.edu/biology/b103/f97/projects97/Newman.html, accessed January 14, 2008.

40. http://www.youtube.com/watch?v=TEG-EBUU7n8, accessed June 2, 2009.

41 "One hundred billion" is Schwartz's number—provided in 2002. Holmes (2005) places the number of adult neurons at one trillion—"each with several thousand synapses (possibly tens of thousands), Kindle locations 412–14.

42. Schwartz, 111.

43. Holmes, Kindle 412–14.

44. Braitenburg and Schuz, 1998, quoted in Holmes, Kindle 412–14.

45. Holmes, Kindle 412–14.

46. Schwartz, 111.

47. "The number of neurons and their possible connections is far more vast than the number of genes coding for the neural system, and so it is impossible for the genes to specify all the needed neural connections." Holmes, Kindle 370–73.

48. Schwartz, 112.

49. My grandfather, a farmer, lived by the rule: "One never eats the seed corn." Regardless of how hungry one might be, the seed corn had to be saved for planting in the spring when each seed would yield hundreds more. A fully matured plant—with multiple ears of corn—resided in each kernel of corn. Given soil, enough rain, and sun, this mere seed grows to six feet tall in a matter of months. American society has grown so accustomed to the lie that a fetus in the womb is "not human" that to say otherwise is to be labeled a religious fanatic. But the "bundle of cells" that begins to turn inward on Day 14 is a human being in the making—far more precious than the kernels of corn my grandfather went hungry to spare.

50. Schwartz, 112.

51. Ibid., 113.

52. Ibid., 114.

53. Ibid.

54 .Neuroplasticity is the ability of the brain to change its structure and wiring.

55. Schwartz, 253.

56. Ibid., 366.

57. Neuroplasticity decreases with age—as we reinforce circuits over time. It becomes increasingly difficult to change long-held values and perspectives, but the brain is not deterministic. Under the right circumstances, brains can remap themselves to think in new ways or to recover from damage—as long as we are alive.

58. Ibid., 253.

59. Ibid., 115–16.

60. Ibid., 116/

61. Ibid., 117.

62. Ibid., 118.

63. See http://www.businessballs.com/kolblearningstyles.htm for an overview of Kolb's system, accessed March 22, 2009.

64. Schwartz, 367.

65. Hardiman's arguments were previously published under the title "Connecting Brain Research with Dimensions of Learning," *Educational Leadership*, Vol. 59, No. 3 (November 2001). Bruer's arguments were previously published under the title "Brain Science, Brain Fiction," *Educational Leadership*, Vol. 56, No. 3 (November 1998). Seeing the 1998 publication date makes me wonder if Bruer has changed his mind in the last ten years.

66. Mariale Hardiman is principal of the Roland Park Elementary/Middle School in Baltimore, Maryland. "Connecting Brain Research with Dimensions of Learning," in Leonard Abbeduto, *Taking Sides: Clashing Views in Educational Psychology*, 4th ed., (Dubuque, IA: McGraw-Hill Contemporary Learning Series, 2006), 251, 257.

67. Ibid., 254.

68. Ibid., 255.

69. His second of three Laws of Learning. See Chapter Six.

70. Ibid.

71. I found this illustration in 2007 while surfing the Web. I have not been able to relocate the location of the report. Perhaps it has been removed since it is such a blatant misuse of brain research in education.

72. Bruer, "Brain Science, Brain Fiction," *Educational Leadership*, Vol. 56, No. 3, (November 1998), in Abbeduto, 260.

73. Ibid., 264.

74. Ibid., 265.

75. Gerry M. Madrazo and LaMoine L. Motz, "Brain Research: Implications to Diverse Learners," *Science Educator* 14, No. 1 (Spring 2005), 56. The authors listed three groups of three; I am combining the statements in one list of nine.

76. Ibid., 57.

77. Ibid., 57–58.

78. Ibid., 58.

79. Ibid., 58–59.

80. Schwartz, 57.

81. One example he gives is having patients bring a "piece of toilet paper soiled with a miniscule amount of fecal material and rub it on their face and through their hair during the therapy session" (Schwartz, 3).

82. The reported success rates of 60 to 70 percent excluded, Schwartz learned years later, the 20–30 percent of patients who refused to "undergo the procedure" and an additional 20 percent who dropped out before success was achieved (Schwartz, 7), dropped the reported success rate to 30 to 42 percent.

83. I encourage you not to let his Buddhist connections put you off just yet. Buddhism focuses on the power of the mind, which places it in opposition to the materialistic self-definition of science. While Buddhism does not accept the supernatural, its engagement of neuroscience—to find "common ground" between the biochemical functions of the brain and the mental force of consciousness—certainly has implications for us. After all, do we not worship the Living God who possesses an omniscient Mind but, being Spirit, has no physical brain at all?

84. I draw the following discussion of Schwartz's treatment from his summary on pages 362–63, but he spends scores of pages detailing the development of his treatment process from 1987 through the writing of his book in 2002.

85. Namely, the "orbital frontal cortex, anterior cingulated gyrus, and caudate nucleus." Schwartz, 362. Brain scans demonstrated these areas are involved in the firing of obsessive thoughts (Schwartz, 93).

86. Ibid., 56.

87. Schwartz's therapeutic treatment of focused attention became known as the Four Steps: Relabel ("Obsessions are false signals, symptoms of a disease"); Reattribute ("This thought represents a malfunction of my brain, not a real need to wash my hands again"); Refocus ("Turning their attention away from the pathological thoughts and urges onto a constructive behavior"), and Revalue ("Obsessions have no intrinsic power or value") (14).

88. Schwartz, 88.

89. Ibid., 89.

90. Schwartz, 79.

91. Most of us think in terms of the classical physics of John Newton. Simply put, classical physics is cause and effect.

Stimulus in, response out. Neurotransmitter in, behavior out. The laws of nature. A real world independent of human choice or observation. Quantum physics lives in probabilities and uncertainties, where "the world comes into being through our knowledge of it." While it seems counter-intuitive to state that a thing does not exist until I observe it, such a notion has been verified in countless experiments over the last century. It is the basis for "explaining the burning of stars, the structure of elementary particles . . . and describes the physics of a newborn universe." And it provides the theoretical basis for the way mental force, attention, can change the physical functioning of neurons in the brain. (Schwartz, 260–63).

92. Schwartz, 362.

93. Schwartz, 217. Another interesting anecdote concerns William F. Straub, a sports psychologist who conducted an experiment in mental training while at Ithaca College. He divided 75 college students into five groups to compete in throwing darts at a regulation dartboard. Each made 50 dart throws to set a baseline (possible points 0–3000). Group 1 was sent home to do nothing except return in eight weeks and throw 50 darts. Group 2 threw darts for 30 minutes a day, five days a week, for two months. The remaining three groups were assigned various mental training exercises: relaxing and listening to mental training tapes. They would do things like mentally visualize holding the dart, focusing on the target, seeing and hearing the dart hit the bull's eye, and experiencing the pride and satisfaction of doing well. Every other day, these three groups would physically practice throwing darts. At the end of eight weeks, 71 subjects returned and threw 50 darts. The control group did not improve. The daily-practice group improved their scores by an average of 67 points. The three mental-practice groups improved their scores by 111, 141, and 165 points, respectively (Blakesee and Blakesee, 55). There are no references given in the book for this story, and I could find none through Google searches.

94. Ibid., 95.

95. Ibid., 90.

96. Holmes, Kindle 451–55, quoting Elbert et al., 1995.

97. Holmes, Kindle 455–59, quoting Pantev et al., 1998.

98. The hippocampus is located in the forward part of the brain and "helps regulate emotion and memory." http://www.medterms.com/script/main/art.asp?articlekey=3757, accessed March 30, 2009.

99. Schwartz, 251.

100. Holmes, Kindle 455–59, quoting Bear et al. (2001), 418.

101. Ibid., Kindle 463–65.

102. Schwartz, 366. Schwartz continues his work in OCD and the relationship between the mind and body. The most recent reference I could find concerning his work was a YouTube video (dated December 12, 2008), which is drawn from his September 11, 2008, appearance at a United Nations Mind-Body symposium.

103. Ibid., 253.

104. Ibid., 368–69.

105. In case my lack of emphasis on spiritual rebirth—through faith and repentance—concerns you, let me encourage you to read on. The next section should feel more comfortable for you. My point is not that brain science has replaced faith as an explanation for Christian living; it certainly has not. My point is that Scripture and brain science now agree that the choices we make matter; we become what we attend to. The revolution in neuroscience helps us in ways it cannot imagine.

106. God does not throw His "pearls to pigs" (Matt 7:6). Spiritual things are discerned by spiritual minds, and spiritual minds are created at conversion—the point in time when one surrenders self and self-direction to the Creator by faith, repenting of sin (rebellion) and sins (evil actions, thoughts, and attitudes) and following Christ. "Then Jesus said to His disciples, 'If anyone wants to come with Me, he must deny himself, take up his cross, and follow Me'" (Matt 16:24). Anyone unwilling to do this demonstrates a mind unable to understand the Bible's message and cannot "live biblically" in the true sense of the phrase.

107. By this, I mean a life focused on God, His Word, and His will and characterized by the fruit of the Spirit, the Sermon on the Mount, and the many descriptions of one in whom Christ lives. I exclude those like A. J. Jacobs who recently made headlines by living according to "every rule in the Bible as literally as possible" for a year. He then wrote a book about the experience. Since he is not "in Christ Jesus," he experienced biblical rules as a spiritual outsider—akin to an avowed bachelor "trying every aspect of marriage for a year" and then writing about how weird the experience was.

I Googled "living biblically" and the first 99 of 100 citations cited Jacobs's work (one sermon found its way into the top 100). There were 692,000 hits; accessed March 9, 2009.

108. Schwartz, 95.

109. The professor was Dr. Frank Martin, Leadership Development: International Turkey Network, part of the Antioch Network, www.antiochnetwork.org. The interview took place in March 2009.

110. Recollections from a visit to the Studebaker Museum in South Bend, Indiana, while teaching a course in Educational Psychology at Notre Dame University, Summer, 2000. See the museum's Web site at http://www.studebakermuseum.org/.

111. Holmes, Kindle 365–67.

112. Normal descriptions of the world flow from Newtonian physics, where objects exist—whether we observe them or not. The "other world" is quantum physics, which operates on the principle that things do not exist until they are observed (Schwartz, 263). While this seems, on its surface nonsensical, many of the things we have come to take for granted in our lives derive from quantum physics and its impact on chemistry and solid-state electronics—"transistors, lasers, semiconductors, light-emitting diodes, PET scans, and MRI machines" (Schwartz, 262).

113. J. M. Schwartz, H. P. Stapp, , and M. Beauregard, (2005). "Quantum Theory in Neuroscience and Psychology: A Neurophysical Model of Mind-brain Interaction," *Philosophical Transactions of the Royal Society of London, Series B,* **360**(1458): 1309–27.

114. An enriched environment, in this case, consisted of "the complex surroundings of the wild" rather than the near-empty cages of the nonenriched. John Bruer would call this a "complex environment" to differentiate it from "enriched," which has another connotation for educators.

115. Schwartz, 252–53.

116. Schwartz, 226. Space and focus do not permit delving into the early history of modern brain research in the 1970s, including Edward Taub, the Silver Spring monkeys, and the birth of PETA (People for the Ethical Treatment of Animals, 1981). Merzenich built on these early discoveries.

117. Ibid., 228.

118. Brains of dyslexics recognize sounds longer than 200 milliseconds but miss shorter ones. The result is an auditory cortex constructed from faulty inputs. This was a problem—given the assumption of experience-driven brain change. How could they change circuits that were tied to faulty inputs? (Schwartz, 228–29).

119. SLI—"Specific Language Impairment." Children with normal intelligence have "great difficulty in reading and writing, and even in comprehending spoken language. Perhaps the best-known form of specific language impairment is dyslexia." Ibid., 226.

120. Ibid., 232.

121. When stroke took away the use of one arm, standard practice was to encourage the use of the good arm, sometimes placing the paralyzed limb in a sling. Edward Taub, basing his reasoning on early discoveries in brain neuroplasticity, placed the *good arm* in a sling, forcing the stroke victim to use the affected arm. What he found was that the brain created new circuits to control the movement of the affected limb, and remarkable recoveries were documented. Still, entrenched professional interests and the opposition to neuroplasticity resisted his findings (Schwartz, 234).

122. Ibid., 189.

123. Ibid., 191.

124. Schwartz describes these studies in some detail, 189–96.

125. Ibid., 234.

126. Ibid.

127. http://www.evidencebasedprograms.org/Default.aspx?tabid=147, accessed March 14, 2009.

128. Ibid. I could not find pricing information at the *Fast ForWord* site, but one site reported in-home use of the CD programs, beginning at $1100, and in-office use at $4000. I did not find information about how long one might use the programs for these sums. See http://specialchildren.about.com /b/2007/04/05/did-fast-forword-work-for-your-child.htm © 2009, accessed March 14, 2009.

129. Ibid., 236.

130. http://www.scilearn.com/, accessed March 15, 2009.

131. Cecilia Elena Rouse and Alan B. Krueger, "Putting Computerized Instruction to the Test: A Randomized Evaluation of a 'Scientifically-based' Reading Program," *Economics of Education Review*, Vol. 23, Issue 4, August 2004; 323. See http://www.evidencebasedprograms.org/Default.aspx?tabid=147 for summary, accessed March 14, 2009.

132. "141 2nd graders and 274 7th graders," G. D. Borman, J. G. Benson, and L. T. Overman, (2005), "Evaluation of the Scientific Learning Corporation's *Fast ForWord* Computer-Based Training Program in the Baltimore City Public Schools," (2005) *Submitted for publication.* See http://www.evidencebasedprograms.org/Default.aspx?tabid=147 for summary, accessed March 14, 2009.

133. G. D. Borman, J. G. Benson, and L. T. Overman, (2009). "A Randomized Field Trial of the *Fast ForWord* Language Computer-based Training Program," *Educatioal Evaluation and Policy Analysis*, 31, 82. See http://teacheffectively.com/2009/03/12/fast-forword-doesnt/, accessed March 10, 2009. *Note:* These findings do not show conclusively that *Fast ForWord* fails to improve reading. It does show that changes, if they exist, are not measurable by standardized testing. While researchers can take pride in what *Fast ForWord* does, educators should take seriously the fact that it is not reflected in instruments designed to measure reading achievement. RY

134. http://www.evidencebasedprograms.org/Default.aspx?tabid=147, accessed March 14, 2009.

135. http://specialchildren.about.com/b/2007/04/05/did-fast-forword-work-for-your-child.htm © 2009, accessed March 14, 2009.

136 Schwartz, 95, 355.

137 Examples: One passage reports a feeding of 4000 and another 5000. Then he discovered there were two feedings. *This* Gospel says two angels, and *that* Gospel says one angel (witness accounts). One Gospel says *one* Gadarene demoniac, and another says *two* (a main character and a lesser known companion).

138. Mike Barnett and R. Yount, *Called to Reach: Equipping Cross-Cultural Disciplers* (Nashville: Broadman & Holman, 2007).

139. Classical "Newtonian" physics holds that objects exist independently of (mental) observation. In quantum physics, "there is no radical separation between mind and world" (Schwartz, 287).

140. Schwartz, 259.

141. Ibid., 18.

142. Ibid., 22.

143. Ibid., 29.

144. Frith, 190.

145. Schwartz, 40–41.

146. Ibid., 322.

147. Ibid., 309.

148. Holmes, Kindle 419–21.

149. Ibid., Kindle 259–62.

150. Humans and chimpanzees share 95 to 98 percent protein identity, which makes humans appear (in terms of DNA) as a slightly remodeled chimpanzee. But human brains are three times larger, making cognitive function in humans 300 percent greater than chimpanzees (Holmes, Kindle 399–404). More importantly, in symbolic reasoning, imagination, moral abstraction, and a sense of God, "humans differ [from apes] by a thousand orders of magnitude" (Holmes, Kindle 409–14).

151. Ibid., Kindle 387–89, quoting Theodosius Dobzhansky, 1956, 121–22.

152. Ibid., Kindle 385–88.

153. Schwartz, 112.

154. Ernst Mayr (1994) as quoted by Holmes, Kindle 434–37.

155. You may wonder how seminaries teach a scientific approach to problems if "God is not part of the system." Ministerial students study the natural connections among people, actions, attitudes, and processes inherent in ministry systems: denominations, churches, small groups, families. We can study teaching methods (and their impact), counseling techniques (and their efficacy), preaching styles (and their impact); but we cannot scientifically study God who operates "as He wills."

156. Hauser et al. (2002), 1576, quoted in Holmes, "Gods, Brains, Minds: The Human Complex," in *Soul, Psyche, Brain: New Directions in the Study of Religion and Brain-Mind Science,* Kindle 249–50. No further reference data is given.

157. Washoe learned over 150 signs. Researchers claimed she was able to initiate human-like language by putting these elements together in primitive sentences. She also was able to use tangible signs (as in "dirty," meaning she needed her diaper to be changed) in abstract ways (as when she became irritated at her trainer for tickling her and she called him "dirty"). Subsequent research shows that Washoe's researchers overstated her language capacity. See http://www.geocities.com/RainForest/Vines/4451/TalkWithChimps.html for a good overview of this analysis.

158. Holmes, Kindle 258–60.

159. Ibid., Kindle 261–62.

160. Ibid., Kindle 271–74.

161. Patricia Wolfe, "Brain Research and Education: Fad or Foundation," *Brain Connection*, August, 2001, www.brainconnection.com/content/160_1/, accessed December 7, 2007, 3.

162. Materialists will never accept the idea of an immaterial mind since immateriality stands outside their sense of reality. Assuming reality to be material and tangible alone, one must, by definition, define *mind* as a product of the material brain—the only "reality."

Epilogue

1. The term "perestroika" means "restructuring," and refers to major changes in Soviet economic policy 1985-1991, but often the term is used to mean the end of the Soviet Union.

INDEX